The United States Congress

Organization And Procedure

by

Floyd M. Riddick

With a Preface
Professor Lindsay Rogers

This volume pictures Congress at work
. . .; it describes the House and Senate legislative machines and their political and parliamentary procedures in action. Committees and their procedures and the political machinery of Congress are also set forth. Professor Rogers in his preface says that these procedures (the standing orders) "determine the efficiency of the legislature, and more frequently than not this is the efficiency of a large part of the governmental machinery."

The United States Congress: Organization and Procedure offers the teacher and students of legislation a comprehensive, yet succinct volume of information necessary to an understanding of Congress at work.

The resumé of House and Senate procedure is based on the official precedents of the two bodies; its authenticity is assured, having been examined by the Senate and House Parliamentarians. In the preface, Professor Rogers says: "Text writers who now hope to deal with Senate procedure more adequately than they have been able to do in the past will have to quote from Mr. Riddick." He concludes: "The internal enemies are not yet formidable but they can be kept few and the threat from without can be made less only if congressional government is efficient government. Efficiency is more likely if there is a full understanding of the rules that the two branches of Congress have and of how they are applied in practice. To this high end Mr. Riddick's volume has made a notable contribution."

THE AUTHOR

Floyd M. Riddick has been close to Congress and its procedure for over 15 years. After receiving his doctorate in political science at Duke University, he became affiliated with the Federal Government and subsequently joined the faculty of the American University. From 1939 to 1943 he was an editor of the Congressional Daily; he began the publication of the *Legislative Daily* for the United States Chamber of Commerce, and edited it from 1943 to 1947; for the last two years he has been the Senate editor of the "Daily Digest" of the *Congressional Record*, created by the Legislative Reorganization Act of 1946.

He has written a number of articles on Congress and its activities, including the annual reviews of Congressional proceedings for the *American Political Science Review*, since 1939. He is presently the Senate editor of the "Daily Digest," and lectures on American Government at George Washington University.

The United States Congress Organization and Procedure

BY

FLOYD M. RIDDICK, Ph.D.

NATIONAL CAPITOL PUBLISHERS, INC.

Manassas, Va.

P. O. Box 7706, Washington 4, D.C.

Copyright
1949

National Capitol Publishers, Inc.

All rights reserved
Printed in the United States

328.735
R543u
3223

Acknowledgments

The purpose of this volume is simply to picture the Congressional machine at work. There is no attempt here to give a history of the development of legislative procedure, nor are any suggestions for a better system proposed. The study is merely a description of the House and Senate legislative machines, and of their political and parliamentary procedures in action.

Many people have helped me in its preparation. I wish to thank them. The Senate and House Parliamentarians, Charles L. Watkins and Lewis Deschler, are the top authorities in their respective chambers; I have turned to them often for the last word on parliamentary questions within their bailiwick. They have given me help freely to aid me in my endeavor of producing an accurate work on this subject. Mr. Watkins allowed me to draw at will from his personal notes on Senate precedents, compiled in several volumes. The *House Manual*, which is edited by Mr. Deschler, is the official volume on House procedure. Edward J. Hickey, Senate Journal Clerk, and William T. Roy, House Assistant Parliamentarian, have been most helpful.

Anyone attempting a dependable study of Congress must of necessity read and digest the monumental volumes (numbering 8) of House precedents compiled by Mr. Asher C. Hinds and Representative Clarence Cannon, and the Precedents of the Senate compiled by Henry H. Gilfry. Representative Cannon, who has won his place in history in the field of congressional procedure, has also compiled an indispensable volume for Representatives, entitled: *Cannon's Procedure in the House of Representatives.* From these works I quoted at length.

My special thanks go to my wife for her constant assistance; to George H. E. Smith, Frederick H. Green, Margaret Faerber, Edna Riddick, and Elizabeth Gilmore for reading the manuscript for comment, or for proofreading, indexing, and secretarial help.

Some other works in the field, exclusive of Government publications, which the author has cited, include: De Alva Stanwood

iii

Alexander, *History and Procedure of the House of Representatives;* Charles R. Atkinson, *The Committee on Rules and the Overthrow of Speaker Cannon;* George Rothwell Brown, *The Leadership of Congress;* Joseph P. Chamberlain, *Legislative Processes;* Chang-Wei Chiu, *The Speaker of the House of Representatives Since 1896;* Marshall Edward Dimock, *Congressional Investigating Committees;* M. P. Follett, *The Speaker of the House of Representatives;* George B. Galloway, *Congress at the Crossroads;* George H. Haynes, *The Senate of the United States;* Paul De Witt Hasbrouck, *Party Government in the House of Representatives;* Ada C. McCown, *The Congressional Conference Committee;* M. Nelson McGreary, *The Developments of Congressional Investigative Power;* Floyd M. Riddick, *Congressional Procedure;* Lindsay Rogers, *The American Senate;* John Thomas Salter, *Public Men In and Out of Office;* Alexander Simpson, Jr., *A Treatise on Federal Impeachments;* Morris B. Ullman, "Apportionment of Representatives in Congress on the Basis of Special Populations," *Journal of the American Statistical Association;* W. F. Willoughby, *Principles of Legislative Organization and Administration;* Roland Young, *This Is Congress;* and annual articles on various sessions of Congress from the *American Political Science Review,* 1943 to date.

Preface

The final sentence of Woodrow Wilson's famous essay, "The Study of Politics," reads as follows: "In order to know anything about government, you must *see it alive;* and the object of the writer on politics should be nothing less than this, to paint government to the life, to make it live again upon his page."

It would not be true to say that to be outstanding political writers must have experience of the institutions that they seek to describe. Wilson himself had his experience after he had written extensively on politics, but men like De Tocqueville, Bagehot, Lord Morley, and Bryce—writers who are still read—fell into Wilson's category of men of affairs. They had seen alive the governments they described.

I shall not attempt to list any scholars who, without emerging from their ivory towers, have produced books worthy of being ranked with those written by the authors I have just mentioned. There are certainly some. But so far as I know, not a single substantial treatise on parliamentary procedure has come from the pen of one who has not been intimately acquainted with the legislature whose workings he attempted to lay bare. Sufficient familiarity cannot come from the most assiduous reading of the *Congressional Record,* or *Hansard,* or the *Journal Officiel.* One must see the chambers at work either from the press gallery, as an official, or as a member.

Thus Sir Thomas Erskine May was first Examiner of Petitions for Private Bills, later Assistant Clerk, and then for fifteen years Clerk of the House of Commons. His *Treatise on the Law of Privileges, Proceedings, and Usage of Parliament* not only described but influenced parliamentary procedure and has been kept up to date by his successors, of whom the last, Sir Gilbert Campion, two years ago published the second edition of his own work, *An Introduction to the Procedure of the House of Commons.* Sir Courtenay Ilbert, Clerk from 1902 until 1921, was more interested in draftsmanship rather than in procedure, and his *Legislative Methods and Forms* became a classic. Eugène Pierre began as a functionary of the Chamber of Deputies in 1866 and served as General Secretary to its Presidency from 1885 to 1925. His great *Traité de droit politique, électoral, et parlementaire* has gone through half a dozen editions.

The rules of the House of Representatives still do lip service to Thomas Jefferson's manual, which he drew up as a guide for himself when he became Vice President and had to preside over the Senate. Asher C. Hinds (long Clerk at the Speaker's table) and Clarence Cannon (Parliamentarian of the House and later Representative from Missouri), whose new edition of *Hinds'* *Precedents* is a monument of legal and parliamentary scholarship, are names well known to American legislators and to students of legislative procedure.

Dr. Floyd M. Riddick, the author of *Congressional Procedure,* which now appears in a revised edition at a time when certain important rules of the House of Representatives have just been changed and some Senate rules are being given careful scrutiny, has seen the House and the Senate *alive* and at work. From 1939 to 1943 he was an editor of the *Congressional Daily,* which made a more detailed analysis of the internal workings of Congress than did any other agency under extra-governmental auspices. For three years he reported for the United States Chamber of Commerce on the progress of bills in Congress and the work of its committees, as editor of the *Legislative Daily.* For the last two years he has been the Senate editor of the "Daily Digest" of the *Record,* which the Legislative Reorganization Act of 1946 established and charged with the "printing in the Daily Record the legislative program for the day, together with a list of congressional committee meetings and hearings, and the place of meeting and subject matter; and to cause a brief résumé of congressional activities for the previous day to be incorporated in the Record, together with an index of its contents." Mr. Riddick has long been so close to the mysteries of legislative procedure that, as the saying goes, he can count the hairs in their nostrils.

Having read continuously, lectured regularly, and written occasionally on public law and government for more years than I care to count, I fear no contradiction when I say that most present-day journalists and students (graduate as well as undergraduate) know little or nothing about the procedure of the Congress of the

United States. This is not surprising. How could they know much? The writers of textbooks may or may not have some knowledge of their own, but what they say has to be boiled down to such small compass and be in such general terms that it makes the subject, as Winston Churchill said of a country which does not bother with legislative procedure, "an enigma wrapped in a mystery." Mr. Riddick unfolds the details of the mystery, but he has written clearly and interestingly of the sometimes highly technical matters with which he must deal.

Text writers quoted from and students of parliamentary procedure made great use of the first edition of his book, which appeared in 1941. Both groups of readers will find that the present volume is much more than a reprint of what Mr. Riddick said seven years ago with the citation of recent chapters and verses to bring precedents down to date. He has recast his work and now deals with congressional procedure as a part of congressional government.

Moreover, the following pages give a wealth of information on one important phase of the subject which has not been re-explored for a good many years. The interest of students of congressional procedure has centered very largely on the House of Representatives and in particular on the position and powers of its Committee on Rules which have been dealt with by the 81st Congress. Procedure in the Senate—save for difficulties in limiting debate and preventing filibusters—has not attracted the same amount of attention as has procedure in the House. Now Mr. Riddick gives a comprehensive treatment of procedure in the Senate—indeed, the first such treatment since forty years ago Gilfry published his volume of *Precedents,* which has long been out of print. Text writers who now hope to deal with Senate procedure more adequately than they have been able to do in the past will have to quote from Mr. Riddick. For the writers, as I have suggested, are not going to spend the time necessary to see the American Senate alive and they will be able to find adequate information nowhere other than in the present volume.

It is unnecessary for me to say anything about the importance of the standing orders of legislative assemblies. It was Pierre's considered opinion that, although the standing orders of assemblies are on their face only internal laws, "in reality the rules of procedure are formidable instruments in the hands of parties; they often have more influence than the constitution itself on the conduct of public affairs"; they determine the efficiency of the legislature, and more frequently than not this is the efficiency of a large part of the governmental machinery.

These words, true when written, are even truer now when enemies without and within threaten the representative institutions which the framers of the Constitution gave us and which have worked successfully for 160 years. The internal enemies are not yet formidable but they can be kept few and the threat from without can be made less only if congressional government is efficient government. Efficiency is more likely if there is a full understanding of the rules that the two branches of Congress have and of how they are applied in practice. To this high end Mr. Riddick's volume has made a notable contribution.

Lindsay Rogers

Columbia University
New York City

Contents

x

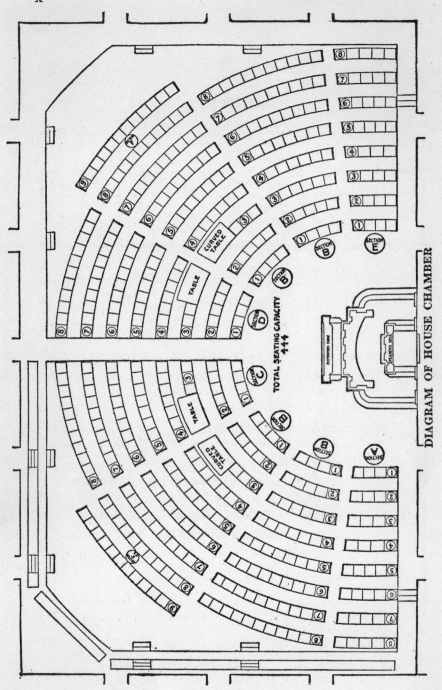

DIAGRAM OF HOUSE CHAMBER

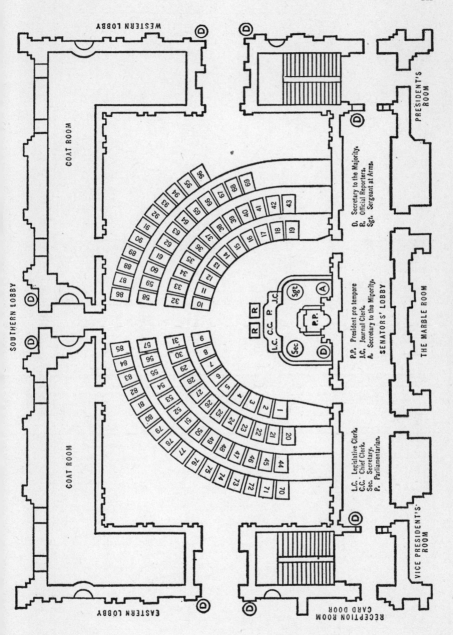

DIAGRAM OF SENATE CHAMBER

CHAPTER I

Introduction

Congress

A properly elected deliberative body is without question the greatest bulwark yet devised to safeguard a free people. The greatest proof of this lies in the evidence of what has happened in countries when their deliberative bodies were permitted to dry up.

Our representative form of government embodies a legislature, an executive, a judiciary, and the people. The legislative arm was designed purposely to make the Government a definite product of the people, with the membership of the House of Representatives allocated according to population and elected for two-year terms of office, and that of the Senate for six years with at least one-third of them coming up for election biennially. This plan proposes to keep Congress close to the "grass roots." [1]

The significance of an unhampered Congress should never be underestimated and every citizen should be vigilant in seeing that Congress functions in the capacity defined for it in the Constitution. The people have a solemn duty of electing capable persons to the House and Senate; the Representatives and Senators have the obligation to voice the will of the people they represent, to act according to their judgment in behalf of their constituencies and the United States in the determination of directions and policies for a way of life.

Anyone endeavoring to follow Congressional procedure or to keep himself posted on legislative activity should be familiar with a few fundamental procedures of the House and Senate and be aware of certain characteristics of the leaderships. For instance, only a small percentage of the bills introduced in the House and Senate is ever considered; a much smaller number is enacted into law. In the 79th Congress a total of 11,656 bills and resolutions were introduced, 4,657 legislative reports were made by com-

[1] All Federal officers are appointive, except the President and Vice President.

1

mittees, but only 1,625 public and private laws were enacted. It is evident that most of the bills and resolutions introduced were never given any consideration at all. In the 71st Congress a total of 25,436 bills and resolutions were introduced, 4,610 reports made, with only 1,524 enacted into law. A very few of the other 20,826 bills and resolutions on which no reports were made received any consideration.[2]

The chances of an introduced bill becoming law are not dependent upon the contents of the bill alone. Far more important are: Who introduced the bill? What groups sponsored the bill? Does the Congressional leadership favor the bill? Did the Administration request the legislation? Is the Administration in full support of the proposal? If these questions can be answered, it is not so difficult to advise whether a bill will be enacted. A comprehension of the legislative and parliamentary procedure, however, in the absence of answers to the above questions, aids one in foretelling what final disposition will be made of any particular measure.

The House of Representatives and Senate share equally in law-making. To carry out their functions and responsibilities derived from the Constitution, or acquired through the years, the House and Senate have developed procedures and modes of conduct to their own liking. The needs of the two, however, are at such great variance that their procedures for transacting business are very different and distinct. The Senate with 96 members, as compared to 435 in the House, has a less rigidly fixed set of rules. Customs and practices have established a parliamentary law for the Senate much looser, less specifically defined, and less regulatory than that of the House. The House of Representatives on the other hand proceeds under very limited debate, with individual consideration giving way to the will of the whole membership in any test case so as to permit the greatest dispatch of business.

No Member of the House may speak for more than an hour on any bill but there is no restriction on how long or the number of times a Senator may speak on a bill, except that a Senator may not speak more than twice on a subject in the same legislative day without leave of the Senate or more than once for five minutes on the same subject under the call of its calendar. The Cloture Rule

[2] See: *Calendars and History of Legislation, House of Representatives*, 76th Congress, final edition, pp. 335-337.

may be invoked in the Senate to limit the debate, but this requires a two-thirds vote of the Senate membership in each instance.

The procedure in the two chambers for calling up business likewise varies. The Senate has not seen fit to establish several legislative calendars and legislative days for the disposition of various classes of bills. Its business has not been classified into various categories according to a privileged status for consideration. Generally all bills reported to the Senate are placed on a "single calendar" known as "General Orders," under Rule VIII. Any bill on the calendar can be brought up at any time by unanimous consent, or if a motion to that effect is entertained and adopted by a majority vote.

The House has established various calendars of business and different legislative days as well as classified its business as to the privileged status for consideration. In pursuance of this procedural maze, controversial public bills which are not privileged cannot be called up for consideration in the House except by unanimous consent, under Suspension of Rules (which requires a two-thirds vote and the approval of the Speaker), under a Calendar Wednesday procedure, by invoking the Discharge Rule, or under a special rule (House resolution) adopted by a majority vote of the House; it is not in order to make a motion, requiring a majority vote, to call up a bill contrary to its defined procedures.

Again, it should be noted that the Congressional committee system is unique as far as the legislatures of all other nations are concerned. Really, the standing committees are powerful creatures of Congress—they can kill, rewrite, or expedite the enactment of legislation. In effect, each of the House and Senate standing committees, of which there are nineteen and fifteen respectively, is a miniature legislature, to the extent of its own jurisdiction. Neither the House nor Senate as a rule will consider legislation until it has been considered by the proper standing committee. Significant is the fact that bills usually pass Congress in much the form they are approved by the committees. The important influence wielded by the chairmen of these committees, both directly with respect to the subjects before their own committees, and indirectly on subjects before other committees, through their position, is seldom overemphasized.

The purpose of this study is to picture our National Legislature at work without any attempt to trace the history of the legislative processes or to propose a better system of procedure. The picture will include a treatment of the legislative and political machines of the two houses, emphasizing the methods used to enact or block the enactment of a bill.

Membership, Sessions, and Place of Meeting

Sessions of Congress: Congress "shall assemble at least once in every year, and such meeting shall begin at noon on the 3rd day of January, unless they shall by law appoint a different day."[3] Likewise, the President of the United States "may, on extraordinary occasions, convene both houses, or either of them . . ."[4] at any time.

The duration of a Congress extends for two years, beginning on January 3 of odd numbered years, but a session cannot last for more than one year. In the case of *sine die* adjournments before the end of the year, a special session might be called, as has often been the case, making two sessions in a single year.[5]

Sessions Held in Capitol: The chambers of the House of Representatives and the Senate are located in the south and north wings of the Capitol Building, respectively.[6] Both chambers are spacious boxes, taking up the second and third floors of the space they occupy. The plans are fundamentally the same; any differences are due to the magnitudes of dimensions, styles and arrangements of doors, and fixtures within each. The galleries, with seating capacities of approximately 600 and 800, elevated some fifteen feet above the level of the floors of the chambers, extend around all four sides. Just under the galleries, adjoining and at the same level of the House and Senate floors, are the cloakrooms, entrances and exits to the chambers, and other rooms into which the Representatives and Senators may retire for discussions, agreements, and the like.

[3] 20th Amendment of Constitution. Until the adoption of the 20th Amendment the meeting date of Congress was the first Monday in December. A great number of annual sessions, however, were convened on other dates. Since adoption of 20th Amendment, several of the sessions were convened at dates other than January 3, as set by special statute. See *Congressional Directory*, Eightieth Congress, first session, pp. 237-41; hereafter cited as 80-1, pp. 237-41.
[4] Article II, section 3 of Constitution. The President has frequently called special sessions (See *Congressional Directory*, 80-1, pp. 237-241) ; he may convene Congress at any location should conditions demand it (*Hinds Precedents*, Volume I, number 2—hereafter cited: Hinds, I, 2.)
[5] At pages 10696-10697 of daily edition of *Congressional Record*, Eightieth Congress, first session, (hereafter cited as C.R., 80-1, pp. 10696-10697—daily edition), is a brief on the meeting of Congress on Nov. 17, 1947, called by the President, to the effect that it was not a special session but a continuation of the same session since both houses were standing in recess to a day definite.
[6] See diagrams of the two chambers.

House Chamber: In the House chamber, the eight complete rows of seats,[7] which have a total seating capacity of 444, are arranged in a semicircle facing the rostrum, divided into eight sections by converging aisles, making a half wheel with the rostrum serving as a hub. The seats have no individual desks;[8] there are four large tables in front of the fourth row of seats, two of which are on either side of the two aisles next to either side of the center aisle. These four tables are occupied by the floor leaders and by members of the committee in charge of the bill under consideration, with the Democrats occupying the two on the right of the Speaker and the Republicans, the two on the left.[9]

The center aisle is known as the line of division. The seats are not assigned,[10] but the Republicans occupy those to the left of the Speaker and the Democrats those to the right. Members of the majority party are entitled to seats on either side of the center aisle sufficient to accommodate its number; regardless of the number of members of the majority, however, the attendance is usually so small that the seats of one side of the center aisle will seat its membership. The rostrum located in the south center of the House chamber is occupied by the Presiding Officer, the Clerk and his assistants, the Parliamentarian, the Doorkeeper, the official reporters, and the Sergeant at Arms.

Senate Chamber: In the Senate chamber, the four rows of desks and chairs, totaling 96, are arranged in a semicircle facing the rostrum; they are assigned individually to the Senators; they are divided by a center aisle known as the aisle of division. The Democrats occupy the seats on the right and the Republicans those on the left. There is sufficient space on either side of the center aisle to accommodate enough desks and chairs to seat the majority. If necessary the chairs and desks are moved from one side of the center aisle to the other at the beginning of each new Congress to meet the needs of any change in party ratios.

Joint Sessions: Congress meets in the House chamber for joint session; joint sessions are held for three purposes: to count the electoral vote, to receive messages delivered by the President of the United States, and to hold formal ceremonies, including state funerals.

[7] There is a ninth row in the two extreme corners back from the Speaker's rostrum.
[8] The House had individual desks until the membership became too large to be thus accommodated.
[9] See Cannon, VI, 4.
[10] Cannon, VI, 4. The last assignment of seats was at the organization of the 62nd Congress.

Evolution of Membership

House: *Reapportionment*: The first House of Representatives had only sixty-five Members. After the first census was taken in 1790, and reapportionment occurred, the number of Representatives was increased to 105; following the next census in 1800, the number was increased to 141. Fulfilling the Constitutional requirement, the census was taken in 1810 and every ten years since,[11] followed by reapportionment each time except in 1920. The House membership was increased on each occasion [12] with one exception,[13] until it reached its present size of 435 in 1911.[14]

Computation of Congressional Districts: Under the present plan adopted in 1941, the number of Representatives allotted each State is based on population [15] and is computed under the method of equal proportions, the objective of which is to assign Representatives "to the States so that the differences in the average number of people per Representative or in the average share of each person in a Representative differs by as small a proportion as possible between any two States." [16] The procedure for finding the number of Representatives to which each State is entitled under this method, is as follows: (1) the first 48 seats are assigned one to each State; (2) second, multiply the population of each State by a series of multipliers taken from the table below; this step is the equivalent of dividing the population of each State by the following quantities (Geometric means or averages) in succession: the

[11] See Article 1, section 2 of Constitution; Cannon, VI, 39-40.
[12] See table in footnote 14.
[13] Only one man ever successfully opposed an increase in the number of Representatives. Representative Millard Fillmore, a New York Whig, in 1840, prior to becoming President, blocked a proposal to make an increase. Since that date various Members of the House at different times have criticized the House membership as being too large and unwieldy, but to no avail.
[14] See Cannon, VI, 40. The evolution of the House membership and its ratio to population has been as follows:

Year	Ratio of Representatives	Number of Congressmen	Year	Ratio of Representatives	Number of Congressmen
1789	one for each 30,000	65	1870	one for each 131,425	293
1790	one for each 33,000	105	1880	one for each 151,911	325
1800	one for each 33,000	141	1890	one for each 173,901	357
1810	one for each 35,000	181	1900	one for each 194,182	391
1820	one for each 40,000	212	1910	one for each 211,877	435
1830	one for each 47,700	240	1920	no reapportionment	435
1840	one for each 70,680	223	1930	one for each 279,712	435
1850	one for each 93,423	234	1940	one for each 302,688	435
1860	one for each 127,381	241			

[15] The Constitutional requirement to exclude Indians not taxed is no longer applicable since court has held that all Indians are now subject to Federal taxation (Superintendent v. Commissioner, 295 U. S. 418; see also House Document No. 45 of 77-1st).
[16] See "Apportionment of Representatives in Congress on the Basis of Special Populations," by Morris B. Ullman, *Journal of the American Statistical Ass'n*, Vol. 40, pp. 484-492; also Senate Doc. 304, 76-3.

square root of (1 x 2), square root of (2 x 3), square root of (3 x 4), etc. (The number of multipliers used for each State should be somewhat greater than the number of Representatives expected to be assigned to that State.)[17]; (3) then, arrange the resulting products in order of magnitude, beginning with the largest, to form what is known as a priority list, which indicates the order in which Representatives in excess of 48 shall be given out to the several States; and (4) Representatives are assigned in that order, until 435 have been given out.[18]

Thus Congress determines the number of Representatives to which a State is entitled, but the actual redistricting is decided by the State legislatures subject to the will of Congress. There is no longer any legal requirement that districts must be composed of contiguous and compact territory, as provided in the law of 1911.[19]

Redistricting: If the House membership remains at 435, reapportionment after each census will only mean redefining existing districts in accordance with population changes. States having no changes in the number of Representatives to which entitled, will not be affected; States in which the number of Representatives is increased or decreased so that the number of Representatives

[17] Table of Multipliers: Method of Equal Proportions:

k	Multiplier	k	Multiplier	k	Multiplier	k	Multiplier
		14	0.0741 2493	27	0.0377 4257	40	0.0253 1848
2	0.7071 0678	15	.0690 0656	28	.0363 6965—	41	.0246 9324
3	.4082 4829	16	.0645 4972	29	.0350 9312	42	.0240 9813
4	.2886 7513	17	.0606 3391	30	.0339 0318	43	.0235 3104
5	.2236 0680	18	.0571 6620	31	.0327 9129	44	.0229 9002
6	.1825 7419	19	.0540 7381	32	.0317 5003	45	.0224 7333
7	.1543 0335—	20	.0512 9892	33	.0307 7287	46	.0219 7935—
8	.1336 3062	21	.0487 9500	34	.0298 5407	47	.0215 0662
9	.1178 5113	22	.0465 2421	35	.0289 8855+	48	.0210 5380
10	.1054 0926	23	.0444 5542	36	.0281 7181	49	.0206 1965+
11	.0953 4626	24	.0425 6283	37	.0273 9983	50	.0202 0305+
12	.0870 3883	25	.0408 2483	38	.0266 6904	51	.0198 0295+
13	.0800 6408	26	.0392 2323	39	.0259 7622	52	.0194 1839

$$k \quad 1/\sqrt{(k-1)} \quad k$$

According to the rule, we are to multiply the population of each State by a series of multipliers taken from the Table of Multipliers for Method EP. In practice, it is convenient to record each of the resulting "products" on a separate card. For example, the State of Mississippi, with population 1,790,618, will yield one series of cards; Tennessee, with population 2,337,885, will yield another series of cards; etc., as follows:

State	k	Product	State	k	Product
Mississippi	2	1,266,158	Tennessee	2	1,653,134
Mississippi	3	731,017	Tennessee	3	954,438
Mississippi	4	516,907	Tennessee	4	674,889
Mississippi	5	400,394	Tennessee	5	522,767
Mississippi	6	326,921	Tennessee	6	426,837
Mississippi	7	276,298	Tennessee	7	360,743
Mississippi	8	239,281	Tennessee	8	312,413
			Tennessee	9	275,522
			Tennessee	10	246,435
			Tennessee	11	222,909

no longer equals the number of districts will have to redefine their districts immediately or elect some or all of their Representatives at large until districts can be redefined.[20] When a State duly redefines its Congressional districts, that number should equal the number of Representatives, thereby allowing the people of each district to elect one Representative.

Automatic Reapportionment: Congress failed to provide for reapportionment following the census of 1920; it was not until 1929 that a law was enacted to overcome that situation. To prevent such delays in the future Congress enacted an automatic redistricting law in 1929, which was amended in 1941. Under this law, the President is required to transmit to each fifth Congress a statement of population and an apportionment of existing number of Members (435) among the several States according to the new census,[21] under the method of equal proportions. Unless

[18] For details on The Method of Equal Proportions see Senate Document 304 for 76th Congress, 3rd Session on Methods of Apportionment in Congress, by Edward V. Huntington, pp. 3-7. To illustrate how the calculation is made note the following from data compiled by Department of Commerce, Bureau of the Census:

Size of House	Priority value as per population	State receiving last assigned Representatives	Cumulative number of Representatives for each state
(The first 48 Representatives are assigned one to each State to fill the Constitutional requirement that each State have at least one Representative)			
49	9,531,193	N. Y.	2
50	7,000,484	Pa.	2
51	5,584,193	Ill.	2
52	5,502,837	N. Y.	3
53	4,884,419	Ohio	2
54	4,884,260	Calif.	2
55	4,535,966	Texas	2
56	4,041,732	Pa.	3
57	3,891,093	N. Y.	4
58	3,716,628	Mich.	2
59	3,224,035	Ill.	3
60	3,052,383	Mass.	2
	Intervening figures omitted		
430	307,081	Ohio	23
431	307,071	Calif.	23
432	304,657	Pa.	33
433	303,016	Mo.	13
434	302,921	N. Y.	45
435	300,797	Ark.	7
436	300,472	Mich.	18
437	299,956	Ky.	10
438	299,157	Wisc.	11
439	299,138	Iowa	9
440	298,620	Ala.	10

[19] See Wood v. Broom, 287 U.S. 3.
[20] If the number of Representatives for a State is decreased, leaving the number of districts greater than the number of Representatives to which it is entitled, the whole delegation will have to be elected-at-large until the State is redistricted; if the number is increased, the additional Representatives may be elected-at-large until redistricted. (See P.L. 291 of 77th Congress.) The candidates to be elected-at-large "shall be nominated in the same manner as candidates for governor, unless otherwise provided . . ." (Cannon, VI, 47; Article I, Section 4 of Constitution).
[21] Cannon, VI, 41.

Congress should make further change in existing law the Clerk of the House after each census will submit to the governor of each State the number of Representatives to which his State is entitled under the new census,[22] and each State shall be entitled to elect that number to the next Congress.[23]

Delegates and Resident Commissioners: In addition to the 435 Representatives, there are two Delegates and one Resident Commissioner, representing Alaska, Hawaii, and Puerto Rico, respectively.[24] These persons enjoy the privileges of a Member except they may not vote or make a motion to reconsider.[25]

Senate: Membership: Since each State is entitled to only two Senators, when the first Congress convened on March 4, 1789, with eleven States [26] in the Union, the total membership could not exceed 22 as contrasted to 65 in the House. In fact, the first session was nearly concluded before the membership exceeded 20.[27] As late as 1888 there were only 76 Senators as contrasted to 325 Representatives. The present ratio of 96 Senators to 435 Representatives was obtained in 1912.

Continuing Membership: The life of a Congress extends for two years, but Senators are elected for six, making the Senate a

[22] See Cannon, VI, 43, for form of notification.
[23] 46 Stat. 26-27.
[24] See *Congressional Directory*, 80-1, pp. 141-142: Alaska has a population of 72,524, Hawaii has 423,330, and Puerto Rico, 1,869,255.
[25] See Cannon, VI, 240-246. Delegates are elected as additional members to a committee.
[26] North Carolina did not come into the Union until November 21, 1789; Rhode Island came in on May 29, 1790.
[27] The names of the States and the dates of their admission into the Union are as follows:

State	Entered Union	State	Entered Union
Vermont	Feb. 18, 1791	Colorado	Aug. 1, 1876
Kentucky	June 1, 1792	South Dakota	Nov. 2, 1889
Tennessee	June 1, 1796	North Dakota	Nov. 2, 1889
Ohio	Nov. 29, 1802	Montana	Nov. 8, 1889
Louisiana	Apr. 30, 1812	Washington	Nov. 11, 1889
Indiana	Dec. 11, 1816	Idaho	July 3, 1890
Mississippi	Dec. 10, 1817	Wyoming	July 10, 1890
Illinois	Dec. 3, 1818	Utah	Jan. 4, 1896
Alabama	Dec. 14, 1819	Oklahoma	Nov. 16, 1907
Maine	Mar. 15, 1820	New Mexico	Jan. 6, 1912
Missouri	Aug. 10, 1821	Arizona	Feb. 14, 1912
Arkansas	June 15, 1836		
Michigan	Jan. 26, 1837		
Florida	Mar. 3, 1845		
Texas	Dec. 29, 1845		
Iowa	Dec. 28, 1846		
Wisconsin	May 29, 1848		
California	Sept. 9, 1850		
Minnesota	May 11, 1858	Alaska was established as a Territorial
Oregon	Feb. 14, 1859	government on May 17, 1884.
Kansas	Jan. 29, 1861	Hawaii was established as a Territorial
West Virginia	June 19, 1863	government on June 14, 1900.
Nevada	Oct. 31, 1864	Puerto Rico was established as a Territorial government on April 12,
Nebraska	Mar. 1, 1867	1900.

continuing body. The Constitution reads: "Immediately after they shall be assembled in consequence of the first election, they shall be divided as equally as may be into three classes. The seats of the Senators of the first class shall be vacated at the expiration of the second year, of the second class, at the expiration of the fourth year, and of the third class, at the expiration of the sixth year, so that one-third may be chosen every second year . . ." [28] In accordance with this provision, in spite of the increased number of States from thirteen to forty-eight, the Senate membership has been divided into classes and thus elected so that at least a third of the Senators would be newly elected at the beginning of each new Congress. The number elected might exceed one-third of the total membership in case there are vacancies resulting from deaths or resignations to be filled.

Elections and Qualifications of Senators and Representatives

Elections: *Regulations by State and Federal Governments*: "The times, places and manner of holding elections for Senators and Representatives, shall be prescribed in each State by the legislature thereof; but the Congress may at any time by law make or alter such regulations . . ." The definition of this clause of the Constitution is still in its making; the relative powers of Congress and States under it have been the subject of much discussion. In recent years the Federal legislature has shown more interest in elections than was the case in the early history of the United States. Presently the Federal Government extends its scope of control to the following subjects: time of elections, the definition of voting instruments, aiding of soldiers to use their voting franchise, what constitutes armed interference at the polls, rights of members of the armed forces to participate in elections, and what constitutes corrupt practices and frauds in an election. Control of primaries is distinctly lodged with the States.[29]

Expenditures for Election: The Federal Corrupt Practices Acts define the amount of money to be spent in elections by candidates for Congress;[30] in order to check the campaign of each it is specified that "unless the laws of his State prescribe a less âmount" a candidate for the Senate may not spend in excess of $10,000 and a candidate for the House may not spend in excess

[28] Article I, section 3.
[29] See *House Manual*, 80-1, sections 42-45.
[30] See Cannon, VI, 67-96.

of $2,500 or "an amount equal to the amount obtained by multiplying three cents by the total number of votes cast at the last general election for all candidates for the office which the candidate seeks, but in no event exceeding $25,000 if a candidate for Senator or $5,000 if a candidate for Representative, Delegate, or Resident Commissioner." [31] Each candidate is required to submit a sworn statement as to the contributions received, amounts expended, and promises made for the purpose of influencing election returns; if he refuses to abide by the law, the House and Senate may refuse to admit him to membership. The statements filed do not have to be published, but there is an obligation to file them.[32] Candidates may not accept contributions from Federal employees to be used in a general election or in a primary.

Vacancies: Vacancies are caused by death, resignation, declination, withdrawal by action of either body declaring a vacancy in its membership or causing one by expulsion.

Vacancies in the House of Representatives may be filled by special election only, called by the executive authority of the State concerned.[33] A person elected to fill a vacancy remains in office only during the remainder of the term of the Representative whose place he takes, unless re-elected at the following general election for another two years.

Vacancies in the Senate may be filled by means of a special election called by the executive authority of the State concerned or "the legislature of any State may empower the executive thereof to make temporary appointments until the people fill the vacancies by election as the legislature may direct." [34] A person elected or appointed to fill a vacancy remains in office only during the remainder of the term of the Senator whose place he takes, unless re-elected at the following general election.

Credentials of Members-Elect: State and Federal laws define in considerable detail the requirements in filing credentials, as to form, time, place, signatories, and the like. The fact that certificates presented by a Congressman-elect are issued in strict accordance with the State law and signed by the proper State executive does not guarantee that the credentials will be accepted and that the Senate or House will not make an investigation; on

[31] U. S. Code, Title 2, section 248.
[32] The law is directory rather than mandatory; failure to comply will not invalidate the election and vacate the seat.
[33] See Constitution, Article I, section 2; Hinds, I, 517.
[34] Constitution, 17th Amendment; see also Hinds, II, 1177-1235.

the other hand, even though the credentials may be defective, if
no doubt is raised in the House or Senate as to their validity, they
will be accepted.[35] If a candidate has been duly elected, precedents
require that disloyalty should be clearly proved before expulsion.[36]

Each House a Judge of its Membership: Under any circumstances, "each house shall be the judge of the elections, returns,
and qualifications of its own Members."[37] Either may impose
qualifications not required in the Constitution or exclude a member-elect even though the Constitutional power of expulsion should
be limited in its application to conduct of Members during their
term of office.[38] If a seat is contested for irregularity the membership of the body concerned may defer giving the oath of office
to the member-elect until an investigation has been made, at
which time it may accept or reject any contested member-elect.
Contestants for a seat are granted the privilege of the floor until
the contested case has been decided in order to defend themselves
or establish their right to serve as a Representative or Senator as
the case might be.[39]

Either house may declare a seat vacant by a majority vote, or it
may expel one of its Members by a two-thirds vote after organization to do business. Briefly, either body is free to receive the credentials of its members-elect, examine them, and decide if they
are to be honored.[40]

Contested Election Cases: The Senate and House have given
considerable attention to contested election cases, respectively,
since 1789.[41] Seldom if ever has a Congress organized without
some losing candidate for a seat in either the Senate or House
contesting the right of the member-elect to be Senator or Representative, as the case might be, as a result of the election in which
the losing candidate participated. Each contest, however, might
not reach the formal stage of consideration by a committee.

Cases may be instituted by a contest filed in accordance with
the law, by protest or memorial from an elector in the district or

---

[35] See Cannon, VI, 57-59, 81-96; Hinds, I, 448, 593, 637.
[36] See Hinds, I, 441-484; Cannon, VI, 56-59.
[37] Article I, section 5 of Constitution.
[38] See Cannon, VI, 56.
[39] See House Rule XXXIII and Senate Rule XXXIII.
[40] Article I, section 2 of Constitution; Cannon, VI, 78: This power is unlimited,
a matter of discretion to be exercised by the two bodies, from which there is no
appeal. The disqualification of the member-elect does not authorize the seating
of a contestant not found to be elected.
[41] There were 56 formal contested cases filed in the House from the 61st through
the 70th Congresses. For breakdown see: *Legislative Establishment Appropriation
Bill*, 1929, Hearings, 70-1, p. 44.

State concerned or by any other person, or on motion of a Senator or Representative as the case might require. The losing candidate might bring his case to the attention of the party officials of his party to get a quicker and more considerate decision, particularly if of the same political faith as that of the party in control.

Contested elections involve many kinds of issues and the decisions are of wide range.[42] When such contests are filed in the House or Senate they are referred to the proper committee for consideration. Reports on them may or may not be made in the early part of the session.[43]

Qualifications for Membership: *For Representatives:* The House is composed of 435 Representatives [44] elected every two years by the people of the several States in accordance with the allocation of Congressional Districts. "No person shall be a Representative who shall not have attained to the age of twenty-five years, and been seven years a citizen of the United States, and who shall not, when elected, be an inhabitant of that State in which he shall be chosen." [45] By practice he must be a resident of the district from which he was elected, but the definition of resident has varied; and he may serve only in the Congress for which he was elected. The voters take care of other qualifications at the polls.

For Senators: The Senate is composed of two Senators from each State elected by the people for terms of six years, so "that one-third may be chosen every second year" [46] at the general election, held on the first Tuesday after the first Monday in November. "No person shall be a Senator who shall not have attained to the age of thirty years, and been nine years a citizen of the United States, and who shall not, when elected, be an inhabitant of that State for which he shall be chosen." [47] A State

---

[42] Cannon, VI, 90-189; Hinds, I, II, 534-1135; Haynes, *The Senate of the United States,* I, pp. 126-127.

[43] Cannon, VI, 75-189. Recent practices in the House require decisions to be made in early part of the session.

[44] The term "Congressman" has been attached to the Representatives as a result of custom. Members of the Senate are just as much Congressmen as are the Representatives. The wrong use of this term has misled many laymen into believing that the House is Congress and that the Senate is entirely separate.

[45] Article I, section 2 of Constitution; See Hinds, I, 413-440 for interpretations of this clause.

[46] Constitution, Article I, section 3.

[47] Senators Clay (in 1806) and Mason (in 1816) were under thirty when they took the oath of office but no question of age was raised in either instance. Senator Rush Holt of West Virginia, a member-elect not of constitutional age, was given the oath of office after he became 30 years of age. Other practices under this section of the Constitution can be found in Hinds and Cannon's Precedents.

may not add to the Constitutional qualifications for a Senator or Representative.

"Public Officer": A "public officer" may not at the same time be a Representative or a Senator. The Constitution reads: "No Senator or Representative shall, during the time for which he was elected, be appointed to any civil office under the authority of the United States . . . and no person holding any office under the United States shall be a member of either house during his continuance in office." Thus the acceptance by a Congressman of any office, the duties of which are incompatible with the duties of a Member of the National Legislature, automatically forces the Congressman to vacate one or the other office. While the Constitution does not specifically prohibit a Congressman from holding a State office at the same time, the duties of a Representative or Senator and the duties of a State governor, for example, conflict sufficiently to make it impossible for the same person simultaneously to discharge the duties of the two offices. Though the decisions have been of wide range, if the duties of a Member of Congress are considered not in conflict with the duties of another office or if an office accepted by a Member of Congress is not classified as "public" as defined by law, the person may retain his membership in Congress and discharge the duties of both offices simultaneously.

Immunities for Congressmen: The Constitution grants the following immunities to Members of each house: "They (the Senators and Representatives) shall, in all cases except treason, felony, and breach of the peace, be privileged from arrest, during their attendance at the session of their respective houses, and in going to and returning from the same; and for any speech or debate in either house, they shall not be questioned in any other place." Obviously the intent of this clause was to prohibit action which might restrain or make the legislative process inoperative; it was not intended, according to accepted practices and decisions, to place Representatives and Senators beyond the realm of the law or to set them up as a privileged class of the citizenry. In practice, "treason, felony, and breach of the peace" have been construed to mean all indictable crimes, leaving little exemption from arrest; and for a defendant to be entitled to what privilege is extended therein, he must have been in good faith on his way to the seat of the government to enter upon the discharge of his public duties. A slight deviation from the usual route, however, "ought not to cause a loss of his privilege, if such deviation was but an incident to the principal journey." [48] Representatives and Senators may not be held responsible for acts done before becoming a Member, nor be removed from Congress for minor things.[49]

The exemption from being questioned for any speech has been held to be absolute, without appeal except to the House and Senate memberships, respectively. The rules of the two bodies do place certain limitations on language used in debate and any Member is subject to be called to order if he fails to abide by them; no Member is subject to libel suits for language used in debate, otherwise it would place a restraint on the legislative process. This right of speech or debate extends generally to things done during the session in relation to business before Congress.[50]

Thus, the Senators and Representatives, once they have campaigned and won the election, meet in Washington in the early part of the following January to begin a new Congress. It then becomes their duty to function as the National Legislature, as set forth in the next chapter.

[48] See Hinds, III, 2673-74.
[49] See Cannon, VI, 238; Hinds II, 1284.
[50] See Hinds, III, 2675.

CHAPTER II

Functions of Congress

In January[1] following each general election a new Congress convenes to perform the duties assigned it by the Constitution. The occasion is a significant one; the people must look to this arm of the Government for the determination of policy and the enactment of law if their general will is to be pursued through the years. The founding fathers at the Constitutional Convention deemed Congress of sufficient importance in the governmental setup to devote Article I to its creation. The opening sentence following the preamble stipulates: "All legislative powers . . . shall be vested in a . . . Senate and House of Representatives." And while this delegation is commonly accepted as the primary raison d'etre, the work of the National Legislature is far more extensive and inclusive.

To carry out its functions, Congress is clothed with particular powers and prerogatives, as follows:

1. To legislate;
2. To propose amendments to the Constitution; \
3. To direct or influence public opinion;
4. To function as a board of directors to the Government and the people;
5. To count electoral votes;
6. To elect President and Vice President by Congress when not duly elected by electoral vote;
7. House to impeach and the Senate to try;
8. Senate to advise and consent to treaties and to confirm certain nominations;
9. To manage its own housekeeping;
10. To receive messages from President on state of Union.

The remainder of this chapter is devoted to a brief discussion of each of these functions of Congress:

(1) To Legislate

In the determination of public policy the Constitution specifies that it shall be the power of Congress to lay and collect taxes,

[1] New Congresses convene on January 3 of odd-numbered years as specified by the Constitution unless Congress, as authorized, should decide upon another date.

duties, imposts and excises, to pay the debts and provide for the common defense and general welfare of the United States; but all duties, imposts, and excises shall be uniform throughout the United States; to borrow money on the credit of the United States; to regulate commerce with foreign nations, and among the several States, and with the Indian Tribes; to establish a uniform rule of naturalization, and uniform laws on the subject of bankruptcies throughout the United States; to coin money, regulate the value thereof, and of foreign coin, and fix the standard of weights and measures; to provide for the punishment of counterfeiting the securities and current coin of the United States; to promote the progress of science and useful arts, by securing for limited times to authors and inventors the exclusive right to their respective writings and discoveries; to constitute tribunals inferior to the supreme court; to define and punish piracies and felonies committed on the high seas, and offenses against the law of nations; to declare war, grant letters of marque and reprisal, and make rules concerning captures on land and water; to raise and support armies, but no appropriation of money to that use shall be for a longer term than two years; to provide and maintain a navy; to make rules for the government and regulation of the land and naval forces; to provide for calling forth the militia to execute the laws of the Union, suppress insurrections and repel invasions; to provide for organizing, arming, and disciplining the militia, and for governing such part of them as may be employed in the service of the United States, reserving to the States respectively the appointment of the officers, and the authority of training the militia according to the discipline prescribed by Congress; to exercise exclusive legislation in all cases whatsoever, over such District (not exceeding ten miles square) as may, by cession of particular States, and the acceptance of Congress, become the seat of the Government of the United States, and to exercise like authority over all places purchased by the consent of the legislature of the State in which the same shall be, for the erection of forts, magazines, and arsenals, dock-yards, and other needful buildings;—and to make all laws which shall be necessary and proper for carrying into execution the foregoing powers, and all other powers vested by this Constitution in the Government of the United States, or in any department or officer thereof.

Thus, Congress was made the supreme power in the determination of policy and in the enactment of legislation. In practice, however, the scope of the executive has been expanded through the use of executive orders and administrative directives in pursuance of the law of the land, in assuming a more active role in initiating and influencing proposed legislation to enactment, and in playing an omnipotent role in setting a stage to "force" legislation.

The courts have outlined in the form of court decisions the confines of the legislative jurisdiction—some in support of the legislature and some to the gain of the administration or the courts. This condition has become so acute as to invite many comments; Representative Howard Smith of Virginia in a statement on March 28, 1945, before the Joint Committee on the Organization of Congress said in part:

> Under our Constitution legislation is supposed to be enacted by the Congress. I want to call your attention to what I assert to be a fact, that we now have not only legislation by the Congress, but we have four other types of legislation . . . We have legislation by sanctions; we have legislation by subsidies; we have legislation by executive regulations, under authority of Congress; and we have legislation by interpretation—interpretations that Congress never dreamed of when we enacted the law. I think that is of very grave moment . . . I do not think the American people realize to what extent our system of government is being changed by these innovations in the way of the four types of legislation that I have enumerated.

Nevertheless, Congress cannot be deprived of the right of legislating if it cares to assert itself; the utilization of this right depends upon the legislative leadership and how it equips itself to that end. Nothing except amendments to the Constitution can deprive either the House or Senate of the right of introducing and enacting bills or resolutions without limitation as to number or content. Any nullification of law written by Congress must come after the House and Senate have acted. The President's veto is not exercised until after Congressional action; the court may not interpret a law until it has been enacted and a case arises in pursuance of its application. On the other hand, within the realm of legislation, the Congress might undo by legislation anything done by the courts or administration.

Congress alone is authorized to amend, modify, or change existing statutes, or to enact a new one. Every bill enacted, however, must have the complete approval of both the House and Senate, including every word and even the punctuation thereof before it is sent to the President for his signature. The President only shares in lawmaking to the extent of signing bills or vetoing them, but Congress may override that veto by a two-thirds majority of each house. The influence that the Administration may exert in the determination of legislation is another thing.

While the functions of Congress include more than the enactment of bills or resolutions, the rules and regulations utilized by the House and Senate are primarily devoted to establishing a mode of procedure for the consideration and disposition of proposed legislation.

Forms and Kinds of Bills Introduced in Congress: All legislative proposals introduced in the House of Representatives take one of the following forms: H.R. *00*, H.J.Res. *00*, H. Con.Res. *00*, or H.Res. *00*; those introduced in the Senate take one of the following: S. *00*, S.J.Res. *00*, S.Con.Res. *00*, or S.Res. *00*. "All bills for raising revenue shall originate in the House of Representatives; but the Senate may propose or concur with amendments as on other bills," and this has been interpreted to include appropriation bills. Such bills can be introduced in the Senate, as is often the case, but if the Senate should pass them, the House would refuse them consideration, on the grounds that such action is an encroachment on its prerogatives. All other bills as to content may be originated in either house without encroachment on the prerogatives of the other.

Concurrent and simple resolutions, however, are not truly legislative proposals even though they are frequently closely connected therewith; they are also used in carrying out the other functions of Congress, mentioned subsequently.

(A) *In House*: H.R. *00*, abbreviation for House of Representatives, designates a *bill* originating in that body, as distinguished from a resolution. The bill may be public or private; no distinction is made in labeling public and private proposals. A bill bearing the designation H.R. *00*, when passed by both houses in identical form and signed by the President, becomes a public or private law, depending upon nature of content; when passed by the House alone and messaged to the Senate it no longer bears the designation "A Bill," from that stage until it goes to the White House, it bears the title "An Act."

H.J.Res. *00*, abbreviation for House Joint Resolution, designates that the resolution originated in the House. A joint resolution when passed by both the House and Senate in identical form, and

80TH CONGRESS
1ST SESSION

S. 1566

IN THE SENATE OF THE UNITED STATES

JULY 3 (legislative day, APRIL 21), 1947

Mr. WHERRY introduced the following bill; which was read twice and refer to the Committee on Armed Services

A BILL

To provide for greater efficiency of the military forces United States in occupied countries, and for other pur

1 Be it enacted by the Senate and House of R
2 tives of the United States of America in Congress
3 That (a) in order to alleviate conditions existing
4 foreign countries occupied by military forces
5 States, which might lead to uprising, rioting,
6 which might endanger the lives and security
7 such forces, and in order to aid in the restora

80TH CONGRESS
1ST SESSION

S. RES. 171

IN THE SENATE OF THE UNITED STATES

NOVEMBER 28 (legislative day, NOVEMBER 24), 1947

Mr. WILEY submitted the following resolution; which was referred to the Committee on Rules and Administration

RESOLUTION

1 Resolved, That the Senate Committee on Rules and
2 Administration, or any duly authorized subcommittee thereof,
3 is authorized and directed to make a study (1) of the
4 desirability and feasibility of installing a mechanical or
5 electrical device for automatically recording roll calls and
6 votes of the Senate and (2), if the installation of such a
7 device is recommended by the committee, of any changes
8 in the Rules of the Senate which might thereby be
9 necessitated.

80TH CONGRESS
1ST SESSION

S. CON. RES. 31

IN THE SENATE OF THE UNITED STATES

JULY 25 (legislative day, JULY 16), 1947

Mr. GURNEY, from the Committee on Armed Services, reported the following concurrent resolution; which was considered and agreed to

CONCURRENT RESOLUTION

1 Resolved by the Senate (the House of Representat
2 concurring), That the War Department, the Navy De
3 ment, and the War Assets Administration are requ
4 to delay until March 15, 1948, in reporting as surpl
5 in disposing of (1) any lands or permanent str
6 located thereon declared by any State, municipal,
7 government, or political subdivision thereof, thro
8 proper authorities, to be suitable and desirable fo
9 for educational, recreational, medical, or scientific

80TH CONGRESS
1ST SESSION

S. J. RES. 87

IN THE SENATE OF THE UNITED STATES

MARCH 14 (legislative day, FEBRUARY 19), 1947

Mr. FLANDERS introduced the following joint resolution; which was read twic and referred to the Committee on Foreign Relations

JOINT RESOLUTION

To prohibit shipment of goods to Russia until that country has fulfilled its obligations under the Yalta and Potsdam agreements.

1 Resolved by the Senate and House of Representatives
2 of the United States of America in Congress assembled,
3 That no further shipments of goods to the Union of Soviet
4 Socialist Republics, whether by private sale or pursuant to
5 agreements made with that country by the United States,
6 be permitted until that country has fulfilled the commitments

---

Sample Copy of First Page of a Senate Bill, a Senate Resolution, a Senate Concurrent Resolution, and a Senate Joint Resolution; House bills take the identical forms and are designated as H. R. —, H. Res. —, H. Con. Res. —, H. J. Res. —, in the House of Representatives.

signed by the President becomes a public or private law, depending upon nature of content, just as in the case of a bill. A joint resolution to amend the Constitution does not require the President's signature.

Theoretically, there is a difference between the content of a bill and the content of a joint resolution; practical usage has left little distinction. Commonly, joint resolutions are legislative proposals involving a single matter which in no way could be considered a comprehensive law. On the other hand, the contents of some House joint resolutions are totally indistinguishable from the contents of some bills bearing the label of H.R. *00*. In fact, the identical language is frequently introduced in both the form of H.R. *00* and H.J.Res. *00*. The most common usage of an H.J.Res. *00* is for continuing the life of an existing law. For example, the original Reciprocal Trade Agreements Act (H.R. 8687, of 73rd Congress, approved June 12, 1934) was introduced in the form of a House bill (H.R. *8687*). That public law authorized the President to enter into trade agreements for the duration of three years; subsequent extensions of that Act have been effected by passing House joint resolutions providing for such extensions.

H.Con.Res. *00* designates a House Concurrent Resolution. Before an H.Con.Res. *00* can become effective, it must have the concurrence of both houses. A concurrent resolution in practice comprehends the authority of Congress as distinguished from that of the Government; in practice it does not require the signature of the President. Legal authorities, however, have argued that whether or not a concurrent resolution requires the signature of the President depends upon the nature of the resolution.

Concurrent resolutions are commonly used by Congress to take a joint action, simply embodying a matter within the limited scope of Congress, to express its intent, purpose or sense. They are not used to enact legislation and are not binding or of legal effect. A common use of this instrument is to correct errors in enrolled bills. In the last several years, Congress has incorporated language in a number of laws authorizing Congress to repeal the law, in each instance, by use of the concurrent resolution, thereby making it possible for Congress to repeal a law by a majority vote since the concurrence of the President in the concurrent resolution would not be necessary (eliminating any veto possibility). Whether or not this use of the concurrent resolution is constitutional remains to be decided by the courts.

H.Res. *00* is an abbreviation for House Resolution. This type of resolution is known as a simple resolution and its authority extends only to that of the House itself. A simple resolution passed by the House does not require concurrence on the part of the Senate; the House action is final. Such simple resolutions are generally used to create special House investigating committees, to authorize the printing of special reports, or additional copies of hearings and reports, to request information from administrative agencies, or to express the will of the House on a particular matter.

(B) *In Senate*: S. *00* designates a *bill* originating in the Senate as distinguished from a resolution. A bill bearing the designation S. *00*, when passed by both houses in identical form and signed by the President, becomes a public or private law, depending upon nature of contents. When passed by the Senate alone and messaged to the House it no longer bears the designation "A Bill"; from that stage until it goes to the White House, it bears the title "An Act." See discussion of H.R. *00* which is also applicable to S. *00*.

S.J.Res. *00* is an abbreviation for Senate Joint Resolution, showing that it originated in the Senate. See discussion of H.J.Res. *00* which is also applicable to S.J.Res. *00*.

S.Con.Res. *00* is an abbreviation for Senate Concurrent Resolution, showing that it originated in the Senate. See discussion of H.Con.Res. *00* which is also applicable to S.Con.Res. *00*.

S.Res. *00* is the abbreviation for Senate Resolution, and action by the Senate on a S.Res. *00* is final. See also discussion of H.Res. *00* which is applicable to S.Res. *00*.

Legislation vs. Appropriations: All legislative proposals divide themselves into two classes, according to whether they provide for legislative authority or actually make an appropriation. In practice, Congress has defined and classified bills and joint resolutions into these two categories; each house has adopted rules and regulations which prohibit the inclusion of legislation in an appropriation bill or an appropriation in a legislative bill. Legislative authority must be enacted before an appropriation for that purpose may be made. To state it another way, if an appropriation bill contains legislation or a legislative bill contains an appropriation, such an attempt to mix the two is subject to a point of order, and action on the part of one Member in either house may prohibit or eliminate the same; this is also true in case an attempt is made to appropriate before enacting the legislative authority. Any of these limitations or procedural restrictions, nevertheless, can be ignored by suspending the rules, which requires a two-thirds vote, by unanimous consent, or in the absence of any opposition. In the House, they can be suspended by use of a special rule reported by the Rules Committee which requires a majority vote. Likewise, an action by one house contrary to such procedure is honored by the other.

The legislative activity of every session is tremendous. Each Congress enacts hundreds of laws, the number varying according to the needs and conditions; thousands of bills and resolutions are introduced. Every session finds the House and Senate enacting at least twelve appropriation bills, and sometimes twice that number, and two or three hundred legislative proposals.

To do this requires endless committee meetings, hearing hundreds of witnesses, and receiving testimony involving thousands of printed pages; the preparation and filing of reports to accompany the bills explaining them; the making of investigations of various types to aid in the enactment of better legislation; and the study and debate of bills in both houses in the various forms they take before clearing both bodies in an identical form. All of this involves the writing and printing of a small library of information during the course of a session or in a period of a year.

To give some definite information on recent sessions note the following data on House and Senate bills and resolutions:

Congress	Number of Bills and Resolutions Introduced	Number of Reports Filed	Total Number of Laws Enacted
78-1	6,539	1,610	384
78-2	2,996	1,882	773
79-1	8,113	2,358	658
79-2	3,543	2,299	967
80-1	7,970	2,043	526
80-2	4,099	2,190	837

(2) To Propose Amendments to the Constitution

Article V stipulates that: "The Congress, whenever two-thirds of both houses shall deem it necessary, shall propose amendments

32223

to this Constitution . . . which . . . shall be valid to all intents and purposes, as part of this Constitution, when ratified by the legislatures of three-fourths of the several States or by conventions in three-fourths thereof as the one or the other mode of ratification may be proposed by the Congress."

The procedure for passing a joint resolution proposing an amendment to the Constitution is the same as that for enacting a law. All proposals to amend the Constitution are introduced in the form of House or Senate joint resolutions and when passed by the House and Senate in identical form by a two-thirds majority vote, they are submitted through the Secretary of State to the various States for ratification. They are not submitted to the President for his signature.

This prerogative of Congress has been seldom exercised, the Constitution having been amended only twenty-one times, with the Twenty-First repealing the Eighteenth Amendment. Others have been approved by Congress but never ratified by the States as was the case with the child labor proposal in 1924. Many proposed amendments have been introduced. From 1789 through January 3, 1941 a total of 4,020 such resolutions were introduced in the two houses, with 740 of them having been thrown in the "hopper" from 1926 to 1941.[2] From 1926 to 1941 there was a numerically strong support for the proposals to tax incomes from governmental securities and salaries, to grant the public a referendum on matters pertaining to war, and to accomplish what later became the twentieth and twenty-first amendments. Other proposals include: limitation on length of service of President and Vice President, granting the President item veto power in appropriation bills, equal rights for men and women, uniform marriage and divorce laws, national representation for the District of Columbia, fixing number and tenure of service of members of the Supreme Court and clarifying the court's power to rule over the constitutionality of legislative acts, enlarge upon the general welfare clause of the Constitution, and to extend the term of office for members of the House of Representatives to four years.

(3) To Direct or Influence Public Opinion

Congress is not charged by the Constitution in so many words to direct or influence public opinion. On the other hand, one of

---

[2] These data are according to a pamphlet issued by the Secretary of the Senate.

the inherent duties of a legislative body is to debate informatively the current legislative proposals. In so doing, it serves as an aid in educating and crystallizing opinions entertained by the people. Congress is a public forum where informed opinions are expressed, policies discussed, and the conduct of the Government exposed and commended or criticized. With the aid of the instrumentalities disseminating information, all activity and debate by the Members of Congress are brought directly to the attention of the people. One must not minimize the importance of Congress in serving as a clearing house of economic, social, and cultural information.

Congress is designed to represent the people, but its membership is not just a weather vane to point the direction of public clamor. Depending on the ability of the individual Members and caliber of the leadership, the people are inclined to give their opinions a decided deference over general opinions, all of which go into the making of public opinion, be it informed or otherwise. History reveals that our national development has been closely tied to the emphasized opinions in Congress.

(4) To Function as a Board of Directors to the Government and People

Investigation of Administration: The supervision of the Administration has always been an important Congressional function, starting off in the very beginning with the rift between Congress and Secretary of the Treasury Hamilton. Congressional investigations and supervision of the Administration have always been emphasized and increased in times of emergencies, as exemplified at the time of the Civil War and in recent years. To perform in this capacity, however, most of the work is undertaken by committees, agents of the parent bodies. The efforts of the House and Senate must of necessity be limited to approval of resolutions authorizing committees or subcommittees to investigate and supervise administrative activity, or by adding restrictive amendments to laws and decreasing or limiting expenditures of funds. Viewing the Administration from this angle also informs the membership as to the needs for constructive legislation.

"Each standing committee of the Senate, including any subcommittee of any such committee, is authorized to hold such hearings, to sit and act at such times and places during the sessions,

prepared legislation, respectively; this has been the accepted conception particularly in the case of the two Committees on Expenditures in the Executive Departments. Nevertheless, such supervision has been periodic and superficial. Certainly, the standing committees as a whole have never been equipped to assume such an undertaking, at least until the Reorganization Act was passed; it is still doubtful if that can be done with the present limited staffs. If the professional personnel of each committee is selected after careful scrutiny and the process of sifting continues until good staffs have been selected, Congress will have gone a long way in equipping itself not only to supervise the work of the Administration, but to enact better legislation.

Administrative Reports to Congress: The power of requiring periodic or special reports describing executive performances is a significant club for Congress to hold over the Administration. Better results are likely to be obtained from requests for special reports than from the reports requested quarterly or annually as stipulated in statutes. These regular reports become habits, with great numbers of them being published every year [6] and the agencies concerned setting up staffs sufficient to prepare long and convincing results, but usually without giving much information needful to Congress in writing better legislation. In fact, Congressmen usually find them dull and without sufficient interest to merit even a casual examination.

Inquiry Resolutions: Resolutions of inquiry requesting information from executive departments are seldom utilized. When the party in control of the two houses is the same as that of the President, few such resolutions can be expected. The fear of embarrassment is too great.

Work of Committees on Appropriations: The Committees on Appropriations are in strategical positions to do the most in the field of supervision of the Administration. These committees must work closely with all of the departments and agencies, making a review of funds needed and spent by each division of the Government at least once a year. Congress has the authority (usually following the recommendations of the two Appropriations Committees) to determine the amount of money to be appropriated for each purpose. Since 1921, in accordance with the Budget and Accounting Act, an annual Budget Message is

[6] See "Reports to be made to Congress," 77-1, House Document 40.

submitted to Congress by the President, setting forth in detail the estimates of appropriations needed for the next fiscal year to defray the cost of operating the Government. While the committees give deference to the recommendations of the Bureau of the Budget, and follow them with slight variances here and there, Congress is free to appropriate more than the estimates call for, refuse to appropriate any funds at all for purposes requested, or modify the requests in any way it sees fit; it may appropriate the amount of money requested but place such limitations on the use of the funds that the hands of the agency concerned will be tied tightly. There are hardly any limits to the conditions under which the money might be appropriated. Should a condition written by Congress be called unconstitutional, that does not have to be the final answer; Congress can refuse funds altogether.

Preventive Medicine: It should be emphasized that the authority Congress has to make investigations and to supervise administrative activity serves as a preventive medicine; it blocks cankerous growths in the form of public scandals from ever getting started.

Serving Their Constituencies: Close to the supervision of the Administration is tied the work of individual Members of the House and Senate to get consideration for their constituents or for group interests. Whether or not the end results are good or bad depend somewhat on the wisdom exercised by the Member making the requests; when used within the realm of good judgment, it has a tendency to make the Administration responsive and alert to the will of the people. In performing in this capacity, Congress reflects State and local interests and plays the part of a mediator between the people and a hard-fixed Administration.

(5) To Count Electoral Votes

Electors and Certificates of Election: The counting of the electoral vote is a routine assignment for Congress; nevertheless, it must be performed every fourth year.

A statute of 1934 provides that the electors shall meet on the "first Monday after the second Wednesday in December" and vote by ballot for the President and Vice President.[7] Six sets of certificates of the votes are made and signed, and cast by the electors of each State. Each certificate consists of two lists of votes, one for the President and the other for the Vice President. One set of these certificates with the attached list of electors' names is sent by registered mail to the President of the Senate; two are delivered to the Secretary of State of the State in which the voting occurred; two are sent by registered mail to the Secretary of State at Washington; and one is delivered to the Federal judge of the district in which the electors voted. If these records are not sent to the President of the Senate in due time, the President of the Senate may send for them.[8] The set of votes sent to the Vice President is opened and counted by Congress in joint session.[9]

Procedure for Electoral Count: The procedure of these sessions is generally the same and only a matter of routine. The Doorkeeper announces the Vice President and the Senate membership upon arrival; the Senators enter preceded by the Sergeant at Arms and headed by the Vice President and the Secretary of the Senate; Members and officers of the House rise to receive them.[10] The Vice President, as President of the Senate, presides at the meeting; he sits in the Speaker's chair with the Speaker immediately on his left. The Senators sit in the body of the Hall in the front seats, and the Representatives take the remaining ones. Debate is not in order at this meeting.

In the 1945 electoral count Vice President Truman presided, and the proceedings of that meeting as printed in the *Record* follow:

COUNTING THE ELECTORAL VOTE

At 12 o'clock and 56 minutes p. m., the Doorkeeper, Mr. Ralph R. Roberts, announced the Vice President of the United States and the Senate of the United States.

[7] 48 Stat. 1, p. 879. The electors are chosen on the first Tuesday after the first Monday in November every fourth year, from the last presidential election. The States are free to define the process of choosing the electors with a few exceptions stipulated in the Constitution. The electors vote for the Presidential and Vice-Presidential candidates, one of whom must not be an inhabitant of the same state as the other. The Constitution debars any one from holding an office of trust and profit under the United States from being an elector. Congress may determine the time of choosing electors and the day on which they shall give their vote.
[8] Cannon, VI, 441.
[9] See Cannon, VI, 442-446; Hinds, III, 1928-1963.
[10] The galleries are no longer reserved for the families of the Members but are given to guests by special cards.

The Senate entered the Hall, headed by the Vice President of the United States and the Secretary of the Senate, the Members and officers of the House rising to receive them.

The Vice President took his seat as the presiding officer of the joint convention of the two Houses, the Speaker of the House occupying the chair on his left.

The VICE PRESIDENT. Mr. Speaker and gentlemen of the Congress, the Senate and the House of Representatives, pursuant to the requirements of the Constitution and laws of the United States, have met in joint session for the purpose of opening the certificates and ascertaining and counting the votes of the electors of the several States for President and Vice President. Under well-established precedent, unless a motion shall be made in any case, the reading of the formal portions of the certificates will be dispensed with. After ascertainment has been made that the certificates are authentic and correct in form, the tellers will count and make a list of the votes cast by the electors of the several States.

The tellers, Mr. Green and Mr. Austin, on the part of the Senate, and Mr. Worley and Mr. Gamble, on the part of the House, took their places at the desk.

The VICE PRESIDENT. The Chair hands to the tellers the certificates of the electors for President and Vice President of the State of Alabama, and they will count and make a list of the votes cast by that State.

MR. GREEN (one of the tellers). Mr. President, the certificate of the electoral vote of the State of Alabama seems to be regular in form and authentic, and it appears therefrom that Franklin Delano Roosevelt, of the State of New York, received 11 votes for President, and Harry S. Truman, of the State of Missouri, received 11 votes for Vice President.

The tellers then proceeded to read, count, and announce, as was done in the case of Alabama, the electoral votes of the several States in an alphabetical order.

The VICE PRESIDENT. Gentlemen of the Congress, the certificates of all of the States have now been opened and read, and the tellers will make final ascertainment of the result and deliver the same to the Vice President.

The tellers delivered to the Vice President the following statement of the results:

The undersigned, Theodore Francis Green and Warren R. Austin, tellers on the part of the Senate, Eugene Worley and Ralph A. Gamble, tellers on the part of the House of Representatives, report the following as the result of the ascertainment and counting of the electoral vote for President and Vice President of the United States for the term beginning on the 20th day of January 1945:

		For President		For Vice President	
Electoral votes of each State	States	Franklin D. Roosevelt, of New York	Thomas E. Dewey, of New York	Harry S. Truman, of Missouri	John W. Bricker, of Ohio
11	Alabama	11	0	11	0
4	Arizona	4	0	4	0
9	Arkansas	9	0	9	0
25	California	25	0	25	0

6	Colorado	0	6	0	6
8	Connecticut	8	0	8	0
3	Delaware	3	0	3	0
8	Florida	8	0	8	0
12	Georgia	12	0	12	0
4	Idaho	4	0	4	0
28	Illinois	28	0	28	0
13	Indiana	0	13	0	13
10	Iowa	0	10	0	10
8	Kansas	0	8	0	8
11	Kentucky	11	0	11	0
10	Louisiana	10	0	10	0
5	Maine	0	5	0	5
8	Maryland	8	0	8	0
16	Massachusetts	16	0	16	0
19	Michigan	19	0	19	0
11	Minnesota	11	0	11	0
9	Mississippi	9	0	9	0
15	Missouri	15	0	15	0
4	Montana	4	0	4	0
6	Nebraska	0	6	0	6
3	Nevada	3	0	3	0
4	New Hampshire	4	0	4	0
16	New Jersey	16	0	16	0
4	New Mexico	4	0	4	0
47	New York	47	0	47	0
14	North Carolina	14	0	14	0
4	North Dakota	0	4	0	4
25	Ohio	0	25	0	25
10	Oklahoma	10	0	10	0
6	Oregon	6	0	6	0
35	Pennsylvania	35	0	35	0
4	Rhode Island	4	0	4	0
8	South Carolina	8	0	8	0
4	South Dakota	0	4	0	4
12	Tennessee	12	0	12	0
23	Texas	23	0	23	0
4	Utah	4	0	4	0
3	Vermont	0	3	0	3
11	Virginia	11	0	11	0
8	Washington	8	0	8	0
8	West Virginia	8	0	8	0
12	Wisconsin	0	12	0	12
3	Wyoming	0	3	0	3
531	Total	432	99	432	99

. THEODORE FRANCIS GREEN,
WARREN R. AUSTIN,
    Tellers on the part of the Senate
EUGENE WORLEY,
RALPH A. GAMBLE,
    Tellers on the part of the House of Representatives

The state of the vote for President of the United States, as delivered to the President of the Senate, is as follows:

The whole number of electors appointed for President of the United States is 531, of which a majority is 266.

Franklin D. Roosevelt, of the State of New York, has received for President of the United States 432 votes;

Thomas E. Dewey, of the State of New York, has received 99 votes.

The state of the vote for Vice President of the United States, as delivered to the President of the Senate, is as follows:

The whole number of the electors appointed to vote for Vice President of the United States is 531 of which a majority is 266.

Harry S. Truman, of the State of Missouri, has received for Vice President of the United States 432 votes;

John W. Bricker, of the State of Ohio, has received 99 votes.

This announcement of the state of the vote by the President of the Senate shall be deemed a sufficient declaration of the persons elected President and Vice President of the United States, each for the term beginning on the twentieth day of January, 1945, and shall be entered, together with a list of the votes, on the Journals of the Senate and House of Representatives.

The VICE PRESIDENT. Gentlemen, the purpose for which the joint session of the two Houses of Congress has been called, pursuant to Senate Concurrent Resolution 1, having been accomplished, the Chair declares the joint session dissolved.[11]

(6) Election of President and Vice President by Congress

The task of electing a President or Vice President as defined by the Twelfth and Twentieth amendments to the Constitution has not fallen on Congress in recent times. Only two elections of the President have been thrown into the House and one election of the Vice President has devolved upon the Senate.[12] In the case of the President, if no person receives a majority, the Twelfth Amendment provides:

. . . then from the persons having the highest numbers not exceeding three on the list of those voted for as President, the House of Representatives shall choose immediately, by ballot, the President. But in choosing the President, the votes shall be taken by states, the representation from each state having one vote; a quorum for this purpose shall consist of a member or members from two-thirds of the states, and a majority of all the states shall be necessary to a choice. [And if the House of Representatives shall not choose a President whenever the right of choice shall devolve upon them, before the fourth day of March next following, then the Vice-President shall act as President, as in the case of the death or other constitutional disability of the President.] [13]—The person having the greatest number of votes as Vice-President, shall be the Vice-President, if such number be a majority of the whole number of electors appointed, and if no person have a majority, then from the two highest numbers on the list, the Senate shall choose the Vice-President; a quorum for the purpose shall consist of two-thirds of the whole number of Senators, and a majority of the whole

---

[11] See C.R., 79-1, No. 3 for January 6, 1945, pp. 90-91.

[12] See the Presidential elections of 1800 and 1824; in 1837 the Senate elected a Vice President (Hinds, III, 1941).

[13] The clause in brackets was superseded by section 3 of XXth Amendment which is quoted also.

number shall be necessary to a choice. But no person constitutionally ineligible to the office of President shall be eligible to that of Vice-President of the United States.

The 20th Amendment supersedes that section of the 12th Amendment having to do with date of election. Sections 3 and 4 of the 20th, which is applicable, is quoted here:

If, at the time fixed for the beginning of the term of the President, the President elect shall have died, the Vice-President elect shall become President. If a President shall not have been chosen before the time fixed for the beginning of his term, or if the President elect shall have failed to qualify, then the Vice-President elect shall act as President until a President shall have qualified; and the Congress may by law provide for the case wherein neither a President elect nor a Vice-President elect shall have qualified, declaring who shall then act as President, or the manner in which one who is to act shall be selected, and such person shall act accordingly until a President or Vice-President shall have qualified.

The Congress may by law provide for the case of the death of any of the persons from whom the House of Representatives may choose a President whenever the right of choice shall have devolved upon them, and for the case of the death of any of the persons from whom the Senate may choose a Vice-President whenever the right of choice shall have devolved upon them.

(7) Impeachment Proceedings

House Impeaches: The Constitution reads: "The President, Vice President, and all civil officers of the United States, shall be removed from office on impeachment for, and conviction of, treason, bribery, or other high crimes and misdemeanors." [14] Judges, at least theoretically, are not subject to impeachment for rendering erroneous decisions, but the House impeached President Johnson for "crimes not indictable." There has been a division of opinion as to whether or not an officer may be impeached for crimes not of a criminal nature; and there are arguments for and against impeaching a judge or other officers for offenses committed prior to accepting office. In the twelve impeachment cases tried by the Senate, "the articles of impeachment as presented by the House in every impeachment except those of Blount and Belknap included other than indictable offenses." [15]

The sole power of impeachment, however, is conferred on the House of Representatives, and there is no appeal from its deci-

[14] Article II, section 4.
[15] Haynes, *The Senate of the United States*, II, p. 860; for other precedents see Hinds and Cannon's Precedents, Volumes III and VI.

sion. Even if the Senate should find the person not guilty that would not alter the fact that he had been impeached by the House.

Impeachments Set in Motion: There has been a wide variance in the manner in which preliminary investigations for impeachment have been set in motion. Proceedings may be started in one of several different ways. Investigations with a view to impeachment have been invoked by one person introducing a formal statement or a resolution, by letter or by a message from the President, by an act of a grand jury forwarded to Congress from a territorial legislature, by a memorial setting forth certain charges, by a resolution authorizing a general investigation of the execution of laws, and by the introduction of a resolution referred to the Judiciary Committee.

Privileged Motion: Any motion proposing an impeachment is highly privileged [16] and permits the proponent recognition for one hour of debate at the time submitted, if in the form of a written resolution.[17] A motion loses this preference, however, when it only proposes an investigation to see whether or not an officer should be impeached.

Resignation: Impeachment proceedings begun are generally terminated if the officer against whom invoked dies or resigns, but not necessarily so. A person may be impeached after resignation, and he does not avoid punishment by resignation.

Procedure: The precedents and practices established in impeachments have not been uniform. A compendium of the procedure most frequently used,[18] variations from which are not particularly significant, includes an introduction in the House of the impeachment charges which are then referred to the Judiciary Committee, or to a special investigating committee. The Judiciary Committee, if the matter is referred to it, instead of creating a select committee for the occasion, considers the charges to decide whether a formal investigation should be ordered, whether the case should be dropped, or whether evidence already in possession is sufficient to justify an immediate impeachment. Any report from the Judiciary Committee is usually acted on by the

---

[16] Impeachment may interrupt the reading of the Journal or business considered under the unanimous consent.

[17] Cannon, VI, 468, 470.

[18] See Alexander Simpson, Jr., *A Treatise on Federal Impeachments;* Hinds III, 2001-2520; Cannon, VI, 454-552.

The principles for conducting an impeachment case laid down here are mainly based on the proceedings of the Judge Swayne and Judge Louderback cases, rather typical cases (See Cannon, VI, 467; Cannon, VI, 513-524; Hinds, III, 2469-2485). Several impeachment charges have been referred to special committees.

House in due time. A report to impeach will be disposed of
without delay or further investigation. If the committee recommends further investigation and the same is adopted by the House,
or if the House decides upon an investigation, the same committee
or a committee created for that purpose will carry out the assignment. Any report returned will be acted on by the House as it
sees fit; it may ignore the majority report and adopt the minority
report, lay the report on the table, or even refuse to dispose of it.[19]
Should the committee refuse to make a report, the House may
discharge it and proceed to impeach.

Drafting Articles: If a resolution to impeach is adopted and
articles have not been already drafted, a select committee is appointed to prepare the articles of impeachment.[20] The members
of the committee may be appointed by the Speaker or by resolution, and the entire committee may be composed of persons favoring the impeachment and of the majority party.[21] In order to
guarantee complete and authentic articles, the House usually
grants the committee the right to compel testimony.

Consideration of Articles and Appointment of Managers:
Articles, returned to the House by the committee, may or may
not be first considered in the Committee of the Whole. When
articles of impeachment have been adopted, managers are selected
to direct the impeachment proceedings in the Senate in behalf
of the House. The managers have been selected in three different ways: (1) by resolution authorizing the Speaker to appoint
managers, fixing their number, (2) by resolution naming both
the number and the persons of the committee, (3) and by election by ballot with a majority vote for each candidate.[22]

The managers should represent the sentiment of the House
since they are the only official representatives of the House at
the trial; the minority party should be given some representation.
Managers may be excused from serving by permission of the
House.

[19] See Cannon, VI, 514-541.
[20] Hinds, III, 2297, 2472. In some cases the Speaker has appointed a select committee to inform the Senate of the impeachment, telling the Senate that the House
will later present the articles of impeachment.
[21] Hinds, III, 2387, 2412.
[22] Cannon, VI, 467; see also Hinds, III, 2323, 2345, 2368, 2412, 2417, 2475, 2448.
A form of the resolution authorizing the Speaker to appoint the managers is as
follows:
"Resolved, That seven managers be appointed by the Speaker of the House to
conduct the impeachment against Charles Swayne, judge of the district court of the
United States in and for the northern district of Florida."

Senate Informed: The Senate is duly informed of each impeachment in advance of trial by message or by special committee selected for that purpose. In the case of Judge Swayne, the chairman of the committee chosen to inform the Senate of the impeachment, appeared in the Senate with his committee and addressed the Vice President thus:

Mr. President, in obedience to the order of the House of Representatives we appear before you, and in the name of the House of Representatives and of all the people of the United States of America we do impeach Charles Swayne, judge of the district court of the United States for the northern district of Florida, of high crimes and misdemeanors in office; and we do further inform the Senate that the House of Representatives will in due time exhibit articles of impeachment against him and make good the same. And in their name we demand that the Senate shall take order for the appearance of the said Charles Swayne to answer the said impeachment.[23]

Senate Receives the Managers: After delivering the message, the managers withdrew from the Senate and reported their actions to the House.[24] The Senate refers the case to a select committee which returns a report on preparation for the trial to the Senate. The Senate keeps the House informed of its progress toward the trial and when all is in readiness for it, the Secretary of the Senate informs the House that the Senate is ready to receive the managers for the trial. At the designated time, the managers appear in the Senate and are introduced at the bar of the Senate by the Sergeant at Arms. The Sergeant at Arms is then ordered by the Vice President to make the proclamation, as follows:

Hear ye, hear ye, hear ye. All persons will keep silence, on pain of imprisonment, while the House of Representatives is exhibiting to the Senate of the United States articles of impeachment against Charles Swayne, judge of the district court of the United States for the northern district of Florida.
Mr. Manager Palmer. Mr. President.
The President Pro Tempore. Mr. Manager.
Mr. Manager Palmer. The managers on the part of the House of Representatives are ready to exhibit articles of impeachment against Charles Swayne, district judge of the United States in and for the northern district of Florida, as directed by the House, in the words and figures following: . . .[25]

Attendance at Trial: Although the entire House membership may attend the trials, it is not always done;[26] it frequently at-

---

[23] Hinds, III, 2473. The House resolution of the impeachment had already been read to the Senate by the Chief Clerk of the Senate.
[24] If the Senate is informed by message these steps are avoided.
[25] Hinds, III, 2476, 2295, 2385, 2390. The articles are signed by the Speaker of the House (Hinds, III, 2302, 2390).
[26] If the House attends, the membership might be announced upon entering.

38 THE UNITED STATES CONGRESS

tends for any important decisions. The managers are the representatives of the House at the trial, and the impeachment arguments may be opened and closed by them.

Procedure: The Constitution rather briefly states that "The Senate shall have the sole power to try all impeachments. When sitting for that purpose, they shall be on oath or affirmation." The Senate, however, has twenty-five special rules to define the procedure for impeachment trials. The more descriptive ones include:

I. Whensoever the Senate shall receive notice from the House of Representatives that managers are appointed on their part to conduct an impeachment against any person and are directed to carry articles of impeachment to the Senate, the Secretary of the Senate shall immediately inform the House of Representatives that the Senate is ready to receive the managers for the purpose of exhibiting such articles of impeachment, agreeably to such notice.

II. When the managers of an impeachment shall be introduced at the bar of the Senate and shall signify that they are ready to exhibit articles of impeachment against any person, the Presiding Officer of the Senate shall direct the Sergeant at Arms to make proclamation, who shall, after making proclamation, repeat the following words, viz: "All persons are commanded to keep silence, on pain of imprisonment, while the House of Representatives is exhibiting to the Senate of the United States articles of impeachment against ——————;" after which the articles shall be exhibited, and then the Presiding Officer of the Senate shall inform the managers that the Senate will take proper order on the subject of the impeachment, of which due notice shall be given to the House of Representatives.

III. Upon such articles being presented to the Senate, the Senate shall, at 1 o'clock afternoon of the day (Sunday excepted) following such presentation, or sooner if ordered by the Senate, proceed to the consideration of such articles . . . .

IV. When the President of the United States or the Vice President of the United States, upon whom the powers and duties of the office of President shall have devolved, shall be impeached, the Chief Justice of the Supreme Court of the United States shall preside; and in a case requiring the said Chief Justice to preside notice shall be given to him by the Presiding Officer of the Senate of the time and place fixed for the consideration of the articles of impeachment . . . .

XII. At 12:30 o'clock afternoon of the day appointed for the trial of an impeachment, the legislative and executive business of the Senate shall be suspended, and the Secretary shall give notice to the House of Representatives that the Senate is ready to proceed upon the impeachment of ——————, in the Senate Chamber, which chamber is prepared with accommodations for the reception of the House of Representatives.

XIII. The hour of the day at which the Senate shall sit upon the trial of an impeachment shall be (unless otherwise ordered) 12 o'clock m.; and when the hour for such thing shall arrive, the Presiding Officer of the Senate shall so announce; . . .[27]

[27] *Senate Manual*, 80-1, pp. 101-112.

The Senate is urged by the rules to proceed with the trial from day to day until finished. Oaths, orders, mandates, writs, precepts authorized by the Senate, rulings on the procedure, and the like are made and issued by the Presiding Officer. The Senate shall have power to force any needed attendance and punish for disorder and so forth. " . . . The Presiding Officer of the Senate, upon the order of the Senate, shall appoint a committee of twelve Senators to receive evidence and take testimony at such times and places as the committee may determine, . . . but nothing herein shall prevent the Senate from sending for any witness and hearing his testimony in open Senate, or by order of the Senate having the entire trial in open Senate." [28]

When any trial begins, a writ of summons shall be issued and delivered to the accused, giving him all details. If the accused fails to appear " . . . the trial shall proceed, nevertheless, as upon a plea of not guilty." [29] In the Senate chamber an oath shall be administered to the accused [30] and all other persons called to the witness stand. The impeached person is tried very much as any person in a court room is tried for a criminal offense. Records just as in the case of a legislative session are kept of the proceedings. All remarks are addressed to the Presiding Officer as in regular procedure.

Voting: After the trial, a separate vote is taken on each article and if a two-thirds vote is not forthcoming on any one of them, the accused is acquitted. One article convicts, and the judgment is deposited in the office of the Secretary of State.

Trials: In practice, the Senate has sat as a court on twelve different occasions of impeachment with these results: four persons were removed from office, one person resigned, one case was dismissed for want of jurisdiction, and six persons were acquitted.[31]

House Informed of Senate Action: The Senate informs the House through the managers, the chairman of the Committee of the Whole, or by report, of its final decision; [32] it may inform the House of each day's sitting. All reports by the managers may be verbal or written.

[28] *Ibid.*, pp. 105-106.
[29] *Ibid.*, p. 104.
[30] *Ibid.*, 104-105.
[31] *Congressional Directory*, 80-1, p. 243.
[32] The House attended the final hearing of Pickering's impeachment to hear judgment against him.

(8) Senate to Advise and Consent to Treaties and to Confirm Certain Nominations

The Constitution provides that the President shall have power, "by and with the advice and consent of the Senate, to make Treaties, provided two-thirds of the Senators present concur; and he shall nominate, and by and with the advice and consent of the Senate, shall appoint Ambassadors, other public Ministers and Consuls, Judges of the Supreme Court, and all other Officers of the United States, whose appointments are not herein otherwise provided for, and which shall be established by law; but the Congress may by Law vest the Appointment of such inferior Officers, as they think proper, in the President alone, in the Courts of Law, or in the Heads of Departments." [33]

The President submits treaties and nominations to the Senate in pursuance of this clause and the Senate approves or disapproves of them under a procedure much the same as that used for disposition of proposed legislation. Disposition of this business is discussed at more length under Chapter X on Senate Procedure, pp. 331-340.

(9) To Manage Its Own Housekeeping

The Constitution authorizes Congress to enact necessary laws providing for its own maintenances, and specifies that "Each House may determine the rules of its proceedings, punish its Members for disorderly behavior, and, with the concurrence of two-thirds, expel a Member." Each is charged with keeping a journal of its proceedings, and "from time to time publish the same, excepting such parts as may in their judgment require secrecy; and the yeas and nays of the Members of either House on any question shall, at the desire of one-fifth of those present, be entered on the Journal."

"Neither House, during the Session of Congress, shall, without the consent of the other, adjourn for more than three days, nor to any other place than that in which the two houses shall be sitting.

"The Senators and Representatives shall receive a compensation for their services, to be ascertained by laws, and paid out of the Treasury. . . . "

[33] Article II, section 2 of the Constitution.

Thus, the House and Senate have established various procedures to serve as guides in the performance of their duties. This volume is devoted primarily to an explanation of the endless rules, regulations, and precedents adopted by the two houses, which they use to keep their houses in order. Each has a printed manual of rules of proceedings as well as compilations of precedents to serve as guides.

(10) Presidential Messages and Formal Ceremonies

The President "shall from time to time give to the Congress information of the State of the Union, and recommend to their consideration such measures as he shall judge necessary and expedient; he may, on extraordinary occasions, convene both Houses, or either of them . . . " Most of the messages from the President are sent down on paper and referred to proper committees for study just as proposed pieces of legislation, but the President may care to deliver the message in person; in which case, he always addresses the two houses in joint session, in the House chamber. Those in attendance are seated in the order prescribed for the electoral count except that the Cabinet members are present, seated in the first row next to the "well" of the House. The Presiding Officer of the body extending the invitation presides; the Vice President, however, sits on the right of the Speaker at all joint meetings.

The President, upon entering the hall, is immediately introduced, and delivers the address. When the message has been concluded, the President and Cabinet withdraw from the floor, followed by the Senators and their Presiding Officer, and the meeting is dissolved. The Speaker then assumes charge and calls the House to order for purposes of adjourning or to continue any business which might be before the House at the particular time.

The seating arrangements for all ceremonial joint sessions are very similar to the sessions for electoral count and to hear the President. If the Supreme Court and the Cabinet officers are guests for the occasion, they sit in the front rows on the right hand side of the hall with the Senators. The Justices are received after the Senators.

Chapter III

Political Organization of the Two Houses

Introduction

Party Government: Congress is not only bicameral, but it also operates under a two-party system. At the polls every two years it is determined which of the two parties is to control the legislative procedure in the House and Senate; and consequently, at that time the people give, in effect, a mandate to the membership as to the legislation the new Congress should consider.

Political and Parliamentary Machines: To carry out the will of the voters, both bodies have developed through the years, with variations of course, a parliamentary legislative machine and a political legislative machine, each of which is controlled by the party commanding the most votes; the two are just as distinct as are the two coordinate branches of Congress.

The two political parties are commonly referred to as the majority and the minority. The majority always assumes control of procedure and concomitantly accepts the responsibility for what is done or what is not done.

This chapter is devoted to a mention of the political legislative machines of the two parties. The parliamentary legislative machines are subject to control by the political, however, being composed of members of both parties in ratio to their respective party strength. The source of party strength over Representatives and Senators of the same political faith is through the use of party organization and incentives. Each member of Congress is concerned with his position in the legislative machine, his ability to get legislation enacted expressing his own political faith, and the power and prestige "in the affairs of the nation" derived from being one of the political group. Political machines must be set up around incentives; Members generally adhere to their party's program and points of view unless their constituents demand sufficiently to the contrary, or unless their own individual convictions dictate otherwise. Customarily, Representatives and Senators acquiesce in the wishes of their political leadership which derives its strength through the party organization.

When the majority party controls both the executive and legislative branches of the government, the President, as the titular head of the party, is able to assist and work with the legislative majority. The Administration, when of the same political faith as that of the majority of Congress, can do a lot to "cement" the party membership together through leadership, administrative controls, and through favors, appointments, and the like available to the Administration. With a well-geared machine, the Executive and Congress are able to work with dispatch and with efficiency, enhancing the position of the political party in power. The President is then able successfully to aid in the preparation of the legislative program. In discharging this duty imposed by the Constitution, he is required "from time to time to give to the Congress information of the state of the Union, and recommend to their consideration such measures as he shall judge necessary and expedient."

When the legislative branch is controlled by one party and the executive by another, the legislative program develops usually without too much cooperation between the Congress and the Executive. The latter, however, waives none of his constitutional prerogatives with respect to recommending legislation. Responsibility for enactment of legislation asked by the President under any circumstances remains with the Congress, as representative of the people.

House and Senate Political Machinery

Two Party Machines: The memberships of the House and Senate divide and organize themselves along party lines into the two major political parties: Republicans and Democrats. Each party of both houses organizes itself into caucuses or conferences so as to act on all legislative matters in unison. In each session of Congress a number of political battles are staged, battles which each party desires to win, but which are won by the party controlling the greatest number of Representatives and Senators. Consequently, impelled by the desire to command a majority, each party encourages the election of members of its own political faith from as many States and districts as possible at each general election as well as in special elections, particularly when a special election is expected to reveal something of the political trends. Activity toward that objective is concentrated and directed through selected Representatives and Senators of each party, operating as committees and known as Republican and Democratic Congressional and Senatorial campaign committees. Any third parties are generally so small in number that it would be impracticable to set up such national committees.

Congressional Campaign Committees: In the House both the Democrats and Republicans have a campaign committee. The Republicans organized their first permanent Congressional campaign committee in 1912; the Democrats in 1915. Both committees maintain their offices in Washington. Each "group" is composed of one member from every State having a Representative who is a member of its party, but only one, even if the State delegation is solidly of the same party. States having both Republican and Democratic Representatives will be represented on both committees.

The State delegations of each party, acting separately, choose one of their number to represent them for two years in their respective party campaign committee. The members of each committee thus elected meet separately to organize themselves.

The Democrats elect directly from among their number a chairman and three vice chairmen, an executive committee of seven, a finance committee of seven, and a speaker's committee (speaker's bureau) varying in number from one Congress to another. The chairmen and vice chairmen are elected by the whole membership of the Democratic Congressional Campaign Committee and the members of the executive, the finance, and speaker's committees are appointed by the chairman in pursuance of custom. The total membership of that committee was 37, in the 80th Congress, first session. The committee works on a coordinate basis with the Democratic National Committee, not as its subordinate.

The Republican Congressional Campaign Committee organizes itself by electing from among its membership a chairman and four vice chairmen who serve ex-officio on an executive committee consisting of themselves, together with five additional members, appointed by the chairman also from among the members of the full committee. Each member of the full committee, in voting on any question presented to them for determination, has the voting power equal to the number of his State delegation. To illustrate: if he represents a State delegation of 10 Republicans, he has a voting power of 10.

These two groups of officers of the full committees do the detail work for their respective Congressional campaign committees.

Senatorial Campaign Committees: The Senatorial Campaign Committees have much smaller memberships than the Congressional, but the size of each may vary from one Congress to another. The Republican Senatorial Campaign Committee, dating from 1916, was composed of 8 members as of the first session of the 80th Congress, appointed for a term of two years by the chairman of the Republican Conference, subject to confirmation by the conference.

The Democratic Senatorial Campaign Committee was composed of 5 designated to serve for an election, or term of two years, by the chairman of the Democratic Conference. In making these selections the chairmen of the conferences usually select Senators from States in which there will be no Senatorial election and they give consideration to geographical representation.

Functions of Senatorial and Congressional Campaign Committees: The Senatorial and Congressional Campaign Committees of the same party work closely together, with the executive committees or chairmen of each directing all of the activities toward the election of Representatives and Senators; each committee of each party works independently of the other, subject to the will of the party membership it represents. The functions of these committees include any activities essential to turning an election, but only after the primaries, which are left to the discretion of the local constituencies. Once the primaries are over, these committees take an active part respectively in the election of Representatives and Senators, which might well include raising and distributing funds, providing political speakers, and other favors which the candidates may request to enhance their political popularity. It is the aim of each committee to perform all services within its power to assure the election of all candidates of its political faith and thereby retain or regain control in the House and Senate as the case might be. The energies of each are concentrated in the doubtful districts or States where a minimum effort will turn the trick.

Caucuses and Conferences

In Washington, all of the Members-elect to the House and Senate before taking the oath of office align themselves into partisan groups, in accordance with the ticket on which they were elected, for the purpose of nominating certain officials of the House and Senate and to effect other plans of organizing that body when Congress convenes. The meetings held by the persons aligning themselves with the Democratic party are usually called caucuses while the meetings held by the persons aligning themselves with the Republicans are usually called conferences.[1] Of recent years, the Democratic Senators call their organization a conference. The objective of each in organizing into partisan groups is the same, namely: to integrate their respective party memberships of each house on a basis which will permit as much political unity as possible to assure the enactment of legislation desired by its party. By the use of this system of integration all members elected to the House and Senate on a particular party ticket are obligated to act collectively on legislative business.

All Republicans in the House are members of the Republican Conference and all Democrats in the House are Members of the Democratic Caucus; all Republican members in the Senate are members of the Republican Conference and all Democrats are members of the Democratic Conference. At the first meeting of these conferences and caucuses just before the opening of a new Congress, each group elects from among itself officers for its party caucus or conferences and nominates certain officers for the House and Senate, respectively. Each caucus or conference has a chairman and a secretary to act as permanent officers and to serve each group at its meetings during the remainder of that Congress. The chairmen act in other capacities for their parties, as set out elsewhere.

If the organizations set up by the caucuses or conferences at the beginning of a Congress fail to produce results, the chairmen of the respective groups may always call other meetings to rectify the "errors." The job, notwithstanding the possibility of a cor-

---

[1] The Farm Labor Party organized and presented a candidate for the Speakership for the Progressive Conference in the 74th Congress (*Congressional Record*, Seventy-fourth Congress, first session, p. 11—hereafter cited as C.R. 74-1, p. 11).

rection, is usually performed so perfectly that reorganization is not necessary. The Members receiving the posts accept their assignments seriously and strive for promotions. If the organization work by each is well done, there will be little use of many other caucuses or conferences during the remainder of the Congress. Occasional conflicts may arise, over certain bills, however, which will invite a meeting of the members of either party to determine what the party position should be on the particular issue. This practice is a last resort [2] by the leaders to achieve party solidarity; and, though it is not a generally popular undertaking, one must concede that agreements reached behind closed doors aid the leaders to demand the support of their party on the floor of the House and Senate.[3] In the case of the Democrats in the House, if a decision is reached as to how the party should vote on a particular bill by a two-thirds vote, every member of the party, with the exceptions laid down in the rules of the Democratic Caucus [4] is "bound" to vote in accordance with the decision reached. The Republicans do not have binding caucuses; in practice, nevertheless, the membership, in pursuance of certain conferences, vote as a unit just as uniformly as do the Democrats.

House Party Caucuses

Procedure of the House Groups: By and large the organization of each group is very similar; the modes of procedure differ in some instances. The following, however, will point out any significant variations on the House side.

The rules of the House, insofar as they are applicable, are regularly adopted by the Republican Conference at its first meeting. Further meetings may be called by the chairman or at the written request of fifty members. The conference proceeds upon the basis that a majority rules.

[2] See C.R., 63-2, pp. 1015-1016.
[3] Haines, *Law Making in America*, p. 16. "A little history in connection with H.R. 21,213, revising the sugar schedule, illustrates the system. This bill was introduced into the caucus March 1, and acted upon by that body in the usual way. Then followed the superfluous formalities, made necessary only because caucus 'legislation' is not legal. After the caucus had approved the measure and bound its members to stand by the program through to its final passage, Mr. Underwood introduced the bill into the House the following day, March 2. To comply with another formality, it was referred to the Ways and Means Committee, from which it was reported back to the House March 5. Eight days later, Mr. Underwood called it up and, after permitting a day of debate, with a number begging for the privilege of being heard, he made the following motion.
" 'I move that all general debate on the bill close in 10 minutes, and on that motion I move the previous question.'
"The previous question itself was not debatable" and the motion was carried by a vote of 163 to 131. The motion to close the debate in 10 minutes carried 157 to 124.
[4] See pp. 352-353 of first edition of *Congressional Procedure*.

The Democratic Caucus, like the Republican, utilizes the parliamentary procedure of the House so far as it is applicable. In addition thereto, a definite set of rules is regularly adopted, including the following: All members of the Democratic party of the House are *prima facie* members, provided they abide by the caucus rules. The chairman may call a meeting on his own initiative or whenever twenty-five members petition for a caucus.[5] A majority of the membership composes a quorum. Special rules may be adopted to substitute for regular parliamentary law. "In deciding upon action in the House involving party policy or principle, a two-thirds vote of those present and voting at a caucus meeting shall bind all members of the caucus; PROVIDED, The said two-thirds vote is a majority of the full Democratic membership of the House; AND PROVIDED FURTHER, That no member shall be bound upon questions involving a construction of the Constitution of the United States or upon which he made contrary pledges to his constituencies prior to his election or received contrary instructions by resolutions or platform from his nominating authority." The debates proceed under the five-minute rule unless the body suspends the rule by vote. No persons shall attend except Democratic Members of the House. A record of all proceedings shall be kept, and the yeas and nays on any question shall, at the desire of one-fifth of those present, be entered on the caucus journal.

Nominations: (a) *Speaker.* At the first general meeting of each party before every new Congress, the first business in order is the election of officers for the caucus or conference, after which, the nomination of candidates for offices in the incoming House are presented and considered. First, a candidate for Speaker is nominated, a nomination which frequently occasions much confusion and compromise. To illustrate: In 1919, Mr. Gillett and Mr. Mann, both of the Republican party, opposed each other for the Speakership. Mr. Mann seemingly was the person directly

---

[5] Form of letter by which the chairman calls a caucus meeting:

Washington, D. C.
Feb. 21, 1933.

"Dear Congressman:

"By virtue of the authority conferred upon me under the rule of the Democratic Caucus, I hereby call a Caucus of the Democratic Members-Elect of the 73rd Congress to meet in the Hall of the House of Representatives, Thursday, March 2, at 4 o'clock in the afternoon, to elect officers of the Caucus, nominate a candidate for Speaker and other House positions to be filled, and to elect a Majority Leader for the 73rd Congress . . .

Wm. W. Arnold,
Chairman."

in line for the post since he had been the Republican floor leader under the Democratic administration, but Mr. Gillett was nominated over Mr. Mann by the Republican Conference to be its candidate for Speaker, and he was elected by the House. The reason given by the Republicans for passing over Mr. Mann was that he had been too dictatorial and commanding as a leader to merit the Speakership. The Mann faction, nevertheless, was compensated for withdrawing from the Speakership race and for supporting Mr. Gillett as Speaker. A total of sixty-seven rewards were placed at the disposal of the Mann faction for their withdrawal from the race, according to a contemporary article.[6] These included: a controlling number of members on the Republican committee on committees, including the chairman; the appointment of a majority of members on the Republican steering committee; the right of naming the floor leader and the whip of the same party; the privilege of designating the ten crucial standing committee chairmanships and many of the lesser chairmanships; and the power of determining thirty-six additional appointments to the ten most important standing committees.

The Speakership position, in fact, is highly cherished and sought for by each Representative; the few Members of each party who are in line for such a preferment put up a fight to obtain the nomination for the office. Usually, however, by the date the caucuses assemble to make nominations the contests are over since nearly all Members will have priorly committed themselves. Some years the conflicts are so well mitigated before the official nominating sessions that only one name for Speakership will be offered in each party assembly when the nominations are in order.

(b) *Floor Leader.* The position of the floor leader is almost equally sought for since it frequently leads to the Speakership; and too, the incumbent enjoys much power and prestige. This election creates much confusion and tension. Incidentally, it should be mentioned that the minority party candidate for Speaker is nominated with the understanding that he will become the minority floor leader in case of his defeat for the Speakership.

(c) *Others.* If all members of the two committees on committees have not been arranged for, each party must provide for the selection of the members to their respective committees.

---

[6] Such conditions obtain, however, only when there is a closely contested fight between two or more candidates.

Finally, all other nominations, as Clerk, Sergeant at Arms, Postmaster, and the like are selected usually without much difficulty.

Meetings of Party Groups During Session: After organizational meetings, but before Congress convenes, other caucuses may be summoned for the purpose of approving the work of the committee on committees, to decide upon broad questions of legislative policy, to settle the question of Capitol patronage,[7] or to reach any other major party decisions.

Senate Party Conferences

Procedure of Senate Groups: In most respects the party caucuses of the Republican and Democratic Senators operate much like those of the Representatives. On the Senate side the meetings are not as formal, perhaps due to the difference in numbers. Most party caucuses or conferences called from time to time during the session of a Congress seldom enjoy full attendance; in fact, most of the policy work of the two parties is undertaken at the meetings of the two policy committees and steering committees. The functions of the caucuses or conferences are partisan in nature.

Nomination: *President Pro Tempore.* Unlike in the House, the regular Presiding Officer of the Senate is not elected to that post; he is elected Vice President. The Democratic and Republican groups, however, do nominate candidates to be President pro tempore, who presides during the absence of the Vice President. This post is desired and sought by the various Senators in line for such recognition. The nominee of the majority is always elected the President pro tempore; both parties nominate candidates at their respective organizational meetings a few days before the new Congress convenes.

Floor Leaders: The position of floor leader is the most cherished political post in the Senate; the incumbent enjoys much power and prestige, particularly if he is the majority leader. Hence, a fight is always staged in selecting a new floor leader for either party. Once a party decides upon its floor leader, whether he be of the majority or minority, his service is continuous from

---

[7] Cannon, VIII, 3627-3629. "The patronage of the House is distributed through a patronage commmittee nominated by the committee on committees and elected by the majority caucus.
"Chairmen of committees control the patronage of their respective committees and do not participate in the genral distribution.
"The paronage of the House, exclusive of the committee assignments, is divided as equitably as may be among the majority Members exclusive of chairmen, the amount . . . varying with the size of the party majority."

one Congress to another unless he should be defeated in the next general election or resigns, or unless "something extraordinary" should occur.

Other Selections: The Republican and Democratic Senators at their respective organizational caucuses consider memberships of their policy committees, their steering committees, and their committee on committees, all of whom are designated in pursuance of their instructions, usually by the Republican Conference chairman, or the Democratic Conference chairman, as the case might be.

Finally, all party nominations for administrative positions, as Secretary of the Senate, Sergeant at Arms and Doorkeeper, Chaplains, secretaries to the majority and minority, are agreed upon for presentation to the Senate at its first meeting of the new Congress. All patronage including any "jobs" on Capitol Hill are distributed by the Patronage Committee under mandate from the party conference.

Importance of the Caucus or Conference

These institutions of the two parties serve to unify the memberships of each for party unison. Of course, even with their aid it is seldom that the memberships divide in yea and nay votes on a strict party basis. So many insist on individualism that party unity is a much sought goal. Without the conferences and caucuses, however, the semblance of party government, particularly in the Senate, would be questionable. The number of general party meetings held by both the Democrats and Republicans during a Congress depends upon a number of things—legislative issues which might arise, conditions facing the country, party unity, and the like.

Committees on Committees

Each party in both houses has a committee on committees to select the memberships of standing committees. The Republican Committee on Committees of the House selects Republican Representatives to the various standing committees of the House ; the Democratic Committee on Committees of that body does the same for the Democrats; the same is true of each in the Senate. The objective of this setup is to provide another aid in the legislative process to assure representative party government, allowing the majority party to control what is or what is not done.

mittee, had been in Congress for only four terms; Tilson when elected floor leader had served only seven terms and they were not consecutive.

The floor leader is the customary person in line for the Speakership; there have been exceptions to this rule, however.. Speaker Henderson was never a floor leader; he had been the chairman of the Committee on the Judiciary and a member of the Rules Committee. More recently, Speaker Gillett was never floor leader; he was chairman of the Committee on Appropriations at the time of his selection. After the death of Speaker Longworth, Representative Tilson of Connecticut was the next Republican in line for Speaker, but the Republicans nominated Snell of New York as their candidate, but the Democrats organized the House.

The seniority rule makes it impossible for a Representative of a closely contested district from becoming Speaker since he is not likely to survive elections long enough, regardless of his ability. Under recent practices, the House has only selected men to such distinction who (1) come from districts dominated by a party boss as was the case of Nicholas Longworth of Ohio or (2) from districts which are overwhelmingly dominated by one party as was the case with Speakers Cannon, Garner, Byrns, and Bankhead.

Another custom which has stamped its imprint on the House in its choice of Speaker is that of re-election. Since 1863 every Speaker has been re-elected at least once, with five exceptions, of which three died before time for election and two were not candidates. Prior to 1863 over a dozen were not re-elected.

To summarize briefly: for a Representative to get himself in a position to be considered for candidacy, he must have been in Congress a long time and have held party preferments sufficient to demand recognition. To get these, a Member not only must be in Congress for some time but also he must exhibit political acumen and leadership.

Qualifications for President of Senate: Of course the Vice President as President of the Senate is under no obligation as far as prior experience in that body is concerned; he is elected by the people on the ticket with the President of the United States and may never have even seen Congress in session. Obviously the people will not elect a man Vice President unless he has gained sufficient recognition to merit consideration; politics, of course, enters into every decision toward his selection. After his arrival in the Senate, his relationships and influence depend on his ability as a party leader and as an individual.

The President pro tempore on the other hand finds himself in much the position as that of the Speaker of the House. The Senate does not confer this honor on a newcomer. In recent years and since the President pro tempore has been made a continuous office, that promotion has been given only to Senators with long terms of service, and who have risen to prominence in that body. The office is given to a man of legislative experience, holding an important committee chairmanship. Party prestige and geographical consideration weigh heavy in that determination; if the majority leader champions one faction of the party, consideration is given to selecting the President pro tempore from another to balance. All choices are made with a view toward strengthening party unity.

Historical Position of the Presiding Officers

Position of Speaker: The very nature of the Speaker's position makes him the leader of the House, and so much so that he gains exceptional increase in stature in his political party; he is actually looked upon as being on a different plane from that of the other Representatives, not in ability necessarily, but in prestige.

Until 1911 the Speaker was "all powerful." His power was so great that he could permit the consideration of a measure or prevent its consideration. This he was able to do mainly because of three prerogatives: (1) he was chairman of the Rules Committee, (2) he had the right of arbitrary recognition, and (3) he had power to name the standing committees and to designate their chairman. Mr. Pou, chairman of the Rules Committee for the 73rd Congress, on December 8, 1931, insisted that the House had been entirely under the control of the Speaker. He said: "I was a member of this House under what I may term a one-man oligarchy. For 10 years following my entrance into the House the House of Representatives had tied itself hand and foot and delivered itself to the Speaker. The House was under the control of the Committee on Rules, composed of three men, the Speaker, a gentleman from his side of the House, and one man from the minority side."

.The practice of placing so much power in the hands of the Speaker was not sudden. It had been a gradual growth dating from the first Congress in 1789, but it had not been altogether continuous nor of progressive growth. The power exerted by the chair always depends to a great extent on who is the Speaker; the office can be made whatever the holder has the capacity to make of it.

It was during the "Cannon regime" that the domination of the Speaker over the membership reached its height, to be taken away by a "revolution" in 1910.[11] The move to curtail this great power of the Speaker, nevertheless, was no sudden thing; and it was not a personal move against the Speaker. One writer stated that Mr. Cannon loved his House and the House loved him.[12] The move was against the system; "The Speaker of the House of Representatives grew in strength as the servant of the people, not their master." [13] It was held that the Speaker was misusing two powers, namely: refusing to recognize Members for unanimous consent, so that they might call up their bills, and abusing the use of the Rules Committee. The Speaker also appointed committees and then sent bills to them as he saw fit.

Since the revolution of 1910, the position of the Speaker has been stripped of some of the great powers formerly at his command; the Rules Committee, which had been one of the main sources of his power, was changed so as to spread out the power of control among the leaders, but the majority party, spearheaded by the Speaker, did not lose any power. The Speaker of the House does more than just preside; his prestige has diminished little if any; he still has sufficient prerogatives to make himself powerful if he so desires and has the capacity. Some of the more recent Speakers have displayed or wielded a strong hand over the House at times, each developing his own method of control. Speaker Gillett at times invoked almost arbitrary authority over recognition. He rendered decisions demanded by the machine

---

[11] Assaults against the great powers of the Speaker were started as early as 1806, when Nathaniel Macon of North Carolina was Speaker. Representative Willis Alston, Jr., of the same State, proposed that members of committees be chosen by ballot. This was the first recorded attempt to take away this power of the Speaker. The motion was defeated by a vote of 44 to 42; the argument was that the election by ballot placed no responsibility in the Speaker and a House with new Members could not ballot intelligently. Though this proposal was defeated, many others were attempted before the revolution in 1910; in fact, the rules had been modified several different times. Criticism of the autocracy displayed by the Speaker was nothing strange even during the Cannon reign prior to time of his overthrow.

[12] Brown, *The Leadership of Congress*, pp. 113-114.

[13] *Ibid.*, p. 12.

and its special friends, as stated by one writer. Later the House witnessed Longworth and Garner using just as much power, but they used it perhaps more diplomatically. Speaker Longworth knew his House and he handled "his men diplomatically, not dogmatically," one author said of him. "Yet the House soon learned that 'for all his jolly non-chalance, his thorough enjoyment of the good things of life . . . beneath the gloved hand would be found an iron grip.' " [14]

In the chair, Speaker Rayburn made no pretense at being overly diplomatic. He always stated his case as he saw it. The House membership learned his firmness and trustworthiness; it became aware of the fact that he knew how to be hard-boiled; and from all appearances, the Representatives feared to abuse their rights and privileges under the rules because of the possible outcome with the Speaker. He first tried to use persuasion with the membership and particularly with his party; if that did not get results he knew how to get tough quickly. Mr. Rayburn was the Administration's chief spokesman and leader in the House.[15]

Position of President of Senate: The Vice President (President of the Senate) and the President pro tempore share alike the powers and prerogatives embodied in the Presiding Officer of the Senate; the former, however, always presides unless absent from day to day or because he has taken over the Presidency of the United States; in the latter case the President pro tempore becomes number one man; in any case, during the absence of the Vice President, the President pro tempore assumes all the powers and prerogatives of the Vice President. The Senate does not always accept the Vice President as one of its family and it always looks upon him with a bit of "suspicion," or with a glance as toward a stranger.

The Constitution makes the Vice President the Presiding Officer of the Senate, but it makes no provision to assume that he will be of the same political faith as that of the party in control of the Senate. He is not subject to the will of the Senate in any way except that it has power to try him if he should be impeached. This is a condition that the Senate cannot forget should the Vice President try to exert influence over the membership in the administration of his duties. The Senate has no assurance as to his personality or ability. Because of this, the

14 *Review of Reviews*, LXXVII (1928), pp. 323-324.
15 *Public Men in and Out of Office*, p. 159.

success of the Presiding Officers in keeping good order and decorum has run from one extreme to another, with some good presiders, others not so good.

The President pro tempore on the other hand is one of the family. To illustrate: during the 80th Congress Senator Vandenberg, as the Presiding Officer and as the Chairman of the Foreign Relations Committee, took quite an important part in the legislative program and no doubt exerted as much influence in what was done or not done as the Speaker of the House. He was firm in his rulings, of which all but one or two stood as the decision of the Senate, even though several appeals were taken; he participated in discussions of the pending legislation from the chair perhaps to an unprecedented extent during any Congress of recent years;[16] John Adams, the first Vice President, talked from the chair at will.

Like the Speaker, the influence the President pro tempore exerts depends upon his personality and ability; he can make of the office what he wills to the extent of his ability. As pointed out by Mr. Haynes in his *The Senate of the United States*, the office has had a varied and an interesting history. For years a President pro tempore was elected on each occasion that the Vice President was absent; if the Vice President was present at the opening of a day's session he enjoyed the authority to designate a Senator to fill the chair for the rest of that day, but not beyond an adjournment. It was not until 1890 that the Senate adopted a resolution giving the President pro tempore permanent tenure of office; since that date with some interruptions caused by "insurgency" it has been the practice to elect a President pro tempore with the Vice President present and in the regular course of organizing the Senate.

Duties and Functions of the Presiding Officers

Duties and Functions of the Speaker: *Definition of the Office:* After the Speaker is elected he immediately takes over his twofold duties, political and judicial. Mr. Richardson of Tennessee said of the Speakership: "The position of Speaker of the House is both judicial and political. It is judicial in this, that the occupant of the Chair is at all times bound by and obedient to a code of rules prescribed for the government and control of the House,

[16] See C.R., 80-1, pp. 3776, 9302-9303 (daily edition).

and in the execution of which he is but its organ and servant. It is at the same time political. In the very nature of things, he is expected in his position to look carefully to the interest of his party, and while he is to administer the affairs of his great office in a manner best to promote the public weal, it is not expected that he will fail to use all legitimate and proper methods to build up his party and fortify it against attack." [17]

When Mr. Longworth was elected Speaker for the Sixty-ninth Congress he said:

The functions and duties of the Speakership as I view them divide themselves into two general classes, the one parliamentary, the other political.

The first I propose to administer with most rigid impartiality. With an eye single to the maintenance in the fullest degree of the dignity and honor of the House, and the rights and privileges of its Members, I promise you that there will be no such things as favoritism in the treatment by the Chair of either parties or individuals. . . .

The political side, to my mind, involves a question of party service. I believe it to be the duty of the Speaker, standing squarely on the platform of his party, to assist in so far as he properly can the enactment of legislation in accordance with the declared principles and policies of his party and by the same token to resist the enactment of legislation in violation thereof. . . . [18]

Party Agent: These quotations suggest that while the Speaker must act within certain parliamentary limits, he will do all that is within his power to aid his party to enact or to block the enactment of legislation according to the needs of his party. There are many ways in which the Speaker may do this. There is a world of play in the system which will permit the Speaker to act within certain bounds and still work in behalf of his party.[19] Tradition and unwritten law require that the Speaker apply the rules of the House consistently, yet in the twilight zone, a large area exists where he may exercise great discrimination and where he has many opportunities to apply the rules to his party's advantage.

On August 12, 1941, Speaker Rayburn's performances were such as to seccure for himself the credit for having made possible the enactment of the bill [20] for the extension of the Draft Act. Had this bill been killed, "the whole defense program of preparedness for World War II would have been disrupted. The Speaker

---

[17] C.R., 56-2, p. 3604.

[18] C.R., 69-1, p. 382.

[19] "I actually saw this, Mr. Speaker," said Mr. Pou. "It is hard to believe, but the records of the House will bear me out. I saw the two majority members of the Committee on Rules report a rule to this House for the consideration of a measure, and when the rule was adopted and the language of the rule was carefully examined, bless goodness, they found it not only provided for the consideration of the measure but actually passed the measure." (C.R., 72-1, p. 72.)

[20] See procedure on H.J.Res. 222 and S.J.Res. 95 for 77th Congress.

knew, with the aid of his party assistants, that it was doubtful if a majority of the Representatives would vote for House passage of the bill; and he knew that it was his responsibility to do something to assure a continuation of the defense program. Thus, he called upon Secretary of State Cordell Hull and the top official of the armed forces for letters to read to the House in order to impress its membership with the seriousness of the situation; and during the closing minutes of the debate before the roll-call vote was taken, he exerted all of his influence as Speaker by taking the floor and appealing to his party membership for support. Beyond that, he utilized his knowledge of parliamentary procedure during the few moments of confusion as to what had happened to freeze once and for all time the announced bare majority vote of 203 yeas to 202 nays, by which the bill passed. This vote was determined by making last minute pleas to doubtful colleagues," [21] involving a recapitulation to get passage.

The Speaker may direct affairs to block the adoption of an issue opposed by the party. Thus, when the conference report on the Independent Offices Appropriation Bill of the 72nd Congress, second session, was under consideration, the veterans pay clause was heatedly contested. When called up, Mr. Connery of Massachusetts moved that the House recede and concur in the Senate amendment (No. 22), and on that motion a record vote was demanded; the membership was closely divided and the leaders knew it. A short verbal war was started over requests for change of votes, parliamentary inquiries, and demands for an announcement of the vote. The Speaker demanded a recapitulation, since the vote had been 190 to 189. This delayed any announcement of the decision and gave the leaders time to bargain; that is, to get someone to reconsider his vote. The final vote was 189 to 190, blocking the amendment opposed by the leaders.

Activity: The Speaker has to be always on the alert, except when the roll is being called. Generally, unless during regular debate, he is answering questions, putting questions, announcing results, and recognizing Members, except when the House is in Committee of the Whole, at which time he does not preside.

The Speaker must take the chair on every legislative day precisely at the hour to which the House shall have adjourned at the

[21] See Chapter on "Speaker Rayburn" in *Public Men in and out of Office*.

last sitting; he must preserve order and decorum and conduct the counting of the quorum. He also receives invitations on behalf of the House; represents that body on public occasions; appoints and removes official reporters; introduces visitors and trustees of public institutions; issues warrants; executes orders; authenticates proceedings; approves bonds; certifies salary accounts for Members; controls committee rooms, corridors, galleries, and House grounds; signs bills which are passed; notifies the proper State officials whenever a vacancy occurs in the House; answers parliamentary inquiries; and decides questions of order.

The real presiding power is found in the right of recognition, which must be lodged with the chair. By the use of this, the Speaker is obviously in a position to favor his party or certain individuals, in line with the American idea of the Speaker. Any Member rising to get recognition must address the chair. It is necessary to address the Presiding Officer, even if the purpose is to interrupt a Member who already has the floor. A Member may not address an employee of the House; all remarks must be prefaced by: "Mr. Speaker," not "Gentlemen of the House" or "Ladies and Gentlemen."

Power of Recognition: The Speaker has the power to name the Member who is entitled to the floor and there is little appeal from this decision. Various Members from time to time have accused the Speaker of arbitrary recognition.

Under the reign of Uncle Joe Cannon, recognition meant that a Member had already had an interview. It has become the practice to notify the Speaker before proposing a unanimous consent request which deviates from the authorized order of business; it is also customary to notify the majority and minority leaders. To illustrate the absoluteness of this power, note the following:

The SPEAKER (announcing the vote sustaining the Chair in refusing to entertain a motion to adjourn) . . . On this vote the yeas are 163 and the nays are none—

Mr. SPRINGER. I move that the House do now adjourn.

The SPEAKER. And accordingly the motion of the gentleman from Ohio (Mr. McKinley) to lay the appeal on the table is agreed to.

Mr. SPRINGER. I move that the House do now adjourn.

The SPEAKER. The gentleman from Pennsylvania, Mr. Dalzell, has the floor.

Mr. SPRINGER. I move that the House do now adjourn. Does the Speaker decline to entertain that motion?

The SPEAKER. The motion of the gentleman from Illinois (Mr. Springer) is not entertained by the Chair.

Mr. SPRINGER. Parliamentary business has intervened since the former motion to adjourn and therefore this motion is in order.
The SPEAKER. Precisely.
Mr. SPRINGER. And therefore another motion to adjourn is in order.
The SPEAKER. But there has also been a decision of the Chair as to that class of motions and the decision had been sustained by the House, and it now becomes the duty of the Chair to execute the will of the House as expressed by its vote.
Mr. SPRINGER. Then when will it be in order for some one to move to adjourn?
The SPEAKER. It will be in order at the proper time.[22]

On July 11, 1946 Representative Luce asked unanimous consent for consideration of a bill to continue rent control, which had been previously introduced by Representative Wolcott, upon which Speaker Rayburn asked: "Did the gentlewoman consult the Speaker about this and notify him that she was going to make this request?" She replied: "I did not, Mr. Speaker." To this Speaker Rayburn replied: "The Chair refuses to recognize the gentlewoman for that purpose." On July 12, Mrs. Luce inquired of the Speaker when she could ask for consideration of the measure. "That resolution will come up in the proper fashion," was the answer she received. Mrs. Luce asked further: "Then this resolution cannot be presented by anyone by unanimous consent?" The Speaker: "It can be presented by unanimous consent, but the Chair is not going to recognize for that purpose at this time." [23]

On June 8, 1942 one Member, Representative Hoffman, had the following to say about the Speaker:

If any think that the Speaker's control of this House has in any way weakened or is less than it should be, they should revise their opinion. The present Speaker, as the two preceding him, whom I knew, never made any attempt to stifle the action of this House.
True, the Speaker has endeavored, as he has the right and as he should, because of his official position, to direct and to control the House procedure. That he has done with an iron hand, even though he wore the velvet glove.
It is true that, on occasion, the present Speaker has taken the floor, as Speakers in the past have taken the floor, as was their right, their duty, and urged the adoption of legislation handed down by the Administration.[24]

Thus, it is always possible to use the power of recognition very autocratically; it is within the power of the Presiding Officer to ignore any Member requesting recognition.

[22] Atkinson. *op. cit.*, pp. 42-43. To rise to make inquiries does not give a Member the floor. While a motion to adjourn is always in order, a Member must first secure recognition in order to present the motion or to appeal (Cannon, VI, 293, 287-288; also Hinds, II, 1442-1444).
[23] See *Congressional Record* for July 11 and 12, 1946, pp. 8726, 8808.

Power to Ask: "For What Purpose Does the Gentleman Rise?":
The authority which permits the Speaker to inquire "for what purpose does the gentleman rise?" fortifies the Presiding Officer
against unexpected moves by individual Members of the House.
By the use of this prerogative, the chair may refuse to recognize
for a unanimous consent request, and protect the planned program.
To illustrate: Representative Howard in 1931, asked unanimous
consent that all business be put aside for two hours and that during this time some consideration be given to the drought and unemployment. The Speaker inquired if the gentleman realized that
there was special order for the morning:

> Mr. HOWARD. But I am asking unanimous consent, Mr. Speaker.
> The SPEAKER. The Chair, under the circumstances stated, and also in
> his intense desire to protect Calendar Wednesday, can not recognize the
> gentleman for that purpose.[25]

Appointment Power: The Speaker selects the chairman of the
Committee of the Whole House and appoints Speakers pro tempore, for not over three days. The Speaker does not always, or
with the approval of the House for a term not to exceed ten days,
name the temporary Presiding Officer in the open House. A
Speaker pro tempore, after being appointed, may designate another Speaker pro tempore. If the time is to exceed ten days the
House elects a Speaker pro tempore, but the House has permitted
the Speaker to designate a Speaker pro tempore for a term longer
than provided for by the rules.[26]

If the Speaker is not present at the opening of a session, he may
designate a temporary Speaker in writing; otherwise, the House
may elect a temporary Presiding Officer, who is not sworn in.
The temporary Presiding Officer may appoint conferees with the
consent of the House; if his designation has received the approval
of the House and he has been sworn, he may sign enrolled bills
and issue warrants for the arrest of absent Members under a call
of the House. A Member called to the chair during the day's
sitting does not sign enrolled bills or appoint committees.

---

[24] C.R., 77-2, p. 5035.
[25] C.R., 71-3, p. 1552.
[26] Cannon, VI, 267, 280. In 1897 the Speaker, desiring to attend certain ceremonies, designated Mr. Charles W. Stone, of Pennsylvania, to be Speaker pro tempore
for the succeeding week, having previously asked and obtained unanimous consent
of the House to make the designation (Hinds, II, 1381). "The House having agreed
to an order for formal sessions on two days only of each week over an extended
period, authorized the Speaker to appoint Speakers pro tempore at will during that
time." (Cannon, VI, 267).

The Speaker does not appoint standing committees, a task assigned the committees on committees. He does appoint members of select and investigating committees and Managers on the part of the House (conferees) on a bill sent to conference. Generally, House Members on joint committees are appointed by the Speaker, as well as those on committees or commissions created by law. The Parliamentarian and certain other officials of the House also owe their appointments to the Speaker.

Order and Decorum: The Speaker is assigned the task of keeping order. This undoubtedly is a real assignment in a body of 435. There are always sufficient Members present who are so indifferent to decorum that they hinder orderly procedure; the Speaker may repress such disorder by calling Representatives by name; he may not censure or punish them; he may call any Member to order, in which case the Representative "shall immediately sit down, unless permitted," to continue on motion; also "he shall be liable to censure or such punishment as the House may deem proper." [27]

One of the duties which Speaker Longworth performed most skillfully was the preservation of order. Longworth never resorted to the extreme use of his power to keep order, though he was put to the tests of restoring order after complications ranging from arguments to fist fights.[28] He knew how to handle a body of men without being militant. Speaker Longworth never thundered out to an individual to keep quiet, he advised in an amicable conversational tone; Speaker Rainey was easy going but did enjoy the respect of the membership; Speaker Byrns was gentle; Speakers Garner, Bankhead, and Rayburn were firm and demanded respect; with each the order was kept reasonably well.

Rulings of Chair: When the Speaker decides points of order, controversy with the chair is not allowed, unless by his consent. This precedent was introduced under Speaker Reed when he declined to hear Representative Mills of Texas. If the chair refuses to reconsider his ruling, the Members of the House must keep silent unless they demand an appeal. Speaker Crisp said: ". . . No Member has a right, after the Chair has decided a point

[27] Rule XIV, Clause 4.
[28] In both sessions of the 79th Congress, various conflicts between different members almost led to fist fights, see *American Political Science Review* for annual articles on the two sessions; *New York Times*, Feb. 13 and 18, 1927. In 1927 a fight occurred in the House of Representatives between Representatives Strong and Tischer. A few days later the boxing gloves which Tunney and Dempsey had used in their Philadelphia fight were sent to Speaker Longworth with the following remarks: "Kindly make use of these, for according to reports they are a necessity in the halls of Congress."

of order, to ask upon what grounds he bases his position." During Reed's historic contest to compel Speaker Crisp to count a quorum, the latter declined to entertain an appeal: "On what grounds?" asked Reed.

> The SPEAKER. The chair declines to make any further statement.
> Mr. REED. I think I can satisfy the chair—
> The SPEAKER. The chair declines to hear the gentleman further.
> Mr. REED. The chair will permit me to explain.
> The SPEAKER. The chair will not.
> Mr. REED. The chair will permit me—
> The SPEAKER. The gentleman from Maine will be seated. The sergeant-at-arms will see that the gentleman takes his seat.[29]

The chair is obligated to give precedence its proper consideration in deciding points of order. If precedents conflict, the chair is required to give the greater weight to the more recent decisions; and his decision is final if no appeal is taken. The Speaker or the chairman always renders his opinion subject to an appeal on motion of any Member; it is very seldom, however, that a decision of the chair is overruled. The chair naturally decides as nearly in line with the wishes of his party as possible, so that he may retain the support of the majority party. Speaker Reed said in 1892: "I have been fifteen years in Congress, and I never saw a Speaker's decision overruled, and you will never live to see it either." [30] Nevertheless, rulings of the chair have been reversed. This power by the House must be retained in order to protect it against arbitrary control by an autocratic Speaker. On one occasion when a Speaker's decision was overthrown, he attempted to resign.

In deciding points of order, the Speaker may decline to rule until he has had time to examine the records. He may require the point of order to be presented in writing, and when a point is raised it is within his power to have debate on the question to inform himself. To entertain filibuster might aid the Presiding Officer in more ways than merely rendering information. He may permit the debate to mark time so that if an appeal is permitted all the force of his party may have been collected. Speaker Clark, in his *My Quarter Century of American Politics,* tells how this practice was used during the Cannon revolution.[31]

---

[29] Alexander, *History and Procedure of the House of Representatives,* p. 49.
[30] Atkinson, *op. cit.,* p. 100.
[31] Clark, *op. cit.,* II, 275-276.

He was waiting for reinforcements enough to outvote us, for everybody knew two things: "First, that when he did rule he would sustain the point of order, thereby holding the Norris resolution not to be privileged; second, that we would appeal from his decision. He could not be forced to rule. He was deferring to get a majority. We were holding on grimly to our majority. He wouldn't rule. We would not let the House adjourn. It was St. Patrick's day, and many members were absent in near-by cities attending banquets of the Ancient Order of Hibernians and making speeches. By sundown every absent Member had been telegraphed for. The Speaker hoped that when the midnight trains arrived his cohorts would muster enough votes to sustain the ruling which he intended to make; but when the midnight trains got in they brought seven of his supporters and six of ours!—not enough to change the status quo ante. We scrapped all that night and all of the 18th until 2 p. m."

Advisory Opinions and Responsibility of Membership: The Speaker does not render advisory opinions, decide hypothetical points of order, or anticipate questions. Before he decides a question an actual conflict must have arisen. It is the duty of every Member to make a point of order, or the chair to demand order, when there is a deviation from the procedure prescribed by the rules. The membership must be willing to call down any person proceeding improperly, if the House is to have order.

Decisions by House: The House, as opposed to the Speaker, reserves for itself the right to decide whether a proposed action is consistent with other acts, whether a Senate amendment to a revenue bill violates the privileges of the House, whether a law conflicts with the Constitution, whether an amendment conflicts with a former amendment, what will be the legislative effect of a proposition under consideration, what will be the propriety or expediency of a proposed course of action, what will be the decision on questions in which the House is concerned as a unit, and whether or not a committee has followed instructions.[32]

Debates and Voting: The Speaker not only presides over the House, but he may debate and vote as every other Member. The right to speak on bills, nevertheless, is not particularly significant from a political point of view. It is only to be expected that the Speaker's words would have a great deal of influence with the House membership but the party membership knows that the floor leaders speak for the party as well as the Speaker. Depending on the issue, the influence of the Speaker might be significant.

The number of times a Speaker participates in debates depends upon the personality of the individual holding the office. Speaker

[32] See Hinds and Cannon's Precedents.

Clark could not understand why a "Speaker has not as much right to make speeches as anybody else, if he feels like it." [33] Speaker Cannon spoke to the House four times from the Speaker's chair, four times on the floor of the House, and six times in the Committee of the Whole within eight years. Speaker Clark spoke eighteen times from the floor and forty-five times in the Committee of the Whole. He never took part in debate from the chair. During one session he spoke twenty-three times. Speaker Gillett took part in debate only five times in six years. Speaker Longworth took the floor in 1927 to aid the navy bloc. This was the first time that any Speaker had taken part in debate against an administrative proposal since Champ Clark opposed Wilson in 1917. Garner took the floor in 1932 to make a long political speech on a tax measure. Longworth took the floor eleven times in six years, Garner seven times in two years, and Rainey one time in two years. Subsequent Speakers have taken the floor at irregular intervals but comparatively frequently.[34]

The Speaker may leave the chair to make a motion, but this has not been the practice of recent years. The other leaders of the party in power are so closely allied with the Speaker that there is no necessity for the Speaker to leave the chair to offer any motion. The Speaker has called other Members to the chair so that he might take the floor to defend himself.[35] The Speaker may make brief explanations from the chair; he has a right to speak from the chair on questions of order and to be heard first; otherwise he may speak from the chair only by leave of the House. Usually he asks consent of the House even to speak on questions of order.[36]

Section six of Rule I reads: "He shall not be required to vote in ordinary legislative proceedings, except where his vote would be decisive, or where the House is engaged in voting by ballot; and in cases of a tie vote the question shall be lost." Due to the implication of this rule, the early Speakers did not take a part in voting. Henry Clay was probably the first Speaker to cast his vote in ordinary proceedings. Clay claimed the right to vote just as any Member.

[33] C.R., 62-2, p. 3705.
[34] On Jan. 31, 1945, Speaker Rayburn took the floor to support the Manpower bill (H.R. 1752), which died in conference.
[35] Hinds, II, 1371. On June 14, 1906 the Speaker called Mr. John Dalzell of Pennsylvania to the chair while he left the chair to reply to a speech reflecting on his conduct.
[36] See Hinds' and Cannon's Precedents.

Prior to 1896 the Speaker seldom voted;[37] since that date, however, the Speakers have been more active in voting;[38] nevertheless, the increase in the use of this right has not been consistent. Cannon and Clark voted often, but then there was a decided drop until the Speakership of Rainey. Speaker Rainey reached an all time mark by voting twenty-three times in one session, during which there were eighty-two votes by roll call. The Speaker's name is not listed on the roll from which the Clerk calls the yeas and nays. His name is not called except by his request. After the roll has been called, if the Speaker intends to cast his vote, he states to the House: "The Clerk will call my name." If the vote is a tie or if it takes one vote to make it a tie, the Speaker has a responsibility to vote and he may vote after other business has intervened.

Signing of Bills: The Speaker signs all bills passed by the House and Senate and enrolled, and incidental transactions approved by the House. The Speaker does not sign a matter, however, until a pending motion to reconsider is disposed of; he is not authorized to sign enrolled bills in the absence of a quorum; he may be authorized to sign bills when the House is not in session.

A Member called to the chair by the Speaker for a temporary sitting does not ordinarily sign bills; if the House approves he may. Any person designated by the House may sign enrolled bills under the same restrictions as the Speaker.

Reference of Bills: The Speaker refers bills to their proper committees; according to Rule XXII:

All other bills, memorials, and resolutions may, in like manner, be delivered, indorsed with the names of Members introducing them, to the Speaker, to be by him referred, and the titles and references thereof and of all bills, resolutions, and documents referred under the rules shall be entered on the Journal and printed in the Record of the next day, and correction in case of error of reference may be made by the House, without debate, in accordance with Rule XI, on any day immediately after the reading of the Journal, by unanimous consent, or on motion of a committee claiming jurisdiction, or on the report of the committee to which the bill has been erroneously referred.

[37] Chiu, *The Speaker of the House of Representatives,* p. 50. "In upward of a hundred years before 1896, votes cast by the Speaker with the minority to make an even division totaled more than twenty; with the majority to make a two-thirds vote, less than ten; and 'unnecessary' votes, less than ten."

[38] Reed voted 7 times in the 55th Congress; Henderson in the 56th and 57th Congresses voted 14 times; during Cannon's 8 years, he voted 121 times and answered present 10 times; Clark voted 96 times and present once. (Chiu, *op. cit.,* pp. 52-58). Gillett voted only 18 times altogether. Longworth did not vote in the 69th Congress.

The assigning, however, is actually done by the Parliamentarian of the House subject to the Speaker's will. If there is a bill to be referred which would gain political advantage by reference to a particular committee, the Speaker handles the situation subject to the will of the House.

Examination of Journal: The Speaker examines and corrects the Journal before it is read to the House for approval. This responsibility, like the referring of bills, is thrown upon the Parliamentarian subject to the will of the Speaker.

Controls House Wing of Capitol: The Speaker has charge of the House side of the Capitol. He has general control of the Hall and corridors in the House wing of the Capitol. The unappropriated rooms are placed in his custody for him to assign. On one occasion the Speaker ordered the removal of a placard posted in the lobby of the House. Finally, during the session of the House, he may order the galleries of the House cleared. His salary is $20,000 per year.

Conclusion: The Speaker, an outstanding official in American legislation, has been subjected to much criticism since the beginning of the first Congress. Thomas B. Reed once said that the office "had but one superior and no peer." Many modern editors have placed him second to the President of the United States. Under the Presidential Succession Act, he follows the Vice President in line of succession to the Presidency. Had he been permitted to continue to gain power, as the tendency was evident during the reign of Cannon, the Speaker would have soon become more powerful in legislation than the President. Today, he neither appoints the membership of the committees nor is he a member of any standing committee.[39] His influence over legislation has been limited to personality and leadership. To summarize briefly, the Speaker as the Presiding Officer, keeps order, decides points of order, and recognizes Members on the floor. The incumbent has a desirable and dignified position.[40]

[39] Though not a member of any standing committee, he might be a member of several political committees.

[40] In 1905, Cannon was invited to a state dinner by President Roosevelt, in honor of the Chief Justice of the Supreme Court. At this dinner the President asked Mr. Cannon if he would object to a seat below the Attorney General. To this Speaker Cannon was unwilling to comply due to the fact that it was not a private dinner. " . . . Were it a private dinner," he replied, "he would be content with any place the most high might assign to him; and were he a private individual he would be equally pleased with whatever course the host might take; but he felt that in attending a state dinner as Speaker of the House he might not waive the position to which he was entitled officially." Rather than waive the position to which he was entitled officially, he would much prefer to be excused from the dinner (Hinds, II, 1309).

It appears that three of the main reasons why this office has gained so much prestige are: first, the President, the Vice President, and the Speaker must all three sign every piece of legislation before it becomes law; secondly, the Speaker is the representative of the people's Representatives, a fact which implies that he must have received, indirectly, a majority of the votes of all the people of the United States—each Representative must receive a majority to be elected and the Speaker must receive a majority of the Representatives' votes; and thirdly, under law passed during the first session of the 80th Congress, the Speaker follows the Vice President in line of succession to become the President of the United States.

Duties and Functions of the President of the Senate: *Definition of Office:* The President of the Senate and the President pro tempore are made the Senate Presiding Officers by Section III, Article I, of the Constitution. This merely provides that the Vice President "shall be President of the Senate, but shall have no vote, unless they be equally divided;" and the "Senate shall choose . . . a President pro tempore, in the absence of the Vice President, or when he shall exercise the office of President of the United States." The rules of the Senate have little additional to say about the office. Thus these men preside fortified with what aid the precedents lend.

These Presiding Officers are charged with maintaining a reasonable parliamentary procedure; in practice, they do not command equal discretion with the Speaker in applying "political and parliamentary law." Rarely the Vice President, but more frequently the President pro tempore, may approach the influence over his chamber that the Speaker exercises over his.

The rule for appointing substitutes to the chair gives more deference to the President pro tempore than to the Vice President; it provides: In the absence of the Vice President, the President pro tempore presides; the President pro tempore on the other hand, is authorized "to name in open Senate, or, if absent, in writing, a Senator to perform the duties of the chair; but such substitution shall not extend beyond an adjournment, except by unanimous consent." [41] In case of vacancy in the Office of the Vice President, the appointive power to the chair by the President

[41] Rule 1, Clause 3.

pro tempore is practically the same as that enjoyed by the Speaker.[42]

The Senate has not been disposed to extend extensive powers to a Presiding Officer not of its own choosing, and sometimes not of the same political faith as that of the majority party. To illustrate: Senator Bacon in protesting a ruling by Vice President Sherman on June 4, 1912, reminded the Presiding Officer that he must not forget that "the Senate is a self-governing body." Thus, since the Vice President presides most of the time, the power exercised by the chair has been confined more so than might have been the case otherwise.

Party Agent: The Vice President may or may not be of the same political faith as that of the party in control; in case they are, the relationship between the Senators of the majority party and the Presiding Officer (Vice President) might or might not be good, to the extent of party unison; when they are of the same party and party unison exists, he might well play the part of a party leader in the legislative process. In recent practice, however, while he might be helpful, the management and direction of the party program devolves upon the majority floor leader.

The President pro tempore is an agent of the party, and when he presides he takes an active part in the enactment of the legislative program, the degree depending on personality and abilities of the individual.

Activity: The Presiding Officer of the Senate must always be on the alert; unlike the House, the Senate no longer uses the Committee of the Whole procedure nor does it set aside so much time for general debate of a measure before it is read for amendments. While it is a practice for Senators to make long speeches, involving hours of time, which delays a vote, the moment a speech is going to be terminated cannot always be anticipated. When a bill is under consideration and a Senator speaking to it concludes his remarks, the question recurs on the adoption of the pending amendment or passage of the bill if no further amendments are offered. Besides, during a long speech, various Senators may interrupt if the Senator having the floor yields for questions; this activity can result in taking the floor from one Senator and giving it to another; hence the proceedings must be watched. Parlia-

[42] In the absence of the Vice President and pending the election of a President pro tempore, the Secretary or, in his absence, the Chief Clerk, shall preside.

mentary inquiries and points of no quorum are continuously commanding the attention of the chair.

Power of Recognition: The Senate rules stipulate that "When a Senator desires to speak, he shall rise and address the Presiding Officer, and shall not proceed until he is recognized, and the Presiding Officer shall recognize the Senator who shall first address him. No Senator shall interrupt another Senator in debate without his consent, and to obtain such consent he shall first address the Presiding Officer; and no Senator shall speak more than twice upon any one question in debate on the same day without leave of the Senate, which shall be determined without debate." [43] The House rule provides that "The Speaker shall name the Member who is first to speak . . ." Obviously the latter stipulation permits more discretion. The Senate rule constrains recognition to the first Senator addressing the chair; there is no power to inquire for what purpose the Senator rises. Of course, the Presiding Officer may go a long way in exercising his own discretion as to who was the first Senator to rise to his feet; he has not always recognized the one rising first. The chair must also protect the rights of the Senator who is holding the floor; since a Senator may not speak more than twice on any question during the same legislative day, a Senator could be easily shut out from debate of a bill if other Senators were permitted continuously to interrupt the Senator who is speaking. Charges of favoritism in granting recognition have been comparatively few.

Before a Senator speaks or interrupts another he must address the chair and get permission. Like a Representative, a Senator is prohibited from referring offensively to any State of the Union or "directly or indirectly, by any form of words impute to another Senator or to other Senators any conduct or motive unworthy or unbecoming a Senator." If the rules are transgressed by any Senator it is up to the Presiding Officer or any Senator to see that the transgressor is called to order, and when called to order he must sit down and not proceed without leave of the Senate, all of which is determined without debate.

Appointment Power: The appointing power has varied from time to time; for a brief period the Presiding Officer was authorized to appoint standing committees as well as special and conference committees, but some of that authority was recalled and

[43] Rule XIX, clause 1.

placed directly in the hands of the Senate. The appointing power of President and President pro tempore is limited to the designation of Senators to select or special investigating committees, conferees (managers on the part of the Senate) on any bill sent to conference, and to certain non-political positions created by law— for example, trustees of philanthropic institutions maintained by the government. The appointment of the Senate conferees by the Presiding Officer is by unanimous consent, "under the custom of the Senate." The same applies to the appointment of select, investigating, and joint committees created by law and concurrent resolutions.[44]

In the selection of conferees or other committee assignments made by the chair, the Presiding Officer does not have a free hand. Senator Gorman in 1905 insisted that "there has grown up another custom, to which there have been exceptions only in very, very rare cases, and that is that the conferees on the part of this body shall be the chairman of the committee who has charge of the bill and usually the senior member of the majority next to him and the senior Senator representing the other side of the Chamber." [45] On the other hand, Vice President Garner on April 8, 1935, said that the Senator in charge of a bill asks for a conference and "sends to the chair the names of the conferees. So far as the Record shows, the occupant of the chair appoints the conferees, whereas, as a matter of fact, he exercises no discretion and does not even see the names of the conferees until they are sent to the chair."

He continued:

Hereafter the present occupant of the chair expects to exercise some discretion in the matter of selecting conferees when the Senate authorizes him to make the appointments.

The Chair mentions this now so that no Senator in the future may think he is slighted or otherwise discriminated against if he asks unanimous consent that the Chair appoint conferees and sends up his list, and those named on the list are not appointed. The Chair merely desires to give notice of his course in the future. If there is any reaction to the contrary the Chair would like to know it, and then some rule ought to be made as to how conferees should be appointed, because the Chair is advised there is no specific rule of the Senate concerning the appointment of conferees.[46]

On October 22, 1945, Senator Bailey, chairman of the Commerce Committee, said:

[44] See *Senate Manual*, 80-1, p. 278.
[45] Gilfry, *Senate Precedents*, I, p. 306.
[46] C.R., 74-1, p. 5296.

I filed with the President of the Senate just now a list of five names. Mine is not on the list, so I am not embarrassed. That is the custom which I have always followed in the Senate, and according to my recollection that is the universal custom. But let no Senator for 1 minute get the impression that I am insisting on any right to name conferees. They are named by the Chair, and I take it if the Chair does not satisfy the Senate, the Senate may name them.[47]

It should be pointed out that the rule (Rule XXIV) authorizing committee appointments has remained the same, but the practice under that rule, because of various possibilities specified, is subject to vary from one Congress to another, depending on the relationship between the majority party and the Presiding Officer. When the relationship is not so good, obviously the Presiding Officer merely reads the list submitted to him, as stated above by Vice President Garner, and then only when a unanimous consent request is made that the Presiding Officer make the appointments. When the relationship is good, the Presiding Officer, depending upon his leadership and the influence he is able to wield, might use more discretion in making such appointments. When the President pro tempore presides, since he is selected by the majority party membership of the Senate, the chair speaking for his party is able to exert much influence. The rule authorizing committee appointments is discussed at pp. 154-171.

Order and Decorum: The chair is charged with maintaining order and decorum, or if any Senator calls another to order in pursuance of the rules, the chair must insist that the proceedings go forward according to the rules. A Senator may be called to order by the chair or by another Senator for proceeding out of order in which case he must sit down, except with leave of the Senate to proceed. If a Senator is called to order for words spoken in debate, "Upon the demand of the Senator or of any other Senator, the exceptionable words shall be taken down in writing, and read at the table for the information of the Senate." [48] The House rule is more severe; it concludes by stating that if the case requires it, "he shall be liable to censure or such punishment as the House may deem proper." [49] The order in the Senate, however, depends a good deal upon who is presiding; through the years there has been a great variation in the strictness with which the rules have been enforced. A Vice President who is a poten-

---

[47] C.R., 79-1, p. 9880, Oct. 22, 1945.
[48] Rule XIX, Clauses 4 and 5.
[49] *House Manual,* 80-1, section 760.

tial candidate for the Presidency might hesitate to rub any Senator the wrong way for fear of the outcome.

"Whenever confusion arises in the Chamber or the galleries, or demonstrations of approval or disapproval are indulged in by the occupants of the galleries, it shall be the duty of the Chair to enforce order on his own initiative and without any point of order being made by a Senator." [50]

Putting Questions and Deciding Points of Order (Rulings): The Presiding Officer of the Senate puts questions and decides points of order in the same manner as does the Speaker. He decides points of order without debate, but he may entertain such debate without objection for his own information; if the point of order is submitted to the membership for decision, it may be debated. Rule XX provides:

A question of order may be raised at any stage of the proceedings, except when the Senate is dividing, and, unless submitted to the Senate, shall be decided by the Presiding Officer without debate, subject to an appeal to the Senate. When an appeal is taken, any subsequent question of order which may arise before the decision of such appeal shall be decided by the Presiding Officer without debate; and every appeal therefrom shall be decided at once, and without debate; and any appeal may be laid on the table without prejudice to the pending proposition, and thereupon shall be held as affirming the decision of the Presiding Officer.

The Presiding Officer may submit any question of order for the decision of the Senate.

Rulings by the chair are binding on the Senate unless the membership takes an appeal, and while appeals are not uncommon, reversals of decisions by the chair are surprisingly few. Appeals from the decision of the chair are debatable. In spite of the lack of experience, with the aid of the Parliamentarian, the President bases his decisions on Senate precedents, or if the question is new or "a tough one," he may voluntarily submit it to the Senate in the first instance for determination. The Presiding Officer does not raise questions of order on his own initiative, nor exercise too much control over dilatory proceedings; he readily blocks motions to adjourn, and the like, if another is offered after one has just been defeated and no legislative business has transpired. When unanimous consent agreements to limit debate on pending issues have been entered into, he parcels out the time, but in accordance with the wishes of the Senate. Under Cloture Rule proceedings,

[50] Rule XIX, Clause 6.

he exercises much control over dilatory motions. But he has no right to call a Senator to order for speaking on irrelevant subjects during debates.[51]

Debates and Voting: The Vice President is not a Member of the Senate and therefore does not participate in debates. Occasionally he makes certain statements from the chair explaining and justifying his own rulings which may or may not have been questioned. The President pro tempore on the other hand is a member of the family and may designate someone else to preside while he takes the floor; also, he, like the Vice President, may make certain statements from the chair. President pro tempore Vandenberg in the 80th Congress assumed more freedom in making explanation from the chair than has been the recent practice of Vice Presidents; it was not uncommon for him to make some comments about the pending legislation from the chair or to designate someone to preside in his stead and take the floor to speak, particularly as chairman of the Foreign Relations Committee.

Article I, Section 3 of the Constitution provides that "The Vice President of the United States shall be President of the Senate, but shall have no vote, unless they be equally divided." Hence he has no vote unless there is a tie,[52] and since a tie vote kills a proposal, the Vice President needs only to cast a vote in cases when he wishes the motion to prevail, by affirmative vote. The President pro tempore or any Senator temporarily presiding has a vote just as any other "member of the family."

Signing of Bills: "The signing, by the President of the Senate and the Speaker of the House of Representatives, in open session, of an enrolled bill is an official attestation by the two Houses that such bill has been passed by Congress, . . ." [53] and made ready for the President's signature. In the absence of the Vice President, bills are signed by the President pro tempore; in his absence, by a Senator duly authorized. While bills are usually signed in open session, the Senate may authorize the Presiding Officer to sign bills during a recess or adjournment of the Senate or after Congress adjourns *sine die.*

[51] Gilfry, *Senate Precedents,* I, p. 401. This precedent was set February 29, 1872 by a vote of 28 to 18; various Senators have held it unfortunate.

[52] For a record of times the Vice President voted from 1789 to June 6, 1938, see Haynes, *The Senate of the United States,* I, pp. 232-239.

[53] Gilfry, *op. cit.,* I, p. 213.

Reference of Bills: The Presiding Officer approves the references of public bills to committees, both bills introduced in the Senate and House-passed bills messaged to the Senate; the Parliamentarian actually makes the references. All references are subject to be questioned, and the final determination of the committee to which a bill shall be referred is lodged with the Senate itself, since decisions of the chair are subject to appeal.

Conclusion: The Presiding Officer of the Senate has not been made as powerful, politically speaking, as has the Speaker of the House. Historically, the significance of the office has varied considerably with the personality in the chair, with some being more dominating than others, some more talkative than others, and some more politically active than others. Under all conditions and at all times, he presides, keeping order and decorum, recognizing Senators to speak, rendering parliamentary rulings when occasions arise, presenting business to the Senate, voting in case of a tie, referring bills to committees, and generally enforcing the rules of the Senate.

CHAPTER V

The Floor Leaders and Whips

Floor Leaders

The floor leaders and whips of the two houses, while not mentioned in the rules of either, play important roles in the enactment of legislation.[1] The floor leaders, to fill their posts successfully, must be truly leaders, and not just in title. Theirs is a thankless task from the point of view of the individual Member; each legislator knows best what he would like to have done, but the floor leaders must speak for the interests of the party which might cut across the desires of the individual Representative or Senator. When bills are brought up for consideration, the majority and minority leaders of the body concerned are expected to pursue a course in keeping with their party's legislative program; they have no parliamentary rules empowering them to accomplish their tasks; theirs is no public office of authority, backed with power to order the members of their parties to hew to the line in voting. Obviously they have the support of their party organizations and can get party favors, particularly for those who are "regulars." But there are never enough "party plums" to exchange for all votes cast.

[1] The office of the floor leader has had a very interesting history. In the early Congresses there was no party official bearing this title but as the amount of work increased, it became necessary to have some person as the acknowledged director of the program. In the House, the early titular floor leaders were at the same time the chairmen of the Ways and Means Committee. Before the division of the work of that committee, the duties of its chairmen were so numerous that they automatically became the actual leaders, since as chairmen of that committee they had to direct the consideration of most of the legislation presented to the House. From 1865 until 1896 the burden of handling most of the legislation was shifted to the chairman of the Appropriations Committee, who then was designated most frequently as the leader. From 1896 until 1910 once again the chairmen of the Ways and Means Committee were usually sought as the floor leaders. During all of these years before the "Cannon revolution" of 1910, the Speaker, who appointed all members to committees, saw to it that his party opponent for the Speakership, some Representative with a large following, or one of his faithful lieutenants was made the floor leader. When in 1911 the Democrats, who had been in the minority since 1895, came back into power, they continued the precedent of designating the chairman of the Ways and Means Committee as the floor leader. The choice of floor leader, as of the Speaker, was made by the Democratic caucus. In 1919 the Republicans came back into power and introduced still another idea. Their new leader, ex-chairman of the Ways and Means Committee and now chosen by the Republican Conference to be floor leader, was made chairman ex-officio of the Republican Committee on Committees as well as that of the Republican steering committee, but he was no longer a member of any legislative committee of the House.

Furthermore, Senators and Representatives are concerned with
the districts they represent. There have been comparativly few
strict party votes in recent Congresses. When the voters of a State
elect a solid party delegation, it does not mean that that State
agrees with all the proposals of the same National political party;
and some Senators and Representatives gain the distinction of
being independent, regardless of their party affiliation. Nevertheless, if party government is to survive there must be present at
all times some semblance of a political organization. All Representatives and Senators cannot ignore their respective political
party, turning to it only for convenience sake, if there is to be
party-government in Congress. Thus the floor leaders with the
aid of their cohorts must reckon with all inconsistencies and
variances and try to hold enough supporters together to maintain
a coherent and powerful organization in cases of showdown.

A floor leader must have real ability to gain the confidence of
the members of his political faith; he must have administrative
and organizational talent; he must be easy to approach, with the
type of personality to which members of his party may feel free
to go and expose their troubles, political positions, and ambitions.

Any close observer visiting in the galleries of either house during a session is most certain to be attracted to the part the majority and minority floor leaders play in the program. The floor
leaders of the Senate are the mediators between the individual
Senator and members of his party as a whole; these relationships,
however, are seldom recorded—the same generalization is true in
the case of the House floor leaders.

Election: All of the floor leaders are chosen by their respective caucuses or conferences; the announcement of their
selection is later made known to the legislative body concerned.
In the House, practice reveals that when a Representative accepts
an appointment to become the majority or minority floor leader,
he relinquishes any right to be a member of a legislative committee; he may continue to serve in certain other strategic political
positions. In the Senate, he continues to serve on standing committees; Senator Wallace H. White, Jr., served as majority leader
in the 80th Congress and also as chairman of the Interstate and
Foreign Commerce Committee.

The leaders serve only during the pleasure of the party membership of the bodies of which they are a member, and while no

leader in recent years has been removed during the term of office for which he was elected, his party's membership retains the right to terminate his services at any time.[2]

Experience Prior to Election: In the House from 1919 to 1947, the Republicans have had six and the Democrats seven different persons to serve as their floor leaders. Of the six Republicans,[3] two of them stood high on the Ways and Means Committee, one on the Appropriations Committee, and three on the Rules Committee. Of the seven Democrats,[4] three stood high on the Ways and Means, one on the Appropriations, two on the Rules, and one on the Interstate and Foreign Commerce committees. Thus, all of them had enjoyed long service in the House before promotion to the office.

The Republican Senators since the early part of the 20th century have stuck closer to the seniority rule in selecting their floor leaders than have the Democrats. Neither party has hewed strictly to the line; both require apprenticeship and ignore first termers who might entertain any such ambition. In the 80th Congress, the Democratic leader was older in term of service than the Republican.

In 1919, the Republicans assumed control of the Senate, this time with the Wilson Administration still in power. Senator Curtis, later to become Vice President of the United States, was soon to become floor leader, having been Vice Chairman of the Republican Conference, Republican whip, and member of the Republican Committee on Committees and of the Steering Committee. Jim Watson, Senate veteran, followed Curtis in that capacity in 1929, retaining that post until replaced by Senator McNary in 1933; Senator White became leader in 1944 at the death of McNary. In the case of the Democrats, Senator Oscar Underwood was elected Democratic floor leader on March 5, 1921, by the Democratic Caucus, after having been in the Senate only seven years; when Senator Underwood retired in 1923, Senator Joe Robinson was promoted to that post on December 3, of the same year instead of one of the senior Senators, to be followed by Senator Alben Barkley on July 22, 1937, who was far down on the seniority list.

[2] In the second session of the 78th Congress (1944), Senator Barkley broke with President Roosevelt on February 23, over his veto of the tax bill, and resigned as floor leader. The next morning at a meeting of the Democratic Conference of the Senate, he was re-elected unanimously.
[3] They were: Mondell, Longworth, Tilson, Snell, Martin, and Halleck.
[4] They were: Garrett, Garner, Rainey, Byrns, Bankhead, Rayburn, and McCormack.

Office of the Leaders: In the House, the position of the floor leader for the Republicans is more inclusive in scope than that of the Democrats; the Republican leader serves on both the Republican Committee on Committees and on the Steering Committee. The Democratic Committee on Committees, on the other hand, is composed of the Democratic members of the Ways and Means Committee, and as this is a legislative committee, the floor leader is not eligible to become a member. In the Senate, the Democratic floor leader in recent years has served as chairman of the Democratic Conference and of its Steering Committee, while the Republican leader has not enjoyed such prestige; Senator McNary served as the Republican leader and chairman of its Conference, but he held no other top post, while Senator White, who succeeded him, was leader and chairman of the Interstate and Foreign Commerce Committee, but held no other top preferment; he was an ex-officio member of the Republican Policy Committee, but not its chairman. Thus it can be seen that there has been little consistency in either of the two parties or houses in the determination of the floor leaders' orbit; the post is subject to change to meet the situation. Actual leadership, particularly in the Senate, is either given to the man most nearly fitted in the qualities of experience and personality or it is lodged in a commission of key party officials, with the floor leader as spokesman.

Floor Leaders—The Party's Agent: The relations between the floor leaders and their party memberships revolve around an exchange basis. Individual Representatives and Senators usually have problems of their own to solve, but which they cannot accomplish singlehanded; these situations can become embarrassing to them, particularly in the absence of leadership support. It is not unbelievable that Members of Congress fear committing themselves on issues over which their constituents seem equally divided. The floor leaders are commonly in positions to reconcile individuals finding themselves in such predicaments. On doubtful issues, if a good party supporter takes his troubles to his floor leader, relief is usually available; to illustrate: it is helpful to a Member for a party official to announce at the time of the vote that Mr. —— was unavoidably absent.

In the House, more so than in the Senate, good party workers find the support of the leadership most helpful in the making of a good legislative record toward re-election; matters worth con-

sidering with the leadership include: how and when to participate
in debates, committee assignments and appointments as well as
political advancements, consideration of particular pieces of legislation, patronage problems, and administrative action in the Federal Government when the President and the party in control of
Congress are of the same political faith. Into the office of the
floor leaders go the troubles of the individual members of the
same political faith. The work of the leader in making party
government function must not be underestimated; he is the great
"mitigator" for individual Members' ills; to the party he is the
cement that holds it together.

Relations With Leadership: The floor leaders work very
closely with all other agents of the party, not to dominate them
but to get cooperation and unity for better results in carrying out
the party's legislative program. He is concerned with integrating
the forces of the party machine toward the objective of making
it possible for the party to work as a unit. He is always an ex-
officio member of the steering or policy committees, and he keeps
in continuous touch with the chairmen of the various standing
committees to keep posted as to the progress being made on proposed legislation, and when it will be ready for consideration by
the Senate or House as the case might be. Depending on how
successfully this is done, the leadership is able to stabilize and
divide the legislative work somewhat equally throughout the
session.

Advisor of Status of Legislation: The leaders' knowledge
of legislation must include any information on when the various
committees will report any of the important bills so that he can
keep his program properly planned, or so that he will be able to
inform the membership at any time when a particular measure
is expected to be reported. The leaders usually have a comprehensive acquaintance with all significant bills which have been
reported from any of the various committees. They usually know
the approximate date when such measures will be called up for
disposition and are ready to give out this information upon request by the Members.

Legislative Program: The chairman of the various committees commonly consult with the majority leaders. They approach him and he them concerning any plans to call up bills or
resolutions which deviate from the planned program. In the

House, the majority leader is usually interviewed by the various chairmen even before they introduce a special rule or request from the Rules Committee. For example, the Revenue bill of 1935 was considered under a special rule. Mr. Doughton, the chairman of the Ways and Means Committee, however, consulted with Majority Leader Byrns before asking the Rules Committee for the rule. After the Ways and Means Committee had voted sixteen to five that a special rule be requested, Mr. Doughton went to Mr. Byrns and discussed party support of such proposition on the floor of the House. The Rules Committee, though usually in accord with the leadership, is free to give a rule or to refuse it, on the merits of the bill *per se,* or on the merits of giving the bill special consideration.

Part in Debate: The leaders' performances on the House or Senate floors, as the case might be, in bringing about the passage or rejection of proposed legislation are primarily political; they are selected to this top political post with that objective. Their speeches, therefore, recommending the passage of a bill are not necessarily confined to the merits of the bill; they might remind the membership of the needs of the party and of party loyalty, the conditions and times, and the legislation under consideration. To illustrate: When Mr. Underwood of Alabama closed debate on the passage of the Panama bill in the Sixty-third Congress, as floor leader, he stated:

I have served from one Democratic administration to another. I have never scratched a party ticket; I have always endeavored to live up to and sustain my party's platform. . . . The Democratic Party, not I, wrote this provision as to free tolls in its platform. I believe this plank of the platform is right. . . . Believing it is right, there is but one position that I can take, and that is to sustain the position of my party as expressed in its convention and in its platform.[5]

From the very beginning as floor leader, Mr. Rayburn conducted himself as a true party leader. He had stated upon accepting the new assignment that he expected to "make it his business to try to put through the program in connection with the Speaker" and other responsible leaders of the House, and he worked closely with the President to see that the administration's legislative program was enacted.

Representative Rayburn as a leader of the House was not very loquacious. He was regularly in attendance when the House was

[5] C.R., 63-2, p. 5616.

good temper, firm will, and the ability to appreciate the services rendered by other men. Joviality and affability enhance his popularity. He must have an interesting personality. He must be a good organizer of men, and above all, know how to work with them. These qualities may make a very successful leader in the absence of attributes of a forceful and persuasive public speaker.

On Senator Barkley's eighth anniversary as floor leader, the longest period of time served in that capacity by any other in the history of the Senate,[7] his colleagues had the following to say: Senator George declared:

Mr. President, I wish to say that the distinguished majority leader has at all times maintained the dignity of his political party in this body, but he likewise has approached the discharge of all his duties, as the President of the United States says, without "semblance of partisanship or desire for party advantage whenever the welfare of our nation required it."

Senator White, the minority leader, declared:

I have wondered many times how it was possible for him to master the intricacies of the many legislative subjects which come before the Senate; how he could discuss them with such force and such clarity as he has done. . . .[8]

Duties of the Floor Leaders

Majority and Minority Leaders: The duties of the floor leaders are very much alike. Any major differences are due to the relative strength of the two parties. The majority floor leader, as an agent of the majority, in effect speaks for his whole house; the minority leader speaks for his party. One majority leader said that his duties were "manifold and diversified. This person assumes an assiduous position which makes him a leader in the true sense of the word. His activities, if not influence, make him the titular leader. . . . He is considered the main agent of his party and defends it or assists it whenever possible." A minority leader stated that his duties:

are hardly less responsible and exacting than those of the majority leader; such difference being only in kind and degree. The position of minority leader is important, not only from a party standpoint but in the interest of public business, requiring in its occupant a high degree of alertness and tact combined with parliamentary knowledge; it involves at least three elements—political, parliamentary, and legislative.

[7] See *American Political Science Review* XL, p. 260, April, 1946.
[8] *American Political Science Review*, XL, p. 260 (April, 1946).

As spokesman for the minority, he gives close attention to all proposed legislation and he may employ any legitimate parliamentary tactics to embarrass the majority party.

Cannon's Precedents quotes from the *Congressional Record* for May 11, 1928, the following statement of functions and duties:

The floor leader, especially the leader of the majority side, has much to do with the legislative program. The majority leader, of course, represents the majority on the floor. Motions he makes are usually passed. He endeavors to represent the majority view and the majority follow his leadership. He leads in debate on administration matters and gives the House and the country the viewpoint of his party on the legislative program.

The leader keeps in touch with proposed legislation, the status of bills of importance, with the steering committee of which he is chairman, and with the attitude of the Rules Committee. He confers with committee chairmen and Members in general. The majority leader often confers with the President and advises with him regarding administrative measures. He takes to the President the sentiment of the party in the House and he brings to the party in the House the sentiment of the President.

Director of Program: The majority and minority floor leaders, in cooperation with the steering and policy committees as the case might be, manage the legislative programs of the two houses.

They proceed to dispose of nearly all noncontroversial business under unanimous consent; many controversial measures are called up for consideration under that procedure. This system saves time and also gives any Member power to block the program. The memberships commonly follow the majority leaders for political purposes; occasionally, however, Members buck the leadership, deeming their own case more important.

All bills under the call of the Calendar in the Senate and on the Unanimous Consent Calendar in the House are disposed of without debate and "without objection." Every Representative or Senator, independent of party organization, is free to object to bills disposed of under this procedure. The leaders watch the passage of bills after this fashion very closely, to protect the party or an individual Member who cannot be present.

Not infrequently, agreements between the majority and minority leaders for the disposition of business are revealed, which bar some measures from being brought up on a particular day; or due to the absence of some Senators or Representatives who are interested in measures coming up in their chamber, the leaders, in accord with their prior agreements, insist that the bill be held over until their return. And while the leaders are unable to rule by arbitrary edicts, the memberships of both houses usually give them deference.

The majority leaders or someone designated by them remain on the floor continuously to see that the program is carried out to the party's satisfaction; the minority leaders or someone designated by them stay to defend the rights of the minority. If at any time it becomes necessary to pass some measure unexpectedly, the majority leader, with the support of other "key" Members in the absence of opposition, quickly changes from the planned program and moves to take care of the emergency.

When proceeding under unanimous consent procedure, "reserving the right to object" to the unanimous consent request is a common practice; this "play" is used to avoid an outright objection and yet allow persons concerned to establish a grievance, or to find out more details about the request before allowing it to be approved. One objection blocks the request, but the majority leaders usually have their way on all reasonable requests, even in the face of "independents." Note this illustration from the second session of the Seventy-third Congress:

Mr. BYRNS. Mr. Speaker, I ask unanimous consent to address the House for 2 minutes on a noncontroversial subject.
The SPEAKER. Is there objection?
Mr. MOTT. Mr. Speaker, I reserve the right to object; and in connection with this I call the attention of the distinguished majority leader to the fact that, in reply to my protest on the 2d of March to sending the Independent Offices bill to the Appropriations Committee, he assured us that the Appropriations Committee—
Mr. O'CONNER. Mr. Speaker, I demand the regular order.
The SPEAKER. The regular order is, is there objection?
Mr. MOTT. Reserving the right to object, and I shall object unless I be allowed to finish my statement—
Mr. O'CONNOR. Mr. Speaker, I demand the regular order.
Mr. BYRNS. The matter I want to talk about is purely noncontroversial, of interest to the gentleman as well as to every other Member of the House.
Mr. MOTT. I just want to call the attention of the majority leader to the assurance that he gave us at that time.
Mr. O'CONNER. Mr. Speaker, I demand the regular order.
The SPEAKER. Is there objection to the gentleman from Tennessee?
Mrs. ROGERS of Massachusetts. Mr. Speaker, I reserve the right to object.
Mr. O'CONNER. I demand the regular order.
The SPEAKER. Is there objection?
Mrs. ROGERS of Massachusetts. Mr. Speaker, reserving the right to object, I ask—

Mr. O'CONNOR. Mr. Speaker, I demand the regular order.
The SPEAKER. Is there objection to the request of the gentleman
from Tennessee?
There was no objection.[9]

Before attempting to call up a bill under unanimous consent out
of the regular order of business, Members generally consult the
leadership; in the House, it is customary for any Member, including chairmen, to notify the leader and the Speaker prior to
making any request to deviate from the planned order of business.
The leaders on the contrary, will object readily to special requests which contravene their program, be they to bring up proposed legislation, to proceed out of order, or to any request that
will delay disposition of the pending business.

On July 17, 1945, Senator Barkley during the consideration of
the Bretton Woods Agreement (H.R. 3314) in the 79th Congress stated:

> I have no objection to the Senator addressing himself to the subject he
> has in mind, but I wish to express the hope that until the pending bill is
> acted upon we may eliminate extraneous discussions which have no bearing
> on the bill. We have now spent 2 days in discussions on the bill. I under-
> stand there are a number of amendments on the desk to be offered to this
> measure which will probably invoke some discussion. It is very important
> that we dispose of this legislation at the earliest possible date. I hope that
> from tomorrow on until this measure is disposed of Senators will not under-
> take to discuss extraneous matters which have no connection with the bill.[10]

In the House, it is a common practice for Representatives to
ask unanimous consent to make brief speeches on various subjects
before completion of the business for the day, but the leaders will
object to these requests on the grounds that they consume too
much time if the legislative program is pressing. The following
quotations will illustrate:

> Mr. CONNERY. Mr. Speaker, I ask unanimous consent to proceed for
> 2 minutes more.
> The SPEAKER. Is there objection?
> Mr. SNELL. Mr. Speaker, reserving the right to object, is any other
> business before the House this afternoon?
> Mr. BYRNS. Mr. Speaker, I reserve the right to object. We have a
> conference report that we desire to consider and dispose of, and then there
> is the legislative appropriation bill; and under general debate on that bill
> the gentleman will have the right to discuss this or any other subject in
> order in general debate. We are then to follow it with the tariff bill; and
> I do think the gentleman should give us an opportunity to proceed with the
> business before the House. I object.[1]

[9] Riddick, op. cit., pp. 71-72.
[10] C.R., 79-1, p. 7626.
[11] C.R., 73-2, pp. 5061-5062 (daily edition) ; see C.R., 71-2, p. 2983.

Mr. Rayburn had not been floor leader long before he introduced the practice of prohibiting endless brief speeches at the beginning of each session before the House proceeded to the day's legislative program. Early in 1937 he served notice on the House membership that he would object to speeches of more than a minute's duration until each day's legislative business had been disposed of. He stated:

Mr. Speaker, reserving the right to object, and I am not going to object this time, but a few days ago Members got in the habit of asking unanimous consent to proceed for 1 minute; then it was 2, then 3, then 4, and now it is 5. There is not a great deal of difference betyeen 5, 6, 7, or 10. I may say that hereafter to requests to address the House for more than 1 minute before the legislative business of the day has been concluded I shall object.[18]

Again, during the consideration of the labor bill (H.R. 4908) in 1946 in the Senate, Senator Barkley warned against the procedure of "yielding time." He told the Senate that he would make a point of order against any Senator who held the floor and "farmed it out" to others for speeches.

The leaders sometime find it necessary to lecture their memberships because of poor attendance or lack of interest shown in the legislative program. The following two quotations from the Seventy-ninth Congress, first session, will emphasize the point: On April 10th, 1945, Senator Barkley lectured the Senators:

I do not know what has happened to the Senate of the United States. I regret to say what I am going to say, but it seems to me that it has reached an all-time peak in irresponsibility of attendance on the floor of the Senate. We can get but few Senators to come here while there is under consideration one of the most important matters that will be before the Senate in weeks, involving billions upon billions of dollars worth of property; and when the debate has been concluded Senators will come trooping in, asking somebody at the door what the Senate is voting on and how they should vote. It does not present a very encouraging picture of deliberation in the Senate of the United States.

On June 22, 1945, Representative Ramspeck, whip, acting as leader, reminded the Democratic Members of the House during consideration of OPA extension, that "it is about time they woke up. It is the responsibility of the Democratic party to legislate and, therefore, more important that Democrats be on the floor than Republicans."

Leader's Responsibility: When the memberships are not supporting the program as they should, it is left to the leaders to rectify the situation. Their power is not absolute, and they may not count on the same Representatives and Senators in every controversy for their vote. Sometimes it is a matter of marching up the hill and down again; various individuals or groups just refuse to cooperate with their leaders in support of certain bills, as in the case with the Southern Democrats when such issues as FEPC or Anti-Poll Tax are brought up for consideration by the Democratic leadership. Some Senators and Representatives just refuse to follow the leadership; they follow their own desires with little regard for party support. By and large, however, the majority leadership nearly always "runs the show." Endless examples, of which the following is but one, are convincing:

On March 20, when the Senate was considering the Naval Appropriation Bill, a vote was taken on the so-called Argentine Beef Amendment, showing yeas 32 (32 Dem.), nays 32 (9 Dem., 21 Rep. ,and 2 others). Vice-President Wallace was entertaining at a luncheon, and hence was not present to break the tie. Without objection, the Senate on March 24 approved a motion by Senator Barkley, the majority floor leader, to correct the roll-call to make the vote 33 to 32 in favor of the amendment—which was then ordered engrossed as a part of the Naval Bill.[13]

If the party is trying to block the consideration of a certain measure, it is expected that the members of the majority party will recognize that fact and act accordingly. If they do not cooperate thus, the leader will warn them. If a member deliberately bucks the party, and this is the practice of the House more so than in the Senate, the leader will advise that it is not the best course for the Member's own good. To cite an extreme case during the leadership of Representative Mann:

Mr. MONDELL. Mr. Speaker, I ask unanimous consent that when the House adjourns today it adjourn to meet on Monday.
The SPEAKER. The gentleman from Wyoming asks unanimous consent that when the House adjourns today it adjourn to meet on Monday next. Is there objection?
Mr. SEARS. Reserving the right to object, Mr. Speaker, what is the request?
The SPEAKER. That when the House adjourns today it adjourn to meet on Monday next. Is there objection?
Mr. SEARS. I object for the present.
The SPEAKER. The gentleman objects for the present.
Mr. MANN. That will not pass your Florida bill (Laughter.).[14]

Expediter of Program: The floor leaders play an important part in the legislative mechanism. They engineer the legislative

[13] *American Political Science Review,* Vol. 36 (April 1942), p. 294.
[14] C.R., 67-2, p. 2717.

programs through the two houses comparably to the way an engineer pilots his train. The engineer is advised when to pull out of a station by the signals from the flagman or conductor, but once the order has been given, the engineer is responsible to pull safely into the next station on schedule. The steering committees, policy committees, and the chairmen of various standing committees play the part of conductor and flagmen, but once the order has been placed in the hands of the floor leaders, it is theirs to see that they are carried out. If the passage of a particular bill is desired by a certain date the leaders are responsible to see that a vote on the bill is reached before the close of that day; in the House, with the motion of the previous question and debate restrictions, such a goal is easily within the grasp of the majority leader.

Relations of the Minority and the Majority Leaders

In debates, the majority and minority leaders appear to the visitor in the galleries to be generals of enemy camps. During heated debates on certain partisan issues or particular conflicts on procedure, one can observe the flushed faces of the two leaders as they stand across the aisle from each other and shake their fists and make emphatic assertions. Their actions on some occasions are so pugnacious that a visitor would assume that they had really never spoken to each other privately, but if the same visitor could see them back of the scene ten minutes later talking things over in a friendly manner, he would change his opinion. Some of the floor leaders of the two parties have been very good friends in private life.

The minority leader keeps in constant touch with the majority leader relative to the program. In this way the two leaders keep their parties in step as far as procedure is concerned. By the use of informal agreements between the leaders, the minority leader is in a position to advise his members in advance as to what the program will be for a few days ahead. Many such agreements are made between these two men off the floor, and in formal sessions they are usually carried out. Of course the majority could ignore the minority, but such action would be unwise. The minority, though powerless in a showdown, can cause the majority no little trouble. It is much better for the majority leader to work with the minority leader as far as feasible, rather than have his opposition. Obstructive tactics by the minority party will always delay considerably the legislative program.

Whips

Position: Each party in both houses has an official designated as the "Whip." [15] The whips are selected by and subject to removal by their respective floor leaders or caucuses. In absence of the floor leaders, their whips act for them.

The whips may or may not appoint assistants; the House whips usually have assistants, with their number and boundary of districts changing with each new regime. When assistant whips are appointed they are allocated to expedite the canvassing of their party membership to obtain opinions or to pass out information. In any case, the whip always establishes a machine or mechanism to make contact upon short notice with any members of his party; this can be done by obtaining all possible addresses as to the whereabouts of each and then arrange them so that each can be contacted in a minimum length of time. In the Senate, the secretaries to the Majority and Minority serve their respective parties to a great extent in this regard.

Expedites Contacts: With this set-up, each floor leader can have contact with every member of his party in a short time. The organization is more formal and planned in the House than in the Senate. On any occasion, should the floor leaders order a tally taken on a partisan issue on which there is doubt, prior to a vote, or just to find how his party members stand on various issues, he will consult with his whip. In the House where the whips have assistants they may call a hurried meeting of the assistants and inform them of the situation. Each assistant then hurriedly informs all members of his party from his district of an immediate assembly to take a tally of opinions, or communicates with them to obtain such opinions. As soon as all such conferences have been held, the assistants report their findings to their whip. By this process, within less than an hour if all Representatives are in town, the whip can obtain accurate information and the leader thereby learns what support he may expect from his party. The same system can be used to pass out information in case of "emergencies," or to acquaint the members of each party with the party desires.

[15] The Whip system was organized about 1900.

The whips are primarily responsible for keeping the members of their party in attendance during consideration of controversial legislation, particularly during a vote or in anticipation of such a vote.

In the House at the end of each week the majority whip sends out a letter outlining the official program for the week ahead. This program is frequently modified to care for issues arising unexpectedly which must be acted on immediately, but usually the program outlined in those letters is followed rather closely.

Though the organizations of the parties may differ at times, and variations are introduced in each house by both parties from one administration to another, the purpose is always to get a unified party. The leaders are always striving to that end. If expediency calls for alteration in the old set-up, the necessary changes will be made in due time. Fellow members always fall into line because of an "uncanny ability" to understand that if they expect to get far in party rank, they must support the party machine.

Membership Follows: The memberships of the parties, depending on how successfully the leader has his party organized, will "about face" to follow their party leaders. In the last decade both houses have completely reversed their votes on particular legislative issues. One of the most classic examples follows: In the House on July 5, 1913, Mr. Mann, minority leader, led his Republican followers in support of the Levy amendment to a resolution to create an investigating committee. Then on the 9th of the same month, Mr. Mann announced that he had changed his mind, and he moved to reconsider the vote whereby the Levy amendment had been adopted. Practically all the Republicans to a man, who had followed him to adopt the amendment, now followed him to reject it. Again on May 23, 1912, the House adopted the Doremus amendment to the canal bill by a vote of 147 to 128. The same issue was before the House again on March 31, 1914, and the amendment (to repeal the tolls exemptions) was repealed by a vote of 247 to 162.[16]

[16] C.R., 62-2, p. 7019; C.R., 63-2, p. 6089.

CHAPTER VI

Instruments For Determination of Legislative Program

Bills on Calendar and Order of Consideration

As already pointed out, after a new Congress has organized for business, the committees play an important part in the selection of proposed legislation for consideration. The bills which are approved by standing committees are reported to their respective houses and placed on a calendar of business. The fact that a bill has been placed on a calendar, however, does not mean that it will be called up for immediate consideration. Many bills reported are never acted on but are permitted to die on the calendar when the Congress adjourns *sine die*. The procedure for consideration is more complex in the House than in the Senate. The House has five such calendars on which bills are placed when they are reported. In addition, definite days of each month are set aside by the rules for the consideration of particular types of bills or for consideration of bills under special procedure, namely: Calendar Wednesday business, District of Columbia business, Suspension of the Rules, and business placed on the Consent Calendar, Discharge Calendar, and Private Calendar. Each of these is discussed in more detail elsewhere in this volume.

In the Senate all bills reported are placed on one calendar known as General Orders; Senate business, however, is divided into the following categories: General Orders, Resolutions and Motions Over Under the Rule, Motions for Reconsideration, and Subjects on the Table. But these classifications are of little significance in a discussion of the Senate program and its order of business.

There is little relationship in either house between the various calendars or types of business, and the order in which bills are brought up for disposition. Though bills and resolutions are placed on all calendars in consecutive order according to the time they are reported, they are not always thus considered. It is true that bills on the Consent and Private Calendars (when these

103

calendars are under call) in the House are called in the order in which they are reported, and passed in that order unless someone objects. Those calendars, however, can be called only on specific days each month and objection by three Members to any bill precludes affirmative action on it by the House. In the Senate during the morning hour when unobjected-to bills are disposed of under the call of the calendar, bills are likewise brought up in the order in which they are reported and they are passed in that order by unanimous consent; one objection prohibits consideration.

Further, all bills passed from the Private and Consent calendars in the House and passed in the Senate without objection under the call of the calendar are either minor or noncontroversial legislative proposals.

Both houses spend comparatively few hours each year passing bills under unanimous consent procedure or "without objection" regardless of the calendar on which they are placed. It is the major issues of each session over which there is controversy that present the problem in making up the legislative program for the session.

Thus the instruments discussed in this chapter concern themselves primarily with the major bills and controversial issues; in effect, they decide the order in which the real debates in each session will be staged.

Instruments for Determining Senate Program

Program Planners: The steering committees and policy committees, together with a combination of the leadership, including all the chairmen of standing committees, speak for the Senate as to what the order of business shall be. Specifically, the instruments of the majority in reality make the determination since in a showdown the majority party is able to command more votes.

While the whole membership has a voice and while the political leadership plans the program subject to the will of a majority, the majority leader of the Senate is usually the mouthpiece for his party as to what the program shall be. The majority leader is always an ex-officio member of the policy and steering committees and frequently is its chairman. He may also be chairman of a standing committee. Thus he is an interlocking agent for all of the instruments determining the program, consequently strategically fitted to be the spokesman.

Steering Committees: The Steering Committee of the Republican party for the 80th Congress was composed of nine Senators of whom the Republican floor leader, the Republican whip, and the chairman of the Republican Conference were ex-officio members. The other six members were appointed by the chairman of the Republican Conference subject to the confirmation of the conference. The Steering Committee selected its own chairman. Its personnel for the first session follows: Senators White, majority leader; Wherry, majority whip; Millikin, chairman of the Republican Conference; and Senators Taft, *chairman*, Brooks, Ferguson, Hawkes, Cordon, and Saltonstall. The Steering Committee is an organ of the Republican party and has no recognition in the Senate rules.

The Democratic Steering Committee was composed of twelve Senators including three ex-officio members: the floor leader, the party whip, and the secretary of the conference. The members in addition to those ex-officio, were appointed by the Democratic leader, who was also chairman of the Democratic Conference and of its Steering Committee. The members for the 80th Congress, first session, were: Senators Barkley, *chairman* and minority leader, Lucas, whip, and McMahon, secretary of the conference, and Senators McKellar, George, Tydings, Green, Wagner, Hayden, O'Mahoney, Thomas (Utah), and Connally. Like the Republican Steering Committee it is a party organ, but is not recognized by the Senate rules.

The objectives of the steering committees,[1] as the name implies, are to steer by studying the legislative problems and policies of their respective parties and then to help to effectuate the program according to their party policy. In the 80th Congress with the introduction of the two policy committees, these committees were practically wheels within wheels—their memberships and the purpose of their creation were much the same.

Policy Committees: The Senate has two policy committees, a Republican and a Democratic; P.L. 663 of 79th Congress set the membership at seven each.[1a] The Republican Policy Committee for the 80th Congress consisted of the first seven Senators appointed

---

[1] The Democratic Steering Committee of the 80th Congress concerned itself almost solely with making committee appointments; discussions of policy were conducted by its Policy Committee.

[1a] Neither party has hewed to the letter of this provision of this law.

to its Steering Committee, already named above, of which three were ex-officio members—the chairman of the conference, the floor leader, and the whip. The conference rules of the Republican party place some restrictions on continuous membership on its committee, which are not applicable to the members ex-officio. Under the practices of the 80th Congress, first session, in addition to the seven members authorized by law, the Republicans permitted two Senators, the last two named to its Steering Committee, to serve in advisory capacity. They were invited to attend each meeting of the group; in effect, making the Republican Steering Committee and the Republican Policy Committee one and the same, but meeting under different names.

The Democratic Policy Committee for the 80th Congress was appointed by its floor leader, who was also chairman of the Democratic Conference, pursuant to a resolution adopted by the conference. The membership for the first session included: Senator Barkley, *chairman,* who was also chairman of the Democratic Conference and of the Steering Committee.[2] The others were: Senators Tydings, Russell, Hatch, O'Mahoney, Green, and Hill; the two following ex-officio members were also invited to attend each meeting: Senators Lucas, the whip, and McMahon, secretary to the Democratic Conference.

The law establishing this organ for each party provides that their purpose is "The formulation of over-all legislative policy of the respective parties . . ."[3] Each committee is authorized a staff "To assist it in study, analysis, and research on problems involved in policy determination, which is to be appointed by the policy committee concerned." The steering committees are not legal creatures.

The Leadership, Including Committee Chairmen: The majority and minority floor leaders are elected by, and responsible to their respective political parties; hence, they are spokesmen for them. The whips, agents of the party, work closely with their own floor leader. They "whip the Senators of their own political faith in line, keep them on the floor of the Senate, or nearby, for voting purposes, and advise the Senators of the party's position on each issue as it comes up in the Senate for consideration." Each of them likewise keeps his floor leader as spokesman for

[2] He was made chairman by the conference.
[3] P.L. 663—79th Congress.

the party advised as to his activities and results, and he works closely with him; in the absence of his floor leader, he acts in that capacity.

The chairmen of the steering and policy committees, who serve the party in determination of party policy and program, obviously keep in close touch with the thinking of the members of their own party and therefore know the type of program their respective membership desires.

The committee chairmen and ranking minority members of each committee know their respective committees and the dates each committee wishes to bring up particular legislation under its jurisdiction. As chairman and ranking minority members of their committees they are able to advise their respective leaders already mentioned of what legislation they deem of sufficient importance to demand immediate disposition.

Hence these two small groups of Democratic and Republican leaders, consisting of some 15 to 20 each, after serious consideration and possible compromises, are able to steer a course which is acceptable to the remaining members of their own party. The Senate is usually moved to action by Members of these "two small groups."

For further discussion of the activities of the floor leaders and whips, in behalf of their own parties, see chapter devoted to a discussion of these officials; see also chapters on "Political Organizations of the Two Houses" and "Committees of Congress."

The Senate procedure is rather simple since all bills are placed on one calendar, and unless the Senate is disposing of unobjected-to bills under the call of the calendar, it works on the unfinished business, on business brought up under unanimous consent, or on business made in order by simply agreeing to put aside temporarily the unfinished business to proceed with some matter deemed more pressing. After one item of unfinished business is completed, the Senate then moves to consider some other, making of it the unfinished business.

The majority party can usually muster more votes, but under the "unrestrained" procedure in the Senate, the minority party can cause the majority endless trouble and even upset the latter's program. Consequently, the minority is usually given consideration in mapping out and executing the program. Without the minority's consent it would be impossible to reach unanimous consent agreements to limit debate on various major bills, and consequently impossible to reach a final vote on passage. Only under unanimous consent procedure may it postpone temporarily the unfinished business and immediately move to consideration of another issue; with the consent of the minority, the majority is able to follow a planned program with the greatest dispatch. These two groups of partisan leaders working together are able to keep the calendar clear of all noncontroversial issues as rapidly as they are reported; likewise they can work full speed ahead on the pending controversial proposals, adopting motions to that effect.

Instruments for Determining House Program

Program Planners: The steering committees, the Rules Committee, and the leadership, including all the chairmen of standing committees, speak for the House as to what the order of business shall be. The majority in reality makes the determinations but in consultation with the minority. The majority and minority leaders are the mouthpieces for their parties.

Like the Senate, the whole House membership has a voice, and the political leadership plans its programs subject to the will of the majority, but the majority leader of the House and the Speaker in collaboration with the Rules Committee, serve the majority party as to what the program shall be. The majority leader is nearly always an ex-officio member of the steering committee and sometimes its chairman; he does not serve as a member of a standing committee. He is never a member of the Rules Committee, the only instrument of the House which can report a privileged resolution for the consideration of non-privileged legislation, which when adopted by a majority vote of the House makes that legislation the pending business before the House. It is true that bills on the Private, Discharge, and Consent Calendars and legislative proposals which come up under Calendar Wednesday, Suspension of the Rules, and District of Columbia Day can be brought up on certain legislative days each month and in the order they are reported, but these legislative proposals do not compose the important program of a session. Likewise, privileged bills can be brought up by motion, but the major bills which are not privileged and which compose much of the work of each session must await a special rule from the Rules Committee before they can be reached.[3a]

Steering Committees: The House unlike the Senate does not have party policy committees; it has a political steering committee for each of its parties which perform much the same for their respective parties of the House as the policy and steering committees of the Senate do for theirs.

The Republican Steering Committee of the House is made up of ten Representatives selected by the Republican Committee on Committees; four ex-officio members: chairman of its Conference, its majority leader, its whip, and chairman of its Congressional Committee; and the Republican members of the Committee on Rules. While the rules of the House do not recognize this committee, it is a significant power in the determination of the House program, particularly when the Republicans are in the majority. The membership for the first session of the 80th Congress follows: Speaker Martin, *chairman;* Representatives Halleck, majority leader; Arends, whip; Woodruff, chairman of the Republican Conference; Representatives Hope, Robsion, Jenkins (Ohio), Simpson (Pa.), Wigglesworth, Knutson, Michener, Gearhart and Ploeser (Mo.); and the Republican members of the Rules Committee.

The Democratic party created its first real policy and steering committee at the first session of the 73rd Congress, calling it the "Democratic Steering Committee." It is composed of fifteen members representing fifteen geographical zones plus six ex-officio members, namely: its floor leader, whip, the chairman of its Caucus, and its highest ranking member of the committees on Appropriations, on Rules, and on Ways and Means. Each of the fifteen members is elected by the Democratic Representatives of his geographical zone. For the first session of the 80th Congress the members of the Democratic Steering Committee follow: the ex-officio members—Representatives Rayburn, minority leader; McCormack, whip; Forand, chairman of the Democratic Caucus; Doughton, ranking minority member of Ways and Means Committee; Cannon, ranking minority member of Appropriations Committee, and Sabath, ranking minority member of the Rules Committee. The fifteen zones and the Congressmen representing them follow:

[3a] See p. 124.

Representative	Zone Number	States in Each Zone
Lane (Mass.)	1	Massachusetts, Maine, Vermont, Rhode Island, Connecticut, and New Hampshire
Byrne (N. Y.)	2	New York
Hart (N. J.)	3	Pennsylvania, Delaware, New Jersey
Kerr (N. C.) and D'Alesandro (Md.)⁴	4	Virginia, Maryland, North Carolina
Peterson (Fla.) and Brown (Ga.)⁴	5	Florida, Georgia, S. Carolina
Brooks (La.)	6	Louisiana, Alabama, Mississippi
Cravens (Ark.) and Chapman (Ky.)⁴	7	Arkansas, Kentucky, Tennessee
Crosser (Ohio)	8	Ohio, West Virginia
Dingell (Mich.)	9	Indiana, Michigan
O'Brien (Ill.), Vice Chairman	10	Illinois, Wisconsin
Bell (Mo.)	11	Minnesota, Missouri, Iowa
Morris (Okla.)	12	Oklahoma, North Dakota, South Dakota, Nebraska, Kansas
Thomason (Tex.)	13	Texas
Murdock (Ariz.), Chairman	14	Montana, Idaho, Wyoming, Utah, Colorado, Nevada, Arizona, New Mexico
Jackson (Wash.), Secretary	15	California, Washington, Oregon

The functions of these committees are in a general way to determine policy and program for their respective parties. Neither ever considers a matter unless it is of vital interest to the party. The members of each committee keep in touch with their own group and if a question involves a matter of great importance they consult the members of the party they represent. In the light of such information these political groups are able to speak to the House for the membership of their party. While their recommendations are not binding, they are persuasive. Their objectives

⁴ These districts selected two representatives to the committee membership but each zone has the voting power of only one.

are to steer for their respective parties after studying their legislative problems and policies. The details of the daily schedule of the House nevertheless are left to the floor leaders, as spokesmen for their parties.

Of particular significance in the House in the determination of the House program is the Rules Committee. The part it plays in mapping out the House program is so important that much space will be devoted here to a discussion of the Rules Committee and its chairman.

The Rules Committee and Its Chairman: The chairman of the Rules Committee is one of the three outstanding leaders in the House due to the extensive power the committee has over the House program and procedure. In order to appreciate the important role assumed by this official in the legislative machine, one must acquaint oneself with the functions and jurisdiction of this committee.

First Rules Committee: Since the first Congress in 1789, the House has had a committee on rules; for a number of years, however, only select committees were authorized to report a system of rules at the beginning of each Congress. Five days after the first select committee on rules was created,[5] it reported a comprehensive set of rules which was immediately adopted.[6] The adoption of a supplemental report from the same committee completed its work [7] and there was no more important assignment for any such group for many years.

Adoption of Report and "Report at any time": On June 18, 1841, a most important precedent in behalf of the Rules Committee was established. Speaker John White, Kentucky, ruled that only a majority vote was required to adopt a resolution from the Committee on Rules changing the rules of the House. An appeal from the decision was taken, but the ruling of the Speaker was sustained. It was further held during the same Congress that

[5] On Motion
"Ordered, That a committee be appointed to prepare and report such standing rules and orders of proceeding as may be proper to be preserved in this House.
"And a committee was appointed of Mr. Gilman, Mr. Gerry, Mr. Wadsworth, Mr. Boudinot, Mr. Hartley, Mr. Smith, Mr. Lee, Mr. Tucker, Mr. Madison, Mr. Sherman, and Mr. Goodhue." (Atkinson, *The Committee on Rules and the Overthrow of Speaker Cannon*, pp. 7-8.)
[6] *Ibid.*, pp. 8-11. The report consisted of about 1,500 words arranged under four headings. Clause 6 of section 1, provided: "The Speaker shall appoint committees unless it be determined by the House that the committee shall consist of more than three members, in which case the appointment shall be by ballot of the House."
[7] Atkinson, *op. cit.*, p. 8. On April 9, 1791, the first Rules Committee, on instruction by the House, made a supplementary report relating to the Sergeant at Arms and his symbol, but the report was ordered to lie on the table. On April 14, however, the report was taken from the Speaker's table and adopted.

since the House had given the committee the right to report at all times, it might report in part at different times. This was the first precedent to make of the Rules Committee an agent through which the House might proceed to consideration of any piece of legislation.

Rules of 1853 and 1858: In 1853 the House adopted a resolution to create a select committee on rules with power to report at any time, and make their reports when presented of high privilege. On June 14, 1858, a Rules Committee, with the Speaker as a member,[8] was created, and was authorized to revise the rules and report the same at an early day in the next session of Congress.

Rule of 1880 and Special Orders: In 1880 the Rules Committee was made a standing committee with a membership fixed at five, which was in accordance with the usual number of Representatives that had served on the select committees. The jurisdiction of the committee was extended to include: "all proposed action touching the rules and joint rules." In pursuance of the above rule, the House began the practice of making special orders by adopting by a majority vote a resolution reported from the Committee on Rules,[9] a practice which was established after the will of the majority to enact certain legislation was defeated on several different occasions under the suspension of the rules. The first orders from the Committee on Rules had been reported in order to block filibuster by the minority and not at all for the purpose of giving a particular bill a special consideration. As late as 1889 Speaker Carlisle said that "The spirit of the special order is to prevent dilatory motions." [10]

Special Rules: Since the first special rule was reported the usage has increased and the scope has been extended to include a setting of the time for debate and defining the method of consideration for particular bills or classes of bills. In 1890 the House adopted a rule providing that the Rules Committee, which had been made a standing committee in 1880, should be given the power to report at any time.[11] During that Congress this right

---

[8] Mr. James L. Orr, of S.C., was Speaker. For the membership of the Committee on Rules from 1789 to 1893, see C.R., 53-1, p. 1042. Speakers had not been chairmen of select committees.

[9] *House Manual*, 80-1, sections 718-719, 730; C.R., 49-1, pp. 6758-6760.

[10] *Cannon's Procedure in the House of Representatives*, p. 381.

[11] Prior to this time the Committee on Rules had exercised the same privilege "and the uniform practice has been to give the same privilege to the Committee on Rules," said Speaker Carlisle in his decision on August 16, 1888. (C.R., 50-1, p. 7641; see also C.R., 50-2, p. 538).

was contested, but the chair decided in favor of the Rules Committee.

Mr. COVERT, rising for a parliamentary inquiry, asked: Would not a motion that the Journal of Saturday's proceedings be now read, be in order?

The SPEAKER. It would not. What is the statement of the gentleman from New York? (Mr. Tracey).

Mr. TRACEY. I raise the question of consideration, Mr. Speaker.

The SPEAKER. The Chair holds that the question of consideration cannot be raised upon the report.

Mr. TRACEY. Why, Mr. Speaker? (Laughter).

The SPEAKER. The rule provides that—it shall always be in order to call up for consideration a report from the Committee on Rules, and, pending the consideration, the Speaker may entertain one motion that the House adjourn. . . . [12]

Even as late as April 29, 1902, the right of the Rules Committee to report a resolution providing a special order for the consideration of a bill (H.R. 14018, ". . . to increase the limit of cost of certain public buildings, to authorize the purchase of sites for public buildings . . .") was questioned on the grounds that it suspended the rules of the House, and therefore such action required a two-thirds vote for adoption. Speaker Henderson decided that "The question has been fought out again and again, and is well settled that the Committee on Rules can bring in a rule providing for order of business in the House . . . There have been many decisions that a rule from the Committee on Rules which fixes the order of business with the approval of the House does not require a two-thirds vote." [13]

Speaker as Chairman of Rules Committee: In 1893 the House extended to the Rules Committee the privilege to sit during the sitting of the House, a right which no other committee enjoys. Thus the power of this committee was rapidly increased after the Speaker in 1858 became a member of the group. The Speaker as chairman of the Committee on Rules rapidly made of it an agent through which the majority party could control legislative procedure and thereby control legislation; and the Speaker as chairman became the "czar" of the House. Eventually the House membership became recalcitrant to this monopoly of power on the part of the Speaker, and in the Sixty-first Congress members of the majority party, known as insurgents, charged that the

[12] C.R., 52-1, p. 1826 (March 7, 1892).
[13] Hinds, IV, 3169; See Hinds, IV, 3170-3172.

House had "degenerated into an assembly showing no other purpose than to register the arbitrary edicts of a too powerful Committee on Rules." At first the insurgent Republicans in order to remedy conditions made allies of several Democrats and adopted a more liberal plan,[14] but the compromise was not permanent. The insurgents were not satisfied, and after a few weeks of playing the part of "watch dog" they caught the regular Republicans without a majority, combined with the Democrats, and forced the election of a new Committee on Rules which was to consist of ten Members, exclusive of the Speaker.[15] The revolution curtailed the power of the ". . . Speaker in his relation with the Committee on Rules, but the power of the committee remains unchanged."[16]

Functions and Jurisdiction of the Rules Committee: Definition of Functions: The Rules Committee is not a legislative group. It is a procedure determining organization, and it is the only committee authorized, "without special leave," to sit when the House is in session. Mr. Snell, chairman of the committee from the 68th through the 69th Congresses and later minority floor leader, said that if he understood the functions of the Rules Committee, "it is to act in harmony with the majority sentiments of the majority party of the House of Representatives. It is to act in coordination and harmony with the steering committee of the House. It is the duty of the Rules Committee, as I understand it, to act, as far as possible, for the protection of the administration and the administration program of legislation." It is the duty of the Rules Committee to feel the pulse, get the opinions and sentiments of the House, and to execute them. The committee does not attempt to dictate legislation to the House or to the country, he added.[17] The jurisdiction of the committee extends to "The rules, joint rules, and order of business of the House" and to "Recesses and final adjournments of Congress."

[14] C.R., 61-2, pp. 3285-3334. See these pages for remarks concerning the autocratic Rules Committee.

[15] C.R., 61-2, pp. 3292-3295, 3305-3434, 3388-3397, 3425-3436. The resolution was adopted by a vote of 191 to 156. The Norris Resolution provided: "There shall be a Committee on Rules, elected by the House, consisting of 10 Members, 6 of whom shall be of the majority party and 4 of whom shall be of the minority party. The Speaker shall not be a member of the committee and the committee shall select its own chairman from its own members."

The number of members on this committee was increased to 11 in the Sixty-second Congress and 13 in the Sixty-fifth Congress; since that date there were 12 until the 76th Congress at which time the number was increased to 14; at the beginning of the 80th Congress the number was decreased to 12.

[16] Chiu, *The Speaker of the House*, p. 146.

[17] C.R., 71-3, p. 3700.

In practice this definition has been interpreted to mean reports on: (1) all changes in the rules of the House, (2) creation of all select and investigating committees, (3) stipulations setting up special orders other than the consideration of legislation, (4) resolutions on recesses and adjournment, and (5) resolutions concerning the consideration of bills or classes of bills.[18] Any of these reports are adopted by a bare majority vote. Now to review these five types of reports in a little more detail:

Change Rules: (1) The Rules Committee was originally created to report all changes in the rules of the House. Any such reports are usually made and adopted at the beginning of a session, particularly at the beginning of a new Congress when there has been a change in parties. On a few occasions the rules of the House have undergone general revisions as in 1880, 1890, 1907, and 1911. Generally, however, many such resolutions are introduced in each Congress, but they die in the committee. There have not been many changes in the rules of the House in recent years;[19] Congress adopted the Legislative Reorganization Act of 1946, but that had little effect on the House rules except for changing the number of standing committees.

Create Select and Investigating Committees: (2) Resolutions to create select and investigating committees are regularly introduced and occasionally reported to the House and adopted. In recent years this procedure was common until the 80th Congress. For further details on special committees see section on Investigating Committees, pp. 150-152.

Set Up Minor Special Orders: (3) The third class of reports (on setting up special orders other than the consideration of legislation) is not so important. The number of such orders is small, and their scope is not of much significance. The effect of such rules on legislation is usually nil.

Recesses and Adjournment: (4) Resolutions effecting recesses and adjournment are handled by this committee, but this jurisdiction is of little significance.

Report Special Rules: (5) Resolutions effecting special consideration of proposed legislation account for most of the com-

---

[18] *Cannon's Procedure in the House of Representatives,* pp. 383-384. No business shall be in order before the reading of the Journal, but the Speaker has ruled it permissible "to call up for consideration a report from the Committee on Rules, and pending the consideration the Speaker may entertain one motion that the House adjourn" before the Journal is read.

[19] In fact the Rules Committee seldom reports out a resolution to change the permanent rules of the House.

mittee's work. Mr. Snell, one time chairman of the Rules Committee, insisted that if the Rules Committee were to try the sheer impossibility of bringing in each individual request, then the work of the committee would sink into utter chaos.[20] Any application must be "based upon either the necessity or the importance of the proposed legislation." [21] If the proposed legislation is of sufficient importance, from a national point of view, or if some emergency or necessity should arise having "preference above other proposed legislation which is already upon the House calendars and awaiting action, then it is within the power of the Rules Committee" to recognize such facts and to give preference to those bills above all others.[22] Under the chairmanship of Mr. Sabath, according to his own statement, the committee followed "the practice of bringing before the House any and all important legislation without having it smothered in the Rules Committee." [23] A rule is usually granted if the leaders or a majority of the committee, think the measure merits such consideration.

Inclusiveness of Special Rules: Special orders of this nature provide for the consideration of a wide range of bills and include a broad jurisdiction of subjects as to how and what may be done to any particular bill.[24] They are strictly construed and they may be worded to provide for: the consideration of a particular bill or series of bills, stipulate the length and control of debate of any measure and how a vote will be taken on the bill, consider a Senate bill in the "Committee of the Whole making in order House committee amendments and providing for separate vote on each," take a Senate bill from the Speaker's table and consider "House bill in lieu thereof in Committee of the Whole," exclude any amendments [25] or define what amendments may be offered to a bill,[26] take bills with Senate amendments from the Speaker's table and send to conference, waive points of order against a conference report, modify or temporarily stay any rule affecting the bill under consideration, exclude intervening motions after the previous question has been ordered, bar all motions to reconsider,

[20] C.R., 71-3, pp. 3699-3703.
[21] *Copyright Bill, Hearings before the Rules Committee*, H.R. 13452, 70-2, p. 32. This is a statement by Representative Charles A. Wolverton, of N. J.
[22] Ibid., p. 32.
[23] C.R., 76-1, p. 13504 (daily edition).
[24] For forms of various kinds of special orders see, Cannon, VII, 797-845.
[25] See House Resolution 205 of 76th Congress.
[26] See House Resolution 149 of 76th Congress; Hinds, IV, 3204-3205.

waive all points of order against any designated bill,[27] make it in order to offer legislation to a general appropriation bill and vice versa, authorize the suspension of the rules at any time "during the remainder of a session," allow non-germane amendments, and the like. In brief, these special orders may in effect suspend any of the rules of the House and prescribe a particular procedure for a certain duration of time.[28] Any such rule must be reported one day before adoption or else a two-thirds vote for adoption is required. Any resolution to exclude the operation of Calendar Wednesday requires a two-thirds vote for adoption and the motion to recommit may never be excluded.[29]

Special Rules of High Privilege: Reports from the Rules Committee are highly privileged. Rule XI, reads: "It shall always be in order to call up for consideration a report from the Committee on Rules (except it shall not be called up for consideration on the same day it is presented to the House, unless so determined by a vote of not less than two-thirds of the Members voting, but this provision shall not apply during the last three days of the session), and, pending the consideration thereof, the Speaker may entertain one motion that the House adjourn; but after the result is announced he shall not entertain any other dilatory motion until the said report shall have been fully disposed of." This clause has been interpreted by the chair to mean: "A report by the Committee on Rules on matters within its jurisdiction is in order at any time . . . and but one motion to adjourn and no dilatory motion may be entertained during the consideration . . ."[30] How-

---

[27] On February 20, 1907, the Committee on Rules offered a special order for the consideration of the Post Office Department Appropriation Bill, providing: ". . . The previous question shall be considered as ordered on said amendments immediately and on the bill to its final passage without intervening motion or appeal." (C.R., 59-2, p. 3493). Mr. Dalzell said in presenting the resolution: "There were certain paragraphs in the Post Office Appropriation Bill which went out on points of order. . . The object of this rule, if adopted, is to restore to the bill the paragraphs which went out on points of order . . ." (C.R., 59-2, p. 3493).

[28] A special rule was once resorted to by Speaker Cannon to evade a ruling made by the chairman of the Committee of the Whole. In 1903 a civil appropriation bill had been considered in the Committee of the Whole. Two amendments were offered for the construction of an office building near the Capitol and also for the extension of the Capitol building. Both were ruled out of order when points of order were made in the Committee of the Whole. Immediately thereafter the Speaker moved that the Committee rise, and he took the chair. Two special orders were offered by the Rules Committee to replace the provisions which had been blocked by the rulings made when points of order had been raised. The two special orders were agreed to and the provisions were added to the bill; the House resolved itself back into the Committee of the Whole to finish the bill (C.R., 57-2, p. 2051).

[29] Rule XI.

ever, of course a question of consideration on the report itself is not in order.[31]

Committee Reports: Reports "on rules, joint rules, and order of business" from the Rules Committee are to be reported to the House within three legislative days from the date decided upon by the committee. If the report is not considered when made, it is referred to the calendar, and "if not called up by the Member making the report within seven legislative days thereafter, any member of the Rules Committee may call it up as a question of privilege and the Speaker shall recognize any member of the Rules Committee seeking recognition for that purpose . . ."[32] The rule, however, does not stipulate what shall be done in case neither of the above condition is fulfilled. There is one recourse. Resolutions to bring up bills already reported, and which have been before the Rules Committee 21 days without being reported may be called up on Discharge days by the chairman of the committee which reported the bill

Adverse Reports: Adverse reports on any resolutions providing for an order of business are placed on the calendar and on Discharge days it is in order for any Member of the House to move the adoption of any such adverse report. The Speaker shall recognize the Member seeking "recognition for that purpose as a question of the highest privilege."[33]

Procedure of Reporting a Special Rule: Introduction and Reference: Special rules reported by the Rules Committee are printed in the form of simple House resolutions, introduced at will by any individual Member. Upon introduction, the Speaker refers them to that committee where they are lodged until reported back to the House. Generally speaking, rules reported out of the Rules Committee are introduced under the direction of the leadership. Of course, it is within the power of the committee membership to make a report on any resolution independent of the leaders.[34]

[30] *Cannon's Procedure in the House of Representatives,* pp. 381-382.
[31] Hinds, V, 4961-4963. The Speaker generally supports the position taken by the chairman of this committee. On one occasion Thomas C. Blanton, of Texas, had raised the point of order that the Rules Committee had no jurisdiction over a particular pending measure, since the bill had neither been introduced in the House nor had been referred to the Committee on Rules for action. Speaker Gillett replied, however, that the Committee on Rules was an executive organ of the majority of the House. If it were held that the committee could not act until the subject had been referred to it, then it would be beyond the capacity of the committee in a morning before a session to make a decision and bring in a rule which is frequently necessary and desirable at the first meeting of the House; therefore, he overruled the point of order (C.R., 67-2, pp. 9576-9577).
[32] Rule XI.
[33] Rule XI.
[34] See House Resolution 205 of 76th Congress.

Committee Consideration: By and large, if for one reason or another a committee reporting a bill desires that it should be granted special consideration, a resolution to that effect is introduced, after the committee has voted for such action and all leaders concerned have been consulted. Then the authorized member of the committee reporting the bill to the House makes the request of the Rules Committee to grant the rule. The Rules Committee may or may not hold "hearings" on the resolution before taking action. If hearings are held, any Representative may make a request to be heard. Each side will stress the merits or demerits of the issue. After all arguments have been heard, the committee usually resolves itself into an executive session to reach its decision, at which time questions of immediate need of the law, whether or not the majority expects to be embarrassed by the minority, the policy of the leadership, whether or not the rule is really needed to block conflicts during consideration, and the like are raised.

Reports: When a report on a resolution is made to the House, it is placed on the House Calendar to await consideration. Being a privileged report it is made from the floor. If the matter is not called up within seven days by the Member making the report, any member of the Rules Committee may call it up thereafter as a question of privilege.

Effects of Special Rule: All special rules are customarily debated for one hour after which a vote on adoption is taken. If adopted, the House usually proceeds immediately to act in accordance with the procedure defined in the rules, for example:

Resolved, That upon the adoption of this resolution it shall be in order to move that the House resolve itself into the Committee of the Whole House on the state of the Union for the consideration of H. R. 12348, "A bill to create a Federal cooperative marketing board, to provide for the registration of cooperative marketing, clearing house, and terminal market organizations, and for other purposes."

That after general debate, which shall be confined to the bill and shall continue not to exceed two hours, the time to be equally divided and controlled by those favoring and opposing, the bill shall be read for amendment under the five-minute rule. At the conclusion of the reading of the bill for amendment the committee shall rise and report the bill to the House with such amendments as may have been adopted, and the previous question shall be considered as ordered on the bill and the amendments thereto to final passage without intervening motion except one motion to recommit.

Usage of Special Rules: Development: It was during the Speakership of Mr. Crisp that the House began the practice which might be termed as "the era" of special orders, by considering legislation under rules reported by the Rules Committee. Since 1910 there has been a gradual though irregular increase in the number of special rules adopted during each Congress. The practice has continued until today practically every major piece of legislation not otherwise privileged is considered under a special rule. One chairman of the committee remarked that "Even the Committee on Ways and Means, the Committee on Appropriations, committees that report privileged business now come to the Committee on Rules for rules governing the consideration of matters." [35]

Usage: No two Congresses, whether controlled by the same party or not, utilize this practice to the same degree. During some sessions the number of rules granted will be insignificant, yet that Congress will enact just as many laws as a session in which there were a number of special rules granted.[36] For example, during the Sixty-eighth Congress there were 39 special rules granted and 996 laws passed, while in the Seventy-third Congress there were 61 rules granted and 976 laws passed. The number of such orders granted during any one session is always dependent upon the circumstances. Of course any explanation

[35] See C.R., 67-2, p. 8051; C.R., 71-3, p. 3702.
[36] Cannon, VII, 762. On March 17, 1910 Mr. Mann gave a list of special rules adopted during the 60th Congress. Below is a complete list of the number of rules, by session, adopted since the first session of the 60th Congress as compiled by Mr. Cannon through the 73rd; data on subsequent Congresses were compiled by the author.

Congress	Session	Number Adopted	Congress	Session	Number Adopted
60	1	6	69	2	13
60	2	3	70	1	22
61	1	5	70	2	17
61	2	6	71	1	3
61	3	5	71	2	24
62	1	3	71	3	11
62	2	11	72	1	32
62	3	4	72	2	13
63	1	6	73	1	27
63	2	17	73	2	34
63	3	5	74	1	54
64	1	14	74	2	37
64	2	11	75	1	33
65	1	7	75	2	2
65	2	25	75	3	16
65	3	8	76	1	33
66	1	21	76	2	1
66	2	19	76	3	47
66	3	9	77	1	58
67	1	26	77	2	41
67	2	29	78	1	40
67	3	1	78	2	49
67	4	12	79	1	64
68	1	14	79	2	57
68	2	8	80	1	58
69	1	22			

of this variation would include the kind and nature of bills to be considered, the demands throughout the country for particular legislation, and the needs of the leadership,[37] as well as a great number of specific and lesser conditions.

Rules not Considered: Many rules are reported to the House which are never called up. For example, in the first session of the Seventy-sixth Congress the Rules Committee reported 52 special rules of which only 35 were considered. Thirty-three of the 52 were adopted and eleven were laid on the table without consideration because the bills for which they provided consideration had been disposed of under some other procedure.[38] Nearly every special rule reported by the Rules Committee and called up means that a certain bill will be granted special consideration; the House usually adopts all of them. Only a very few of the bills for which rules provide consideration ever fail to pass the House; a larger number never become law. In the first session of the Seventy-sixth Congress nine bills considered under special rules were lost in the legislative machine, of which two died in Conference and four were never considered in the Senate. Three were even defeated in the House. This was an unusually large number to be lost in the House.[39] To illustrate the practice, the second session of the 79th Congress was a regular session, and here is what it reveals: fifty-nine special rules providing for the consideration of 54 bills were called up and acted on by the House, but only 57 were adopted.[40] The Rules Committee actually reported 91 rules providing for the consideration of particular pieces of legislation; but one was recommitted (H.Res. 625), one failed

---

[37] During the 68th Congress there were: 707 public laws and 289 private laws; during the 73rd Congress there were: 540 public laws and 436 private laws. Note the following quotation: "Yes. This committee could bring in a special rule at any time. But I want to say on that, Mr. Fassett, that my idea has always been that we ought to have just as few special rules from the Committee on Rules as possible, and that the Committee on Rules ought never to bring in a special rule unless there is a very great demand for it, or a necessity for it, and then take advantage of the emergency to act with fearlessness." (*Hearings on House Resolutions* 884, 887, 888 *and* 892 *to amend Rules XI and XXVII of the House of Representatives*, 61-3, p. 7.)

[38] *American Political Science Review*, XXXIII, p. 1038, December, 1939.

[39] Twenty-six of them, or a bill in lieu thereof, became law. Nine were lost along the way, of which two died in conference (S. 2009 and H.R. 4929), two were never debated since the rules for their consideration were rejected (S. 591 and H.R. 7120), one was voted down by the House (H.R. 6466-Townsend Bill), and four were never considered in the Senate (H.R. 5643, H.R. 3794, H.R. 5138, and H.J.Res. 306).

[40] Two rules were granted on each of five bills, making the total number of bills considered under special rule 54 instead of 59. During the last previous session, the House adopted 64, the largest number ever adopted during a single session of Congress.

of passage (H.Res. 452), 19 were "laid on the table," [41] and 13 were left on the calendar when Congress adjourned.

"An analysis of the 57 rules adopted shows that 48 provided for the immediate consideration of 48 bills. All but 13 were open rules, merely giving otherwise unprivileged business the right of way for House consideration; two were absolutely closed (so-called "gag" rules) [42] with 11 others waiving points of order against the bills for which the rules provided consideration. Of the 54 bills and resolutions for which rules were reported to the House, 42 became public law, three passed the House but died in the Senate, two passed both houses in amended form but were never cleared for the President, three passed both houses but were vetoed, three were killed by the House, and one rule was defeated, thus preventing consideration of the bill.

"On the positive side, these results show that the Rules Committee was not used solely to carry out the program of the majority party; on the negative side, the Committee refused to grant rules on various bills including the FEPC and the Kefauver bill to amend the anti-trust law relative to the purchase of assets (H.R. 4810 and H.R. 5535). In several other instances, the committee granted rules only after prolonged fights."

The Chairman and His Powers: Position: It is customary for the Rules Committee to entrust to its chairman nearly all of its business for reporting to the House, over which, according to precedents, he carries "a pocket veto." This power, in addition to the regular prerogatives of a chairman of any standing committee of the House, explains in part the unusual power embodied in this person. It was not until January 18, 1924 that the House adopted an amendment to the rules which provided that

[41] These were laid on the table because the legislation for which they provided was brought up under a more expeditious procedure; 14 becoming public law, 4 passing the House only, and the other one being killed by veto.

[42] The rule (H. Res. 500) which provided for the consideration of H.R. 4908, the Labor Fact Finding bill, not only waived points of order, but provided that after the first paragraph of H.R. 4908 had been read, it should be in order to move to strike out all after the enacting clause and substitute H.R. 5262 therefor and then read it for amendments, waiving all points of order against it. H.R. 5262 had not been considered by any committee; H.R. 4908 had been reported by the Labor Committee. This rule was criticized on the ground that it took away the jurisdiction of the other standing committees. Another rule (H. Res. 710) not only waived points of order and set the general debate at one hour, but provided: "The bill shall be considered as having been read for amendment. No amendment shall be in order to said bill except amendments offered by direction of the Committee on Ways and Means, and said amendments shall be in order, any rule of the House to the contrary notwithstanding. Amendments offered by direction of the Committee on Ways and Means may be offered to any section of the bill at the conclusion of the general debate, but such amendments shall not be subject to amendment." *C.R.*, 79-2, July 24, 1946, pp. 9961-2. This analysis is taken from *The American Political Science Review*, Vol. XLI, No. 1, February, 1947, pp. 17-18.

the Committee on Rules should present to the House reports concerning the rules, the joint rules, and the order of business within three legislative days of the time when ordered reported by the committee. Even today, the rule does not prescribe a definite relief in case the moral obligation is not met. Some Representatives have complained that certain special rules were not called up for consideration even after they were reported.

Autocratic Powers: Understanding the great powers of the committee one can readily see why the chairman of this committee is so powerful and influential in the House procedure. He is in a position to be autocratic in behalf of his party if he so desires, with his political party supporting him. "Why has he not brought forward the rule which replies to the retirement bill," inquired one Member. "Because I have not seen fit to," replied the chairman of the Committee on Rules. Mr. Moore of Virginia once stated on the floor: "In April I introduced a resolution which was sent to the cemetery which is operated by the gentleman from Kansas, Mr. Campbell, the chairman of the Rules Committee, a cemetery where all Democratic measures are interred." [43] One Member added that he really meant a "morgue." Mr. Campbell, on another occasion, speaking with reference to the Woodruff resolution in 1923, declared with an unusual air: "Even though every Member wants this investigation, what will that avail you? I have the resolution in my pocket and shall keep it there." [44] He made this statement a little stronger to the Committee on Rules at their meeting. "You can go to ——;" he said, "it makes no difference what a majority of you decide; if it meets with my disapproval, it shall not be done; I am the Committee; in me reposes absolute obstructive powers." [45]

Past Criticisms of Chairman: Mr. Howard, in 1931, charged that Mr. Snell had more power in the affairs of the government than the President himself. His powers are "so far-reaching that he can choke to death any piece of legislation" before it can even get a chance for consideration on the floor of the House. He continued: No Member, "no matter how charming his personality, should be vested with such vast powers. . . . Often now

43 C.R., 71-3, p. 3891.
44 The Searchlight, VI (1922), No. 12, p. 6.
45 Ibid., No. 12, pp. 5-6. Mr. Walsh of Mass. made a point of order that Johnson could not question Campbell's right to carry the investigation in his pocket. Speaker Gillett ruled in favor of Walsh. Johnson appealed from the decision. Mr. Mondell moved to lay the appeal on the table. By a vote of 149 to 114, the House approved the position of Campbell and Mondell.

I am wishing that but for a moment I might have a tithe of the courage displayed by Andrew Jackson when he spoke to Nicholas Biddle. In that moment I would look BERTRAND SNELL squarely in the eye, and my Quaker lips would paraphrase the speech of Andrew Jackson long enough to make them say: 'Chairman Snell, the power which, under the House gag rule you exercise, is too damned much power'." [46] In the first session of the Seventy-sixth Congress, Representative Barden of North Carolina stated: " . . . I regret exceedingly that the chairman of the Rules Committee saw fit to keep in his pocket the rule granted by the Rules Committee until it made it practically impossible to realize the passage of this bill during this session." [47] Many such statements can be found in the *Record,* but the reader should remember that these remarks may or may not be completely dependable. They are expressions by individuals to gain a political advantage or to gain a cause. It all comes in the game of politics.[48]

Present Restraint on Chairman: On the other hand, an amendment to the rules at the beginning of the 81st Congress [48a] (Jan. 3, 1949) offers some relief to chairmen of committees reporting bills for which the Rules Committee will not give special rules. It stipulates that resolutions providing for immediate consideration of public bills already reported and which have been before the Rules Committee 21 days without being reported may be called up on Discharge days (second and fourth Mondays each month) by the chairman of the committee which reported the bill. ". . . The Speaker shall recognize the Member seeking recognition for that purpose . . ."

The Leadership Including Committee Chairman: The majority and minority floor leaders are elected by and responsible to their respective political parties, and are spokesmen for them in the House. The majority floor leader and the Speaker are most influential in the determination of the detailed program. The whips work closely with their respective floor leaders. It is the duty of each whip to keep his floor leader as spokesman of the party, advised as to the standing of his party and what

[46] C.R., 71-2, p. 5536.
[47] C.R., 76-1, p. 15328 (daily edition).
[48] "Snell is very unpopular," Blanton said. "He was always trying to play the part of a demagogue." In fact, he said, he is the biggest demagogue in the House (C.R., 71-3, pp. 4073-4079). See C.R., 71-3, p. 4083. Snell replied: "It is a very difficult thing for a man constituted as I am to take the pounding that the Chairman of the Rules Committee receives . . . when I know the Member is demagoguing . . ." (C.R., 71-2, p. 3894).
[48a] Paragraph (2) (c) of Rule XI.

he might expect from his party's membership on any particular piece of legislation.

The chairman and members of the steering committees serve their party in the determination of their general policy and program by keeping in touch, after direct or indirect contact, with their fellow party members.

The standing committee chairmen and the ranking minority members of each know their own committees as to membership and program. They are able to speak for their committees to their own party officials; they can advise as to what legislation proposed by their committees they deem of sufficient importance to demand immediate disposition.

With this set up, two small groups of Democratic and Republican leaders, consisting of a very small percentage of the total membership of the House, are able after serious calculation and compromises to direct a program acceptable to a majority of the Representatives. The House is generally moved to action by three or four members of each party, with those of the majority taking the initiative and those of the minority defending the rights and interests of the Representatives of their political faith. For further discussions of the floor leaders and whips, the Speaker, political organizations of the two houses, and standing committees of Congress, see chapters devoted to the same subjects.

The House procedure is quite complex with the hands of the leaders being restrained somewhat by the specific rules, which procedures can be ignored only by unanimous consent, by a special rule, or sometimes by a two-thirds vote. Such a vote is usually difficult to command; impossible on some issues.

The House unlike the Senate does not necessarily proceed with unfinished business until completed. Business brought up under one calendar, or upon a specific calendar day, and not finished at the end of that day must wait over until another such day for the consideration of the same such business—at least a week in case of Calendar Wednesday business and for longer periods of time under other procedures. Consequently, while this is not unfinished business in one sense, it is proposed legislation on which some action has been taken, but which the House cannot turn to again except in pursuance of the rules defining that type of procedure. The leaderships, however, serve to tie all such loose ends together.

Nearly all of the minor or noncontroversial bills in the House are disposed of under Consent or Private Calendars, unanimous consent procedure, or special calendar days, such as District of Columbia day, Calendar Wednesday, and Suspension of the Rules. These bills, however, do not make up the real legislative program for the session. While they compose the large numbers of legislative measures enacted, they occupy very little of the House's time. The real debates are on privileged proposals and major bills which are nonprivileged, brought up in pursuance of special rules reported by the Rules Committee and adopted by the House, or in accordance with a general program determined by the leadership. The major bills are those the leaders are concerned with in making up the legislative program. The majority leaders can usually muster the most votes in the case of a showdown, and although the House utilizes the "previous question" procedure, permitting a vote to shut off debate and reach a vote on passage with greatest dispatch, the majority is usually considerate of the minority's rights. The minority is usually consulted for expediency's sake in making up the House program. The minority can cause the majority plenty of trouble in case of closely contested fights or otherwise delay the program.

Bills Banned From Legislative Program

The leaders were aided somewhat in the determination of their legislative programs by the "Legislative Reorganization Act of 1946." That law banned the introduction of certain types of bills, which only cluttered the calendars of the committees and of the two houses without being of too much significance to the public. The Act provides that "no private bill or resolution (including so-called omnibus claims or pensions bills), and no amendment to any bill or resolution, authorizing or directing (1) the payment of money for property damages, for personal injuries or death for which suit may be instituted under the Federal Tort Claims Act, or for a pension (other than to carry out a provision of law or treaty stipulation); (2) the construction of a bridge across a navigable stream; or (3) the correction of a military or naval record, shall be received or considered in either the Senate or the House of Representatives." [48b] Jurisdiction over these matters are transferred by this Act to the Administration and the courts.

[48b] See p. 231 for more discussion of private bills; also sections 123, 131, 207, 402-404, 410-412, 502-511 of the Act.

CHAPTER VII

Officers and Employees of the House and Senate

Capitol Hill Employees and Their Employment

The Constitution delegates to each house the power to choose its own officers. This of course has been interpreted in practice to include the selection of employees necessary to carry out its duties. Either the House or Senate acting separately may create or abolish for itself at will any post, but neither may abolish an office provided for by virtue of joint action; it may remove any officer from office over whom it has the power of appointment.

The officers of the two houses include those persons elected directly at the beginning of each new Congress. In the House they are: the Speaker, the Clerk, the Sergeant at Arms, Doorkeeper, Postmaster, and Chaplain.[1] In the Senate they include: the President pro tempore, the Secretary, Sergeant at Arms and Doorkeeper, Chaplain, Secretary for the Majority, and Secretary for the Minority.[2]

[1] In 1947 the House adopted the following resolution on the first day, after electing Joseph W. Martin, Jr., Speaker:
"Resolved, That John Andrews, of the State of Massachusetts, be, and he is hereby, chosen Clerk of the House of Representatives;
"That William F. Russell, of the State of Pennsylvania, be, and he is hereby, chosen Sergeant at Arms of the House of Representatives;
"That M. L. Meletio, of the State of Missouri, be, and he is hereby chosen, Postmaster of the House of Representatives.
"That Rev. James Shera Montgomery, D.D., of the District of Columbia, be, and he is hereby chosen, Chaplain of the House of Representatives."
The recent practice is to present a resolution electing officers after the election of the Speaker but before notifying the President and Senate of organization to do business (C.R., 80-1, p. 36).
[2] The recent practice in the Senate is to elect the following officers by adopting resolutions to that effect, as follows:
"Resolved, That Hon. Arthur H. Vandenberg, a Senator from the State of Michigan, be, and he is hereby, elected President of the Senate pro tempore, to hold office during the pleasure of the Senate, in accordance with the resolution of the Senate adopted on the 12th day of March, 1890 on the subject.
"Resolved, That Carl A. Loeffler, of Pennsylvania, be, and he is hereby, elected Secretary of the Senate.
"Resolved, That Edward F. McGinnis, of Illinois, be, and he is hereby, elected Sergeant at Arms and Doorkeeper of the Senate.
"Resolved, That Rev. Peter Marshall, D. D., of the District of Columbia, be, and he is hereby, elected Chaplain of the Senate.
"Resolved, That J. Mark Trice, of Maryland, be, and he is hereby, elected Secretary for the majority of the Senate.

127

The employees of Congress include legislative clerks and experts of the two houses, staffs of standing and special committees, staffs of legislative councils, experts, administrative assistants and secretaries, clerks, and clerical help in the offices of Representatives and Senators, pages and doorkeepers, laborers, and others participating in the legislative process. All told there are employed in nonelective positions at the Capitol more than 3,500 persons.

Generally speaking all nonelective positions on Capitol Hill are authorized by law (directly or indirectly through adoption or passage of resolutions or bills) ; the actual appointments are made by several hundred different persons. All appointments on the House side can be placed in the following four categories: (1) Each Representative selects his own office force, limited in number and maximum salary only. (2) Each standing committee by a majority vote selects not more than four professional staff members and not more than six clerks "to be attached to the office of the chairman, to the ranking minority member, and to the professional staff, as the committee may deem advisable." (3) The Speaker appoints the House Parliamentarian and approves appointments in the office of the legislative counsel. (4) House officials and Representatives acting as officers of the House or of a party make particular appointments. The system is much the same on the Senate side: (1) Each Senator selects his own office force. (2) Each standing committee by a majority vote selects not more than four professional staff members and not more than six clerks "to be attached to the office of the chairman, to the ranking minority member, and to the professional staff, as the committee may deem advisable." (3) The Vice President, and/or the President pro tempore, appoints his own staff and members of the legislative council. (4) Senate officials and Senators acting as officials of the Senate or of the party make party appointments in much the same way as in the House.

None of the legislative employees are subjected to civil service examinations for their appointment. That does not mean, however, that merit and ability are not used as criteria for selecting them.

The tenure of legislative employees varies. Some of the positions filled by experts are permanent, surviving party changes; some change with every change in party control, others owe their

"Resolved, That Felton M. Johnston, of Mississippi, be, and he is hereby, elected Secretary for the minority of the Senate." (C.R. 80-1, pp. 105-108).

jobs to their respective Representative or Senator and survive as long as he is a member of Congress. Many of the positions through the years have developed into what might be called career assignments.

The activities of the legislative employees may be divided into public relations, research and drafting, and clerical. The first include: the making of all contacts with the public relative to status and content of legislation; when, where, and what kind of meetings the committees will hold on certain bills as well as answers to questions asked Congress in general or Representatives and Senators individually. Public relations activities also include keeping the membership notified as to dates of various meetings by Congressional committees and the two legislative chambers and the subjects to be considered; to post witnesses testifying on a bill as to date, place, and time of public hearings; and to assist the chairmen of the committees when any bill by their committees is up for consideration.

Research and drafting activities include the preparation of committee reports on reported bills; the drafting of bills and material on pending bills and resolutions; writing of speeches; the filing of all data of value for future use by the committee; accumulation of hearings, reports, bills, communications on legislation from the various departments, the President and the public, and cataloging them so that any such information can be made available to any committee member in a short time; and the assembling of information requested by the public.

Clerical duties include pretty much what the term implies: the management of correspondence, filing, reference, and disposition of all daily communications and other routine chores in regular office procedure.

Committee Staffs: Before describing the functions and duties of the various officers elected by the two houses and enumerating the officials appointed by each, it is essential to make the following generalizations about the committee staffs and office forces of Representatives and Senators. Under the Legislative Reorganization Act of 1946 each committee of the House and Senate "is authorized to appoint by a majority vote of the committee not more than four professional staff members in addition to the clerical staffs on a permanent basis without regard to political affiliation and solely on the basis of fitness to perform the duties of the office; and said staff members shall be assigned to the chairman and ranking minority member of such committee as the committee may deem advisable. Each such committee is further authorized to terminate by a majority vote of the committee the services of any such professional staff member as it may see fit." It is further provided that:

The clerical staff of each standing committee, which shall be appointed by a majority vote of the committee, shall consist of not more than six clerks, to be attached to the office of the chairman, to the ranking minority member, and to the professional staff, as the committee may deem advisable; and the position of committee janitor is hereby abolished. The clerical staff shall handle committee correspondence and stenographic work, both for the committee staff and for the chairman and ranking minority member on matters related to committee work . . . The professional staff members of the standing committees shall receive annual compensation, to be fixed by the chairman, ranging from $5,000 to $8,000 and the clerical staff shall receive annual compensation ranging from $2,000 to $8,000.[3]

The Appropriations Committees are given larger staffs.

To force a gap between the legislative and administrative staffs the law prohibits a committee from appointing "to its staff any experts or other personnel detailed or assigned from any department or agency of the Government, except with the written permission of the Committee on Rules and Administration of the Senate or the Committee on House Administration of the House of Representatives, as the case may be." Professional staff members of a committee are not eligible for appointment in the Executive branch of the Government for a period of one year "after he shall have ceased to be such a member" of a committee.[4] The Legislative Reorganization Act of 1946 has been so recently enacted that comment on practices thereunder is not justified.

Office Force of Senators and Representatives: Each Senator and Representative is free in selecting his or her office force, limited, however, as to number and amounts of salaries. Each Representative is authorized up to $9,500 to be used for base salaries, but he may employ no more than 5 employees simultaneously, no one of whom may draw in annual base salary in excess of $5,000. No Senator is limited in the number of employees except to the extent of the total funds allotted him for his office force. In practice each Senator generally has from 8 to 12 employees; no one of them may draw a base salary in excess

[3] P.L. 601—79th Congress, Sec. 202.
[4] Senate Manual, 80-1, p. 156.

of $5,040 a year, except that the administrative assistant is authorized a base salary of $8,000 per year. The variations in the number of employees each Senator is authorized are due in part to the increased allowances permitted a Senator because of the large population in his State. For example Senators from States with populations in excess of 3 million are entitled "to an additional clerk."

Retirement and Civil Service Advantages to Employees: Recently Congress has shown interest in the tenure of office of its employees and what happens to those who are displaced "involuntarily and without prejudice" by new political appointments. The Civil Service Act has been amended to give a classified civil service status to Capitol Hill employees filling secretarial or clerical jobs for Members of Congress and committees or for the House and Senate, if they have held their posts for 4 years [5] and were separated from service without prejudice; they must pass "such suitable non-competitive examination as the Civil Service Commission may prescribe." The transfer to an administrative agency, however, must be obtained within one year from the date of separation from service on Capitol Hill, but professional staffmen on committees are excluded since they must be out of committee service one year before affiliating with an administrative agency. Also the Civil Service Retirement Act has been amended to make employees of the legislative branch of the government eligible to participate in the Federal retirement plan; this is not compulsory.

House and Senate Officials

The officials elected by the House and Senate are enumerated below with a discussion of their duties respectively as well as an account of certain nonelective Senate and House officials.

Election and Oath of Office: In accordance with Rule II, of the House, "There shall be elected by a viva voce vote,[6] at the commencement of each Congress, to continue in office until their successors are chosen and qualified, a Clerk, Sergeant-at-Arms, Doorkeeper, Postmaster, and Chaplain, each of whom shall take an oath to support the Constitution of the United States, and for

[5] See P.L. 880 of 76th Congress and P.L. 295 of the 79th Congress. Certain advantages are extended to persons separated from Capitol Hill employment for military services.

[6] The Speaker in recent practice is elected by yeas and nays after nominations have been made.

the true and faithful discharge of the duties of his office to the best of his knowledge and ability, and to keep the secrets of the House; and each shall appoint all of the employees of his department provided for by law." [7] The Senate has no such rule, but its practice is generally the same; its officers, the number of which is determined by custom, have no definite term of office; usually they hold their offices without re-election during the pleasure of the Senate. Their services may be terminated at any time by a majority vote of that body by simply electing others to replace them. This practice is in keeping with the fact that the Senate has a continuing membership; but while these officers serve until their successors are elected, they are usually changed with each shift in political control of the Senate. Sometimes they are re-elected at the beginning of a new Congress even though there has been no change in political control. This may be done to avoid re-electing a particular officer of the prior Congress.

In both houses at the organization of a new Congress (in the Senate only when there is a change in political control or positive action to replace an incumbent), the majority floor leaders or officials of the majority party,[8] (after it has been agreed to proceed to the election of officers) offer resolutions providing for the election of the various officers of the House and Senate, respectively. The minority party always submits substitute nominations for those offered by the majority, except in the case of Senate secretaries to the Majority and to the Minority. In the House all officers are elected by adoption of a single resolution; in the Senate, a resolution is presented for each officer. In both bodies it is practically a matter of re-electing, or of continuing the existing officers except when there is a change in political control.

Each house not only selects its officers but retains the incidental power to remove them. Any Member of either body may make a motion to remove an officer or employee; in the House it does not necessarily present a question of privilege unless the motion is to remove for misconduct. Each body is the sole judge of whether or not its appointees are properly discharging the duties of their office.[9]

---

[7] Rule II; see *Legislative Appropriation Bill, 1929*, Hearing, 70-1, p. 45.
[8] In the House the resolution is usually offered by the chairmen of the Democratic Caucus and Republican Conference.
[9] Cannon, VI, 36. An elective officer of the House may remove any persons under him. See Cannon, VI, 30.

Resignation of Officers: Any officer may submit his resignation at any time; it is read to the body concerned but not accepted or rejected. The resignation is customarily laid on the table and a successor is elected.

Chaplains

The Chaplains of the House and Senate take no part in the legislative process; their tasks require only a brief attendance. At the hour of opening each session in their respective houses they merely start the day off with a prayer while the membership stand in solemn austerity. The Chaplains are paid a salary.

Clerk of the House and Secretary of the Senate

Clerk of House: *Development of Office:* The Clerk has been an officer of the House since the beginning of the first Congress. Today his office occupies an important place in the legislative machine. Although it was originally modeled after the office of the Clerk in the House of Commons, the present position of the office reflects developments by the House of Representatives. There has been a number of decided modifications in the functions of that office since 1789 [10] but the services performed by the Clerk have remained fundamentally the same. While he is an official of the House, he is always selected by the majority party and goes out of office with every change in party control.

There is no continuity between two Congresses; one dies and another is born; further, the House does not have a continuing membership. Most of the Representatives are re-elected. But to provide at least a clerical continuity, the House adopted a rule at the beginning of its history to make the Clerk of the outgoing Congress the Clerk of the incoming Congress until another could be elected to replace him.[11] This was purposely done to provide for a Presiding Officer until the Speaker of each new Congress could be elected.

At the beginning of each Congress, the Clerk of the previous House calls the membership to order at noon on the date fixed for

[10] *Legislative Establishment Appropriation Bill, 1929, Hearings,* 70-1, p. 46.

[11] By this action the House endeavors to perpetuate its authority beyond its own existence (Hinds, I, 235).

the House to convene,[12] and calls the roll prepared by himself.[13] Just as soon as the roll has been called, the Clerk places the question of electing a Speaker before the House and presides during the election.[14] Following the election he appoints the committee to escort the newly elected Speaker to the chair.

During this short period, while the Clerk is acting as the Presiding Officer, he may refuse to entertain a motion to refer to a committee a matter concerning the election of a Member, to entertain any matter not consistent with the organization of the House, to consider a question of order, or "an appeal pending the motion to proceed to the election of the Speaker." In brief, the position of the Clerk, pending the election of its Presiding Officer is similar to that of the Speaker.

Duties: After the House is organized, the Clerk assumes his regular duties, which are administrative and quasi-judicial in their nature. He derives his authority from the rules of parliamentary law, from rules of practice having the force of common law, from express statutes, and from the rules of the House. Mr. Page, a former Clerk of the House, stated that his duties "ramify from the Clerk's desk in the House where the journal clerk, reading clerks, and tally clerk handle in part in its initial stages the legislative routine business of the House to other branches scattered throughout the House wing of the Capitol and the House Office Building." In addition to the work on the floor of the House, Mr. Page listed as under his supervision the following:

The engrossment and enrollment of all bills and resolutions.
The office of the chief bill clerk and four assistants.
The hall library.
The disbursing office, in which salaries of all employees, including clerks to Members, are paid, and various specific and contingent fund appropriations are disbursed by check.
The office of the property custodian and assistants, and the furniture repair shop, partly in the Capitol (formerly Chief Clerk's office) and partly in the House Office Building.
The House library, of which the hall library is a part.
The stationery department.

[12] On one occasion the Speaker died during recess of the House; when the House met again, the Clerk presided until a new Speaker was elected (Hinds, I, 234). The position of the Clerk during organization of the House is debatable. (See Hinds, I, 73.)

[13] As already shown the Clerk makes up the roll of Representatives-elect. See *Legislative Establishment Appropriation Bill, 1929, Hearings,* 70-1, p. 47. In the absence of the Speaker, the Clerk presides until the Speaker pro tempore is appointed (Cannon, VI, 272) ; in his absence, the Sergeant at Arms presides.

[14] See Hinds, I, 211-217. In accordance with recent practices the Speaker is elected by yeas and nays.

The Clerk's document room.
The telephone switchboard and operators.
The bathrooms.

Persons under his direction, as of the 80th Congress, include: Assistant to the Clerk, Journal Clerk, Reading Clerks, Ass't Reading Clerk, Tally Clerk, Ass't Tally Clerk, Enrolling Clerk, Disbursing Clerk, File Clerk, Chief Bill Clerk, Stationery Clerk, Librarian, Property Custodian, Ass't Custodian, and the *Daily Digest* staff.

The Clerk has such additional duties as furnishing stationery, blank books, and the like, to the committees, to the officers of the House, and to the Representatives. He has discretionary authority to reprint bills and documents, to receive and print the testimony taken in election contests, to compensate the Members during recesses of Congress, compile information filed by lobbyists, and to prepare the budget for the House and submit the annual budget estimates to the House Appropriations Committee.[15] He is the property custodian for the House; in short, he is the general housekeeper for the House part of the Capitol.

Some of his duties which are connected directly with the House procedure are as follows: preparing and overseeing the preliminary approval of the Journal, after which it is submitted to the Speaker for his approval; making records of bills referred to the standing committees; and attending to clerical matters largely delegated to him by the Speaker at the Speaker's table. All reports made to Congress by committees are printed under his supervision and delivered to each Member.[16] He makes notations on all questions of order, with the decisions, and has them printed as an appendix to the *Journal*; he supervises the printing and distribution of the *Journal*. He must attest and sign all warrants, writs, and subpoenas issued by the order of the House, and certify all bills passed by that body. He is required by law at the commencement of each session to file in the House a statement showing names of all persons employed by his office together with time of service and pay of each. All of these assignments must be done by the Clerk personally or under his supervision. Finally, the seal of the House is placed in the custody of the Clerk.[17]

[15] *Legislative Establishment Appropriation Bill, 1929, Hearings,* 70-1, pp. 47, 48.
[16] Hinds, I, 252. Non-privileged reports are delivered to him for reference to the calendars; a record of the report filed with the Clerk is entered in the Journal and printed in the Record.
[17] Hinds, I, 254. If absent, he may appoint a Clerk pro tempore by written message. For the written form see Cannon, VI, 26.

Secretary of the Senate: *The Office*: The Secretary of the Senate holds a post comparable to that of the Clerk of the House. Since the Senate is a continuing body he does not serve in a presiding capacity at the beginning of each Congress as does the Clerk of the House; he enjoys such a prerogative only when there is neither a Vice President nor a President pro tempore of the Senate.

The Secretary is selected by the majority party, and casually approved by the Senate. Under recent practices he is continued in office from one Congress to another, barring death or other casualty, unless there is a change in party control of the Senate; it is considered a partisan post, but it is also the top administrative office in the Senate.

Duties: The Secretary, unlike the Clerk of the House, does not make up a temporary Senate Roll for organization purposes. The credentials of each new Senator, however, are filed with the Secretary, who merely keeps "a record of the certificates of election of Senators by entering in a well-bound book kept for that purpose the date of the election, the name of the person elected, and the vote given at the election, the date of the certificate, the name of the governor and the secretary of State signing and countersigning the same, and the State from which such Senator is elected." [18]

[18] See *Senate Manual*, 80th Congress, (Rule VI, clause 2). The form of the Certificate of Election and Certificate of Appointment are as follows:

Certificate of Election
"TO THE PRESIDENT OF THE SENATE OF THE UNITED STATES:
"This is to certify that on the .... day of ...., 19......, A............
B .... was duly chosen by the qualified electors of the State of .... a Senator from said State to represent said State in the Senate of the United States for the term of six years, beginning on the 3d day of January, 19......
"Witness: His excellency our governor ...., and our seal hereto affixed at .... this .... day of ...., in the year of our Lord 19.......
"By the governor:

"C.................... D....................,
"Governor.
"E............ F....................,
"Secretary of State."

Certificate of Appointment
"TO THE PRESIDENT OF THE SENATE OF THE UNITED STATES:
"This is to certify that, pursuant to the power vested in me by the Constitution of the United States and the laws of the State of ...., I, A............
B ...., the governor of said State, do hereby appoint C............ D.................... a Senator from said State to represent said State in the Senate of the United States until the vacancy therein, caused by the .... of E............ F...................., is filled by election as provided by law.
"Witness: His excellency our governor ...., and our seal hereto affixed at .... this .... day of ...., in the year of our Lord 19.......
"By the governor:

"G.................... H....................,
"Governor.
"I............ J....................,
"Secretary of State."

The Secretary has no power to shut out any Senator-elect from voting on the grounds of improper election or appointment. These are questions to be decided by the other "two classes" of Senators (who compose two-thirds of the Senate membership) when the Senators-elect present themselves for membership. Persons presenting themselves to the Senate for membership for the first time may be excluded by a majority vote of the continuing membership. "The oaths or affirmations required by the Constitution and prescribed by law shall be taken and subscribed by each Senator, in open Senate, before entering upon his duties," which is administered by the Presiding Officer.[19]

His duties are much like those of the Clerk, already enumerated above. He processes bills to enactment for the Senate, just as the Clerk does for the House; additionally, he is responsible for disbursing all money in the Senate; the compilation of information filed by lobbyists; supervises the Executive Clerk who receives dispatches, and accounts for all nominations and treaties sent down from the White House; he is keeper of the Senate seal and has jurisdiction over the Senate Library and Document Room. Offices under his jurisdiction follow: Chief Clerk, Parliamentarian, Journal Clerk, Ass't Journal Clerk, Legislative Clerk, Financial Clerk, Ass't Financial Clerk, Chief Bookkeeper, Principal Clerk, Enrolling Clerk, Executive Clerk, Ass't Executive Clerk, Printing Clerk, Clerk of Enrolled Bills, Keeper of Stationery, Librarian and Ass't Librarian, Superintendent of Document Room and his First Assistant, Registration Clerk, and the *Daily Digest* staff.

Postmasters

Each house has a postmaster to superintend the House and Senate post offices in both the Capitol and House and Senate Office Buildings, respectively. The House postmaster is an elected official along with the Clerk, Doorkeeper, Chaplain and Sergeant at Arms. In the Senate he is an appointed official. The function of these two offices is to supervise the mail services to the Representatives and Senators respectively, as well as to the offices of the House and Senate as expeditiously as possible. The

[19] Rule II.

law requires that these postmasters account to the House and Senate for the government property in their possession at the beginning of each session.

Sergeant at Arms and Doorkeepers

House Sergeant at Arms: The statutes and rules define the duties of the Sergeant at Arms, who is the police officer of the House and in the Committee of the Whole. He continuously attends all sittings to maintain order and decorum at the request of the Presiding Officers.[20] He disburses the pay of Members of the House and accounts for their mileage.

When there is a call of the House, it is his duty to detain Members who are already present and return those who are absent. The Speaker may authorize the Sergeant at Arms, by presenting him with duly signed warrants attested and sealed, to arrest absent Members and bring them to the bar of the House. He may bring any person to the bar by order of the House when the Speaker duly signs warrants for that purpose. Finally, the Sergeant at Arms of the two houses appoint the police for the Capitol grounds and the office buildings, and they enforce the regulations set by Congress for the National Capitol. The symbol of the office is the mace "which shall be borne by him while enforcing order on the floor."

House Doorkeeper: The Doorkeeper holds a conspicuous position. He introduces the bearers of all messages, official guests, and Members attending joint sessions.

He is made custodian of all House furniture, books, and public property in the committee rooms or other rooms under his charge. The folding and document rooms come under his jurisdiction, as well as general charge of the quarters occupied by the House during recess. At the beginning of each session he must submit to the Administration Committee for examination an inventory of things in his custody. He supervises janitor service. In case the Clerk and the Sergeant at Arms are absent, he makes up the roll of Members.

The Doorkeeper is required to enforce strictly the rules relating to the hallways and to keep unprivileged persons from the floor of the House; he is responsible for the official conduct of the

---

[20] In the absence of the Sergeant at Arms his duties are discharged by sworn deputies.

persons performing the task. Under the rules of the House, it is left to him to see that the House and all official entrances to the immediate floor of the House are cleared of all unauthorized persons fifteen minutes prior to each assembly and kept cleared until ten minutes after adjournment. The Doorkeeper performs this duty, and he may make any rules necessary to achieve the desired end, subject to the will of the House. Some of his assistants attend all doors to both the galleries and the floor to prevent any conflict between visitors and Members, and the House pages, under his direction, stay in attendance at sessions of the House to run errands for the Representatives and authorized persons, in expediting the legislative process.

Senate Sergeant at Arms and Doorkeeper: The Sergeant at Arms and Doorkeeper elected by the Senate is the police of that body; it is his duty, or of some person designated by him, to be in attendance when the Senate is in session to see that the Senate's orders of decorum in the chamber and the galleries are administered. When so ordered he brings absentees into the chamber to make up a quorum; he takes into custody persons accused of contempt of the Senate; and he makes any other necessary arrests or detentions.

The Sergeant at Arms under the direction of the presiding officer "Shall be the executive officer of the body for the enforcement of all rules made by the Committee on Rules and Administration for the regulation of the Senate wing of the Capitol and Senate Annex. The Senate floor shall be at all times under his immediate supervision, and he shall see that the various subordinate officers of his department perform the duties to which they are especially assigned." [21] He is custodian of public property under the jurisdiction of the Senate committed to his care. He appoints Senate messengers, pages,[22] laborers, and may delegate any of his duties to assistant doorkeeper, as well as appoint special deputies to assist him.

The Capitol police, under the direction of the Sergeants at Arms of the Senate and House of Representatives and of the architect of the Capitol "shall police the Capitol building and the

[21] Rule I for regulation of Senate Wing. *Senate Manual*, 80-1, p. 121.
[22] The nonstatutory standing orders not embodied in the rules provide that "it shall be the duty of the Sergeant at Arms to classify the pages of the Senate so that at the close of the present and each succeeding Congress one-half of the number shall be removed"; and in no case shall a page be appointed younger than 14 years, or remain in office after the age of 17 years.

Capitol grounds." The Sergeants at Arms are authorized "to make such regulations as they may deem necessary for preserving the peace and securing the Capitol from defacement, and for the protection of the public property therein, and they shall have power to arrest and detain any person violating such regulations until such person can be brought before the proper authorities for trial." [23]

Senate Deputy Sergeant at Arms and Storekeeper: The Deputy Sergeant at Arms and Storekeeper is responsible for the execution of many of the duties of the Sergeant at Arms. This officer travels over the country to investigate ballot boxes or to bring certain witnesses or other persons before the Senate. And finally he is the storekeeper of United States property used by the Senators.

Senate Secretaries for the Majority and for the Minority: The Senate also elects a Secretary for the Majority and a Secretary for the Minority, both of whom are "assigned during the daily sessions of the Senate, to duty upon the Senate floor. They shall see that the messengers assigned to the doors upon the Senate floor are at their posts, and that the floor and cloakrooms are cleared at least five minutes before the opening of daily sessions of all persons not entitled to remain there. In the absence of the Sergeant at Arms the duties of his office, so far as they pertain to the enforcement of rules, shall devolve upon the secretary for the majority and the secretary for the minority in the order of their rank."

These persons are truly secretaries to their respective parties on the Senate floor, keeping the Senators to whom they are responsible informed of the pending business—motions or amendment under consideration—and informed as to the need of their presence on the floor at any time from the party point of view. The Senators call on these men for individual consideration; that is, if they must be absent from the floor on other business it is up to these secretaries to keep those of their political faith posted of any developments, or if their presence is demanded for a roll call or for any other purpose.

House and Senate Legislative Counsels: Each body has a legislative counsel to assist its committees, individual Members or groups thereof in the drafting of proposed legislation or even

[23] From the general and permanent laws relating to the Senate, *Senate Manual*, 80-1, p. 191.

interpretation of existing law. In the Senate the office consists of a legislative counsel, assistant counselors, law assistants, a clerk and assistant clerks. In the House the office consists of a legislative counsel, assistant counsels, an assistant counsel and administrative assistant, law assistants, a clerk, and assistant clerk.

Members of the counsel work closely with the legislators to facilitate the preparation of legislation. They work with the Representatives and Senators individually, with groups of legislators or with the committees. Generally when an important public bill is under consideration by one of the standing committees one member of the counsel or several of them attend the committee hearings and sessions to aid the committee in writing a bill.

Frequently, members of a committee or subcommittee have a general idea of legislation needed to correct certain social and economic conditions or to combat certain social injustices, but they are not trained to draft the technical legal language necessary to accomplish that end. In such cases it is the duty of these legislative experts to attend the committee hearings and to acquaint themselves with the problems and acquire an exact understanding of what the legislators have in mind; subsequently, the counselors draw up different proposed drafts to express the full intent of the committee and present them for consideration. Before the drafts can be perfected, the counsel must investigate the existing law, the Constitution, Federal court decisions, and the Statutes so as to avoid the possibility of loopholes and conflicts. This procedure protects the legislators by giving them a correctly drafted bill for enforcement in accordance with the existing law. The counselors and the legislators thus working together are able to satisfy themselves that the proposed draft correctly reflects the will of the committee or subcommittee.

Once the committee has reached a final accord as to what is to be reported, the counsel perfects the product for presentation to the parent body concerned.

To illustrate: if the bill arises in the House, the counsel will work with the committee having jurisdiction of it in the manner outlined above until it has been reported to the House. If the bill successfully passes that body, the same members of the counsel will follow the measure through the Senate and any conferences between the two houses until final enactment. During that period, the counsel might find it essential to consult legal experts in the Executive departments to obtain the benefit of their administrative experience and knowledge. On the other hand, proposed drafts submitted to Congress by the Administration, and drafted by the administrative experts, undergo the same scrutiny and possible redrafting by the counsel.

House and Senate Parliamentarians: The parliamentary law of the House and Senate entails endless complexities. For one to be able to preside without expert assistance would necessitate several years of observation and study. To accommodate the Presiding Officer and the Representatives and Senators called to the chair to preside temporarily, each body has accepted the practice of appointing a permanent Parliamentarian to assist in rendering correct parliamentary decisions, thus keeping the practices and precedents uniform within each body. The Parliamentarian is seated in the House immediately to the right of the Speaker's chair and in the Senate just in front of the Presiding Officer; he must be so well acquainted with the practice of his body that he can render a decision to the chair on a moment's notice.

This office, like all others of long duration, has had an interesting evolution. Not until after the beginning of the 20th century did either house have a permanent Parliamentarian, designated as such. The person performing these duties in earlier years held other titles, performing other duties simultaneously. Likewise for short periods the office was partisan, and subject to change with each change in party control. Today the job is considered that of an expert and the person filling it has a permanent assignment. In recent years some of the tasks formerly performed by the Presiding Officers have been assumed by the Parliamentarians. In the name of the Presiding Officers the two Parliamentarians refer bills and resolutions to the proper committees, and in the House places reports from committees on the proper calendars of business. They examine records and the *Journal* before they are read to their respective bodies. They act in an advisory capacity to committees as well as to individual Members, concerning the legislative processes of bills through the Congress. They assist the party in control toward the enactment of their legislative program through giving parliamentary advice.

In the House, he renders special service to the Rules Committee, attending meetings of that group, and upon request he drafts rules to expedite bills through the House. In both bodies, when the houses are in session they advise the Presiding Officer as to the order of business, the proper decisions in case of parliamentary inquiries or in case a point of order is raised as to the mode of procedure, or as to the next order of business.[24]

Principal Clerks of the Two Houses: *Reading Clerks:* The duties of the reading clerks (in the Senate, both the Chief Clerk and the Legislative Clerk perform this function) are to read all matters, formal and informal, presented to the House and Senate respectively. Included therein are: messages from the President; letters from the various governmental officials; letters, telegrams, and newspaper articles; documents; bills; and resolutions of all kinds; or any other matter that the Senators and Representatives may call upon them to read. The reading clerks have no opportunity to examine much of the material before reading it, yet they are supposed to read all subject matter intelligently so as to give the membership the full intent and content. Their major task of course is reading bills and resolutions, and proposed amendments thereto, when they are under consideration. Calling the rolls for yea and nay votes and quorums are their most severe

[24] The following remarks were made by the late Speaker Longworth when the House adopted a resolution to create the office of Assistant Parliamentarian.

"Mr. LONGWORTH. My colleagues, I think it is incumbent upon me to say just a word about this resolution, because it was introduced by the gentleman from New York at my request.

"The object of this resolution is to create a new office in the House, to be known as assistant parliamentarian. The reason for it, I think, I can express in a very few words. The duties of the parliamentarian of this House are many and various, and they are among the most important duties performed by any man in the Capitol. They are growing daily; they are becoming more important and multifarious, and the situation at present is that it is almost impossible for one man to do all the routine work necessary; and, more important still, if that man resigns or anything should happen to him, there is no one qualified to take his place. We have been very fortunate, I think, certainly during the time I have been in Congress, in always having capable parliamentarians, none of whom resigned or died suddenly or were ill for a day, so that there has been time to train another man to fill that position. However, I do not think I exaggerate when I say no man, however able he may be, can in less than two years of intense study become entirely capable of fully carrying out the duties of the parliamentarian.

"Under the rules of the House it is the duty of the Speaker to refer all bills to appropriate committees but, of course, it is physically impossible for any Speaker of the House, with the other many duties that he has imposed upon him to actually make those committee references. Before the end of this Congress there will be 18,000 or 19,000 bills introduced, and they must be referred by some one who has read those bills. That is one of the duties of the parliamentarian.

"Of course, all of you are familiar with the fact that it is absolutely impossible for any Speaker or any Chairman of the Committee of the Whole House on the state of the Union, no matter how great his experience may be, to decide all parliamentary questions without some study of the precedents and unless he has a competent man beside him. While the Speaker or the Chairman of the Committee of the Whole must, of necessity, listen to arguments, it is necessary that those precedents should be looked up by one who is competent to lay his hands on them very speedily."

tasks, as far as patience is concerned. In the House it takes from 25 to 45 minutes to call the roll. In the Senate it takes about 10 minutes. All amendments offered and adopted to pending bills must be incorporated in the bill at the proper place by these clerks, an important task because the work must be done accurately. Their work is performed under the supervision of the Clerk of the House and Secretary of the Senate respectively.

Journal Clerks: The Journal clerks perform their duties respectively under the direction of the Clerk of the House or the Secretary of the Senate. Each prepares a Journal of the proceedings of his legislative chamber, to be read for approval at its next session. These journals of necessity must be carefully prepared. A uniform system of procedure must be followed making the record of the meetings give a full story and in proper sequence of action taken. The Journal clerks handle all papers and bills acted on by the House and Senate, respectively, endorsing them and passing them on to the other clerks participating in the legislative process. In brief, they must determine the status of all official papers and keep the records of their whereabouts; they must be careful with their records, which are the only official records of the proceedings of the two houses recognized by law as evidence in the courts.[25]

Enrolling Clerks: Bills passed and noted by the Journal Clerk are submitted to the Enrolling Clerk for engrossment. The House enrolling clerk ascertains that the proper messages on House-passed bills and resolutions are sent to the Senate and in return receives those coming from the Senate; the Senate enrolling clerk ascertains that the proper messages on Senate-passed bills and resolutions are sent to the House and in return receives those coming from the House. They prepare every bill passed by their respective bodies for printing and presentation to the other. The revised printed copy of a bill which has passed one body must correspond exactly to its original. To assure this they must be read very carefully to eliminate all possible errors. After a bill has passed both houses it must likewise be prepared for transcribing on parchment paper, and enrolled to be sent to the President.

Bill Clerks: The bill clerks (including the Tally Clerk in the House) are really the custodians of data on the history of all bills introduced in their respective bodies. For example, when a bill

---

[25] The Journal clerks have assistant clerks.

is introduced in the Senate it is sent to the Senate bill clerk, who records the number and data thereon. Bills and each type of resolution are numbered in a separate series. After recording the proper information, including the bill number, the committee to which it was referred, and by whom introduced, the bill clerk sends the bill to the Government Printing Office for publication. The following morning the bills are available in printed form in the House and Senate document rooms.

Each time the Senate takes action on a bill or resolution, be it a Senate measure, or a House measure, it comes back to the Senate bill clerk for recording data in the bill book on action taken. Hence, after the bill has run the gauntlet to final enactment, the bill clerk has a complete history on the bill. The bill clerk of the House performs comparably for the House.

House Tally Clerk: In addition to the work performed by the bill clerk of the House, that body has a tally clerk who prepares the following information for the convenience of the House membership: A subject index on reported legislation, a numerical index on reported legislation, the calendars of the House which are printed daily, roll calls in the House, voting records of the Representatives, an index to these voting records, individual lists of Representatives and their committee assignments, and a list of Representatives by States.

CHAPTER VIII

Committees of Congress

Kinds of Committees

Classification of Committees: The committees of Congress may be divided into the following classes: political committees, committees of the whole, joint committees, including conference committees, select and special investigating committees, and standing committees.

Political Committees: The political committees include the congressional campaign committees, the steering and policy committees, committees on committees, patronage committees, and any *ad hoc* political groups set up from time to time to meet the needs of the two parties. These are discussed elsewhere in this volume.

Joint Committees: *Conference Committees:* Conference committees, special joint committees created by concurrent resolutions, and what might be called statutory joint committees, compose the types of joint committees of Congress.

Conference committees, in one sense, are not considered as truly joint committees; the conferees vote separately as units of each house in the determination of their reports. They are appointed by the presiding officers of their respective houses and the first named Senator presides as chairman. Conference committees are created to iron out any differences on the various bills which have passed the two houses in different forms and usually on which a stage of disagreement is evident or has been reached; such a committee is appointed *de novo* in each instance that a bill is sent to conference; in each case when a report on the particular bill is made to and acted upon by the two houses the committee passes out of existence. This type of committee is discussed in detail at pages 269-278, 388-391.

Special Joint Committees: Special joint committees created by concurrent resolutions to undertake an assignment for the two houses, usually to make an investigation, act as a single unit; they vote per capita and not as members of the two houses, although there is precedent for the membership from one house being larger than that of the other. The resolution of creation sets out the committees' jurisdiction. Though usually confined to investigations and recommendations, it may be extended to the reporting of legislation as was done in the case of the First Reorganization Act under the Roosevelt Administration. The resolution stipulates the number of members of each house, nearly always dividing them equally. Each house is responsible for selecting that number of persons to which it is entitled from its own membership. The appointments, however, are usually made by the presiding officers of the two bodies respectively as stipulated in the resolution. The actual determination is made after consultation with the various party officials concerned.

A quorum of a joint committee is a majority of its total membership instead of a majority of the Members representing each house. The chairman is ordinarily selected by the committee but the first Senator named in making the assignments is usually chairman. There are exceptions.

The number of special joint committees created during a Congress varies from one to another; many sessions have passed without a single joint committee being created. The will of the two houses is final since a concurrent resolution is not binding on either house until it has been agreed to in identical form by both. Such a resolution does not have to be submitted to the President for his signature as its scope does not extend to legislative authority.

Statutory Joint Committees: Statutory joint committees are created by law. Their functions, lives, and jurisdictions are defined in each instance, but they "are used infrequently in the legislative practice . . ." Such committees are created from time to time to make continuing studies of particular subjects, or to work and check with certain administrative units in an advisory capacity. The committees are composed of Members from both houses.[1] Like the joint committees created by concurrent resolutions, the memberships vote as single units or per capita rather than as a majority of either house. The law specifies the number of members to be appointed by each house. A quorum is a majority of the whole membership. The committee usually selects its chairman, but the first named of the Senators is most frequently the chair-

[1] There are occasionally some administrative officials appointed to statutory committees.

man. The law specifies "That there shall be a Joint Committee on Printing, consisting of the chairman and two members of the committee on Rules and Administration of the Senate and the chairman and two members of the Committee on House Administration of the House of Representatives, who shall have the powers hereinafter stated." "The Joint Committee of Congress on the Library shall hereafter consist of the chairman and four members of the Committee on Rules and Administration of the Senate and the chairman and four members of the Committee on House Administration of the House of Representatives."

Another illustration is the Joint Committee on the Economic Report consisting of seven Senators and seven Representatives created by the Employment Act of 1946, to study, analyze, and report on the Economic Report of the President.

The law stipulates: "It shall be the function of the joint committee—

"(1) to make a continuing study of matters relating to the Economic Report;

"(2) to study means of coordinating programs in order to further the policy of this Act; and

"(3) as a guide to the several committees of the Congress dealing with legislation relating to the Economic Report, not later than March 1 of each year (beginning with the year 1947) to file a report with the Senate and the House of Representatives containing its findings and recommendations with respect to each of the main recommendations made by the President in the Economic Report, and from time to time to make such other reports and recommendations to the Senate and House of Representatives as it deems advisable."

The Joint Committee on Internal Revenue was established in 1926 by the Revenue Act of that year; the committee consists of five Representatives and five Senators of the Ways and Means and Finance Committees, fortified with a staff of experts. The functions of the Joint Committee on Internal Revenue are as follows:

(1) To investigate the operation and effects of the Federal system of internal-revenue taxes.

(2) To investigate the administration of such taxes by the Bureau of Internal Revenue or any executive department, establishment, or agency charged with their administration.

(3) To make such other investigations in respect of such system of taxes as the Joint Committee may deem necessary.

(4) To investigate measures and methods for the simplification of such taxes, particularly the income tax.

(5) To publish from time to time for public examination and analysis proposed measures and methods for the simplification of such taxes; and

(6) To report from time to time to the Committee on Finance and the Committee on Ways and Means and, in its discretion, to the Senate or the House of Representatives, or both, the results of its investigations, together with such recommendations as it may deem advisable.

"To the above, section 710 of the Revenue Act of 1928 added the duty of examining refunds in excess of $75,000 of income, war-profits, excess-profits, estate, and gift taxes and of making annual reports thereon to the Congress."

The statute confers upon the Joint Committee certain powers necessary for the performance of its duties. The experts of this committee are highly respected and given great deference. The committee as an arm of the legislature occasionally moves into conflict with the Treasury Department over the determination of tax policy; the proposals by each to Congress at different times have been at great variance. On the other hand, it cooperates and works very closely with the Treasury officials, particularly in the supervisory activities assigned it relative to refunds in excess of $75,000 income.

Other important joint committees include those on Atomic Energy, Labor Study Committee, and Reduction of Nonessential Federal Expenditures.

Appointments to joint committees may be effected after the regular fashion used to select standing committee memberships, as is the case in determining membership of the Joint Committee on Printing and the Joint Committee on the Library. The law may stipulate that the membership will be designated by the Speaker of the House and the Presiding Officer of the Senate, as is the case with the Joint Committee on the Economic Report, which provides: "to be composed of seven Members of the Senate, to be appointed by the President of the Senate, and seven Members of the House of Representatives, to be appointed by the Speaker of the House of Representatives. The party representation on the joint committee shall as nearly as may be feasible reflect the relative membership of the majority and minority parties in the Senate and House of Representatives." Obviously the presiding officers consult with, if they do not accept the recommendations of, the party organizations of the two houses.

Each new Congress of course has authority to appoint Members to its committees *de novo*; resignation of a member from a joint committee created by law is made either to the House or Senate as the case may be, or to the committee and, while neither house has power to accept or refuse such resignation, it may fill the vacancy so occasioned.[2] The Employment Act of 1946 provides: "Vacancies in the membership of the joint committee shall not affect the power of the remaining members to execute the functions of the joint committee, and shall be filled in the same manner as in the case of the original selection. The joint committee shall select a chairman and a vice chairman from among its members."

The procedure followed by joint committees at their meetings is practically the same as that utilized by the standing committees.

Joint committees have joint jurisdiction; they are not subject to control or change by one house. To alter their jurisdiction requires an amendment to the law or to the concurrent resolution which created them.

Investigating Committees: Investigating committees, either joint or select, are created by the adoption of a concurrent or simple resolution as the case may be. Such committees are created to make an examination, study, or scrutiny of a particular matter. Their powers, duration, and duties are defined in each instance. The resolution commonly provides that the committee is "authorized to sit and act during the present Congress at such times and places, whether or not the House (or Senate) is sitting, has recessed, or has adjourned, to hold such hearings, to require the attendance of such witnesses and the production of such books, papers, and documents, and to take such testimony, as it deems necessary. Subpoenas shall be issued under the signature of the chairman of the committee or any member designated by him, and shall be served by any person designated by such chairman or member. The chairman of the committee or any member thereof may administer oaths to witnesses." The subpoena power as provided above is not always granted to House investigating committees.

[2] Cannon, VI, 371.

The lives of investigating committees are terminated when they report finally to their parent body on their assignment. The principal objectives of these, their *raison d'etre*, are to make inquiries concerning Members, to obtain information for better lawmaking, and to check administrative departments to find out if they are carrying out the will of the legislature.[3]

Under law, any investigating committee of either the House or Senate, or a joint investigating committee "is empowered to administer oaths to witnesses in any case under their examination." Any person "who having been summoned as a witness by the authority of either House of Congress" and "willfully makes default," or refuses to answer any question pertinent to the inquiry "shall be deemed guilty of a misdemeanor, punishable by a fine of not more than $1,000 or less than $100 and imprisonment in a common jail for not less than one month nor more than twelve." When a summoned witness fails to testify, fails to produce any books, papers, records, or documents requested of him, or whenever "any witness so summoned refuses to answer any" pertinent question, the matter may be referred to the appropriate U. S. attorney, "whose duty it shall be to bring the matter before the grand jury for its action."[4] In the final analysis, the courts, of course, must decide whether or not a witness must answer a question. If the courts should decide that an answer to a question would be self-incriminating, the defendent would be excused for refusing to answer. If it were decided that the committee was seeking information within its scope as an aid to legislate more intelligently, even if the answer reflected on the character of the witness, the witness would be guilty and subject to punishment under the above law. The witness must be his own judge as he stands before the committee as to whether or not he should answer the question; his decision, however, is subject to review by the courts.

Witnesses are invited to testify or summoned to give testimony in pursuance and by virtue of the authority conferred on the committee to send for persons and papers. The resolution may specify that the committee will have the power of subpoena. The House with certain exceptions does not give such general authority to its committees. Joint investigating committees and investigating

[3] For more details on investigating committees, see Dimock, *Congressional Investigating Committees*, also McGreary, *Developments of Congressional Investigative Power* (1940).

[4] *U. S. Code*, Title 2, sections 191-194.

committees of the Senate are nearly always so fortified. Likewise, each standing committee of the Senate has subpoena power.[5] Under House practice, a witness can be summoned by a committee; if he refuses, the committee, by use of another resolution, requests and usually gets permission of the House to subpoena a witness. House permission must be sought in each instance. Three standing committees of the House have continuous authority to issue subpoenas. They are the committees on Appropriations, on Expenditures in the Executive Departments, and on Un-American Activities.

From 1940 to 1947, the Senate and House of Representatives adopted many resolutions during each session [6] authorizing various investigations by each House individually, or occasionally jointly. During the first session of the 80th Congress, the number of investigations authorized was decreased; some proponents of the Reorganization Act of 1946 had hoped that no further investigating committees would be created; instead, they favored extension of investigatory power to the standing committees. A Senate standing committee under the Legislative Reorganization Act does have power to make "investigations into any matter within its jurisdiction," subject to additional funds being granted by the Senate. Under the practice of the first session of the 80th Congress, each House standing committee went back to its parent body for authority before undertaking an investigation, but not for each separate study under that authorization.

Investigating committees as a rule have never enjoyed the power to report legislation. Generally their authority has been limited to a study, an analysis, or an investigation of a particular subject or subjects with a view to making a report or reports on findings, accompanied by various and sundry recommendations. Each committee of course reports to its own parent body; a joint committee to both bodies.

Standing Committees: *Importance in Legislative Process:* Standing committees, created by the rules of the House and Senate, respectively, play a very vital role in the legislative process. All legislation, with occasional exceptions, is born in them. Practice and the rules dictate that all bills and resolutions, or proposals, shall be referred to some standing committee for consideration.

[5] See P. L. 601 of 79th Congress for standing committee authority of subpoena.
[6] For a breakdown of such investigating committees see the annual review articles of various sessions of Congress in the *American Political Science Review.*

After committees have been appointed it is not in order except by unanimous consent to offer legislative or financial measures to either house until they have been duly reported by or discharged from the appropriate standing committee.

Officially the House and the Senate legislate; in reality they do little more than approve or disapprove what the committees report to them. Many minor and occasionally a few major amendments other than committee amendments are added to each important bill before final enactment. Most major bills are amended in various respects and sometimes a new bill is substituted for the one reported by the committee, but to take reverse action on a reported bill is the exception rather than the rule.

Importance of Committee Assignment: Congressmen are vitally concerned with their committees assignments and committee rank. These are matters of major importance to their congressional careers. The power and influence each Senator or Representative wields in national legislative affairs are derived primarily through his committee position or positions.

Committee appointments and promotions are made by the committees on committees in the House and Senate in accord with certain precedents and political practices and in pursuance of a well established "seniority rule." The rules of the House stipulate: "There shall be elected by the House, at the commencement of each Congress," the membership to each of the nineteen standing committees. It continues:

At the commencement of each Congress, the House shall elect as chairman of each standing committee one of the Members thereof; in the temporary absence of the chairman the Member next in rank in the order named in the election of the committee, and so on, as often as the case shall happen, shall act as chairman; and in case of a permanent vacancy in the chairmanship of any such committee the House shall elect another chairman.

All vacancies in standing committees in the House shall be filled by election by the House. Each Member shall be elected to serve on one standing committee and no more; except that Members who are elected to serve on the Committee on the District of Columbia or on the Committee on Un-American Activities may be elected to serve on two standing committees and no more, and Members of the majority party who are elected to serve on the Committee on Expenditures in the Executive Departments or on the Committee on House Administration may be elected to serve on two standing committees and no more.[7]

[7] Rule X.

The Senate rule provides:

In the appointment of the standing committees, the Senate, unless otherwise ordered, shall proceed by ballot to appoint severally the chairman of each committee, and then, by one ballot, the other members necessary to complete the same. A majority of the whole number of votes given shall be necessary to the choice of a chairman of a standing committee, but a plurality of votes shall elect the other members thereof. All other committees shall be appointed by ballot, unless otherwise ordered, and a plurality of votes shall appoint.

When a chairman of a committee shall resign or cease to serve on a committee, and the Presiding Officer be authorized by the Senate to fill the vacancy in such committee, unless specially otherwise ordered, it shall be only to fill up the number on the committee.[8]

The practice varies slightly from the above rules.

Committees on Committees and Standing Committees

Selection of Committee Membership: Standing committee appointments and promotions are determined by the committees on committees, limited only by precedents. The committees on committees of both houses for both parties are agents of their respective political parties. They are not directly responsible to their legislative bodies nor do the rules and practices of the two chambers define their procedures, powers, and duties. These committees are political creatures charged primarily with the duty of selecting Congressional standing committee memberships for their respective party from among their own members.

House Republican Committee on Committees: The Republican Committee on Committees of the House consists of one Representative from each State having Republican representation. Each Republican State delegation, meeting separately, selects its member. If a State has only one Republican Representative that person automatically serves as a member of the committee.

Each member of the committee on committees in voting for a nomination has as many votes as there are Republican Representatives from his State. Thus, the appointive power is based directly on numerical representation.[9]

The slate of Republican nominations for standing committee memberships prepared by this committee on committees must also be submitted to the Republican Conference of Representatives for

[8] Rule XXIV.

approval. Subsequently, it is presented to the House by the Republican floor leader in the form of a resolution for confirmation.

Vacancies filled from time to time during the same Congress are usually made by the Republican floor leader, who is chairman ex-officio of the committee on committees, after consultation with key men of his party.

Senate Republican Committee on Committees: The Senate Republican Committee on Committees has a small membership as contrasted to that of the same party in the House; its size, however, has varied from one Congress to another. In 1877 the number of members on that committee was nine, in the Seventy-sixth Congress, five; in the seventy-seventh, six; and in the eightieth, eight.[10] The membership is appointed by the conference chairman under the authority vested in him by the Republican Conference, but he himself is not even a member of the group.

[9] For the 80th Congress, the membership together with their respective voting strength follow:

State	Representative	Number of Votes
California	Bertrand W. Gearhart	14
Colorado	William S. Hill	3
Connecticut	William J. Miller	6
Delaware	J. Caleb Boggs	1
Idaho	John Sanborn	2
Illinois	Leo E. Allen	20
Indiana	Gerald W. Landis	9
Iowa	Karl M. LeCompte	8
Kansas	Edward H. Rees	6
Kentucky	John M. Robsion	3
Maine	Frank Fellows	3
Maryland	Edward T. Miller	2
Massachusetts	Charles L. Gifford	9
Michigan	Roy O. Woodruff	14
Minnesota	Harold Knutson	8
Missouri	Walter Ploeser	9
Montana	Wesley A. D'Ewart	1
Nebraska	A. L. Miller	4
Nevada	Charles H. Russell	1
New Hampshire	Norris Cotton	2
New Jersey	Fred A. Hartley, Jr.	12
New York	James W. Wadsworth	28
North Dakota	William Lemke	2
Ohio	Thomas A. Jenkins	19
Oklahoma	George B. Schwabe	2
Oregon	Lowell Stockman	4
Pennsylvania	Richard M. Simpson	28
South Dakota	Francis Case	2
Tennessee	Dayton Phillips	2
Utah	William A. Dawson	1
Vermont	Charles A. Plumley	1
Washington	Walt Horan	5
West Virginia	Hubert S. Ellis	4
Wisconsin	Frank B. Keefe	9
Wyoming	Frank A. Barrett	1

Total _____ 245

[10] In the 80th Congress, the committee for the Republicans was composed of Senators: Robertson of Wyoming, *Chairman*, Taft of Ohio, Brooks of Illinois, Butler of Nebraska, Bushfield of South Dakota, Capehart of Indiana, Donnell of Missouri, and Knowland of California.

While this power to name the committeemen who assign the Republicans to the various standing committees places great party control in the hands of the conference chairman, the final authority is lodged with all of the Republican Senators in conference who may question any assignment.

The slate of nominations made up by this Committee on Committees is submitted to a conference of Republican Senators at the beginning of each new Congress for its approval. The list is then turned over to the party floor leader for presentation to the Senate for formal confirmation. Committee assignments made subsequently from time to time as vacancies occur during the same Congress are usually determined by the Committee on Committees and casually approved by the Senate.

House Democratic Committee on Committees: The Democrats on the House Ways and Means Committee have dual functions. In one instance they sit with the Republican members of the same standing committee to study legislative proposals for raising revenue to defray governmental operating costs. At other times, they sit separately as the Democratic Committee on Committees of the House; in this capacity they assign Democratic Representatives to the other standing committees.

The size of the Democratic Committee on Committees is smaller than that of the Republicans. The number of members varies from one Congress to another, depending on the party ratio to the total House membership. The number of Democrats as against the number of Republicans on the Ways and Means Committee is determined in accordance with the strength of the two parties, the same formula used for determining the party ratio on the other standing committees. Since the Committee on Ways and Means is composed of 25 members, the number of Democrats on that committee, or the number of members of the Democratic Committee on Committees, can be expected to vary between seven and seventeen.

In the 80th Congress this committee consisted of ten members,[11] all of whom enjoy continuous service as long as they are members of the Committee on Ways and Means.

The Democratic members of the Committee on Ways and Means are selected by the Democratic Caucus and approved by the House,

---

[11] The membership consisted of the following Democratic Representatives of the Ways and Means Committee: Representatives Doughton, Cooper, Dingle, West, Mills, Gregory, Camp, Lynch, Forand, and Eberharter.

when submitted in the form of a resolution by the chairman of the Democratic Caucus. The Democrats on that committee in a previous Congress are always reappointed to their berths in the same order unless in the case of death, resignation, or election casualty. The number of Democrats may be decreased, through cutting off some of the old members at the bottom of the list due to declining strength of that party as a result of election returns. New appointments are made to fill vacancies or to fill new berths created as a result of increased party strength.[12]

The Caucus in selecting Democratic Members to the Ways and Means Committee or its Committee on Committees takes into consideration geographical allocation of party strength.

In the 80th Congress the Democratic Steering Committee, selected geographically, worked closely with the Democratic Committee on Committees in making the Democratic assignments to standing committees. This was done to emphasize geographical representation. The number of Democrats on the Ways and Means Committee had been curtailed to such an extent that geographical representation also had been greatly reduced. The seniority rule had aggravated the situation by striking the Democratic Representatives off the committee in the order of their service without regard to the geographical area they represented. The ten Democrats left on the committee, the number allowed the party under the new ratios of political strength, were all from east of the Mississippi except in the case of Representatives West (Texas) and Mills (Arkansas). Each member of the Democratic Committee on Committees has one vote in determining an appointment to a standing committee. The number of Democratic Representatives from a State has no bearing on the voting strength.

The slate of nominations for standing committee assignments prepared by this committee is always submitted to the Democratic Caucus for its approval before it is reported to the House in the form of a resolution for confirmation. Any appointments to fill vacancies occurring after this date and until the beginning of a new Congress are not presented to the Democratic Caucus for approval. Nominations made after general organization are presented directly to the House by some member of the Committee on Committees without formal caucus approval.

[12] Since members of the Ways and Means Committee may not serve on any other standing committee of the House, the members of the Democratic Committee on Committees may not name themselves to any other standing committee.

Senate Democratic Committee on Committees: The Senate Democratic Steering Committee serves as the Senate Democratic Committee on Committees. Its membership is appointed by the Democratic floor leader as authorized by the party caucus. In making the appointments, the floor leader takes into "consideration whether they are liberal or conservative, their position and prestige, and the geographical location of their State," as stated by one member of the committee. The committee in closed session meets regularly at the beginning of a new Congress until a slate has been made up, which is then turned over to its floor leader for presentation for Senate confirmation.[13]

Committees Each Member Serves: Each Committee on Committees considers many factors in the determination of standing committee appointments. First the total number of committee appointments to be made, together with the number assigned each party, restrict each committee on committees in its selections. The majority party in accordance with the Legislative Reorganization Act of 1946 makes these decisions.

Under existing rules, every Representative "shall be elected to serve on one standing committee and no more; except that members who are elected to serve on the Committee on the District of Columbia or on the Committee on Un-American Activities may be elected to serve on two standing committees and no more, and members of the majority party who are elected to serve on the Committee on Expenditures in the Executive Departments or on the Committee on House Administration may be elected to serve on two standing committees and no more." [14]

In the Senate, "Each Senator shall serve on two standing committees and no more; except that Senators of the majority party who are members of the Committee on the District of Columbia or of the Committee on Expenditures in the Executive Departments may serve on three standing committees and no more." [15]

[13] The number of members on this committee is determined by the party floor leader. The original resolution creating the committee stipulated that a committee of fifteen members should be appointed; in all subsequent resolutions authorizing the floor leader to make the appointments, the number to be appointed has been omitted. For the 80th Congress, the floor leader only appointed two ex-officio members and ten others, including himself, even though in the prior session there had been a total of seventeen members; the floor leader just did not fill the vacancies which had occurred—he reappointed the old membership which had been returned to the 80th Congress. They follow: Senators Barkley, *Chairman*, McKellar, George, Tydings, Green, Wagner, Hayden, O'Mahoney, Thomas (Utah), and Connally. Senator Lucas, Democratic whip, and Senator McMahon, Secretary of the Conference, were ex-officio members.
[14] House Rule X, (3).
[15] Senate Rule XXV, (4).

Standing Committees and Their Size: The size of each committee is fixed by the rules of the House and Senate, respectively, but the party ratio is determined by the majority party.

The number of standing committees has varied through the years. In the 69th Congress the House had 61 standing committees; in the 79th it had 47; and in the 80th it had only 19, as redefined under the Reorganization Act of 1946. The Senate had 42 standing committees in the 51st Congress; 73 in the 67th, 33 in the 79th Congress, and 15 in the 80th.

The Reorganization Act curtailed the number of committees drastically, consolidating some and redistributing the jurisdictions of others. The following table sets forth these changes:

HOUSE

79th Congress	*80th Congress*
Agriculture	Agriculture
Appropriations	Appropriations
Expenditures, Executive Depts.	Expenditures, Executive Depts.
Banking and Currency Coinage, Weights, and Measures	} Banking and Currency
Civil Service Census Post Offices and Post Roads	} Post Office and Civil Service
District of Columbia	District of Columbia
Flood Control Public Buildings and Grounds Rivers and Harbors Roads	} Public Works
Interstate and Foreign Commerce	Interstate and Foreign Commerce
Judiciary Patents Revision of the Laws Immigration and Naturalization	} Judiciary
Foreign Affairs	Foreign Affairs
Labor Education	} Education and Labor
Merchant Marine and Fisheries	Merchant Marine and Fisheries
Military Affairs Naval Affairs	} Armed Services
Pensions Invalid Pensions World War Veterans' Legislation	} Veteran's Affairs
Public Lands Territories Irrigation and Reclamation Mines and Mining Insular Affairs Indian Affairs	} Public Lands

Ways and Means..Ways and Means
Rules ....Rules

Accounts ⎫
Disposition of Executive Papers ⎪
Enrolled Bills ⎪
Library ⎬ House Administration
Memorials ⎪
Printing ⎭

Election of President, Vice President, ⎫
and Representatives of Congress ⎪ Would abolish these and transfer
Elections No. 1 ⎪ the jurisdiction of the Elections
Elections No. 2 ⎬ Committees to the Committee on
Elections No. 3 ⎪ House Administration
Claims ⎪
War Claims ⎭

Un-American Activities ....Un-American Activities

SENATE

79th Congress	80th Congress

Agriculture and Forestry........................Agriculture and Forestry
Appropriations ....Appropriations

Military Affairs ⎫
Naval Affairs ⎬ Armed Services

Banking and Currency..........................Banking and Currency

Civil Service ⎫
Post Offices and Post Roads ⎬ Post Office and Civil Service

District of Columbia................................District of Columbia
Expenditures, Executive Depts..............Expenditures, Executive Depts.

Finance ⎫
Pensions ⎬ Finance

Foreign Relations....................................Foreign Relations

Interstate Commerce ⎫
Commerce ⎪
Interoceanic Canals ⎬ Interstate and Foreign Commerce
Manufacturers ⎭

Judiciary ⎫
Patents ⎬ Judiciary
Immigration ⎭

Education and Labor................................Labor and Public Welfare

Public Lands and Surveys ⎫
Mines and Mining ⎪
Territories and Insular Affairs ⎬ Interior and Insular Affairs
Irrigation and Reclamation ⎪
Indian Affairs ⎭

Public Buildings and Grounds................Public Works

Rules ⎫
Audit and Control ⎪
Library ⎪
Privileges and Elections ⎬ Rules and Administration
Printing ⎪
Enrolled Bills ⎭

Claims ....Abolished

The nineteen standing committees of the House together with the number of members on each are as follows:

Committee on Agriculture, to consist of twenty-seven Members.
Committee on Appropriations, to consist of forty-five Members.
Committee on Armed Services, to consist of thirty-three Members.
Committee on Banking and Currency, to consist of twenty-seven Members.
Committee on Post Office and Civil Service, to consist of twenty-five Members.
Committee on the District of Columbia, to consist of twenty-five Members.
Committee on Education and Labor, to consist of twenty-five Members.
Committee on Expenditures in the Executive Departments, to consist of twenty-five Members.
Committee on Foreign Affairs, to consist of twenty-five Members.
Committee on House Administration, to consist of twenty-five Members.
Committee on Interstate and Foreign Commerce, to consist of twenty-seven Members.
Committee on the Judiciary, to consist of twenty-seven Members.
Committee on Merchant Marine and Fisheries, to consist of twenty-five Members.
Committee on Public Lands, to consist of twenty-five Members.
Committee on Public Works, to consist of twenty-seven Members.
Committee on Rules, to consist of twelve Members.
Committee on Un-American Activities, to consist of nine Members.
Committee on Veterans' Affairs, to consist of twenty-seven Members.
Committee on Ways and Means, to consist of twenty-five Members.[16]

The fifteen standing committees of the Senate together with the number of Senators on each are as follows:

Committee on Agriculture and Forestry, to consist of thirteen Senators.
Committee on Appropriations, to consist of twenty-one Senators.
Committee on Armed Services, to consist of thirteen Senators.
Committee on Banking and Currency, to consist of thirteen Senators.
Committee on the District of Columbia, to consist of thirteen Senators.
Committee on Expenditures in the Executive Departments, to consist of thirteen Senators.
Committee on Finance, to consist of thirteen Senators.
Committee on Foreign Relations, to consist of thirteen Senators.
Committee on Interior and Insular Affairs, to consist of thirteen Senators.
Committee on Interstate and Foreign Commerce, to consist of thirteen Senators.
Committee on the Judiciary, to consist of thirteen Senators.
Committee on Labor and Public Welfare, to consist of thirteen Senators.
Committee on Post Office and Civil Service, to consist of thirteen Senators.
Committee on Public Works, to consist of thirteen Senators.
Committee on Rules and Administration, to consist of thirteen Senators.[17]

The Senate Appropriations Committee is composed of both a permanent and an alternating membership. The "permanent members" are appointed in the same manner as that used for making

[16] *House Manual*, 80-1, Rule X, sec. a pp. 303-305.
[17] Rule XXV.

all other committee appointments, but the alternating members are cared for by a different procedure. The system was created to give certain legislative committees of the Senate some representation in preparing appropriation bills. The legislative committees concerned choose some of their own members respectively to serve on the Appropriations Committee as ex-officio members during the consideration of the appropriation bill comparable to the legislative bills handled by themselves. For example: The Committee on Agriculture and Forestry shall select three of its members who "shall be ex-officio members of the Committee on Appropriations, to serve on said committee when the bill making appropriations for the Department of Agriculture is being considered by the Committee on Appropriations, and at least one Member of the Committee on Agriculture and Forestry shall be a member of the conference committee appointed to confer with the House upon said agricultural appropriation bill. . . ." The table below sets forth the names of all legislative committees allowed representation on the Appropriations Committee when considering certain of the different appropriation bills. The representation together with the names of each respective appropriation bill also follow:

Name of Committee	Number of Members	Name of Appropriation Bills	Number to Serve on Conference Committees
Committee on Agriculture and Forestry	3	Department of Agriculture	1
Committee on Civil Service	3	Post Office Department	1
Committee on Armed Services	3	Department of War and the Department of the Navy	1
Committee on the District of Columbia	3	District of Columbia	1
Committee on Public Works	3	Rivers and Harbors	1
Committee on Foreign Relations	3	Diplomatic and Consular Service	1

Party Ratios on Committees: The total committee membership having been decided upon,[18] the number of committee appointments allotted either party in the House or Senate is determined by a formula generally giving each party a voice on every committee in ratio to its party strength. The majority party can make exceptions in any case since the power for making the final determination of all party ratios is lodged with the majority party of each house,

[18] This number is fixed under the Legislative Reorganization Act of 1946; either house can make changes.

respectively. In the case of the House Rules Committee, for example, a policy forming committee for the party in control, there is an exceptional variation.[19] Representatives and Senators, affiliated with third parties, receive their committee assignments through one of the two major parties, usually the minority.

Mathematically the formula provides that the number of members of the party is to the number of its committee appointments as the total membership of the legislative body is to the total number of committee appointments. To illustrate: as applied to the House in the 80th Congress, the 246 Republicans are to their total number of committee appointments (x) as the 435 Representatives are to the 484 standing committee positions.[20]

For the 80th Congress, the 19 standing committees of the House had a total membership of 484 of which 283 were allotted to the majority party and 201 to the minority. The House membership at the beginning of the 80th Congress consisted of 188 Democrats, 246 Republicans, and 1 American Laborite (who was not assigned a committee), or 201 appointments went to the 188 Democrats and 283 appointments to the 246 Republicans. The Senate committee assignments are figured accordingly. The 15 committees of the Senate had a sum total membership of 203 of which 113 were allotted to the majority party and 90 to the minority. The Senate membership at the beginning of the 80th Congress consisted of 51 Republicans and 45 Democrats.

The reason the party ratio on some committees is not always mathematically accurate as per the formula is self evident. The party in power needs a controlling majority at all times, even should one or possibly two of its members see fit not to support their party on a particular issue. Such discretionary variations are limited under the present rules as contrasted to the situation before the Reorganization Act of 1946, because now each Member of Congress can have only a definite number of committee berths and no more. There are meagre exceptions in the rules which have already been mentioned. Under existing rules the assignments allowed each party on each committee are closely tied to its ratio of the total membership. The total number of committee berths was even determined by multiplying the number of appointments allowed each Representative or Senator by the total number of

[19] The Rules Committee of the 80th Congress consisted of eight Republicans and four Democrats.
[20] The formula as applied to the 80th Congress would work out as follows: $246:x :: 435:484; 435x = 246 \times 484$ or $188:x :: 435:484; 435x = 188 \times 484.$

Representatives and Senators. It is possible under all circumstances, however, for slight exceptions from the mathematical formula to be made, giving the majority party more members than it is entitled to under the determined ratio. This procedure is frequently resorted to in the case of a few committees.[21]

Consideration in Making Appointments: Significant is the fact that senior Representatives and Senators in point of service are granted their requested committee assignments over any preferences made to "freshman" Congressmen—with exceptions, of course. Briefly, the Committees on Committees really concern themselves only with transfers from one committee to another and the placement of "freshmen" Representatives and Senators or those returned after having been defeated in some prior election.

Members of standing committees in continuous service returning to a new Congress retain their old committee appointments unless they request otherwise. When a ranking member of a committee is defeated, not up for re-election, resigns, or is promoted to another committee, leaving a vacancy, all of the committee membership of the same political faith below his rank, are moved up one step toward the chairmanship.[22] Such promotions are to the same degree as there are vacancies. Chairmanship vacancies are filled by promoting the ranking majority member of the committee with all members below his rank of the same party moving up one step. In case of party change, the ranking member of each committee of the old minority becomes the chairman. The filling of a Democratic vacancy does not affect the Republican members of the same committee or vice versa.

The members of a committee are ranked according to the order in which they are enumerated in the lists presented to the House and Senate respectively for approval. The first named on the majority list becomes the chairman.

In case of temporary absence of the chairman, the next ranking member serves as acting chairman; in case of a permanent vacancy,

---

[21] C.R., 80-1, p. 113. At the beginning of the 80th Congress, when the appointments of Senators to committees were made, the ratio question came up. Senator Barkley, minority leader said: ". . . I cannot help but deplore the fact among the entire list of 15 committees the majority conference decided there should be a disproportionate ratio on the Appropriations Committee, the Committee on Rules and Administration, and the Labor and Public Welfare Committee."

[22] In speaking of how he became chairman of a subcommittee after having been appointed to the Appropriations Committee, Representative Umstead in the 75th Congress stated: "When I was appointed to a place on the Committee on Appropriations 2 years ago I did not ask to be assigned to the Subcommittee on Appropriations for the Navy Department. If I could have selected the subcommittees to which I was to be assigned, I confess I would not have selected the Subcommittee on Appropriations for the Navy Department." (C.R., 75-1, p. 6222, daily edition.)

a new chairman is selected by the parent body, usually the ranking majority member.

Thus, the seniority rule has a very definite and strong influence on all committee appointments and promotions, including the appointments of chairmen, but it is neither absolute nor invariable. On occasions both houses have ignored the seniority rule and designated members of lower committee rank as chairmen. One outstanding case occurred in the House when Mr. Good, chairman of the Appropriations Committee in the early 1920's, resigned and Mr. Madden who was holding third place in point of service was made its chairman. Custom and practice insist upon a wide geographical distribution of committee appointments, party factions must be recognized or placated, and individual leadership cannot be completely overlooked in spite of the seniority rule.

The seniority rule always limits the selections made by the committees on committees and aid Members of long service to obtain their pet committee posts. The application of the seniority rule, however, does not prevent any member of a committee in one Congress from requesting a new committee appointment in a subsequent one. In fact many of the most sought for committee appointments, particularly in the House, have been obtained by the promotions of old Members from lesser important committees to the more desired committees. Members of Congress already on lesser important committees do not generally get promotion to other committees except by request. Occasionally the party officials take cases in their own hands and promote certain individual Congressmen with little regard for the seniority rule.

Length of service is an important factor in the determination of transfers from lesser to more important committees. Of course, one must not discount the influence a national reputation or "political prominence" commands in either the House or Senate in securing a particular committee assignment.

Any committee vacancies not filled by promotions or transfers are open to freshmen Congressmen. The committees on committees, however, weigh many factors in behalf of the various candidates before making a nomination. In the Senate for example, a man who has been a Governor or State legislator is granted preference to a major committee over politically inexperienced men, other factors remaining the same. Some factors always taken into consideration are: "political fitness" and party loyalty, education and training together with the Members' particular interests in certain matters to which they may have devoted long years of study, length of service of the Member, geographical location, and the committees requested. Tied up with all of this are the human elements of personalities and friendships.

Some members of committees on committees have asserted that they assume responsibility for all elements of society; that they endeavor to appoint members to represent the consumer, labor, and industry, to committees handling controversial social issues. For example: the committees on committees make some effort to avoid appointing to the Armed Service Committee only men favoring big armies and navies; otherwise Congress would always be laden with the job of acting on army and navy bills, one Representative said.

Geographical allocation is important in the selection of committee personnel, and in some cases is the determining factor. While the committees on committees do not hew to the line in all cases, they endeavor to see that all sections of the country are represented on committees acting on legislation directly affecting the public weal.

By practice no two Members from the same State serve on the same major committee. That is more so the case in the Senate than in the House. The procedure of necessity places limitations on committee appointments, but exceptions to the rule are made if the cases seem justifiable.

The requests for particular assignments by a Congressman have some weight. A request, however, by no means assures that the preference will be granted. The late Representative West, on the House Democratic Committee on Committees stated that application for a particular appointment weighs heavily in the determination of to whom an assignment shall be given and that all newcomers should make application for their committee preferences. In the Senate more so than in the House, the new Members are consulted individually. Should three requests be made for a particular committee on which there were three vacancies, he continued, they would be granted, other things being equal. There have been instances, however, in which only three applications were made for three vacancies and not one of the requests was granted.

Selection of Committee Members: The procedure of the different committees on committees to select members of the standing committees varies but not sufficiently to justify a separate discussion of each. At the beginning of every Congress each one holds a series of sessions for making nominations to fill any committee vacancies. The number of sessions held by each depends on the number of appointments to be made, the contests for the various posts, and the number of candidates for each vacancy.

The first two problems confronting the committees involve finding out the number of vacancies and applications. The first is simple, merely a totaling of the committee vacancies to be filled resulting from political casualties in the preceding election, resignations of old appointments by the re-elected Representatives or Senators, increases in size of committees, or increased representation by one party as opposed to that of the other.

The second task necessitates requesting each new Congressman to file formally or informally his committee preferences. Old Members in point of service desiring to be transferred from one committee to another must also file requests for changes and campaign to get such preferments, or both. Senior Members in point of service desiring a change from one committee to another are free to file applications for a new committee with the understanding that they will resign their old posts if assigned to the new ones requested. These requests will be given prior consideration over those by the new Congressmen.

Many or most committee nominations presented to the respective committees on committees in formal session are agreed upon in the absence of any opposition and without taking secret ballots. The names of the candidates are merely presented and without opposition or in the absence of any contest, they are confirmed by unanimous consent or by a voice vote. Many decisions are "prearranged affairs," i.e. the "slate" is made up informally among members of a certain committee on committees and presented at a later formal session of that group for approval. In the House, all Representatives of a party from the same State frequently caucus in order to prevent competition among themselves for a certain vacancy. This practice gives the request of each Representative for a particular committee assignment more force when it is presented to the personnel committee for consideration.

Other cases involve more consideration, some more controversial than others. Several closely contested applications might be up for the same vacancy, thus involving discretion on the part of the committee on committees concerned. The procedure in reaching a decision in such cases may differ. Usually it includes the presentation of the nominations for a particular vacancy, each of which is offered by the member of the committee on committees working in behalf of a particular candidate. In the House, each member of the committee on committees is a champion for the cause of each Representative of the same party from the geographical district he represents. In the Senate, the committees on committees are small and function as units. Individual Senators may strongly support certain nominations. After a free discussion, regardless of how the case is to be handled, or whether in the House or Senate, the members of the committee vote secretly by ballot. This procedure is more formal in the House than in the Senate due to the larger number of Members participating in the balloting. Should there be three persons up for three vacancies the case is simple; should there be 5 applicants for 3 vacancies, the three persons receiving the highest number of ballots, provided that number is a majority of all the votes cast, would be selected for the assignments. Each member of the committee would cast one vote for each of three candidates.[23]

In the House if three are put on the committee at the same time their rank will be determined by their seniority. If they are "freshmen" Congressmen or of equal seniority, the committee rank will be determined by drawing the names out of a box or alphabetically. The procedure in the Senate as stated by one Senator is as follows: "Where seniority of service is equal as between applicants desiring the same assignment priority is given to the applicant who may have seniority either as former Senator, Member of the House, or Governor of a State. If this does not exist the final determination of seniority as well as seniority assignment on a given committee will be given alphabetically as applied to the name."

In the House after the slate has thus been made up it is turned over to the chairmen of the committees on committees who present these assignments in the form of a resolution to their respective

[23] In the case of the House Republican Committee on Committees, which uses a plural voting procedure, each Member is entitled to three times the number of votes he is allowed for one candidate.

caucuses for approval. Subsequently they are submitted to the House for confirmation.

At the beginning of the 80th Congress, first session, the two resolutions providing for the election of the Republican and Democratic members to all standing committees, except the Committees on Appropriations and Ways and Means, both of which had already been named, were presented as follows:

On January 14, 1947, Representative Halleck, majority leader, offered H.Res. 47, providing for election of the Republican representatives to committees, which was adopted as follows:

Resolved, That the following-named Members be, and they are hereby, elected members of the following standing committees of the House of Representatives:
Committee on Agriculture: Clifford R. Hope (chairman), Kansas; August H. Andresen, Minnesota; etc.
(*Personnel of other committees were listed accordingly.*)

On January 16, 1947, Representative Forand, chairman of the Democratic Caucus, offered H.Res. 49, providing for election of the Democratic Representative to committees, which was adopted as follows:

Resolved, That the following-named Members be, and they are hereby, elected members of the following standing committees in the House of Representatives:
Committee on Agriculture: John W. Flannagan, Jr., Virginia; Harold D. Cooley, North Carolina; etc.
(*Personnel of other committees were listed accordingly.*)

In the Senate, the slate by the Democratic Committee on Committees is submitted to its floor leader and by him directly to the Senate. The slate of the Republican Committee on Committees is submitted to a conference of Republican Senators for approval and then submitted by the floor leader to the Senate for confirmation. The complete slate of both parties is offered in open Senate in the form of an order, which upon adoption by the Senate itself constitutes the membership of the standing committees of the Senate. At the beginning of the 80th Congress, the procedure for election of its standing committees was as follows:[24]

The PRESIDENT pro tempore. The Chair inquires whether the majority and minority leaders wish to submit their committee lists before the Senate proceeds with the morning hour.

[24] Senator Barkley later withdrew the minority members temporarily which were resubmitted and approved, but this shows the typical procedures.

Mr. WHITE. Mr. President, I understand that both the majority and minority lists were prepared, and that Senators were ready to offer them. I understand the Senator from Wyoming (Mr. Robertson) would present the majority list.

Mr. ROBERTSON of Wyoming. Mr. President, I send to the desk a resolution and ask for immediate consideration.

The PRESIDENT pro tempore. The clerk will state the resolution.

The resolution (S.Res. 18) was read, as follows:

"*Resolved,* That the following shall constitute the standing committees of the Eightieth Congress."

Mr. BARKLEY. A parliamentary inquiry.

The PRESIDENT pro-tempore. The Senator will state it.

Mr. BARKLEY. Does the Chair wish that both lists be read simultaneously so as to show the complete membership of each committee as it is called?

The PRESIDENT pro tempore. The Chair thinks it yould be preferable if both lists were presented together, and the full list of each committee announced.

Mr. BARKLEY. I present the minority list, by direction of the Democratic steering committee.

Thereupon the Chief Clerk read the list of committees and the assignments thereto, as follows:[25]

"On Agriculture and Forestry: Messrs. Capper (*Chairman*), Aiken, Bushfield, . . ." etc.

Note the following remarks by a Representative concerning the influence of an individual Member in obtaining a particular committee appointment for himself. Congressman Pittenger said:

I learned that the rule of seniority prevailed and that a new Member started at the bottom of the ladder. Members are assigned a room or office. But Congressmen older in point of service have a preference or first choice as to the office they will occupy. The new Member takes what is left . . .

I talked to one of the veteran Members of the House about a committee assignment . . . He told an interesting story of his first experience in Congress. At that time the Speaker selected the committees. My friend was asked to designate the committees on which he wanted to be placed. He did so. He was then asked to name the committees on which he would refuse to serve. He did so, and said that under no circumstances would he work on those committees. When the appointment was made, to his surprise, he received committee appointments he had indicated he would refuse to take. But he swallowed his disappointment, changed his mind, and accepted. Today he is chairman of one of the leading committees of the House. Of course, the members of the minority political party are assigned to membership on the various committees, and that is done by the House upon designation by their party leaders.[26]

A committee appointment can only be refused by permission of the parent body;[27] a Member may resign his committee assign-

---

[25] C.R., 80-1, pp. 111-13.
[26] C.R., 72-1, p. 259.
[27] Floor leaders and Speaker are excluded from committee service in the House.

ment. Proposals making committee assignments are privileged, debatable, and amendable; in the House the previous question can be moved to their adoption.

Position of Chairmen

Agent of Majority Party: The chairmen of committees usually receive their appointments in accordance with the seniority rule, but actual preferments are conferred by the House and Senate respectively. Senators and Representatives when promoted to chairmanship become the parliamentary officials as well as the party heads of their respective committees. As agents of the majority party, it is expected they will support measures favored by but not those opposed by the party; they are generally the instrumentalities through which the party in power "speaks," and generally determines the destiny of partisan legislation.[28]

Presiding Officer: The chairmen of committees preside at the meetings of their groups; in case of their absence, the next ranking members preside without special authorization from the committee. As the presiding officers of the committees, the chairmen fill a post very much like that of the Presiding Officers of the two houses, since their rules apply at the meetings of the committees so far as they are applicable. The chairmen present the business to the committees; they put questions; they determine quorums; they keep order and decorum; they administer oaths

[28] Referring to the power of the chairmen of the House committees, Mr. Anderson of Minnesota said: "Of course the chairman of a committee can not report a bill without the consent of a majority of the committee, but under the unwritten, and, I believe, the unbroken, rule no majority has ever reported a bill without the consent of the chairman. On the floor the bill is absolutely in his hands.

"It is obvious that the power to say that legislation shall not be considered is the power to legislate. It is the negative power which lends real significance to these chairmanships. This negative or obstructive power rests in the hands of a few men and may be exerted at any of the various stages of the bill's progress toward final passage." (C.R., 63-1, p. 4761. See C.R., 62-3, p. 4845.)

On March 24, 1941, when Senator Adams was chairman of Appropriations subcommittee reporting the National Defense Supplemental Appropriation Bill for 1941 (Lend Lease), he directed the bill through the Senate even though he had opposed the Lend Lease law. Note his following comments:

"MR. ADAMS. Mr. President, I am presenting this bill to the Senate under direction of the Committee on Appropriations. As a Member of the Senate, I voted against the lease-and-lend bill. I appreciate that my individual votes and opinions are of no concern, but I wish to make my position clear. I voted against the lease-and-lend bill because I thought, as I still think, that it was unsound in principle and apt to bring my country not only danger but catastrophe and disaster. However, the Congress of the United States, in whose power rests the making of policies, passed the bill, and I regard myself as much bound by the legal requirements of the lease-and-lend measure as are those who voted for it. Therefore, as an individual Senator and as chairman of the subcommittee of the Committee on Appropriations, I am presenting the bill now before us upon the premise that Congress having declared the principle, having laid down the policy, Congress should, and I think must, implement the lease-and-lend law by providing adequate financing." (C.R., 77-1, p. 2499, March 24, 1941.)

to witnesses appearing before their committees; they call sessions of the groups; and they, as spokesmen for their groups, file or submit reports (reported bills) by their committees to the House or Senate as the case may be, unless the committees in each case direct otherwise. The rules state: "It shall be the duty of the chairman of each such committee to report or cause to be reported promptly to the Senate or House of Representatives, as the case may be, any measure approved by his committee and to take or cause to be taken necessary steps to bring the matter to a vote." [29]

Seniority Rule: The seniority rule has a very definite and strong influence on all committee promotions; in fact, it is usually the determining factor. There have been some exceptions. A case in point occurred on the occasion when Mr. Good, chairman of the House Appropriations in the early 1920s, resigned and Mr. Madden who was holding third place in point of service was made its chairman.[30]

Custom and practice insist upon a wide geographical distribution of committee appointments, but under the operation of the seniority rule the chairmanships are not so distributed. When the Democrats have been in power most of the committee chairmanships have gone to men from the South and when the Republicans have been in power most of them have gone to men from the North. Dividing the country up roughly into four geographical areas,[31] North, South, West, and Southwest, and tabulating the chairman of the House and Senate committees for different years selected at random, one gets the following picture:

Geographical location	Republicans 1928		Republicans 1930		Democrats 1933		Democrats 1938		Republicans 1948	
	House	Senate	House	Senate	House	Senate	House	Senate	House	Senate
North	28	15	28	14	14	6	16	5	14	9
South	2	1	2	1	22	13	19	13	0	1
West	16	17	17	18	4	7	5	9	5	5
Southwest	0	0	0	0	7	7	7	6	0	0

Reference of Bills to Standing Committees

Committee Jurisdiction and Reference: After committees are organized at the beginning of a new Congress to do business, all bills and resolutions introduced are referred to a standing committee according to its jurisdiction. The Speaker refers to House

---

[29] Sec. 133 of P.L. 601 of the 79th Congress.
[30] See Brown, *op. cit.*, p. 209; Willoughby, *Principles of Legislative Organization and Administration*, pp. 330-408.
[31] See *Congressional Directory* for the various years cited. Included in the North are all States east of the Mississippi and North of the Mason and Dixon Line. Included in the Southwest are Arkansas, Oklahoma, Texas, Arizona, and New Mexico.

committees all bills and resolutions introduced in the House, or Senate bills and resolutions passed by the Senate and sent to the House, subject to the will of the House. The Presiding Officer of the Senate refers to Senate committees Senate bills and resolutions and House bills and resolutions passed by the House and sent to the Senate, subject to the will of the Senate. Actually, the references are made by the Parliamentarian of each house under supervision of the presiding officers. In the House a bill can be referred to only one committee; it can be re-referred but only one committee ever makes a report on the same bill. In the Senate bills are referred to only one committee but sometimes action is taken to send a bill to two or more committees with each making a report on the bill.

The task of referring bills is a confusing one. So many bills can seemingly be referred to two or more standing committees. This was the case before the 80th Congress when the House had 47 committees and the Senate 33; it is still the case, the House having 19 committees and the Senate 15. To illustrate: on one occasion during the 80th Congress, Senator Vandenberg, in referring S. 758, the Army-Navy merger bill, to the Senate Committee on Armed Services, had the following to say:

Knowing that this question of reference would arise, the Chair has given serious study to the matter. It is typical of several other problems of reference which have confronted the Chair. Decisions frequently are difficult under the Legislative Reorganization Act, because of conflicting interpretations which can be put upon the language of the act. It is not unusual that a thoroughly persuasive argument can be made, on the basis of the language of the act, for jurisdiction in one of two or three of the new standing committees of the Senate. Under such circumstances, the decision of the Chair unavoidably becomes a policy decision. When the Chair finds no explicit and indisputable instructions in the Reorganization Act, the Chair must weigh the rival interpretations which are possible and base his decision upon the preponderance. This becomes then a matter of judgment. It is not a matter of serious import in the ordinary routine, but it may become a major decision in policy in such instances as the present one. In such case the Chair believes the Senate itself should decide, in the final analysis. The Chair will not seek escape from responsibility in such instances. The Chair will make his ruling and his reference, but he will immediately bring such decisions to the direct attention of the Senate so that the Senate itself can decide on the basis of an appeal from the ruling of the Chair if there is disagreement.

In the present instance, the Army-Navy-Air merger bill, in the opinion of the Chair, can, under the language of the Reorganization Act, be referred either to the Committee on Expenditures in the Executive Departments or to the Committee on Armed Services, within the meaning of the act.

The jurisdiction of the Committee on Expenditures in the Executive Departments might seem to be specifically established by the language of the act which assigns "reorganizations in the executive branch of the Government" to this committee. The merger bill clearly involves reorganization in the executive branch.

On the other hand, the jurisdiction of the Committee on Armed Services would seem to be just as specifically established by the language in the act which assigns "the common defense generally." [32]

This same over-all problem confronts the Speaker to the same degree in making references to House committees. The problem became more acute at the beginning of the 80th Congress than prior thereto, particularly because the number of committees had been reduced, and their jurisdictions broadened, requiring new definitions for committee jurisdictions, and current precedents to serve as a guide had not been established. The House of Representatives met this problem in part by modifying Rule XI as follows: "All proposed legislation, messages, petitions, memorials, and other matters relating to the subjects listed under the standing committees named . . . shall be referred to such committees, respectively: *Provided,* That unless otherwise provided herein, any matter within the jurisdiction of a standing committee prior to January 2, 1947, shall remain subject to the jurisdiction of that committee or of the consolidated committee succeeding generally to the jurisdiction of that committee."

The Senate rules give the Presiding Officer the following directive in making references:

In any case in which a controversy arises as to the jurisdiction of any standing committee of the Senate with respect to any proposed legislation, the question of jurisdiction shall be decided by the Presiding Officer of the Senate, without debate, in favor of that committee which has jurisdiction over the subject matter which predominates in such proposed legislation; but such decision shall be subject to an appeal."

The appeals from the decision of the chair are debatable. In the absence of objection, the Senate may proceed in any order it may desire. The Presiding Officer may entertain debate on a reference for his own information.

In the House an appeal may be taken from the decision of the Speaker in making a reference; the appeal is debatable, unless the previous question has been moved; but it is customary when an appeal from the decision of the chair is made for someone to move to table the motion, which motion is not debatable.

In any case the decision of the House or Senate is final concerning the committee to which a particular bill or resolution shall

[32] C.R. 80-1, p. 1413 (daily edition).

be referred. Positive action by either house rightly refers any bill to any committee without regard to precedents.

Change of Reference: In both houses the reference of any bill may be questioned, recalled, or re-referred. Generally the question of recalling and re-referring a bill is not raised until the members of the committee concerned are consulted, and then usually by the chairmen. The recalling and re-reference of a bill is usually routine; it may involve much debate and roll call votes.

In the House such a motion is privileged only when formally authorized by the committee to which the measure was referred or by the committee claiming jurisdiction thereof. The motion where a public bill is involved can be made immediately after reading the *Journal,* but it is not debatable—an appeal from the decision of the chair is debatable. The motion may be made by unanimous consent, on the authorized motion of the committee claiming jurisdiction, or on report of the committee to which the bill was erroneously referred. A motion is applicable to a single bill at a time. Errors in reference of private bills are corrected at the Clerk's desk without action by the House. The question of incorrect reference can be raised in the House on a public bill at any time until it is reported; it may be raised on private bills at any time prior to passage.

Standing Committees of the House and Senate

The standing committees play a vital role in legislating; they determine to a great extent just what legislation shall be written. The committees are creatures of their respective houses, but once they have been created and their memberships appointed, they are living entities for the duration of a single Congress unless the legislative chamber concerned takes action to the contrary. Practice and the rules of the two Houses of Congress dictate that all proposed legislation shall be referred to some standing committee in accordance with its jurisdiction. After committees have been appointed at the beginning of each new Congress, legislative or financial bills are not considered by either chamber unless and until they have been duly reported by or discharged from one of the authorized committees. Exceptions are made frequently in the case of minor noncontroversial bills under unanimous consent when they are acted on in one or both houses without being referred to a committee. Standing committees never report out all bills referred to them; in fact, hundreds of bills could be referred to a single committee in one session and it may not report out a bill; it may report only a few; or it may report many. The others die in the committee files.

Committees of House and Their Jurisdictions: In the House "All proposed legislation, messages, petitions, memorials, and other matters relating to the subjects listed under the standing committees named below shall be referred to such committees, respectively":

Provided, That unless otherwise provided herein, any matter within the jurisdiction of a standing committee prior to January 2, 1947, shall remain subject to the jurisdiction of that committee or of the consolidated committee succeeding generally to the jurisdiction of that committee.

"(a) **Committee on Agriculture.**
"1. Agriculture generally.
"2. Inspection of livestock and meat products.
"3. Animal industry and diseases of animals.
"4. Adulteration of seeds, insect pests, and protection of birds and animals in forest reserves.
"5. Agricultural colleges and experiment stations.
"6. Forestry in general, and forest reserves other than those created from the public domain.
"7. Agricultural economics and research.
"8. Agricultural and industrial chemistry.
"9. Dairy industry.
"10. Entomology and plant quarantine.
"11. Human nutrition and home economics.
"12. Plant industry, soils, and agricultural engineering.
"13. Agricultural educational extension services.
"14. Extension of farm credit and farm security.
"15. Rural electrification.
"16. Agricultural production and marketing and stabilization of prices of agricultural products.
"17. Crop insurance and soil conservation.

"(b) **Committee on Appropriations.**
"1. Appropriation of the revenue for the support of the Government.

"(c) **Committee on Armed Services.**
"1. Common defense generally.
"2. The War Department and the Military Establishment generally.
"3. The Navy Department and the Naval Establishment generally.
"4. Soldiers' and sailors' homes.
"5. Pay, promotion, retirement, and other benefits and privileges of members of the armed forces.
"6. Selective service.
"7. Size and composition of the Army and Navy.
"8. Forts, arsenals, military reservations, and navy yards.
"9. Ammunition depots.
"10. Conservation, development, and use of naval petroleum and oil shale reserves.

"11. Strategic and critical materials necessary for the common defense.

"12. Scientific research and development in support of the armed services.

"(d) Committee on Banking and Currency.

"1. Banking and currency generally.

"2. Financial aid to commerce and industry, other than matters relating to such aid which are specifically assigned to other committees under this rule.

"3. Deposit insurance.

"4. Public and private housing.

"5. Federal Reserve System.

"6. Gold and silver, including the coinage thereof.

"7. Issuance of notes and redemption thereof.

"8. Valuation and revaluation of the dollar.

"9. Control of prices of commodities, rents, or services.

"(e) Committee on Post Office and Civil Service.

"1. The Federal civil service generally.

"2. The status of officers and employees of the United States, including their compensation, classification, and retirement.

"3. The postal service generally, including the railway mail service, and measures relating to ocean mail and pneumatic-tube service; but excluding post roads.

"4. Postal-savings banks.

"5. Census and the collection of statistics generally.

"6. The National Archives.

"(f) Committee on the District of Columbia.

"1. All measures relating to the municipal affairs of the District of Columbia in general, other than appropriations therefor, including—

"2. Public health and safety, sanitation, and quarantine regulations.

"3. Regulation of sale of intoxicating liquors.

"4. Adulteration of food and drugs.

"5. Taxes and tax sales.

"6. Insurance, executors, administrators, wills, and divorce.

"7. Municipal and juvenile courts.

"8. Incorporation and organization of societies.

"9. Municipal code and amendments to the criminal and corporation laws.

"(g) Committee on Education and Labor.

"1. Measures relating to education or labor generally.

"2. Mediation and arbitration of labor disputes.

"3. Wages and hours of labor.

"4. Convict labor and the entry of goods made by convicts into interstate commerce.

"5. Regulation or prevention of importation of foreign laborers under contract.

"6. Child labor.

"7. Labor statistics.

"8. Labor standards.

"9. School-lunch program.

"10. Vocational rehabilitation.

"11. United States Employees' Compensation Commission.

"12. Columbia Institution for the Deaf, Dumb, and Blind; Howard University; Freedmen's Hospital; and Saint Elizabeths Hospital.

"13. Welfare of miners.

"(h) (1) Committee on Expenditures in the Executive Departments.

"(A) Budget and accounting measures, other than appropriations.

"(B) Reorganizations in the executive branch of the Government.

"(2) Such committee shall have the duty of—

"(A) receiving and examining reports of the Comptroller General of the United States and of submitting such recommendations to the House as it deems necessary or desirable in connection with the subject matter of such reports;

"(B) studying the operation of Government activities at all levels with a view to determining its economy and efficiency;

"(C) evaluating the effects of laws enacted to reorganize the legislative and executive branches of the Government;

"(D) studying intergovernmental relationships between the United States and the States and municipalities, and between the United States and international organizations of which the United States is a member.

"(i) Committee on Foreign Affairs.

"1. Relations of the United States with foreign nations generally.

"2. Establishment of boundary lines between the United States and foreign nations.

"3. Protection of American citizens abroad and expatriation.

"4. Neutrality.

"5. International conferences and congresses.

"6. The American National Red Cross.

"7. Intervention abroad and declarations of war.

"8. Measures relating to the diplomatic service.

"9. Acquisition of land and buildings for embassies and legations in foreign countries.

"10. Measures to foster commercial intercourse with foreign nations and to safeguard American business interests abroad.

"11. United Nations Organization and international financial and monetary organizations.

"12. Foreign loans.

"(j) (1) Committee on House Administration.

"(A) Employment of persons by the House, including clerks for Members and committees, and reporters of debates.

"(B) Expenditure of the contingent fund of the House.

"(C) The auditing and settling of all accounts which may be charged to the contingent fund.

"(D) Measures relating to accounts of the House generally.

"(E) Appropriations from the contingent fund.

"(F) Measures relating to services to the House, including the House Restaurant and administration of the House Office Buildings and of the House wing of the Capitol.

"(G) Measures relating to the travel of Members of the House.

"(H) Measures relating to the assignment of office space for Members and committees.

"(I) Measures relating to the disposition of useless executive papers.

"(J) Except as provided in paragraph (o) 8, matters relating to the Library of Congress and the House Library; statuary and pictures; acceptance or purchase of works of art for the Capitol; the Botanic Gardens; management of the Library of Congress; purchase of books and manuscripts; erection of monuments to the memory of individuals.

"(K) Except as provided in paragraph (o) 8, matters relating to the Smithsonian Institution and the incorporation of similar institutions.

"(L) Matters relating to printing and correction of the Congressional Record.

"(M) Measures relating to the election of the President, Vice President, or Members of Congress; corrupt practices; contested elections; credentials and qualifications; and Federal elections generally.

"(2) Such committee shall also have the duty of—

"(A) examining all bills, amendments, and joint resolution after passage by the House; and in cooperation with the Senate Committee on Rules and Administration, of examining all bills and joint resolutions which shall have passed both Houses, to see that they are correctly enrolled; and when signed by the Speaker of the House and the President of the Senate, shall forthwith present the same, when they shall have originated in the House, to the President of the United States in person, and report the fact and date of such presentation to the House;

"(B) reporting to the Sergeant at Arms of the House the travel of Members of the House;

"(C) arranging a suitable program for each day observed by the House of Representatives as a memorial day in memory of Members of the Senate and House of Representatives who have died during the preceding period, and to arrange for the publication of the proceedings thereof.

"(k) **Committee on Interstate and Foreign Commerce.**

"1. Interstate and foreign commerce generally.

"2. Regulation of interstate and foreign transportation, except transportation by water not subject to the jurisdiction of the Interstate Commerce Commission.

"3. Regulation of interstate and foreign communications.

"4. Civil aeronautics.

"5. Weather bureau.

"6. Interstate oil compacts; and petroleum and natural gas, except on the public lands.

"7. Securities and exchanges.

"8. Regulation of interstate transmission of power, except the installation of connections between Government water power projects.

"9. Railroad labor and railroad retirement and unemployment, except revenue measures relating thereto.

"10. Public health and quarantine.

"11. Inland waterways.

"12. Bureau of Standards, standardization of weights and measures, and the metric system.

"(l) **Committee on the Judiciary.**

"1. Judicial proceedings, civil and criminal, generally.

"2. Constitutional amendments.

"3. Federal courts and judges.

"4. Local courts in the Territories and possessions.

"5. Revision and codification of the statutes of the United States.

"6. National penitentiaries.

"7. Protection of trade and commerce against unlawful restraints and monopolies.

"8. Holidays and celebrations.

"9. Bankruptcy, mutiny, espionage, and counterfeiting.

"10. State and Territorial boundary lines.

"11. Meetings of Congress, attendance of Members, and their acceptance of incompatible offices.
"12. Civil liberties.
"13. Patents, copyrights, and trade-marks.
"14. Patent Office.
"15. Immigration and naturalization.
"16. Apportionment of Representatives.
"17. Measures relating to claims against the United States.
"18. Interstate compacts generally.
"19. Presidential succession.

"(m) **Committee on Merchant Marine and Fisheries.**
"1. Merchant marine generally.
"2. Registering and licensing of vessels and small boats.
"3. Navigation and the laws relating thereto, including pilotage.
"4. Rules and international arrangements to prevent collisions at sea.
"5. Merchant marine officers and seamen.
"6. Measures relating to the regulation of common carriers by water (except matters subject to the jurisdiction of the Interstate Commerce Commission) and to the inspection of merchant marine vessels, lights and signals, lifesaving equipment, and fire protection on such vessels.
"7. The Coast Guard, including lifesaving service, lighthouses, lightships, and ocean derelicts.
"8. United States Coast Guard and Merchant Marine Academies.
"9. Coast and Geodetic Survey.
"10. The Panama Canal and the maintenance and operation of the Panama Canal, including the administration, sanitation, and government of the Canal Zone; and interoceanic canals generally.
"11. Fisheries and wildlife, including research, restoration, refuges, and conservation.

"(n) **Committee on Public Lands.**
"1. Public lands generally, including entry, easements, and grazing thereon.
"2. Mineral resources of the public lands.
"3. Forfeiture of land grants and alien ownership, including alien ownership of mineral lands.
"4. Forest reserves and national parks created from the public domain.
"5. Military parks and battlefields, and national cemeteries.
"6. Preservation of prehistoric ruins and objects of interest on the public domain.
"7. Measures relating generally to Hawaii, Alaska, and the insular possessions of the United States, except those affecting the revenue and appropriations.
"8. Irrigation and reclamation, including water supply for reclamation projects, and easements of public lands for irrigation projects, and acquisition of private lands when necessary to complete irrigation projects.
"9. Interstate compacts relating to apportionment of waters for irrigation purposes.
"10. Mining interests generally.
"11. Mineral land laws and claims and entries thereunder.
"12. Geological survey.
"13. Mining schools and experimental stations.
"14. Petroleum conservation on the public lands and conservation of the radium supply in the United States.
"15. Relations of the United States with the Indians and the Indian tribes.

"16. Measures relating to the care, education, and management of Indians, including the care and allotment of Indian lands and general and special measures relating to claims which are paid out of Indian funds.

"(o) **Committee on Public Works.**

"1. Flood control and improvement of rivers and harbors.

"2. Public works for the benefit of navigation, including bridges and dams (other than international bridges and dams).

"3. Water power.

"4. Oil and other pollution of navigable waters.

"5. Public buildings and occupied or improved grounds of the United States generally.

"6. Measures relating to the purchase of sites and construction of post offices, customhouses, Federal courthouses, and Government buildings within the District of Columbia.

"7. Measures relating to the Capitol Building and the Senate and House Office Buildings.

"8. Measures relating to the construction or reconstruction, maintenance, and care of the buildings and grounds of the Botanic Gardens, the Library of Congress, and the Smithsonian Institution.

"9. Public reservations and parks within the District of Columbia, including Rock Creek Park and the Zoological Park.

"10. Measures relating to the construction or maintenance of roads and post roads, other than appropriations therefor; but it shall not be in order for any bill providing general legislation in relation to roads to contain any provision for any specific road, nor for any bill in relation to a specific road to embrace a provision in relation to any other specific road.

"(p) **Committee on Rules.**

"1. The rules, joint rules, and order of business of the House.

"2. Recesses and final adjournment of Congress.

"(q) (1) **Committee on Un-American Activities.**

"(A) Un-American activities.

"(2) The Committee on Un-American Activities, as a whole or by subcommittee, is authorized to make from time to time investigations of (i) the extent, character, and objects of un-American propaganda activities in the United States, (ii) the diffusion within the United States of subversive and un-American propaganda that is instigated from foreign countries or of a domestic origin and attacks the principle of the form of government as guaranteed by our Constitution, and (iii) all other questions in relation thereto that would aid Congress in any necessary remedial legislation.

"The Committee on Un-American Activities shall report to the House (or to the Clerk of the House if the House is not in session) the results of any such investigation, together with such recommendations as it deems advisable.

"For the purpose of any such investigation, the Committee on Un-American Activities, or any subcommittee thereof, is authorized to sit and act at such times and places within the United States, whether or not the House is sitting, has recessed, or has adjourned, to hold such hearings, to require the attendance of such witnesses and the production of such books, papers, and documents, and to take such testimony, as it deems necessary. Subpenas may be issued under the signature of the chairman of the committee or any subcommittee, or by any member designated by any such chairman, and may be served by any person designated by any such chairman or member.

"(r) Committee on Veterans' Affairs.
"1. Veterans' measures generally.
"2. Pensions of all the wars of the United States, general and special.
"3. Life insurance issued by the Government on account of service in the armed forces.
"4. Compensation, vocational rehabilitation, and education of veterans.
"5. Veterans' hospitals, medical care, and treatment of veterans.
"6. Soldiers' and sailors' civil relief.
"7. Readjustment of servicemen to civil life.
"(s) Committee on Ways and Means.
"1. Revenue measures generally.
"2. The bonded debt of the United States.
"3. The deposit of public moneys.
"4. Customs, collection districts, and ports of entry and delivery.
"5. Reciprocal trade agreements.
"6. Transportation of dutiable goods.
"7. Revenue measures relating to the insular possessions.
"8. National social security." [33]

Committees of the Senate and Their Jurisdictions

The following standing committees of the Senate shall be appointed at the commencement of each Congress, with leave to report by bill or otherwise on the subjects listed under each committee, respectively:

"(a) **Committee on Agriculture and Forestry,** to consist of thirteen Senators, to which committee shall be referred all proposed legislation, messages, petitions, memorials, and other matters relating to the following subjects:
"1. Agriculture generally.
"2. Inspection of livestock and meat products.
"3. Animal industry and diseases of animals.
"4. Adulteration of seeds, insect pests, and protection of birds and animals in forest reserves.
"5. Agricultural colleges and experiment stations.
"6. Forestry in general, and forest reserves other than those created from the public domain.
"7. Agricultural economics and research.
"8. Agricultural and industrial chemistry.
"9. Dairy industry.
"10. Entomology and plant quarantine.
"11. Human nutrition and home economics.
"12. Plant industry, soils, and agricultural engineering.
"13. Agricultural educational extension services.
"14. Extension of farm credit and farm security.
"15. Rural electrification.
"16. Agricultural production and marketing and stabilization of prices of agricultural products.
"17. Crop insurance and soil conservation.

"(b) **Committee on Appropriations,** to consist of twenty-one Senators, to which committee shall be referred all proposed legislation, messages, petitions, memorials, and other matters relating to the following subjects:
"1. Appropriation of the revenue for the support of the Government.

[33] Rule XI, *House Manual,* 80-1, pp. 307-331.

"(c) **Committee on Armed Services,** to consist of thirteen Senators, to which committee shall be referred all proposed legislation, messages, petitions, memorials, and other matters relating to the following subjects:

"1. Common defense generally.

"2. The War Department and the Military Establishment generally.

"3. The Navy Department and the Naval Establishment generally.

"4. Soldiers' and sailors' homes.

"5. Pay, promotion, retirement, and other benefits and privileges of members of the armed forces.

"6. Selective service.

"7. Size and composition of the Army and Navy.

"8. Forts, arsenals, military reservations, and navy yards.

"9. Ammunition depots.

"10. Maintenance and operation of the Panama Canal, including the administration, sanitation, and government of the Canal Zone.

"11. Conservation, development, and use of naval petroleum and oil shale reserves.

"12. Strategic and critical materials necessary for the common defense.

"(d) **Committee on Banking and Currency,** to consist of thirteen Senators, to which committee shall be referred all proposed legislation, messages, petitions, memorials, and other mateers relating to the following subjects:

"1. Banking and currency generally.

"2. Financial aid to commerce and industry, other than matters relating to such aid which are specifically assigned to other committees under this rule.

"3. Deposit insurance.

"4. Public and private housing.

"5. Federal Reserve System.

"6. Gold and silver, including the coinage thereof.

"7. Issuance of notes and redemption thereof.

"8. Valuation and revaluation of the dollar.

"9. Control of prices of commodities, rents, or services.

"(e) **Committee on the District of Columbia,** to consist of thirteen Senators, to which committee shall be referred all proposed legislation, messages, petitions, memorials, and other matters relating to the following subjects:

"1. All measures relating to the municipal affairs of the District of Columbia in general, other than appropriations therefor, including—

"2. Public health and safety, sanitation, and quarantine regulations.

"3. Regulation of sale of intoxicating liquors.

"4. Adulteration of food and drugs.

"5. Taxes and tax sales.

"6. Insurance, executors, administrators, wills, and divorce.

"7. Municipal and juvenile courts.

"8. Incorporation and organization of societies.

"9. Municipal code and amendments to the criminal and corporation laws.

"(f) (1) **Committee on Expenditures in the Executive Departments,** to consist of thirteen Senators, to which committee shall be referred all proposed legislation, messages, petitions, memorials, and other matters relating to the following subjects:

"(A) Budget and accounting measures, other than appropriations.

"(B) Reorganizations in the executive branch of the Government.

"(2) Such committee shall have the duty of—

"(A) receiving and examining reports of the Comptroller General of the United States and of submitting such recommendations to the Senate as it deems necessary or desirable in connection with the subject matter of such reports;

"(B) studying the operation of Government activities at all levels with a view to determining its economy and efficiency;

"(C) evaluating the effects of laws enacted to reorganize the legislative and executive branches of the Government;

"(D) studying intergovernmental relationships between the United States and the States and municipalities, and between the United States and international organizations of which the United States is a member.

"(g) **Committee on Finance,** to consist of thirteen Senators, to which committee shall be referred all proposed legislation, messages, petitions, memorials, and other matters relating to the following subjects:

"1. Revenue measures generally.

"2. The bonded debt of the United States.

"3. The deposit of public moneys.

"4. Customs, collection districts, and ports of entry and delivery.

"5. Reciprocal trade agreements.

"6. Transportation of dutiable goods.

"7. Revenue measures relating to the insular possessions.

"8. Tariffs and import quotas, and matters related thereto.

"9. National social security.

"10. Veterans' measures generally.

"11. Pensions of all the wars of the United States, general and special.

"12. Life insurance issued by the Government on account of service in the armed forces.

"13. Compensation of veterans.

"(h) **Committee on Foreign Relations,** to consist of thirteen Senators, to which committee shall be referred all proposed legislation, messages, petitions, memorials, and other matters relating to the following subjects:

"1. Relations of the United States with foreign nations generally.

"2. Treaties.

"3. Establishment of boundary lines between the United States and foreign nations.

"4. Protection of American citizens abroad and expatriation.

"5. Neutrality.

"6. International conferences and congresses.

"7. The American National Red Cross.

"8. Intervention abroad and declarations of war.

"9. Measures relating to the diplomatic service.

"10. Acquisition of land and buildings for embassies and legations in foreign countries.

"11. Measures to foster commercial intercourse with foreign nations and to safeguard American business interests abroad.

"12. United Nations Organization and international financial and monetary organization.

"13. Foreign loans.

"(i) **Committee on Interior and Insular Affairs,** to consist of thirteen Senators, to which committee shall be referred all proposed legislation, messages, petitions, memorials, and other matters relating to the following subjects:

"1. Public lands generally, including entry, easements, and grazing thereon.

"2. Mineral resources of the public lands.

"3. Forfeiture of land grants and alien ownership, including alien ownership of mineral lands.

"4. Forest reserves and national parks created from the public domain.

"5. Military parks and battlefields, and national cemeteries.

"6. Preservation of prehistoric ruins and objects of interest on the public domain.

"7. Measures relating generally to Hawaii, Alaska, and the insular possessions of the United States, except those affecting their revenue and appropriations.

"8. Irrigation and reclamation, including water supply for reclamation projects, and easements of public lands for irrigation projects.

"9. Interstate compacts relating to apportionment of waters for irrigation purposes.

"10. Mining interests generally.

"11. Mineral land laws and claims and entries thereunder.

"12. Geological survey.

"13. Mining schools and experimental stations.

"14. Petroleum conservation and conservation of the radium supply in the United States.

"15. Relations of the United States with the Indians and the Indian tribes.

"16. Measures relating to the care, education, and management of Indians, including the care and allotment of Indian lands and general and special measures relating to claims which are paid out of Indian funds.

"(j) **Committee on Interstate and Foreign Commerce,** to consist of thirteen Senators, to which committee shall be referred all proposed legislation, messages, petitions, memorials, and other matters relating to the following subjects:

"1. Interstate and foreign commerce generally.

"2. Regulation of interstate railroads, busses, trucks, and pipe lines.

"3. Communication by telephone, telegraph, radio, and television.

"4. Civil aeronautics.

"5. Merchant marine generally.

"6. Registering and licensing of vessels and small boats.

"7. Navigation and the laws relating thereto, including pilotage.

"8. Rules and international arrangements to prevent collisions at sea.

"9. Merchant marine officers and seamen.

"10. Measures relating to the regulation of common carriers by water and to the inspection of merchant marine vessels, lights and signals, life-saving equipment, and fire protection on such vessels.

"11. Coast and Geodetic Survey.

"12. The Coast Guard, including life-saving service, lighthouses, lightships, and ocean derelicts.

"13. The United States Coast Guard and Merchant Marine Academies.

"14. Weather Bureau.

"15. Except as provided in paragraph (c), the Panama Canal and interoceanic canals generally.

"16. Inland waterways.

"17. Fisheries and wildlife, including research, restoration, refuges, and conservation.

"18. Bureau of Standards including standarization of weights and measures and the metric system.

"(k) **Committee on the Judiciary,** to consist of thirteen Senators, to which committee shall be referred all proposed legislation, messages, petitions, memorials, and other matters relating to the following subjects:

"1. Judicial proceedings, civil and criminal, generally.
"2. Constitutional amendments.
"3. Federal courts and judges.
"4. Local courts in the Territories and possessions.
"5. Revision and codification of the statutes of the United States.
"6. National penitentiaries.
"7. Protection of trade and commerce against unlawful restrains and monopolies.
"8. Holidays and celebrations.
"9. Bankruptcy, mutiny, espionage, and counterfeiting.
"10. State and Territorial boundary lines.
"11. Meetings of Congress, attendance of Members, and their acceptance of incompatible offices.
"12. Civil liberties.
"13. Patents, copyrights, and trade-marks.
"14. Patent Office.
"15. Immigration and naturalization.
"16. Apportionment of Representatives.
"17. Measures relating to claims against the United States.
"18. Interstate compacts generally.

"(l) **Committee on Labor and Public Welfare,** to consist of thirteen Senators, to which committee shall be referred all proposed legislation, messages, petitions, memorials, and other matters relating to the following subjects:
"1. Measures relating to education, labor, or public welfare generally.
"2. Mediation and arbitration of labor disputes.
"3. Wages and hours of labor.
"4. Convict labor and the entry of goods made by convicts into interstate commerce.
"5. Regulation or prevention of importation of foreign laborers under contract.
"6. Child labor.
"7. Labor statistics.
"8. Labor standards.
"9. School-lunch program.
"10. Vocational rehabilitation.
'11. Railroad labor and railroad retirement and unemployment, except revenue measures relating thereto.
"12. United States Employees' Compensation Commission.
"13. Columbia Institution for the Deaf, Dumb, and Blind; Howard University; Freedmen's Hospital; and Saint Elizabeth Hospital.
"14. Public health and quarantine.
"15. Welfare of miners.
"16. Vocational rehabilitation and education of veterans.
"17. Veterans' hospitals, medical care and treatment of veterans.
"18. Soldiers' and sailors' civil relief.
"19. Readjustment of servicemen to civil life.

"(m) **Committee on Post Office and Civil Service,** to consist of thirteen Senators, to which committee shall be referred all proposed legislation, messages, petitions, memorials, and other matters relating to the following subjects:
"1. The Federal civil service generally.
"2. The status of officers and employees of the United States, including their compensation, classification, and retirement.

"3. The postal service generally, including the railway mail service, and measures relating to ocean mail and pneumatic-tube service; but excluding post roads.

"4. Postal-savings banks.

"5. Census and the collection of statistics generally.

"6. The National Archives.

"(n) **The Committee on Public Works,** to consist of thirteen Senators, to which committee shall be referred all proposed legislation, messages, petitions, memorials and other matters relating to the following subjects:

"1. Flood control and improvement of rivers and harbors.

"2. Public works for the benefit of navigation, and bridges and dams (other than international bridges and dams).

"3. Water power.

"4. Oil and other pollution of navigable waters.

"5. Public buildings and occupied or improved grounds of the United States generally.

"6. Measures relating to the purchase of sites and construction of post offices, customhouses, Federal courthouses, and Government buildings within the District of Columbia.

"7. Measures relating to the Capitol building and the Senate and House Office Buildings.

"8. Measures relating to the construction or reconstruction, maintenance, and care of the buildings and grounds of the Botanic Gardens, the Library of Congress, and the Smithsonian Institution.

"9. Public reservations and parks within the District of Columbia, including Rock Creek Park and the Zoological Park.

"10. Measures relating to the construction or maintenance of roads and post roads.

"(o) (1) **Committee on Rules and Administration,** to consist of thirteen Senators, to which committee shall be referred all proposed legislation, messages, petitions, memorials, and other matters relating to the following subjects:

"(A) Matters relating to the payment of money out of the contingent fund of the Senate or creating a charge upon the same; except that any resolution relating to substantive matter within the jurisdiction of any other standing committee of the Senate shall be first referred to such committee.

"(B) Except as provided in paragraph (n) 8, matters relating to the Library of Congress and the Senate Library; statuary and pictures; acceptance or purchase of works of art for the Capitol; the Botanic Gardens; management of the Library of Congress; purchase of books and manuscripts; erection of monuments to the memory of individuals.

"(C) Except as provided in paragraph (n) 8, matters relating to the Smithsonian Institution and the incorporation of similar institutions.

"(D) Matters relating to the election of the President, Vice President, or Members of Congress; corrupt practices; contested elections; credentials and qualifications; Federal elections generally; Presidential succession.

"(E) Matters relating to parliamentary rules; floor and gallery rules; Senate Restaurant; administration of the Senate Office Building and of the Senate Wing of the Capitol; assignment of office space; and services to the Senate.

"(F) Matters relating to printing and correction of the Congressional Record.

"(2) Such committee shall also have the duty of examining all bills, amendments, and joint resolutions after passage by the Senate; and, in cooperation with the Committee on House Administration of the House of Representatives, of examining all bills and joint resolutions which shall have passed both Houses, to see that the same are correctly enrolled; and when signed by the Speaker of the House and the President of the Senate, shall forthwith present the same, when they shall have originated in the Senate, to the President of the United States in person, and report the fact and date of such presentation to the Senate. Such committee shall also have the duty of assigning office space in the Senate Wing of the Capitol and in the Senate Office Building.

Committees at Work

Facilities and Hearings: Each committee of each house is assigned a room on its respective side of the Capitol in which to hold hearings and to prepare legislation for reporting. All supplies including stationery and office equipment up to a certain amount are furnished, and up to one thousand copies of hearings on each legislative proposal (bills or resolutions) up to one thousand copies may be ordered printed by the proper chairman for committee use and committee distribution; permission of the house concerned is required for additional copies. Each committee is furnished with facilities to file and keep its records and papers. The rules require: that "Each such committee shall keep a complete record of all committee action. Such record shall include a record of the votes on any question on which a record vote is demanded." The Secretary of "the Senate and the Clerk of the House . . . are authorized and directed, acting jointly, to obtain at the close of each Congress all of the non-current records . . . of each committee . . . and transfer them to the National Archives for preservation, subject to the order of the Senate or the House, respectively.[34] "The Librarian of the Library of Congress is authorized and directed to have bound at the end of each session of Congress the printed hearings of testimony taken by each committee of the Congress at the preceding session."[35]

Clerks and employees are furnished to each committee. The clerk keeps the committee membership posted as to its sessions and as to actions taken on items of legislation; he prepares the committee calendar and keeps all pertinent data filed, and supervises routine office tasks. The Clerk takes care that any witnesses who are to be examined at the hearings appear at the proper time, likewise sending out invitations to prospective witnesses. Official stenographers furnish transcripts of any testimony at the request

[34] Section 140 (a) of P.L. 601 of the 79th Congress.
[35] Ibid., sec. 141.

COMMITTEE ON
AGRICULTURE AND FORESTRY
UNITED STATES SENATE

LEGISLATIVE CALENDAR

EIGHTIETH CONGRESS

CALENDAR
SENATE BILLS REFERRED TO THE COMMITTEE ON AGRICULTURE AND FORESTRY

Docket No.	By Whom Presented to the Senate, and Date of Reference to the Committee	Number of Bills	Title	Date	Action
1	Mr. McCarran____ Jan. 6, 1947.	S, 2	To provide for the use of 10 percent of the receipts from national forests for the making of range improvements within such forests.	Jan. 10, 1947 Feb. 24, 1947	Referred to Department of Agriculture for report. Favorable if amended report from Department of Agriculture.
2	Mr. Hill._____ Jan. 6, 1947.	S. 43	To amend the Rural Electrification Act to provide for rural ᵗ'ᵉphones, and f⸍ ᵗher pur-	Jan. 9, 1947	Referred to Department of Agriculture for report.

A Sample of the Heading of Title Page and a Part of the Contents of a Senate Committee Calendar; House Committee Calendars Take Comparable Forms

of the chairman of the committee concerned. For further details on committee employees, see chapter on "Officers and Employees of the House and Senate."

Meeting Days of Committees: The rules of the two houses provide that "Each standing committee of the Senate and the House of Representatives (except the Committees on Appropriations) shall fix regular weekly, biweekly, or monthly meeting days for the transaction of business before the committee, and additional meetings may be called by the chairman as he may deem necessary."[36] Or in the House if the chairman refuses or fails for three days to call a meeting it may be called by request of at least three members within 7 calendar days of request (Rule XI). The committees of the Senate for the 80th Congress established the following regular program for committee meetings, which is subject to be changed by the committee at any time [36a] or the chairman may cancel any such scheduled meeting by announcement:

Committees	Days of Meeting
Agriculture and Forestry	First and third Wednesday
Appropriations	Upon call of chairman
Armed Services	Tuesday
Banking and Currency	First and third Wednesday
District of Columbia	First Tuesday
Expenditures in the Executive Departments	First Thursday
Finance	Second and fourth Thursday
Foreign Relations	Tuesday
Interior and Insular Affairs	First and third Monday
Interstate and Foreign Commerce	Second and fourth Thursday
Judiciary	Monday
Labor and Public Welfare	Second and fourth Thursday
Post Office and Civil Service	Tuesday
Public Works	Tuesday
Rules and Administration	Second and fourth Wednesday

The chairman of each committee may also call meetings at will.

The committees of the House established the following regular program for committee meetings for the 80th Congress, subject to change under the same conditions applicable to Senate committee meetings:

Agriculture	First Tuesday
Appropriations	Upon call of chairman
Armed Services	Tuesday
Banking and Currency	Upon call of chairman

[36] Sec. 133 P.L. 601, 79th Congress.
[36a] Some changes were in prospect for the 81st Congress at the time this volume went to press.

District of Columbia	First Monday
Education and Labor	Upon call of chairman
Expenditures in the Executive Departments	First and third Wednesday
Foreign Affairs	Upon call of the chairman
House Administration	Second Wednesday
Interstate and Foreign Commerce	Upon call of chairman
Judiciary	Tuesday and Thursday
Merchant Marine and Fisheries	Upon call of the chairman
Post Office and Civil Service	Thursday
Public Lands	First Tuesday
Public Works	Second and fourth Tuesday
Rules	Upon call of chairman
Un-American Activities	Upon call of chairman
Veterans' Affairs	Tuesday
Ways and Means	Upon call of chairman

These are the published schedules of the standing committees of the two houses for 80th Congress, but they were not always adhered to. The chairman of each committee may also call additional meetings at will. The committee programs from day to day. and week to week are printed in the "Daily Digest" of the *Congressional Record.*

Time of Committee meetings: Regular committee meetings are held in the morning hours since the meeting hour of both houses is at 12 o'clock noon. The rules provide: "No standing committee of the Senate or the House, except the Committee on Rules of the House, shall sit, without special leave, while the Senate or the House, as the case may be, is in session." [37] It is a frequent practice of both houses, however, to extend a special "leave to sit at any time" to any committee upon reasonable request by an authorized committeeman. These requests to sit at pleasure within a specific duration of time are made and granted under unanimous consent procedure. The motion has no privileged status and may be blocked at any time by a single objection, and occasionally is blocked in the face of certain personal or political considerations, or if attendance in the chambers is unusually bad while important business is under consideration.

Quorum and Procedure: In the House, a majority of the total of each full committee membership constitutes a quorum; in the Senate, "Each standing committee is authorized to fix the number of its members (but not less than one-third of its entire membership) who shall constitute a quorum thereof for the transaction of such business as may be considered by said committee." [38]

[37] Section 134 (c) of P.L. 601 of 79th Congress.
[38] Senate Rule XXV (3).

In either case, "no measure or recommendation shall be reported from any such committee unless a majority of the committee were actually present."[39]

The election of the majority members to a committee is sufficient to permit it to organize and consider business even though the minority members have not been elected.[40] At any meeting of a committee, the chairman, or any other authorized person in his absence, presides and may present business to the committee for its disposition. No action taken by a committee is valid in the eyes of the House unless it is accomplished at a formal meeting, with a quorum present; proxies are not in order. In the Senate, proxies are quite a common practice. In the House if a committee should adjourn for the lack of a quorum it may not on that day hold a session for transacting business, even if a majority at a later hour be present.

When a bill will be considered is generally determined by its chairman; a majority of the committee, assuming that a quorum is present, may refuse to consider a particular bill. While a majority of the committee actually could overrule the chairman in calling up or blocking consideration of a particular bill, or even hold a meeting against his will, it just isn't done.

Transaction of Business: Several bills can sometimes be disposed of at a single session of a committee, several or many sessions may be necessary to finish up with one. The meetings are normally called to dispose of a particular bill or bills; that is, to consider them and report them to the House or Senate, as the case may be, recommending their passage or defeat. The committee could kill a bill and never order it reported, but if a bill is reported it is generally with recommendations that the measure be enacted.

Both public and executive (closed) sessions are held. Rules provide: "All hearings conducted by standing committees or their subcommittees shall be open to the public, except executive session for marking up bills or for voting or where the committee by a majority vote orders an executive session."[41] In practice some bills are completely disposed of in executive sessions, some in public session, and others involve both. Proceedings in the executive session are strictly confidential unless the group agrees

---

[39] Sec. 133 (d), P.L. 601 of 79th.
[40] Committee reports have been delayed in the House pending election of minority members (Cannon, VIII. 2176-2177).
[41] Section 133 (f) of P.L. 601 of the 79th Congress.

to divulge its actions; the subjects under consideration are usually announced. Confidential business of the committees is not divulged even to the parent body.

General Committee Procedure: The procedure by a committee toward the disposition of a bill is usually as follows: The committee announces that hearings will be held on a particular piece of legislation beginning on a certain day. If the bill is of little importance, the committee often acts on it in the absence of any hearings. At the public hearings, if they are held, public-spirited citizens or interested groups and authorized persons in behalf of the Government appear at invitation or at their own request. Witnesses appear to defend or oppose the particular measure. The hearings run for an indefinite length of time, depending on how popular or controversial the particular measure is, how many persons wish to be heard, how urgently the law is needed, and what the committee decides. After the hearings have been concluded, the committee meets in executive or closed sessions to study the testimony and bill, and to draft the measure in a form satisfactory to the committee membership. The committee at this stage is free either to report the bill as is, entirely re-write the bill, just add amendments to it, or possibly kill the whole thing. Finally, the committee takes a vote on the bill as perfected, to determine if it is is to be reported.

Committee Amendments: Amendments proposed to the bill by a committee do not become a part of the bill at this point, and therefore, when a bill is reported with amendments it is designated as "reported with amendments." All of the introduced bill will be printed in Roman type and the proposed amendments will appear in italics. The committee amendments do not become a part of the bill until the bill has been considered by the chamber to which it was reported, and that body votes to accept them as such. Either chamber is free to reject the whole bill or any committee amendment.

In practice, the work of the committees is generally accepted by the House and Senate, respectively. When any committee reports a bill, a written report accompanies it. That written report explains the work of the committee and its recommendations. If the committee proposes amendments to the bill, the report will explain the contents of the amendments and give the reasons why they were ever proposed.

Calendar No. 76

80TH CONGRESS }
1st Session }
SENATE
{ REPORT
{ No. 78

NATIONAL SCIENCE FOUNDATION

MARCH 26 (legislative day, MARCH 24). 1947.—Ordered to be printed

Mr. SMITH, from the Committee on Labor and Public Welfare, submitted the following

REPORT

To accompany S. 526

The Committee on Labor and Public Welfare, to whom have been referred two bills for the support of scientific research, including provision for schol~~~~ ~~~~ and f~llowshi~~ ~~ ~~~~~~~ (S. 525 intro-

---

80TH CONGRESS }
1st Session }
HOUSE OF REPRESENTATIVES
{ REPORT
{ No. 864

NATIONAL SCIENCE FOUNDATION ACT OF 1947

JULY 10, 1947.—Ordered to be printed

Mr. WOLVERTON, from the Committee on Interstate and Foreign Commerce, submitted the following

REPORT

[To accompany H. R. 4102]

The Committee on Interstate and Foreign Commerce, to whom was referred the bill (H. R. 4102) to promote the progress of science; to advance the national health. pr~~~~~~ty. and w~~~~~~ to secur~~

Sample Copy of the First Page of a Senate and of a House Committee Report

Union Calendar No. 534

80TH CONGRESS
1ST SESSION

S. 1361

[Report No. 1019]

SENATE-PASSED
BILL
READY FOR HOUSE
CONSIDERATION

IN THE HOUSE OF REPRESENTATIVES

JUNE 24, 1947

Referred to the Committee on Banking and Currency

JULY 21, 1947

Reported with amendments, committed to the Committee of the Whole House on the State of the Union, and ordered to be printed

[Omit the part struck through and insert the part printed in italic]

HOUSE COMMITTEE
REPORTS SENATE
BILL

1   Be it enacted by the Senate and House of Representa-
2   tives of the United States of America in Congress assembled,
3   That section 15 of the United States Housing Act of 1937
4   is amended by adding at the end thereof the following new

HOUSE COMMITTEE
ACCEPTS SENATE
LANGUAGE

7   pay, or cause to be paid by the State or political subdivision,
8   the difference between the cost limitations prescribed in sub-
9   section (5) of this section and the actual cost of construc-
10 tion per family dwelling unit or per room during the period

HOUSE COMMITTEE
REJECTS SENATE
LANGUAGE

11 of building construction such proportion of the total develop-
12 ment cost of the project as the amount of the average actual
13 cost per family dwelling unit of the items covered by the
14 applicable cost limitations prescribed in subsection (5) of
15 this section in excess thereof bears to such average actual cost:
16 Provided, That the amount of any such payment shall be

HOUSE COMMITTEE
SUBSTITUTES NEW
LANGUAGE

A Sample Copy of the First Page of a Senate-passed Bill Reported in House

Committees in Charge of Debate of Their Bills: When an important bill is called up in either chamber for consideration, the chairman of the committee which handled the bill becomes a sort of manager of the debate on it; he assumes responsibility to see that the measure gets favorable action. Generally, he works to get the committee amendments adopted and to prevent the addition of any other amendments, and frequently that is what is done. Usually all committee amendments are adopted, with comparatively few others which are offered from the floor, unless the chairman of the committee, speaking for his group, assures the chamber that his committee is agreeable to the proposed amendments offered from the floor. The committees thus become specialists and the remaining members of the House and Senate give deference to the committee's decisions. The committees are actually little lawmaking bodies.

Witnesses Testify: At public hearings, witnesses are called in to give expert advice or to render lay opinions on the subject under consideration; witnesses may make request to be heard or may insist that the committee give their points of view consideration before making a final determination on the pending question.

The Senate rules provide that "each standing committee . . . including any subcommittee of any such committee, is authorized to hold such hearings, to sit and act at such times and places during the sessions, recesses, and adjourned periods of the Senate, to require by subpena or otherwise the attendance of such witnesses and the production of such correspondence, books, papers, and documents, to take such testimony and to make such expenditures (not in excess of $10,000 for each committee during any Congress) as it deems advisable. Each such committee may make investigations into any matter within its jurisdiction, may report such hearings as may be had by it, and may employ stenographic assistance at a cost not exceeding 25 cents per hundred words. The expenses of the committee shall be paid from the contingent fund of the Senate upon vouchers approved by the chairman."[42] In the House, only the Committees on Appropriations, Expenditures in the Executive Departments, and on Un-American Activities enjoy the use of the subpoena power unless they go to the House and get that permission in each instance. In either house, if a witness refuses to

[42] Section 134 (a) P.L. 601 of 79th.

respond to a subpoena he may be cited for contempt by action on the part of either house. The law provides:

Every person who having been summoned as a witness by the authority of either House of Congress to give testimony or to produce papers upon any matter under inquiry before either house, or any joint committee established by a joint or concurrent resolution of the two Houses of Congress, or any committee of either House of Congress, willfully makes default, or who, having appeared, refuses to answer any question pertinent to the question under inquiry, shall be deemed guilty of a misdemeanor, punishable by a fine of not more than $1,000 nor less than $100 and imprisonment in a common jail for not less than one month nor more than twelve months.

Whenever a witness summoned as mentioned in section 192 of this title fails to appear to testify or fails to produce any books, papers, records, or documents, as required, or whenever any witness so summoned refuses to answer any question pertinent to the subject under inquiry before either House, or any joint committee established by a joint or concurrent resolution of the two Houses of Congress, or any committee or subcommittee of either House of Congress, and the fact of such failure or failures is reported to either House while Congress is in session, or when Congress is not in session, a statement of fact constituting such failure is reported to and filed with the President of the Senate or the Speaker of the House, it shall be the duty of the said President of the Senate or Speaker of the House, as the case may be, to certify, and he shall so certify, the statement of facts aforesaid under the seal of the Senate or House as the case may be, to the appropriate United States attorney, whose duty it shall be to bring the matter before the grand jury for its action.[43]

Any Member of either House of Congress may administer oaths to witnesses on any matter pending in "either House of Congress of which he is a Member, or any committee thereof."[44]

The Rules of both houses also provide:

To assist the Congress in appraising the administration of the laws and in developing such amendments or related legislation as it may deem necessary, each standing committee of the Senate and the House of Representatives shall exercise continuous watchfulness of the execution by the administrative agencies concerned of any laws, the subject matter of which is within the jurisdiction of such committee; and, for that purpose, shall study all pertinent reports and data submitted to the Congress by the agencies in the executive branch of the Government.

Each such standing committee shall, so far as practicable, require all witnesses appearing before it to file in advance written statements of their proposed testimony, and to limit their oral presentations to brief summaries of their argument. The staff of each committee shall prepare digests of such statements for the use of committee members.[45]

Legislative Budget: The Reorganization Act of 1946 also provides for a Legislative Budget, as follows:

[43] *Senate Manual*, 80-1, pp. 174-5.
[44] Title 2, section 191 of U.S. Code.
[45] Secs. 133e and 136 of P.L. 601 79th Congress.

The Committee on Ways and Means and the Committee on Appropriations of the House of Representatives and the Committee on Finance and the Committee on Appropriations of the Senate, or duly authorized subcommittees thereof, are authorized and directed to meet jointly at the beginning of each regular session of Congress and after study and consultation, giving due consideration to the budget recommendations of the President, report to their respective houses a legislative budget for the ensuing fiscal year, including the estimated overall Federal receipts and expenditures for such year. Such report shall contain a recommendation for the maximum amount to be appropriated for expenditure in such year which shall include such an amount to be reserved for deficiencies as may be deemed necessary by such committees. If the estimated receipts exceed the estimated expenditures, such report shall contain a recommendation for a reduction in the public debt. Such report shall be made by February 15.

The report shall be accompanied by a concurrent resolution adopting such budget, and fixing the maximum amount to be appropriated for expenditure in such year. If the estimated expenditures exceed the estimated receipts, the concurrent resolution shall include a section substantially as follows: "That it is the sense of the Congress that the public debt shall be increased in an amount equal to the amount by which the estimated expenditures for the ensuing fiscal year exceed the estimated receipts, such amount being $_____." [46]

Hearings and Reports by Appropriations Committees: The 1946 Act embodies specific provisions on hearings and reports by the Appropriations Committees.

No general appropriation bill shall be considered in either house unless, prior to the consideration of such bill, printed committee hearings and reports on such bill have been available for at least three calendar days for the Members of the house in which such bill is to be considered.

The Committees on Appropriations of the two houses are authorized and directed, acting jointly, to develop a standard appropriation classification schedule which will clearly define in concise and uniform accounts the subtotals of appropriations asked for by agencies in the executive branch of the Government. That part of the printed hearings containing each such agency's request for appropriations shall be preceded by such a schedule.

No general appropriation bill or amendment thereto shall be received or considered in either house if it contains a provision reappropriating unexpended balances of appropriations; except that this provision shall not apply to appropriations in continuation of appropriations for public work on which work has commenced.

The appropriations committees of both houses are authorized and directed to make a study of (1) existing permanent appropriations with a view to limiting the number of permanent appropriations and to recommend to their respective houses what permanent appropriations, if any, should be discontinued; and (2) the disposition of funds resulting from the sale of Government property or services by all departments and agencies in the executive branch of the Government with a view to recommending to their respective houses a uniform system of control with respect to such funds.[47]

[46] P.L. 601 of 79th Congress.
[47] P.L. 601 of 79th Congress.

Subcommittees

Most of the committees of both houses divide themselves into subcommittees for the dispatch of business, particularly under the Reorganization Act of 1946. The number of committees of course have been reduced and so as to expedite action on the many bills pending before each, most of them have subdivided themselves into smaller groups according to a classification in accordance with the jurisdiction of the full committee; frequently subcommittees are created to handle a particular bill and once it is disposed of the subcommittee automatically dissolves. At the first session of the 80th Congress, a tabulation showed the standing committees of the two houses had divided themselves into over 125 subcommittees.

The subcommittees usually do all of the preliminary work on bills assigned to them. When a committee assigns a bill or bills to its subcommittee, that group functions for all practical purposes, just as a full standing committee, but any action taken by a subcommittee must be presented to its parent committee for approval before the matter is reported to its chamber. The full committees generally approve the recommendations of their subcommittees.

The two appropriation committees function primarily as subcommittees. The full committees meet only to approve the bills as prepared by their respective subcommittees. Of course, the full committees can either kill the subcommittee bill, re-write it or report it in the form recommended.

When a major bill which was handled by a subcommittee comes up in one of the houses for consideration, the chairman of the subcommittee usually takes charge of handling it on the floor of the body concerned just as does the chairman of a full committee in all other instances.

CHAPTER IX

Order of Procedure in the House

Introduction

The procedure in the House is more complex than that in the Senate. There are endless parliamentary mazes in the House through which bills may and sometimes must pass before final enactment. An explanation of them must of necessity be involved —different calendars of business, specified days each month for consideration of particular kinds of bills, privileged business as opposed to non-privileged business, precedence of one type of privileged business over that of another, privileged status of possible motions in order during the disposition of all legislative proposals, and the Committee of the Whole House procedure are important factors which must be touched upon in any attempt to explain the order of business in the House of Representatives.

The Senate has done away with the Committee of the Whole procedure; the House still utilizes it. In the House of Representatives all bills involving an expenditure, the raising of revenue, or dealing with finances in any way on the part of the Federal Government (that is, bills on the Union Calendar) must first be considered in the Committee of the Whole;[1] the Committee then resolves itself back into the House; the House receives the recommendations of the Committee, and proceeds to pass or reject the recommended bill. Most of the legislative time of each session is spent in the Committee, the procedure generally used for preparing bills in a form to be accepted or rejected by the House. Sometimes the House proceeds "as if in the Committee of the Whole" under unanimous consent. The House, as contrasted to the Committee of the Whole, spends a small proportion of its time considering legislation; all routine proceedings and speeches made under special orders are made in the House as such.

This chapter will be devoted to a discussion of House procedure in the following order: "Characteristics of Business before the

---

[1] See *House Manual*, 80-1, section 742; Hinds IV, 3115, 3136-3151, 4704-4935; *Cannon's Procedure in the House of Representatives*, pp. 95-112.

House of Representatives and Procedure under Rule XXIV"; "Committee of the Whole"; "Certain Days for the Consideration of Particular Legislation"; "Precedence of Other Classes of Legislation"; "Precedence of Motions Affiliated with Legislation and Certain Other Aspects of Procedure"; and the Discharge Rule. Following the next chapter, which is devoted to "Order of Procedure in the Senate," a resumé will be given of the "Steps of Passage of a Bill Through the House and Senate."

I. Characteristics of Business Before the House and Procedure Under Rule XXIV.

Parliamentary Procedure in House: To the average visitor in the gallery, the House of Representatives is a noisy playhouse. To persons familiar with its legislative procedure and parliamentary law, the House in session is indeed something more fascinating. The complicated proceedings requires plenty of mental activity for a comprehension. The few Representatives who are expert in parliamentary law can cause endless trouble to the leadership by insisting on delay tactics.

Growth of House Procedure: The development of procedure in the House has had a growth somewhat comparable to that of any organism. Many of the practices utilized in the very first Congress are still in existence in spite of the fact that each new House of Representatives is free to adopt any set of rules it desires; previous Congresses may not determine procedure for a subsequent one. On the first day of each new Congress, the rules and procedure of the previous House apply only as justified by custom. Customarily, however, each new House, after the Speaker is elected, adopts the rules and practices of the former one and they remain in force until the Rules Committee brings in and the House adopts a resolution or resolutions of alteration.[2] Many sessions pass, however, without any significant change.[3] Rarely are the fundamental rules changed.[4]

Procedure According to Rules: After the rules are adopted they govern the procedure of the House. Variances and temporary

[2] See Cannon, VI, 191; Hinds, IV, 3060. Before rules for a new House are adopted, general parliamentary law applies (*House Manual*, 80-1, section 60).

[3] Rulings by the chair may disclose new applications of rules and precedents.

[4] The number of Representatives is so great that unrestricted individual participation would be impossible. This realization, founded on experience, has invited the establishment and development of a set of practices in the form of rules or precedents.

waiving of the rules, however, are made from time to time under the directorship of the leaders; the rules while fixed in one sense of the word, are sufficiently flexible to meet any emergency or situation which may arise.

Plan of Explanation: The preceding chapters have been devoted to a descriptive analysis, separately, of the more outstanding instruments which compose Congress. This and the next two chapters will disclose a picture of the legislative procedure in the House and Senate. This one will point out the maze of endless rules and regulations, labeled as rules and precedents, by which the membership of the House works to enact law. Their number, their modifications, and the variations in their utilization are complicated, and the rules even conflict in their prescriptions for the order of various classes of business. The plan here will endeavor to outline how all business pending before the House is classified for disposition, and the order of motions.

Calendars of House: Generally speaking, all bills introduced are first referred to and considered by standing committees from which they are returned to the House for further consideration if favorably acted on by one of the committees. All bills reported are printed in list form by title according to defined classifications and chronologically. These compilations are known as House calendars, and they give the following information on each measure: bill number, report number, calendar number and title, name of Representative reporting the bill, and date reported.

All reports made to the House by its committees are first placed on one of three calendars.[5] There are, all told, however, five calendars, as published in the *Calendars of the United States House of Representatives and History of Legislation,* namely: Union, House, Private, Consent, and Discharge Calendars. Bills on the Consent Calendar are at the same time printed on either the Union or House Calendar. All calendars are printed daily and distributed to each Member. They contain valuable information; they supply Congressmen with a brief history on every bill pending before the House.[6]

---

[5] Hinds, IV, 3115-3116. Bills on the Discharge Calendar never reach one of the three calendars.

"Adverse reports do not go to the calendars except by direction of a committee or request of a Member.

"Unless request for other disposition is made within three days a bill reported adversely is automatically tabled and may be taken from the table and recommitted or placed on the calendar by unanimous consent only." (Cannon, VI, 750).

EIGHTIETH CONGRESS

CALENDARS

OF THE UNITED STATES
HOUSE OF REPRESENTATIVES

—AND—

HIST____ _____ _____

LEGISLATIVE I

1. UNION CALENDAR

Clause 1, rule XIII:
"First. A calendar of the Committee of the Whole House on the State of the Union, to which shall be referred bills raising revenue, general appropriation bills, and bills of a public character directly or indirectly appropriating money or property."

1947				No.
H. Rept. 1 Jan. 3	Mr. Bland...... Merchant Marine and Fisheries.	A report pursuant to H. Res. 38 (79th Cong.)...		1
H. Rept. 2 Jan. 3	Mr. Bland............. Merchant Marine and Fisheries.	A report pursuant to H. Res. 38 (79th Cong.)....		2

2. HOUSE CALENDAR

Clause 1, rule XIII:
"Second A. House Calendar, to which shall be referred all bills of a public character not raising revenue nor directly or indirectly appropriating money or property."

1947				No.
I. Res. 21 Mar. 17	Mr. Allen of Illinois......... Rules. Report No. 131	A resolution to continue the Special Committee To Investigate All Matters Pertaining to the Replacement and Conservation of Wildlife. (By Mr. August H. Andresen.)		47
H. Res. 173 Apr. 23	Mr. Allen of Illinois......... Rules. Report No. 299	A resolution to create a Select Committee on Foreign Aid. (By Mr. Herter.)		74

3. PRIVATE CALENDAR

Clause 1, rule XVIII:
"Third. A calendar of the Committee of the Whole House, to which shall be referred all bills of a private character."
Clause 6, rule XXIV:
"6. On the first Tuesday of each month after disposal of such business on the Speaker's table as ___ references ___ Speaker shall ___ the Clerk to call the bills and resolutions on the Pri ___ force and effect as if each Dennis and House bill or ___ therein contained or referred to were considered by the House as a separate and distinct bill or resolution."

1947				No.
S. 851 July 2	Mr. Reeves.............. Judiciary. Report No. 773	An act for the relief of Belmont Properties Corp...		193
H. R. 4381 July 24	Mr. Jennings.............. Judiciary. Report No. 1054	A bill for the relief of Bertha M. Rogers. (By Mr. Boggs of Delaware.)		259

CONSENT CALENDAR

Clause 3, rule XIII:
"3. After a bill has been favorably reported and shall be upon either the House or Union Calendar any Member may file with the Clerk a notice that he desires such bill placed upon a special calendar to be known as the 'Consent Calendar.' On the first and third Mondays of each month immediately after the reading of the Journal, the Speaker shall direct the Clerk to call the bills in numerical order which have been for three legislative days upon the 'Consent Calendar.' Should objection be made to the consideration of any bill so called it shall be carried over on the calendar without prejudice to the next day when the 'Consent Calendar' is again called, and if objected to by three or more Members it shall immediately be stricken from the calendar, and shall not thereafter during the same session of that Congress be placed again thereon: Provided, That no bill shall be called twice on the same legislative day."

1947				No.
H. R. 1436 May 21	Mr. Keating.............. Judiciary. Report No. 408 (Union Calendar No. 199)	A bill to repeal the prohibition against the filling of a vacancy in the office of district judge in the southern district of New York. (By Mr. Celler.) (Passed over without prejudice June 9, 1947, June 16, 1947, July 7, 1947, July 21, 1947.)		132
H. R. 210 June 6	Mr. Weichel.............. Merchant Marine and Fisheries. Report No. 515 (Union Calendar No. 261)	A bill to establish rearing ponds and a fish hatchery at or near Rogers City, Mich. (By Mr. Bradley of Michigan.) (Passed over without prejudice June 16, 1947, July 7, 19__)		178

Sample Copy of the Heading on Front Page of Calendars of the United States House of Representatives and History of Legislation

Each Monday the calendars carry special information, including a complete index of all legislative matters pending; by this index, the status and history of all legislative matters already reported are available.[7]

Bills on Calendars: Bills are placed on each calendar according to particular classifications, and if any bill is printed on the wrong calendar, it may be correctly transferred at request of any Member to the place to which it would have been entitled when originally reported.[8]

If a bill is on the wrong calendar, a Member may raise a point of order against it when it is called up for consideration.[9] The Speaker himself may make a change in reference before consideration begins or while the question of consideration is pending;[10] after the consideration has begun, it is too late to raise a point of order against any improper reference.[11]

As early as 1820 a rule was adopted to create calendars for the Committee of the Whole, and bills not considered in the Committee of the Whole were considered when reported to the House. This method proved inadequate to meet the needs of the House as business increased, and, by 1880, calendars [12] were created to avoid delay in making reports.[13]

The names of the three calendars to which all bills and resolutions are referred when first reported to the House and the nature of the bills and resolutions going to each are as follows:

[6] *Legislative Establishment Appropriation Bill*, 1929, *Hearings*, 70-1, p. 55. The calendars treat the following subjects each day: "Legislation in order on each special day; Call of committees under the Calendar Wednesday rule, and committees having the call; Special orders of business made by the House; Unfinished business; Excerpts from the rules applicable to the calendars; Bills in conference: History of daily changes; Bills through conference: Completed history of bills from the point of disagreement between the Houses; Union Calendar; House Calendar; Private Calendar; Consent Calendar; Laws: Complete list by number and titles of all bills and resolutions, House and Senate, enacted during the current session; Numerical index of legislation; Calendar of special legislative days; Status of appropriation bills for the session." (The semicolons have been inserted in this quotation in order to clarify the above enumeration of matters included in the daily calendars).

[7] *Ibid.*, p. 55. The weekly addition to the calendar includes: "General subject index of Legislation; Complete record of all reported bills, House and Senate, in each stage of progress each day of the session. Prepared each day. Printed weekly.

"Several of the subjects listed above are more or less of a permanent nature and are only listed to show somewhat the scope of the work, but the calendars of business and the indexes of legislation are constantly being changed and represent a great volume of work."

[8] Cannon, VI, 745.

[9] Cannon, VI, 744-745.

[10] Cannon, VI, 746.

[11] Cannon, VII, 856.

[12] When the calendars were first created they were not exactly the same as they are today.

[13] See McCown, *The Congressional Conference Committee*, p. 135. Before adoption of the calendars of the House the Speaker's table was one of the calendars of the House, and the business there was reached in precisely the manner as the business on any other calendar, by motion to proceed to its consideration.

(1) *Union Calendar:* To the Calendar of the Committee of the Whole House on the state of the Union go all "bills raising revenue, general appropriation bills, and bills of a public character directly or indirectly appropriating money or property." This calendar is commonly known as the Union Calendar.[14] All measures in this category are normally considered first in the Committee of the Whole. While all business on this calendar is placed there in the chronological order reported to the House, its consideration need not be in that order.

(2) *House Calendar:* To the House Calendar go all "bills of a public character nor raising revenue nor directly or indirectly appropriating money or property." Business on this calendar is listed in the chronological order reported, but is not necessarily so considered; it is considered in the House as contrasted to Committee of the Whole procedure.

(3) *Private Calendar:* To a Calendar of the Committee of the Whole go all "bills of a private character." They are listed there in the order reported to the House, and considered in that order. It is better known as the Private Calendar.

Relation Between Calendars and Consideration of Business: This system of classifying bills does not determine the time and manner of House consideration. But all bills and resolutions reported by committees and all other matters laid before the House (whether on calendars, Speaker's table, or a privileged motion in order when it comes to the attention of the House) are pending business until finally disposed of or until the last session of a Congress adjourns *sine die.* The House over a number of years has set up a system for the consideration of all types of business.

Mr. Cannon in his work on *Procedure in the House of Representatives* has enumerated the precedence of business considered by that body as follows: the order of business coming before the House under, "Precedence of Business," and the order of motions during debate under, "Precedence of Motions."[15] Mr. Cannon stated that while the rules of the House conflict and make it impossible to lay down any arbitrary order of precedence, the House by custom has established certain tentative principles of priority designed to preserve the status of privileged matters and at the same time give the House a wide latitude of determination. He arranged them in the order of their importance as follows:

[14] See *House Manual,* 80-1, section 865.
[15] Cannon, *Cannon's Procedure in the House of Representatives,* pp. 240-263.

206   THE UNITED STATES CONGRESS

      I.   Reception of messages.
     II.   Oath.
    III.   Quorum.
     IV.   Presentation of conference reports.
      V.   Adjournment.
     VI.   Entering motion to reconsider.
    VII.   Organization of House.
   VIII.   Impeachment.
     IX.   Journal.
      X.   Election cases.
     XI.   Vetoed bills.
    XII.   Electoral vote.
   XIII.   Adjournment or recess of Congress.
    XIV.   Privilege.
     XV.   Change of reference to calendars.
    XVI.   Calendar Wednesday.
   XVII.   Call of Private Calendar.
  XVIII.   Change of reference to committees.
    XIX.   Consideration of conference reports.
     XX.   Reconsideration.
    XXI.   Report from Committee on Rules.
   XXII.   Special orders.
  XXIII.   Suspension of rules.
   XXIV.   Propositions coming over with previous question ordered.
    XXV.   Resolutions of inquiry.
   XXVI.   Amendments in disagreement.
  XXVII.   Motions to go into Committee of Whole for consideration of
            revenue and appropriation bills.
 XXVIII.   Bills privileged under right to report at any time.
   XXIX.   Census.
    XXX.   Motions to discharge committees.
   XXXI.   District Monday.
  XXXII.   Consent Calendar.
 XXXIII.   Senate bills on Speaker's table similar to bills on House
            Calendar.
  XXXIV.   Disposition of Messages.[16]

He arranged the list of Precedence of Motions when a question
is under debate as follows:

      I.   Adjourn.
     II.   Lay on the table.
    III.   Previous question.
     IV.   Postpone to day certain.
      V.   Refer.
     VI.   Amend.
    VII.   Postpone indefinitely.
   VIII.   Discharge.
     IX.   Motions without privilege.
            1. Rescind.
            2. Recess.
            3. Leave for committee to sit during sessions of House.

[16] *Ibid.*, p. 241.

4. Alter procedure of House.
5. Change hour of daily meeting.
6. Motion to print, even privileged reports.
7. Motion for reading of Washington's Farewell Address.
8. Motion to recapitulate vote.
X. Motions not entertained.
1. Admission to the floor.
2. Delegate use of Hall of the House.
3. Relating to order of business.
4. To fix time to which to adjourn.
5. Expunge the Journal.[16a]

This discussion on House procedure will not cover the various procedural subjects in the order quoted above. The following outline will attempt to set forth the House procedure with major emphasis on the daily schedule and minor emphasis on precedence of motions.

Rule XXIV: *Development*: Originally there was no rule for the daily order of business; gradually, a fixed procedure grew up. The first rule to be adopted was in 1811; it was subjected to subsequent alterations with a view to working out a simple formula for an order of business and at the same time to give the House sufficient freedom to select and consider measures which it might deem most important. With this object in mind, the House continued to alter Rule XXIV until the adoption of its present form in 1890, namely:

The daily order of business shall be as follows:

First.   Prayer by the Chaplain.
Second.   Reading and approval of the Journal.
Third.   Correction of reference of public bills.
Fourth.   Disposal of business on the Speaker's table.
Fifth.   Unfinished business.
Sixth.   The morning hour for the consideration of bills called up by committees.
Seventh.   Motions to go into Committee of the Whole House on the state of the Union.
Eighth.   Order of the day.

Nature: This rule gives a general daily order of business without regard to the importance of the bills. After a consideration of this general order there will be mention of the specific methods used to get bills and resolutions up because of their privilege, their importance, and the like. The rule under examination here is very elastic and it can hardly be called binding on the House at all

[16a] *Ibid.,* pp. 256-259.

since nearly all the business going before the House can be granted precedence over the daily order of business defined by this rule. Any alterations in the plan set forth in Rule XXIV, however, need the sanction by a majority or more of the membership if the question of consideration is raised. In practice, the House has practically abandoned the full use of the rule; for a complete picture of procedure this rule needs to be mentioned and briefly examined.

An Elastic Rule: Any interruption by privileged business in the daily program as defined in the rule above merely stays that business from the point of interruption. When the privileged matter making the interruption is disposed of, if the House has not adjourned, the business that was in order at the point of interruption is in order.[16b] The elasticity of this rule, however, allows privileged matters to interrupt in the order of their privilege at any time and remain the business before the House for days without complications. On the other hand certain portions of this order are followed each day that the House adjourns.

Prayer and Reading of Journal: Each morning the Chaplain offers prayer, and the *Journal* is read, but the other steps are not generally followed. Usually, after the *Journal* is read, the House proceeds to consider some privileged matter.

Correction of Reference of Public Bills: The third step of procedure seldom requires any time. The House is not frequently consulted about the problem of changing a bill from one committee to another. *The Congressional Record* regularly shows the change of references of various bills but the attention of the House as a body is not called thereto. For clerical errors, and frequently otherwise, the Speaker merely authorizes the change and a mention thereof is made in the *Record* immediately following the proceedings of the days' session. If the House is confronted with the task of making a change of reference, it is done by the Speaker, with or without debate thereon, but his decision can be overruled by a majority vote.

Disposition of Business on the Speaker's Table: ". . . Messages from the President shall be referred to the appropriate committees without debate. Reports and communications from heads of de-

16b Hinds, IV, 3070-3071. When a privileged matter is completed the order of the House goes back to where it was when that privileged business superseded the regular order, unless the House adjourns, on which occasion the procedure begins over just as set forth in the above rule. This procedure may be altered by a majority vote.

partments, and other communications addressed to the House, and bills, resolutions, and messages from the Senate may be referred to the appropriate committees in the same manner and with the same right of correction as public bills presented by Members; but House bills with Senate amendments which do not require consideration in a Committee of the Whole may be at once disposed of as the House may determine, as may also Senate bills substantially the same as House bills already favorably reported by a committee of the House, and not required to be considered in Committee of the Whole, be disposed of in the same manner on motion directed to be made by such committee." [17] For detailed consideration of the disposition of business on Speaker's table, see pp. 289-293.

Unfinished Business: As early as 1794 the House adopted a rule to dispose of unfinished business, but not until 1890 did the body adopt the rule as it exists today.[18] This rule provides that all unfinished business, as defined by the rule and by custom, shall be resumed each day as soon as the Speaker's table is cleared.[19] The unfinished business [20] includes only that which the House considers during its general legislative time, as distinguised from unfinished business before the Committee of the Whole,[21] or unfinished business from a specific time which has been set aside for consideration of particular business.[22] This procedure has little significance in practice; it is seldom applicable unless the previous question has been moved on passage of a bill. The House usually adjourns after consideration of business in order on specific days or at a specific time or shortly after the Committee of the Whole has risen. Unfinished business in order on a specific day must go over to another such day. Hence, after the House convenes and transacts certain routine business, it proceeds to the business in

[17] Rule XXIV, clause 2.
[18] See Hinds, IV, 3112.
[19] Rule XXIV, clause 3; *House Manual*, 80-1, sections 885-888.
[20] A motion relative to the procedure of the House is not considered as unfinished business on the following day (Hinds, IV, 3114), and the question of consideration does not recur as unfinished business (Hinds, V, 4947-4948).
[21] Hinds, IV, 4735-4736. The unfinished business in the Committee of the Whole is different from that of the House. If the previous question has been moved on a proposition, it comes up the following day immediately after the reading of the *Journal* (Hinds, V, 5510-5517).
[22] Certain matters which may appear to be unfinished business of the House under this rule but which have been defined to the contrary are: (1) bills unfinished which were brought over from the morning hour or Calendar Wednesday; (2) bills under consideration in the Committee of the Whole; (3) bills which have been under consideration under suspension day, Consent Calendar day, and the Discharge Calendar; (4) business from the District of Columbia Day; (5) and bills considered under the Private Calendar. Under normal procedure, business coming under these classifications is not considered on the following legislative day, but it goes over until the next legislative day when that business is in order.

order "on a specific day" or "specific time," because of its privileged nature, or resolves itself into a Committee of the Whole to work on the unfinished business before the Committee, or to proceed with new business which must be considered in the Committee. The unfinished business of the House is determined in its general legislative time as distinguished from special periods set aside for classes of business such as call of committees, private bills, Consent Calendar, etc.

Call of Committees: (A) Morning Hour: There are two distinct rules for the call of committees: one is for the call of committees on Calendar Wednesday and the other is for the call of committees in the morning hour. The rules are unrelated, and unfinished business from one may not be considered under the other.[23] The call is known as "the morning hour for the call of committees." By 1880 the House had established the practice of devoting the morning hour to a call of committees for a consideration of House Calendar business.[24] The call is in order each day that the House completely follows Rule XXIV; but this procedure has become obsolete since the adoption of Calendar Wednesday. The leaders assume the responsibility for determination of the program, and the House proceeds accordingly.

(B) Interruption of Call: The call, if it were used, would not necessarily end in sixty minutes;[25] nevertheless at the end of sixty minutes the call could be interruped by a privileged matter or by a motion to go into the Committee of the Whole.[26]

(C) Bills in Order Under the Call: "A bill on the Union Calendar may not be brought up under the call of committees";[27] this is a call for non-privileged business. Only matters which have been reported to the House by a committee at least one day previously and placed on the House Calendar[28] may be called up,[29] and it must be by authority of a committee.[30] Once the House pro-

---

[23] Cannon, VI, 752; see Cannon, VII, 944.
[24] Hinds, IV, 3118.
[25] Hinds, IV, 3119, 3130, 3132. Unrelated motions would not be in order during this call.
[26] See Hinds, IV, 3132-3134.
[27] Cannon, VI, 753.
[28] Rule XXIV, clause 4; Hinds, IV, 3118.
[29] Hinds, IV, 3122-3126.
[30] Hinds, IV, 3127. In case of disputes as to the authorization by the committee, the Speaker may decide the fact. The Speaker accepts in good faith statements by Members in regard to the matter.

ceeds with one of such bills under this procedure it becomes the
unfinished business, but it is privileged only during that particular
morning hour.[31]

Motions to go into the Committee of the Whole: After the call
of committees has proceeded for one hour, it is then in order for
some Member to move that the House resolve itself into the Committee of the Whole on the state of the Union[32] for the consideration of such business. Under current practices, the House does
not follow any such program each day; to the contrary, on specified
days each month, discussed elsewhere, it considers private bills,
District of Columbia business, Calendar Wednesday business,
proposals under Suspension of the Rules, bills on the Consent
Calendar, bills on the Discharge Calendar, and the like—if there
is such business and it is not dispensed with to consider something else. The remaining days of each month are devoted to the
consideration of bills in an order determined by the leaders and
approved by the House. These bills usually are either privileged
measures and "may be called up at any time" or they are brought
up under special rules. At any rate they are first considered in the
Committee of the Whole and then recommended to the House by
the Committee for passage. When a bill is brought up thus, the
House in Committee generally continues on it from day to day,
immediately after the reading of the *Journal,* until it is completed;
a report is then made to the House and a vote on adoption of
amendments and passage of bill is immediately taken; the House
then moves to the next bill. A bill considered may take one or
several days or several bills may be disposed of in a single day.
If one of the specified days of each month for the consideration
of certain classes of bills intervenes, the pending bill is put aside
for that day. A subsequent section is devoted to "certain days for
the consideration of particular legislation." The next section of
this chapter is devoted to "Committee of the Whole," since most of
the legislative time of the House is spent in Committee on bills
brought up under special rules,. measures privileged for consideration because of their nature, or considered under unanimous consent or by agreement. This is without regard to selection for
order of consideration.

31 Hinds, IV, 3113. A committee may recall its bills from further hearing at
any time until reading for amendments begins (Hinds, IV, 3129).
32 Rule XXIV, clause 5.

Orders of the Day: After the business under the above steps of procedure has been disposed of, the House considers orders of the day,[33] which is really business the House has priorly agreed to consider.

II. The Committee of the Whole

Origin of Committee: The Committee of the Whole is a far more ancient parliamentary institution than are American deliberative bodies. It is a creation of the English Parliament. As used in the United States House of Representatives today, however, it is definitely American. As first used in the Continental Congress, the Committees of the Whole handled important business and gave audience to foreign ministers.[34] The characteristics, the functions, and the jurisdiction of it since that date have been developed and extended to include a procedure for disposing of nearly all important legislation considered by Congress. Many bills are considered in the House "as in the Committee of the Whole."

Committees of the Whole: There is a Committee of the Whole House and a Committee of the Whole House on the state of the Union. The first was used for considering business on the Private Calendar, but it has fallen into disuse. The present rule establishing the Private Calendar, which is discussed elsewhere, provides that "bills and resolutions" on that calendar, "if considered, shall be considered in the House as in the Committee of the Whole."

Bills on the Union Calendar are first considered in the Committee of the Whole House on the state of the Union before the House as such acts on them. Business on the House calendar is considered in the House, and not in the Committee of the Whole.

"In House As In Committee of Whole": The consideration of legislation "in the House as in the Committee of the Whole" is a practice which has grown up for the sake of convenience as contrasted to what would be involved if the bills were considered in either the House or in a Committee of the Whole House and then in the House. To proceed in this manner, however, requires a special rule or unanimous consent approval to that effect.[35] This method of legislating means simply that all debate will be under

---

[33] Rule XXIV.
[34] See *Journal of Continental Congress*, Feb. 13, 1779.
[35] Hinds, IV, 4923.

the five-minute rule while the bill is being read for amendments;[36] and general debate is not in order.[37]   Bills called up for consideration under this procedure are read by title when first called; immediately thereafter the clerk begins to read the bill by sections or paragraphs under the five-minute rule for amendments.[38]   The Speaker remains in the chair and no report is made to the House of actions taken on the various bills; as soon as the reading has been finished and amendments disposed of, he puts the question on engrossment and third reading of the bill [39] and then on passage.

Characteristics of "House As in Committee of Whole": A quorum to do business is a majority of the House and not a hundred Members as required in the Committees of the Whole House.   Disorderly proceedings can be dealt with, yeas and nays can be taken, messages from the President and Senate can be received, bills can be committed to standing committees, motions to reconsider may be entertained, amendments to bills may be withdrawn at any time until action on them is taken, the previous question can be moved, and the motion to adjourn is in order.[40] In brief, the procedure is much the same as it is in the House.

The Committee of the Whole and Its Relation to the House: *Definition*: To the layman, the Committee of the Whole is the House in regular session; to a student of legislation, this mode of procedure used in the House of Representatives in the enactment of law is something definite and different from any other step of lawmaking.   The Committee is really the whole House membership sitting as a committee with some Member other than the Speaker presiding; it is an agent of the House and it serves that body in the expedition of legislation.   Purposely, the institution has been developed to hear all legislation over which it has jurisdiction, to read and amend bills to its satisfaction, and to decide if it will recommend the passage of bills to the House. Generally speaking, all bills considered by the Committees of the Whole and approved by them are as good as law so far as the House is concerned.   It is the common practice for the Committee to spend anywhere from two hours to a week or more in consider-

---

[36] Cannon, VIII, 2565.
[37] Hinds, IV, 4924-4925; Cannon, VIII, 2431-2432.
[38] Cannon, VIII, 2433.   As to the time when substitutes are in order, see Hinds, IV, 4933-4934.
[39] See *House Manual*, 80-1. sec. 424.
[40] Hinds, IV, 4926-4932, 4935; Cannon, VIII, 2431, 2793.

ation of each bill, debating and amending it, after which the bill is reported back to the House for approval, which generally takes from five to thirty minutes.

Creature of House: Created by and subordinate to the House,[41] the Committee of the Whole, over a long period of time, has been given a defined position within which it must work while performing its task in legislating. The rules by which it must operate can be classified into action which it must take or cannot take; and, secondly, motions which are or are not in order. The House is omnipotent in its relations with the Committee; and it has prescribed its own rules to be utilized by the Committee of the Whole as far as they are applicable.[42] Consequently, the procedure is much the same with the exceptions mentioned here.

Procedure: The significant differences in the Committee procedure as contrasted with that of the House are: A quorum consists of one hundred Members instead of a majority of the House membership,[43] tellers may be requested by twenty Members instead of by forty-four (one-fifth of a majority of the House),[44] the yea and nay vote may not be taken,[45] amendments may not be withdrawn or modified except with unanimous consent,[46] debate may be both general and under the five-minute rule for amendments,[47] and leave to extend remarks may be given only by unanimous consent since general leaves may only be granted by the House.[48]

House Prescribes Orders: The rules and practices provide that the House may give to the Committee specific orders which are absolutely binding[49] and neither the chairman nor the Committee may change them.[50]

To illustrate: When a Committee of the Whole receives an assignment from the House to consider a particular bill, it can do one of two things: either consider the measure as prescribed or rise and go back into the House for the purpose of changing the said order.[51]

---

[41] Hinds, IV, 4705-4706.
[42] *House Manual*, 80-1, secs. 340, 877; Hinds, IV, 4737; Cannon, VIII, 2553.
[43] *House Manual*, 80-1, sec. 329; Rule XXIII, clause 2.
[44] See *House Manual*, 80-1, secs. 629-631.
[45] *Ibid.*, secs. 75-76; Hinds, IV, 4722-4723.
[46] *House Manual*, 80-1, secs. 824, 870; Hinds, V, 5221; Cannon, VIII, 2465, 2859, 3405.
[47] *House Manual* 80-1, sec. 870.
[48] Hinds, V, 7009-7010; Cannon, VIII, 3488.
[49] Hinds, IV, 4712-4713; Cannon, VII, 786; Cannon VIII, 2321, 2323.
[50] The Committees may not change time for debate fixed by the House even with unanimous consent (Cannon, VIII, 2321, 2550).
[51] See Hinds, IV, 4734.

Questions Beyond Committee's Jurisdiction: A few of the more outstanding actions beyond the jurisdiction of the Committee of the Whole are: general questions of privilege,[52] the right to grant leaves of absence, the control of admission to the floor,[53] questions of consideration,[54] and the disposition of words taken down in debate in the Committee.[55]

Committee's Jurisdiction: Generally, most motions for disposition of business in the House are in order in the Committees of the Whole. Many motions which have been excluded from the Committee's jurisdiction can be accomplished indirectly. If the Committee finds itself confronted with a problem over which it cannot offer a motion, it can usually rise and report the business under consideration back to the House with recommendations that certain actions be taken. For example: The Committee may not make motions to recommit but it is in order to rise and report bills back to the House with the recommendations that the bills be recommitted.[56] While motions to adjourn may not be entertained, the Committee may rise and report the business under consideration to the House.[57] The motion to lay business on the table or to lay aside (which is not debatable) is not in order except to report to the House at a later hour;[58] after general debate on a bill is over, however, the Committee may rise and report the business to the House with recommendations that it be laid on the table.[59] Finally the following actions are not in order in the Committee of the Whole: to appoint or discharge a committee,[60] to originate legislation,[61] to order a call of the House in the absence of a quorum,[62] to recess,[63] to limit general debate except by unanimous consent and then when it was not fixed by the House,[64] to send

---

[52] Hinds, II, 1657. If a situation occurs in a Committee of the Whole which is peculiar to that committee and a question of privilege is raised, the matter can be handled without reporting it back to the House (See exceptions: Hinds, III, 2540-2544). All such matters of the committees must be reported back to the House for it to assume jurisdiction even though it be a general question of privilege (Hinds, IV, 4912).

[53] *House Manual*, 80-1, sec. 919.

[54] Hinds, V, 4973-4976; see also Cannon, VII, 952-953.

[55] Hinds, II, 1257-1259, 1348.

[56] Cannon, VIII, 2324, 2326-2329, 2375; Hinds, IV, 4714.

[57] See *House Manual*, 80-1, sec. 334. The Committees do not adjourn; they rise and make a report to the House; the House adjourns.

[58] Hinds, IV, 4719-4720, 4763-4765; Cannon, VIII, 2330, 2366, 3455.

[59] Hinds, IV, 4777.

[60] Hinds, IV, 4697, 4710.

[61] Hinds, IV, 4707-4708.

[62] Cannon, VIII, 2369.

[63] Hinds, V, 6669-6671; Cannon, VIII, 3357, 3362.

[64] Cannon, VIII, 2321, 2550; Hinds, V, 5208, 5232; *Cannon's Procedure in the House of Representatives*, pp. 104-105.

matters to conference, to recommend a conference, to instruct conferees,[65] or to reconsider an issue.[66] These are matters to be attended to by the House.

Committees of the Whole and Standing Committees: The Committee of the Whole and the standing committees have about the same relationship to the House.[67] Mr. Cannon wrote: "There are two Committees of the Whole, in effect standing committees." [68] Business can be referred by the House to either the standing committees or the Committee of the Whole or both, but only business which shows on its face that it involves an expense on the government is referred to the Committee of the Whole.[68a] The House may recommit a proposition to either; but both serve in different capacities for the House. They have no immediate relationship to each other; both are creatures of the House; and they must work through their creator to reach each other in any capacity.[69]

Business Before the Committees of the Whole: *Bills*: According to Rule XXIII, the House resolves itself into a Committee of the Whole to consider all "propositions involving a tax or charge upon the people; all proceedings touching appropriations of money, or bills making appropriations of money or property, or requiring such appropriation to be made, or authorizing payments out of appropriations already made, or releasing any liability to the United States for money or property, or referring any claim to the Court of Claims . . ." [70] This test is applied to all amendments as well as to bills,[71] and the practices and customs under this rule have defined in detail just what kind of business comes within its scope.[72] Bills which involve an appropriation,[73] the adjudicating and paying of claims,[74] the leasing of government property,[75] increasing the number of officers in a branch of the government,[76]

[65] Cannon, VIII, 2319-2320.
[66] Hinds, IV, 4716-4718; Cannon, VIII, 2324-2325.
[67] Hinds, IV, 4706. In 1826 Mr. Speaker Taylor held the Committee of the Whole to be but a committee of the House, "though a large one."
[68] *Cannon's Procedure in the House of Representatives*, p. 95.
[68a] Hinds, V, 4709.
[69] See Hinds, IV, 4710-4711; Hinds, V, 5552.
[70] Rule XXIII, clause 3; see Hinds, IV, 4792.
[71] Hinds, IV, 4793, 4825; Cannon, VIII, 2381.
[72] *Cannon's Procedure in the House of Representatives*, p. 105.
[73] This holds true even if the undertaking is to be handled by a governmental agency (Cannon, VIII, 2399, 2401; Hinds, IV, 4824).
[74] Cannon, VIII, 2414.
[75] Cannon, VIII, 2399.
[76] Hinds, IV, 4847.

distributing rations among sufferers,[77] and the like,[78] must be first considered in the Committee of the Whole. Bills which merely change the manner of spending,[79] apparently involve a charge upon the government,[80] raising an officer to a higher grade,[81] spending money when it is a mere matter of speculation,[82] and the like do not have to be considered in the Committee of the Whole.[83] To come within the scope of the rule, the bill must show on its face that a definite charge on the Treasury will be made if passed;[84] if the charge is speculative, conditional, or doubtful, the rule does not apply.[85]

Amendments: The nature of a Senate amendment, as is the case with bills introduced in the House, determines whether or not it must be considered in the Committee of the Whole House, and the same tests are applied to it as are applied to business originating in the House. The fact that the bill originated in the House does not imply that any Senate amendment thereto will be referred to the Committee of the Whole; that decision is determined by the nature of the amendments;[86] if it does not involve a new charge upon the government, it does not have to be considered in the Committee.[87] The House is very particular, however, to see that all new appropriations are first given a hearing in

---

[77] Hinds, IV, 4851.

[78] Other subjects include: waiving a lien of the government (Cannon, VIII, 2406), increasing the number of cadets (Hinds, IV, 4850), extending the time of a grant (Hinds, IV, 4839), granting of easements across military reservations (Cannon, VIII, 2403), erecting of a memorial on land belonging to the United States Government (Cannon, VIII, 2405), dedicating public lands for public use (Hinds, IV, 4837), confirming grants of public lands (Hinds IV, 4843), releasing "a lien of the government while increasing the security of the government's claim" (Cannon, VII, 746-747), increasing the rate of pay of postage (Hinds, IV, 4861), creating a new office (Hinds, IV, 4846), authorizing cession of territory which belongs to the United States (Cannon, VIII, 2404), increasing the number of persons entitled to pensions (Hinds, IV, 4849), paying money into the Treasury and making an appropriation of the same (Hinds, IV, 4834), and the like (Cannon, VIII, 2381-2416; Hinds, IV, 4792-4868).

[79] Hinds, IV, 4830.   [80] Hinds, IV, 4809-4810.   [81] Hinds, IV, 2828.

[82] Hinds, IV, 4818. The chair stated, quoting from the ruling: "It may be possible that it will increase the expenses, but that is a mere matter of speculation as to whether they will be larger or not . . ."

[83] Some things which do not have to be considered in the Committee of the Whole are: authorizing payment of money out of the contingent fund (Hinds, IV, 4862), issuing military equipment (Hinds, IV, 4852), investigating certain funds in the Treasury (Hinds, IV, 4836), disposing of funds held as a trust under the control of the government but not the property of the government (Hinds, IV, 4853), spending money which is to be provided otherwise than by the government (Hinds, IV, 4831), matters relating to the printing for the two houses, and the like (See Cannon, VIII, 2381-2416; Hinds, IV, 4792-4868).

[84] Hinds, IV, 4811-4817; Cannon, VII, 2391.

[85] Hinds, IV, 4809-4810, 4818-4821; Cannon, VIII, 2388.

[86] "A Senate amendment being under consideration, and a proposition being made to concur with an amendment requiring consideration in Committee of the Whole, the entire bill goes to the Committee of the Whole, although only the proposed amendment is considered." (Hinds, IV, 4808).

[87] This is true even if the Senate amendment altered the original amount provided for in the House bill but did not add a new expense.

the Committee. If a Senate amendment is under consideration in the House which does not involve an expenditure on the part of the Government, and the House adds to the Senate amendment an amendment which provides for an expense, it must be considered in the Committee of the Whole.[88] Should a Member make a point of order that a Senate amendment must first be considered in Committee of the Whole because on its face it "apparently placed a charge upon the Treasury," the responsibility of citing proof that the amendment may first be considered in the House falls upon the Representative opposing the point of order.[89]

Privilege of Motion to Go into Committee of the Whole and the Speaker's Participation Therein:. *Precedence of Motion*: The motion to go into the Committee of the Whole House on the state of the Union is highly privileged nearly every day after the reading of the *Journal* if the bill to be considered is a revenue or general appropriation measure,[90] and if authorized by the committee reporting the bill. There are a few exceptions on certain days each month which are set aside for special business.[91] After the adoption of a special rule providing for the consideration of a particular bill, it is in order to move to go into the Committee of the Whole to consider that bill, and such motion is privileged. A motion to go into the Committee of the Whole is always privileged if the bill prompting that motion is privileged. These motions are not debatable;[92] they are not subject to amendments;[93] they may not be indefinitely postponed;[94] and they may not be laid on the table.[95]

The House no longer resolves itself into the Committee of the Whole to consider bills on the Private Calendar. Besides, the Private Calendar is considered only on the first and third Tuesdays of each month after the disposition of business on the Speak-

---

[88] Hinds, IV, 4795. It is the rule of the House to refer directly from the Speaker's table to a standing committee a Senate amendment which must be considered in the Committee of the Whole (Cannon, VI, 731-732).

[89] Cannon, VIII, 2387.

[90] The motion to go into the Committee of the Whole House on the state of the Union is in order on District Mondays (Cannon, VI, 716-718; Cannon, VII, 876, 1123), and it takes precedence over the motion to go into the Committee of the Whole to consider Private Calendar (Hinds, IV, 3082-85; Cannon, VI, 719-720).

[91] Rule XVI, clause 9; Hinds, IV, 3072-3073; Cannon, VI, 3. Motions to consider either an appropriation or a revenue measure are equally privileged (Hinds, IV, 3075-3076). Privileged motions may not be amended by non-privileged propositions, and the previous question may not be demanded on them (Hinds, IV, 3077). A motion to consider a specific bill is privileged if reported by a committee under its leave to report at any time (Hinds, IV, 3086, 3074).

[92] Hinds, IV, 3062; Cannon, VI, 716.

[93] Hinds, IV, 3078-79; Cannon, VI, 52.

[94] Cannon, VI, 726.   [95] Cannon, VI, 726.

er's table,[96] on which days bills on the Private Calendar are privileged for consideration.

Speaker Determines Business: When any motion to go into the Committee of the Whole is made, it is the duty of the Speaker to decide whether or not the bill proposed for consideration must be considered in the Committee.[97] In making his decision, however, he confines himself to the provisions of the bill; he must restrain himself from being influenced by what he personally knows about the bill, not included in its text.[98]

Going into Committee: When a bill is called up which must be acted on by the Committee of the Whole, an authorized Representative addresses the Speaker and states: "Mr. Speaker, I move that the House resolve itself into the Committee of the Whole House on the state of the Union for the (further) consideration of the bill H.R. _____." [99] Should the Representative desire that the House set the time for the general debate on the bill at this moment, he should add: "And pending that, I ask unanimous consent that general debate be limited to _____ hours, one-half to be controlled by the gentleman from _____, Mr. _____, and one-half by myself." [100] If this request is not made simultaneously, the motion to set the time for debate comes too late. The same result could be obtained at a later hour should the Committee resolve itself back into the House and receive such instructions from the House, or by unanimous consent agreement. After the motion to go into the Committee has been decided in the affirmative, the Presiding Officer will decline to recognize for a unanimous consent request, a motion to adjourn, or any question of order that arose in the House.[101] The order is mandatory and the Speaker retires from the chair, having designated some Member as chairman.[102] The Sergeant at Arms removes the

[96] Rule XXIV, clause 6. Private bills under the present rule are considered in the "House as in the Committee of the Whole."
[97] The Speaker's decision is subject to appeal. ". . . A point of order under this rule shall be good at any time before the consideration of a bill has commenced." (Rule XXIII, clause 3; *House Manual*, 80-1, sections 865-6).
[98] Cannon, VIII, 2386, 2391.
[99] If a special rule has been adopted providing for the consideration of a bill in the Committee of the Whole, it is not necessary that a Member make such a motion. At the set time, it is in order for the Speaker to announce: "Under the (special) rule the House automatically resolves itself into the Committee of the Whole House on the state of the Union, with the gentleman from _____, Mr. _____, in the chair."
[100] *Cannon's Procedure in the House of Representatives*, p. 95.
[101] After the vote on the motion to go into the Committee of the Whole has been taken, other business is not in order. On one occasion the Chair refused to entertain a motion to adjourn but he did entertain an appeal from his decision. (See Hinds, V, 5208, 4725-4728).
[102] Until 1794 the chairman was nominated from the floor and elected but the inconvenience of this practice led to its abandonment.

mace from its stand. In the *Congressional Record,* describing this action, appears the following: "Accordingly the House resolved itself into the Committee of the Whole House on the state of the Union for the (further) consideration of the bill H.R. _____, with Mr._____, of _____ in the chair." [103]

Order of Business: The House nearly always resolves itself into a Committee of the Whole House on the state of the Union for the consideration of one specific measure; if it fails to finish the bill in one sitting, having risen "without coming to a resolution thereon," it returns to further consideration of the same measure at the next sitting; when the Committee has completed this assignment, it rises and reports its actions back to the House. This procedure is not absolute. The Committee not having specific orders may take action on measures at its discretion. If the House resolves itself into a Committee in the absence of a specific order, the unfinished business, if there is any, is first in order;[104] the Committee may then dispose of business as it sees fit.[105] This, however, is only a possibility; under current practices, the House never resolves itself into Committee except to carry out a specific order.

Procedure in the Committee of the Whole: *Chairman of Committee:* A Committee of the Whole having been organized, it immediately proceeds to the consideration of pending business with a Chairman presiding. The Chairman performs duties comparable to those of the Speaker.[106] His powers are more limited, however, than those of the Speaker; this is true because the jurisdiction of the Committee is not so broad as that of the House. The Chairman, nevertheless, acting as the Presiding Officer, is obligated to assume certain responsibilities; he must, even in the absence of any suggestion from the floor, call to order any Member who violates the rules of decorum or the privileges of debate,[107] but he is without power to inflict punishment. In case disorderly words spoken are ordered "taken down" by the Committee or some Member assaults the Presiding Officer, the Chairman is personally responsible to see to it that the Committee goes

---

[103] It is assumed that the chairman announces: "The House is in the Committee of the Whole House on the state of the Union for the (further) consideration of the bill H.R. _____, which the Clerk will report (by title)." See *Cannon's Procedure in the House of Representatives,* p. 96.
[104] Hinds, IV, 4735-4736.
[105] Hinds, IV, 4730-4731.
[106] See Hinds, IV, 4704, also C.R., 46-2 pp. 205-206, 1208. The Chairman may have the galleries or lobby cleared in case of disturbances or disorderly conduct.
[107] Hinds, I, 257; Cannon, VIII, 2515, 2520.

"back into the House" and informs the Speaker of what has occurred. The Speaker having returned to the chair, he disposes of the case as the House determines. While it is then within the power of the House to proceed to other business, customarily, the Committee of the Whole is immediately reorganized for further consideration of its unfinished business without other intervening business.[108]

Consideration of Business before the Committee: Bills found on the Union Calendar comprise the business considered in the Committee of the Whole House on the state of the Union.[109] These bills are public and generally involve much time and work. In practice, each sitting of the Committee is confined to a single bill. The Committee begins consideration of a bill under general debate which varies from a few minutes to many hours. During this general debate the Members can talk on any subject under the sun.[110] The time is equally divided among the Members favoring and opposing the bill.[111] After general debate has been finished the bill is read under the five-minute rule for amendment.[112] All debate under this procedure, including debate on pro forma amendments, is confined to the subject under discussion. All of the proceedings are taken down verbatim by the official reporters of the House and printed in the *Congressional Record*, just as if the proceedings were in the House as such. The time under general debate is placed equally at the disposal of the chairman and the ranking minority member of the committee in charge of the bill. These two persons yield the time to their respective supporters, generally in accordance with the precedents.

Quorum: A quorum to carry on business in the Committee of the Whole consists of 100 Members,[113] and during the consideration of business it is in order at any time for any Member of the House to rise and make a point of order that a quorum is not

[108] See Cannon VIII, 2533; Hinds, II, 1348-1351. Only business reported to the House will be considered.

[109] *House Manual* 80-1, secs. 742, also 891, 892.

[110] While the House is in the Committee of the Whole on the state of the Union under general debate, the debate need not be relevant (Cannon, VIII, 2590).

[111] Cannon, VII, 766.

[112] *House Manual*, 80-1, sec. 870. Debate under the five-minute rule gives the Member offering the amendment five minutes to argue in favor of the amendment and the Member opposing the amendment five minutes to oppose it. If Members want more time to discuss the amendment they begin to offer pro forma amendments. See *Cannon's Procedure in the House of Representatives*, p. 142.

[113] In the absence of a quorum no further business is in order but the Committee may rise. See Cannon, VI, 665; Cannon, VIII, 2379; Hinds, IV, 2966, 2968-2971; *House Manual*, 80-1, sec. 329. In the House or in the House as in the Committee of the Whole a quorum consists of a majority of the House membership.

present.[114]   The absence of a quorum may be ascertained by some Member demanding a count, by taking cognizance of a vote in which less than 100 Representatives participate, or by the Chairman on his own initiative making a count and announcing no quorum.[115]   If a point of order is made the Chairman is obliged to secure the attendance of 100 Representatives, and no further business is in order until this has been done.[116]   The Chairman does the counting and his count is not subject to verification by tellers.[117]   When the fact is established that 100 Members are not present a motion to rise is in order, and if a quorum develops as evidenced by the negative vote on the motion to rise, the roll is not called and the Committee proceeds with its business;[118] if the Committee rises, the roll is called.   It is not in order for anyone to move a call of the House in the Committee of the Whole.[119] When the absence of a quorum is ascertained, the Chairman orders the doors closed, the Sergeant at Arms to notify the absentees, and the Clerk to call the roll.   The Committee rises, the Speaker having taken the chair, and the Chairman goes to the floor of the House and addresses the Speaker, stating: "The Committee having under consideration the bill H.R. _____, and finding itself without a quorum, I caused the roll to be called, when _____ Members responded to their names, a quorum, and I hand in the names of the absentees for printing in the *Journal*."   The Speaker announces the presence of a quorum and the Committee resumes its sitting.

Voting: Voting in the Committees of the Whole is such that one not observing the session cannot identify how his or her Representatives vote on an issue.   Yea and Nay votes may not be taken,[120] the only method of voting in the House by which the Representatives go on record as to how they voted.   Tellers (at the request of twenty Members in Committee or forty-four in House), division, and viva voce are in order upon a motion to that effect, but they only disclose the total number for and against an issue.

[114] Cannon, VI, 666.
[115] Cannon, VI, 641.
[116] See Cannon, VI, 665. Hinds, IV, 2966.
[117] Cannon, VIII, 2369, 2436.   He may count any Members in the Chamber regardless of whether or not they voted (Cannon, VI, 641).
[118] Cannon, VIII, 2369; also Cannon, VI, 671.
[119] Cannon, VIII, 2369.
[120] Hinds, IV, 4722; *House Manual*, 80-1, sec. 76.

Recognition: Prior recognition is given at all times to the chairman and the ranking minority member of the standing committee reporting the bill, which is under consideration.[121] In debate under the five-minute rule, preference over the general membership is grantd to all members of the standing committee reporting the bill.[122] The general membership is theoretically recognized without discrimination, alternating where practicable between those favoring and those opposing the business before the House.[123] Members recognized for general debate may yield their time to others; this is not true under the five-minute rule. A Member using any time under the five-minute rule, regardless of how brief, is charged with having exhausted his full five minutes. The Representative in charge of the bill and not necessarily the proponent is entitled to close debate in the Committee of the Whole.

Reading for Amendments: The reading of a bill for amendments is the most interesting and constructive part of the Committee consideration; it does not occur until general debate has been exhausted.[124] The Clerk then begins to read under the five-minute rule, by sections or paragraphs as determined by the Chairman subject to the Committee's approval.[125] In practice, most bills are read by paragraphs.[126] As soon as a paragraph or a section, as the case may be, has been read, that portion is open for amendments,[127] committee amendments having priority. A paragraph or section having been read, amended, and passed over (by beginning the reading of the following one or any new one), it is completed, and a motion to return to that portion of the bill or any other is not in order; the same can be accomplished only by unanimous consent request.[128] A motion to proceed with a new section or paragraph is not in order until the

---

[121] Hinds, II, 1457.

[122] Hinds, II, 1438, 1448.

[123] Hinds, II, 1439-1444; Cannon, VIII, 2558, 3455.

[124] If no Member desires to enter into general debate, the reading for amending begins as soon as the said bill is called up for consideration. Each bill must be read for amendment before it is finished (Hinds, IV, 4759, 4761).

[125] Cannon, VIII, 2340-2350.

[126] See Cannon, VIII, 2340; Hinds, IV, 4739. Tariff bills are read by paragraphs (Cannon, VIII, 2341-2349).

[127] All amendments are to be reduced to writing (Cannon, VIII, 2827-2828). The right to amend has precedence over the right to rise and report (Hinds, IV, 4751-4758; Cannon, VIII, 2364-2365).

[128] Hinds, IV, 4742; Cannon, VIII, 2354-2355. A section or paragraph is considered finished when an amendment in the form of a new section or paragraph is taken up for consideration or when the next paragraph has been read. "Amendments in form of new sections or paragraphs are not considered until all amendments to the pending section or paragraph have been disposed of." (Cannon, VIII, 2358-2362).

pending one has been disposed of;[129] and the right to explain or oppose an amendment has precedence over a motion to amend it. A Member who has consumed five minutes explaining an amendment under a pro forma amendment, may not get five additional minutes to make further explanation thereof by offering another pro forma amendment. To get the floor for the first time for five minutes during the consideration of any portion of a bill, a Member may offer a pro forma amendment. An example of a pro forma amendment: "Mr. Speaker, I move to strike out the last word."

Amendments may not be withdrawn or modified in the Committee except by unanimous consent.[130] All amendments must be germane to the portion of the bill to which they are offered.[131] And finally, the Committee may report an amendment in the nature of a substitute.[132] All other significant characteristics of amending bills in the Committees of the Whole are general and are discussed in another section under the general topic of *amendments*.

Finished Bills: When the Committee consideration of a bill has been completed, it is reported back to the House with recommendations for disposition.[133] The question before the House, if the Committee recommends the passage of the bill,[134] is the rejection or adoption of any amendments which the Committee approved, separately or *en grosse*,[135] and secondly the passage or defeat of the bill.[136] All amendments are on an equal basis and must be disposed of in the order reported. Both the bill and the amendments reported by the Committee of the Whole are subject to amendments by the House if the previous question has not been ordered.[137] Any amendments rejected or portions of the bill stricken out in the Committee are not reported back to the House,[138] but any clauses or proposals voted down in the Com-

---

[129] Cannon, VIII, 2356.
[130] Cannon, VIII, 2859; *House Manual*, sections 822, 824. Any Member offering an amendment in the House may withdraw it or modify it at any time until it has been acted on (Hinds, V, 5753); the same is true with an amendment offered in the House as in the Committee of the Whole (Hinds, IV, 4935).
[131] Hinds, V, 5811-5820; *House Manual*, 80-1, sec. 794.
[132] Hinds, IV, 4899. If the substitute is for the entire bill, it will be subject to amendments unless the previous question has been ordered (Cannon, VIII, 2419).
[133] *Cannon's Procedure in the House of Representatives*, pp. 100-102.
[134] The Committee may recommend adverse disposition.
[135] Hinds, IV, 3225, 4872, 4896. It is not in order to demand a separate vote on each of the perfecting amendments (Cannon, VIII, 2422-2424, 3211).
[136] Cannon, VIII, 2419.
[137] See *House Manual*, 80-1, sections 337, 423; Cannon, VIII, 2419.
[138] Hinds, IV, 4877; Cannon, VIII, 2421, 2429. Hinds, IV, 4869-4870. Amendments are not necessarily placed before the House in the order considered in the Committee (Cannon, VIII, 2417, 2418).

mittee may be offered as amendments in the House,[139] if the previous question is not operating.

The Committee may adopt and report an amendment in the nature of a substitute, but amendments added to the substitute are not noted in the report; only the agreed upon substitute is noted. If the substitute is for the entire bill, only the substitute as a single amendment is reported to the House, but it is subject to further amendment unless the previous question is operating. If the House rejects a substitute to a bill reported by the Committee of the Whole, the original bill without amendment is before the House; or if the substitute is for a section of the bill, that section of the original bill remains in the bill in its original form. A matter alleged to have arisen in the Committee of the Whole but not reported may not be brought to the attention of the House. '

Purposes for Which Committee of the Whole May Rise: Should certain conditions arise in the Committee while it is at work which demand the immediate attention of the House of Representatives, any Member may make a motion to rise and go back into the House. This motion is privileged and in order at any time that no one is on his feet participating in debate. If a Committee is dissatisfied with an order it has been given, it may rise and have the House change this order. The Committee of the Whole may rise at any time to receive special messages, as messages from the President and the Senate. It may rise and report any disorderly words spoken during debate. It may rise to adjourn until the next day's sitting. The Chairman reports to the Speaker that the Committee "had come to no resolution thereon." Generally, the Committee rises at the close of each day and reports the situation to the House until the particular bill has been completed; at the next meeting of the House, it is reconstituted to resume that unfinished business. Finally, when a bill has been completed in Committee, it rises and reports it to the House, with any recommendations.

Termination of the Committee of the Whole House: *Way of Terminating*: The termination of general debate in the Committee of the Whole may be effected either by the decision of the Committee or by order of the House. Normally, the House fixes

---

[139] Hinds, IV, 4878.

the time for debate;[140] when that time has been consumed, the
Chairman directs the clerk to read the bill for amendments [141] even
if some Member has the floor. In case the time for general
debate on a measure has not been determined by the House, the
Committee of its own accord may do so by unanimous consent.[142]
This is not in order if some Member has the floor.[143] Consideration of the bill in Committee having been finished, the motion
to rise is in order, and it is not debatable. The motion to rise
has precedence over a motion to proceed to the consideration of
another measure; the simple motion to rise has precedence over
the motion to amend; and the motion to report a measure back
to the House with recommendations that it be recommitted has
precedence over a motion to rise and report with recommendations
that the bill pass.[144] The Committee may make a report to the
House with recommendations that the measure be postponed;
such a recommendation has precedence over a recommendation that
it pass.[145]

Motion to Rise: When a motion is made that the Committee
rise and report its actions on a bill, it must either be accepted or
voted down, and is not debatable. If the motion is accepted the
Committee rises; if it is rejected, the Committee continues in session until affirmative action is taken. When the Committee rises the
Chairman goes to the floor, the Speaker having taken the chair,
and addresses the Speaker, announcing the decision taken on the
bill. The report on a bill might include: no resolution,[146] resolution with [147] or without [148] amendments, adverse disposition,[149] a

[140] See Hinds, IV, 3229 for form of a special order to fix time of debate in the
Committee of the Whole.
[141] Hinds, IV, 4712; Cannon, VIII, 2550-2552.
[142] Cannon, VIII, 2554.
[143] Cannon, VIII, 2370.
[144] Cannon, VIII, 2329. Favorable recommendation has precedence over an unfavor-
able recommendation (Hinds, IV, 4776; See also 4766, 4767, and 4770).
[145] Hinds, IV, 4774.
[146] An example: "Mr. Speaker, the Committee of the Whole House on the state
of the Union, having had under consideration the bill H.R. ___, directs me to
report that it has come to no resolution thereon." This and the forms in footnotes
147 to 150 are taken from *Cannon's Procedure in the House of Representatives*.
[147] The form: "Mr. Speaker, the Committee of the Whole House on the state of
the Union, having had under consideration the bill H.R. ___, directs me to report
the same back to the House with (an amendment) sundry amendments and with
the recommendation that the amendments be agreed to, and that the bill, as
amended, do pass."
[148] The form: "Mr. Speaker, the Committee of the Whole House on the state of the
Union, having had under consideration the bill H.R. ___, directs me to report the
same back to the House with the recommendation that the bill do (not) pass."
[149] The form: "Mr. Speaker, the Committee of the Whole House on the state of the
Union, having had under consideration the bill H.R. ___, directs me to report the
same back to the House with the recommendation that (the enacting clause be
stricken out), (the bill be laid on the table), (consideration of the bill be postponed
indefinitely), (consideration of the bill be postponed until ___), (the bill
be recommitted to the Committee on ___)."

combination recommendation, or a report on a bill considered under a special order.[150]

The following is an example of the regular report at the completion of a bill:

Mr. ARNOLD. Mr. Chairman, I move that the Committee do now rise and report the bill back to the House with the amendments, with the recommendation that the amendments be agreed to and that the bill, as amended, do pass.

The motion was agreed to.

Accordingly the Committee rose; and the Speaker having resumed the chair, Mr. Bulwinkle, Chairman of the Committee of the Whole on the state of the Union, reported that that Commitee had had under consideration the bill H.R. 4442, the Treasury and Post Office appropriation bill, and had directed him to report the same back to the House with sundry amendments, with the recommendation that the amendments be agreed to and that the bill, as amended, do pass.[151]

Special Order May Alter the Normal Procedure: All of the principles and regulations mentioned above can be altered at any time if the House adopts a special rule to that effect. Special rules adopted to provide for the consideration of particular bills may waive temporarily any of the House rules, including the requirement that a bill be considered in the Committee of the Whole,[152] change or limit the time for debate, set the time for the Committee of the Whole to report,[153] instruct what actions are to be taken,[154] hold the bill open for amendments which will prevent a motion to strike out the enacting clause, waive points of order against the contents of the bill, or purge the bill of all unauthorized items. A special order may set the time for the House to go into the Committee of the Whole. In such a case the motion does not have to be made, and it is not debatable or amendable. When the set time arrives the Speaker merely makes his declaration, appoints a Chairman, and retires from the chair. Finally, the regular pro-

---

[150] "It is now 3 o'clock p. m. Under the special rule the Committee of the Whole House on the state of the Union will now rise.

"Mr. Speaker, the Committee of the Whole House on the state of the Union having had under consideration the bill H.R. _____, reports it back to the House with sundry amendments and with a certain amendment specified in the rule, which amendment has been disagreed to, for further consideration in the House under the rule."

[151] C.R., 74-1, p. 1394.

[152] Hinds, IV, 3217-3225.

[153] The time as set by the rule having arrived, the Chairman directs the Committee to rise even if some Member has the floor (Hinds, IV, 4785; Cannon, VIII, 2376). All special orders are literally interpreted. For example: a rule providing for consideration of a measure until a time certain precludes a motion to rise and report prior to that time (Cannon, VII, 794).

[154] See Hinds, IV, 3238. The time for debate having been fixed by the House, the Committee may not extend it even by unanimous consent (Cannon, VIII, 2321-2322).

cedure may be ignored when the House is considering measures under unanimous consent. A bill enacted by unanimous consent does not have to be considered in the Committee of the Whole.[155]

III. Certain Days for the Consideration of Particular Legislation

Special Calendars for Expedition of Business: As already pointed out all measures reported by standing committees to the House are placed on one of three calendars in the order reported. With the exception of bills on the Private Calendar, however, they are not considered for passage in that order. To expedite business and at the same time allow flexibility in the program, the House has set aside certain days each month to consider particular kinds or minor and noncontroversial bills.

These legislative and calendar days and characteristics of their procedure are discussed under the following headings: Unanimous Consent Calendar, Private Calendar, Discharge Calendar, Calendar Wednesday, Suspension of the Rules, and District of Columbia Day.

Unanimous Consent Calendar: *History of Calendar*: The Consent Calendar was created in 1909 to replace the old cumbersome method of asking the Speaker's permission to call up petty bills.[156]

The change came as a part of the Cannon Revolution and has been classed as one of the principal changes in the House rules of that time; it did away with the necessity of consulting the Speaker on every bill before it could be given consideration by common consent.[157] It has relieved the Speaker of the burden of entertaining so many motions for the consideration of bills by unanimous consent. The device expedites the passage of noncontroversial legislation.

Bills on Calendar: Noncontroversial bills which have already been printed on either the House or the Union Calendar may also be placed on the Consent Calendar by filing such a request with

[155] Cannon, VII, 788; Cannon, VIII, 2393-2394; Hinds, IV, 4823. Consent may be conditionally given so that the measure may be considered in the Committee of the Whole.

[156] This calendar was first established on March 15, 1909, and amended January 18, 1924, December 7, 1925, December 8, 1931, and April 23, 1932.

[157] See *House Manual*, 80-1, sec. 746.

the Clerk. Only legislative matters, however, are referred to this calendar; "matters of routine and convenience purely formal in nature" are excluded.[158]

Status of Business: All bills and resolutions printed on the Consent Calendar for three legislative days[159] are in order for consideration on two days each month. On these days that business is highly privileged, and usually is made the order of the day. The Speaker is not obliged on these days to recognize for unanimous consent, motions to go into the Committee of the Whole House on the state of the Union to consider a revenue or appropriation bill, or any of certain other highly privileged motions.[160]

Procedure Under Calendar: Immediately after the *Journal* is read on the first and third Mondays of each month, the Speaker informs the House: "This is Consent Calendar day. The clerk will call the first bill on the Calendar." After the clerk reports the first bill by title, the Speaker inquires: "Is there objection to the present consideration of the bill?" If no objection is forthcoming, the clerk reports the bill. If no one objects to the passage, a question which is immedtely put after the bill has been reported, the Speaker announces that "The bill was ordered to be engrossed and read a third time, was read the third time, and passed, and a motion to reconsider was laid on the table." A bill heard under this procedure is just that quickly on its way to becoming a law as far as the House is concerned. A single objection against the consideraton of a measure when it is first called has the effect of blocking its immediate passage. When the calendar is next called and the same bill is reached for a second time, three objections must be heard instead of one, to block passage. If three are forthcoming the bill is immediately stricken from the calendar for the remainder of the session. It may be restored by unanimous consent, and striking a measure from the calendar one session does not exclude it for the following one. The official objectors, three or more for each the majority and minorty parties, are assigned the task of watching the bills under this precedure for their respective political parties. The setup and how it functions is discussed under the Private Calendar.

---

[158] Rule XIII, clause 3; Cannon, VII, 980-982.
[159] Holidays or days on which the House is not in session are not included. The three-day requirement does not apply to a bill which, having been objected to once, is again placed on the calendar (Cannon, VII, 1003).
[160] On one occasion, the Speaker held that the bill on which the previous question was pending from the prior day was of equal privilege (Cannon, VII, 990). It has been held that contested election cases may not subordinate the consideration of the Consent Calendar (Cannon, VII, 988, 989, 986-987).

If some Representative does not desire to object outright to the passage of a bill but is unwilling to see it approved by the House at the moment for lack of certain explanation, for want of particular information, or for absence of some concerned Member, or the like, he may request that the measure be "passed over without prejudice" or he may "reserve the right to object." In the case of the. latter, after any discussion between Members is finished, the person who reserved the right to object is still free to object outright or withdraw the reservation. Reservation of . objections by one Representative does not block another from making a definite objection. In case objection has been reserved and some one demands the regular order, the person reserving the right to object must either object outright or withdraw his reservation. Motions to pass over without prejudice or to reserve objections may be entertained at any time before consideration of the bill begins or before objection has been made.[161] If a bill is passed over without prejudice, it remains on the calendar, and when next called can be blocked by a single objection; it retains the same status as if it were being called for the first time.

The status of a bill on the Consent Calendar is not affected by actions taken on it on other calendars. For example: if a measure has already been discussed as business on the House Calendar, when it is called up under the Consent Calendar the proceedings are as if no prior hearings or discussion had been extended. When passed from either calendar, it is stricken from the other. A bill can be considered on the Consent Calendar while it is pending as unfinished business in the Committee of the Whole.

Unfinished Business: Unfinished business on the Consent Calendar is not privileged for continued consideration on any day but the first and third Mondays of each month,[162] if not finished one Monday, it does not come up the next legislative day; it must lie over until the next Consent Calendar day. If the previous question on a bill has been moved and adopted, however, it becomes the unfinished business of the House and may be completed the following day.

House Bill Similar to Senate Bill: A House bill on the Consent Calendar similar to a Senate bill, which is pending in the House or House committee, may, by unanimous consent, be disposed of at

---

[161] Cannon, VII, 996, 998. After debate begins it is too late to reserve objections or to object.
[162] The bill might be brought up under some other rule independent of the Consent Calendar.

the same time. It is in order to substitute the language of the House bill for that of the Senate and then pass the Senate bill, as is frequently done; it may pass a House bill which is a companion to a Senate bill and ignore the latter; it may pass the Senate companion bill without amendment, clearing it for the President.

A Calendar of the Committee of the Whole (Private Calendar): *Ban on Private Bills:* This calendar, to which is referred all bills of a private nature, is better known as the Private Calendar; the procedure is very interesting; in the past nearly half, or more, of the laws enacted in each session of Congress have been passed from this Calendar.[163]

In accordance with Section 131 of Public Law 601 of the 79th Congress, no private bill or resolution and no amendment to any such bill or resolution involving money for property damages or personal injuries for which suit may be instituted under the Federal Tort Claims Act, may be received or considered in either the Senate or the House of Representatives. This was an attempt to remove from Congress the burden of handling private bills. According to the Federal Tort Claims Act, however, the claim must have arisen after January 1, 1945, to fall in this category. Private claims that arose prior to January 1, 1945, are not banned from introduction in Congress under Section 131, and the one-year statute of limitation is stipulated in the Federal Tort Claims Act as not applicable to such claims prior to January 1, 1945. Hence, bills involving claims that arose prior to January 1, 1945, may be introduced at any time from now on under the existing law without contravening Section 131 of Public Law 601. Claims which have arisen after January 1, 1945, involving less than one thousand dollars are to be settled by the administrative agencies concerned; those involving over one thousand dollars must be instituted in the Federal courts, as set forth in Public Law 601. It should be emphasized, however, that there are exceptions under the Federal Tort Claims Act which will permit certain private bills to be introduced in the future without contravening Section 131. In the 80th Congress, 458 private laws were enacted as contrasted with 892 in the 79th Congress, which shows a decrease in the number enacted.

[163] See *Calendars of the House,* final editions of various sessions.

Nature of Calendar: All bills and resolutions on the calendar may be called upon two days each month for a hearing.[164] The consideration of this calendar on the first Tuesday of each month is highly privileged; the rule makes it mandatory unless determined to the contrary by a two-thirds vote.[165] On the third Tuesday, the Speaker is free to use his own discretion, and he may entertain motions for other privileged business instead.[166] The rule prescribes that the bills shall be considered in the House as in the Committee of the Whole. Debate must be confined to the subject of the motions permitted under the rule. Motions to strike out the last word,[167] to reserve objections,[168] to obtain time for debate by unanimous consent,[169] and to request for recognition to make statements [170] are not admitted under the rule.

The Presiding Officers have rendered many decisions concerning the old rules defining the procedure for consideration of private bills, but, obviously, most of them became obsolete with the adoption of the present rule.[171]

Procedure Under Rule: The rule in its present form was adopted on March 27, 1935, setting aside the first and third Tuesdays of each month for this business.[172] On these days immediately after the disposition of business on the "Speaker's table as requires reference only," the Speaker directs the call of the Private Calendar. He announces that the day is the first (or the third) Tuesday and "Under the rules, today is Private Calendar day. The clerk will call the first individual bill on the Private

---

[164] Note the following remarks as to the efficiency of this procedure under the new rule adopted on Mar. 27, 1935. Mr. Pittenger said: "I do this, Mr. Speaker, to call the attention of the Members of the House to the fine procedure which we have here this afternoon in connection with private bills. I do not think it was better illustrated than 3 or 4 minutes ago when I tried to get the floor and when I was absolutely ruled off the floor, and very correctly so, by the distinguished Presiding Officer, the gentleman from New York (Mr. O'Connor). I want to say to the Members of this House that up until the time the Rules Committee changed the rule so as to provide for the procedure which we now have, and also to provide for omnibus bills, people having claims against this Government were neglected and received practically no consideration of the kind to which they were entitled.

"Thanks to the chairman of the Rules Committee and his associates, this House is now proceeding in an orderly and business like way in connection with private claims. The interests of claimants are receiving fair consideration and the distinguished gentleman from California (Mr. Costello) and his associates are protecting the Government wherever it needs protection, so that I think everybody is happy.

"I think the gentleman from New York (Mr. O'Connor) is entitled to this little tribute this afternoon . . ." (C.R., 74-2, p. 3158).

[165] Rule XXIV, clause 6; see C.R., 74-1, pp. 9548-9549.

[166] C.R., 74-1, p. 9548. Debate on question of consideration is limited to ten minutes, equally divided between pro and con.

[167] C.R., 74-2, p. 3158.

[168] *House Manual*, 80-1, sec. 893.

[169] C.R., 74-1, p. 7100.

[170] C.R., 74-2, p. 6691.

[171] See Hinds, IV, 3266-3303.

[172] *House Manual*, 80-1, secs. 893-894.

Calendar." After the first bill is reported by title, he inquires if there is objection to the consideration of the bill. If no objection is heard the clerk reads the bill, with committee amendments, if any.[173] The period for amending a private bill is generally very short. The Speaker then announces that "The bill was ordered to be engrossed and read a third time, was read a third time, and passed, and a motion to reconsider was laid on the table." Should objection be heard by two or more Members to the consideration of a measure when it is called up the first Tuesday of a month, ". . . it shall be recommitted to the committee which reported the bill or resolution and no reservation of objection shall be entertained by the Speaker." [174] The standing committee to which the bill was recommitted is free to reconsider it and report it back to the House in an omnibus bill, and on the third Tuesday of each month the Speaker is authorized to give preference to consideration of omnibus bills. The omnibus bills [175] are called up in the same general manner described for individual private bills; they generally consume much time for consideration. They are read by paragraph for amendments.[176] After a paragraph has been read it is in order to offer amendments to that paragraph but the amendment is not in order unless it strikes out, reduces, or places limitations on the amounts of money stated in the original bill. The common practice is to offer an amendment to strike out the paragraph, which in effect kills that private bill since no item or matter stricken from one omnibus bill may be included in another during the same session of Congress. All issues are decided by a majority vote. The omnibus bill, consisting of two or more

[173] C.R., 75-3, pp. 4763-68. Customarily there are few amendments except committee amendments. The following is an extract from the *Record* showing the form of procedure under this rule:
"The Speaker. The Clerk will call the first bill on the private calendar.
Rosalie Rose
"The Clerk called the first bill of the Private Calendar, H.R. 2261, for the relief of Rosalie Rose.
"There being no objection, the Clerk read as follows: Be it enacted, etc., That the Secretary of the Treasury be, and he is hereby, authorized and directed to pay . . . in a collision with United States Coast Guard truck no. 1001.
"With the following committee amendments:
"Page 1, line 6, strike out '$11,454.50' and insert '$1,454.50 in full settlement of all claims against the United States . . .'
"The committee amendments were agreed to.
"The bill as amended was ordered to be engrossed and read a third time, was read the third time, and passed, and a motion to reconsider was laid on the table."
Paul Burress
"The Clerk called the next bill, H.R. 3252, for the relief of Paul Burress. . . ." (C.R., 74-2, p. 3148).
[174] Rule XXIV, clause 6.
[175] An omnibus bill as used here consists of private claims proposals pending before the House for consideration, consisting of two or more bills designated as titles.
[176] Individual private bills are read by sections.

private bills,[177] when passed is resolved into its original parts and engrossed as if they had passed in the House severally.[178]

Where a House bill included in an omnibus bill is similar to a Senate bill on the Speaker's table, it is in order to call up the Senate bill for consideration and substitute it for the House bill.[179]

Unfinished Business: Unfinished business from this calendar does not come up the next legislative day; it must wait until a Tuesday on which such bills are in order. If the previous question has been moved on the bill to final passage, it becomes the unfinished business of the House and may be completed on the next legislative day.[180]

Official Objectors: Generally speaking, the individual Representative is concerned only with the private bills introduced by himself. Consequently, seldom are more than fifty Members present at a time during consideration of private bills. To the observer there seems to be no interest in these bills passed by the House, but the political parties are very much interested, and they see to it that some check is placed on the number and nature of private bills to be enacted. If no check existed, many billions of dollars would be drawn from the Treasury to pay off alleged claims. To prevent this each party has three or more "official objectors." The majority floor leader designates three to five official objectors; the minority leader to check the majority party does likewise. In each case these objectors are charged by the leaders of their party with respect to the kind of bills and resolutions they should oppose. These men are obligated to read all of the measures carefully and pass judgment by either remaining silent or objecting when each bill is called up for disposition. These men stay on the floor constantly while the Private Calendar is under consideration, and when each bill is brought up, they readily object if it fails to meet the test.[181]

This system, utilizing official objectors, has been subject to much criticism from time to time.[182] It has been argued that it places

[177] Each bill is really independent of every other; any point of order must be made against a section to the bill and not against the whole omnibus bill (C.R., 74-2, p. 5894.).

[178] Rule XXIV, clause 6. "In the consideration of any omnibus bill the proceedings as set forth above shall have the same force and effect as if each Senate and House bill or resolution therein contained or referred to were considered by the House as a separate and distinct bill or resolution."

[179] C.R., 74-1, p. 13993.

[180] Cannon, VII, 854; Cannon, VIII, 2694.

[181] See *Hearings before the Committee on Rules,* H. Res. 31, 47, 93, 72-1, pp. 19-32 for a discussion of the position of these persons.

[182] See Luce, "Petty Business in Congress," *American Political Science Review,* XXVI (1932), pp. 815-827.

too much power and discretion in the hands of a few Representatives not responsible to the whole people, and that it tends to breed conflicts between the individual Members and the official objectors. A good illustration occurred in the 73rd Congress.

Mr. ZIONCHECK. The bonding companies are perfectly familiar with the rules of the court in the matter of the production of defendants; if they do not produce them when needed there must be some negligence. Mr. Speaker, I object.

Mr. SNELL. Mr. Speaker, may I ask the gentleman if he is one of the official objectors on his side?

Mr. ZIONCHECK. Yes; I am one of these that have been so designated.

Mr. SNELL. If that is going to be the attitude of the objectors on the majority side, we can object as well as they; and I serve notice that there will be no more bills passed here this morning or this session by unanimous consent.

Mr. ZIONCHECK. That is entirely up to the gentleman from New York.

Mr. SNELL. Here we have an absolutely legitimate bill, but the gentleman objects to it merely because he does not like bonding companies.

Mr. BLANTON. Mr. Speaker, the minority leader ought not to get angry because a posted and very valuable youngster, whom we have well trained on this side, is able to answer him.

Mr. SNELL. But the youngster is not answering me.

Mr. BLANTON. I think the youngster took care of himself pretty well when he answered the minority leader.

Mr. SNELL. He made certain statements that should not have been made and have nothing to do with the bill under consideration.

Mr. BLANTON. The youngster made a mighty good argument; and when the minority leader cannot make an argument in reply, he gets angry.

Mr. SNELL. I am not trying to make an argument; but the gentleman from Washington says he objects to the bill because he is against bonding companies.

Mr. BLANTON. Mr. Speaker, I demand the regular order.

The SPEAKER. The regular order is, the Clerk will call the next bill on the calendar.

(After the Clerk had called a few bills and objections were heard to each one, the following occurred.)

Mr. COCHRAN of Missouri. Mr. Speaker, I have a bill coming up on the Private Calendar. I want it considered on its merits. I feel it is going to be objected to; in fact, that is plainly evident, and if it is once objected to, it will not be reached again during this Congress.

As I said, I want my bill considered on its merits. The gentleman from New York (Mr. Snell) insists that he will let no more bills pass; that he will object to them as fast as they are reached. In view of his determination to prevent further consideration of the Private Calendar, I see no reason why we should remain in session.

The regular order was demanded.

Mr. COCHRAN of Missouri. Mr. Speaker, for the reason just stated, I move that the House do now adjourn.[183]

[183] C.R., 73-2, pp. 2291-2292.

The Discharge Rule: *Introduction*: Certainly one of the greatest possible weapons the House leadership commands in the determination of legislation is the control it exercises over the program. The easiest place to block or defeat a bill in the legislative process is in committee. To offset this possibility, a majority of the House membership adopted in 1910, and has retained almost continuously since that date, a rule to force bills out of reluctant committees.

With certain exceptions, bills which have not been reported out of a standing committee to the House may not be included in any legislative program; all bills must be considered by a committee before the House as a legislative body may act on them.[184] Hence, committees can be used as "legislative burying grounds."

The House, however, has nearly always placed certain limitations on its standing committees with a view toward preventing their absolute control over the destiny of bills referred to them, regardless of the desires of the whole House membership. Prior to the adoption of the Discharge Rule, the following restraints on committees had been adopted from time to time, and are still retained as part of the rules of the House. Any bill incorrectly referred to a committee may be recalled and assigned to another committee by unanimous consent, by authorized motion from the committee claiming jurisdiction, or as a result of a report from that committee to which the bill was erroneously referred.[185] All resolutions of inquiry may be recalled by the House seven days after their respective references, and motions for such action are privileged.[186] Resolutions affecting the personal privilege of a Member of the House or the House itself and veto messages are almost always in order to be called up irrespective of which committee may have jurisdiction over them.[187] Finally, under unanimous consent any Member if recognized by the Speaker for that purpose may make a motion to discharge any committee from further consideration of a bill.[188] To supplement these limitations as a protection to the membership, the House has developed a new

---

[184] Bills brought before the House under the Discharge Rule are not considered by a standing committee (see Rule XXVII, clause 4). Senate bills on the Speaker's table if there is a like House bill on the Calendar do not have to be considered by a standing committee (*House Manual*, 80-1, sec. 883).
[185] *House Manual*, 80-1, secs. 854, 878; Hinds, IV, 4377.
[186] Hinds, III, 1865-1871; matters of equal privilege may delay such business at the discretion of the Speaker (*House Manual*, 80-1, secs. 856, 858, 859).
[187] *House Manual*, 80-1, secs. 105, 106, 399; Hinds, IV, 3532.
[188] C.R., 62-2, pp. 2775-2807. On this day several committees were discharged from further consideration of bills, the rules were suspended, and the bills were passed; the action was taken under unanimous consent procedure.

procedure known as the Discharge Rule, a rule which has apparently found a permanent place in the parliamentary procedure of the House of Representatives. Adopted in 1910 for the first time, it has experienced periods of lethargy; on different occasions it has withstood the House leadership's antagonistic attacks and criticisms, but it has survived some of the most severe parliamentary storms. The first and only bill ever to become a law which was considered in the House under the procedure prescribed by the Discharge Rule was the Wages and Hours bill [189] enacted into law during the last session of the Seventy-fifth Congress. Others have become law after passing the House under such a threat.

History of the Rule: The Discharge Rule has taken six distinct forms since its adoption in 1910.[190] Three of these were adopted by Republican majorities [191] and three by Democratic majorities.[192]

The first rule was adopted on June 17, 1910,[193] when the minority membership of the House joined with the "Insurgents" of the majority party.[194] Individually, Representatives had for many years at various times protested against the Speaker's power to control the destiny of legislation by dictating which bills the House might consider. Likewise, many chairmen of standing commit-

---

[189] C.R., 75-3, pp. 7274-7279, 7279-7326, 7373-7448, 7450; the bill was approved on June 25, 1938 (see C.R., 75-3, p. 9616).

[190] The six rules were adopted on the following dates: (1) June 17, 1910, C.R., 61-2, pp. 8439-8445; (2) April 5, 1911, C.R., 62-1, pp. 18-19, 54-80; (3) February 3, 1912, C.R., 62-2, pp. 1684-1690; (4) January 18, 1924, C.R., 68-1, pp. 943-975, 994-1016, 1048-1069, 1099-1118, 1122-1144; (5) December 7, 1925, C.R., 69-1, pp. 383-391; (6) December 8, 1931, C.R., 72-1, pp. 10-14, 72-83. For the amendment to the present rule, see: January 3, 1935, C.R., 74-1, pp. 13-21.

[191] The Republicans supported the first (adopted in 1910), the fourth (adopted in 1924), the fifth (adopted in 1925).

[192] The Democrats supported the second (adopted in 1911), the third (adopted in 1912), and the sixth (adopted in 1931). The Democrats in 1935 amended their 1931 rule by changing the number of signatures from 145 to 218.

[193] The first rule is included here in its entirety to show how inadequate it was then as contrasted to the present status. The vote on the adoption of the first rule showed, 201 yeas and 1 nay (C.R., 61-2, p. 8445). The rule reads as follows: Rule XXVIII, clause 4. "Any Member may present to the Clerk a motion in writing to discharge a committee from further consideration of any public bill or joint resolution which may have been referred to such committee. All such motions shall be entered in the *Journal* and printed on the Calendar under an appropriate heading. Immediately after the Unanimous Consent Calendar shall have been called on any Monday, it shall be in order to call up any such motion which shall have been entered at least seven days prior thereto. Recognition for such motion shall be in the order in which they have been entered. Such motions before being submitted to the House shall be seconded by a majority by tellers. If a second be ordered debate on such motions shall be limited to 20 minutes, one-half thereof in favor of the proposition and one-half in opposition thereto. Such motions shall have precedence over motions to suspend the rules and shall require for adoption an affirmative vote of a majority of the membership of the House.

"Whenever such a motion shall prevail the bill so taken from the consideration of the committee shall thereupon be placed upon its appropriate calendar and upon call of the committee from which any bill has been so taken it may be called for consideration by any Member prior to any bill reported by said committee at a date subsequent to the discharge of said committee." (C.R., 61-2, pp. 8439-8445).

[194] The composition of the House at this time was as follows: 217 Republicans and 173 Democrats.

tees had played the part of little autocrats over their respective committees. This system of "autocracy" invited change in spite of the "leadership." [195] As early as 1884 there was a proposal for a "Discharge Rule." In that year, Mr. Turner, of Kentucky, offered a proposal providing that it should be in order to call up any bill for consideration on any Monday provided it had been thirty days in a committee.[196] In 1908 one Member dramatically inquired: "Has it come to pass that the Speaker of the House of Representatives has brought us to the level of the Russian peasants who have no privilege but that of revolutions?" [197] In 1909, a Member arrested the attention of the House by urging a change in procedure so as to act on popular legislation, stating that there was no Member of the House who could not go back to "his constituency tomorrow and protest his earnest enthusiasm for my measures and blame his refusal to vote for them upon the procedure of the House. Now, that is an abuse and a serious one. Anything that can be interposed between the discharge of a Representative's duty and full knowledge by his constituents of how he discharges it is a grave abuse upon the representative system." [198] Many similar statements may be found in the *Congressional Record* dating from the early 1880's. These feelings had crystallized by 1910 into an articulate protest by a majority of the Representatives with a view to the overthrow of "Cannonism" and to the adoption of a new system of leadership. One of the reforms proposed and adopted was a check on the standing committees, forcing any committee to make a report on any bill which had been before it for a certain length of time, and on which no report had been made to the House when a majority of the Representatives demanded it.

[195] C.R., 69-1, p. 387: Mr. Pou said of such leadership: "I was here a long time . . . You were forced to go into the Speaker's office, hat in hand, bowing and scraping, and begging for favors if you ever accomplished anything. The Speaker was in fact the czar of the House. He could make or break the Members. His will was always ratified." A good illustration of this can be found in the work by Joseph P. Chamberlain, *Legislative Processes*, at p. 115. On one occasion when the House was proceeding under the "Consent Calendar," Congressman Terry passed the Speaker's chair on his way out of the House chamber. Speaker Reed called to him: "You are not going to quit now, Terry, as I am about to recognize you to call up your church bill?"

"There is no use of calling up my bill, Mr. Speaker," replied Terry, "when you had already arranged with Dalzell to object to its consideration."

"Why," the Speaker exclaimed, "I thought you would like to call the bill up anyhow, so as to convince your folks at home that you are doing the best you can."

[196] C.R., 48-1, pp. 964, 973 (February 7, 1884): The motion was changed to read from 30 to 40 days. The amendment was defeated by a vote of 56 to 115. Mr. Thomas B. Reed opposed the amendment at that time, although he was then a member of the minority.

[197] C.R., 60-1, p. 1087.

[198] C.R., 60-2, p. 610.

The second rule, replacing the first one, was adopted the following year by a House composed of 228 Democrats and 160 Republicans. The introduction of the measure was a party decision reached in the Democratic Caucus.[199] The resolution itself was not subject to amendment but a substitute to the resolution was in order. The new rule was presented with other reforms in the rules, all of which were debated four hours and adopted en bloc without a record vote.[200]

The third rule was adopted on February 3, 1912. The Democrats held that Mr. Mann, a Republican, had abused the use of the second rule so much that the Democrats finally had to change the rule in order to carry on their legislative program. Mr. Garrett, of Tennessee, one time floor leader of the House, stated that the change, which came in Febuary of the session, became necessary in order to do the business of the House, as the rule had not been used in good faith.[201] Mr. Henry, of Texas, chairman of the Rules Committee at this time, reported the new measure to the House and after much heated debate it was adopted in the House by a vote of 153 to 102. The House composition at the time was 229 Democrats and 162 Republicans.

The fourth rule, more liberal and more comprehensive than the three preceding ones, was submitted by the Republicans and adopted by the House composed of 225 Republicans and 206 Democrats. The resolution embracing this Discharge Rule as well as a number of other changes in the rules of the House was adopted by a vote of yeas 253 to nays 114.[202] These proposals for change were so many and far-reaching that much division of opinion among the membership was discernible. The issues involved were considered so important that the House devoted five whole days of debate to them. In speaking of these proposed changes at this time, Mr. Snell, the chairman of the Rules Committee which reported the resolution, said:

[199] Mr. Pou, of North Carolina, one time chairman of the Rules Committee, in speaking on the rule said: "You gentlemen pursued your policy of centralization of power until you made the American House of Representatives well-nigh the laughing stock in the eyes of the world." (C.R., 62-1, p. 62). Mr. Mann, of Illinois, in defiance of the majority party, threatened the new proposal. He said, "I may undertake to demonstrate if I choose, and I make no promises that I will not choose, to show the utter absurdity, not to say idiocy, of the rule that is now proposed." (C.R., 62-1, p. 79).

[200] C.R., 62-1, pp. 54-80.

[201] This new rule was not sufficient for the new Democratic majority; on June 3, 1913, the entire rule was suspended for the rest of the session to assure the Democratic leadership of no embarrassment (C.R., 63-1, pp. 1879-1880). This action was severely criticized by the Republicans.

[202] The vote is found at p. 1143 of C.R., 68-1; the resolution was H.Res. 146.

We know we have regular Republicans, insurgent Republicans, and Democrats. We fully appreciate that to get any report adopted at the present time it must represent all of these elements. As I have said before, we have taken a middle-of-the-road compromise position on every proposition and on every one of the contested points. When the revision of the rules was taken up in 1910 the late and beloved Champ Clark, at that time the leader on the Democratic side of the House, said that he would never advocate on the floor of the House as a member of the minority a proposition that he would not be willing to stand for as a member of the majority. He said that he would never recommend the adoption of any rule that would help to clog legislation, and beyond that he had supreme confidence in the common sense of the House itself. I solemnly subscribe to those sentiments.[203]

Sam Rayburn, later to become Speaker of the House, said that he would not support the rule if his party were in power, and "I shall not support it when my party is not in power . . . I do not support this rule because I do not believe in half-baked legislation."[204] Mr. Crisp, of Georgia, one time Parliamentarian of the House, maintained that all of the old rules had been unworkable even at face value; "I have been here 10 years and I do not remember one single instance where any legislative bill has been discharged from a committee."[205] But there was a need for a good rule, he insisted. In pursuance of such arguments a fairly liberal rule was adopted by a vote of yeas 253 and nays 114,[206] but it was not to survive long.

The fifth rule, adopted on December 7, 1925, replaced the liberal rule of 1924. Many of the leaders wanted every trace of the rule erased, but even the Republicans with their new majority were unable to muster enough support within their own ranks to accomplish that end. Realizing that fact, the Rules Committee set about to work out a compromise. The rule was adopted by a vote of 206 yeas and 196 nays [207] by a House composed of 247 Republicans and 183 Democrats.

The sixth and present Discharge Rule was adopted on December 8, 1931 by a House composed of 218 Democrats and 214 Republicans.[208] The Democrats who had been the minority party for a number of years had returned to power at the beginning of the Seventy-second Congress with a bare majority. The situation

[203] C.R., 68-1, p. 954 (January 14, 1924). Mr. Crisp, of Georgia, speaking on the measure said that there were only a few changes made in the rule as originally drafted by himself (C.R., 68-1, p. 966).
[204] C.R., 68-1, p. 999.
[205] C.R., 68-1, p. 966.
[206] C.R., 68-1, p. 1143.
[207] C.R., 69-1, pp. 390-391.
[208] The rule was amended in 1935, changing the number of signatures from 145 to 218.

demanded a very liberal rule. Practically the same arguments which had been offered in times past to defend or to oppose the adoption of the preceding rules were restated or reviewed. The resolution,[209] including the Discharge Rule as well as other alterations in the rules of the House, however, was not discussed so heatedly nor so long as some prior ones had been. The vote on the resolution showed 227 yeas and 193 nays.[210]

The succeeding Congress had an increase in the number of Democratic Representatives and the leadership of the House began to feel them out in anticipation of a change in the number of signatures necessary before the petition became effective; it urged a removal of the liberal rule.[211] The "leaders" wished every trace of the rule removed but they knew this was impossible. The Democratic party enjoyed an unprecedented majority in the Seventy-third Congress [212] but sentiment within the party would not give up the idea of a Discharge Rule. The leaders in the 74th Congress, however, were able to get the House to change the liberal clause of 145 signatures. On the opening day of the Seventy-fourth Congress a resolution was reported and adopted by a vote of 245 yeas to 166 nays to amend the Discharge Rule by substituting the number of 218 [213] for 145, with the rule otherwise remaining as of the Seventy-third Congress. The amendment was debated in rather a partisan spirit.[214]

An Analysis of the Discharge Rule: Introduction: An analysis of the six discharge rules, as considered in this section, will show the history, the scope (which has been always more inclusive if not always more practical) and application of the procedure. In order to disclose the intricacies, the extent, and the development of this kind of parliamentary procedure most clearly, the different clauses of the present Discharge Rule will be considered separately, showing in each instance its history.

Name of Calendar: The present Discharge Rule provides that all motions shall be placed on a calendar to be known as a "Cal-

---

[209] House Resolution 5.
[210] C.R., 72-1, pp. 72-83.
[211] C.R., 73-2, pp. 6490-6491.
[212] Composition of House was: 322 Democrats, 102 Republicans, and 10 others.
[213] The rule reads: "When a majority of the total membership of the House shall have signed the motion. . ."
[214] C.R., 74-1, pp. 13-21.

endar of Motions to Discharge Committees." This has been the name of the calendar under each of the rules with two exceptions.[215]

Petition to Discharge: When any Member wishes to discharge a committee from further consideration of any bill,[216] he must file a written petition [217] at the Clerk's desk [218] to be signed [219] by a majority of the House membership [220] before the discharge may occur. When duly signed by as many Representatives as are stipulated in the rule, it is entered in the *Journal* and printed "with signatures thereto" [221] in the *Congressional Record,* and referred to the "Calendar of Motions to Discharge Committees" where it awaits consideration in pursuance of the rule. Under this rule a majority of the Members must go on record for a hearing of the measure before any official record is made of the situation, or before any action to discharge a committee is in order. Prior to 1924, only a written motion was required, without any signatures, which was to be recorded in the *Journal* when filed.[222]

To call a motion before the House under the first three rules mentioned (all prior to 1924) signified practically nothing as far as the desire to pass such a bill on the part of the House membership was concerned. It would mean that one Member of the House was in favor of such a law or that some scheme by one or more Members to stage a filibuster to prevent the operation of the rule was under way. Before any action could be taken which would show the sentiment of the House toward the bill, the membership had to second the motion by tellers, and since no

---

[215] The two exceptions were: The first rule provided that all motions to discharge were to be printed on "a calendar" under an appropriate heading. The fifth rule provided a calendar to be known as the "Calendar of Motions to Instruct Committees."

[216] The bill which is discharged from the committee must be the bill originally referred to the committee and not as the committee may have amended it (Cannon, VII, 1015).

[217] The Member filing a petition may notify the House from the floor or send letters to the individual Members of the House of his action (Cannon, VII, 1008).

[218] "Motions to discharge committees are signed at the Clerk's desk during the session of the House and not otherwise." (Cannon, VII, 1009). See also C.R., 68-1, pp. 951-953; C.R., 73-2, pp. 6491-6492, 6643.

[219] Rule XXVII, clause 4.   Some convenient place must be arranged to place signatures to the petition.

[220] Signatures may not be given by proxy (Cannon, VII, 1014).

[221] In the Seventy-third Congress the Speaker made a ruling designating which persons were eligible to have their names included in the list printed in the *Journal* and *Record*. The Speaker made it clear to the Members of the House that no one would be permitted to sign the petition after the specified number had affixed their names thereto.   If a Member fears his constituency but opposes the measure, he must take a definite position.   After a petition has been duly signed, the names of the signers will be placed in the *Record* and no name not included in the specified number may be published.

[222] A Member may withdraw his signature in writing at any time before the motion is entered in the *Journal* (*House Manual,* 80-1, sec. 908).

such motion ever had a fair trial or was ever seconded,[223] the sentiment of the House toward bills for which such motions had been filed could not be known through the use of this rule until after 1924.

Number to Sign Petition: The question of how many Members should sign the petition before the motion to discharge a committee was in order has been the bone of much contention.[224] The first rule to include a clause concerning signed petitions required the signatures of 150 Representatives. Many argued during the consideration of this rule, adopted in 1924, that 218 should have been the number, but to no avail.[225] Mr. Snell, chairman of the Rules Committee reporting the rule, said that 100 were too few, that 218 were perhaps a bit conservative, and that 150 would be the best since it was the middle ground; he personally, however, preferred 218.[226] Sam Rayburn, who later became Speaker, said that it did not make any difference in his opinion whether the dignity of the House was manslaughtered with the figure of 100 or murdered with the number of 150. "I can not support this rule because I believe it is a fatal mistake." [227]

The figure was changed from 150 to 218 in 1925. When this change was under consideration Mr. Snell stated to the House that "There is no use in going through the preliminary proceedings and wasting all the time, if you do not have the votes to adopt the main proposition." [228]

He continued: if the importance of a bill is demonstrated by the appearance of 218 signatures on the petition, the Rules Committee deems it wise to allow forty minutes debate on the issue before any vote is taken to discharge the committee concerned from further consideration of the issue and to bring it before the House. He added that no single piece of legislation which had been brought out of a committee by this procedure has ever been passed. Mr. Crisp, of Georgia, opposed the number 218; the old rules, he said, had not required any such great number.[229] To understand the significance of the arguments against the number

---

[223] Twelve petitions were called up under this procedure but the circumstances did not permit a vote on the merits of the bills; each situation elicited a vote according to party strength.
[224] C.R., 73-2, p. 10159.
[225] C.R., 68-1, pp. 1100, 995-1016.
[226] C.R., 68-1, p. 995. A vote on whether the number should be 100 or 150 disclosed that the House was for the number of 150 by a vote of 164 to 224 (C.R., 68-1, p. 1116).
[227] C.R., 68-1, p. 999.
[228] C.R., 69-1, p. 386.
[229] C.R., 69-1, pp. 387-388.

of 218 signatures as opposed to 150, one should contrast it with the requirements for lawmaking. Suppose there are 218 Members present, a quorum of the House to do business. One hundred and ten of these Members could pass a bill, as far as the power of the House extends, entangling our country in a world war; they could pass an appropriation act for billions of dollars to be drawn from the United States Treasury; they could levy any tax upon the people.

In 1931, under the leadership of Mr. Crisp, the number was changed once again, this time to 145. The Democrats had returned to power with a very small majority, and the decision was reached in the face of heated debate. The liberal decision was retained only until 1935. Even in 1933 the Democrats with an increased membership tried to change the number back to 218.[230] A resolution to the same effect was sent to the Rules Committee, but it was never reported out because of dissension within the party.[231] The present number was changed back to a majority of the House membership in the 74th Congress.[232]

Bill in Committee 30 Days—Resolution in Rules Committee 7 Days: Any bill or resolution must have been referred to a committee at least thirty days before a motion to discharge the said committee from further consideration of the measure may be filed with the Clerk; or "That said resolution from which it is moved to discharge the Committee on Rules has been referred to that committee at least seven days prior to the filing of the motion to discharge." [233] The first rule included no such limit of time. The second rule stipulated that the bill or resolution must have been referred to such a committee fifteen days prior thereto. The fourth rule incorporated the next change by increasing the length of time to thirty days; this specification has not been changed [234]

---

[230] C.R., 73-2, p. 6490.
[231] C.R., 73-2, pp. 6490-6491.
[232] Rule XXVII, clause 4. "A signature may be withdrawn by a Member in writing at any time before the motion is entered in the *Journal*." The names of Representatives who have signed the petition may not be made public until the petition has been completed, for the petition is the property of the House, and no one Member has a right to dispose of it (C.R., 73-2, p. 6490, Cannon, VII, 1008). For a review of the number of signatures needed to place petitions on Discharge Calendar at different times, note the following: From Sixty-Eighth Congress, first session to Sixty-ninth Congress, first session (Jan. 18, 1924-Dec. 7, 1925) 150 signatures were required. From Sixty-ninth Congress, first session to Seventy-second Congress, first session (Dec. 7, 1925-Dec. 8, 1931) 218 signatures were required. From Seventy-second Congress, first session to Seventy-fourth Congress, first session (Dec. 8, 1931-Jan. 3, 1935) 145 signatures were required. Since the Seventy-fourth Congress, first session (Jan. 3, 1935-   ) 218 signatures have been required.
[233] Rule XXVII, clause 4.
[234] Cannon, VII, 1019. The time that a bill has been referred to a committee does not start running until the committees are appointed and organized.

but the clause affecting the Rules Committee was an innovation of the Seventy-second Congress.

Jurisdiction of Rule: The jurisdiction of the present rule extends to the discharge of any committee from any "public bill or resolution," as well as "it shall also be in order for a Member to file a motion to discharge the Committee on Rules from further consideration of any resolution providing either a special order of business, or a special rule for the consideration of any public bill or resolution favorably reported by a standing committee, or a special rule for the consideration of a public bill or resolution which has remained in a standing committee thirty or more days without action: *Provided,* That said resolution from which it is moved to discharge the Committee on Rules [235] has been referred to that committee at least seven days prior to the filing of the motion to discharge."

These stipulations designating the jurisdiction of what issues may be discharged and from which committees, are far more specific and inclusive than the clauses defining jurisdiction found in any of the preceding rules. The first rule permitted the discharge of "any public bill or joint resolution" from committees; no mention was made of the Rules Committee. The status of the first rule in this respect was re-written in each subsequent rule until a fourth one, in 1924. In that year the clause was changed to read: "a public bill or resolution." The present jurisdiction was not innovated until 1931, and as defined in the above quotation, it included not only the discharge of standing committees from further consideration of "public bills and resolutions" but also extends to a discharge of the Rules Committee from any resolution determining the time and the order of procedure on legislative measures, both as to bills already reported by a standing committee to the House and placed on a calendar or to bills which have already been referred to a standing committee for thirty days, on which no action has been taken.[236] The resolution from

---

[235] Rule XXVII, clause 4. "If the motion prevails to discharge the Committee on Rules from any resolution pending before the committee, the House shall immediately vote on the adoption of said resolution, the Speaker not entertaining any dilatory or other intervening motion except one motion to adjourn, and, if said resolution is adopted, then the House shall immediately proceed to its execution."

[236] This present control over the Rules Committee does not extend to motions to discharge the Rules Committee from further consideration of resolutions concerning investigations. A good illustration of this occurred in 1934. On this occasion Mr. DePriest, of Illinois, filed a motion to discharge the Rules Committee from further consideration of a resolution to investigate a certain situation. After the motion had been printed on the Discharge Calendar to discharge the Rules Committee from further consideration of the resolution to investigate the use of the House Restaurant by Negroes, and before the discharge had occurred, the Rules

which the Rules Committee may be discharged must have been already referred to it at least seven days. If the Rules Committee is discharged from a resolution to grant a privileged status and provide a special procedure for the consideration of a bill already reported to the House by a standing committee, the proceedings are practically the same as those followed in discharging a standing committee from a bill which has been before it for thirty days, except the resolution must have been referred to the Rules Committee only seven or more days previously. If the Rules Committee on the other hand is discharged from a resolution providing a special order of business for a bill before a standing committee, which has already been in that committee thirty days without action, it has the effect of bringing the bill out of the standing committee, and also, the resolution out of the Rules Committee. The adoption of the resolution under the Discharge procedure, after the Rules Committee has been discharged, sets up a special procedure, as defined in the resolution, for the consideration of the bill brought out of the standing committee. By this process the House may accomplish with one petition what otherwise would require two petitions and more time. This latter use of the Discharge Rule is becoming the practice of the House.[237] Without this procedure when a petition had received enough signatures to discharge a standing committee, the committee before the seven days of grace had elapsed could make a report on the bill.[238] Thereupon, it would then become necessary to file another petition, this time against the Rules Committee, in order to get the bill up before the House,[239] unless it was otherwise highly privileged business.

Committee reported the resolution to the House. A strong opinion existed in the House that the committee had made the report to prevent its own discharge from further consideration of the resolution. Later the chair had an occasion to make a ruling on this situation which cleared up the point. The chair stated that the resolution provided: "That a committee of five Members of the House be appointed by the Speaker to investigate by what authority the Committee on Accounts controls and manages the conduct of the House resaurant and by what authority said committee or any Members thereof issued and enforced rules or instructions whereby any citizen of the United States is discriminated against on account of race, color, or creed in said House restaurant—" The discharge Rule provides, he said: "Under this rule it shall also be in order for a Member to file a motion to discharge the Committee on Rules from further consideration of any resolution providing either a special order of business, or a special rule for the consideration of any public bill or resolution favorably reported by a standing committee, or a special rule for the consideration of a public bill or resolution, which has remained in a standing committee 30 or more days without action." He added that it is therefore apparent that this particular resolution does not come within the purview of the Discharge Rule (C.R., 73-2, p. 7162).

[237] For example, see C.R., 775-1, pp. 3386-3387.

[238] See C.R., 73-2, p. 7162. The Speaker rules on the right of a committee to make a report to the House during the seven days of grace.

[239] See C.R., 73-2, pp. 6604-6605, 7156-7160.

Business in Order : Discharge business is in order on the "second and fourth Mondays of each month, except during the last six days of any session of Congress, immediately after the approval of the *Journal*." [240] Each petition printed on the calendar, however, must have been there at least seven legislative days before its consideration is in order. If it has been on the calendar seven legislative days,[241] on the second or fourth Monday of each month, immediately after the *Journal* has been approved, it will inevitably be granted some kind of a hearing since "any Member who has signed a motion to discharge . . . , and seeks recognition, shall be recognized for the purpose of calling up the motion, and the House shall proceed to its consideration in the manner herein provided without intervening motion except one motion to adjourn." [242] Some person interested in the discharge, however, must call up the motion since the business does not arise of its own accord ;[243] it is merely privileged business for these two days each month.

If a motion to discharge prevails, the House shall proceed to its execution,[244] i.e., grant consideration to the bill concerned until its completion. If the House determines not to consider the bill immediately the bill will be placed on the proper calendar as if it had been reported to the House by its standing committee.[245]

The first two rules did not give to such business the privileged status as defined above. They merely provided that the business on the Discharge Calendar should be in order for consideration

---

[240] Motions to discharge take precedence over business merely privileged under the rules of the House (Cannon, VII, 1011).

[241] The first Discharge Rule was not tested because no bill had been on the calendar seven legislative days on June 20, 1910, the first day that any discharge business was ever in order, following the adoption of the first Discharge Rule. Since Congress for that session adjourned on June 25th of the same year no business was brought up under that procedure (see C.R., 61-2, p. 8545).

[242] When a Member properly rises and calls up a motion to discharge a committee the motion is not debatable (See *Cannon's Procedure in the House of Representatives*, pp. 158-162).

[243] The first attempt to discharge a committee under the first rule came on December 19, 1910; between twenty and twenty-nine motions were on the desk ready for consideration (C.R., 61-3, p. 499). On that day, after the business on the Unanimous Consent Calendar was disposed of, Mr. Fuller, of Illinois, arose to suspend the rule and pass a bill. Mr. Sherley, of Kentucky, made a point of order. Others rose to their feet to interrupt but the Speaker ruled that the Discharge Calendar business did not arise of its own accord; if no one moves the consideration of the business on the calendar it is in order to pass to the next business in order. Mr. Fuller has a right to move to suspend the rules, he said, and pass his bill, if no one objects. Immediately Mr. Fitzgerald asked to discharge the Ways and Means Committee, but the adroit Mr. Mann had seen to it that his measures were placed first on the calendar. He therefore objected and moved to consider his motion to "discharge the Committee on Post Office and Post Roads from further consideration of the House bill 21321, to codify, revise, and amend the postal laws of the United States . . ." (C.R., 61-3, pp. 498-499.)

[244] This principle has always been included in each rule except the one of 1925. The motion to proceed to consideration is not debatable (*House Manual*, 80-1, sec. 908).

immediately after the consideration of the Unanimous Consent Calendar, a position which could not be reached in the face of an antagonistic leadership. The third rule made the situation even worse by placing the business after the Unanimous Consent Calendar and motions to suspend the rules. The fourth rule greatly improved the privileged status of the business when it provided for its consideration "On the first and third Mondays of each Month, except the last six days of any session of Congress, immediately after the approval of the *Journal*."[246] The fifth rule, adopted in 1925, which was in existence until the present status obtained, changed this privileged position by providing "the third Monday of each month, immediately after the approval of the *Journal*" but committees could only be instructed, not discharged.

Order of Recognition: The order of recognition has always been fixed in the order in which the motions were entered on the calendar and in the *Journal*.[247]

Bills Read by Title: "When any motion under this rule shall be called up, the bill or resolution shall be read by title only." The purpose of this clause is to block filibuster. The first rule carried no such limitation at all. The first attempt to discharge a committee under the Discharge Rule showed this definfiite loophole when Mr. Mann[248] took advantage of the situation and insisted that his bill, a bill to codify, revise, and amend the postal laws of the United States, which had an unusually long title, must be read in its entirety.[249] To avoid this situation the second rule provided

---

[246] See Rule XXVII, clause 4, of the 68th Congress, first session.

[247] Cannon, VII, 1018. To illustrate: Mr. Mann took advantage of this situation when the rule was first tried and saw to it that his motions were the first motions on the calendar and that his bill to codify, revise, and amend the postal laws of the United States was the very first one. The purpose of this was to have a bill with such a long title that the clerk would never finish reading the title, and the House, under the rule could not move to another.

[248] The rule was not foolproof and Mr. Mann of Illinois set out to make a fool of those who had sponsored the measure. He hated the rule. He said: "Now, Mr. Speaker, I was not the father of the rule for the discharge of committees. I did not vote for it. It is true I did not vote against it, but as soon as it was reported from the Committee on Rules I went and prepared a motion which would demonstrate its utter absurdity." He further added, "Mr. Speaker, there is a simple method of bringing matters before the House. We have a Committee on Rules, which has the right to report at any time that motions to suspend the rules shall be in order. The Committee on Rules may now report a resolution providing that today or tomorrow, or the next week, not Wednesday, but any day except 'holy Wednesday,' the balance of the session, it shall be in order to move to suspend the rules. They may further report that suspension may be had by a majority instead of by a two-thirds vote." (C.R., 61-3, p. 680).

[249] The title was so long and business was so delayed that there were an endless number of motions made, but the Speaker ruled that the title had to be read first, that the bills were to be considered in the order in which they were on the calendar, and that "Such motions shall have precedence over motions to suspend the rules." During this classic filibuster, there were motions to second the bill, recommit it, request why the Clerk was reading so slowly, suspend the rule that made such procedure in order, to adjourn, to recess, and to bring the bill before the House since it had not been taken from the Committee. There were six roll calls, but Mr. Mann

that the title of any bill must not contain more than 100 words
and that any bill must have been referred to a committee fifteen
days before any action to take the bill away from the committee
could be put in the form of a motion. But this proved inadequate
to avoid an abuse of the intent of the rule. This weak guard was
insufficient to block Mr. Mann from calling up a series of bills
which had been referred to committees fifteen days but which
the committees had not had time properly to consider and make a
report on them to the House. Therefore, on January 15, 1912
when Mr. Mann attacked the rule by calling up eleven motions
consecutively, he naturally defeated the purpose of the rule since
the majority party was forced to vote the motions down in order
to carry on their program.[250]

insisted that the bill must be read in its entirety. Finally at 5:55 p.m. the House adjourned in despair; only a little over a fifth of the bill had been read (C.R., 61-3,
pp. 498-507).

[250] The second rule had been adopted at the beginning of a special session, and the
leaders of the Democratic party had decided to limit their program to certain specified
subjects, and by caucus action the committees were directed not to report any other
measures. Therefore, the Discharge Rule was not given a chance. Nearly every
week-end prior to the first and third Mondays the House would adjourn over until
Tuesday. Only on two occasions when they did not adjourn was there any evidence
that the Members planned to call up motions on the Discharge Calendar; on each of
these occasions, at the request of Mr. Underwood, the House adjourned. This action
blocked any consideration of the Discharge Calendar during the whole five months of
the special session. On August 21, the last possible Monday of the session, the Rules
Committee presented a special order for a tariff reduction bill. This special rule, as
a sort of a rider, provided that no business be in order on that day under the Discharge Calendar. But in the regular session of 1912, Mr. Mann resumed his attack.
On December 18, the first Discharge Monday of the Month, the House immediately
adjourned; on January 1, the second Monday of the session for Discharge business,
the House had adjourned over—having adjourned from December 21, to January 3.
On January 15, the following proper day, eleven motions were stricken from the
Calendar. On this day Mr. Mann called up consecutively eleven motions to bring out
of committees important bills which the Democrats had advocated during the campaign but which they were not yet ready to report (C.R., 62-2, pp. 952-956). The
subjects of the bills and the vote by tellers were as follows:

1. Physical valuation of railroad properties. (vote: 71-101).
2. Regulation of hours of work of post office clerks. (vote: 76-88).
3. Pensions to soldiers confined in Confederate prisons. (vote: 72-89).
4. Legal rights of laborers before the Court of Claims under the national eight-
   hour law. (vote: 63-90).
5. Penny postage rate for "drop letters." (vote: 39-75).
6. Pensions to widow, minor children, etc., of deceased soldiers, etc. (vote:
   62-130).
7. Creation of a tariff board. (vote: 69-111).
8. Fixing the price of gas in the District of Columbia. (vote: 42-102).
9. Additional compensation to the R.F.D. carriers. (vote: 62-94).
10. Compensation for injuries to employees of the United States. (vote: 50-88).
11. Second-class mail privileges to publications of benevolent societies. (vote:
    45-74). (See C.R., 62-2, pp. 952-956).

On the fourth discharge day of the session, the first bill called was not considered
since a second was refused by a vote of 51-90. The bill was not stricken from the
calendar, however, since the question of no quorum was raised and the vote was never
finished. By the third of February the third Discharge Rule had been adopted
putting Discharge business in the third place (C.R., 62-2, pp. 1684-1685). This action
had defeated the purpose of the rule as the above votes show: this had been Mr.
Mann's idea. By February 3rd, of this session, the Discharge Rule became a dead
issue for several years; in fact, it was never again brought before the House for
consideration until Mr. Mann was no longer a Member of Congress.

The third rule limited the title of bills to 100 words but the business had lost its privileged status. The Discharge Calendar was to be called after the Unanimous Consent Calendar and the suspension of the rules—third place on these calendar days. Under this condition the Discharge Rule became a dead issue until 1924.[251] The fourth rule altered this situation by removing all limitations on the number of words in a title to the bill. It set up a new requirement, however; it provided that a certain number of Representatives must sign a petition before a motion to discharge a committee was in order. But this too was insufficient to prevent filibuster supported by the leadership. Under that rule the Discharge business was limited to one day a month [252] and a minority or the leadership could demand enough votes on various dilatory motions to consume one complete sitting of the House.[253] In 1925 the rule was altered considerably but there was no change to prevent a filibuster.

Business Privileged Until Completion: Under the rule of 1931, which is still in operation, the situation was corrected to exclude filibusters. Once the House begins the consideration of a bill under the present rule that business becomes the unfinished business of the House and remains so until final disposition.[254] Under this condition it is almost useless to attempt a filibuster.

[251] Mr. Hayden on Monday, December 18, 1922, started to utilize the Discharge Rule once more; he stated he had been in Congress for ten years and had not seen it work. But his motion was refused by a vote of sixty to ninety. The motion was to discharge a bill from the Committee on Interstate and Foreign Commerce (C.R., 67-4, pp. 639-640).

[252] Under this situation the business was privileged only on Discharge days. If the business was unfinished at the end of the day it had to wait over until the next discharge day.

[253] The consideration of the Barkley-Howell bill (H.R. 7358, to provide for the expeditious and prompt settlement, mediation, conciliation, and arbitration of disputes between carriers and their employees and subordinate officials, and for other purposes) was in pursuance of the procedure prescribed by the Discharge Rule. It was easily defeated under this procedure and yet it was not considered on a partisan basis. The vote to discharge the committee showed twenty-seven Democrats voting against the motion and forty Republicans voting for it. The rule was abused on this occasion, however. Points of order were raised against its consideration but the Speaker overruled them; the committee was then discharged (C.R., 68-1, p. 7874; the vote was 194 to 181) and the House proceeded to its consideration with an obstinate leadership. A vote was first demanded on consideration which was adopted by a vote of 197 to 172; then there was a vote to see if the House should resolve into the Committee of the Whole; other questions raised were: no quorum, vote to adjourn, to lay motion on table, no quorum, etc. All told there were 17 roll calls and 16 of them were record votes. This defeated the operation of the Discharge Rule (see C.R., 68-1, pp. 7866-7902).

[254] Rule XXVII, clause 4. "If the motion prevails to discharge one of the standing committees of the House from any public bill or resolution pending before the committee, it shall then be in order for any Member who signed the motion to move that the House proceed to the immediate consideration of such bill or resolution (such motion not being debatable), and such motion is hereby made of high privilege; and if it shall be decided in the affirmative, the bill shall be immediately considered under the general rules of the House, and if unfinished before adjournment of the day on which it is called up it shall remain the unfinished business until it is fully disposed of. Should the House by vote decide against the immediate consideration of such bill

Debate on Discharge Motion: When a motion to discharge a committee is brought up before the House, it will be debated twenty minutes, "one-half in favor of the proposition and one-half in opposition thereto," before the vote is taken to see if the House will make the discharge. This provision has been the same in each rule except the 1925 rule, which provided for forty minutes of debate, "one-half in favor of the proposition and one-half in opposition thereto." [255]

"Seven Days of Grace": The discharge rules have always incorporated the stipulation, "which shall have been entered at least seven days prior thereto." This is known as the seven days of grace. If a motion has been filed and signed by the proper number of Representatives, it still must have been printed on the calendar at least seven days before the House may consider it. During this time the committee having jurisdiction of the bill against which the motion to discharge was filed may make a report on the bill to the House and thereby block a consideration of the Discharge petition,[256] unless it is to discharge the Rules Committee. Further, when a committee makes such a report to the House, if the bill is not otherwise privileged it may lie on the calendar for the remainder of that Congress without consideration unless a resolution to grant the bill a privileged status is introduced and then discharged from the Rules Committee. The leadership has used these seven days of grace to block the consideration of measures under this procedure by recessing from day to day after the petition had been printed on the calendar but before discharge day had arrived. By this means when Discharge day arrived the peti-

---

or resolution, it shall be referred to its proper calendar and be entitled to the same rights and privileges that it would have had had the committee to which it was referred duly reported same to the House for its consideration."

[255] The rule of 1925 was never utilized. The time is limited in the rule and the Speaker is constrained to extend it. See Cannon, VII, 1010.

[256] A committee may report a bill after a motion to discharge has been printed on the calendar but before the discharge day arrives, and at least seven days after the motion is printed. In 1934 a certain bill was referred to the Banking and Currency Committee. The committee refused to report the measure to the House since the leaders and the administration were against the bill. After the proper lapse of time, a motion was signed by 145 Members and placed on the Discharge Calendar. Before the discharge day arrived and after the motion had been placed on the calendar, the Banking and Currency Committee made a report on the bill (H.R. 7908). When the discharge day arrived, a Member moved to discharge the committee, basing his rights on the petition signed by 145 Representatives. His motion was ruled out of order; the Speaker stated that the Banking and Currency Committee had already made a report on the bill and that there was no reason for discharging the committee. The purpose of the rule is to force a report from recalcitrant committees, not to prevent a committee from making a report, he said. The seven days of grace are provided so as to give the committee concerned time to decide whether it prefers to make a report on the bill or to be discharged (C.R., 73-2, p. 7160).

tions would not have been on the calendar for seven legislative days, since each day the House recesses does not count as a legislative day.[257]

Limitation of One Bill on Same Subject Each Session: Only one piece of legislation of substantially the same subject matter may be acted on by the House in the same session of Congress [258] under the Discharge Rule procedure. When one motion to consider a certain bill has been disposed of all other motions substantially the same "or from the Committee on Rules of a resolution providing a special order of business for the consideration of any other such bill or resolution" shall be stricken from the calendar for the rest of that session. The Speaker is constrained to entertain two motions during the same session under the Discharge Rule procedure seeking the passage of the same or similar bill or resolution.[259] The intent behind this clause was included in all the rules with the exception of the first one.[260]

Procedure to Discharge: "If the motion prevails to discharge the Committee on Rules from any resolution pending before the committee, the House shall immediately vote on the adoption of said resolution, the Speaker not entertaining any dilatory or other

[257] In the Seventy-third Congress, two motions to discharge committees were placed on the Discharge Calendar by June 2, 1934; they were to be considered on June 11, the following discharge day. On June 1, the House adopted a special rule making a motion to recess a motion of high privilege. After that day and before June 11, the House began recessing from day to day instead of adjourning. On June 11, when a Member arose and asked that a committee be discharged from further consideration of a bill for which a petition had been placed on the Discharge Calendar, the Speaker held the motion out of order. The Speaker said that calendar days June 4, 5, 6, 7, and 8 were one legislative day. (When the House takes recesses, the legislative day remains the same. Just as soon as it adjourns the legislative day becomes the same day as the calendar day. Therefore, if the House recesses over a certain legislative day, when it adjourns it just passes over that legislative day, or until the House adjourns regardless of how many calendar days may have elapsed the legislative day remains the same). He added that Speaker Longworth had ruled that a bill had to be on the Consent Calendar three legislative days and not three calendar days, that the wording of the two rules was exactly the same in the above respect, and that the decision made by Speaker Longworth was therefore applicable. Since seven legislative days had not elapsed since the petition was placed on the Discharge Calendar, the measure could not be considered under the Discharge Rule on that day but must go over to the next—Congress had adjourned before another discharge day was reached (C.R., 73-2, pp. 11063-11065).
[258] Rule XXVII, clause 4. *"Provided further,* That if before any one motion to discharge a committee has been acted upon by the House there are on the Calendar of Motions to Discharge Committees other motions to discharge committeee from the consideration of bills or resolutions substantially the same, relating in substance to or dealing with the same subject matter, after the House shall have acted on one motion to discharge, the remaining said motions shall be stricken from the Calendar of Motions to Discharge Committees and not acted on during the remainder of that session of Congress." Many petitions for similar bills may be on the Clerk's desk until one of them receives 218 signatures.
[259] Rule XXVII, clause 4. "Any other bill or resolution substantially the same, relating in substance to or dealing with the same subject matter, or from the Committee on Rules of a resolution providing a special order of business for the consideration of any other such bill or resolution, in order that such action by the House on a motion to discharge shall be res adjudicata for the remainder of that session:"
[260] The first rule carried no statement on the subject; see also C.R., 61-2, p. 8439.

intervening motion except one motion to adjourn, and, if said resolution is adopted, then the House shall immediately proceed to its
execution. If the motion prevails to discharge one of the standing
committees of the House from any public bill or resolution pending before the committee, it shall then be in order for any Member
who signed the motion to move that the House proceed to the
immediate consideration of such bill or resolution . . ."[261] The
motion in either instance is not debatable and is made of high
privilege. The Speaker does not entertain other business when the
Discharge procedure is in order.[262] The rules, in their early stages,
allowed too much delay and so many destructive motions during
the consideration of this business that the House would finally
adjourn out of disgust.

The Rule in Operation: Rule in Practice: The adoption and
development of this unique procedure is such that when a committee refuses to make a report on an issue already thirty days
before the committee, and on which a majority of the Representatives desires a vote, any Member may file a petition at the Clerk's
desk requesting the House to recall that measure from the committee. When 218 Representatives have signed the petition, it is
immediately placed on the Discharge Calendar. After having
been on the Calendar for seven days, any Member who signed
the petition may move, on the second and fourth Mondays of each
month immediately after the reading of the *Journal*, that the
House consider the motion. If the decision is made in the negative the cause is lost and the bill remains in the committee; if the
motion is decided in the affirmative the issue is recalled from the
committee and the House may immediately consider the measure
with a view toward passage, or it may place the measure on one
of the House calendars. The whole object of the rule is to give
to the House the power to have a hearing on any issue it wishes,
regardless of what may be the program of the leaders or of any
particular committee. This is assured by two possible methods.
Firstly, it holds a threat over the leaders to compel them to select
a program acceptable to the House membership; and secondly, it

---

[261] Rule XXVII, clause 4.

[262] The motions are of higher privilege than a motion to resolve the House into the
Committee of the Whole for the consideration of revenue or appropriation bills
(Cannon, VII, 1016-1017) ; it has precedence of a motion to suspend the rules. In
fact, this business on that day is of highest privilege (Rule XXVII, clause 4; Cannon,
VII, 1007, 1011). The Speaker declines to recognize for any matter not directly re-
lated to the proceedings (Cannon, VII, 1010). It has precedence over unfinished
business coming over from the preceding day with the previous question ordered
(C.R., 74-2, p. 7010).

provides that the Representatives themselves may take charge of the situation and demand a vote on measures which for one reason or another have been held up.

Difference of Opinion on Rule: The practices under the rule have revealed somewhat different results from those hoped for, but the success of the rule cannot be completely estimated. The rule has initiated much discussion and conflict in House procedure and has forced slight alteration of the leadership's legislative plan on different occasions. The leaders generally have been able to get their measures before the House for consideration; but with their opposition, large segments of the House membership have not been too successful in getting some issues up for a vote. The leaders, who are responsible for the business of the House, oppose any check on themselves; if members of the minority party who might later become responsible for the program vote for or support any such rule it is usually to embarrass the party in power. The men in charge of the program know that a liberal discharge rule is a source of much trouble to them if bills contrary to the Majority's program are to be successfully blocked.[263] In their opinion this rule is only a hindrance to legislation because it might upset the plans of the Majority, who after all are responsible for what the House does or fails to do.[264] They say it is not a liberalization; it merely causes a waste of time.[265]

"Dangerous Procedure": Many good legislators further maintain that the rule is dangerous; if the bill is discharged from a committee, they add, it is thrown open to the House without any of the safeguards that come from committee consideration.

Value of Rule: How much good has come out of this procedure is unknown; perhaps much is derived from it in the form of compromise.[266] One can find many statements in the *Record*

[263] See proceedings for the bills H.R. 2855, H.R. 7430, H.Res. 332, and H.Res. 236, all of the Seventy-third Congress.
[264] See *Hearings, Revision of the Rules,* 68-1, (1924), pp. 6-13; *World's Work,* LX (1930), p. 20.
[265] See C.R., 73-2, pp. 6640-6646; *Editorial Research Reports,* I (1931), pp. 73-80.
[266] Champ Clark, Speaker of the House during the Wilson Administration, said at the time the first rule was introduced that the rule simply provides the machinery by which the House can consider a bill which a committee fails, refuses, or neglects to report when the House desires it. He further added, if the rule is adopted it will not have to be used; it will be held over the heads of the members of the committee as a *Terrorem* (C.R., 61-2, pp. 8441-8442). The threat to discharge House Resolution 241 from the Rules Committee for consideration of H.R. 6995, of the Seventy-fourth Congress apparently had some influence on the destiny of that bill. The petition was filed on June 15, 1935 and by 2:15 that afternoon the bill had passed the House. H.R. 1 of the Seventy-fourth Congress was discharged from the committee and never passed, but the Vinson Bonus Bill (H.R. 9870) was substituted therefor and it became law. In 1945, after the necessary 218 signatures had been affixed to the

accusing the leadership of preventing passage of certain bills. It is common for a Representative to state on the floor of the House that his bill would have passed long ago had it been given a hearing; it has been stated that two-thirds of the House membership was in support of certain legislation but that the men in charge would not allow the House to vote on the measures.[267]

It is questionable, nevertheless, if any of the bills on which such campaigns have been promoted, and on which no action was taken, would have been enacted into law even if they had been brought up for consideration. Rash statements made on the floor of the House about how many Members are in favor of the passage of certain bills are not always dependable or well-founded; they may be made for political purposes or emphatically to establish an altruistic protest against an autocratic leadership. No one can know how the membership is going to vote until a tally of some kind is taken. Of course it is quite possible that certain bills which were never granted a hearing would have passed if they had been brought up for a vote; it is quite possible that certain bills on which committees made no report, and for which petitions to discharge were filed, expressed the will of a majority of the House membership; but any such inaction was not due to the weakness of the present Discharge procedure *per se*. Such results, if so, are due to the whole parliamentary system pursued by the House. Certainly there have been instances when bills for which no agitation was made would have passed had they been brought up for a vote. In fact, it is quite natural to expect that Congress operating under a system of party government will so organize itself that the party in control can, within certain limitations, defeat any particular proposed legislation, not sponsored by that party. The result might be accomplished by abuse of parliamentary law or by control of votes on final passage—that is party government.

petition on H.R. 1362, to increase and extend coverage of unemployment and retirement benefits for railroad employees, the Interstate and Foreign Commerce Committee reported out its version of the bill, blocking operation of the Discharge Rule. It is interesting to note, however, that the House finally passed the introduced version of the bill instead of the one reported by the committee, and the bill finally became law, much in the form as passed by the House. H.R. 4051, to grant personnel of armed forces equal treatment in the matter of leave, was likewise disposed of and became public law.

[267] C.R., 68-1, p. 995. Mr. Snell, chairman of the Rules Committee, said: "If you had given me this rule in the last Congress, with 150 or even with 200 Members, I would have taken from the Committee on Military Affairs and passed the Bursum bill, and it would today be a law, and I would have taken from the Rules Committee, of which I am a member, the so-called Woodruff-Johnson resolution, and you would have had an investigation of war frauds, which would have been a real investigation, and the facts would have been given to the public." For other such comments see: C.R., 61-1, p. 389; C.R., 71-3, pp. 2406-2407; see references for H.R. 4497 of the Sixty-ninth Congress, and H.R. 7825 of the Seventy-first Congress.

Criticism by Leaders: The leaders on different occasions have accused the membership of signing petitions and then refusing to vote for the passage of the bill. The late Speaker Byrns once complained on the floor of the House [268] that many who sign these petitions never vote for the passage of the bill and thereby consume the time of the House without getting any legislation.

Actually, only on two occasions has the vote on a motion to discharge a committee been smaller than the number of signatures then required to make the discharge in order.[269] Further, one can assume that more party pressure is brought on the membership in an attempt at final passage of a bill than during the preliminaries.

Table on Use of Rule: While the true value of the Discharge Rule is not completely revealed by the following table, it is helpful in obtaining the picture on the use of the Rule.

Congress	Discharge Motions Filed	Number Printed on Calendar	Number Granted Discharge Hearing Under Rule	Number of Bills Discharged from Committees	Number of These to Pass House
61	223				
62	82				
63	68				
64	37				
65	34				
66	10				
67	10				
68	4	1	1	1	0
69	4	0	0	0	0
70	2	0	0	0	0
71	5	0	0	0	0
72	12	5	5	1	1
73	31	6	1	1	1
74	33	3	2	2	0
75	43	4	4	3	2
76	37	2	2	2	2
77	15	1	1	1	1
78	21	3	3	3	3
79	35	3	1[270]	1	1
80	20	1	1	1	1

[268] "Mr. Byrns. I simply want to make this statement in reply to our friend the gentleman from Texas (Mr. Patman). In the Seventy-second Congress there were, as I recall 12 bills which were sought to be brought up under discharge petitions signed by 145 Members. Only 5 of those bills were voted on, and only 1 of them passed upon final roll call. One of those bills received only 113 votes, although 145 had signed the petition." (C.R., 73-2, p. 6646).

[269] Only on two occasions did the vote on the motion to discharge show a smaller vote than the required signatures to place the petition on the Discharge Calendar for consideration. House Resolution 117 of the Seventy-second Congress, first session, showed only 133 voting to discharge the committee. The number of required signatures at that time was 145. House Resolution 165 of the Seventy-fifth Congress, second and third session, showed only 188 voting to discharge the committee. The number of required signatures at that time was 218.

Review of Rule in Practice: From 1924 through 1948 twenty-nine motions to discharge committees obtained sufficient signatures to be printed on the Discharge Calendar. Twenty-one of these were granted consideration by the House, and sixteen were adopted. That means that sixteen bills have been discharged from committees under the Discharge Rules. Twelve of these sixteen were passed by the House of Representatives but only one ever became law. In only two instances by yea and nay vote was the number of those voting in favor of passage under this procedure as large as the number favoring the adoption of the motion to discharge. This difference has always been small; in every instance the number not voting has been large enough to account for any differences. Finally the table shows that the use of the Discharge Rule has been popular and practical since the Seventy-second Congress.

All petitions prior to the Sixty-eighth Congress signified nothing since they required the action of only one person. They did not serve to show the opinion of the House on the bill any more than the act of introducing a bill. A negligible number of the petitions, other than those finally printed on the calendar, ever receive more than 25 to 50 signatures. Comparatively speaking, many of the petitions never receive as many as ten signatures.

Conclusion: In conclusion, several bills have been granted a hearing in the House under this kind of procedure. A number of compromises have been forced by the use of the rule; one bill has become law. The rule seems to have gained in popularity; it certainly has become more practical; and it has apparently found a permanent place in the House procedure.

Calendar Wednesday: *Nature of Calendar:* The rule for Calendar Wednesday was adopted by the House on March 1, 1909.[271] It provides that each Wednesday shall be set aside exclusively for the various standing committees to call up for enactment bills and resolutions [272] not otherwise privileged.[273] The bills or resolutions must have been printed on either the House or

---

[270] Two were placed on the Calendar but the two bills (H.R. 1362 and H.R. 4051) were reported and considered under Special Rules prior to being reached under the Discharge Rule; both became public law. For details on various bills involved under this procedure from 61st through 75th Congresses, see Riddick, *Congressional Procedure*, pp. 297-299.

[271] *House Manual*, 80-1, sec. 898. The rule was amended March 1909; additional amendments were attached on January 18, 1916 and again on December 8, 1931.

[272] Committees are recognized only for the purpose of calling up bills and resolutions (Cannon, VI, 754).

[273] *House Manual*, 80-1, sec. 897; Cannon, VII, 881, 932-935. This includes specific appropriation bills.

Union Calendars for one or more days.[274] If there is a Calendar Wednesday before all the committees are appointed, the rule includes only those in existence. Committees are absolutely forbidden to yield or attempt to exchange their order of consideration and the House is not bound by any agreement made off the floor between committees.

Status of Bills: The status of any measure under this call has no relation to that on another calendar. Bills or resolutions called up for consideration under this rule, even though they have been debated at another time under another rule, will be heard as if no prior action has been taken on them, and vice versa.

Procedure: Under this rule the Speaker is authorized on the mid-week day of each week to announce to the House: "This is Calendar Wednesday. The Clerk will call the roll of the committees." No other business shall be in order on that day "except as provided by paragraph 4" of the same rule "Unless the House by a two-thirds vote on motion to dispense therewith shall otherwise determine." By practice the business is commonly dispensed with by unanimous consent; motion to dispense with Calendar Wednesday is limited to 10 minutes, five for and five against. The floor leader, who is responsible for the program, generally the day before, makes a unanimous consent request that the proceedings on Calendar Wednesday be dispensed with. If this business is not dispensed with before a Wednesday, the Speaker may decline to recognize on Wednesday a Member making a unanimous consent request to establish a special order for the day.[275] In recent years most of the Calendar Wednesdays have been passed over and replaced by other business. There has been complaint against the practice. One Member of the Committee on Immigration and Naturalization complained in 1931 that his committee had not been given a Calendar Wednesday since 1922.[276] This is an extreme case, but it is true that most of the Calendar Wednesdays have been dispensed with by unanimous consent.

The committees are called in the order in which they appear in Rule X, that is, alphabetically. Each committee is called twice; if there is no response, the call passes on to the next committee. When a committee is passed over it loses its chance to offer a bill under this procedure until it is reached again on the next

[274] *House Manual*, 80-1, sec. 897; Cannon, VII, 881, 938.
[275] Cannon, VII, 888, 915-916, 964.
[276] *Immigration, Hearings before the Committee on Rules*, 71-3, H.J. Res. 473, p. 43.

round of calls. A committee, recognized for the consideration of its measures, may consume the entire day. But one committee is not entitled to more than one Wednesday, unless the House by a two-thirds vote decides to the contrary.[277]

Committees Call up Business: Each committee determines the order in which its measures shall be called, but the question of consideration on each bill may be raised.[278] The committee may withdraw any bill it has called at any time until the House begins to add amendments; at this time the House assumes complete jurisdiction.[279]

Classes of Bills and Consideration: All bills called up for consideration under Calendar Wednesday rule are divided into two classes, namely: bills and resolutions from the Union Calendar and bills and resolutions from the House Calendar. Bills or resolutions authorizing money or property or a charge on the Federal Treasury (from the Union Calendar), must be first considered in the Committee of the Whole, if unanimous consent to consider in the House as if in the Committee has not been requested and granted.[280] When a bill of the first class is called up, if the bill is not considered in the House as if in the Committee of the Whole, the House automatically resolves itself into the Committee.[281] The House determines whether or not a bill must be considered in the Committee.[282]

Method of Calling Up for Debate: When any committee is called, the Member properly authorized by it,[283] addresses the Speaker: "Mr. Speaker, by direction of the Committee on _____, I call up the bill (H.R. _____)" etc. Depending on whether the bill is from the House or Union Calendar, the Speaker replies: "This bill is on the House Calendar. The clerk will report the bill"; or he states: "This bill is on the Union Calendar, and under the rule the House automatically resolves itself into the Committee of the Whole House on the state of the Union, with the gentleman

---

[277] Rule XXIV, clause 7; Cannon, VII, 945. If the previous question on a bill has been reached, it becomes unfinished business of the House (Cannon, VII, 895, 967-969; Cannon, VIII, 2680). All pending business not House unfinished business must go over to the next Wednesday (Cannon, VII, 965).

[278] Cannon, VII, 947. The House may not, by an extension of a general rule grant priority to bills on the House Calendar over those on the Union Calendar (Cannon, VII, 938).

[279] Cannon, VII, 930.

[280] This is quite a common practice; it simplifies procedure and saves time.

[281] See Cannon, VII, 939-942, 966.

[282] If the House disapproves of a report made by the Committee of the Whole, it will resolve itself back into the Committee for reconsideration (Cannon, VII, 943, 951); the bill is open to further amendments and the motion to strike out the enacting clause is in order (Cannon, VIII, 2633-2640).

from _____, Mr. _____, in the chair." General debate is limited to two hours;[284] time allotted may not be extended in Committee even by unanimous consent.[285] The purpose of this procedure is to expedite legislation.

The maximum of two hours of debate to be equally divided does not apply to bills on the House Calendar; the time does not have to be as much as two hours nor does it have to be equally divided. Debate on bills on the House calendar is governed "by the same rules as prevail on any other day." A person calling up a bill from the House Calendar is recognized for one hour, but he may move the previous question after less than a minute discussion;[286] the same is true with any measures considered in the House as if in the Committee of the Whole. Bills considered in Committee of the Whole should be debated, pro and con, each side consuming one hour; if no Member of the committee claims the time in opposition, the chair may use his discretion in granting time. Generally, if no person claims the time in opposition, the bill is immediately read for amendment at conclusion of the first hour, or even before.[287] The time allowed for general debate can be increased beyond two hours under unanimous consent agreement.

Debate: In recognizing for debate, as in all debate in the House, the Speaker must give preference first to Members reporting the bill, and secondly to the members of the committee responsible for it. If no member of the said committee opposes the bill any Member may be recognized in opposition.[288] With the above exceptions, the general rules for debate apply.

Reading Bills for Amendments: In the Committee of the Whole the bill is read under the five-minute rule for amendments (see section on reading for amendments); the same is true when in the "House as in the Committee of the Whole"; when a person offers an amendment to a bill in the House, he is recognized for an hour. Bills or resolutions are read in Committee of the Whole by sections for amendments; as soon as each section is read, committee amendments thereto are considered, followed by individual amendments. In the House a bill is read in full, without reference

---

[283] Business is not in order except when authorized by the committee in charge. The committee may authorize any Member to call up a measure (Hinds, IV, 3127-3128) ; authority having been granted one Member, another may not be recognized if objection is heard (Cannon, VII, 928-929).

[284] *House Manual*, 80-1, sec. 897; Cannon, VII, 959.

[285] Cannon, VII, 959.

[286] Cannon, VII, 955-957.

[287] Cannon, VII, 960-962.

[288] Cannon, VII, 958.

to sections or paragraphs. When the amending process in the House is over, the previous question for passage of the measure is moved. In the Committee of the Whole, the committee rises and reports the bill back to the House with recommendation; if no amendments are offered in the House, the bill is immediately passed or defeated.

Precedence of Business: If the business is not dispensed with before Wednesday, the business defined by this rule is of high privilege. The call of committees will take precedence over a request for a unanimous consent.[289] "The Speaker is constrained to recognize on Wednesday any Member proposing a motion to dispense with proceedings in order on that day," [290] and privileged questions are not in order.[291] On exceptional occasions veto messages have been considered as a constitutional mandate superseding the business in order under the rules.[292] Questions of privilege,[293] reference of reports to proper calendars,[294] and moving the previous question [295] are in order.

On Calendar Wednesdays when there is no business to consider as defined by the rule the House proceeds with other business; a motion to dispense with the regular business for the day is not even necessary.[296] Further, on any occasion, when the call of committees is completed before the close of the day, business otherwise in order will be considered.

Unfinished Business: Unfinished business from Calendar Wednesdays goes over until a following like day if the previous question has not been reached. If the previous question has been

---

[289] Cannon, VII, 882-887.

[290] Cannon, VII, 915. "While a bill may be reported for printing on Wednesday, the right to call up for immediate consideration is not thereby implied." (Cannon, VII, 907).

[291] Business which has been held not to be in order: consideration of motion to reconsider (Cannon, VII, 905), privileged bills (Cannon, VII, 932-934), contested election cases (Cannon, VII, 903), motions for recess (*House Manual*, 80-1, section 897), conference reports (Cannon, VII, 901), "motions to discharge a committee from consideration of a privileged resolution of inquiry" (Cannon, VII, 896-897), resolutions of inquiry (Cannon, VII, 898), propositions relating to impeachment (Cannon, VII, 902), motions to change reference of bills to other committees (Cannon, VII, 883-884), motion to go into Committee of the Whole to consider revenue or appropriation bills (Cannon, VII, 904), Senate bills which are privileged because of similarity to some bill already on the House Calendar (Cannon, VII, 906), measures coming over from Tuesday on which the previous question has been moved (Cannon, VII, 890-894), and motions of unanimous consent not concerned with Calendar Wednesday (Cannon, VII, 882-888).

[292] Cannon, VII, 912.

[293] Cannon, VII, 908-911.

[294] Hinds, III, 2614-2615.

[295] Cannon, VII, 955-957.

[296] Cannon, VII, 918-920.

ordered, the issue comes up the next legislative day as unfinished business of the House, but the question of consideration can be raised.[297]

This rule does not apply to the proceedings of the last two weeks of a session, and if all the committees are not called during one session the call begins the next session where it was last left off. With a new Congress everything begins *de novo*.

Suspension of the Rules: *Nature of Business and Recognition by Speaker*: Suspension of Rules procedure is in order on two Mondays each month. The business is not of any particular classification nor does it arise from any one Calendar. The determination of what issues shall be entertained is placed at the discretion of the Speaker. He has absolute power of recognition;[298] he may entertain or refuse to entertain a motion to suspend the rules. The rule prescribes, however, that preference shall be given to individuals to make motions in their own behalf on the first Mondays and to the committees on the third ones. These motions may not be divided, amended, postponed, tabled, reconsidered, or recommitted.

Procedure under the Rule: On the first and third Mondays,[299] immediately after disposition of the business on the Consent Calendar,[300] it is in order for a Member to address the chair: [301] "Mr. Speaker, I move to suspend the rules and pass the bill, H.R. _____ . . ." [302] On these days this motion is highly privileged, but it yields to certain motions, as special orders,[303] questions of privilege, motions to adjourn, and the like.

When a bill is called up under this procedure, if no question of second is raised, the bill will not be debated, but the vote will be taken immediately. If a two-thirds vote is forthcoming, the rules are suspended and the bill is passed at the same time. If, after the bill is read,[304] someone opposes or demands a second on the bill, a vote by tellers is taken.[305] A yea and nay vote may not be demanded on the second, but if the teller vote discloses

---

[297] Cannon, VIII, 2447.

[298] Hinds, V, 6790-6862; Cannon, VIII, 3397-3426.

[299] The motion is in order at any other time should a special rule to that effect be adopted by the House, and motions are in order any time on the last six days of a session (Cannon, VIII, 3393, 3399; see H.Res. 410 of the Seventy-third Congress).

[300] While the rule does not stipulate this, the practice reveals it.

[301] Customarily, agreements as to whom the Speaker will recognize are reached before the day's session begins.

[302] For all types of forms concerned with Suspension of Rules see: Cannon, *Cannon's Procedure in the House of Representatives*, p. 398.

[303] See *Ibid.*, p. 400; Hinds, V, 5743-5746, 6825-6839.

lack of a quorum, an automatic call of the House with a yea and nay vote is in order. A negative vote defeats the consideration of the measure; if the vote is in the affirmative by a bare majority or better, the measure will be debated forty minutes,[306] twenty minutes by each side, after which another vote is ordered. The Representative demanding the second is entitled to recognition against the motion to suspend, and debate is equally divided between him and the mover, each of whom may yield time. There will be no debate unless a second is ordered.[307] If a two-thirds vote is forthcoming, after the consideration of the measure is finished, the bill is passed and the rules are suspended at the same time. If the vote does not show a 2/3 majority in favor of the proposition, the motion to suspend fails [308] and the bill is defeated. The object of the stipulation permitting one to demand a second before the debate begins, is to save time on measures which have no chance of passing under this procedure.[309]

Bills not Amendable: The House may, as it wills under unanimous consent procedure, allow more time for debate if the bill under consideration seems to justify the extension. Speaker Longworth once said: "Suspension of the rules is not a normal legislative procedure. In a sense it is a trifle unfair in that it limits debate and does not permit the right of amendment. But there are times when suspension of the rules is vitally necessary to dispatch public business, and the Chair must use his discretion, when he believes it is in the interest of a large majority of the House." [309a] All measures must be either accepted or rejected *in toto* after forty minutes of debate. On one occasion during the second session of the Seventy-third Congress a bill came up appropriating $950,-000,000 for relief under the suspension of the rules. There was an attempt to increase the time for the debate. Mr. Cochran of Missouri objected to the increase. The colloquy was as follows:

Mr. BOILEAU. Reserving the right to object, I would ask the gentleman from Texas whether there will be opportunity to amend this bill?

[304] Cannon, VIII, 3413.
[305] *House Manual*, 80-1, sec. 906; see Cannon, VIII, 3109, 3416; Hinds, V, 6802-6804.
[306] Hinds, V, 5405, 6823-24; *House Manual*, 80-1, sec. 907. If the previous question is ordered on a measure before any debate, it is then in order to debate the previous question forty minutes.
[307] Hinds, V, 6799.
[308] See *House Manual*, 80-1, sections 902-903; Hinds, V, 6797.
[309] This count is made by tellers, and the constitutional demand for yeas and nays does not exist (Hinds, V, 6032-6036). If a quorum is absent, a roll call is taken (Hinds, IV, 3053-3055).
[309a] *Cannon's Procedure in the House of Representatives*, p. 398.

Mr. BLANTON. No.

Mr. BUCHANAN. Suspension of the rules is asked for and amendments will not be in order.

Continuing the discussion, one Member inquired why the measure should be debated at all if it could not be amended.[310] Mr. Cannon said: "The motion to suspend the rules is not subject to amendment. . . . Amendments are incorporated and read as a part of the original bill, and the matter as read is the proposition before the House. If amendment is desired after the reading, the remedy is to withdraw and reoffer to be again read as modified."

Use of the Rule: The Suspension of the Rules has become less important with the increased importance of special rules reported by the Rules Committee. By adopting a special rule which requires only a majority vote, the House may accomplish the same end that it would realize by suspending the rules, which requires a two-thirds vote, and the party in power doesn't often have a sufficient majority to muster a two-thirds vote.

Unfinished Business: A motion to suspend the rules on which a second has been ordered, remaining undisposed of at adjournment, recurs as unfinished business on the next day when such business is again in order, according to Mr. Cannon. If the second fails it is not unfinished business.

District of Columbia Day: *Nature of Business and Consideration:* "The second and fourth Mondays in each month, after the disposition of motions to discharge committees and after the disposal of such business on the Speaker's table as requires reference only, shall, when claimed by the Committee on the District of Columbia, be set apart for the consideration of such business as may be presented by said committee." [311] This rule applies to both revenue and legislative measures.[312] Bills considered in the House proper are called up by the authorized Member and reported to the House by the clerk. Debate and amendments are then in order under the general rules, unless some agreement to to contrary is reached. As soon as time for debate has been consumed, it is in order for the person in charge to move the previous question on the bill to final passage. If a "money" measure is

[310] C.R., 73-2, p. 1939.

[311] *House Manual*, 80-1, section 899; Cannon, VII, 872. The first rule giving a fixed day for the District of Columbia business was adopted in 1870. In 1890 the rule was amended. The rule was again amended December 8, 1931.

[312] Rule XXIV, clause 8; see Cannon, VII, 873; Hinds, IV, 3311. The District of Columbia Committee must have made the reports to the House.

called up, the House resolves itself into the Committee of the Whole for general debate, after which the bill is read for amendments under the five-minute rule.

Question of Consideration: On this day there can be no "question of consideration" raised against the District business as such; however, a question against the consideration of a particular measure is in order.[313] The District of Columbia Committee is privileged to call up its bills in the order it sees fit, provided they have already been reported.[314]

Debate: General debate in the Committee of the Whole on this business is fixed by the House for each measure, following which it is read under the five-minute rule for amendments. In the House a Member recognized to speak on any measure is recognized for one hour.[315] Of course the time for any debate may be limited or extended by agreement, usually reached under unanimous consent. If the time is fixed, the Members in charge yield time, and the procedure is that of regular debate.

Precedence of Business: On this day the measures reported by the District of Columbia Committee are granted the right-of-way for consideration unless the House acts to dispense with District of Columbia business. It has been held, nevertheless, that a motion to go into Committee of the Whole for the consideration of a general appropriation bill [316] or a motion for the House to go into the Committee to consider a measure made in order by a special rule are of equal privilege with one to go into the Committee to consider a District of Columbia bill. Recognition is at the discretion of the chair.[317]

Unfinished Business: Any business unfinished at the close of the day is not in order on the next legislative day; it must go over until the next District of Columbia day.[318] If the previous question on a bill to final passage has been decided in the affirmative, it becomes the unfinished business of the House, and it is in order on the next legislative day.

[313] Hinds, IV, 3308, 3309.
[314] Hinds, IV, 3311.
[315] Cannon, VII, 874.
[316] C.R., 67-2, p. 1585.
[317] Cannon, VII, 877-878.
[318] Cannon, VII, 879.

IV. Precedence of Other Classes of Legislation

Explanation: The preceding section describes the order of business on specific days of each month. This one is concerned with the order in which classes of business arise from day to day, excluding the specific legislative days of each month, because of their privileged status. The order in which these classes of business are considered are practically according to the precedence of business most frequently recognized, as enumerated by Mr. Cannon in his work on *Procedure in the House of Representatives.*

Business Under Unanimous Consent: *Procedure:* Unanimous consent procedure is used for many purposes, such as leave to print, to vacate actions already taken by the House, to make special orders, to change the regular order of business as prescribed by the rules, to bring a bill before the House for immediate action, and the like. Briefly, the adoption of a unanimous consent request obligates the House to take actions in accordance with the directions contained in that agreement. The House finds it quite expedient to proceed by unanimous consent. It enables the House to take rapidly many actions which otherwise would consume much of its time, and it enables the membership to dispose of bills which otherwise would not be in order. The body has adopted the practice of letting personal explanations be made only by unanimous consent, and of requiring that the remarks be confined to the subject.[319] The majority floor leader uses this method of presenting his requests to the House. Finally, motions to vacate or undo what has already been done can only be reached by unanimous consent.[320]

Privileged Status: Matters presented to the House under this procedure are highly privileged and remain the unfinished business until disposed of if the request so implies or so stipulates.[321] Proceedings admitted under unanimous consent may supersede those provided for by a special rule.[322]

[319] Hinds, V, 5064.
[320] Cannon, VI, 711.
[321] Cannon, VII, 770.
[322] Cannon, VII, 771. The following is an example of a special order found printed on the *Daily Calendars of the House* for Thursday, February 22, 1934: "On motion of Mr. Byrns, by unanimous consent, ORDERED; That on Thursday, February 22, 1934, after the reading of the Journal and completion of business on the Speaker's table, Mr. Smith of Virginia be permitted to read George Washington's *Farewell Address* (agreed to February 21, 1934)." See C.R., 73-2, p. 3009 for adoption of the order by the House.

Motions: "Unanimous consent requests should not be coupled." They should be offered separately so that one will not be made dependent on the granting of another.[323] It is regular order, however, to include in one request the right to dispose of several bills, and any restrictions on that procedure depend entirely on custom.

Scope of Motions: Consideration of legislation under unanimous consent is a very expeditious and all-inclusive method of legislating provided the Speaker will entertain and Members will grant unanimous consent requests. A Representative is free at almost any time that another Member does not have the floor to address the chair and ask: "Mr. Speaker, I ask unanimous consent for the present consideration of the bill H.R. ————" etc.; it is the customary practice for everyone to consult the Speaker and inform the majority and minority floor leaders of his intentions prior to making any significant unanimous consent request. It is not considered good parliamentary ethics in the House for individuals to resort to this type of procedure except for emergency and formal matters.[324]

Suspends Rules: The granting of a unanimous consent for the consideration of a particular bill frees it from the normal rules of the House. For example: a Member might ask for the consideration of a bill from the Union Calendar under this procedure and then supplement the request by asking that the bill be considered in the House as in the Committee of the Whole.

Recognition and Debate: The Speaker's refusal to entertain any unanimous consent motion is his method of objecting to the request, but if the request is entertained and no objection is forthcoming, it is granted. While the Member calling up a bill in the House under unanimous consent is entitled to control at least one hour of debate on that measure, he does not generally consume much time due to the lack of any controversy. Had there been much opposition to the bill the unanimous consent request would never have been granted in the first place.

Consideration of Vetoed Bills: Veto messages are offsprings of bills which have already been passed by both the House and Senate but rejected by the President. Under constitutional mandate, a message accompanying a vetoed bill is sent back to the house in which the bill originated, and in the absence of further

[323] Cannon, VI, 709.
[324] Cannon, VII, 980-983.

action on the message, the measure is dead. In effect, if a veto is not overridden by a two-thirds vote of both houses, the original efforts of the legislature on the bill are lost. A vetoed bill if acted on further is considered first in the house of origin.

Reception of Message: The reception of such a message is always in order and an examination thereof for passage over the President's opposition is highly privileged.[325] Though this deference is determined by the rules of the House, it is a constitutional mandate. A veto message supersedes a special order;[326] it takes preference over a motion to suspend the rules;[327] the question of consideration may not be raised against it;[328] and generally it may not be superseded by other privileged matters.[329] Customarily, a veto message is heard the same day it is received, but the Speaker may use his own discretion as to what time of the day.[330] Generally, the House accepts each message, enters it in the *Journal*, and if further action is to be taken proceeds to its immediate consideration. A message not immediately disposed of is placed on the Speaker's table for reference to committee for further study. The committee is free to report the same bill again, rewrite the bill in accordance with the President's veto and report it, or let it die without further action.

Dispositon of Veto Message: When the Speaker calls the attention of the House to a veto message, one of three motions is in order, namely: to lay on the table, postpone to a day certain, or refer to a committee; and preference is given in the order listed.[331] If no one of these motions is offered the House proceeds to dispose finally of the message by overriding or sustaining the veto.

A message is considered under the hour rule; the previous question may be ordered; but if no debate has occurred, forty minutes of debate confined to that motion will be allowed. If a few minutes of debate have expired and the previous question is moved and adopted, any further discussion is cut off. Debate is in order on any one of the motions in order, but it must be confined to the subject.[332] The vote to override a President's veto requires a

[325] Cannon, VII, 1096.
[326] Hinds, III, 2554.
[327] Hinds, III, 2553.
[328] Hinds, V, 4969-4970.
[329] Hinds, III, 2552.
[330] Cannon, VII, 1100.
[331] Cannon, VII, 1100, 1114; Hinds, IV, 3542-3550.
[332] See Cannon, VIII, 2740.

two-thirds majority of those present [333] according to a yea and nay vote,[334] and at least a quorum must be present.

Conference Committees and Conference Reports: *To Expedite Legislation:* Conference reports are offspring of bills or resolutions which have been passed in different forms by both houses. Their *raison d'etre* arises out of the necessity for reaching some kind of an agreement over differences between the two bodies. The plan is not a development to introduce new legislation; to the contrary, it is a device to put on the statute books that which is already an act as far as Congress is concerned, if certain differences between the two houses over proposed legislation can be ironed out. If a complete compromise is impossible any bill sent to conference is lost. While the consideration of conference reports is not a method of getting up original legislation many bills on which much time and effort have been spent would be lost if there were no conference committees. An expeditious hearing of conference reports dispatches legislation.

It would not be feasible to permit bills to go from one house to another in the hope that sometime in the future the two bodies would accidentally strike upon an accord. By the use of conferences a few Members of each house can come together and very effectively reach compromises over any differences on a proposed bill between the two houses.

History of Conferences: This idea of utilizing conferences to settle disagreements was no innovation on the part of the American Congress in 1789. England had employed them very much earlier. One is recorded in the English *Journal* in 1554.[335] With the loss of power of the House of Lords during the last century, however, they have been eliminated in England since need for them no longer exists.[336]

In this country, the early colonial legislatures, following the example set by England, used conferences long before the adoption of the Constitution.[337] The benefits derived from the use of them were rather significant, sufficient to cause the first Congress to follow the same practice. Since 1789 a gradual development of this institution has been experienced in the absence of any elaborate rule or rules to define its functions and characteristics. A

---

[333] A majority must be present to carry on business, if the question is raised.
[334] Cannon, VII, 1110 ; Hinds, IV, 2726, 3520.
[335] McCown, *The Congressional Conference Committees*, p. 24.
[336] *Ibid.*, pp. 23-33.
[337] The practice was not general; see *Ibid.*, pp. 33-38.

very brief resolution sanctioning the institution was adopted in the very first Congress. It reads:

RESOLVED, That in every case of an amendment to a bill agreed to in one House and dissented to in the other, if either House shall request a conference, and appoint a committee for that purpose, and the other house shall also appoint a committee to confer, such committee shall, at a convenient time, to be agreed on by their chairman, meet in the conference chamber, and state to each other verbally, or in writing, as either shall choose, the reason of their respective houses for and against the amendment and confer freely thereon.[338]

One author commenting on the situation prior to 1880 said:

As had been said before, the Conference Committee System had evolved almost without any definite rules governing it in either house. The first joint rule providing for conference committees in cases of disagreement between the two houses had been followed by a number of others, none of them relating specifically to conferences but dealing largely with the treatment of bills. All of these joint rules were allowed to lapse in 1876, and outside the general parliamentary law there were for a time no rules in House or Senate governing either the conference committee or any of the relations between the two houses. Perhaps this is part of the reason why, in 1880, the House passed its first definite rule in regard to conferences.[339]

First Rule: In 1880 the House adopted its first definite rule on conferences. The rule is as follows:

1a. The presentation of reports of committees of conference shall always be in order, except when the *Journal* is being read, while the roll is being called, or the House is dividing on any proposition.

Since 1880 the rule has been amended to include the following:

1½a. After House conferees on any bill or resolution in conference between the House and Senate shall have been appointed for twenty calendar days and shall have failed to make a report, it is hereby declared to be a motion of the highest privilege to move to discharge said House conferees and to appoint new conferees, or to instruct said House conferees; and, further, during the last six days of any session of Congress, it shall be a privileged motion to move to discharge, appoint, or instruct House conferees after House conferees shall have been appointed thirty-six hours without having made a report. 1b. And there shall accompany every such report a detailed statement sufficiently explicit to inform the House what effect such amendments or propositions will have upon the measures to which they relate. 2. It shall not be in order to consider the report of a committee of conference until such report and the accompanying statement shall have been printed in the *Record* except on either of the six days preceding the end of a session.

338 *Ibid.*, p. 39.
339 *Ibid.*, p. 100.

This above rule is the present form of Rule XXVIII, and other rules affecting conferences are few, but practice has defined the system very clearly.

Secret Sessions: What goes on in the conference is little known outside of Congress. Conference meetings are not open to the public, the press, or the general membership of the two houses of Congress, and the proceedings of the conferences are not published. The chairman or some Member often holds press conferences after meetings of the conferences to tell what was accomplished. At any rate, only a prepared formal report on what took place is made available to the public. The meetings are usually held in the Senate wing of the Capitol.

Voting Procedure: The first named Senate manager is frequently referred to as the chairman of the conference committee, but the representatives of each house act and vote separately on all issues. The majority of each group in conference determine the attitude or position for its house and at least a majority of each house must sign the report. The minority may file a report with their signatures.[340]

Bills in Conference: This institution today is very significant to the legislative branch. A large proportion of all major bills passed by both houses and cleared for the President are ultimately considered in conference. A study of the House calendars will show this.

Customs Define Procedure: Customs and precedents define the system.[341] When a conference shall be called, the extent of its jurisdiction, who the conferees are to be and their rank, how a conference shall be conducted, and when it shall be terminated are almost completely determined by practices.

Agree or Disagree to Amendments: The motion to ask for a conference is unlike and distinct from a motion to agree to or disagree with amendments of the other body to a bill,[342] and a motion to agree or disagree takes precedence over a motion to send to conference.[343] For example: The House, having passed one of its bills, (H.R.——), sends the measure to the Senate. If that body approves the same with amendments, it may return the bill to

[340] Hinds, V, 6497-6498; Cannon, VIII, 3295; *Cannon's Procedure in the House of Representatives,* pp. 126-130.
[341] Cannon, VIII, 3209-3218; Hinds, V, 6254-6325.
[342] Hinds, V, 6268.
[343] Hinds, V, 6270; Cannon, VIII, 3193-3194. The general statement, "agree to or disagree with," includes the motions: lay on the table, refer, amend, concur, and disagree.

the House where it will be placed on the Speaker's table. When a Member of the House (usually the person in charge of the bill) calls it up for immediate disposition, the following motions are in order: (a) lay on the table, (b) refer, (c) amend, (d) agree, (e) disagree, or (f) send to conference. They take precedence in the order listed,[344] and any one of them may be offered by addressing the chair, for example, "Mr. Speaker, I desire to offer a preferential motion. I move to (recede and) concur in the amendments of the Senate." The motion having been entertained, the House acts on it as it sees fit. If the amendments are not accepted or the bill is not left to die, any differences will be sent to conference. For the details as to the dispostion of such business on the Speaker's table see the section on: "Disposition of Business on the Speaker's Table," pp. 289-293.

"Ask for Conference:" If no one makes one of the preferential motions, customarily the Member in charge of the bill makes one of two motions, namely: recede and concur in the Senate amendments, or "Mr. Speaker, I ask unanimous consent to take from the Speaker's table the bill H.R. ——, etc., with the Senate amendments thereto, disagree to the Senate amendments, and ask for a conference with the Senate . . ." Note that this procedure is under unanimous consent.[345]

According to practices, a conference is requested when a state of disagreement has been reached, i.e., the first house passes the bill and messages it to the other; the latter passes the bill with amendments, and sends it back to the house of origin, with the amendments.[346] The first house to pass the bill refuses to accept the amendments (disagreeing to them) and asks for a conference. It is not infrequent in recent practice for the second house passing the bill to request a conference without sending the bill back to the first to see if the amendments will be accepted. This is nearly always done in the case of general appropriation bills. To illustrate: The House passes one of its bills or resolutions and sends it to the Senate; the latter passes the same with amendments and insists upon them;[347] at this point, the Senate requests a conference without waiting to send the measure back to the House for

---

[344] Hinds, V, 6164-6172, 5575, 6219-6323; Cannon, VIII, 3200, 3203, 3179, 3201, 3213.

[345] See pp. 290-292. This is the procedure if the issue would regularly be heard in the Committee of the Whole.

[346] Cannon, VIII, 3213; see also pp. 388-391.

[347] See Cannon, VIII, 3216.

its disagreement thereto.[348] The request is then forwarded to the House as a message and placed on the Speaker's table. The message, if the Speaker does not act on his own, is disposed of when some Member addresses the chair: "Mr. Speaker, I ask unanimous consent to take from the Speaker's table the bill H.R. ——, with Senate amendment thereto, disagree to the Senate amendment and agree to the conference requested by the Senate."

Unanimous Consent Procedure: Bills with Senate amendments requiring consideration in the Committee of the Whole can be taken from the Speaker's table and sent to conference by unanimous consent [349] or by a special rule to that effect, reported by the Rules Committee; the latter procedure requires only a majority vote. A rule takes the following form: "RESOLVED, That immediately upon the adoption of this resolution the bill H.R. —— with Senate amendments thereto be, and the same is hereby, taken from the Speaker's table; that the Senate amendments be, and they are hereby, disagreed to by the House; that the conference requested by the Senate on the disagreeing votes of the two Houses on the said bill be, and hereby is, agreed to by the House; and that the Speaker shall immediately appoint conferees without intervening motion." [350]

Chamber Asking Conference: In any instance and under any condition as to how and when a bill is sent to conference, the body making the request for the conference must be in possession of the papers [351] concerning the bill, immediately after which they are forwarded to the other house. The house agreeing to the conference sends the papers back to the house asking for the conference, the managers of which take them to the conference chamber. If the conferees fail to make a report within twenty calendar days, it is a matter of high privilege for any Member in the House to move to discharge its conferees from further consideration of the measure assigned them and appoint new ones. ". . . During the last six days of any session of Congress, it shall be a privileged motion to move to discharge . . . conferees after House conferees

[348] Cannon, VIII, 3214-3217.
[349] See pp. 289-293, "Disposition of Business on the Speaker's Table."
[350] See H.Res. 233 of the 76th Congress.
[351] See Hinds, V, 6518-6522. The papers are composed of the "original engrossed copy of the bill attested by the Clerk of the House or the Secretary of the Senate, the engrossed amendments, any special acts concurring in amendments with amendments, and the messages transmitting them between the two Houses, all similarly attested, and later the conference report signed by the managers. The statement is signed by the House conferees only." (*Cannon's Procedure in the House of Representatives*, p. 117).

shall have been appointed thirty-six hours without having made a report." [352]

After a successful conference has been held the papers change hands; the managers of the house agreeing to the conference receive them and present them to their body, which considers the conference report first.[353] Neither body may call up a report for consideration until the conferees have formally reported the matter back. A majority of the conferees of each house must have signed the report;[354] the report must have been accompanied by the papers [355] and the statement;[356] and they must have been written in duplicate.[357]

Conference Report: Every report must be accompanied by a "detailed statement sufficiently explicit to inform the House what effect" the adoption of it will have upon the bill to which it is related,[358] and in the House the report is required to be printed in the *Record* one day before it may be considered,[359] except by unanimous consent.

Consideration of Report: A Representative presents the matter to the House by addressing the chair as follows: "Mr. Speaker, I call up the conference report on the bill H.R. ——, and ask

[352] Rule XXVIII, clause 1½a.

[353] "When a conference occurs before a vote of disagreement, the managers of the House asking the conference retain the papers and bring them back to their House." (Hinds, V, 6254). ". . . In exceptional cases when managers on the part of the House agreeing to conference have surrendered the papers, inadvertently or otherwise, the report has been first received by the other House." (Cannon, VIII, 3330).

[354] Hinds, V, 6497-6498; Cannon, VIII, 3295.

[355] See Hinds, V, 6518-6522.

[356] See Hinds, V, 6504, 6514-6515. The statement is an explanation of decisions by the conferees.

[357] In practice triplicates are prepared (Cannon, VIII, 3296). The Senate managers sign first the Senate copy and the House managers sign first the House copy (Hinds, V, 6426, 6499, 6500-6504).

[358] Rule XXVIII, clause 1 b.

[359] Rule XXVIII, clause 2. *House Manual,* 80-1, section 974. "The general form of a report of a committee of conference is as follows:
"The committee of conference on the disagreeing votes of the two Houses on the amendments of the Senate to the bill (H.R. 10) 'making appropriations,' etc., having met, after full and free conference, have agreed to recommend and do recommend to their respective Houses as follows:
"That the Senate recede from its amendment numbered ——.
"That the House recede from its disagreement to the amendment of the Senate numbered —— and agree to the same.
"That the House recede from its disagreement to the amendment of the Senate numbered —— and agree to the same with an amendment as follows: —— etc., and the Senate agree to the same.
"That the House recede from its amendment to the amendment of the Senate numbered ——.

Managers on the part of the House.

Managers on the part of the Senate."

unanimous consent that the statement be read in lieu of the report."
The reports are called up directly from the table and they take
precedence over other business by virtue of their position.[360]

Procedure on Adoption of Report: The first business confronting the House when a conference report is called up is to agree,
disagree, or recommit it. The reports may not be tabled, referred
to a committee, or amended except by concurrent resolution.[361]
If the report is rejected, it may or may not go back to conference;
if it does not, the bill is dead.

Debate: The reports in the House are debated under the hour
rule, but the previous question may be moved at any time after
the discussion begins. The Member in charge has prior recognition
and may not be taken from his feet even by a preferential
motion.[362]

Amendments in Disagreement: Each conference report may or
may not have accompanying it certain of the original amendments in disagreement on which the conferees could not reach a
compromise. If there are such differences remaining, after the
report has been disposed of, the amendments will be called up
for further consideration. For example: The Member in charge
may address the chair: "Mr. Speaker, I move that the House
recede and concur in amendments of the Senate Nos. ———." Or
he may say: "Mr. Speaker, I move that the House further insist
on its disagreement to the Senate amendment." [363] At this stage,

[360] Rule XXVIII, clause 1 a. In practice they are presented at any time considered
opportune by the leaders. See also Hinds, V, 6443-6515; Cannon, VIII, 3291-3297;
House Manual, 80-1, section 909. "Under the language of the rule a conference report
may be presented while a Member is occupying the floor in debate . . . , while a bill
is being read . . . , after the yeas and nays have been ordered . . . , after the
previous question has been demanded or ordered . . . , and during a call of the
House if a quorum be present . . . It even takes precedence of the motion to reconsider . . . and to adjourn . . . , although as soon as the report is presented the
motion to adjourn may be put . . . Also the consideration of a conference report
may be interrupted, even in the midst of the reading of the statement, by the
arrival of the hour previously fixed for a recess . . . While it may not be presented while the House is dividing, it may be presented after a vote by tellers and
pending the question of ordering the yeas and nays . . . It also has precedence of
a report from the Committee on Rules . . . , and has been permitted to intervene
when a special order provides that the House shall consider a certain bill 'until the
same is disposed of' . . . Of course, a question of privilege which relates to the
integrity of the House as an agency for action may not be required to yield precedence to a matter entitled to priority merely by the rules relating to the order of
business . . .
     "While the rule provides that the managers of the House asking a conference shall
leave the papers with the managers of the other . . . , if the managers on the part
of the House agreeing to a conference surrender the papers to the House asking
the conference, the report may be received first by the House asking the conference . . . The conferees are limited to the differences between the two Houses and
can not insert in their report new matter not germane thereto, but where an
amendment strikes out all after the enacting clause of a bill, the conferees have the
entire subject before them."
[361] See Hinds, V, 6536, 6558; Cannon, VIII, 3306-3308.
[362] Cannon, VIII, 3259.

the House membership may recede from its former position and concur in that of the Senate, concur with an amendment, or it may insist upon further disagreement to the said amendment and send it back to conference for further action thereon. This procedure might continue indefinitely, until the bill is lost or passed.

Appointment of Conferees: The Speaker appoints the Members of the House to serve on conference committees [364] in accordance with a rule which was first adopted in 1890.[365] The Vice President or President pro tempore appoints Senators thereto. The Presiding Officers are supposed to appoint persons who will voice the opinions of their respective houses. The number of Representatives appointed is determined by the Speaker,[366] but by precedent the number is three, five, seven, or nine.[367] The Senate determines the number of Senators to be appointed. The number appointed by one house does not determine the number to be appointed by the other. One house may have three members and the other nine.[368]

Conferees: The personnel of these committees generally consists of the chairman, the ranking members of the Majority and Minority of the committee in charge of the particular bill, with other members from the same committee if the number chosen is greater. The same general rule applies to a subcommittee when a bill is handed by a subcommittee of the standing committee. While the tradition of seniority has a profound effect upon the personnel of the committee, it does not always operate. These members should be chosen to voice the opinion of the House regardless of seniority. On July 17, 1935, Mr. Byrns said:

In appointing the conferees, the Chair is always willing to accept the suggestions of the chairman of the committee which has charge of the bill, assuming that the Members who are appointed will stand for the House measure because they represent the House in conference. The Chair would not assume that gentleman would accept a position as a conferee and not stand for what the House wants.[369]

The rank of the members of a conference committee is fixed by the order in which they are appointed; the Senator first named

---

[363] Two or more amendments can be acted on *en bloc* under unanimous consent.
[364] See Hinds, V, 6326-6378; Cannon, VIII, 3219-3229. Members may decline to serve.
[365] Cannon, VIII, 2192.
[366] Cannon, VIII, 3219-3221.
[367] Cannon ,VIII, 3221; Hinds, V, 6336, 6331-6333. There have been one or two exceptions.
[368] Cannon, VIII, 3221.
[369] *Cannon's Procedure in the House of Representatives*, p. 122.

usually presides as chairman. Both parties are represented, the majority party having the major representation.

Instructing Conferees: The House on certain occasions has followed the policy of instructing its conferees [370] as to the position they are to take. The instruction must be given before the managers are appointed [371] and the motions may be debated and amended, if germane.[372] Conferees having been instructed, further motions to that effect are not in order,[373] and whether instructed or not, they may disregard all instructions and the report is not subject to a point of order unless matters extraneous to the differences are included.[374] In any instance, the managers are confined to the disagreement;[375] the rules deprive the conferees of the power to alter legislation agreed to by both houses, and they may not add new matters.[376]

Legislation by Conferees: Under present practices one house may pass a substitute bill for the measure passed by the other by striking out all after the enacting clause and substituting its language for that approved by the other house, and then both houses send the two bills to a conference committee which is permitted in turn to write a third bill. This procedure permits the conferees to write the legislation since conference reports are "high privilege," and both houses must accept or reject them *in toto.*

Legislating: This legislative instrument sometimes aids the leaders of the majority party in the two houses to get proposed legislation in the form they want it before final enactment.

Two examples occurred in the first session of the Seventy-sixth Congress. The parity amendment offered to the Agriculture Appropriation bill (H.R. 5269) in that session was defeated in the House by a vote of 191 yeas to 204 nays. In the Senate, an almost identical amendment was added to the bill. The bill was returned to the House and by means of a special rule the whole matter was sent to conference. There the parity amendment was placed in the conference report. Hence, once again the issue came before the House and was adopted by a vote of 180 yeas to 175

[370] Each house can instruct only its managers (Cannon, VIII, 3241).
[371] Cannon, VIII, 3233, also 3231-3251.
[372] Cannon, VIII, 3231, 3240. The Senate on one occasion declined further conference when the House instructed its conferees. For such practices in the Senate see Gilfry, *op. cit.,* 1, pp. 292-302.
[373] Cannon, VIII, 3236.
[374] The matter is not subject to the point of order that it is in violation of instructions (Cannon, VIII, 3247).
[375] See Hinds, V, 6407-6442 ; Cannon, VIII, 3252-3290.
[376] This statement is not absolute if no point of order is made. New legislation has been inserted at times ; C.R., 63-2, p. 1430.

nays. Representative Jenkins of Ohio, when speaking on the subject said: "It is an absolute insult to our parliamentary procedure whereby four or five men, conferees, can vote $225,000,000 on this country when one house of Congress had voted it down before." [377]

The Senate had an identical experience with the Stabilization bill (H.R. 3325) in the same session. The Senate altered the bill as it had passed the House by striking out the section giving the President power to devalue the dollar and adding a clause to set the price of silver by law. In conference the bill was changed back to its original form as passed in the House. Certain groups in the Senate were very much opposed to this action, but the report was adopted by a vote of 43 yeas, 39 nays. "In effect, the Members turned around and accepted what they had already rejected."

For further discussion of conference procedure and adoption of conference reports as utilized in the Senate, see pp. 388-391.

Reports from Committee on Rules: As pointed out in Chapter VI, one of the most important functions of the Rules Committee is to report special rules, which are adopted by a bare majority vote, to grant the right of way for the immediate consideration of a bill or resolution not otherwise privileged. It is always in order to call up reports from the Committee on Rules. Questions of consideration may not be raised. The number of times the House resorts to the use of special rules each year depends upon the needs of the majority party; the number has ranged from 1 to 64 each session. The Rules Committee insists that the application for a special rule must be "based upon either the necessity or the importance of the proposed legislation." [378] If the committee decides that a piece of legislation has sufficient merit, it will report a resolution to the House with recommendation that it be adopted, granting the right of way to some proposed legislation. Any such resolution must be reported to the House one or more days before its consideration; otherwise it requires a 2/3rds vote for adoption.[379a] When presented to the House, it is generally discussed one hour,[379] the time equally

---

[377] *New York Times*, June 23, 1939.

[378] *Copyright Bill, Hearings before the Rules Committee.* H.R. 13452, 70-2, p. 32.

[379] The previous question can be moved at any time after the debate begins. See section 884 of *House Manual;* C.R., 65-3, p. 3142.

[379a] See pp. 118, 124, for recent change in rule.

divided, before adoption or rejection; the proposed legislation considered thereunder is usually approved by the House.

These resolutions are highly privileged and may be considered at almost any time; once adopted, the bill granted preferential consideration therein is called up immediately. The House membership proceeding under such orders ignores the normal procedure to the extent of the stipulations contained in the resolutions. For details and further information on the importance of this kind of procedure see Chapter VI, pp. 111-124.

Special Orders of the House: Special orders of the House authorize the Representatives to ignore the regular rules of procedure and clear the way for transacting some particular business or they may provide that some Representative be given time to address the House.

Adoption: Special orders for the House are made by three different methods: unanimous consent, suspension of the rules, and adoption of a resolution from the Rules Committee.[380]

In its early history the House frequently found it necessary to adopt the use of special orders for the sake of expediency;[381] but it was not until 1883 that the House began the practice of making special orders by adopting special rules reported by the Rules Committee. Today, the special orders are made either by unanimous consent or by the adoption of a special rule reported from the Rules Committee. The practice of adopting special orders under the suspension of the rules has been practically abandoned. All three of these methods for presenting legislation to the House have been considered under their respective headings and will not be reviewed here separately.

Scope and Jurisdiction: A special order in effect suspends the rules of the House [382] and its scope may include many subjects in varying degrees of absolutism. If an occasion arises for a Member to raise a point of order against or a parliamentary inquiry concerning a special order or a rule, the Speaker always interprets the words of it as literally as possible,[383] without regard to practicability;[384] and they are strictly construed even to the abrogation

---

[380] Hinds, IV, 3152-3160; 3165-3166. In the early history special orders were adopted only by the suspension of the rules, which required a two-thirds vote, and by unanimous consent, which requires that no one object (Hinds, IV, 3161-3162); see also pp. 118, 124.
[381] See Hinds, IV, 3155-3159.
[382] A motion to proceed with the regular order is not in order under procedure by special orders (Hinds, IV, 3170-3172).
[383] Cannon, VI, 779.
[384] See Cannon, VI, 789-794.

of regular procedure if there is conflict.[385]   If a special order
states that all intervening motions between the amending process
and the final vote be excluded, the motion to reconsider will be
prohibited; or if it provides that the previous question shall be
ordered without intervening motions except one, i.e., the motion
to recommit, all debate and amendments are excluded.   If the
previous question has been moved on the motion to recommit,
amendments and debate on that motion are prohibited.   A rule to
block intervening motions bars all motions, and an order to consider a bill until disposed of means consideration straight through
to completion, even to the exclusion of normal business provided
for by House rules, unless exceptions to that effect are stipulated
in the order.[386]   If the rule states that a bill shall not have precedence beyond a fixed time, the bill may be completed before that
time, but an order providing that the consideration shall continue
until a definite time, prevents completion until that time expires.[387]
When a special order specifies a definite hour for the consideration of a measure, its privileged status is lost if it is not called up
at that time, but a bill thus in order immediately after the reading
of the *Journal* does not lose its privileged position if it is called
up at a later hour during the same day.[388]   Finally, when an order
declares that a bill must be finished on a specific day and it has
not been completed, the bill is no longer privileged under the
order.[389]

In practice, special orders may be far reaching in their effect
on procedure.   For example: They may waive all points of order
against a bill,[390] exclude dilatory motions to recess, to adjourn,
and to appeal,[391] committees may be given certain days for
consideration of their measures,[392] amendments to a bill may be
specified by enumerating and describing those allowed,[393] an
amendment to replace the original bill may be authorized,[394] the

---

[385] Cannon, VI, 780. If a special order has been made to permit a committee to call
up a certain bill at a certain time, the committee may do so regardless of whether
or not the House is in the Committee of the Whole or if the bill is on the calendar.
A special order has preference over a continuing one (Hinds, IV, 3197-3199).   If two
special orders are in conflict for the consideration of two bills, the first order adopted
has preference (Hinds, IV, 3193-3195).   The House may determine the order by
raising the question of consideration.
[386] Hinds, IV, 3201-3202; Cannon, VII, 763, 773.
[387] See Cannon, VII, 793-794.
[388] Hinds, IV, 3184.
[389] Hinds, IV, 3186-3191.
[390] Cannon, VII, 769.
[391] Hinds, IV, 3210-3213.
[392] Hinds, IV, 3200.
[393] Hinds, IV, 3204-3205; Cannon, VII, 782.
[394] Cannon, VII, 784.   In such a case, the amendment is read and not the bill.

time for debate may be set,[395] and the time for a recess may be fixed.[396]   A motion to rescind a special order is not privileged.[397]

Business on Which the Previous Question Has Been Ordered: The "previous question motion" is a procedure designed to shut off debate and proceed immediately to a vote on disposition of the pending business. The disposition of a bill or resolution on which the previous question to final passage has been moved involves two things: the motion to recommit and the final vote on the passage of the bill,[398] neither of which is debatable. All incidental questions at this stage are put and immediately decided without debate.[399] The business is highly privileged and if not finally disposed of on the day the previous question is moved it comes up the next day immediately after the reading of the *Journal.* It takes precedence over special orders, providing for immediate consideration,[400] disposition of veto messages,[401] business in order on Mondays and Fridays, and the like.[402] It does not take precedence over Calendar Wednesday business. If several measures are called up in this manner, they are taken up in the order in which the previous question on them was moved.[403]

Amendments in Disagreement: Bills of one house with amendments by the other which the first house will not accept are privileged business for immediate consideration, and this stage must obtain before the measure may be sent to conference. Should these amendments be accepted when first called up or before the stage of disagreement obtains, there would be nothing to send to conference. This stage of procedure on a bill is comparable to conference reports, and it is business on the Speaker's table. For further information as to character and the disposition of this type of business, see the section below on "Disposition of Business on the Speaker's Table."

Appropriation and Revenue Measures (Motion to Go into the Committee of the Whole): *Scope of Business:* Appropriation and revenue measures, apparently, present more confusion and trouble for the House membership than any other

[395] Cannon, VII, 765.
[396] Hinds, IV, 2965. Even though a quorum may be absent at the time, the Speaker will declare the House in recess.
[397] Hinds, IV, 3173-3174.
[398] *Cannon's Procedure in the House of Representatives,* pp. 264-268.
[399] *House Manual,* 80-1, sections 782, 811; Hinds, V, 5448-5449.
[400] Hinds, V, 5520.
[401] Cannon, VIII, 2693.
[402] See Hinds, V, 5511, 5512.
[403] Hinds, V, 5518.

class of business. The rules, practices, and decisions made by the chair [404] have been so extensive and so numerous that they involve a real study in themselves. No attempt will be made here to discuss all of the peculiarities of money and revenue bills. Only a resumé will be made, sufficient to give general ideas of their place in the procedure of the House.

Originate in House: The Constitution definitely states that all revenue·measures [405] must arise in the House of Representatives and practice has extended this to appropriation measures. The Senate, however, seldom fails to use its prerogative of amending. It uses this right to such a great extent that on certain occasions a complete Senate bill is substituted for the House bill by way of amendment. Generally speaking, however, both bodies are mindful of the prerogatives of each other. The Senate itself on occasions has refused to consider certain measures which it thought beyond its jurisdiction according to the constitutional mandate.[406] Should the Senate send a bill to the House infringing on the rights of the latter, a point of order can be made against its consideration in that body, and if sustained the bill would be returned to the Senate.[407] The scope is not all-inclusive. On December 18, 1920, the Speaker decided that a measure which raises revenue incidentally does not infringe upon the constitutional prerogatives of the House to originate revenue measures.[408] The House is very jealous of its rights and prerogatives and frequently it discloses this attitude.

Jurisdiction of Ways and Means and Appropriations Committees: The Appropriations Committee has jurisdiction over appropriations,[409] and the Ways and Means Committee· handles all revenue bills.[410] The rule defining revenue bills is rather liberal; the clause: "Revenue measures generally" is broadly construed to cover any bills relating to the revenue.[411] Rule XI specifically gives

[404] When one of these measures is being read for amendments, it is quite common for some Member to raise a point of order on which the Speaker must render a decision.
[405] Article I, section 7 of Constitution.
[406] Cannon, VI, 316, 320.
[407] Cannon, VI, 319.
[408] Cannon, VI, 315.
[409] This committee is not a legislative committee. See Cannon, VII, 2133-2162.
[410] *House Manual,* 80-1, sections 724-725.
[411] *House Manual,* 80-1, section 728. "Raising revenue" is broadly construed. The privilege of the Committee on Ways and Means to report "bills raising revenue" is broadly construed to cover bills relating to the revenue (IV, 3076, 4624, 4625), and if the major feature of the bill relates to revenue other matters in the bill not relating to the revenue but incidental to its main purpose do not destroy the privilege. (Speaker Longworth, Jan. 22, 1927, 69th Congress, 2d. session). A bill providing for a tariff commission (IV, 4626), a declaratory resolution on the subject

the Appropriation Committee jurisdiction over appropriations. The rule reads: "Appropriation of the revenue for the support of the Government." But Rule XXI states: "No bill for the payment or adjudication of any private claim against the Government shall be referred, except by unanimous consent, to any other than the following named committees, namely: To the Committee on Foreign Affairs and to the Committee on the Judiciary." Quoting further: "No bill or joint resolution carrying appropriations shall be reported by any committee not having jurisdiction to report appropriations, nor shall an amendment proposing an appropriation be in order during the consideration of a bill or joint resolution reported by a committee not having that jurisdiction. A question of order on an appropriation in any such bill, joint resolution, or amendment thereto may be raised at any time." [412]

Privileged Status: General appropriation bills and revenue bills share equally [413] a privileged status for consideration.[414] The dates on which measures of this nature are reported and placed on the calendar have no effect upon their relative preference.[415] The rule reads: "At any time after the reading of the *Journal* it shall be in order, by direction of the appropriate committees, to move that the House resolve itself into the Committee of the Whole House on the state of the Union for the purpose of considering bills raising revenue, or general appropriation bills." [416] Note that this gives privileged consideration to general appropriation bills and not to specific appropriation measures. While all appropriation measures are placed on the Union Calendar and first considered in the Committee, they are not all privileged for immediate consideration under the motion defined above.

relating to the revenue (IV, 4626, 4627), a bill extending the time of payment of a debt incurred by Austria for the purchase of flour from the United States (Speaker Gillett, Mar. 29, 1922, p. 4736, 67th Cong., 2d. sess.), a bill amending the Drug Importation Act (Speaker Gillett, May 4, 1922, p. 6332, 67th Cong., 2d sess.), and a bill permitting the admission under parcel post of cigars and cigarettes in smaller packages (Speaker Longworth, Jan. 22, 1927, 69th Cong., 2d sess., p. 2121) were held not to be within the privilege. In order to come within the privilege the bill must show on its face that it relates to the revenue (Speaker Longworth, Jan. 22, 1927, p. 2121, 69th Cong., 2d sess.).

[412] The rule does not apply to private bills since the committees having jurisdiction of bills for the payment of private claims may report bills making appropriations within the limits of their jurisdiction (*House Manual*, 80-1, p. 401).

[413] Hinds, IV, 3075-3076; Cannon, VI, 722.

[414] Hinds, IV, 3073. These bills are privileged until completed (Hinds, IV, 3148). A motion to consider a bill in this classification on the second and fourth Mondays, District of Columbia days, is more privileged than a motion to move that the House resolve itself into the Committee of the Whole to consider a bill reported by the District of Columbia Committee (Cannon, VI, 717-718).

[415] Cannon, VI, 722.

[416] Rule XVI, clause 9.

General Appropriation Bills and Drafting Procedure: With the exception of the general deficiency bills, general appropriation bills provide for expenses of the various departments of the Government for the coming fiscal year.[417] The annual general appropriation bills include one each for the Agriculture Department; District of Columbia; Independent Offices; Interior Department; Legislative Establishment; Navy; State, Justice, Commerce and Judiciary; Treasury and Post Office Departments; Military; War Department Civil Functions; Labor-Federal Security; Government Corporations; and Deficiency.[418] In preparing these bills, the House depends upon each of the respective branches of government for information. Under the Budget Act, each department must submit to Congress a statement of its needs through the Bureau of the Budget.   At its hearings on these bills the Appropriations Committee examines officials of the various divisions of the Government to obtain data as to how much money should be spent. Since the mechanism of government has become exceedingly complicated, the House generally follows the pattern outlined by the Bureau of the Budget; it must be remembered, however, that all final decisions lie with the Congress. It is within the power of the House, in drawing up such bills, to request the President or any executive department of the government to effect a reduction of its estimates or to make any desired reports.[419]

Jurisdiction of Ways and Means versus Appropriations: The Ways and Means Committee may not report bills making appropriations and the Appropriations Committee may not include legislation in a general appropriation bill, except by unanimous consent or under special rules. A point of order can be made against a bill reported by either committee containing such prohibited subject matter.[420]

If a point of order against an appropriation in a legislative bill or legislation in a general appropriation bill, is sustained, the effect is to strike that provision from the bill.

Privileged Business: Bills defined in Rule XVI, clause 9, and authorized by the proper committee may be called up each day for

---

[417] Hinds, IV, 3554-3561. Expenditures for preceding years are not in order on any bill reported by committees other than the Appropriations Committee.
[418] *Cannon's Procedure in the House of Representatives*, p. 22.
[419] See Hinds, IV, 3577.
[420] See Cannon, VII, 2133; *House Manual*, 80-1, section 678. All committees are creatures of the House and therefore can have no authority or jurisdiction not conferred on them by the rules or by special consent of the House itself (see Cannon, VII, 780). The Rule of Germaneness applies, see *Cannon's Procedure in the House of Representatives*, pp. 190-202.

consideration at nearly any time, with certain exceptions, after the reading of the *Journal*.[421] Some of the exceptions: A motion to go into the Committee of the Whole for the consideration of a revenue or general appropriation bill yields to business on Calendar Wednesday,[422] questions of privilege,[423] conference reports,[424] resolutions affecting the organization of the House,[425] Discharge Calendar Business,[426] Consent Calendar business,[427] and the motion to reconsider.[428] When the motion is in order, a Representative, wishing to call up a revenue or general appropriation bill, merely addresses the chair: "Mr. Speaker, I move that the House resolve itself into the Committee of the Whole on the state of the Union for consideration of the bill H.R. ——, and pending that motion, I ask unanimous consent that general debate may continue —— hours, one half the time to be controlled by the gentleman from —— (Mr. ——) and the other half by myself." [429]

General Debate: Bills thus called up are first open to general debate. They are then read for amendment under the five-minute rule during which time points of order may be made against parts of the bills or amendments offered thereto, if they are not germane or do not accord with restrictions on each type bill mentioned subsequently.

Ways and Means without Appropriations Jurisdiction: Revenue measures must not carry appropriations since the Ways and Means Committee has no such jurisdiction. All amendments must be germane to the bill and to the section of the bill to which they are offered.[430] Otherwise the procedure on this type of legislation is as that described in the section on Committee of the Whole House on the state of the Union.

Legislation Prohibited in Appropriation Measures: For the sake of clarity, it should be emphasized here that the following principles do not apply to specific appropriation measures. Rule XXI, section 2 specifically states: "No appropriation shall be reported in any general appropriation bill, or be in order as an amendment

---

[421] See Rule XI, clause 45; Rule XVI, clause 9; Rule XXIV, clause 7; Rule XXVII, clause 4; C.R., 61-3, pp. 965-976; Hinds, IV, 3072-3074.
[422] Cannon, VII, 904.
[423] Cannon, VIII, 3461.
[424] Cannon, VIII, 3291.
[425] Cannon, VI, 3.
[426] Cannon, VII, 1016-1017; Rule XXVII, clause 4.
[427] Cannon, VII, 986-987.
[428] Hinds, IV, 3087.
[429] The motion to go into the Committee of the Whole may not be amended or debated, and the previous question may not be demanded on it (Hinds, IV, 3077-3079); it is either accepted or rejected by direct vote.
[430] See Hinds, V, 5806, 5825.

thereto, for any expenditure not previously authorized by law, unless in continuation of appropriations for such public works and objects as are already in progress. Nor shall any provision in any such bill or amendment thereto changing existing law be in order, except such as being germane to the subject matter of the bill shall retrench expenditures by the reduction of the number and salary of the officers of the United States by the reduction of the compensation of any person paid out of the Treasury of the United States, or by the reduction of amounts of money covered by the bill: *Provided,* That it shall be in order further to amend such bill upon the report of the committee or any joint commission authorized by law or the House Members of any such commission having jurisdiction of the subject matter of such amendment, which amendment being germane to the subject matter of the bill shall retrench expenditures." "The rule applies to general appropriation bills only." [431] The specific appropriaton bills, however, are subject to the same tests defined in the above paragraph concerning revenue bills, and generally speaking, all expenditures must be authorized by law.

Exceptions to "no legislation in appropriations": The limitations placed on general appropriation bills are far more specific, inclusive, and complex than on revenue bills. An infinite number of decisions relative thereto has been made by the Presiding Officer with the approval of the House, setting forth characteristics of amendments in order on these measures.[432]

Legislation with certain exceptions may not be included in general appropriation bills, and any provision which repeals or alters existing law will be defined as legislation.[433] Some of the exceptions to the rule include: amendments to propose the repair of a building,[434] stipulations reenacting word for word an existing law,[435] provisions which stipulate that no part of the appropriation

---

[431] See *Cannon's Procedure in the House of Representatives,* p. 20.

[432] See Cannon, VII, 1116-1720; Hinds, IV, 3553-4018.

[433] See Cannon, VII, 1628, 1630; Hinds, IV, 3580-3810.

[434] Cannon, VII, 1384. It is not in order in the consular and diplomatic appropriation bills to propose acquisition of sites or buildings for embassies in foreign countries (Hinds, IV, 3606-3608).

[435] Hinds, IV, 3814-3815. A slight variation in the wording of the law may subject the amendment to a point of order (Hinds, IV, 3817).

shall be used for certain purposes,[436] and clauses which are germane and effect a retrenchment of the expenditures.[437]

Retrenchment of Expenditures: The House rules definitely stipulate that amendments which are germane and which retrench expenditures shall be in order to a general appropriation bill,[438] and decisions have defined retrenchment as a "reduction in amounts taken from the Federal Treasury" [439] to be spent by the Federal Government. Usually the House is very liberal in defining retrenchment if it favors cutting down expenses. The House has permitted as a retrenchment amendments which actually repealed existing law,[440] but the retrenchment must be a certainty.[441] In deciding whether or not an amendment will operate to retrench expenditures, note the following decision by the chair:

. . . The Chair can look to the pending bill, the specific section or amendment under consideration, the law of the land so far as applicable, and the parliamentary rules and practices of the House . . . The mere fact that the Chair may think that it is likely that a section, or an amendment will very probably save a considerable sum of money to the Treasury of the United States, is not a sufficient ground on which to hold that such an amendment, or section, is in order . . . If it requires evidence to establish such conclusion, then it does not appear from the provision itself that it will work a retrenchment, and the same will not be in order . . . Hence, the mere fact that the effect of a proposition may be assailed in debate will not operate to establish its invalidity or put it beyond the pale of the Holman rule. The true doctrine is that with or without discussion the Chair must be satisfied, as a condition precedent to holding an amendment to be in order, that the necessary effect of the same operating by its own force will be a retrenchment of expenditures in one of the three ways indicated by the rule.[442]

It must be obvious that the expenditures will be reduced,[443] that the cutting down of expenses will be actual and not that sufficient profits will be made to cover the additional expenses.[444]

Unobjected-to Amendments: Amendments not objected to, regardless of content, will not be stricken out, and it is in order to

[436] Hinds, IV, 3917-3926. Such a stipulation may only apply to the bill under consideration (Hinds, IV, 3927-3928) and such limitation may not be used to insert legislation proper (Cannon, VII, 1636). A provision repealing an existing limit of salary is legislation and not a limitation (see Cannon, VII, 1642). It is in order to provide that no part of an appropriation may be used for the purchase of typewriters at a price in excess of a certain standard (Cannon, VII, 1713).
[437] Hinds, IV, 3889-3891; Cannon, VII, 1481-1560; *House Manual*, 80-1, sec. 846.
[438] See *House Manual*, 80-1, sections 834-846; Cannon, VII, 1481.
[439] Cannon, VII, 1502.
[440] Cannon, VII, 1552.
[441] See Cannon, VII, 1483, 1538; *House Manual*, 80-1, sec. 834-846.
[442] Cannon, VII, 1490. This was a ruling by chairman Edward W. Saunders (Va.).
[443] Cannon, VII, 1543.
[444] Cannon, VII, 1565.

perfect them with germane amendments,[445] but the perfecting amendments may not add new legislation or permit additional legislation.[446]

Appropriations and Legal Authorization: No appropriations may be made unless they are authorized by law,[447] except for the continuation of public works, projects already in progress,[448] or authorized by implication. Many decisions have been made by the Presiding Officer to define what was and what was not authorized by law. The decisions are fairly uniform and exact in scope,[449] and they provide that such projects must be held "actually in 'progress' according to the usual significance of the words." [450] The decisions have, nevertheless, been interpreted sufficiently broad to permit discretion on the part of the Presiding Officer. The purchase of adjoining land to complete a work already established,[451] the provision of money to equip vessels "already possessed by the Coast and Geodetic Survey," [452] the completion of tangible projects like buildings, ships, and roads,[453] the continuation of projects which are capable of completion within a definite time [454]—all of these have been interpreted as continuation of works in progress. Finally, no money may be appropriated for a continuation of public works or for other projects already in progress in violation of an existing law.[455]

Authorization by Implication: If an existing law implies an appropriation, the implication is sufficent to justify the inclusion of an appropriation to pay off that implied charge against the government. For example, a law creating a department must of necessity authorize "contingent expenses incidental to its maintenance." [456] Unless reported by the Committee on Appropriations, deficiencies are not in order on a general appropriation bill,[457] and the appropriation of a salary does not create an office and thereby justify appropriations in succeeding years.[458]

[445] Cannon, VII, 1269, 1416-1419; Hinds, IV, 3823-3835.
[446] Cannon, VII, 1420, 1425-1434.
[447] Cannon, VII, 1125, 1128-1134, 1144; Hinds, IV, 3701.
[448] Hinds, IV, 3578; Cannon, VII, 1125-1131. These citations will give rulings on what are projects in continuation.
[449] Hinds, IV, 3701-3809; Cannon, VII, 1332-1390.
[450] Cannon, VII, 1334; Hinds, IV, 3705-3706.
[451] Hinds, IV, 3766.
[452] Hinds, IV, 3800.
[453] Hinds, IV, 3709-3713. The erection of a new school building in the District of Columbia was held not to be continuation of public works (Hinds, IV, 3790).
[454] Hinds, IV, 3714.
[455] Hinds, IV, 3702.
[456] Cannon, VII, 1273.
[457] Hinds, IV, 3563-3564.
[458] Hinds, IV, 3687-3698.

Burden of Proof: When any of these points of order are raised against any item of an appropriation measure,[459] the burden of proof falls upon the committee reporting the bill to prove the authorization of the appropriation by law.[460] It is left to the Members of the House to see that the bills on the floor meet the requirements briefly outlined above.

Special Rules: A special rule reported by the Rules Committee to waive points of order against a bill, and adopted by the House, except where it might be in conflict with law, will exempt that bill from all of the above limitations, and permit a procedure on the particular proposal concerned [461] exactly as provided for in the resolution.

Disposition of Business on the Speaker's Table: *Type of Business:* As early as 1832, the House adopted a rule to govern the disposition of business on the Speaker's table.[462] Business of this kind had become so great that it was necessary to adopt some uniform mode of disposition. Gradually, the custom grew up of referring to the Speaker's table when received all messages, bills, and resolutions from the Senate, messages from the President,[463] and communications and reports from the heads of the departments. All of these are disposed of at some subsequent time according to Rule XXIV, clause 2.

Reference of Business: Messages from the President are referred to the proper committees without debate;[464] messages which require no further action by the House are not referred.[465] "Reports and communications from heads of departments, and other communications addressed to the House, and bills, resolutions, and messages from the Senate. . ." [466] according to the rules are to be referred to standing committees [467] by the Speaker just

---

[459] See Cannon, VII, 2143.

[460] Cannon, VII, 1233.

[461] Cannon, VII, 769; see also pp. 118, 124.

[462] See *House Manual,* 80-1, secs. 882-884.

[463] Rule XXIV, clause 2   Veto messages are not included.

[464] Hinds, V, 6631. The President's annual messages are generally referred to the Committee of the Whole House on the state of the Union (Hinds, V, 6621-6622). Portions of these messages from time to time have been referred directly to select committees (Hinds, V, 6628). Messages from the President are generally referred at the discretion of the Speaker, but they may be referred by the House on the motion of any Member (Hinds, IV, 4053).

[465] C.R., 70-1, p. 1603.

[466] Rule XXIV, clause 2.

[467] House bills which are returned by the Senate with such amendments as require consideration in the Committee of the Whole are properly referred to the appropriate committee, a step which can be by-passed by sending it to conference under unanimous consent or by adopting a special rule (Hinds, IV, 3094-3095, 3106-3110).

as any bill introduced by a Member.[468]   Included in "bills, resolutions, and messages" from the Senate are all Senate and House
bills with Senate amendments, together with any messages, which
according to the rules are to be considered in the Committee of
the Whole, and Senate amendments to a House bill adding new
appropriations even though there is a request for a conference on
them.   The Speaker, at the time of referring matters to committees, for example, merely announces: "The bill H.R. _____
with the Senate amendments thereto is taken from the Speaker's
table and referred to the Committee on _____."   Measures thus
referred to a standing committee are heard, reported back to the
House, (if the committee takes favorable action on them) and
then are first considered in the Committee of the Whole.[469]

Disposition of the Business: Regardless of the specified rules,
bills with Senate amendments which are privileged for immediate
consideration, and the ones not privileged under unanimous consent, are frequently disposed of from the Speaker's table.   Because
of understanding between the Speaker and the chairmen of the
committees in charge of the bills, the measures are not sent back
to standing committees at all.   House bills with Senate amendments which do not require consideration in Committee of the
Whole may be disposed of directly from the Speaker's table as
the House may see fit.   After a bill with Senate amendments which
require consideration in the Committee of the Whole has been
placed on the Speaker's table, the chairman of the committee in
charge of the bill may say: "Mr. Speaker, I ask unanimous consent to take from the Speaker's table the bill (H.R. 5765 of the
76th Congress) to authorize commissioning aviation cadets in the
Naval and Marine Corps Reserves upon completion of training,
and for other purposes, with Senate amendments thereto, and
concur in the Senate amendments," or a unanimous consent request
may be made to disagree with the Senate amendments and ask for
a conference.   The bill is finally passed and cleared for the President at this point if all the amendments thereto are thus concurred in.

[468] Hinds, IV, 3107, 3111, 4053. This business is referred to the appropriate standing committee at discretion of the Speaker without action by the House. Reference
may be made by the House (Hinds, V, 6631-6634).

[469] See Hinds, IV, 3090-3095, 3108-3110. When measures are reported by the Committee of the Whole back to the House, any amendments added in the Committee are
voted on en bloc, and only on demand by a Member are they voted on separately.
See "Disposition of Business in the Committee of the Whole."

If a bill on the Speaker's table with Senate amendments is heard in the Committee of the Whole first, it is then reported back to the House for further determination. In the House as in the Committee of the Whole, Senate amendments to bills are considered in the order reported to the House and not in the order of their importance.[470] Amendments are read when considered and not the whole bill.[471] The motions to lay on the table, refer, amend, agree (recede and concur), disagree (insist on further disagreement), and send to conference are in order when each amendment is called up for disposition.[472] The motion to table a proposed amendment to a bill is always in order, and if adopted it carries with it the bill.[473]

In practice, all measures [474] with Senate amendments in which the House will not concur and measures on which the stage of disagreement has been reached, which must be considered in Committee of the Whole, are usually called up from the Speaker's table and by *unanimous consent* sent to conference. The Member in charge addresses the chair, for example: "Mr. Speaker, I ask unanimous consent to take from the Speaker's table the bill H.R. 6577, with Senate amendment thereto, disagree to the Senate amendment and agree to the conference requested by the Senate." [475] One objection blocks the request. When the situation is such as to demand further attention by the majority party, the Rules Committee may report a resolution which if adopted by a majority vote has the effect as stated therein, for example: "RESOLVED, That immediately upon the adoption of this resolution the bill H.R. 3325 with Senate amendments thereto be, and the same is hereby, taken from the Speaker's table; that the Senate amendments be, and they are hereby, disagreed to by the House; that the conference requested by the Senate on the disagreeing votes of the two Houses on the said bill be, and hereby is, agreed to by the House; and that the Speaker shall immediately appoint conferees without intervening motion." [476]

---

[470] Hinds, V, 6151-6156, 6197-6198.
[471] Hinds, IV, 3407.
[472] See Hinds, V, 6201-6203, 6225; Cannon, VIII, 3177, 3193-3195, 3199, 3208, 3218, 3259.
[473] Hinds, V, 5423-5424.
[474] The exceptions are described in the following paragraph.
[475] See H.R. 6577 of the Seventy-sixth Congress. If there is no intention of sending the matter to conference, the Member may address the chair as follows: "Mr. Speaker, I ask unanimous consent to take from the Speaker's table and consider the bill H.R. —— with the Senate amendments thereto."
[476] See House Resolution 233 of the Seventy-sixth Congress.

Disposition of Bills Directly from "Table": There are exceptions, however, to the general rule that all measures which require consideration in committee will be referred to standing committees: House bills with Senate amendments and Senate bills "substantially the same" [477] as House bills already on the House Calendar which do not require consideration in the Committee of the Whole are privileged and may be disposed of at once as the House sees fit by a majority vote.[478] Of course they must be called up at the request of a committee. A Senate bill to be given immediate consideration must meet four conditions: it must be substantially the same as a House bill, come to the House after and not before the House bill is placed on the calendar, the House bill must be correctly on the House Calendar, and the committee of the House reporting the similar bill must authorize the calling up of the Senate bill from the Speaker's table.[479] In the event a Senate bill coming over to the House is similar to a House bill already passed, it may be substituted for the House bill on a motion directed by the committee having jurisdiction thereof.[480] If no other disposition is made of this privileged business, it is disposed of by the Speaker as he sees fit.[481]

Business on the Speaker's table is generally disposed of soon after it is received, but the practice is only a result of custom since the rule is not mandatory in this respect. The length of time that matters are permitted to be on the table is at the dis-

---

[477] Hinds, IV, 3098. "Substantially the same" has been interpreted thus: "In ascertaining whether a Senate bill proposed to be taken from the Speaker's table was sufficiently similar to a House bill already on the calendar, a bill limiting certain banks to loans of $15,000 was deemed not substantially the same as a bill limiting such banks to loans of $25,000." (Cannon, VI, 737).

The Speaker making a ruling relative to this subject said: "This bill having come over from the Senate, the question arising is, therefore, whether it shall be retained on the Speaker's table as being substantially the same as one already reported to the House. In order that it may be so kept upon the table, the Chair must be notified that a committee has passed upon the subject and made a report to the House and asks that the bill be retained on the table for action. The next question to be considered is whether the bill upon the Speaker's table from the Senate is 'substantially' the same as the House bill which has been reported. The reason it ought to be substantially the same is that the House may be notified of the subject that is to come up, that it may have due information as to what is to be brought before it, and if it is so informed by a bill having been considered and reported by its committee, that is enough." (Hinds, IV, 3099).

[478] Cannon, VI, 728-729.

[479] *Cannon's Procedure in the House of Representatives*, pp. 396-397.

[480] C.R., 69-1, p. 5749.

[481] Cannon, VI, 730, 733. In order for these bills to be privileged they must have been favorably reported by a committee, and the motions to call them up must have committee sanction (Cannon, VI, 739). In *House Manual* 80-1, section 883, will be found the following quotation: "Although a committee must authorize the calling up of the Senate bill, the actual motion need not be made by one of the committee . . . The authority of a committee to call up a bill must be given at a formal meeting of the committee."

cretion of the Speaker if they are not privileged for immediate consideration.[482]

Right to Report at Any Time: *"Reports in order at any time":* The Rules Committee may report at any time on rules, joint rules, and the order of business;[483] "The Committee on House Administration—on the right of a Member to his seat, enrolled bills, on all matters referred to it of printing for the use of the House or the two Houses, and on all matters of expenditure of the contingent fund of the House; the Committee on Ways and Means—on bills raising revenue; the Committee on Appropriations—on the general appropriation bills; the Committee on Public Works—on bills authorizing the improvement of rivers and harbors; the Committee on the Public Lands—on bills for the forfeiture of land grants to railroad and other corporations, bills preventing speculation in the public lands, bills for the reservation of the public lands for the benefit of actual and bona fide settlers, and bills for the admission of new States; the Committee on Veterans' Affairs—on general pension bills." [484]   In addition, the House

[482] On one occasion a message from the Senate was detained on the Speaker's table for ten months.

[483] "The Committee on Rules, 'by uniform practice of the House,' exercised the privilege of reporting at any time as early as 1888. The right to report at any time is confined to privileged matters . . . This was probably the survival of the practice which existed as early as 1853 of giving the privilege of reporting at any time to this committee for a session . . . In 1890 the committee was included among the committees whose reports were privileged by rule. The present rule was adopted in 1892 . . . , amended on March 15, 1909, and the matter in parentheses was adopted January 18, 1920." (*House Manual,* 80-1, section 730).
"It shall always be in order to call up for consideration a report from the Committee on Rules (except it shall not be called up for consideration on the same day it is presented to the House, unless so determined by a vote of not less than two-thirds of the Members voting, but this provision shall not apply during the last three days of the session), and, pending the consideration thereof, the Speaker may entertain one motion that the House adjourn; but after the result is announced he shall not entertain any other dilatory motion until the said report shall have been fully disposed of. The Committee on Rules shall not report any rule or order which shall provide that business under paragraph 7 of Rule XXIV shall be set aside by a vote of less than two-thirds of the Members present; nor shall it report any rule or order which shall operate to prevent the motion to recommit being made as provided in paragraph 4 of Rule XVI." (Rule XI).
"The privilege given by this rule to the Committee on Rules is confined to 'action touching rules, joint rules, and order of business,' and this committee may not report as privileged a concurrent resolution providing for a Senate investigating committee . . . , or provide for the appointment of a clerk . . . ; but the privilege has been held to include the right to report special orders for the consideration of individual bills or classes of bills . . . , or the consideration of a specified amendment to a bill and prescribing a mode of considering such amendment." (*House Manual,* 80-1, section 728).

[484] Rule XI, section (2)(a). "The beginnings of this rule appear as early as 1812, but it was in 1880 that the various provisions were consolidated in one rule. At the time these privileges originated all reports were made on the floor, and often with great difficulty because of the pressure of business . . . By giving this privilege the most important matters of business were greatly expedited. In 1890 a rule was adopted providing that reports should be made by filing with the Clerk; but privileged reports must still be made from the floor . . . Thus the privilege of itself would now be a disadvantage were it not for the fact that the right of reporting at any time gives the right of immediate consideration by the House. . . ." (*House Manual,* 80-1, section 727).

may at any time refer a matter to a select committee or a standing committee and authorize that committee to report the said matter at any time.[485]

"Report at any time" Means Immediate Consideration: The House has defined the right to report at any time to mean an immediate consideration of the measure when reported,[486] if such action is not in conflict with other business of superior precedence.[487] For example: business privileged under this franchise yields to: Calendar Wednesday, questions of privilege, and special orders. Once called up, these issues remain privileged until disposed of.[483] The House will not proceed to consider any such reports unless made from the floor by the committee calling up the particular business.[489] If the question is tainted with non-privileged matter, it loses its privileged status.[490]

Census Bills: Formerly bills on this subject were given privileged status as coming under a constitutional mandate to take census or to provide for reapportionment of Representatives. This has dropped into disuse and a Committee on the Census is no longer included among the standing committees.

V. Precedence of Certain Motions and Other Aspects of Procedure

Explanation of Section: The subjects under consideration in this section are concerned with legislating but do not constitute actual procedure for getting measures up for consideration. They involve bills already up for debate, and a discussion of them is important to an explanation of the procedure. Frequently, this type of business consumes much time during the passage of a bill, and may be used to effect its final disposition. Motions affiliated with legislation will be first reviewed somewhat in the order of their precedence.

Reception and Disposition of Messages: The Constitution provides that the President shall from time to time send messages

---

[485] H.R. 4425 of the 76th Congress was so considered—This was the 1939 Reorganization Bill.
[486] Hinds, IV, 3131-3132, 3142-3145.
[487] Cannon, VIII, 2291.
[488] Hinds, IV, 3145. Such matters adversely reported have the same privilege as those favorably reported (C.R., 68-2, p. 605).
[489] See C.R., 68-2, p. 605.
[490] Hinds, IV, 4622-4624, 4633, 4640; Cannon, VIII, 2289, 2299. Privileged business interrupts the regular order of business as established by Rule XXIV, but after privileged business is disposed of, procedure continues on from the point of interruption (Hinds, IV, 3070-3071).

to Congress,[491] and by practice each house exchanges messages regularly while in session. Reception of such matters according to the precedents is not business,[492] but may interrupt the highest privileged proceedings of the House.[493] The practice of the House is to receive messages, with certain exceptions, when they are presented regardless of what privileged business is under consideration, unless the Speaker decides of his own accord to delay the action. The Speaker may even ask some Member participating in debate to yield the floor for a moment in order to receive a message, or if the House is in the Committee of the Whole the committee rises informally long enough for the reception.[494]

Messages are not generally considered when received. Usually they are placed on the Speaker's table and disposed of at some subsequent time by the Speaker at his own discretion. For further details see the section on "Disposition of Business on Speaker's Table," pp. 289-293.

Roll Calls to Obtain Quorum: *Procedure of Calling Roll:* The roll of the House, consisting of all the names of active Members,[495] is called for two purposes, namely: to ascertain a quorum and to have a record vote. The yea and nay vote is discussed under "voting." The roll is prepared and kept up to date by the clerk, in accordance with Rule XV which states: "Upon every roll call the names of the Members shall be called alphabetically by surname, except when two or more have the same surname, in which case the name of the State shall be added; and if there be two such Members from the same State, the whole name shall be called, and after the roll has been once called, the clerk shall call in their alphabetical order the names of those not voting. . ."

---

[491] Article II, section 3. "He shall from time to time give to the Congress information of the state of the Union. . . ."

[492] Hinds, V, 6600.

[493] *Cannon's Procedure in the House of Representatives*, pp. 241-242. It is in order to send messages to the House only after a quorum has appeared in both houses to do business. Messages have been received in the House when the Senate was not sitting. The procedure of receiving a message is: "The messenger is introduced by the Doorkeeper at the bar of the House, with the words 'Mr. Speaker, a message from the President' (or the Senate, as the case may be). Thereupon the messenger bows and addresses the Speaker as 'Mr. Speaker.' The Speaker, with a slight inclination, addresses the messenger as 'Mr. Secretary,' since such is his title whether he be from the President or the Senate. Thereupon the messenger delivers the message in a distinct voice that should be heard by all the Members present." (Hinds, V, 6591). When a message is received, it is entered in the *Journal* and printed in the *Record*.

[494] *House Manual*, 80-1, sections 561-563; Hinds, IV, 4786.

[495] See Cannon, VI, 638: See: Hinds, IV, 2885-2888: Members elected, living, and who have not resigned.

Quorum: A quorum consists of a majority of the ". . .Members chosen, sworn, and living, whose membership has not been terminated by resignation or by the action of the House." [496] And the House proceeds upon the assumption that that number is present unless it is established to the contrary.[497] The lack of a quorum might be brought to the attention of the membership by a Representative making a point of no quorum,[498] by the Speaker on his own initiative taking cognizance of the number absent, or by a vote disclosing that too few were participating. When the roll call is not automatic,[499] the Speaker counts to determine the number present,[500] and his count which is announced without delay is not subject to verification by tellers.

Rule for Obtaining Quorum: There is no reason for a "call of the House" unless a majority necessary to do business is not present. What this number is and how to keep it has caused the membership much trouble since 1789. It was not until more recent years that the precedent of what constituted a quorum was established.[501] The rule reads: "In the absence of a quorum, fifteen Members,[502] including the Speaker, if there is one, shall be authorized to compel the attendance of absent Members, and in all calls of the House the doors shall be closed, the names of the Members shall be called by the clerk, and the absentees noted; and those for whom no sufficient excuse is made may, by order of a majority of those present, be sent for and arrested, wherever they may be found, by officers to be appointed by the Sergeant at Arms for that purpose, and their attendance secured and retained; and the House shall determine upon what condition they shall be discharged. Members who voluntarily appear shall, unless the House otherwise direct, be immediately admitted to the Hall of the House, and they shall report their names to the clerk to be entered upon the *Journal* as present." [503]

---

[496] Cannon, VI, 638.

[497] Cannon, VI, 624, 565. It is too late to raise a point of order that a quorum was not present after an action has been taken (Cannon, VI, 655).

[498] By a count of the Speaker, the absence of a quorum is established if such is the condition. If fifteen Members are present they may demand or order a call of the House by a majority vote of the fifteen (Hinds, IV, 2983-2984).

[499] If the lack of a quorum is determined by the number voting on an issue, the roll call should be automatic.

[500] The Speaker may count all members he can see, even if they are in the cloak room.

[501] See Hinds, IV, 2884-2979.

[502] Fifteen must be present to order a call of the House (Hinds, IV, 2983) and a minority of those present may not order a call or force Members to attend (Hinds, IV, 2984).

[503] Rule XV, clause 2.

Warrants for Bringing in Absentees: Should the House resort to forcing absent Members to attend, a prerogative seldom used, the Speaker or the Speaker pro tempore issues and signs the warrants; and the Sergeant at Arms or his agent arrests the Members and brings them to the House.[504] A Representative so arrested may not question the authority of the House. The House, if a Member is wrongfully arrested, may consider the matter and order the "Sergeant at Arms to investigate and amend the return of his writ." [505] All decisions relative thereto are determined by a majority of those present. The power to compel attendance is not confined to a time when a quorum is not present.[506]

When the roll is called to ascertain a quorum, the Representatives usually appear to answer to their names of their own accord. After the call of the roll has been completed, a motion is generally made without opposition, that further proceedings concerned therewith be dispensed with. The House then proceeds with the unfinished business or the next business in order. Should it become necessary to make arrests, the Representatives would not be held at the bar under the present practice; they would merely report to the clerk and have their names recorded.[507]

The Motion on "Absence of a Quorum": A motion "to call the House" is not debatable;[508] if entertained by the Speaker, some Member addresses the chair, thus: "Mr. Speaker, I move a call of the House." [509] This motion is highly privileged since the House must obtain a quorum before considering further business.[510] Only two motions are in order: to call the House or to

---

[504] See *House Manual*, 80-1, sections 769-773.
[505] Hinds, IV, 3021.
[506] Hinds, IV, 2985.
[507] Cannon, VI, 684; See Hinds, IV, 3012. The old rule requiring Members to present themselves at the bar during the call of the House is obsolete.
[508] Cannon, VI, 683, 688.
[509] See *Cannon's Procedure in the House of Representatives*, pp. 281-282. Methods of addressing the chair vary with the existing conditions in the House.
[510] Cannon, VI, 675; Hinds, IV, 2935-2952. In the absence of a quorum it is not in order for the House to transact business or to do the following things: fix a day to which to adjourn (Hinds, IV, 2954), order the previous question (Hinds, IV, 2964), or fix a recess (Hinds, IV, 2955). Business is not in order even by unanimous consent (Hinds, IV, 2958-2960; Cannon, VI, 660-661). The House may attend to the following matters in the absence of a quorum: prayer (Cannon, VI, 663), administration of oath to a Member (Cannon, VI, 22), reception of messages (Cannon, VIII, 3339), motions incidental to call of the House (Cannon, VI, 681; Hinds, IV, 3029), and motions to adjourn (Cannon, VI, 700). "A recess differs from an adjournment in its effect upon pending business and the House resumes consideration of unfinished business under conditions obtaining at the time recess was taken." (Cannon, VI, 664.) While the House may not fix a recess in the absence of a quorum, it may recess if the hour for recess has already been fixed (Cannon, VI, 664). The absence of a quorum having been recognized, the House must cease debate until a quorum has been obtained (Cannon, VI, 659).

adjourn. Furthermore, if a point of no quorum has been made and established, it may not be withdrawn except by unanimous consent; it may be withdrawn before that stage obtains.[511] If a point of no quorum is raised and sustained, if the Speaker orders a call on his own initiative, or if the roll call is automatic, the Presiding Officer orders the doors closed [512] and the call begins.

Voting: *Ways of Voting:* In voting on any issue before the House, the Representatives may use one or more of the five possible methods, namely: viva voce, division, tellers, yeas and nays, and ballot.[513]

Viva Voce and Division: When a proposition is originally put before the House viva voce is the method of voting used unless some Member requests another or the issue is such that a roll call vote is required by the Constitution; it is within the power of the House to demand any one of the several possibilities in the first instance. The viva voce is as follows: the Speaker says: " 'As many as are in favor (as the question may be), say 'Aye'; and after the affirmative voice is expressed, 'As many as are opposed, say No.' " [514] If the first attempt is by viva voce, and there is doubt, or if for various reasons a group wishes the matter to be voted on in another way, a division, tellers, or the yeas and nays for the second test is in order; the vote by division is as follows: The Speaker says: "As many as are in favor will rise and stand until counted. After the count of the affirmative, the ayes will be seated and the noes will stand." [515]

Tellers and Yeas and Nays: If the first two trial decisions are unsatisfactory to one-fifth of a quorum, either tellers [516] or the yeas and nays may be ordered, depending on whether in the House or in the Committee of the Whole; yeas and nays are not in order in Committee. Each of the first three methods having been exhausted, one-fifth of a quorum may order the yeas and nays, but not in Committee. In case of a viva voce the Speaker decides if the yeas or nays have it. The counting on a division vote is done by the Speaker and his decision may not be contested; in effect, an appeal may be taken by requesting tellers or yeas and nays after the division vote is announced.

---

[511] Cannon, VI, 656.
[512] Cannon, VI, 703.
[513] The use of the ballot is obsolete.
[514] Rule I, clause 5.
[515] The fact that a Member demanded tellers does not *per se* prevent him from demanding a division (Cannon, VIII, 3102).
[516] Tellers may be ordered by the Speaker in the House.

When the House votes by tellers, "he shall name one from each side of the question to tell the Members in the affirmative and negative. . . ." [517] The Members of the House pass between them to vote, with the tellers standing on either side of the center aisle to count the Representatives as they pass.[518] The ayes pass through first and then the nays. The count is then sent to the Presiding Officer and announced.[519]

The yeas and nays consume much of the time of the House. The roll is called twice on the occasion of each record vote, and the average number of names called is approximately six hundred.[520] The time consumed in a call of the House is generally seventeen minutes, while the time for a record vote consumes from twenty-three to forty-five minutes, depending in part on the number of Members answering the first call.[521] A roll call ordered by the House must be continued until finished; it may not be interrupted by a question of privilege, a parliamentary inquiry,[522] a point of order,[523] an appeal, conference report, motion to adjourn, and the like. Votes may be changed after the roll has once been called and the Speaker may even demand a recapitulation of it,[524] but any changes must occur before the Speaker announces the vote. After the vote is announced, a Member may not change his vote even if it was in violation of a pair.

Pairs: The House has a custom of pairing for record voting,[525] a system by which a Member may register his opinion on a particular vote even though he be absent. This is possible by right of any two Representatives to enter into a personal contract (pair) to the effect that one will not vote if the other one is absent. This having been done on a particular vote or votes, their names will be printed at the foot of the record vote each time or so long as

[517] Rule I, clause 5.
[518] See Cannon, VIII, 3100-3101.
[519] See Cannon, VIII, 3096-3106. "In a vote by tellers it is a matter of mutual agreement as to whether each teller shall count his own side" or the opposing side (Cannon, VIII, 3096).
[520] The second call repeats only the names of the ones failing to respond to the first call. Usually there are many Members in the "well" of the House to be recorded after the second call; at times as many as 96 have been in the well of the House for this purpose.
[521] *Legislative Establishment Appropriation Bill,* 1929, Hearings, 70-1, p. 52. In the 67th Congress, when the so-called Voight Filibuster was staged, there were 29 roll calls in three days.
[522] Inquiries have been made.
[523] Cannon, VIII, 3131. The Speaker has entertained points of order at his own discretion.
[524] Cannon, VIII, 3128, 3160. A Member present at the roll call may vote after the call is completed (Hinds, IV, 2907), but it is the duty of the Speaker to qualify him. The Member concerned and not the Speaker, says whether he was in the hall and listening; unless he so states, he may not vote.
[525] Pairs are contracts between Members recognized by the House.

the two are paired, showing one for and one against the issue, however they are contracted. The House has no jurisdiction over these contracts. The terms of the contract are determined by the contracting Members,[526] although the rules of the House [527] do permit such arrangements. In practice, the pair clerks representing the two parties arrange pairs for absent Members, which are announced after the roll call.[528] The pairs are not counted in the calculation of how many voted for and how many against the issue in a record vote.

There are various kinds of pairs, and the names imply their limitations, namely: "live," "general," "further notice," and "session." The "live" pairs are pairs made between Members themselves. If one Member is absent, the other is obligated to respect the pair and not vote, though he may answer present. The "general" pairs are arranged by clerks in the absence of both parties. The "session" pairs are made for the whole session unless mutually suspended. "Further notice" pairs may be terminated upon notice by either party.

Certain Questions Require a Two-Thirds Vote: To expel a Member, to impeach, to override a veto, to suspend the rules, to consider immediately a report from the Rules Committee, to pass a resolution to amend the Constitution, to dispense with Calendar Wednesday, etc., all require a two-thirds vote for affirmative action. A pair on these questions requires two Members favoring the measure to each opposed.

Entering a Motion to Reconsider, and Reconsideration: *Its Application:* The motion to reconsider involves two distinct actions, the one to enter a motion that a certain amendment, bill or action be reconsidered, and the other, the consideration of that amendment, bill or action, after the motion has been entered.[529] According to Rule XVIII, it is in order for any Member of the majority [530] at any time "on the same or succeeding day" [531] on

---

[526] Cannon, VIII, 3077. Members involved determine the termination of their pair, and they indicate their attitude on the question for which their pair was made.
[527] Rule VIII, clause 2.
[528] Rule VIII, clause 2. "Pairs shall be announced by the clerk, after the completion of the second roll call, from a written list furnished him, and signed by the Member making the statement to the clerk, which list shall be published in the *Record* as a part of the proceedings, immediately following the names of those not voting. . ." if the list is announced only once during a single legislative day.
[529] Cannon, VIII, 2785. For many details on the subject see: *House Manual*, 80-1, sections 813-819; Hinds, V, 5605-5705; Cannon, VIII, 2774-2795.
[530] *House Manual*, 80-1, section 813. "A delegate may not make the motion. . . . The provision of the rule that the motion may be made 'by any member of the majority' is construed, in case of a tie vote, to mean any member of the prevailing side. . . . and the same construction applies in case of a two-thirds vote. . . . Where the yeas and nays have not been ordered recorded in the *Journal*, any Member, irre-

which an issue before the House was carried or lost to enter a motion to reconsider the said question,[532] and such action shall have precedence over all other business except conference reports and motions to adjourn.[533] The Representative wishing to take this action addresses the chair: "Mr. 'Speaker, I desire to enter a motion to reconsider the vote by which bill —— (motion, conference report, or any other proposition) passed the House (was agreed to, sent to conference, or action otherwise taken)." If one such motion has been made and lost, a second motion to the same effect is in order, but usually when offered the motion is adopted and then laid on the table in order to make a final and immediate disposition. Motions to reconsider, however, may not apply to a negative decision to adjourn, a refusal to go into a Committee of the Whole, a vote on suspending the rules, and the like—such issues are presented anew on each occasion.[534] Matters referred to committees in the first instance also may not be called back to the House for reconsideration as that would be another way of discharging a committee. [535]

Disposition of the Motion and Its Privileged Status: Should a motion to reconsider be entered properly, it "shall not be withdrawn after the said succeeding day without the consent of the House, and thereafter any Member may call it up for consideration . . ." [536] The phrase "shall not be withdrawn" means pending indefinitely until disposed of, "even until a succeeding session of the same Congress." [537] Bills are not considered passed nor amendments thereto agreed to if a motion to reconsider is pending.

spective of whether he voted with the majority or not, may make the motion to reconsider . . .; but a Member who was absent. . ., or who was paired in favor of the majority contention and did not vote, may not make the motion. . . ."
[531] Rule XVIII, clause 1; See *Cannon's Procedure in the House of Representatives*, p. 307.
[532] This does not include right of considering the motion.
[533] Rule XVIII, clause 1. Such a motion may be entered while questions of highest constitutional privilege are pending (Hinds, V, 5673; Cannon, VIII, 2785), while previous question is operating (Hinds, V, 5657-5662), on Calendar Wednesday (Cannon, VII, 905), pending a motion to resolve into a Committee of the Whole for consideration of an appropriation bill (Cannon, VIII, 2785), and the like (see: *House Manual*, 80-1, sections 813-819).
[534] See *House Manual*, 80-1, sections 812-819; Hinds, V, 5605-5705; Cannon, VIII. 2774-2795.
[535] See *House Manual*, 80-1, section 820-821. For a detailed account of application thereof see: *Cannon's Procedure in the House of Representatives*, pp. 307-308.
[536] Rule XVIII, clause 1: "PROVIDED, That such motion, if made during the last six days of a session, shall be disposed of when made."
[537] Hinds, V, 5684. "A motion to reconsider may be entertained, although the bill or resolution to which it applies may have gone to the other House or the President . . . . The fact that the House had informed the Senate that it had agreed to a Senate amendment to a House bill was held not to prevent a motion to reconsider the vote on agreeing. . . . When a motion is made to reconsider a vote on a bill which has gone to the Senate, a motion to recall the bill is privileged. . ." (*House Manual*, 80-1. sec. 815.)

These motions are privileged business and may be called up for disposition at pleasure after they have been entered.[538] A bill which has passed both houses and gone to the President for his signature may be reconsidered if the House can recover jurisdiction;[539] it is the practice of the Speaker, however, not to sign an enrolled bill until a pending motion to reconsider has been finally disposed of. These motions are not debatable unless the proposition to be reconsidered was debatable.[540]

Use of the Motion: The prerogative of reconsideration is seldom utilized.[541] In practice, if a measure is controversial, one of the Members in charge will likely enter a motion to reconsider it, and immediately move to lay that motion on the table, thereby precluding reconsideration.

Questions of Privilege: *Definition:* "Questions of privilege" and "privileged questions" are definitely distinct matters. Privileged questions are rather inclusive in scope and relate to the order of business, while questions of privilege relate to the safety and dignity of the House and its Members. The latter composes only one type of the many kinds of privileged business.

Two Classes of Questions of Privilege: Questions of privilege divide themselves into two classes: ". . . Those affecting the rights of the House collectively, its safety, dignity, and the integrity of its proceedings . . ." and those affecting ". . . the rights, reputation, and conduct of Members, individually, in their representative capacity only . . ." [542] These two statements broadly but vaguely outline what matters may be presented to the House as questions of privilege. Since 1789, however, the House by practice has more clearly defined what it will accept in these two categories. The present rule was adopted in 1880, and practices in the House in pursuance thereof supplement it.[543]

---

[538] Certain business takes precedence over these motions; for the details see: *Cannon's Procedure in the House of Representatives,* pp. 308-309.

[539] "But when the Congress expires leaving unacted on a motion to reconsider the vote whereby a simple resolution of the House has been agreed to, it is probable that the resolution would be operative; and where a bill has been enrolled, signed by the Speaker, and approved by the President, it is undoubtedly a law although a motion to reconsider may not have been disposed of. . . ." *House Manual,* 80-1, section 816.

[540] *Cannon's Procedure in the House of Representatives,* p. 308.

[541] *Hearings, Revision of the Rules,* 62-1, parts 1, 2, p. 91. "So my own judgment is that our fathers were wise in incorporating reconsideration into our system, and that we have invited grave dangers by abandoning it. But if it is to be abandoned, what is the use of maintaining it in the rules, to deride and deceive the novice, and make him think it is possible to reconsider anything? Why not cut it out and say 'your vote is final.' " These were the remarks of Congressman Luce of Massachusetts.

[542] Rule IX, Cannon, VI, 580.

[543] See Hinds, III, 2521-2725; Cannon, VI, 553-623.

General "Questions of Privilege": The questions of privilege with which the House as a whole is concerned, are of highest privilege.[544] These matters are presented to the House by means of a resolution which must be read before a discussion of the grievance. A Member addresses the chair: "Mr. Speaker, I rise to a question of the privilege of the House, and offer a resolution which I send to the Clerk's desk." The Speaker announces that the Clerk will report it to the House.

This practice permits the House to judge whether or not a matter is vital enough to justify an interruption of the normal procedure and a delay of regular proceedings.

Scope of General "Questions of Privilege": The general "questions of privilege" include such constitutional prerogatives of the House as the power of originating revenue bills, its part in treaty-making, the power to censure a Member, the power to punish for contempt, and the power to summon witnesses to obtain information.[545] The alleged violation of the right of admission to the floor of the House, the accuracy and propriety of reports in the Congressional Record, the conduct of representatives of the press, an accusation that a Member has been influenced by executive patronage, a resolution alleging that the rights and dignity of the House have been invaded by the Executive, the right of a Member to his seat, the protection of papers and files of the House, questions concerning the protection of records and documents of the House, errors in newspapers concerning House proceedings, the conduct of employees, the comfort and convenience of Members and employees, and the integrity of the processes by which a bill is enacted, and the like—all of these present general questions in which the House as a whole is concerned.

Personal "Questions of Privilege": The second class of questions of privilege must involve the conduct of the Member in his representative capacity.[546] Unlike the "general questions," these do not require that a Member must offer a resolution in order to present a grievance.[547] The Representative concerned merely addresses the chair: "Mr. Speaker, I rise to a question of personal privilege." This motion must be put by the Member concerned. Members rising to a point of personal privilege should have sound

---

[544] See Cannon, VI, 558.
[545] See Hinds, II, 1502-1537; 1641-1665; III, 1668-1724.
[546] Cannon, VI, 604.
[547] Cannon, VI, 566; Hinds, III, 2546-2547.

reasons on which to base it, or if the question is presented in the form of a resolution, there must be on its face a statement that there has been an invasion of the Member's rights.

Scope of "Questions of Personal Privilege": Questions of "personal privilege" include: the right of a Member-elect to his seat, the question of support received in elections, matters concerning elections, the act of a Member accusing another of a falsehood in debate, the right of freedom of debate in the House, the assurance of personal safety in the House, false criticisms in newspapers and magazines reflecting unduly on any Member, the publication of circulars which affect a Member in his representative capacity, and many other questions of the same nature.[548]

Privileged Status of These Questions: The House has reserved for itself the right to call up these matters at any time, and they have precedence over all other matters except motions to adjourn.[549] Such business may not take from the floor a Member who has been recognized for debate.[550] When such business is called up it does not have to be considered immediately; the House may postpone it. To reserve the right to call up such business at any time does provide for the House an opportunity to take cognizance of any situation which would reflect on itself or its Members—the law of self-preservation.

(1) Presentation of: Only one question of privilege may be put before the House at a time, but a Member may offer one question and before discussing it submit another; the House may then consider the two questions at the same time. This practice, however, is used only to save time.[551] Unlike most privileged questions, a question of privilege does not forfeit its status through the manner in which it is reported, but the content of the matter must meet the test. The invasion of rights must be actual and not prospective.[552]

(2) Debate of: The debates on this business vary from the regular debates in some respects, while they are true to form in others. The hour rule applies and the time is given to the Member presenting the question, who must confine his remarks to the

[548] Hinds, III, 2557-2725; Cannon, VI, 553-622.
[549] *Cannon's Procedure in the House of Representatives*, pp. 274-275.
[550] Cannon, VIII, 2459.
[551] Cannon, VI, 562.
[552] The Speaker may pass on whether or not a question presents a matter of privilege instead of presenting it directly to the House, but the Speaker may consult the House for its decision. (Cannon, VI, 617; Hinds, III, 2641).

question of privilege; he may not use this time for the discussion of extraneous matters; and he may not yield to another for irrelevant questions.[553]

Change of Calendar Reference: The matter of changing the reference of bills from one calendar to another is not generally of much importance. Mere clerical errors do not raise a privileged question, and all changes of minor bills are made without presenting them formally to the House. Any changes of significance occur very seldom. Should such an occasion arise, the Members concerned with the situation would present the matter to the House, and by unanimous consent request that the proper change be made; otherwise, the situation would have to be presented by motion. In any case, the privileged status for transacting this business is high.[554]

Change of Committee Reference: The changing of the reference of bills from one committee to another is not very significant. All clerical errors are corrected without consulting the House. The Speaker may even re-refer bills without formally presenting the matter to the House. Most other improper references not so cared for are very simply corrected. Generally, the chairman of the committees concerned merely ask unanimous consent that the changes be made. If a political question is involved, which is not the general case, there may be a real fight and much debate before a solution is reached. The disposition of such business is extremely privileged.[555]

If a committee has given consideration to a bill erroneously referred, the House may re-refer it to another,[556] and a point of order may be made against a committee reporting to the House any bill over which it does not have jurisdiction. This action may be taken on private bills reported by improper committees at any time prior to the beginning of consideration.[557] Such points of order against public bills must be made before the committee reports them back to the House.[558]

Resolutions of Inquiry: One of the important prerogatives of the House is to request information from the President or one

[553] Cannon, VI, 617, 576. If the question before the House concerns the conduct of several Members, one person may not claim the floor by calling it a question of personal privilege. (Hinds, III, 2534).
[554] Cannon, VII, 2124, 2128.
[555] *Cannon's Procedure in the House of Representatives*, pp. 248-249.
[556] See Cannon, VII, 2128.
[557] Hinds, IV, 4382-4389.
[558] Hinds, IV, 4365-4371. Such motions are not in order on Calendar Wednesday (Cannon, VII, 883, 2117-2118).

of the executive departments at any time it sees fit; the purpose is to aid Congress in writing better legislation. The requests may be in the form of a simple resolution or a concurrent resolution,[559] but to acquire a privileged status they must be to obtain facts and not opinions.[560] A resolution of this type introduced in the House is referred to a committee which is required to report the same back to the House within a week;[561] it may, however, be returned and considered at any time after it has been referred[562] whether reported favorably or otherwise.[563] Resolutions of inquiry may be debated and amended. The Representative calling up such a resolution addresses the chair as follows: "Mr. Speaker, I call up House Resolution, H.Res. ——, a privileged resolution of inquiry."

If a committee fails to return such a resolution within a week, it may be discharged from further consideration of that resolution, and the motion is privileged.[564] After the committee has been discharged, the resolution may be brought up just as any other of this nature.

Requests for Leave of Absence: Requests for leave of absence are usually laid before the House just prior to adjournment. Whether or not they are privileged is a matter of opinion.

Call of Order: When the House procedure is contrary to the rules, or when it is boisterous or noisy in the Chamber, any Representative may demand the regular order, by addressing the Speaker to that effect. The Speaker may call on the Sergeant at Arms to aid him in obtaining order.[565] The regular order may be demanded at any time.

Question of Consideration: *The Rule:* The question of consideration is well established in the House by practice and custom over a long period of time.[566] It was established to provide

[559] Hinds, III, 1860, 1875. A simple resolution to become effective only requires adoption by the house in which it was introduced, and its jurisdiction is limited to the powers of that body acting separately. A concurrent resolution to become effective requires adoption by both houses but not the signature of the President, and its jurisdiction is limited to the powers of Congress acting independently of the Executive Department of the Government. A joint resolution must be approved by both houses and requires signature of the President to become effective, and it has the force of law.

[560] Cannon, VI, 413, see also 418-432.

[561] *House Manual,* 80-1, section 856; Hinds, 1856. "Committees are required to report resolutions of inquiry back to the House within one week of the reference, and this week's time is construed to be seven days, exclusive of either the first or last day . . ." (*House Manual,* 80-1, section 859).

[562] Hinds, III, 1870. The committee in charge of it must authorize that it be called up.

[563] Cannon, VI, 410-413.

[564] Hinds, III, 1857, 1865-1871.

[565] For details see other sections of this work and *Cannon's Procedure in the House of Representatives,* pp. 73-80.

[566] Hinds, V, 4936-4977; Cannon, VIII, 2436-2447.

the House with a means of protecting itself against business which it does not wish to hear and at the same time give the House a way of moving to the business it wishes to consider. Under this procedure, whenever any Member makes a motion that the House consider a proposition, the question is : "Will the House now consider it ?" The question is never put unless a Member demands it.[567] Under any circumstances the right exists even if the business comes up automatically, leaving no necessity for anyone to make a motion to consider any proposition. There are some questions against which the "question of consideration" may not be raised. The three methods by which the House may protect itself against business which it does not wish to consider are : (1) by voting on the motion to lay on the table, (2) by voting on the motion to go into the Committee of the Whole, and (3) by raising the question of consideration.

Effect of Negative Vote on the Motion: The negative vote on a motion to consider a certain measure has no effect on the bill except to delay its consideration. Any Member may continue to move that the House consider a particular bill, when he can get recognition, until it has been disposed of or until Congress adjourns for the session.[568]

Precedence of the Motion: The question of consideration may be demanded by a Member even though another Member, in charge of the bill, claims the floor for debate. If the debate has already begun, the motion comes too late.[569] The question of consideration may be raised on any business [570] with a few exceptions ;[571] and it is not debatable.[572]

The Motion to Lay on the Table: *Effect of the Motion:* Much of the business going before the House may be laid on the table before or at any time during its consideration until the

[567] See Rule XVI, clause 3 ; *House Manual,* 80-1, secs. 778-781.
[568] A motion to consider a privileged question having been rejected, the House permitted it to be brought up again the same day (Hinds, V, 4942). See *Cannon's Procedure in the House of Representatives,* pp. 138-139.
[569] Hinds, V, 4937-4939 ; see *House Manual,* 80-1, section 779.
[570] A question of consideration may be raised on Calendar Wednesday as on other days (Cannon, VII, 952) ; it may be raised on the right of a Member to his seat (Hinds, V, 4941) ; it may be raised against a bill which has been made a special order (Hinds, IV, 3175 ; Hinds, V, 4953-4957) unless the order provides for immediate consideration (Hinds, V, 4960).
[571] Questions of consideration may not be raised against reports from the Committee on Rules (Hinds, V, 4961-4963), bills returned with the President's veto or objectons (Hinds, V, 4969-4970), and a motion to discharge a committee (Hinds, V, 4977 ; see Cannon, VIII, 2442).
[572] "A point of order which, if sustained, might prevent the consideration of a bill should be made and decided before the question of consideration is put." (*House Manual,* 80-1, section 781.) If the point of order relates merely to the matter of considering, it should be passed on after "the House has decided the question of consideration." (Hinds, V, 4950.)

previous question has been moved,[573] a process by which the House effects a final adverse disposition.[574] When a proposition is laid on the table, it remains there until called up "by unanimous consent or the motion to suspend the rules" unless it is a matter of privilege.[575]

Application of the Motion: Senate bills, House bills with Senate amendments, vetoed bills, motions to reconsider, postpone to a day certain, and discharge committees from resolutions of inquiry,[576] resolutions presenting questions of privilege, appeals from the decisions of the chair, and like matters may be laid on the table. Conference reports, previous questions, motions to recommit, to suspend the rules to go into Committee of the Whole, and generally motions relative to the order of business may not be laid on the table. A motion to discharge a committee can be laid on the table.

Jurisdiction of the Motion: The motion is not in order in the Committee of the Whole and it may not be amended. If a bill is laid on the table, pending motions connected with the bill accompany it;[577] if a proposed amendment is laid on the table, the pending bill accompanies the amendment.[578] There are some exceptions: a proposed amendment to the *Journal,* if laid on the table, is not accompanied by the *Journal;* one resolution is not accompanied by another one with which it is connected; appeals are not accompanied by the original question; a motion to instruct conferees is not accompanied by the bill; and a motion to receive a petition is not accompanied by the petition itself.

The Previous Question: *Devlopment of the Rule and Its Effects:* The previous question was not adopted in 1789 [579] as a procedure to close debate, and it could be used only on the main question. Soon, however, the leaders found it advantageous to apply the rule as it is utilized today. By 1811, in pursuance of several rulings by the Speaker which had been overruled, the Rules Committee reported and the House adopted a rule on the

---

[573] Rule XVI, clause 4; *House Manual,* 80-1, section 785; Hinds, V, 5415-5422; see also Hinds, V, 5391-5395.
[574] Hinds, V, 5389-5442; Cannon, VIII, 2649-2660; *Hearings, Revision of the Rules,* 68-1, parts 1, 2, pp. 65-96.
[575] *Cannon's Procedure in the House of Representatives,* pp. 404-405.
[576] Cannon, VI. 415; Cannon, VIII, 2652, 2659-2660, 2654, 2657.
[577] Hinds, V, 5426-5427; *Hearings, Revision of the Rules,* 68-1, part 2, pp. 65-96. Congressman Luce said: "It does seem as if it were illogical and unreasonable that a motion to lay an amendment on the table should carry with it the whole bill; it is an indirect method of killing it."
[578] Hinds, V, 5423. It applies to House bills with Senate amendments (Hinds V, 5424). See Cannon, *op. cit.,* p. 405.
[579] *House Manual,* 80-1, sections 463, 805.

previous question to close debate and have a vote on the main issue when adopted. By 1840 the House adopted the following rule: ". . . Its effects shall be to put an end to debate, and bring the House to direct vote upon amendments reported by a committee, if any, upon pending amendments, and then upon the main question." Since that time each addition or change has been in keeping with its present intent.

Nature of the Motion: Previous questions can be divided into two classes, namely: On the passage of a bill and on the adoption of any amendment to a bill. They all have the effect, however, of cutting off debate. The ordering of the previous question on a bill to final passage cuts off all debate and makes the vote on the bill privileged business until final disposition; the motion itself is not debatable. The previous question ordered on an amendment or amendments does not per se determine the time at which the bill will be completed, but it precludes further discussion on the said amendments.[580]

Termination of Debate: The use of the previous question is very popular in the House. This is the only method that the House has for closing debate.[581] The adoption of such a motion orders the House to take a vote on the pending question immediately, shutting out any interference, making a vote certain. The rule provides: "A call of the House shall not be in order after the previous question is ordered, unless it shall appear upon an actual count by the Speaker that a quorum is not present."[582] Questions will not be entertained. Modifications or amendments may be made only with unanimous consent, except one motion "to commit to a standing or select committee, without instructions."[583] The motion for the previous question may not be laid on the table. All incidental issues arising after the previous question has been ordered but before the vote is taken are decided without debate.[584]

---

[580] Hinds, V, 5443-5444. "There shall be a motion for the previous question, which, being ordered by a majority of Members voting, if a quorum be present, shall have the effect to cut off all debate and bring the House to a direct vote upon the immediate question or questions on which it has been asked and ordered. The previous question may be asked and ordered upon a single motion, a series of motions allowable under the rules, or an amendment or amendments or may be made to embrace all authorized motions or amendments and include the bill to its passage or rejection." (Rule XVII, clause 1.)

[581] Hinds, V, 5456, 5473, 5490; Cannon, VIII, 2662.

[582] Rule XVII, clause 2.

[583] Hinds, V, 5443-5444.

[584] "Under the present practice, since debate on points of order is entirely within the control of the chair, he may recognize and respond to a parliamentary inquiry although the previous question may have been demanded." (*House Manual*, 80-1, section 811).

The Forty-minute Rule: The previous question may not preclude all debate when there has been no debate of any question which is debatable. If the previous question is moved on a debatable proposition before there is any discussion, forty minutes of debate is in order,[585] the time being equally divided with all remarks confined to the merits of the bill and to the subject. If there has been any discussion, regardless of how brief, no further time is allowed.[586] The 40 minutes may not be demanded on motions not originally debatable, incidental motions, propositions which have been debated in the Committee of the Whole, and conference reports if the subject was debated before it was sent to conference.

Its Application: In any case, if the motion to move the previous question is rejected the order of business returns to the debate on the main question as if the vote had never been taken. Any Member may offer the motion but preference is given to persons in charge of the bill.[587] It can be applied to almost any question [588] so long as it is the main question.[589] Customarily, it applies to only one question or one bill at a time.[590] The motion may not include any subject matter which is foreign to the immediate problem.[591]

Unfinished Business: Legislation on which the previous question has been ordered becomes the unfinished business of the House and is highly privileged until final disposition. If unfinished at the end of one day it will be disposed of on the following legislative day; there are a few exceptions.[592] To illustrate: If the previous question has been ordered on a bill just prior to adjournment on Tuesday, it will not be in order on Calendar Wednesday, but on Thursday;[593] on the other hand, a bill considered on Wednesday on which the previous question has been ordered will also come up on Thursday. If several bills are thus carried over

---

[585] Rule XXVII, clause 3.
[586] Hinds, V, 5499-5501.
[587] See Hinds, V, 5475-5480; *Cannon's Procedure in the House of Representatives*, p. 265.
[588] See Cannon, VIII, 2673-2694. This includes privileged as well as non-privileged business. For things to which it may not be applied see: *Cannon's Procedure in the House of Representatives*, pp. 264-265.
[589] The previous question does not apply to incidental questions arising from the question to which it applies (Hinds, V, 5467). For a list of things to which it applies see *Cannon's Procedure in the House of Representatives*, pp. 266-267.
[590] Hinds, V, 5461-5464. By unanimous consent the motion may be applied to several bills at once. It may apply to the main question and a pending motion to refer at the same time (Hinds, V. 5466).
[591] For example see Hinds, V, 5457.
[592] C.R., 67-4. p. 4009; see *House Manual*, 80-1, sections 885-886; Hinds, V, 5510-5517; See Cannon, VII, 854.
[593] C.R., 62-2, p. 2292. Calendar Wednesday business is more privileged than vote on a bill on which the previous question has been moved.

to the following day, they will be considered in the same order in which the previous question on them was ordered.

Motions to Postpone: There are two distinct motions to postpone, namely: to a day certain and indefinitely. Both are subject to amendments.[594] To postpone indefinitely can be debated without limit, opening all the merits of the question;[595] the motion to postpone to a day certain is debatable within narrow limits only,[596] confined to the advisability of postponement without merits of the question.[597] The motion applies to any measure until the previous question has been moved, or until the time for a vote on passage has arrived. Neither motion is in order in the Committee of the Whole.[598] In practice these motions are not used very much, particularly to postpone indefinitely. To postpone indefinitely is about the same as an adverse disposition of a bill and there are many simpler and more common ways of defeating legislation. Besides, the House commonly uses the motion to table. The advantage gained by using the motion to postpone to a day certain can be obtained by use of the question of consideration or special orders.

Refer: The motion to refer is merely one part of the threefold rule providing for "commit," "recommit," or "refer." [599] A portion of one rule states: "When a question is under debate, no motion shall be received but to adjourn, to lay on the table, for the previous question (which motions shall be decided without debate), to postpone to a day certain, to refer, or to amend or postpone indefinitely; which several motions shall have precedence in the foregoing order; and no motion to postpone to a day certain, to refer, or to postpone indefinitely, being decided, shall be again allowed on the same day at the same stage of the question." [600] For a discussion of this topic, see the section on Recommit, p. 319.

Amending Bills in General: In House (Not Including Revenue and Appropriation Bills): Under normal procedure after all time yielded for general debate only has expired, the pending measure is thrown open for amendments. It is read, not under the five-minute rule; the entire proposal is first read and then amendments

[594] Hinds, V, 5754; Cannon, VIII, 2824.
[595] Hinds, V, 5316.
[596] Hinds, V, 5309-5310.
[597] Cannon, VIII, 2372, 2615, 2640; Hinds, V, 5311-5315.
[598] The Committee of the Whole may rise and report recommendations to the House that a matter be postponed (Hinds, IV, 4765, 4915).
[599] See Rule XVI, clause 4; Rule XVII, clause 1; XXIII, clause 7.
[600] Rule XVI, clause 4.

to all parts of it are in order by any Member, preference being
extended to the Member in charge. Any Member offering an
amendment is recognized for an hour to discuss it.

*In Committee of Whole and "in House as in Committee of
Whole"* : In the Committee of the Whole and in the House as in
the Committee of the Whole, after the termination of all general
debate on a bill or resolution, the clerk reads it by sections or
paragraphs,[601] under the five-minute rule. After any section or
paragraph has been read, any Member, preferably the Member in
charge,[602] is free to offer an amendment to it.[603] The committee
amendments, of course, are disposed of first. This procedure is
also discussed under the section on "The Committee of the Whole."

Limitations on Amendments : All amendments according to the
rules, are to be in writing when offered; in practice, they are
frequently offered orally.[604] They may not be presented by
proxy;[605] they must have been agreed to before they become a
part of the bill;[606] and the title of a bill is not amendable until after
the bill has passed.[607]

All amendments must be germane to the bill and to that portion
of it to which they are offered;[608] if an amendment has been rejected once it may not be offered again in identical form, although
a similar one is in order;[609] and it is not in order to amend or
strike out an amendment which has been accepted by the House.[610]

Substitute Amendments: The House or Committee frequently
follow the practice of adopting substitute amendments,[611] even to
the extent of replacing the entire original proposal. The substitutes,
as is true with all other amendments must be germane ; that is, they
must not only intend to accomplish the same end, but they must
not be foreign to the nature of the bill or that portion of it to

---

[601] Hinds, IV, 4738-4740
[602] Cannon, VI, 296.
[603] Rule XXIII, clause 5, for further details on amending in the Committee of the
Whole see: Chapter VIII.
[604] Cannon, VIII, 2826.
[605] Cannon, VIII, 2830.
[606] Cannon, VIII, 2832-2833.
[607] Amendments to amend the title of the bill are not debatable (Cannon, VIII,
2907).
[608] Rule XVI, clause 7; see Hinds, V, 5753-5924, 5811-5822; Cannon, VIII, 2824-
3064, 2925-2929.
[609] "It is for the House rather than the chair to decide on the legislative effect of
a proposition." (Cannon, VIII, 2841).
[610] Cannon, VIII, 2851-2856.
[611] If a substitute for an amendment or a bill is offered, it is not voted on for
adoption until after amendment to the substitute amendment has been acted on
(Cannon, VIII, 2895).

which they are offered.[612] Legislation to achieve a definite end may not be substituted for that to achieve the same end by a different method.[613] For example: A bill which provides relief for one person may not be amended to provide similar relief for another person. The fundamental purpose of the amendment must be germane to the fundamental purpose of the bill to which it is offered;[614] a portion of a proposed amendment being out of order, the whole amendment will be ruled out.[615] When offering a substitute amendment for an entire bill under consideration, it is in order to submit it after reading the first paragraph, if notice is given at that time, that the remaining paragraphs will be stricken out provided the House agrees to the substitute. Any amendments to the substitute must be disposed of before the substitute to the entire bill is voted on by the House. A replaced section of any measure, in effect a stricken out section, may not be amended.

Number of Amendments in Order at One Time: Four amendments may be pending in House or Committee at the same time,[616] but it is not in order to offer an amendment in the third degree.[617] For example: An amendment may be offered to the original bill, an amendment to the amendment, a substitute for the original amendment, and an amendment to the substitute, but no more. To dispose of them, the House votes first on the amendment to

[612] C.R., 73-2, pp. 284-285 (daily edition). An example: The Committee on the District of Columbia offered a bill for the control of whiskey in the District of Columbia. Mr. Smith of Virginia offered a substitute amendment; Mr. Black of New York made a point of order, holding that the amendment was not germane. The Chair stated: "The amendment offered by the gentleman from Virginia by way of a substitute for the entire bill provides for the sale of alcoholic beverages under a system commonly known as the dispensary system. It is admitted that the provisions of the two measures are for the accomplishment of the same object; that is, the sale of alcoholic beverages in the District of Columbia. It will be apparent, however, to all Members that the methods used are widely different from each other. The Chair has before him a number of decisions holding that to a bill seeking to accomplish a purpose by one method—an amendment proposing to accomplish the same purpose by another method is not germane. The Chair will allude to the most recent of the decisions wherein this principle was enunciated . . ."

[613] "To a bill undertaking to advance the price of agricultural commodities through the operation of a Federal agency with power to control marketing conditions an amendment proposing to secure such advance by granting a bounty to exporters of agricultural commodities was held not to be germane.

"To a bill proposing measures to meet a declared emergency and limited in operation to a period of five years an amendment proposing permanent legislation of the same character was held not to be germane." (Cannon, VIII, 2912).

[614] Cannon, VIII, 2911.

[615] Cannon, VIII, 2878.

[616] Cannon, VIII, 2831. Amendments offered by a committee have priority over amendments offered from the floor (Cannon, VIII, 2862). If a motion to strike out certain words has been defeated, it is then in order to strike out a portion of those words (Cannon, VIII, 2858) ; a motion to perfect has precedence over a motion to strike out. "A motion to strike out and insert is not in order as a substitute for a simple motion to strike out."

[617] "If an amendment be moved to an amendment, it is admitted; but it would not be admitted in another degree, to wit, to amend an amendment to an amendment of a main question" (*House Manual*, 80-1, sec. 454).

the amendment, secondly, on the amendment to the substitute, thirdly, on the substitute for the amendment, and fourthly, on the amendment to the original bill as amended, if any. As fast as one in any of the four categories is disposed of another may be offered in its stead, and offered seriatim until all amendments in each category have been exhausted. At no time may an amendment be offered in the third degree. If a substitute to the amendment should be agreed to, the fourth step becomes a vote on the amendment as amended by the substitute. *Cannon's Procedure in the House of Representatives* diagrams it as follows:

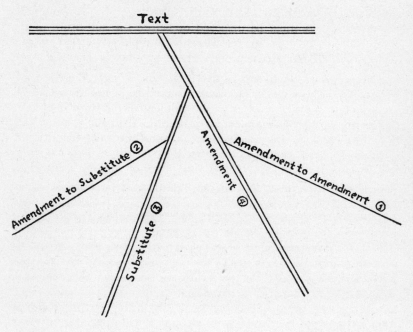

Pro Forma Amendments: The use of pro forma amendments is very popular in the House. It is the common practice when a bill is being read under the five-minute rule for amendments for any Member to rise after a paragraph or section has been read and move to strike out the last word. He thereby obtains five minutes to discuss that particular portion of the bill. After five minutes have been so consumed, another Member may move to strike out the last two words. Thus the Members may continue *ad infi-*

nitum, increasing each time the number of words to be stricken out, each obtaining five minutes to place his grievances before the House concerning the immediate subject. A pro forma amendment is not in order if in the third degree. Each time a pro is recognized, a con is entitled to recognition. This procedure is generally terminated, however, after fifteen or twenty minutes; even if there are further requests for time under this procedure the Member in charge will ask unanimous consent that all debate on the particular portion pending and all amendments thereto be closed in so many minutes.

Motion to Discharge: The motion to discharge is entirely a separate motion from that of considering the Discharge Calendar. This motion to discharge some committee from the further consideration of an ordinary piece of legislation has no privileged status, and it will yield to a demand for the regular order.[618] The motion is privileged if it is to discharge a committee from further consideration of a privileged matter, as in the case concerning a motion to discharge a committee from further consideration of a resolution of inquiry after it has been referred to the said committee as long as seven days. Whenever the motion is offered, it is not subject to the question of consideration.

Recognition and Conduct of Debate: It is obvious to a close observer of the House procedure that a few leaders occupy the floor most of the time. The increase both in the number of Members and in the amount of business has invited the establishment of "seniority" recognition. With 435 Representatives, unlimited participation would be out of the question.

Priority Recognition of Men in Control: The ranking members of the committees in charge of the pending business and the few party leaders manage the procedure of business. The Member reporting or in charge of a measure is entitled to prior recognition at all stages of its consideration; he is responsible for proposing all motions intended to expedite its passage;[619] he may not be taken from the floor by a motion of higher privilege.[620] The adoption of an amendment contrary to his support does not cause him to lose the right of prior recognition during the other stages of that bill.[621] On the other hand, if the chairman opposes a bill in the

618 Cannon, VIII, 2316.
619 Cannon, VI, 301; Hinds, II, 1457.
620 Cannon, VI, 297; Hinds, II, 1460.
621 Hinds, II, 1479. The defeat of an amendment offered by a committee does not cause the Member in charge to lose his right to prior recognition (Hinds, II, 1478; Cannon, VI, 309).

committee, a member of his committee who favored it has prior recognition;[622] if the House decides adversely against the will of the chairman on a bill, prior recognition passes to a member of the committee opposing it;[623] or if the House takes adverse action on a conference report, a conferee opposed to the report is put in control.[624] Commenting on this, Mr. Speaker Randall in 1880 said:

Now, what the Chair wants to say is this: It has always been conceded that the chairman of the Committee on Ways and Means, when a tariff bill is pending, has the floor until he offers the amendments which he sends up in behalf of the majority of the committee. That was not controverted during the pendency of the discussion on the McKinley bill. As long as Mr. McKinley offered amendments they were considered; if he let in other amendments in the meantime and then desired to recur to his own amendments the Committee of the Whole permitted him to do so until he was through with the amendments which he desired to offer. Now, passing away from the question that has just been considered by the Chair and referred to in debate, the question of recognition is absolutely in the discretion of the Chair, as all gentlemen concede. The Chair wants to be fair in exercising this discretion. Shall the Chair stop, before this bill is perfected by the gentlemen who have it in charge, and permit a number of amendments to be offered and possibly adopted to different sections, and then have the Committee on Ways and Means afterwards calling up those different sections for further amendment: The Chair thinks that such a course ought not to be pursued . . . The Chair thought yesterday, and still thinks that the gentleman from West Virginia, representing the majority of the committee, has the right to offer these amendments, and the Chair recognizes him.[625]

Length of Debate on a Bill: Debate on a measure is not in order until the House has decided to consider it by assertion or by silent assent. The length of time a measure will be discussed is generally agreed upon before debate begins; the decision may be postponed.[626] A special rule or a mutual agreement between the Members in charge with a casual approval of the House are the methods of determining the length of general debate. On minor bills, the placing of a time limit may be avoided; the Member in charge is then free to close the debate after the first speech by moving the previous question.[627] General debate is used only in Committee of Whole; in House a Member is recognized for an hour.

[622] Hinds, II, 1449.
[623] Hinds, II, 1465.
[624] Hinds, II, 1473-1477.
[625] Hinds, II, 1450.
[626] The House may have general debate on a measure for a day or so before it decides when the discussion will be terminated. An agreement may be reached on the outside and adopted on the floor.
[627] A Member presenting a bill in House is entitled to an hour to discuss it (Cannon VIII, 2470).

Time of General Debate Equally Divided: The time for general debate of a subject is equally divided between the two sides,[628] those opposing it and those favoring it. The time consumed by the minority is generally given to persons opposing the bill, and the time consumed by the majority to Members favoring it. Customarily, no Member may be allowed more than an hour.[629] When a person is recognized to call up a bill in the House he is recognized for an hour; he may discuss the bill for a few minutes and move the previous question without hearing the opposition; if the previous question is voted down, the bill will be open to further debate.

The "Control" Yields Time: The time of general debate is lodged with the "control" of the two sides, usually the chairman and ranking minority member of the committee reporting the bill, and is yielded by them to the general membership.[630] If a Member in charge of the time yields only a few minutes at first to one of of his colleagues, that does not mean that more time will not be given him. If the "control" sees fit, he may grant additional time to a person when the first allotment has expired, or the person speaking may make a unanimous consent request to proceed for a few additional minutes. The total time allowed one Member in general debate of a bill may not exceed one hour except under unanimous consent.

Practice of "Yielding" Time: A Member is free to consume any time yielded under general debate in the Committee of the Whole as he sees fit. The time granted one Member may be yielded by him to another, and by the second person to a third;[631] in this way, a Member who has already consumed the time allotted him, has an opportunity to discuss a matter during the time allotted another. The person in possession of the "floor" may let an amendment be read,[632] refer to another Member as a source of information, allow questions to be asked, and yield to adjourn without losing the floor.[633] If he yields the floor to another

[628] The control men are generally the chairman and the ranking minority member of the committee reporting the bill (Hinds, V, 5004-5005).
[629] Hinds, V, 4978; Cannon, VIII, 2460.
[630] *Hearings, Revision of the Rules*, 68-1, parts, 1, 2, p. 70. Mr. Luce said: "I dc not think, since I have been here, I have seen a man refused an extension of time unless it was quite palpable that it was a sheer waste of time to let him go on any longer."
[631] Cannon, VIII, 2470-2471.
[632] Cannon, VIII, 2477.
[633] Hinds, V, 5009. If the House adjourns, he resumes the floor when the House next convenes.
[634] Cannon, VIII, 2474-2475.

Member and that Member offers a motion during that time [634] or proposes any other business [635] the Member yielding the time loses the floor. In the House, as opposed to the Committee of the Whole, a Member offering a motion during the time of another gains the the floor for one hour.[636]

Debate Relevant to Subject: A Representative participating in debate in the House should confine his remarks to the subject under consideration,[637] but in general debate in the Committee of the Whole House on the state of the Union, a Representative may talk on any subject he desires. If a Member insists on talking about irrelevant things when he should confine his remarks to the particular subject, the Presiding Officer may require him to relinquish the floor,[638] but this does not take away his right to offer and to debate subsequent amendments. A Member may speak on the main question only once, but he may speak a second time on an amendment to the main question.[639]

Remarks Addressed to Chair and Occupant of Floor: If a Member seeks the "floor" while another is speaking, he may address the chair to make a request. The person speaking does not have to yield.[640] He may exercise his own discretion except when a point of order well taken is made.[641] The "floor" belongs to the Member recognized by the chair, and no one else may wrongfully deprive him of or disturb him in the use of this privilege.[642]

A Member not deprived of the floor by means of a technical rule of parliamentary law, does not lose the floor until he has resumed his seat.[643] A Member rising after another is seated and recognized by the Speaker, by silent assent or in spoken word, or if he breaks in without objection, obtains the floor.[644]

Limitations on Remarks: Certain restrictions have been placed upon the freedom of debate in the House. A Representative may

[635] Cannon, VIII, 2468.
[636] Cannon, VIII, 2471, 2478.
[637] Hinds, V, 5043-5048.
[638] Cannon, VIII, 2594.
[639] Cannon, VIII, 2449.
[640] "If a Member having the floor yields for interruption the remarks of the Member yielded to must appear in the *Record*, but if the Member having the floor declines to yield he may strike from copy for the *Record* remarks so interjected.
"If a Member transgresses the rules . . . in speaking the Chair may call him to order, but in the later practice the Speaker does not pass upon the question as to whether words requested to be taken down in debate are within the rule." (Cannon, VIII, 2465)
[641] Cannon, VIII, 2466-2467.
[642] Cannon, VIII, 2463-2464.
[643] Cannon, VIII, 2451. A Member resuming his seat while a paper is read in his time does not forfeit his right to the floor.
[644] A Member loses his claim to the floor if he neglects to utilize it in due time (Hinds, II, 1435).

not personally criticize the President, except with regard to how he is discharging his duties;[645] it is not in order to refer in disparaging terms to a State of the Union; and no Member may refer to the proceedings in a committee unless it has formally reported them to the House.[646] A Representative may not refer in debate to a Senator in terms of personal criticism, but he may refer to him in accordance with the rules. The rules do not permit the House to criticize the functions or actions of the Senate.[467] One house may not use records of the other by reading them in their debates concerning the subject under discussion.[648]

Members of the House may not address their colleagues in the first person;[649] a Representative should refer to another as the "Gentleman from New York." What one Member may say about another is restricted; the remarks may not be personal or disparaging.[650]

If a Member fails to live up to these precedents, it is always proper to call him to order; in fact, it has always been considered a duty of the Speaker to see that these requirements are met,[651] but it is too late to raise questions of order after other business has intervened.[652] When a demand is made that words be taken down, the person speaking must take his seat, but he proceeds if a unanimous request to that effect is made and granted.

Motion to Recommit: *Definition*: Three different rules of the House [653] provide for the motion to "commit," "recommit," or "refer," all of which are practically the same.[654] The motion offers to the House membership an opportunity of returning business to some one or more of its committees.[655] The motion is applicable to almost any legislative business;[656] it is in order against any such matter which has been debated, amended, and is ready for passage;[657] provided, however, a more privileged motion does not

[645] Cannon, VIII, 2497, 2499-2500.
[646] Cannon, VIII, 2522-2525, 2485-2494.
[647] Hinds, V, 5114-5120. 5127.
[648] Cannon, VIII, 2485-2525, 2501-2503.
[649] Cannon, VIII, 2526.
[650] Hinds, V, 5131-5358.
[651] Hinds, V, 5130.
[652] Cannon, VIII, 2537-2539.
[653] Rule XVI, clause 4; Rule XVII, clause 1; Rule XXIII, clause 7.
[654] *House Manual*, 80-1, section 787; see Cannon, VIII, 2695-2741; Hinds, V, 5521-5604.
[655] Hinds, V, 5558.
[656] It is applicable to: bills, simple and joint resolutions, concurrent resolutions, motions, impeachment charges, Senate amendments to House bills, and the like.
[657] Mr. Cannon enumerates the time to make motions as: "Either pending demand for . . . or after ordering of previous question . . . Either before . . . or after engrossment and third reading . . . After engrossment and third reading, even though previous question is not ordered . . . The motion to refer is in order before

exclude it momentarily, and the issue has not already been disposed of by a negative vote.[658] Under the following conditions, recommitment is automatic: (1) "When the House disagrees to an adverse recommendation from the Committee of the Whole" the matter is automatically recommitted to the Committee of the Whole; (2) "When instructions recommended by Committee of the Whole are ruled out of order," the issue is recommitted to the Committee of the Whole; (3) and "When failing to conform to requirements of clause 2a of Rule XIII . . . providing for comparative print showing omissions and insertions in existing law sought to be amended." [659] In the last case the bill is recommitted to the standing committee reporting it. By and large, the motion to recommit is offered after the previous queston on the passage of the bill has been ordered but before the vote is taken.

Application and Procedure: The motion is highly privileged in its due time and it may not be postponed indefinitely, divided,[660] offered a second time,[661] or laid on the table after the previous question has been ordered.[662] The motion may be withdrawn at any time prior to final disposition.[663] It may be amended by including instructions if the previous question on it is not operating,[664] provided the amendments are germane to the part of the motion to which they are offered.[665] The motions are not debatable

the previous question is demanded, but after the previous question has been ordered on a bill to final passage, the motion to refer is not admissible until after the third reading . . . The motion to recommit a simple resolution may be made at any time before the question is put on the passage of the resolution and is not in order after the resolution has been agreed to . . . . The previous question having been ordered on a motion to agree to a Senate amendment to a House bill, a motion to recommit is in order. . . ." See: *Cannon's Procedure in the House of Representatives*, pp. 297-298.

[658] The motion to recommit is not admitted: "In the Committee of the Whole . . . On report from Committee on Rules after previous question has been ordered . . . When engrossment and third reading are refused . . . When report has been adversely disposed of . . . When previous question is ordered on simple amendment in House . . . On motion to suspend the rules . . . Pending the question of consideration . . . Pending point of order against reception of report . . . If one proper motion to recommit has already been considered . . . On conference report if Senate has acted on report . . . If accompanied by preamble . . . When dilatory . . . If it strikes out an amendment just inserted by the House . . . If accompanied by instructions to include a provision which would have been subject to a point of order if offered as an amendment during consideration in Committee of the Whole . . . If embodying argument . . . If proposal is to recommit to a subcommittee and not committee en banc . . ." See: *Cannon's Procedure in the House of Representatives*, pp. 298-299.

[659] Cannon, *Ibid.*, p. 295.

[660] Cannon, VIII, 3170; Hinds, V, 5528.

[661] Cannon, VIII, 2737-2738, 2770; Hinds, V, 5577, 5582-5585.

[662] Hinds, V, 5412, 5414.

[663] Cannon, VIII, 2764.

[664] Cannon, VIII, 2695, 2698, 2712, 2738, 2741, 2762, 2790; Hinds, V, 5582-5584. The instructions can be amended. A substitute to the motion is in order, and one striking out all proposed instructions cannot be ruled out as interfering with the right of the minority to move to recommit.

[665] See Cannon, VIII, 2707-2711; Hinds, V, 6888.

if ordered on a bill to final passage.[666] Any possible debate on simple motions to recommit is narrowly limited [667] without discussion on the merits of the proposition to be referred.[668] The motion to recommit with instructions is debatable if the previous question has not been ordered,[669] but all incidental matters involving decisions after the previous question to final passage has been adopted are decided without debate. [670]

Recommit with Instructions: Motions to recommit with instructions or recommendation may be rather extensive in scope, provided they are germane to the bill.[671] The instructions may advise the committee as to what must be altered, changed, or added. The House may not recommit with instructions to strike out an amendment adopted by the House; it may instruct to strike out the text perfected by such an amendment,[672] or to add an amendment stricken out by the Committee of the Whole.[673] The motion may not include language to instruct a committee to report the bill back at any time,[674] but it may include provision to report "forthwith." [675] These motions may not include: to report at a time certain, to report out measures other than the one under consideration,[676] to provide a substitute for an entire bill adopted by the House,[677] to change nature of a bill from private to general,[678] to do indirectly what may not be done directly by amendments,[679] nor to include amendments not otherwise in order.[680]

Special Rules: Special rules may not operate to shut these motions out where they would otherwise be in order.[681]

Person Eligible to Make Motions: Any Member unconditionally

[666] Cannon, VIII, 2741.
[667] See Hinds, V, 5054.
[668] Hinds, V, 5564-5568; Cannon, VIII, 2740.
[669] Hinds, V, 5561.
[670] Hinds, V, 5448.
[671] See Hinds, V, 5527-5529, 5541; Cannon, VIII, 2704-2711.
[672] See Cannon, VIII, 2427, 2698, 2712-2725, 2743, 2854.
[673] Cannon, VIII, 2700, 2728.
[674] That privilege is determined by the nature of the bill. Hinds, V, 5543, 5544.
[675] "A bill may be committed with instructions that it be reported 'forthwith'; and in such a case the chairman of the committee to which it is committed makes a report at once without awaiting action of the committee." In 1891 the Chair ruled: "The House of Representatives, considering the bill that was before it, passed it with sundry amendments. The rules of the House provide that after a bill has been ordered to a third reading—that is, after it passes the amendment stage—then the House has an opportunity to look at the bill as amended, and if not satisfied with it, it has a right under the rules to recommit with specific instructions. That is only another method of reconsidering its action." (Hinds, V, 5545).
[676] Cannon, VIII, 2729.
[677] Cannon, VIII, 2426.
[678] Hinds, IV, 3295.
[679] Hinds, V, 5529-5541, 5834, 5889.
[680] See Hinds, V, 5806-5808, 6888; Cannon, VIII, 2704, 2708-2710.
[681] *House Manual*, 80-1, secs. 734, 782; Cannon, VIII, 2260; See Cannon VII, 774; Cannon, VIII, 2264.
[682] See Rule XVI, clause 4.

opposed to the bill as it exists may make the motion.[682] He merely addresses the chair: "Mr. Speaker, I move to recommit the bill (resolution, or conference report) to (standing, select or conference committee) with (or without instructions), and on that motion I demand the previous question." If adopted, it generally has the effect of killing the issue, at least for that session. The re-reference of one section of a bill carries with it the entire bill,[683] and the committee takes up the subject anew without regard to former actions.[684] Any instructions will confine the committee's action to the said stipulations.[685]

Status of Recommitted Bills: A committee, having reconsidered a bill recommitted to it, may make a second report on the same bill. If the bill was recommitted with instructions to report "forthwith," the bill is entitled to immediate consideration when reported;[686] otherwise, it must await its turn in accordance with the regular rules. When presented to the House a second time the Representative in charge addresses the chair: "Mr. Speaker, acting under the instructions (if there are any) of the House, and in behalf of the Committee on ——, I report back to the House the bill H.R. ——, with amendments." During the second consideration of the issue by the House, the priority of recognition passes from the Member who was in charge to the one who made the motion to recommit.[687] A bill recommitted after engrossed and read a third time must be a second time engrossed and read before its passage.[688]

Points of Order and Appeals: *Privileged Motions:* At any time during the proceedings in the House, any Member is free to raise a pertinent point of order against the actions of the House as to content or as to its method of procedure. This action is highly privileged and may interrupt a Member who has the floor;[689] it may not interrupt a roll call.[690] The motion is made thus: "Mr. Speaker, I make a point of order against . . ." or "I make a point of order that . . ." If he does not wish to make an outright point of order, he may reserve the point of order to ask certain questions or get certain information. A demand for the regular order,

[683] See Cannon, VIII, 2326.
[684] Hinds, IV, 4557 ; Hinds, V, 5558.
[685] Hinds, IV, 4404 ; Hinds, V, 5526.
[686] Hinds, V, 5550.
[687] See Hinds, II, 1465-1468.
[688] Hinds, V, 5551, 5591.
[689] See Cannon, VIII, 2466.
[690] Cannon, VIII, 3131.

however, prevents any such reservations by forcing the objector to object outright or to withdraw his objections.

Application of Motion: A point of order having been established, it has the effect of stopping that which is being done contrary to the rules or blocking out that portion of a bill against which it was made. The motion may be made to apply to the whole matter or to a portion of the matter. Debate on a point of order may be entertained to give the chair information on which to base his decision, but other business is not in order until after its disposition.

Chair Makes Decision: Rulings or decisions on points of order raised are rendered by the chair,[691] but appeals may be taken from the decision of the chair, and a majority vote rules. If no appeal is taken from the decision of the chair, it is binding on the House. The Speaker in rendering his rulings is constrained to give precedent its proper influence.

Administration of the Oath: Immediately after a newly elected Speaker assumes the chair at the beginning of each new Congress, he administers en masse the oath to the Members-elect.[692] If some of the Representatives are not present for the occasion the House may authorize the Speaker to swear in those Members at some future convenient time. The act may be performed away from the House and by some one authorized by the Speaker. The Speaker nevertheless possesses no arbitrary power to do this. All such questions of the right to have the oath administered are decided by the House.[693] It is the custom to swear in Members by unanimous consent if there is no question of improper election, even though the credentials have not arrived;[694] if a question is raised the Speaker may request the persons against whom the question was raised to stand aside. The oath as defined in the statute is:

I, A. B., do solemnly swear (or affirm) that I will support and defend the Constitution of the United States against all enemies, foreign and domestic; that I will bear true faith and allegiance to the same; that I take this obligation freely, without any mental reservation or purpose or evasion, and that I will well and faithfully discharge the duties of the office on which I am about to enter. So help me God.[695]

[691] See Hinds, V, 6927-6928.
[692] Cannon, VI, 8. This was formerly done by State delegations.
[693] The oath has been administered in the absence of a quorum (Hinds, I, 174; Cannon, VI, 21-22).
[694] Cannon, VI, 12, 13; Hinds, I, 162, 176.
[695] Hinds, I, 127, 128.

Naturally, since the House could not operate without Members, it makes this business highly privileged. And in practice, when any Member is not sworn in on the first day of the session, he will be sworn in on the day the proper credentials are presented immediately after the reading of the *Journal*.[696]

Adjournment: The House may adjourn from one day to another, recess (not to exceed three days without consent of the other body), or adjourn *sine die* with the consent of the Senate.[697] The simple motion to adjourn from one day to another is one of the highest privileged motions of the House,[698] but the Speaker may refuse to recognize a Member for that purpose when it is dilatory.[699] The simple motion to recess is without privilege,[700] but it can be entertained without objection. To adjourn for more than three days, a concurrent resolution must be adopted, but it is highly privileged.[701] To adjourn *sine die* a concurrent resolution is used, which is highly privileged. None of the motions to adjourn are debatable, including resolutions for *sine die* adjournment.[702]

Organization of the House: Motions relative to the organization of the House are of high privilege. In fact, any actions having to do with the election or disposition of the Speaker, Clerk, Chaplain, officers of the House, officials of the House, personnel of standing committees, and the like are very highly privileged and are generally considered when presented.[703]

Impeachment: Impeachment proceedings are of constitutional mandate, and they may be acted on at almost any time when presented to the House. For details on Impeachment Proceedings, see the section of this work devoted to same.[704]

Election Cases: Election cases present highly privileged business. Propositions relative to the right of a Member to his seat may come up at any time, either before or after reference to a committee, and even after the case has been closed. For details on this see section devoted to Election Cases.[705]

Electoral Vote: Matters relating to count of the electoral vote, fraud or irregularities therein, and questions connected there-

[696] Hinds, I, 172-173; Cannon, VI, 22.
[697] *Cannon's Procedure in the House of Representatives*, pp. 1-4.
[698] *House Manual*, 80-1, secs. 439, 782, 783; Hinds, III, 2521; Hinds, IV, 5605, 5359, 5366, 6451-6453.
[699] *Cannon, Op. Cit.*, p. 3.
[700] See *House Manual*, 80-1, sec. 586; Hinds, V, 6663; Cannon, VIII, 3354.
[701] Hinds, V, 6701-6706.
[702] Cannon, *Op. Cit.*, p. 2.
[703] See: Hinds, I, 212, 214, 237, 189; Cannon, VI, 3, 35.
[704] See pp. 34-39, of Chapter II.
[705] See pp. 10-14.

with have the highest constitutional and parliamentary privilege. See section on Electoral Vote.

Dilatory Motions: Practice has made it the duty of the Speaker to rule a motion dilatory if it is seemingly offered to delay business. To be rejected as such, however, it should manifestly be directed toward blocking the business of the House. Under this prerogative, the Speaker commonly rules as dilatory such highly privileged motions as to adjourn, points of no quorum, and demands for tellers.

The Journal and Record of the House: *Name of Journal:* The Constitution provides that each House shall keep a *Journal*,[706] which has been established as the official record of the House, and it is always produced in preference to the *Congressional Record* in courts or elsewhere as evidence of what occurred in the House.[707] The *Journal* has been preserved either in original draft or in duplication since 1789. The title of this record is illustrated as follows: *Journal of the House of Representatives—Congress of the United States—Begun and held at the Capitol, in the city of Washington, in the District of Columbia, on Monday the fourth day of December, in the year of our Lord nineteen hundred and five, being the first session of the Fifty-ninth Congress, held under the Constitution of the United States, and in the one hundred and thirtieth year of the Independence of said States.*

Procedure for Consideration of Journal: The *Journal* is approved at the beginning of each legislative day. Each day during the session when the House convenes after an adjournment, the transaction of business is not in order until the *Journal* has been approved, having already received the sanction of the Speaker. The reading of the *Journal* may not be interrupted except by a parliamentary inquiry, a point of no quorum,[708] or a motion to amend it.[709] The consideration of the *Journal* is of high privilege. Even during the interim between the time Congress convenes and before the Speaker is elected or the rules of the House adopted,

---

[706] Article I, section 5.

[707] Hinds, IV, 2810. The Record of the House since 1789 has been compiled in the following collections: *Annals of Congress of the United States*, 1-18 Congresses (March 3, 1789-May 27, 1824; *Congressional Debates*, 18-25 Congresses (December 6, 1824-October 16, 1837) ; *Congressional Globe*, 23-42 Congresses (December 2, 1833-March 3, 1873) ; *Congressional Record*, 43- Congresses (March 4, 1873-to date).

[708] See Cannon, VI, 625; Hinds, IV, 2732, 3009.

[709] "An error in a vote may be corrected in the *Journal* of the succeeding day, even though the result be changed thereby." (Hinds, IV, 2829). No changes may be made after the *Journal* is printed (Cannon, VI, 632). "The Speaker has held out of order a motion to expunge a portion of the *Journal*." (Hinds, 1V, 2790).

the *Journal* of the proceedings is read and approved on each legislative day.[710]

Generally it takes only a few minutes to read and approve the *Journal;* it is usually not read in its entirety; and the approval is by unanimous consent without the formal putting of the question.[711] It is possible for a minority to use this step of procedure to obstruct the business in the House.[712] It is in order for the membership to demand the reading of the *Journal* in full,[713] offer amendments to it during the reading, and demand the yeas and nays periodically thereon.[714] But further action may not be taken on the *Journal* after it has been approved.[715]

Contents of Journal: The House decides what is included in the *Journal* even to the exclusion of things which actually occurred and adding actions which did not take place. The general practice of what will be included, however, is fixed by custom. The *Journal* is a record of proceedings and not of opinions, an account of acts and not of reasons for the acts, a record of facts, and not an explanation of the facts.

Congressional Record and Reporters: In addition to the *Journal,* the House and Senate keep a daily record of their proceedings, which is called the *Congressional Record.* All actions taken in the House, all speeches made, and all official remarks by the Representatives are taken down verbatim by official reporters; in addition, matters which did not occur on the floor may be incorporated.[716] The reporters take down the proceedings at alternate periods of a few minutes each; as soon as one of these men has recorded the proceedings for a definite period, he retires from the floor and reads his stenographic notes to a dictaphone. This record is then transcribed and a copy given for correction to each Member concerned. This arrangement provides for the public an amazingly accurate account of what really occurred in the House. It is not absolutely exact, however, for Members may obtain permission from the House to revise and extend their remarks. The proceedings of one day are available in the *Record* early the next morning.

[710] Cannon, VI, 623.
[711] Cannon, VI, 625.
[712] See C.R., 73-2, pp. 10535-10541 (daily edition).
[713] Hinds, IV, 2741; Cannon, VI, 627-628.
[714] Hinds, IV, 2794; *South Atlantic Quarterly,* XXXIV, p. 88.
[715] Hinds, IV, 2781.
[716] The control of the *Record* is by concurrent resolution and law. The House separately can only control what goes in the *Record* on the House side. *Cannon's Procedure in the House of Represntatives,* p. 311.

Contents of Record: The *Record* has greatly increased in size in recent years. In addition to the regular proceedings, many speeches and related matters which had little or nothing to do with the House proceedings are daily incorporated in the *Record,* to say nothing of the speeches written by the Members themselves but never made in the House. The Appendix of the *Record,* including all types of material printed in the *Record* under the right "to leave to print" is as voluminous at times as the *Record* itself.

The Three Readings of a Bill: Rule XXI obligates the House to read each bill three times before its passage. It states that "Bills and joint resolutions on their passage shall be read the first time by title and the second time in full, when, if the previous question is ordered, the Speaker shall state the question to be: Shall the bill be engrossed and read a third time? and, if decided in the affirmative, it shall be read the third time by title, unless the reading in full is demanded by a Member, and the question shall then be put upon its passage."[717] The rule no longer defines the practice. "Formerly a bill was read for the first time by title at the time of its introduction, but since 1890 all bills have been introduced by filing them with the clerk, thus rendering a reading by title impossible at that time . . . The titles of all bills introduced are printed in the *Journal* and *Record,* thus carrying out the real purposes of the rule . . . The second reading now occurs for bills considered in the House alone when they are taken up for action, and, for bills considered in Committee of the Whole, when they are taken up in that Committee. A bill read in full in Committee of the Whole and reported therefrom is not read in full again when acted on by the House . . ." [718] The second reading is really the only time the bill is read, at which time it is read for amendments.[719] The third reading is usually by title only and comes after the order for engrossment.[720] A Member may demand that the reading be in full,[721] in which case the bill must lie over a day before passage.

[717] Rule XXI, clause 1.
[718] *House Manual,* 80-1, secs. 830-831.
[719] *Cannon's Procedure in the House,* p. 289.
[720] *Ibid.,* p. 289.
[721] Cannon, VII, 1061.

Procedure in the Senate

CHAPTER X

Introduction: The order of business in the Senate is simpler than that of the House. While the procedure of both bodies is basically founded on *Jefferson's Manual of Parliamentary Practice,* the practices of the two bodies are at considerable variance. The order and privileged status of motions and the amending procedure of the two are at less variance than their method of calling up business. The business of the Senate (bills and resolutions) is not divided into classes as a basis for their consideration nor are there calendar days set aside each month in the Senate for the consideration of particular bills and resolutions. The nature of bills has no effect on the order or time of their initial consideration. The Senate like the House gives certain motions a privileged status over others and certain business as conference reports command first or immediate consideration, but a bill which has reached the conference stage has been moved a long way toward enactment compared with the position it occupied when first reported.

Basis of Senate Procedure: In the Senate, the method of reaching a bill for consideration and the procedure followed in its passage are determined by the rules and precedents which have varied through the years. The practices and precedents, however, have been changed even more frequently than its adopted rules. There has been a tendency, nevertheless, toward uniformity of procedure. Jefferson, in the preface to his *Manual,* the basis of Senate procedure, stated:

> The Constitution of the United States, establishing a legislature for the Union under certain forms, authorizes each branch of it 'to determine the rules if its own proceedings.' The Senate has accordingly formed some rules for its own government; but these going only to few cases, it has referred to the decision of its President, without debate and without appeal, all questions of order arising either under its own rules or where it has provided none . . . The law of proceedings in the Senate as composed of the precepts of the Constitution, the regulations of the Senate, and, where these are silent, of the rules of Parliament, I have here endeavored to collect

and digest so much of these as is called for in ordinary practice, collating the Parliamentary with the Senatorial rules, both where they agree and where they vary. I have done this as well to have them at hand for my own government as to deposit with the Senate the standard by which I judge and am willing to be judged . . .

I am aware that authorities can often be produced in opposition to the rules which I lay down as parliamentary. An attention to dates will generally remove their weight. The proceedings of Parliament in ancient times, and for a long while, were crude, multiform, and embarrassing. They have been, however, constantly advancing toward uniformity and accuracy, and have now attained a degree of aptitude to their object beyond which little is to be desired or expected.

Yet I am far from the presumption of believing that I may not have mistaken the parliamentary practice in some cases, and especially in those minor forms, which, being practiced daily, are supposed known to everybody, and therefore have not been committed to writing. Our resources in this quarter of the globe for obtaining information on that part of the subject are not perfect. But I have begun a sketch, which those who come after me will successively correct and fill up till a code of rules shall be formed for the use of the Senate, the effects of which may be accuracy in business, economy of time, order, uniformity, and impartiality.

The Senate is a Continuing Body: The Senate is a continuing body as contrasted with that of the House. Legally, two-thirds of the, Senators of an old Congress return to the subsequent new one without having to be re-elected,[1] but all Representatives must stand for re-election every two years. Thus the manner and extent of organizing each new Senate have not been established under the influence of definite breaks between each Congress as has been the experience of the House, nor have the parliamentary rules of the Senate been equally subjected to alterations. The Representatives re-adopt their old rules of procedure at the inception of each Congress, sometimes with slight modification, while the Senators have not given a general reaffirmation to their rules since 1789. The identical rules adopted by the Senate in the first Congresses have remained in force continuously with the exceptions of particular additions or abolishments from time to time. Any such changes are made by amending the rules to meet new needs of that august and esoteric group. Changes have not been frequent as seen by the fact that a codification of the accumulated alterations have occurred on only five different occasions.[2]

[1] This is under the assumption that no Senator dies or resigns during the interim.
[2] They are:

Date Adopted	Citations	Senate Membership at the time	Number of rules
April 16-18, 1789	Senate Journal, p. 16	20	20

The continuity of sessions of the same Congress is provided for by the following rule:

At the second or any subsequent session of a Congress, the legislative business of the Senate which remained undetermined at the close of the next preceding session of that Congress shall be resumed and proceeded with in the same manner as if no adjournment of the Senate had taken place; and all papers referred to committees and not reported upon at the close of a session of Congress shall be returned to the office of the Secretary of the Senate, and be retained by him until the next succeeding session of that Congress, when they shall be returned to the several committees to which they had previously been referred.[3]

The Senate manual embodies 826 printed pages but the Senate rules are set forth in only 61 pages of that volume. Twelve pages of the 61 are devoted to naming the standing committees and defining their jurisdictions. Seven additional pages of the 61 were added to the rules in 1946 by passage of the Legislative Reorganization Act of 1946. The rules number 40. The present practices evolved from the predominant customs, traditions, and usages of the Senate since 1789. This evolutionary process has given the Senate a mosaic parliamentary edifice. Three of the Senate rules are concerned with executive sessions, treaties, and nominations.[4] These subjects are not within the jurisdiction of the House of Representatives.

Senate Calendar: Under its orthodox procedure, all business presented to the Senate for its consideration and disposition is first referred to one of its standing committees for study and report; this step can be by-passed. All reported business is placed on one of two Senate calendars in the chronological order reported and there awaits Senate consideration and disposition. The reported legislative proposals (bills and resolutions) are printed on the "Calendar of Business" * and treaties and nominations are printed on the "Executive Calendar."

Proposed legislation approved by a committee or ordered placed on the calendar by the Senate is placed on the "Calendar of Business" under the heading of "General Orders." Each bill or resolution is not only placed there in the order reported but is given a calendar number, and is set forth in one of the following

---

March 26, 1806	*Ibid.*, pp. 65-66	34	40
January 3, 1820	*Ibid.*, pp. 61-69	46	45
March 25, 1868	*Ibid.*, pp. 340-347	68	53
January 11, 1884	*Ibid.*, pp. 145-160	76	40

[3] *Senate Manual.* p. 44.
[4] Also Rule XXXV could be added to this group since such sessions are always concerned with closed sessions.
* For illustration of Senate Calendar see page 444.

categories: (1) "General Orders," (2) "Resolutions and Motions Over Under the Rule," (3) "Motions for Reconsideration," (4) "Subjects on the Table," and (5) "Calendar of Special Orders." Before discussing the legislative business brief mention will be made of business on the Executive Calendar.

Executive Calendar

Business on the Senate Executive Calendar consists of reported nominations and treaties. Briefly, treaties and nominations are sent to the Senate by the President and disposed of as follows:

Nominations: *Submitted by President:* The Constitution provides that the President:

. . . Shall nominate, and by and with the advice and consent of the Senate, shall appoint Ambassadors, other public Ministers and Consuls, Judges of the Supreme Court, and all other Officers of the United States, whose appointments are not herein otherwise provided for, and which shall be established by law; but the Congress may by law vest the appointment of such inferior officers, as they think proper, in the President alone, in the courts of law, or in the heads of departments.

The President shall have power to fill up all vacancies that may happen during the recess of the Senate, by granting commissions which shall expire at the end of their next session.

On the day the Senate receives such a proposed nomination from the President, it is printed in the *Congressional Record* at the very end of the Senate proceedings, unless the Senate should otherwise order. Likewise, a record of confirmations or rejections of nominations is printed at the end of the Senate proceedings in the *Record* of the day the action was taken.

Committee Reference: Under the rules, nominations when received are referred to the appropriate standing committee for consideration, unless otherwise ordered. The committee of reference is determined in accordance with its jurisdiction over legislation. To illustrate, since matters of foreign relations go to the Committee on Foreign Relations, that committee has jurisdiction over nominations to Foreign and Diplomatic Posts; the Committee on the District of Columbia has jurisdiction over nominations to offices in the District of Columbia Government. Nominations to Federal judgeships go to the Committee on the Judiciary; civil service appointments and postmasters to the Committee on Post Office and Civil Service; nominations to offices administering laws to do with interstate commerce, such as the

Interstate Commerce Commission, the Federal Trade Commission, Securities and Exchange Commission, and the like, to the Committee on Interstate and Foreign Commerce; and nominations to fiduciary agencies such as the Federal Reserve Board, Federal Deposit Insurance Corporation, and Reconstruction Finance Corporation, to the Committee on Banking and Currency. Rule XXV, defining the jurisdiction of the standing committees, does not specify which committees shall receive which nominations, but through the years the line of demarcation for their reference to the various committees has been definitely drawn. Thus each nomination for a Federal office submitted to the Senate by the President is referred by well established precedent to the committee having jurisdiction. If a reference is questioned, the committee to which the nomination was sent can be discharged and the nomination re-referred. If there is a question of reference in the first instance, the final determination is lodged with the Senate after the same procedure utilized in the reference of legislation.

Nominations not Confirmed: Nominations having been received by the Senate but neither confirmed nor rejected during a session to which they were submitted, are not pending business at any succeeding session and will not be considered further unless the President re-submits them. Likewise, when the Senate adjourns or takes a recess for more than thirty days, all pending nominations not finally acted upon as of that date are returned by the Secretary of the Senate to the President, and they must be re-submitted to the Senate if they are to get further consideration. The Senate may vacate the application of this rule to particular nominations and hold them over for consideration at the beginning of a new session or after a 30-day recess.[5]

Committee Consideration: A nomination is referred to a standing committee for study and approval just as a proposed piece of legislation. The committee, usually a sub-committee of the standing committee to which the nomination is referred, is free to hold public hearings, and generally does so in the case of controversial nominations.

When a nomination is referred by a standing committee to one of its subcommittees for study and decision, it is first acted on by that group, and then reported back, favorably or unfavorably,

---

[5] This was done under unanimous consent procedure at the end of the First Session of the 80th Congress in the case of several hundred military nominations Rule 38, paragraph 6 was suspended.

to the full committee. Under this procedure, the subcommittee becomes the high hurdle; the full committee approval of its subcommittee decision is generally perfunctory, but not necessarily so. The full committee is free to open up every phase of action taken by its subcommittee. Or the subcommittee may vote to report inaction and request further instructions from its parent committee.

The normal practice in the disposition of a controversial nomination is as follows: it is referred to a subcommittee for study. The subcommittee may or may not hold hearings. If hearings are held, the nominee may be the only witness; or many persons might be called to testify, including the nominee, his former associates, independent informants, and proponents and opponents. Following the hearings, the subcommittee holds an executive session or sessions to reach a decision—to vote to report the nomination favorably or unfavorably to the full committee. The nomination may die in the subcommittee without action, or without action beyond hearings.

Noncontroversial nominations are generally approved after a brief executive session, either by the full committee, or after brief executive sessions by the subcommittee and then by the full committee; they are usually considered en bloc, when presented to the committee in numbers. The full standing committees commonly act on nominations, reporting them favorably to the Senate, after an executive session, without subcommittee consideration; occasionally this is the case when they are controversial.

In any case, the committees take action on nominations by studying them, by refusing to consider them, by rejecting them, by reporting them unfavorably, or by reporting them favorably to the Senate. A nomination reported to the Senate is placed on the Executive Calendar, where it awaits final disposition.

Nominations are considered in open executive session "unless the Senate in closed session by a majority vote shall determine that a particular nomination . . . shall be considered in closed executive session, in which case all subsequent proceedings with respect to said nomination . . . shall be kept secret." [6]

Senate Consideration: In practice the legislator in charge of the program, generally the majority floor leader, toward the close of the day or near the end of a legislative sitting, moves that the

[6] Rule XXXVIII.

Senate "proceed to the consideration of executive business." A motion to proceed to the consideration of such business is in order at any time [7] and is not debatable. Upon the adoption or approval of the motion, the Senate proceeds with the executive business, in this case nominations. The Clerk merely reports the nominations one after another without awaiting a motion from the floor. They are reported or called in the order listed on the Executive Calendar, namely: The chronological order in which they were reported to the Senate.

In the case of a controversial nomination, the Senate often spends a short time in debate before voting to confirm it, or the debate may be drawn out over several days before a final vote of disposition is reached. Once a controversial nomination has been brought up for debate, either by adoption of a motion to that effect or on call of calendar, it becomes the unfinished executive business, but the consideration of one nomination can be displaced by the adoption of a motion to consider another. If an unfinished nomination is not displaced when the Senate terminates a day's session, if it recesses in executive session, the first order of business on reconvening the next day is further consideration of that nomination. This procedure may be continued indefinitely, even to the extent of calling up and acting on additional nominations without going back into legislative session. When the Senate does go back into legislative session, without final action on an unfinished nomination, that question goes over until the next session for consideration of executive business. The two classes of business are considered independently of each other—one in "executive session", the other in "legislative session."

The amount of debate the Senate may devote to a nomination is without limit. "No Senator shall speak more than twice upon any one question in debate on the same day without leave of the Senate." [8] But, in practice, this is hardly a limitation. The cloture rule, on the other hand, is not applicable to nominations; its application is to "pending measures." [9]

Noncontroversial nominations are frequently considered en bloc, but the procedure must be under unanimous consent. Likewise, it is not in order to move to recommit nominations en bloc. Regular procedure requires that a motion be confined to one nomination.

[7] See C.R., 77-1, p. 3129 (daily edition).
[8] Rule XIX.
[9] See ruling by Chair on August 2, 1948, when question of application was raised as to a motion to bring up H.R. 29, Anti-poll Tax bill.

A nomination may not be confirmed the day it is submitted "unless by unanimous consent." But a nomination which has gone over one day under the rule, cannot be postponed, as a matter of right, by a single objection.[10] The rule provides that the "final question on every nomination shall be, 'Will the Senate advise and consent to this nomination?' which question shall not be put on the same day on which the nomination is received, nor on the day on which it may be reported by a committee, unless by unanimous consent."

Nominations are considered and acted on in the Senate chamber in open session unless the membership in closed session by a majority vote decides to the contrary. In the case of a closed executive session, the proceedings "shall be kept secret," but the injunction of secrecy "may be removed" by a majority vote in closed session. *"And provided further,* That any Senator may make public his vote in closed executive session." [11]

Confirmations may be reconsidered and any Senator who voted with the majority may make that motion, but it must be made on the same day or within two days following an actual executive session. It is in order, of course, to lay any such motion on the table. If the confirmation has been sent to the President, then the motion to reconsider shall be accompanied by a motion to request the President to return such notification to the Senate. The Senate gives up its right to reconsider a nomination when it orders the President to be notified of that confirmation; in effect, such action waives the rule on reconsideration. It may adopt a motion to reconsider the approval of a nomination, but the President may refuse to return it.[12] Senate decisions on nominations are not sent to the President, except when otherwise ordered, until the time has elapsed for making a motion to reconsider them, or until any pending motions to reconsider have been disposed of.

In the case of nominations, the question of "Senatorial courtesy" is frequently raised. Various nominations have been fought on the grounds that they were personally obnoxious to a Senator

[10] See C.R., 80-1, p. 2064 (daily edition) ; March 12, 1947.

[11] Rule XXXVIII.

[12] The Senate in 1939 confirmed the nomination of Elmer D. Davies, to be district judge. Senator Warren Barbour of N. J., holding that the nomination had been disposed of unexpectedly, offered a motion to recall it from the President, which was adopted. The following day the President replied that he was unable to accede to the request since the appointment had already been sent out (see APSR, 76-1, Vol. XXXIII, Dec. 1939, p. 1043).

of the nominee's State. Some have been rejected on that ground
alone; others have been approved, the objections of the Senator
to the contrary notwithstanding, particularly where the Senators
of the same State were divided in the matter. Some of the
instances when personal objections were raised against nominations
follow:

Some which were confirmed

Objections by:	*Date*	*Nominee and Office*
1. Senator Brookhart	1930	Hanford MacNider, minister to Canada
2. Senator Bilbo	1936	Edwin R. Holmes, Circuit Judge of 5th Circuit
3. Senator Holt	1938	F. Roy Yoke, Collector of Internal Revenue
4. Senator O'Daniel	1947	Joe B. Dooley, U. S. District Judge for northern District of Texas

Some which were rejected

1. Senator Bailey	1932	C. A. Jonas, U. S. Attorney for Western District of N. C.
2. Senator Long	1932	Ernest A. Burguieres, Commissioner of Immigration at Port of New Orleans.
3. Senators of La.	1934	Daniel A. Moore, Collector of Internal Revenue, La.
4. Senator Glass	1939	Floyd H. Roberts, U. S. District Judge, Western District of Virginia
5. Senator McCarran	1939	Wm. S. Boyle, U. S. District Attorney for Nevada.

Treaties: *Submitted by President:* Treaties like nominations
are submitted to the Senate by the President. The Constitution
provides that the President "shall have power, by and with the
advice and consent of the Senate, to make treaties, provided two-
thirds of the Senators present concur." The Senate, of course, is
free to adopt resolutions, recommending to the President that he
negotiate a treaty or take action to make certain international
settlements. Constitutionally, however, any document meeting the
definition of a treaty must be negotiated under direction of the
Executive Branch, presented to the Senate by the President, and
concurred in by that body before it can become effective.

Reference to Committee: Under the rules, treaties before ratification must be read three times on separate days, except by unanimous consent. When first presented for Senate concurrence, it is
read a first time, and only for the information of the Senate; at
this time motions to reject, ratify, or alter the whole or any part
thereof are not in order. Only the motions to refer to the Committee on Foreign Relations, to print in confidence for the use of

the Senate, to remove the injunction of secrecy, or to consider in open executive session, may be entertained.[13]

Treaties Not Ratified: All treaties are referred to the Committee on Foreign Relations for study and recommendation, unless the Senate by unanimous consent orders otherwise. Once referred, a treaty becomes the pending business of that committee and remains so until voted down (tabled) or until reported favorably or unfavorably to the Senate. An unfinished treaty at adjournment of a session or of a Congress "shall be resumed" at the next session of the same or of a new Congress. Proceedings on a treaty, however, terminate with a Congress, "and they shall be resumed at the commencement of the next Congress, as if no proceedings had previously been had thereon." Rule XXXVII provides: "Treaties transmitted by the President to the Senate for ratification shall be resumed at the second or any subsequent session of the same Congress at the stage in which they were left at the final adjournment of the session at which they were transmitted; but all proceedings on treaties shall terminate with the Congress, and they shall be resumed at the commencement of the next Congress as if no proceedings had previously been had thereon." To illustrate this procedure: On April 17, 1947, Senator Vandenberg reported on behalf of the Committee on Foreign Relations, a resolution which was passed without objection, directing the Secretary of the Senate to return 19 obsolete treaties which in his message to the Senate on April 8, 1947, the President asked to have withdrawn. On that occasion Senator Vandenberg told the Senate;

Mr. President, under the law and practice, whenever the President of the United States sends treaties to the Senate they remain on the calendar of the Senate Committee on Foreign Relations from one Congress to another. As a result, when the Committee organized for the Eightieth Congress, I found innumerable old treaties carried currently on the calendar of the committee, some of them going back to as far as 1923. For instance, on the current calendar of the committee one treaty is still in the hands of a subcommittee consisting of the Senator from Idaho, Mr. Borah; the Senator from Wisconsin, Mr. LaFollette; the Senator from Illinois, Mr. Glenn; the Senator from Arkansas, Mr. Robinson; and the Senator from Montana, Mr. Walsh.

I find another treaty, Mr. President, which is still currently carried on the calendar and is in the hands of a subcommittee consisting of the Senator from Wisconsin, Mr. Duffy; the Senator from Indiana, Mr. Van Nuys; and the Senator from New Mexico, Mr. Cutting.

[13] Note discussion of procedure for considering treaties at the following references: C.R., 79-1, pp. 2701-2702, 3210, 3226 (daily edition).

It occurred to me that it would be a good idea to clean up the calendar, and, in accordance with instructions of the Committee on Foreign Relations, I addressed a communication to the Department of State, suggesting that it recommend some course of action to bring the calendar down to date. As a result, we received a Presidential message last week, recommending the return to the President of all treaties submitted prior to 1941.[14]

Committee Consideration: The Committee on Foreign Relations in its consideration of treaties follows a procedure much the same as it utilizes in the disposition of legislation. In recent practice, nearly all treaties are studied and acted on by the committee in closed session; public hearings are infrequently held. There is little or no popular demand for them.

The committee is free to kill the treaty, report it adversely, report it with amendments or reservations, or report it in the identical form submitted to the Senate by the President.

On the date a treaty is transmitted to the Senate, its receipt is noted in the *Congressional Record.* Information and details on the treaty are kept secret until the Senate removes "the injunction of secrecy" by motion, or unless considered in open executive session. Of late years, the injunction of secrecy has almost invariably been removed at time of reference to committee. The rule provides: ". . . all treaties which may be laid before the Senate, and all remarks, votes, and proceedings thereon shall also be kept secret, until the Senate shall, by their resolution, take off the injunction of secrecy, or unless the same shall be considered in open Executive session."

After committee action, including a vote to report favorably or to report unfavorably, treaties are printed on the Senate Executive Calendar in the order reported; there they await Senate consideration and final disposition. The Committee having reported a treaty loses jurisdiction over the subject; the Senate reacquires jurisdiction.

Senate Consideration: Except by unanimous consent a reported treaty must lay over one day before it is in order to be called up for consideration. A treaty under consideration is displaced by agreement to take up a nomination.[15] A motion to proceed to the consideration of executive business is in order at any time and is not debatable.[16] When a treaty is reached on the call of the

14 C.R., 80-1, p. 3756 (daily edition).
15 C.R., 79-1, pp. 2142-2143 (daily edition).
16 See Senate proceedings for April 7, 1941.

Executive Calendar a motion for its consideration need not be made from the floor; it is before the Senate and is presented by the clerk for disposition.[17]

When called up, the treaty is read a second time. Debate follows if it is controversial; otherwise it is concurred in without debate or "without objection." If there are any proposed reservations or amendments by the committee, they are acted on first, at the time when each are in order. Thereafter, amendments or reservations from the floor are in order.

Treaties are "considered as in Committee of the Whole" when "it shall be proceeded with by articles." After the amending process has been concluded the proceedings had "as in the Committee of the Whole shall be reported" to the Senate and, if amended the question shall be "will the Senate concur in the amendments made in Committee of the Whole?" The amendments may be voted on separately or in gross "if no Senator shall object; after which new amendments may be proposed." Reservations are in order only after the amending process has been concluded; they are offered to the resolution of ratification as distinguished from the treaty itself. Amendments or reservations are added to any treaty by a majority vote. The title of the treaty, with any amendments or reservations set out in full, are then "reduced to form of a resolution of ratification . . . It shall be proposed on a subsequent day, unless, by unanimous consent, the Senate determines otherwise; at which stage no amendment shall be received unless by unanimous consent." The requirement for the lapse of one day is met by a recess of the Senate taken in legislative session.

"On the final question to advise and consent to the ratification in the form agreed to, the concurrence of ⅔ of the Senators present shall be necessary to determine it in the affirmative." Also motions to postpone indefinitely must be decided by a two-thirds vote. All other questions upon a treaty are decided by a majority vote.

A transcript of proceedings by the Senate on treaties are incorporated in the body of the *Congressional Record*, unless the Senate determines that they shall be kept secret. In the case of closed sessions on treaties, which are determined by a majority vote, the secrecy of the proceeding may be removed by adopting a motion to that effect, which also requires only a majority vote.

[17] C.R., 80-1, p. 4061 (daily edition).

Any Senator is free to make public his vote even in a "closed" executive session.[18]

The Senate may go into a closed session at will for the "discussion of any business which may . . . require secrecy" by adopting a motion to that effect. Immediately upon motion being made and seconded, the Presiding Officer orders the galleries cleared and doors closed. The discussion of a motion to go into closed session, which has been seconded, is held behind closed doors.

"When acting upon confidential or Executive business, unless the same shall be considered in open Executive session, the Senate Chamber shall be cleared of all persons except the Secretary, the Chief Clerk, the Principal Legislative Clerk, the Executive Clerk, the Minute and Journal Clerk, the Sergeant at Arms, the Assistant Doorkeeper, and such other officers as the Presiding Officer shall think necessary; and all such officers shall be sworn to secrecy."

"Any Senator or officer of the Senate who shall disclose the secret or confidential business or proceedings of the Senate shall be liable, if a Senator, to suffer expulsion from the body; and if an officer, to dismissal from the service of the Senate, and to punishment for contempt.[19]

Legislative Business

Introduction: The first portion of the remainder of this chapter is devoted to the order of consideration of legislative business; that is, the time when it is in order to bring up "what business." These are questions entirely separate from: precedence of motions when a bill is pending, the precedence of motions to the final disposition of a conference report and amendments reported in disagreement, or what motions are in order at any time, because of a certain condition which has obtained, such as a motion to call the roll to obtain a quorum—assuming the Senator who has the floor yields for that purpose or that no Senator has the floor—or that the question is privileged, thus taking the Senator's right to the floor away or temporarily suspending it. The latter part of the chapter is devoted to these last-mentioned motions and matters which intervene because of their nature.

Business on Calendar: All business printed on the "Calendar of Business" is set forth under one of the following heads:

18 Rule XXXVIII, clause 2.
19 Rule XXXVI.

(1) General Orders, (2) Resolutions and Motions Over Under the Rule, (3) Motions for Reconsideration, (4) Subjects on the Table, and (5) Calendar of Special Orders.

The business listed under "General Orders" is composed of all bills and resolutions reported by Senate standing committees or ordered placed on the calendar when received by the Senate. In effect, practically all proposed legislation awaiting Senate action is listed under this portion of the calendar. Business listed under "Resolutions and Motions Over Under the Rule" consists of resolutions or motions which were introduced or made during the legislative day but not laid on the table or referred. They are in order for disposition during the morning hour at the beginning of the next legislative day. Under "Motions for Reconsideration" are listed all motions made to reconsider particular actions already taken by the Senate, be they the passage of bills or resolutions or the vote on disposition of any matter coming before the Senate. This business is not privileged but may be brought up by motion having the support of a majority of the Senators present, if a quorum. Comprising "Subjects on the Table" is all business placed there at request, which at a later date may be called up by motion for immediate consideration, or for reference to a committee as the case may require. The "Calendar of Special Orders" is composed of decisions made by the Senate as to order of business at a time specific. Any subject, including the consideration of a bill, may, by a two-thirds vote of the Senators present, or by unanimous consent, be made a special order.

Legislative and Calendar Days: A compendium of the daily order of business in the Senate is set forth primarily by Rules VII, VIII, IX, and X. These rules, however, contemplate a legislative day, whereas the Senate has very few legislative days during a session. Experience shows that the Senate when it has unfinished business, frequently recesses at the close of a calendar day instead of adjourning; it has reduced a whole regular session to five legislative days.

Every time it takes a recess instead of adjourning, the legislative day remains the same and when the Senate reconvenes, even though it be one calender day later, it returns to the business left unfinished at the time of taking the recess. Any deviation from this procedure must be accomplished under unanimous consent or the Senate must take formal action to the contrary. It may adopt a motion to stay further action on the bill under consideration and proceed to another; by unanimous consent it may put aside the bill under consideration until it can pass one it deems more urgent; it may act on privileged business such as a conference report without displacing the unfinished business; or under unanimous consent it can ignore its orthodox procedure completely.

The legislative day and calendar day remain the same only when the Senate adjourns at the end of each day's sitting. When it recesses from day to day for a number of calendar days, the legislative day remains the same as that of the last calendar day to which it last adjourned. When it adjourns following a series of such recesses, the legislative day immediately catches up with the calendar day, skipping over all of the intervening calendar days.

This is significant in Senate procedure because so many of the rules are tied to the legislative day. To illustrate: Rule XIV provides that "whenever a bill or joint resolution shall be offered, its introduction shall, if objected to, be postponed for one day." Rule XIX provides that "no Senator shall speak more than twice upon any one question in debate on the same day without leave of the Senate . . ."

Morning Hour: (A) *Chaplain Offers Prayer*: The daily sessions of the Senate begin at 12 o'clock meridian unless that body decides upon another hour. At 12 noon each day the Senate sits, following an adjournment or recess, the Presiding Officer, accompanied by the Chaplain, occupies the rostrum. The Presiding Officer takes the gavel and raps once for order.[20] The Chaplain opens the session with a prayer.[21]

Business Dependent Upon a Recess or Adjournment: The remaining procedure of each day's sitting is dependent upon whether or not the Senate recessed or adjourned at the end of its prior meeting. If the meeting follows a recess, the next order of business is a return to the unfinished business under consideration at the time the recess was taken; the *Journal* need not be read on a day following a recess.[22] The Senate may transact routine business.

[20] Legend has it that the same gavel has been in *continuous* use since the first Congress.
[21] The Senate on February 6, 1939, adopted S. Res. 8, of that Congress, which was agreed to as follows:
"*Resolved*, That the Chaplain shall open each Calendar day's session of the Senate with prayer." (*Senate Journal*, 76-1, p. 93, Feb. 6, 1939). Prior to this time prayer was offered only at the beginning of each legislative day.
[22] See C.R., 79-2, p. 9839 (daily edition).

While any regular morning hour business following a recess is transacted under unanimous consent and is only justified by practice, such business is transacted at almost every sitting following a recess. Frequently after the prayer is offered, under unanimous consent procedure, the *Journal* of proceedings of the preceding day's session is read by the clerk; reports, messages, and communications on the Vice President's table are disposed of; petitions and memorials are presented, and bills, resolutions, and amendments are introduced or submitted for reference to committees before the Senate returns to the unfinished business coming over from the preceding day. Commonly the regular proceedings of the day are interrupted from time to time for the Senate to dispose of some routine or noncontroversial unanimous consent request. The unfinished business coming over from the preceding day, however, is privileged for immediate consideration after the prayer unless the session follows an adjournment instead of a recess.

Following an adjournment the Senate begins a new legislative day at its next sitting. On this occasion the morning business defined by Rule VII is in order during the morning hour. According to a resolution adopted August 10, 1888, the morning hour terminates at the expiration of two hours after any meeting of the Senate.[23]

(B) *Correction of Journal:* The Presiding Officer having called the Senate to order and the Chaplain having opened the session with prayer, "and a quorum being present, the *Journal* of the preceding day shall be read, and any mistake made in the entries corrected. The reading of the *Journal* shall not be suspended unless by unanimous consent; and when any motion shall be made to amend or correct the same, it shall be deemed a privileged question, and proceeded with until disposed of." [24] A motion to approve the *Journal* is not in order until it has first been read; furthermore, the motion has been ruled unnecessary since Rule II does not require that it be approved; only a "correction" of the *Journal* is stipulated.[25] A motion to suspend the reading of the *Journal* is not in order [26] but the reading is regularly dispensed with under unanimous consent procedure.

[23] See *Senate Journal*, 50-1, p. 1266.
[24] Rule III; see also *Senate Journal*, 72-1, p. 126 for Jan. 6, 1932.
[25] See C.R., 77-2, p. 9196 (daily edition).
[26] *Senate Journal*, 69-2, p. 253.

This step usually takes only a moment. On motion of the Senator accepting the responsibility, generally the majority floor leader, "and by unanimous consent," "the *Journal* of the proceedings of yesterday" are approved without objection. The business is transacted just that quickly; it doesn't have to be, however. It has been used to block action on legislation. In the second session of the 79th Congress, the very first bill called up for consideration was S.101, to make the FEPC a permanent governmental agency. The Southern Senators immediately mobilized to engage in a protracted filibuster, which continued from January 18 through February 9, at which time the bill was put back on the calendar after a motion to invoke the cloture rule had been rejected by a vote of 48 to 36.[27]

The bill, however, was pending before the Senate for a very short time; actually most of the debate was directed to procedural motions instead of to the bill. The Senate having adjourned instead of recessing at the end of the first day after the FEPC bill had been brought up for consideration, the next day, the *Journal* had to be approved before any other business was in order. But when the *Journal* was read for correction, Senator Overton made a motion to amend it to include the Chaplain's prayer. This motion occupied the Senate until Senator Hoey of North Carolina moved to amend the *Journal* to insert the names of Senators who failed to answer a certain quorum call. This motion remained the pending business until Senator Barkley moved to act on a petition to invoke the cloture rule. Senator Barkley's motion was ruled out of order on the basis that the bill on which the petition was presented was not before the Senate.[28] An appeal was taken from the decision of the chair which occupied the Senate through February 7.[29]

In the 80th Congress, on April 3, 1947, the Committee on Rules and Administration reported Senate Resolution 25, to amend the Cloture Rule, to make motions relating to the approval of the

---

[27] Senator Chavez obtained recognition on Jan. 17 after the morning business was dispensed with and moved consideration of S. 101; the motion having been made before 2 p.m., it was not debatable and upon a roll-call vote, the motion carried by 49 to 17. In the vote on cloture, 22 Democrats, 25 Republicans, and 1 other voted for, while 28 Democrats and 8 Republicans voted against.

[28] When Senator Barkley endeavored to invoke the cloture rule the first time, Senator Russell made a point of order that a motion to conclude debate on Senate Bill 101 was not in order since the Senate was debating the *Journal* and not S. 101.

[29] The appeal was never voted on, since at a later date Senator Barkley was given unanimous consent to withdraw his appeal. See C.R., 79-2, p. 1089 (daily edition), for Feb. 7, 1946.

Journal a subject for "cloture." The Senate did not act on the resolution, leaving the rule unchanged.

(C) *Presiding Officer Presents Business to Senate:* Each legislative day following the approval of the *Journal,* the Presiding Officer lays before the Senate for disposition "messages from the President,[30] reports and communications from the heads of departments, and other communications addressed to the Senate, and such bills, joint resolutions, and other messages from the House of Representatives as may remain upon his table from any previous day's session undisposed of."

The *Congressional Record* records samples of such business as follows:

The PRESIDENT pro tempore laid before the Senate a letter from the Acting Secretary of Agriculture, reporting, pursuant to Public Law 657, Seventy-ninth Congress, second session, on the settlement of claims filed in cases where work, supplies, or services have been furnished to the Government under contracts during the war by the Fresno Dehydrating Co., of Fresno, Calif., amounting to $110,234.61, and the Visalia Dehydrating Co., of Visalia, Calif., amounting to $132,956.82, which was referred to the Committee on the Judiciary.

The PRESIDENT pro tempore laid before the Senate a letter from the Secretary of the Navy, transmitting a resolution adopted by the 1948 session of the Guam Congress, favoring the establishment of a national cemetery on Guam, which, with the accompanying resolution, was referred to the Committee on Interior and Insular Affairs.

The PRESIDENT pro tempore laid before the Senate a resolution adopted by the Pennsylvania Society of Sons of the Revolution, Philadelphia, Pa., favoring the enactment of legislation providing universal military training, which was referred to the Committee on Armed Services.

A message from the House of Representatives, by Mr. Swanson, one of its reading clerks, announced that the House had agreed to the amendments of the Senate to the amendments of the House to the bill (S. 1393) to increase the permitted rate of allowance and compensation for training on the job under Veterans Regulation No. 1 (a), as amended.

The PRESIDENT pro tempore laid before the Senate the following letters, which were referred as indicated:

Investment of Certain Funds in Obligations of International Bank for
Reconstruction and Development

A letter from the Chairman of the National Advisory Council on International Monetary and Financial Problems, transmitting a draft of proposed legislation to permit investment of funds of insurance companies organized within the District of Columbia in obligation of the International Bank for Reconstruction and Development (with accompanying papers); to the Committee on Banking and Currency.

As in executive session.

The PRESIDENT pro tempore laid before the Senate messages from

[30] Under custom, a message from the President transmitting a report to the Senate is read and not the report itself (C.R., 80-2, p. 9710-9711—daily edition).

the President of the United States submitting sundry nominations, which were referred to the appropriate committees.

Thus under the morning hour procedure, the Presiding Officer is authorized to lay before the Senate for appropriate disposition any of the above defined matters as remain "upon his table from any previous day's session." But the Presiding Officer is not confined to the morning hour in making references of bills or other matters sent to the Senate by the President or the House of Representatives; he may "at any time lay, and it shall be in order at any time for a Senator to move to lay, before the Senate" such matters or bills.[31] The disposition of this business, except under unanimous consent procedure, is confined to its reference to one of the standing committees for study, or to placing it on the Senate calendar for subsequent consideration. Rule XIV provides that bills and joint resolutions "introduced on leave," or from the "House of Representatives, shall be read once, and may be read twice, on the same day, if not objected to, for reference, but shall not be considered on that day nor debated, except for reference, unless by unanimous consent."[32] Always, the reference, or motions to that effect, shall be decided without debate.[33] Any question pending when such an issue is raised shall be suspended for this purpose, and an appeal may be taken from the decision of the chair by the Senate, which question is debatable. Section 137 of the Legislative Reorganization Act provides: "In any case in which a controversy arises as to the jurisdiction of any standing committee of the Senate with respect to any proposed legislation, the question of jurisdiction shall be decided by the Presiding Officer of the Senate, without debate, in favor of that committee which has jurisdiction over the subject matter which predominates in such proposed legislation; but such decision shall be subject to an appeal."[34] In brief, the Presiding Officer is authorized to lay such business before the Senate at this stage of the morning hour or at any other stage of the Senate proceedings and any decisions incident to the reference of such bills or other matters shall be made without debate; the decisions are made by

[31] See Rule VII, paragraph 7. Messages from the President or the House may be received at any stage of Senate proceedings, "except while the Senate is dividing, or while the *Journal* is being read, or while a question of order or a motion to adjourn is pending" (Rule XXVIII; C.R., 77-2, p. 7049—daily edition).

[32] On May 3, 1948, a House-passed bill was read twice and after objection to further proceedings was heard it was placed on the calendar.

[33] Rule VII, paragraph 7.

[34] Under Senate precedents, appeals on nondebatable motions are not debatable.

the Presiding Officer; an appeal from the decision of the chair is in order and it is debatable; debate may be entertained under unanimous consent before any decisions are made by the chair, or until some Senator demands the regular order. Consideration and debate on an appeal from the decision of the chair are without limit and may interrupt the remaining morning business, but it only suspends, does not displace the unfinished business coming over from the preceding day, which is in order after the morning hour.

Bills and resolutions coming within the above category are either referred to the appropriate committee or placed directly on the calendar under certain conditions. Rule XIV, paragraph 4 reads: " . . . Every bill and joint resolution of the House of Representatives which shall have received a first and second reading without being referred to a committee, shall, if objection be made to further proceedings thereon, be placed on the calendar." This was illustrated in the procedure of May 3, 1948, when objection was raised to further proceedings on H.R. 5992, ownership of tideland waters, after it had been read twice. No question of reference was raised. The bill was then automatically placed on the calendar, even though a motion to take it from the calendar and refer it to a committee would be in order.[35]

Under the Legislative Reorganization Act of 1946 (section 137), the Presiding Officer is required to refer a bill without debate; the decision of the chair is subject to appeal;[36] and the appeal is debatable.

The application of this rule as contrasted to paragraph 4 of Rule XIV was illustrated in the proceedings of May 4, 1948, over the reference of H.R. 2245, to repeal the tax on oleomargarine.[37] In this case a question of reference of the bill was raised and under section 137 of the Reorganization Act of 1946, it is stipulated that "in any case in which a controversy arises as to the jurisdiction of any standing committee of the Senate with respect to any proposed legislation, the question of jurisdiction shall be decided by the Presiding Officer," which decision shall be subject to appeal. The chair did make a decision, which was not debatable, but an appeal was taken from the decision of the chair. After debate, the chair's decision was sustained, establishing a precedent

[35] See C.R., 80-2, pp. 5296-5297 (daily edition).
[36] See C.R., 80-2, p. 5318 (daily edition).
[37] C.R., 80-2, pp. 5350-5360 (daily edition).

supporting the dominance of section 137 of the Act as opposed to Rule XIV, paragraph 4, when the question of reference is raised. That is, if the question of reference is raised after the second reading of a bill which has passed the House and been messaged to the Senate, the bill will be referred to the appropriate committee instead of being placed on the calendar. Of course, all bills and resolutions must be read three times on different days previous to their passage.[38] Hence, it requires unanimous consent to have the first and second reading in a single day. A single objection forces the issue of reference automatically "until tomorrow or the next legislative day." [39]

(D) *Presiding Officer Calls for Morning Business:* Rule VII further provides that during the morning hour following the above business "the Presiding Officer shall then call for" petitions and memorials, reports, introduction of bills and joint resolutions and other resolutions, "all of which shall be received and disposed of in such order, unless unanimous consent shall be otherwise given." [39a] As specified by the rule, the Presiding Officer calls for these steps of procedure and does not wait for a motion from the floor to that effect. The order of receiving the business follows:

1. "The presentation of petitions and memorials."
This takes the following form:
A SENATOR. Mr. President—
The PRESIDING OFFICER. The Senator from _____
The SENATOR. I present the petition (or memorial) of (naming some of the leading petitioners and briefly stating its contents, which should also be indorsed upon the paper), which I move be referred to the Committee on _____
The PRESIDING OFFICER. Without objection it will be so ordered.

2. "Reports of standing and select committees."
Reports made by committees take one of the following forms:

a. *A regular report on a bill or resolution*
The PRESIDING OFFICER. The reports of standing and select committees are now in order (The authorized person of each committee making a report follows the following procedure).
A SENATOR. Mr. President _____
The PRESIDING OFFICER. The Senator from _____
The SENATOR. I am instructed (or directed) by the Committee on _____ to whom was referred (reciting the number and title of the bill

---

[38] Rule XIV, paragraph 2.
[39] C.R., 80-2, p. 5300 (daily edition).
[39a] Rule VII, paragraph 1.

or joint resolution), to report the same to the _____ with certain amendments, favorably.

The PRESIDING OFFICES. The Senator from _____, from the Committee on _____, to whom was referred (the number and title of bill or joint resolution is again stated by the Secretary), submits a favorable report. The report will be printed, and the bill (or joint resolution) placed on the calendar.[40]

b. *A report for a change of reference*

A SENATOR. Mr. President, I report from the Committee on _____ the bill _____ and ask that the committee be discharged from its further consideration and the bill referred to the Committee on _____.

The PRESIDING OFFICER. That order will be made, without objection.

c. *Report and asking unanimous consent for its immediate consideration*

A SENATOR. Mr. President, by direction of the Committee on _____, I report favorably the following bill, and ask unanimous consent for its present consideration:

The PRESIDING OFFICER. The Senator from _____, from the Committee on _____, reports favorably the following bill, and asks its present consideration:

The title of the bill will be reported. Is there objection? The Chair hears none, and the bill will be read at length for the information of the Senate, and subject to objection.

d. *Report a new bill in lieu of an original*

A SENATOR. Mr. President _____

The PRESIDING OFFICER. The Senator from _____

The SENATOR. I am directed by the committee to whom was referred (cite number and title), to report a new bill and ask that the same be read the first and second times, and placed on the calendar.

The PRESIDING OFFICER. The Senator from _____, from the Committee on _____, reports the following bill, which will be read by the Clerk.

(The Clerk reads the title of the new bill.)

The PRESIDING OFFICER. First reading of the bill. This bill will be considered as having been read the second time, and will be placed on the calendar.

e. *Report adversely with recommendation to indefinitely postpone*

The SENATOR. I am instructed (or directed) by the Committee on _____, to whom was referred (reciting the number and title of the bill), to report the same to the Senate adversely, and to move that the bill be indefinitely postponed.

The PRESIDING OFFICER. The Senator from _____, from the Committee on _____, to whom was referred _____

(The Clerk recites the number and title of the bill or joint resolution.)

[40] See Rule XIV, paragraph 4. "Every bill and joint resolution reported from a committee, not having previously been read, shall be read once, and twice, if not objected to, on the same day, and placed on the calendar in the order in which the same may be reported; and every bill and joint resolution introduced on leave, and every bill and joint resolution of the House of Representatives which shall have received a first and second reading without being referred to a committee, shall, if objection be made to further proceeding thereon, be placed on the calendar."

The PRESIDING OFFICER. Reports the same adversely, and moves that the bill be indefinitely postponed. Is there objection? (If there be no objection.) The chair hears none. It is so ordered, and the bill is indefinitely postponed.

On objection the bill goes to the calendar with the adverse report.

(It is customary, when it appears that all reports under this call have been made, for the Presiding Officer to make the inquiry.)

The PRESIDING OFFICER. Reports of standing and select committees are still in order. Are there further reports of committees? If there be none, the introduction of bills and joint resolutions is now in order.

(Reports of select committees are made and disposed of in the same manner as are the reports of standing committees.)

3. "The introduction of bills and joint resolutions."

This procedure takes the following form:
A SENATOR. Mr. President.
The PRESIDING OFFICER. The Senator from _____.
The SENATOR. I ask leave to introduce the following bill (or resolution), which I ask may be read the first and second times by unanimous consent and referred to the appropriate committee.
Or, I introduce the following bill, or resolution, which I ask may be read the first and second times and referred to the appropriate committee.
The PRESIDING OFFICER. The Senator from _____ introduces the following bill, which will be read by title.
(The Clerk reads the bill by title.)

The PRESIDING OFFICER. First reading of the bill. This bill will be considered as having been read the second time, if there be no objection, and referred to the Committee on _____.

4. "Concurrent and other Resolutions." [40a]

At this stage the Presiding Officer is required to announce that "the introduction of bills and joint resolutions is still in order. Are there other bills and joint resolutions? If there be none, that order of business is closed. Concurrent and other resolutions are now in order." This procedure takes the following form:

a. *Resolution submitted for reference*:
A SENATOR. Mr. President.
The PRESIDING OFFICER. The Senator from _____.
The SENATOR. I submit the following resolution for appropriate reference.

b. *Resolution submitted for present consideration*:
A SENATOR. Mr. President.

[40a] On motion by Mr. Hoar:
"*Ordered.* That until otherwise ordered, the chair shall proceed with the call for resolutions to be newly offered before laying before the Senate resolutions which came over from a former day." (*S. Journal* 49-1, p. 102.)

The PRESIDING OFFICER. The Senator from ....
The SENATOR. I submit the following resolution, for which I ask present consideration.
The PRESIDING OFFICER. The resolution will be read.
(After reading)
The PRESIDING OFFICER. The Senator from .... asks unanimous consent that the resolution just read may be now considered. Is there objection? (If there be none.) The chair hears none. The question is on agreeing to the resolution just reported. As many as are in favor of agreeing to the resolution will say "aye"; those of a contrary opinion will say "no".
The resolution is agreed to.

(When objection is made)
The PRESIDING OFFICER. The Senator from .... asks unanimous consent that the resolution may be now considered. Is there objection?
A SENATOR. I object.
Or, I ask that the resolution lie over.
Or, I object to present consideration.
The PRESIDING OFFICER. The resolution, being objected to, will lie over and be printed.

After resolutions have been called, and immediately upon the completion of the routine morning business, resolutions whose consideration on the day offered had been objected to are laid before the Senate in their order by the Presiding Officer.

The PRESIDING OFFICER. The chair lays before the Senate the resolution submitted on a previous day by the Senator from ...., which was objected to and went over.
(The resolution is read by the Clerk.)
The PRESIDING OFFICER. The question is on agreeing to the resolution.

(Debate may ensue; the resolution is open to amendment and all the motions to commit, postpone, etc., are in order. After which—)

The PRESIDING OFFICER. Shall the resolution be agreed to?
(Putting the question—)
The PRESIDING OFFICER. The resolution is agreed to, or disagreed to, as the case may be.

Consideration of Resolutions: Resolutions or motions on the Calendar of "Resolutions and Motions Over Under the Rule" might be disposed of at this time, but not until the routine morning business (discussed above) has been completed. A resolution coming over from a previous day which is under debate at 2 o'clock p. m. goes to the calendar,[40b] even though there be no un-

_____
[40b] Jan. 12, 1903; C.R., 57-2, p. 671; C.R., 69-2, pp. 4653-4660 (daily edition).

finished business; [40c] it may go over another day only by a majority vote or by unanimous consent.[40d]

Reference of Business to Committee: After "petitions and memorials" and "bills and joint resolutions and other resolutions"
are received (introduced), it falls upon the Presiding Officer to
refer them to the appropriate standing or select committees.[41] As
already stated the Presiding Officer makes the reference, and in
any case where a controversy over the reference arises, the question of committee jurisdiction shall be decided by the Presiding
Officer, without debate, but the Senate can take an appeal from
his decision, sending the bill to any committee it might choose.[42]
The preference of committee reference by a Senator has no effect
as to which committee a bill will be sent, unless such desire is put
in the form of a unanimous consent request and granted, or unless a motion to that effect is made and adopted.[43]

A House-passed bill may be considered when received without
referring it to a standing committee provided a similar Senate
bill has been reported and is on the calendar.[44] Likewise, as
already pointed out, a bill under certain conditions can be placed
directly on the calendar. On the other hand, on March 3, 1947,
the chair ruled that when a bill has been reported from a committee, a motion is in order as a matter of right, to refer that

---

[40c] C.R., 77-1, p. 9150 (daily edition).
[40d] C.R., 77-2, p. 253 (daily edition).
[41] Rule VII provides that petitions or memorials shall be referred, "without putting the question, unless objection to such reference is made; in which case all motions for the reception or reference of such petition, memorial, or other paper shall
be put in the order in which the same shall be made, and shall not be open to
amendment, except to add instructions."
  "Only a brief statement of the contents, as provided for in Rule VII, paragraph
five, of such communications as are presented under the order of business 'presentation of petitions and memorials' shall be printed in the *Congressional Record;* and
that no other portion of such communications shall be inserted in the *Record* unless
specifically so ordered by vote of the Senate, as provided for in Rule XXIX, paragraph one; except that communications from the legislatures or conventions, law-
fully called, of the respective States, Territories, and insular possessions shall be
printed in full in the *Record* whenever presented, and the original copies of such
communications shall be retained in the files of the Secretary of the Senate." (Rule
VII, paragraph 6).
[42] The following citations (all from daily editions) give decisions by the chair,
making references of different bills under the Legislative Reorganization Act of
1946; (1) Portal to portal pay bill: Jan. 13, 1947, C.R., 80-1, pp. 279-280. Jan. 15,
1947, C.R., 80-1, p. 381.
  (2) Single Department of National Defense, Jan. 27, Feb. 26, and March 3, 1947,
      C.R., 80-1, pp. 627. 1465-1466, 1658, 1666.
  (3) Automobiles to disabled G.I.'s, Jan. 31, 1947, C.R., 80-1, p. 766.
  (4) Constitutional Amdt. proposal, Feb. 10, 1947, C.R., 80-1, p. 957.
  (5) Interstate compact, June 2, 1947, C.R., 80-1, p. 6277.
  (6) Interstate Waterights of Colorado, July 3, 1947, C.R., 80-1, pp. 8448-8450;
      8591-8599.
  (7) Oleomargarine, May 3, and 4, 1948, C.R., 80-2, pp. 5361-5382, 5426.
  (8) Resolution on Voice of America, May 27, 1948, C.R., 80-2, pp. 6728-6737.
[43] See proceedings for Jan. 8, 1947 at C.R., 80-1, p. 177-178 (daily edition).
[44] See *Senate Journal*, 77-1, p. 476 for Dec. 10, 1941.

bill to another committee. When a bill is offered and objected to, its introduction must be postponed for one legislative day.[45]

Business Placed on Calendar: Reports on bills and resolutions are received by the Senate from the committees and cleared for printing, and the bills and resolutions themselves are reprinted in the reported form. The reported bills and resolutions and their accompanying reports are placed on the Senate calendar.[46] Special reports are likewise received and ordered printed. Unanimous consent is required to report a bill after the expiration of the morning hour. All resolutions and all reports of committees and motions to discharge committees shall lie over one day for consideration, unless by unanimous consent the Senate shall otherwise direct.[47] A motion to consider a resolution submitted on a previous calendar day, but in the same legislative day, is not in order.[48]

Presentation of Matters after Morning Hour: It is further provided in Rule VII that "Senators having petitions, memorials, pension bills, or bills for the payment of private claims to present after the morning hour may deliver them to the Secretary of the Senate, indorsing upon them their names and the reference or disposition to be made thereof, and said petitions, memorials, and bills shall, with the approval of the Presiding Officer, be entered on the Journal with the names of the Senators presenting them as having been read twice and referred to the appropriate committees, and the Secretary of the Senate shall furnish a transcript of such entries to the official reporter of debates for publication in the *Record.*"[49] Actually, all measures relating to claims against the United States are referred to the Judiciary Committee.

Conclusions: Under Rule VII the above routine business is in order each legislative day that the Senate sits following an adjournment as contrasted to each calendar day following a recess; any variation from this procedure is in order only by unanimous consent and a demand for the regular order during a departure from Rule VII under unanimous consent, requires the Presiding Officer to lay before the Senate the order of business

45 See proceedings for June 29, 1946 for illustration.
46 Unanimous consent is required to report a bill after the expiration of the morning hour (C.R., 77-2, p. 9118—daily edition).
47 Resolutions here refer to all resolutions other than joint resolutions; however, concurrent resolutions for final adjournment are privileged and do not have to lie over. See Rule XXVI and Rule XIV.
48 See *Senate Journal*, 69-1, p. 104 for Jan. 22, 1926.
49 Rule VII, paragraph 2.

as defined in the Rule. "Until the morning business shall have been concluded, and so announced from the chair, or until the hour of 1 o'clock has arrived, no motion to proceed to the consideration of any bill, resolution, report of a committee, or other subject upon the calendar shall be entertained by the Presiding Officer, unless by unanimous consent; and if such consent be given, the motion shall not be subject to amendment, and shall be decided without debate upon the merits of the subject proposed to be taken up: *Provided, however,* That on Mondays the calendar shall be called under Rule VIII, and during the morning hour no motion shall be entertained to proceed to the consideration of any bill, resolution, report of a committee, or other subject upon the calendar except the motion to continue the consideration of a bill, resolution, report of a committee, or other subject against objection as provided in Rule VIII." [50] On any day other than Monday, at the close of the morning business, a motion to take up a bill has precedence over a call of the calendar.[51]

Passage of Unobjected-to Bills (Call of Calendar): At the conclusion of the morning business of each legislative day, immediately after the call for "concurrent and other resolutions," or resolutions or motions on the Calendar of "Resolutions and Motions Over Under the Rule," unless the Senate by motion decides to proceed with the consideration of some other business, the disposition of unobjected-to bills and resolutions on the call of the "Calendar of General Orders" is the next order of business. Following the morning business on a calendar Monday, a motion to take up a bill is not in order; the call of the calendar is the regular order in case of such a demand. The call of the calendar during the morning hour takes precedence of unfinished business, but special orders may interrupt until 2 o'clock p. m. The Presiding Officer asks if there is further morning business; "if there be none, that order is now closed, and the calendar under Rule VIII is in order. The Clerk will report the first bill on the calendar."

(The Clerk reports the bill)

"The Presiding Officer. This is now under consideration and

[50] Rule VII, paragraph 3.
[51] See *Senate Journal,* 78-1, p. 491; C.R., 75-1, p. 8786 (daily edition). Note the distinction between the morning business and the morning hour. The morning business may be terminated at any time after 1 o'clock by making the motion to consider a particular bill, which motion is in order and supersedes the morning business; the morning business may be concluded before 1 o'clock; the morning hour runs for two hours after the Senate assembles.

is open to amendment." (If bill is reported with amendments, the first question is on agreeing to the committee amendments.)

During the call of the calendar, all Senators are entitled to speak once for five minutes on each question; objection to the consideration of any such bill or resolution when called is in order at any stage of the proceedings prior to its passage. If an objection is forthcoming, the bill will not be considered unless the Senate membership by a majority vote on motion should decide to the contrary. Such a motion is in order but is not debatable.[52] While considering unobjected-to bills under an agreement on June 17, 1948, the chair ruled that a motion to consider a bill which was objected to was not in order.

The Senate having decided to continue the consideration of a bill in spite of an objection, the five-minute rule no longer applies. Further, it is in order by unanimous consent to call up any bill on the calendar regardless of its relative position, and any motions entertained prior to 2 o'clock concerning that business shall be determined without debate.[53] The call of the calendar is terminated at 2 o'clock, and the right of a Senator to the floor is temporarily suspended and the Presiding Officer announces the termination of the morning hour. According to most precedents, however, the Senator does not lose his right to the floor, but is permitted to continue after the announcement. With unanimous consent the Senate may continue with consideration of unobjected-to bills. A bill objected to during the call of the calendar may be taken up on motion after the call of the calendar has been completed. Likewise, when a motion is made during the morning hour to take up a bill, it is not debatable. When such a motion is made prior to 2 o'clock but unacted upon before that time, it is questionable if the motion becomes debatable. There are precedents both ways,[54] but a preponderance of them holds that the motion is not debatable. A matter unfinished at 2 o'clock goes on the calendar if unfinished business is pending; otherwise, its consideration will be continued, becoming the unfinished business if not disposed of before adjournment.

The above order of business according to the rules continues for two hours after a meeting of the Senate following an adjourn-

[52] Bills on the calendar, when objected to on call are passed over instead of withdrawn.
[53] Rule VIII. All motions made in the morning hour to take up a matter are not debatable.
[54] See Senate proceedings for March 23, 1939; Nov. 13, 1942; and Oct. 12, 1943.

ment. In practice, the majority leader, supported by the majority party, is in charge of the legislative program, and he proceeds with a program mapped out by the majority policy committee or by the leaders. The above procedure may or may not be followed each new legislative day. The Senate on request of the leader may dispense with one or all of the steps under unanimous consent. The unobjected-to bills and resolutions on the "Calendar of General Orders" are seldom called more than twice a month, regardless of how often the Senate adjourns. On the other hand, even if the Senate continues in a single legislative day for more than a month, the calendar is generally called from time to time by unanimous consent, provided there are a number of unobjected-to bills on the calendar and no other business is more pressing. It is not uncommon for the Senate so to proceed to a call of the calendar in mid-afternoon of a session or even later. That depends to a great extent on the program of the leadership.

The above order of business is known as the morning hour, and during that time no other business except privileged matters and that defined in Rules VII and VIII is in order, except by unanimous consent. Likewise, after the termination of the morning hour, or two hours after the meeting of the Senate, the business in order during the morning hour is no longer in order during that legislative day except by unanimous consent or unless there is no unfinished business pending, in which case a bill which was under consideration before 2 o'clock may be continued. By adoption of motion to consider a bill, the unfinished business can be displaced. It is not in order to introduce public bills or resolutions after the morning business has been disposed of, but it can be done by unanimous consent.[55] On the other hand, the morning hour is subject to be stopped or altered in any manner if an agreement (unanimous consent) is reached to that effect or if such a special order should be made.

Under unanimous consent, the Senate may consider legislation during the morning hour, or the Presiding Officer may present, or a Senator may move to lay before the Senate any bill or other matter from the President of the United States or the House of Representatives and "any question pending at that time shall be suspended for this purpose."[56] All such motions shall be determined without debate.

[55] See C.R., 79-1, p. 7059 (daily edition).
[56] Rule VII, clause 7.

The practice of calling the Calendar of General Orders under Rule IX has become obsolete. The rule provides that if the Calendar of Bills and Resolutions is granted consideration and the business thereon has been disposed of or if it has been passed over, at an hour not later than 2 o'clock, provided there are not special orders for that time, the Calendar of General Orders shall be taken up. It is within the power of the Senate to make the Calendar of Bills and Resolutions a special order for the remainder of the day. Special orders do not have to lie over a day before disposition,[57] and the Senate may postpone any previous orders.[58] Assuming that the business on the Calendar of General Orders is taken up under Rule IX, the proceedings begin "with the first subject on the calendar next after the last subject disposed of in proceeding with the calendar. . . ." The business consists of making certain motions to take any action or to consider bills. They shall be in order at any time as privileged motions, save as against a motion to adjourn, or to proceed to the consideration of executive business, or a question of privilege, to wit:

"First. A motion to proceed to the consideration of an appropriation or revenue bill.
"Second. A motion to proceed to the consideration of any other bill on the calendar, which motion shall not be open to amendment.
"Third. A motion to pass over the pending subject, which if carried shall have the effect to leave such subject without prejudice in its place on the calendar.
"Fourth. A motion to place such subject at the foot of the calendar." [59]

Rule IX concludes that "Each of the foregoing motions shall be decided without debate and shall have precedence in the order above named and may be submitted as in the nature and with all the rights of the questions of order."

Unfinished Business: The unfinished business coming over from a previous legislative day is privileged for consideration on a subsequent one immediately following the morning hour,[60] or immediately following prayer by the Chaplain, on any calendar day after the Senate convenes following a recess instead of an adjournment. Though privileged at this stage of Senate proceedings, the unfinished business can be displaced by the adoption of a motion

[57] Gilfry, op. cit, I, p. 535.
[58] Ibid., p. 219.
[59] Rule IX.
[60] The rule provides that the unfinished business coming over from the preceding day is privileged for consideration on each legislative day after the lapse of two hours.

to take up another matter; [61] it may be temporarily laid aside by unanimous consent to consider another measure.[62]   A motion to lay aside the unfinished business and consider another bill is not in order; but the adoption of a motion to consider another bill displaces the unfinished business as opposed to laying it aside under unanimous consent procedure.   If the unfinished business has been laid aside by unanimous consent, the Senate automatically returns to a consideration of the unfinished business upon a demand for the regular order or when the bill which was brought up under unanimous consent has been disposed of.[63]

The Senate has established the precedent of taking up and disposing of privileged business without displacing the unfinished business; this does not have to be done by unanimous consent, though it may be so done to save time.   The adoption of a motion to consider a conference report or House amendments to a Senate bill, both privileged matters, does not displace the unfinished business—it merely suspends it.

If there is not enough business under the morning hour following an adjournment to occupy the Senate for two hours, the Senate, either on motion or by unanimous consent may proceed to the unfinished business.   Of course, if the next meeting is only a new calendar day and a continuation of the same legislative day, the morning hour procedure is not in order, except under unanimous consent.   To start a new legislative day, even though the Senate had recessed the night before, the Senate could adjourn at any time, and reconvene a few minutes later.   To illustrate: on April 30, 1948 it was proposed to consider S. 2565, to provide one-month extension of mortgage loan insurance under Title VI of the National Housing Act, and to authorize an additional $250 million for that purpose.   There was opposition to consideration of the bill; some held that a maneuver was under way to amend the bill by substituting "1-year" for "1-month," thereby eliminating in part the need for the passage of S. 866, the so called T-E-W Long Range Housing Bill.   Objection was made to bringing the bill up; it had been reported on calendar day April 28 or legislative day April 22; April 30 also was legislative day April 22. To make the business in order, the Senate adjourned at 1:11 p. m.

---

[61] *Senate Journal*, 72-1. p. 126 for Jan. 6, 1932; see also proceedings for May 15, 1944. pp. 4553-4560 (daily edition).

[62] *Senate Journal*, 68-2. p. 165 for Feb. 7, 1925.

[63] See C.R., 75-3. p. 8560, 76-3. p. 4045 (daily edition).

by vote of 44 yeas to 17 nays; it reconvened at 1:12 p. m. and after morning business proceeded to the consideration of S. 2565— this was then a new legislative day and the bill having been on the calendar one legislative day as required by the rules, no point of order could be raised against consideration of the bill.[64]

Motions and Other Business in Order During Consideration of a Bill: *Rules Flexible:* The above paragraphs briefly set forth the defined daily order of business. While that procedure is specific it is sufficiently flexible to allow the Senate to proceed to the consideration of any particular piece of business at will. Each procedure has its price, nevertheless. Anything can be done under unanimous consent, even to the extent of ignoring all rules and precedents. Certain business, contrary to the normal rule, is in order by suspending the rules, which action requires a 2/3 vote.[65] A motion to suspend the rules must be in writing and must lie over one day if there is a single objection; it is a debatable question and "one day" has been interpreted to mean "one calendar day." [66]

When it is in order to move to the consideration of a bill by a majority vote the Senate can select any proposed piece of legislation which has already been on the calendar for one legislative day. Before the Senate proceeds to the consideration of a bill by a majority vote, however, a motion to that effect must be adopted, and that motion is debatable if made after 2 o'clock. A motion to proceed to the consideration of a general appropriation bill after 2 o'clock is debatable, but such motion is not privileged over a motion to take up any other bill. Since the Senate permits unlimited debate and the existing cloture rule is not applicable to such motions, the consideration of a bill can be blocked by filibuster.[67]

A bill under consideration can be displaced by a majority vote and a new one brought up. Under an agreement merely to take up a bill, pending its consideration, it is in order to make a motion to take up another bill.

[64] See C.R., 80-2, p. D426, April 30, 1948.
[65] There are numerous decisions by the chair to this effect, and also rulings by the Senate itself.
[66] Decisions by chair can be found in Senate proceedings for Feb. 14, 1935 and July 24, 1947.
[67] S.Res. 25 of the 80th Congress, reported to Senate on April 3, 1947, proposed to change that situation by extending cloture to motions to consider a bill, or amendments or motions relating to the *Journal*. The Republicans on August 4, 1948 announced that a revision of the rules to this extent would be the first order of business of the 81st Congress.

Any parliamentary procedure, however, is somewhat at the mercy of the majority control, and rightly so. If the majority party is to be held responsible by the voters for the legislation enacted that party must have a machinery that allows it a selection sufficient to bring up and consider bills on which it wishes to act. Accordingly, the political machinery—primarily the majority policy committee backed by the majority conference—maps out the legislative program and proceeds to its consideration within the frame work of the defined parliamentary machinery, even if it means resort to the flexible portions of the rules and precedents.

The method of selecting bills and the decision as to what business is next in order are different questions from that of what can be done to a particular bill under consideration or of what is the next step toward the disposition of any pending bill.

The Senate of its own free will since 1789, during the consideration and disposition of any business, out of necessity has developed a mode of procedure to pursue when it is confronted with a question of "how shall we go from here or what shall we do about that?"

Amending Process: As already pointed out when bills or resolutions are brought up for disposition under the call of the calendar, debate by any Senator is limited to five minutes on any question. An objection to a bill by any Senator blocks its consideration under the five-minute procedure, but on adoption of a motion the Senate may continue with the bill under regular procedure.[68] Amendments to bills passed under this procedure, those by committees and individual Senators, are in order although it is infrequent for any other than committee amendments to be offered. Likewise individual Senators are free to offer amendments to any proposed committee amendments. Committee amendments are first in order, followed by amendments offered by individuals from the floor. Amendments to committee amendments are acted on before adoption or rejection of the committee amendment to which they are offered.

According to Rule XIV, amendments are not in order to any bill until it has been read a second time.[69] In practice, unless

---

[68] See pp. 354-359.
[69] Rule XIV, clause 3. "No bill or joint resolutions shall be committed or amended until it shall have been twice read, after which it may be referred to a committee; bills and joint resolutions introduced on leave, and bills and joint resolutions from the House of Representatives, shall be read once, and may be read twice, on the same day, if not objected to, for reference, but shall not be considered on that day nor debated, except for reference, unless by unanimous consent."

otherwise ordered by the Senate, only the title of a bill is read prior to the stage of amending.[70] Bills brought up for consideration by the adoption of a motion as contrasted to "under the call of the calendar" are open to unlimited debate and amendments. The Senate does not necessarily debate bills before proceeding to amend them. Unlike in the House, there is no period for general debate of a bill before the amending process begins. After the title of a bill is reported, the first question is on the adoption of the first committee amendment, if any. Several long speeches may be had before a vote is taken on the first committee amendment but that depends upon the decisions of the individual Senators. The Senate may adopt all of many committee amendments to the bill before any general debate, or it may debate each of the committee amendments as well as those offered from the floor before acting on them.

Under any procedure when a bill is called up for consideration in the Senate the first order of business, as sanctioned by practice,[71] is to dispose of committee amendments proposed to the bill, acting first on any amendments offered from the floor to each respective committee amendment. During the consideration of committee amendments, amendments from the floor to the text of the bill not affected by such amendments are not in order.[72] Thus, if any amendments are proposed to a committee amendment when it is considered, they are first adopted or rejected as the Senate wills, followed by the question recurring on the final disposition of the committee amendment as amended, if any. This extends to a substitute for a committee amendment, if it is in order;[73] it has been held that an amendment from the floor to a committee amendment which proposes to strike out a part of the text is not a substitute. Of course, a committee amendment which has been adopted is not open to further amendment. Likewise an amendment is not in order when proposed to a committee amendment not pending before the Senate. The acceptance of an amendment to a committee amendment by the chairman of the

[70] See Gilfry, p. 214; Rule XIV, clause 2. "Every bill and joint resolution shall receive three readings previous to its passage, which readings shall be on three different days, unless the Senate unanimously direct otherwise; and the Presiding Officer shall give notice at each reading whether it be the first, second, or third: *Provided,* That the first or second reading of each bill may be by title only, unless the Senate in any case shall otherwise order."

[71] There is no rule to this effect; it is only practice. See C.R., 78-4, p. 5392 (daily edition); C.R., 80-2, p. 10112 (daily edition).

[72] *Senate Journal,* 72-1, p. 649.

[73] C.R., 75-3, p. 10400 (daily edition).

committee handling the bill, or by the Senator in charge of the bill, is not binding on the Senate; it might have influence on the outcome, but the Senate must vote all amendments up or down to make the action effective or final. A committee amendment may be withdrawn just as may an amendment offered by an individual Senator, when the action is authorized by the committee.[74] A motion to refer a pending bill to a committee is in order and has precedence over an amendment, but the motion is debatable.[75]

The speed with which committee amendments are disposed of depends upon how controversial they are, including the number of amendments to be offered to the committee amendments. If no amendment is offered to a committee amendment, it becomes a question of adopting it or rejecting it as is, and, in the absence of any long debate, the question can be disposed of very quickly. Each amendment from the floor by an individual Senator to the committee amendment, presents the same problem. Each such amendment from the floor may be quickly disposed of or debated at long length; it might be approved or rejected "without objection" or entail one or more roll call votes. Thus the time given to each subject by the Senate depends upon its controversial nature. The rejection of a committee amendment to strike out has the effect of restoring the original text of the bill.

After committee amendments have been disposed of, the Senate proceeds to the consideration of amendments offered from the floor by individual Senators. The procedure is orderly. A Senator cannot offer an amendment unless he has first been recognized. Each amendment offered is subject to be amended, but a *second amendment* to the bill, as contrasted to being offered to the pending amendment, while another is under consideration, is not in order.[76] The sponsor of an amendment may modify or withdraw it at any time before some action has been taken; [77] the same is true in the case of a committee amendment when such request has the sanction of the committee; [78] but unanimous consent is required to make any modification in an amendment on

---

[74] See Senate proceedings for March 24, 1944.
[75] See Senate proceedings for April 9, 1940.
[76] See proceedings of Senate for June 11, 1941.
[77] See C.R., 78-1, p. 2156 (daily edition); also C.R., 76-1, pp. 15373-5 (daily edition). The amendment may not be withdrawn by the mover if the rules were suspended for the purpose of offering it.
[78] See C.R., 78-1, p. 9175 (daily edition). An individual Senator has no such authority (C.R., 77-2, pp. 6361-6364 (daily edition).

which the yeas and nays have been ordered, on which an agreement has been reached for a vote, or after it has been amended.[79]

As in the House, amendments may not be offered in the third degree but four or more amendments may be pending at any one time: namely, an amendment to the bill, an amendment to the amendment,[80] a substitute amendment to the amendment, and an amendment to the substitute. A substitute amendment, like any other, is open to amendment until it has been adopted, following which any further amendments are precluded. Likewise a bill is not open to further amendments after a substitute therefor has been agreed to. A substitute amendment may be offered to the text of a bill at any time after committee amendments have been disposed of,[81] or a substitute amendment is in order to any committee amendment when it is pending, but perfecting amendments to both the original bill and substitutes have precedence in disposition.[82] Any bill and all amendments thereto are open to amendments as long as they are before the Senate and until "a conclusive stage" has been reached.[83] An amendment or bill already acted on by the Senate is subject to be reconsidered in accordance with the rules; when such reconsideration has been ordered, the bill or amendment is again before the Senate and open to further amendment. It is not in order to offer an amendment to a bill which is identical to one already offered to the same bill and rejected; the same is true in the case of proposing the same substance.[84] But the rejection of an amendment does not preclude a Senator from offering amendments with reference to a different amount of money for a purpose for which another amount has been rejected. The re-offering of an amendment previously rejected with certain material language deleted, is in order; the same is true if the identical language of a rejected amendment is embodied in a new amendment to another section of the bill. An amendment striking out a portion of a bill and inserting a substitute having been rejected, the same substitute may be offered to another portion of the bill, as its effect if adopted would be

[79] *Senate Journal,* 75-3, p. 443.
[80] An amendment to an amendment, to an amendment is in the third degree and not in order as ruled by chair on June 18, 1940.
[81] A substitute may not be offered while a perfecting amendment to the original bill is pending; that would be two independent amendments pending at the same time. See proceedings for April 27, 1942.
[82] C.R., 75-1, pp. 6119-6120; June 22, 1937.
[83] After the third reading of a bill, further amendments to it are in order only under unanimous consent.
[84] See *Senate Journal,* 71-2, p. 387; *Senate Journal,* 75-1, p. 455.

materially different.[85]   Generally if an amendment which has been rejected is offered in a modified form it is in order.

Perfecting amendments have precedence over a motion to strike out; [85a] a motion to strike out and insert has precedence over a motion to strike out; [86] and when a motion to strike out a section of a bill is made, perfecting amendments to the part to be stricken out have precedence.[87]

A negative vote on an amendment or on passage of a bill has the effect of killing it. If the Senate recommits a bill, that nullifies any action that has been taken on amendments to that bill.[88] An amendment can be laid on the table without prejudice to the bill, but an amendment to the amendment would also go to the table.

Amendments are voted on in the following order: first an amendment to the amendment is voted on, secondly an amendment to the substitute, thirdly the substitute, and fourthly the amendment as amended. For example, if a substitute for an amendment is adopted, the vote recurs on agreeing to the amendment as amended by the substitute.[89] As fast as action is taken on an amendment in either category another such amendment in its stead is in order; no amendment in the third degree is in order. An amendment may be offered even after the yeas and nays have been ordered.[90]

The pro forma amendment procedure is not used in the Senate as it is in the House since debate is not limited.[91] On December 14, 1937, during the consideration of S. 2787, farm relief bill, under limitation of debate by agreement (one speech on amendment and one on bill), Senator Connally had consumed his time on pending amendment and moved to strike out "$500,000,000" (a pro forma amendment). He was recognized. A later Presiding Officer opposed the practice as abusing the intent of the Senate in limiting debate, even though within the letter of an agreement.

Where a committee proposes a substitute for an entire bill, an amendment to the committee amendment is under Rule XVIII,

[85] See C.R., 78-1, pp. 1408-1409 (daily edition) for Feb. 8, 1944.
[85a] See Senate proceedings for July 28, 1939; C.R., 76-1, pp. 14439 (daily edition).
[86] C.R., 76-1, p. 1276 (daily edition).
[87] C.R., 75-3, p. 5307 (daily edition). Where the Senate strikes out a section of a bill, a substitute amendment therefor is not in order; an independent amendment to accomplish the same end is in order. See also C.R., 80-2, p. 4604 (daily edition).
[88] See Senate proceedings for May 9, 1906.
[89] C.R., 79-2, p. 8963 for July 12, 1946 (daily edition).
[90] For an example, see C.R., 79-2, p. 6411.
[91] For comment on use of pro forma amendment in Senate see C.R., 75-2, p. 2075 (daily edition).

in the first degree, an amendment to that amendment is in the second degree and thus is not open to an amendment—third degree.[92]

As pointed out above, when a committee reports a substitute bill [93] for the original bill, the substitute is not considered as an amendment but as the original text and must be voted on as a whole. Perfecting amendments to the substitute have precedence over final disposition of the substitute. In other words there can be pending at any one time to such a reported bill in the nature of a substitute, an amendment, an amendment to the amendment, a substitute to the committee substitute and an amendment to the substitute.[94]

The Senate Parliamentarian, Charles L. Watkins, diagrammed the amendments pending at one time during the consideration of H.R. 3896, adjusted compensation bill, as follows:

Patman Bill (H.R. 3896) Committee Substitute (Harrison Bill)

1	3	5
		Clark substitute (1st degree) (Vinson Bill)
Perfecting amendments take precedence over amendments to committee amendment (are in 1st degree only).		6
	Perfecting amendments take precedence over Clark substitute or amendments thereto (and are in first degree only)	Open to amendment, either perfecting or by way of a substitute (in 2nd degree only).
2 Amendments are open to amendment (are in 2nd degree)		
	4 Perfecting amendments to perfecting amendments also in order (and are in second degree).	

[92] See proceedings for Jan. 23, 1948, C.R., 80-2, p. 506 (daily edition).
[93] In 76th Congress, a committee reported a bill by recommending a substitute amendment and then subsequently reported another substitute for the first one prior to consideration of the bill, see p. 12615 of daily edition for 3rd session.
[94] A substitute for a committee amendment as amended, may be amended in one degree, as can the original committee amendment (See C.R., 77-2, p. 7837 for Sept. 29, 1942.)

The rules of the Senate do not require that amendments proposed to a bill be germane to it except in the case of general appropriation bills and to bills on which the Cloture Rule has been invoked.[95] To illustrate: in 1913 the President pro tempore (Mr. Gallinger) gave the following ruling: "This not being a general appropriation bill, the question as to whether an amendment is germane or not does not apply; nor is there any inhibition against a private claim being attached to any bill except an appropriation bill. Hence the point of order is overruled." [96]

On March 27, 1947, the chair overruled a point of order raised against the "inconsistency of amendments," holding that the Senate itself should pass on the question; it has been held that the question of submission to the Senate of the relevancy of an amendment has priority over a point of order that the amendment is general legislation to an appropriation bill.[97] It has also been held that an amendment consisting of two or more provisions, proposing to modify a bill at different places is in fact not a single amendment and cannot be offered together against objection.[98] Under a ruling of June 30, 1941, an amendment to strike out and insert is not devisible, under Rule XVIII, but it is subject to amendment. It is in order to offer a bill as an amendment to another bill.[99]

It is not in order to offer an amendment to an amendment which has already been adopted,[100] but the adopted amendment can be reconsidered and then amended. The reconsideration of one part of a bill does not affect any other part of it.[101] The adoption of an amendment to a part of a section of a bill does not exclude a motion to strike out the entire section as amended,[102] but an amendment to the section proposed to be stricken out has precedence over the motion to strike out.[103]

With respect to appropriation bills, the rule regulating amendments is definitely detailed. It states that all appropriation bills

[95] See *Senate Journal*, 71-2, p. 376 for May 23, 1930; and *Senate Journal*, 75-1, p. 439.
[96] Gilfry, p. 53. "No amendment, the object of which is to provide for a private claim, shall be received to any general appropriation bill, unless it be to carry out the provisions of an existing law or a treaty stipulation, which shall be cited on the face of the amendment." (Rule XVI, clause 5).
[97] *Senate Journal*, 78-1, pp. 280-281: also C.R., 78-1, pp. 5628-43 (daily edition).
[98] C.R., 76-3, pp. 4194, 4203 (daily edition).
[99] Gilfry, *op. cit.*, I. p. 43.
[100] *Senate Journal*, 74-1, p. 206.
[101] Where an amendment has been rejected and a motion to reconsider it is pending, a modification of the amendment can only be made by unanimous consent. C.R., 77-2, p. 3145 daily edition.)
[102] C.R., 76-1, pp. 14232, 14250 (daily edition).
[103] *Senate Journal*, 72-1, p. 505.

shall be referred to the Appropriations Committee and that no amendments to any one of them shall be in order "to increase an appropriation already contained in the bill, or to add a new item of appropriation, unless it be made to carry out the provisions of some existing law, or treaty stipulation, or act, or resolution previously passed by the Senate during that session; or unless the same be moved by direction of a standing or select committee of the Senate, or proposed in pursuance of an estimate submitted in accordance with law." [104] Precedents in pursuance of this rule support a point of order against any amendment to a general appropriation bill not authorized by law.[105] The chair has ruled that an amendment which is of legislative character is not in order even though the proposed appropriation was requested by the Bureau of the Budget.[106] Some points of order have been sustained by the chair on the grounds that no specific law authorized a proposed appropriation, that the item had not been reported by the appropriations committee, and that it had not been estimated for by the Bureau of the Budget.[107] It has been held that an amendment is in order if it would merely increase the proposed amount for carrying out an existing law where no specific amount is authorized.[108]

An amendment to a general appropriation bill is not legislation, however, and subject to a point of order if it merely expresses a "pious hope." [109] Also if the House had added general legislation to an appropriation bill, the Senate has a right to perfect such amendment involving legislation. Vice President Marshall ruled that: "notwithstanding the rule of the Senate to the effect that general legislation may not be attached to an appropriation bill, still when the House of Representatives opens the door and proceeds to enter upon a field of general legislation which has to do with a subject of this character, the Chair is going to rule . . . that the House having opened the door the Senate of the United States can walk in through the door and pursue the field." [110]

[104] Rule XVI, clause 1.

[105] See C.R., 79-1, p. 5347; 79-2, pp. 6221, 7072 (daily edition) for illustrated cases.

[106] C.R., 76-1, pp. 15387-88 (daily edition).

[107] C.R., 76-3, p. 4931 (daily edition) ; Senate Journal 75-3, p. 572; 76-3, p. 104.

[108] This ruling was given on March 6, 1935 during consideration of H.R. 5913, War Department Appropriation Bill.

[109] See Senate proceedings for March 5, 1947 on H.R. 1968, Urgent Deficiency Appropriation, including funds for OPA.

[110] This ruling by Vice President Marshall was quoted in a later ruling to be found in Senate Journal 74-2, p. 333.

Limitations on the use of funds are also in order and are not considered as legislation.[111] A limitation on the use of funds, however, is effective only for the year for which the appropriations are made.[112]

When a question of germaneness is raised on a Senate amendment to a general appropriation bill it is submitted to the Senate under Rule XVI for decision.[113] When an amendment is submitted under the suspension of the rules the question of germaneness of an amendment offered thereto is likewise submitted to the Senate and decided without debate by a majority vote just as if it were an original amendment.[114] Finally Rule XVI applies to general appropriation bills only. Special appropriation bills are open to any amendment just as any piece of legislation.[115] A deficiency appropriation bill is regarded as a general appropriation bill.[116] Rule XVI provides:

All amendments to general appropriation bills moved by direction of a standing or select committee of the Senate, proposing to increase an appropriation already contained in the bill, or to add new items of appropriation, shall, at least one day before they are considered, be referred to the Committee on Appropriations, and when actually proposed to the bill no amendment proposing to increase the amount stated in such amendment shall be received; in like manner, amendments proposing new items of appropriation to river and harbor bills, establishing post roads, or proposing new post roads, shall, before being considered, be referred to the Committee on Public Works.[117]

All amendments to general appropriation bills must be germane and relevant to the subject matter contained in the bill and to the particular "item or clause of such bill" to which it is offered. Any restrictions on an expenditure of funds appropriated, proposing a limitation not authorized by law, shall not be received if such restriction is to take effect or cease to be effective upon the happening of a contingency. Any question of relevancy of amendments, when a point of order is raised, shall be submitted to the Senate for decision, without debate. Any such proposed amendment may be laid on the table without prejudice to the bill.

Debate: When bills are up before the Senate for consideration (except those disposed of under call of the calendar or under some

---

[111] C.R., 76-3, p. 2327; 79-2, p. 1835 (daily edition).
[112] C.R., 79-1, p. 7634 (daily edition).
[113] See paragraph 4, Rule XVI. For precedents see *Senate Journal*, 72-1, p. 320 and 72-2, p. 160.
[114] C.R., 76-1, p. 15373; 15375 (daily edition).
[115] See proceedings for Jan. 25, 1932; *Senate Journal*, 72-1, pp. 180-181.
[116] C.R., 77-2, pp. 1368-1369 (daily edition).
[117] Rule XVI, paragraph 3.

special agreement) debate on them and amendments thereto are unlimited. The Senate may invoke the Cloture Rule. Under Rule XIX, "When a Senator desires to speak, he shall rise and address the Presiding Officer, and shall not proceed until he is recognized, and the Presiding Officer shall recognize the Senator who shall first address him. No Senator shall interrupt another Senator in debate without his consent, and to obtain such consent he shall first address the Presiding Officer . . ." [118] Under the precedents, however, he loses the floor if he yields for more than a question. But after he has been recognized by the Presiding Officer, he can retain the floor as long as he sees fit, speak on any subject, and may not be interrupted against his will unless he transgresses the rules of the Senate. The question of recognition is a prerogative of the chair, and no one is entitled to the floor until he is recognized. [119] Under the practice, however, lists of the Senators who are to speak each day are put on his desk, and he recognizes them in that order, with exceptions, of course. For example, on July 25, 1945, Senator McKellar then President pro tempore stated his intention to recognize the first Senator to rise regardless of any such "list."

A Senator having the floor in his own right and as long as he complies with the rules, may refuse to yield to another Senator for any purpose; he may not be taken off his feet except for a violation of the rules. He may refuse to yield for a parliamentary inquiry, a point of order, or a question of personal privilege; [120] a quorum call over his objection is not in order, and an appeal will not lie as long as he refuses to yield; [121] if he yields to another Senator for a question he has a right to withdraw his consent at any time, [122] and is duty bound to stop the Senator to whom he has yielded if that one starts to make a speech. [123] It has been held that if a Senator yields to another conditionally, the former does not lose the floor even if a point of order is made. [124] Under practices of recent years, if he obtains the floor while no business is pending he cannot be deprived of it upon objection. Without objection, he may yield temporarily for the consideration of other than the pending business; on objection, he can yield only for a

---

[118] See C.R., 80-1, p. 10613 (daily edition).
[119] See *Senate Journal*, 69-2. p. 265.
[120] *Senate Journal* 75-1, p. 404; also *Senate Journal* 74-1, p. 435.
[121] C.R., 80-1, pp. 10230-10235 (daily edition).
[122] See proceedings for July 19, 1947.
[123] C.R., 75-3, p. 1410 (daily edition).
[124] C.R., 78-1, p. 8098.

question.[125] It has been held that a Senator may yield for the consideration of a message received from the House or for laying a privileged matter before the Senate without losing his right to the floor.[126] A Senator having the floor and yielding for the consideration of a conference report resumes the floor after the report has been disposed of.[127] A Senator having the floor can yield for a quorum call without losing his right to the floor,[128] but his resumption of the floor counts as a second speech during that legislative day.[129]

The Rule provides that "no Senator shall speak more than twice upon any one question in debate on the same day without leave of the Senate, which shall be determined without debate." [130] This restriction has been interpreted to mean that a Senator may speak twice on the pending bill as well as twice on any amendments thereto in the same legislative day; this includes amendments to amendments.

During the morning hour, a Senator is not entitled to the floor for debate upon objection; the delivery of a speech is not in order prior to the conclusion of the morning business upon a demand for the regular order of business.[131] Debate on a report submitted during the morning business is not in order.

Relevancy or germaneness of debate to the subject under consideration is not required in the Senate. A Senator may read a paper which is irrelevant to the subject under discussion. But "if a Senator be called to order for words spoken in debate, upon the demand of the Senator or of any other Senator, the exceptionable words shall be taken down in writing, and read at the table for the information of the Senate." "If any Senator, in speaking or otherwise, transgress the rules of the Senate, the Presiding Officer shall, or any Senator may, call him to order; and when a Senator shall be called to order he shall sit down, and not proceed without leave of the Senate, which, if granted, shall be upon motion that he be allowed to proceed in order, which motion shall be determined without debate." This includes disorderly language. "No Senator in debate shall refer offensively to any State of the Union" nor "directly or indirectly, by any form of words impute to another

[125] C.R., 80-2, p. 9400 (daily edition).
[126] See Senate Journal, 70-1, p. 563; C.R., 72-2, p. 2018 (daily edition).
[127] C.R., 77-2, pp. 9712-9713 (daily edition).
[128] Senate Journal, 74-1, p. 434.
[129] See proceedings for July 13, 1937.
[130] For an application of rule, see Senate proceedings for Feb. 18, 1927.
[131] C.R., 74-1, p. 2938 (daily edition).

Senator or to other Senators any conduct or motive unworthy or unbecoming a Senator." Senators should not address each other in the second person.[132] Under the practices, Representatives and Senators may not refer to the action of the other chamber; such procedure is not in order. "It is a breach of order . . . to read extracts of proceedings of the House of Representatives relating to the same subject matter."[133] A Senator holding the floor in debate loses it if he yields to another for the transaction of business or to offer a motion,[134] even though it be a privileged or preferential motion.[135] He may not yield even for the introduction of a bill except by unanimous consent.[136] A Senator cannot make a motion himself and retain the floor; when the chair puts the question, no one has the floor; the chair must again recognize someone.[137] A Senator may not hold the floor and ask for a vote on the pending amendment;[138] he may not hold the floor while a series of amendments by him are being considered, or even while a subsequent one is being offered by him.[139] When a Senator offers an amendment another may be recognized since the chair interrupts the continuity by stating that the question is on agreeing to the amendment.[140] A Senator can not hold the floor while an amendment is being acted upon, and "the chair shall recognize" the Senator who first addresses him.[141]

A Senator may not parcel out his time and one who has the floor cannot interrogate one who does not. Ordinarily one Senator yields briefly to another without losing the floor or without any one making an objection, but the practice of yielding time which prevails in the House of Representatives has no place in Senate procedure. A Senator can always yield for a question, and for a question only in test cases; he may not yield for a short speech.

Cloture: The debate on any bill or amendments thereto may be limited under unanimous consent agreements or by the use of the Cloture Rule. Today it is a regular practice of the Senate for the Senators to tie their own hands by unanimously agreeing to limit

---

[132] See *Senate Journal,* 74-1, p. 339.
[133] Gilfry, *op. cit.,* p. 406.
[134] *Senate Journal,* 73-1, p. 133.
[135] See C.R., 75-3, p. 1937 (daily edition).
[136] C.R., 80-1, p. 11619 (daily edition).
[137] C.R., 77-2, p. 9231 for Nov. 18, 1942 (daily edition).
[138] C.R., 76-1, p. 15361 (daily edition).
[139] C.R., 75-3, p. 10684 (daily edition).
[140] For example see proceedings for August 3, 1937.
[141] C.R., 75-3, p. 12078 (daily edition).

the debate of an issue to a specified time.[142] A single objection blocks any such agreement.

The House uses the "previous question" procedure effectively to terminate debate but the Senate does not; in its first code of rules adopted on April 16, 1789, the "previous question" was recognized. In its revision of the rules on March 26, 1806, the previous question was dropped and since that time has not been readmitted.[143] Instead of developing procedures to curtail debate, the Senate has championed the cause of unlimited debate. For its lack of restrictions, the Senate has made itself famous for freedom of debate on all issues coming before it for disposition. It is the only significant deliberative body in the world in which legislation can be filibustered to death; on the other hand, every Senator is assured an unlimited discussion of every issue before a final vote of disposition is reached.

Many filibusters have been staged in the Senate for the sole purpose of defeating or delaying the passage of the pending proposed legislation To expedite business and to reach a final vote on passage of any controversial proposals on which a filibuster is being staged, the Senate on March 8, 1917, by a vote of 76 to 3 adopted its present Cloture Rule. The sole purpose of the rule is to prevent a small group of Senators from "talking an issue to death."

The Cloture Rule is designed to bring debate on a pending measure to a close. It provides that sixteen Senators may at any time sign a petition "to close the debate" and present it to the Presiding Officer, who is required to state the motion to the Senate immediately.[144] The motion may be presented to the Senate over the objection of any Senator who has the floor. This does not take that Senator's right to the floor away from him, but merely suspends it during the time necessary for calling the membership's attention to the petition.[145] For more than a day following the notification of the Senate membership of the petition, the debate can be continued just as if nothing had happened to restrain debate. But one hour after the Senate convenes two calendar days later that the Senate is in session, the Presiding Officer "shall lay the motion before the Senate and direct that the

---

[142] When a Senator is speaking under a limitation of debate, a quorum call would be charged against his time.
[143] See Gilfry, op. cit., I, p. 402.
[144] It has been ruled that unanimous consent is necessary to affix the name of a Senator to a cloture petition after it has been signed.
[145] See C.R., 69th Congress, special session, p. 154.

Secretary call the roll, and, upon the ascertainment that a quorum is present," shall "without debate submit [146] to the Senate by an aye-and-nay vote the question: Is it the sense of the Senate that the debate shall be brought to a close?" [147] The vote on the petition, according to a decision on July 29, 1946, will be had at the hour required by the rule, even though the bill may have been displaced in the meantime.

A two-thirds affirmative vote is required to invoke cloture, which makes the pending measure "the unfinished business to the exclusion of all other business until disposed of." If a two-thirds vote is not forthcoming, the attempt fails and the debate remains unrestrained. In effect, the bill is killed by a negative vote since further consideration of the measure will be called off and the bill will be left on the calendar without disposition. That has been the recent practice.

If the Cloture Rule is invoked, a two-thirds vote having been cast in support of bringing the debate to a close, no Senator may speak more than one hour "on the pending measure, the amendments thereto, and motions affecting the same." The Presiding Officer keeps the time of each Senator who speaks. The rule and decisions of the chair in pursuance thereof, prohibit the offering of any amendment after the vote "unless the same has been presented and read prior to that time," except by unanimous consent. It has been interpreted that "unanimous consent to submit and print in *Record*" meets the requirement of having been "presented and read prior to that time." "No dilatory motion, or dilatory amendment, or amendment not germane shall be in order." Hence, any amendment offered to a bill on which cloture has been invoked must meet the acid test of being germane, and if it is not, a point of order prohibits its consideration and adoption.[148] All questions of procedure—"points of order, including questions of relevancy, and appeals from the decisions of the Presiding Officer" [149]—shall be decided without debate. The adoption of a cloture petition does not modify the effect of Rule XVI as applied to appropriation bills.

The precedent has been well established in the Senate that the application of the Cloture Rule has been limited to "debate upon

---

[146] The vote on a cloture petition has been postponed by unanimous consent.
[147] See Rule XXII. A vote on a cloture motion filed after midnight will be had on the second calendar day thereafter that the Senate is in session.
[148] *Senate Journal*, 75-1, p. 439-440.
[149] Rule XXII.

any pending measure." In the 79th Congress, during the discussion of S. 101, to make the FEPC a permanent government agency, the chair ruled that a motion by Senator Barkley, majority leader at that time, to invoke the Cloture Rule on a motion to amend the *Journal,* was out of order. It was held that the rule did not apply to matters pertaining to the *Journal.*[150] In the latter part of the second session of the 80th Congress, the chair held that the Cloture Rule did not apply to *motions to consider* a particular piece of legislation.[151] This decision was made in connection with an attempt to call up H.R. 29, anti-poll tax bill. The scope of the rule, as stated by the Presiding Officer, is limited to "debate upon any pending measure" at the time the motion was filed. A resolution (S. Res. 25 of the 80th Congress) to extend the Cloture Rule to include procedural motions and amendments to the *Journal* was reported by the Senate Committee on Rules and Administration, but the resolution was never acted on by the Senate.

In spite of the cloture instrument available to the members of the Senate, the use of it has not been successful; that is, if the standard is to limit debate and bring the pending measure to a vote. Mr. Watkins, the Senate Parliamentarian, in his unprinted volumes on Senate precedents, lists only four cloture motions which have been adopted, and these were all prior to 1928.[152] He lists 15 as having been rejected.[153] Eight motions were filed and later withdrawn.[154]

Non-debatable Questions: Even though debate is unlimited in the Senate and a Senator cannot be taken off his feet unless he yields or transgresses the rules of the Senate, there are certain questions which are not debatable. Once a Senator is recognized to put one of these questions, it must be decided by the Senate without discussion; in effect, immediately. A Senator having the floor may not be taken off his feet for the presentation of a non-debatable question, but whenever a Senator is recognized for this

[150] The decision by the chair was made when a point of order was raised against the Barkley motion to the effect that the Senate was debating the *Journal* and not S. 101.

[151] See C.R., 80-2, pp. 9749-9754 (daily edition). The chair stated that "the existing Senate rules regarding cloture do not provide conclusive cloture. They still leave the Senate . . . at the mercy of unlimited debate *ad infinitum.*" Hence it was held that the motion was not in order.

[152] The four adopted were acted on on: Nov. 15, 1919; Jan. 25, 1926; Feb. 15, 1927; and Feb. 28, 1927.

[153] The 15 were rejected on the following dates: Feb. 2, 1921; July 7, 1922; June 1, 1926; Feb. 26, 1927; Feb. 26, 1927; Jan. 19, 1933; Jan. 27, 1938; Feb. 16, 1938; Nov. 23, 1942; May 15, 1944; Feb. 9, 1946; May 7, 1946; May 25, 1946; July 31, 1946.

[154] For speech on filibusters see C.R., 79-2, pp. 653-662, for Jan. 31, 1946 (daily edition).

purpose, he may submit such a question for decision. Each non-debatable question is not always in order since some of them must be tied to the particular parliamentary situation on a bill, and hence, hinge on what business is under consideration as well as the stage of consideration. The Parliamentarian lists the following non-debatable questions:

1. Quorum proceedings (Rule V).
2. Presentation and reference of petitions or memorials (Rule VII, Par. 5).
3. Motion to lay before the Senate a bill or other matter sent to the Senate by the President or the House of Representatives (Rule VII, Par. 7).
4. Motions made before 2 o'clock to proceed to consideration of any matter (Rule VIII).
5. Motions under Rule IX as to order of business—which are seldom if ever used.
6. Motions to change or displace special orders (Rule X, Par. 2).
7. Reading of paper when called for by Senator (Rule XI).
8. Request of Senator to be excused from voting and reasons for excusing (Rule XII, Par. 2).
9. Motions to request the House of Representatives to return a bill or other matter on which the Senate has acted when there has been entered a motion for reconsideration (Rule XIII, Par. 2).
10. Questions of relevancy of amendments to general appropriations bills (Rule XVI, Par. 4).
11. Motions to allow Senators to proceed in order when called to order for violation of rules (Rule XIX, Par. 4).
12. Questions of order arising on appeals, incidental appeals thereto, and questions of order not submitted to Senate for decision (Rule XX, Par. 1).
13. Motions to adjourn (Rule XXII).
14. Motions to adjourn to a day certain or that when Senate adjourns it shall be to a day certain (Rule XXII).
15. Motions to take a recess (Rule XXII).
16. Motions to proceed to the consideration of executive business (Rule XXII).
17. Motions to lay a matter on table (Rule XXII).
18. Questions on adoption of motion signed by 16 Senators to invoke Cloture Rule (Rule XXII).
19. Points of order, questions of relevancy of amendments, and appeals after cloture has been invoked (Rule XXII).
20. Motions to proceed to the consideration of conference reports (Rule XXVII, Par. 1).
21. Questions of closing of doors on discussion of business on which some Senators think secrecy is required; not applicable to open executive sessions (Rules XXXV and XXXVIII).
22. Leave of the Senate to allow a Senator to speak more than twice on any one question in one day (Rule XIX).

Motions in Order When Question Is Pending: During the course of the daily procedure when the Senate is working on a bill or amendments thereto, various motions for their disposition may be entertained. No motion intended to effect their disposition "shall be received" except those listed in Rule XXII. This does not, however, exclude certain matters or questions which might be raised because of their nature, and which do not necessarily relate to the disposition of the pending business. To illustrate: it is always in order during the consideration of a bill and amendments thereto—brought up under a motion and not under the call of the calendar—to raise the following questions: the presence of a quorum, order and decorum in the Senate Chamber, whether the Senator speaking is complying with the rules, and consideration of a conference report. The chair may refuse to entertain some of these questions or he may rule points of no quorum out of order if raised too frequently; that is, before the transaction of business since the same motion was offered. In recent years, it has b̶ repeatedly held that debate was not intervening business. Ea decision of the chair, however, is subject to appeal, but all appeals must be taken before other business intervenes.

The motions which "shall be received" under Rule XXII when "a question is pending" "and which shall have precedence as they stand arranged" are:

"To adjourn.
"To adjourn to a day certain, or that when the Senate adjourn it shall be to a day certain.
"To take a recess.
"To proceed to the consideration of executive business.
"To lay on the table.
"To postpone indefinitely.
"To postpone to a day certain.
"To commit.
"To amend."

All but the last four of these motions are not debatable.

1. "Motion to adjourn" and "adjourn to a day certain."

The motion to adjourn should be distinguished from a resolution to adjourn both houses of Congress. Neither is debatable.[155] But the resolution is not effective until acted on by both houses and does not necessarily provide for the termination of business. The Senate may adopt an adjournment resolution to adjourn the Senate or both houses of Congress for a few days or *sine die,* a

---

[155] The resolution can be amended. A resolution providing for a conditional adjournment is in order; the Senate reassembled on Sept. 5, 1945 in pursuance of such adjournment (see C.R., 79-1, p. 8459—daily edition).

few hours or several days before the action becomes effective. The adoption of the motion to adjourn is generally the remedy for breaking up of a day's sitting of the Senate; that is, the termination of a legislative day. As stipulated above, there are two such motions, namely: (1) to adjourn, and (2) to adjourn to a day certain. The first is a simple motion to terminate immediately a legislative day as contrasted to recessing, in which case the Senate will reconvene the next calendar day (Sundays excepted) at the regular meeting hour; it takes precedence over the motion to adjourn to a day certain.[156] The latter is more complex with the adjournment motion specifying the hour to which the Senate adjourns. For example, it might provide that when the Senate closes its day's work, it adjourn until 1 p.m. tomorrow. Such a motion might be adopted at 2 p.m. with the day's sitting terminating at 5 p.m.[157] At any rate, a motion to adjourn is generally referred to as an action on the part of the Senate to terminate a legislative day, as distinguished from a recess.

This motion is in order at any time during the consideration of legislation provided a Senator can get recognition for that purpose. One such motion may be offered after another has been rejected if business has intervened. While it might delay final action on the pending measure, it does not displace its consideration; it merely suspends it temporarily until the unfinished business is again in order. Adjournment does displace a motion.

The Senate may adjourn for as long a period of time as it sees fit up to the Constitutional limitation of three days without the consent of the other House, or it may adjourn for only a few minutes, and reconvene on a new legislative day in the same calendar day. On April 30, 1948, the Senate adjourned for only one minute, in order to effect a new legislative day and thus make in order for consideration a bill which had not been on the calendar for a legislative day.[158]

The motion to adjourn is not debatable and is not in order when no business has intervened since an identical such motion was made and rejected. But one such motion may be offered after another has been rejected provided business has intervened. It is not in order if a Senator refuses to yield to a Senator trying to

---

[156] C.R., 75-3, p. 4345 (daily edition).
[157] Senate has adjourned after a joint session of the two houses without returning to the chamber.
[158] A committee report must likewise lie over a legislative day instead of a calendar day.

get the floor for that purpose.[159] A motion to adjourn to a day certain is not in order in the absence of a quorum;[160] it is in order to adjourn in the absence of a quorum.[161] Where an order for a recess has been made, a subsequent motion to adjourn is not in order in the absence of a quorum; a motion to adjourn having been adopted by yeas and nays cannot be withdrawn later except by unanimous consent.[162]

2. "To take a Recess."

Next to a motion to adjourn, a motion to recess is preferential, and takes precedence over a motion to "lay on table."[163] The motion is not debatable. The motion is not in order while the Senate is dividing.[164] But less than a quorum may take a recess,[165] if ordered in the presence of a quorum. This procedure is commonly used for terminating a day's sitting of the Senate; in fact, the Senate recesses from day to day far more often than it adjourns. When it recesses, the legislative day remains the same, with the unfinished business coming up for consideration the first thing at the next meeting of the Senate. Any action to the contrary, or intervening matters that are not privileged must be transacted under unanimous consent unless the Senate by motion should displace the unfinished business.

3. "Consideration of executive business."

Next in line is the motion to proceed to the consideration of executive business. This is not the transaction of business; it is a change in the status of Senate proceedings. Once the Senate is in executive session, it proceeds with one of the following types of business: messages from the President, executive reports of committees, or business on Executive Calendar. Business on this calendar is divided into nominations and treaties. After referring messages from the President and receiving committee reports, the Senate moves to business on the Executive Calendar, and in the order listed there unless passed over. It may first consider either nominations or treaties; usually nominations are first.

---

[159] Senate Journal, 71-1, p. 78.
[160] See Senate Journal, 70-1, p. 565.
[161] See proceedings for July 15, 1942 and Nov. 14, 1942. The Senate has adjourned to a day certain in absence of a quorum when no point of order was made (See C.R., 76-1, p. 13786 daily edition).
[162] See Senate Journal, 70-2, p. 211.
[163] Senate Journal, 70-2, pp. 270-271.
[164] Gilfry, op. cit., p. 503.
[165] Ibid., p. 503.

4. "Motion to lay on table."

The motion to lay on the table is a simple way of taking final action on pending business on which the Senate wishes to take a negative position. It is applicable to a bill and amendments thereto as well as to certain motions. An amendment can be laid on the table without prejudice to the bill to which it was offered, but an amendment to the amendment would also go to the table. Since the motion is not debatable, the question can be brought to a vote in a hurry. The motion is used generally to reach a final disposition on motion to reconsider, or appeals from the decision of the chair. While the motion is applicable to pending business, it is not commonly used for the disposition of legislation—bills and amendments thereto are generally either voted up or down. The preamble to a bill or resolution may be laid on the table without carrying the bill or resolution with it.[166] The Senate rules specify that "any such amendment or restriction to a general appropriation bill may be laid on the table without prejudice to the bill."

5. "Motions to postpone indefinitely and to a day certain."

The motion to postpone indefinitely is the next in order, but it is rarely used to dispose of bills except in the case of companion bills, i.e., the Senate passes a House-passed bill and indefinitely postpones a companion Senate bill which has been reported and placed on the calendar. It is a way of effecting a final disposition of a measure. The motion to postpone to a day certain is also used by the Senate. These motions are debatable and amendable and take precedence over a motion to refer or commit. A motion to take up another bill while unfinished business is pending has precedence over a motion to postpone the unfinished business to a day certain.

6. "Motion to Commit."

The motion to commit or recommit may or may not effect a final disposition of a matter, depending on whether or not the committee to which committed takes further action on the matter and reports back. The motion may be offered by any one opposed to a matter and is in order at any time prior to passage,[167] while Rule XIX particularly provides for presentation of the motion to recommit after the third reading and before passage. Any such motion, which is in order, is debatable but cannot be amended

[166] Rule XXIII.
[167] See C.R., 76-3, p. 18446 (daily edition).

except to add instructions.[168] The number which can be ordered in the course of disposing of a single matter is not limited under the Senate rules;[169] the motion to recommit a bill is in order only when it is before the Senate.[170]

A motion to recommit with instructions to report the bill back forthwith with an amendment, if agreed to, requires that the committee report the bill back immediately.[171] The Senate has recommitted conference reports, but it is not a current practice; the same purpose can be accomplished by a rejection of the report, when another conference can be ordered, and, in accordance with usage, the same conferees appointed. It is in order to move to recommit a conference report with instructions [172] at the proper time; the motion is not in order when the other house has agreed to the report.

7. "To Amend."

The last of this series of motions which shall be received under Rule XXII, "when a question is pending," and in the order listed above, is "to amend." Any bill, or amendment thereto, before the Senate is open to amendment. The time, conditions, and kind are discussed elsewhere.[173]

Order in Chamber and Galleries: During the consideration of a bill or amendments thereto, certain other questions might also be raised without regard to the series of motions mentioned above. A Senator may demand that order be maintained in the Senate or in the galleries, and the Presiding Officer is required to interrupt the business until order is restored. Rule XIX provides that "whenever confusion arises in the chamber or the galleries, or demonstrations of approval or disapproval are indulged in by the occupants of the galleries, it shall be the duty of the chair to enforce order on his own initiative and without any point of order being made by a Senator." Of course if the Presiding Officer does not give the Senate satisfaction, an appeal may be taken from the decision of the chair.

---

[168] Rule XXVI, paragraph 1; also C.R., 80-1, p. 4265 (daily edition). A point of order against a committee amendment, and not against a bill itself, under Rule XVI, if sustained, does not send the bill back to committee (C.R., 76-3, p. 1618 daily edition).

[169] *Senate Journal*, 74-1, p. 289.

[170] C.R., 78-1, p. 5733 (daily edition).

[171] C.R., 76-3, p. 15411 (daily edition).

[172] Gilfry, *op. cit.*, p. 261.

[173] See pp. 360-368.

Decorum: At no stage of the proceedings may a Senator "refer offensively to any State of the Union." "No Senator in debate shall, directly or indirectly, by any form of words impute to another Senator or to other Senators any conduct or motive unworthy or unbecoming a Senator." "No Senator shall interrupt another in debate without his consent, and to obtain such consent he shall first address the Presiding Officer; and no Senator shall speak more than twice upon any one question in debate on the same day without leave of the Senate, which shall be determined without debate." "If any Senator, in speaking or otherwise, transgress the rules of the Senate, the Presiding Officer shall, or any Senator may, call him to order; and when a Senator shall be called to order he shall sit down, and not proceed without leave of the Senate, which, if granted, shall be upon motion that he be allowed to proceed in order, which motion shall be determined without debate." [174]

"Privileged Matters," Including Vetoes: At any time the Presiding Officer may lay or a Senator may move to lay before the Senate any bill or other matter sent to the Senate by the President or the House of Representatives, and any pending question or business at that time shall be suspended,[175] but not displaced.

Included in this category are veto messages, which constitute privileged business and which may be brought up at almost any time; a Senator, however, cannot be deprived of his right to the floor for this purpose nor may certain business be interrupted, such as approving the *Journal*,[176] while the Senate is dividing, "or while a question of order or a motion to adjourn is pending." [177] The message must be spread upon the *Journal* before it can be considered. A motion to refer a veto to the proper standing committee has precedence over a demand for a vote thereon; the question is debatable.

A veto message having been received by the Senate [178] the Presiding Officer calls it to the attention of the Senate. Any Senator, generally the floor leader, may request its immediate consideration; depending on the question and the program, the time for consideration is determined. Three preferential motions are in order before a vote is taken to override or sustain the veto. They are here

---

[174] Rule XIX.
[175] Rule VII.
[176] See C.R., 80-2, p. 8588 (daily edition).
[177] Rule XXVIII.
[178] Veto messages are sent to the house in which the vetoed bill originated.

listed in the order of preference: (1) lay on table, (2) postpone, (3) or refer to a committee. The last two are debatable. The veto message itself is debatable, without limit on time. The vote to override a President's veto requires a two-thirds majority of those present, by yea and nay vote, with at least a quorum present.

Motion to Consider: The adoption of a motion to proceed to the consideration of a particular bill displaces the consideration of the unfinished business, and hence, may be used at any time to interrupt and dispose of the pending question regardless of the precedence of the series of motions in order "when a question is pending."

Suspension of Rules: The motion to suspend, modify, or amend any rule (except paragraph 1, Rule XII) or part thereof, after one day's notice, shall be in order at any time. The notice must be in writing and specify precisely the rule or part thereof to be affected. With unanimous consent, the same action can be taken without notice.[179]

Credentials of Senators Elect: "The presentation of the credentials of Senators elect and other questions of privilege shall always be in order, except during the reading and correction of the *Journal,* while a question of order or a motion to adjourn is pending, or while the Senate is dividing; and all questions and motions arising or made upon the presentation of such credentials shall be proceeded with until disposed of." [180]

Conference Reports and House Amendments: Included in "other questions of privilege" are reports of conference committees, the presentation of which shall "always be in order, except when the *Journal* is being read or a question of order or a motion to adjourn is pending, or while the Senate is dividing; and when received the question of proceeding to the consideration of the report, if raised, shall be immediately put, and shall be determined without debate." [181] The consideration of a conference report does not displace the unfinished business; it merely suspends it. The same is true in the case of House amendments to a Senate-passed bill, which is also privileged business. For a further discussion of conference reports, see pp. 388-391.

Quorum: "If, at any time during the daily sessions of the Senate, a question shall be raised by any Senator as to the presence of a quorum, the Presiding Officer shall forthwith direct the

179 Rule XL.
180 Rule VI.
181 Rule XXVII, paragraph 1.

Secretary to call the roll and shall announce the result, and these proceedings shall be without debate.

"Whenever upon such roll call it shall be ascertained that a quorum is not present, a majority of the Senators present may direct the Sergeant at Arms to request, and, when necessary, to compel the attendance of the absent Senators, which order shall be determined without debate; and pending its execution, and until a quorum shall be present, no debate nor motion, except to adjourn, shall be in order." [182] A quorum to do business shall consist of a "majority of the Senators duly chosen and sworn."[183] The Senate proceeds under the assumption that a quorum is present unless the question is raised; in which case, the bells are rung to inform the "absentee" Senators and the Presiding Officer directs a call of the roll. All decisions incident thereto are made without debate, and if a quorum is not present by the time the results from the roll call are announced, a majority of the Senators present may direct the Sergeant at Arms to request, or to compel the attendance of the absent Senators. Senators may be forced to attend, unless granted a "leave of absence" or by authority of the Senate, even if a quorum is present. Senators who do not reach the chamber when the roll is being called in time to answer to their names may gain recognition after the call and have their presence or vote recorded, provided the results have not been announced.

Under the practice of this rule, anyone, once recognized, can request a quorum call, but a Senator who has the floor cannot be forced to yield to another for that purpose; the chair is not permitted to count the quorum; it must be determined by roll call. A Senator having the floor may yield to another for the purpose of requesting a quorum without losing his right to the floor, but the action has the effect of terminating his first speech on that subject during the same legislative day, if a point of order is made. While a vote by a division is being taken, a quorum call is in order prior to the announcement of the result of the vote. Upon demand after the prayer and approval of the *Journal*, following each convening of the Senate, a quorum must be called. Where a unanimous consent agreement has been proposed and objected to after a quorum call, the submission of a new agreement requires the roll to be called again unless it is dispensed with by unanimous consent; and a second for the yeas and nays not being sufficient,

[182] Rule V.
[183] Rule III, paragraph 2.

a quorum call is in order.[184] A call is not required to act on a request for limitation of debate; a proposed unanimous consent agreement submitted immediately following a quorum call, requires another under the rule;[185] but a call is not required in case of a unanimous consent request for a vote on an amendment at a certain time. Rule XII provides: "No request by a Senator for unanimous consent for taking of a final vote on a specified date upon the passage of a bill or joint resolution shall be submitted to the Senate for agreement thereto until, upon a roll call ordered for the purpose by the Presiding Officer, it shall be disclosed that a quorum of the Senate is present; and when a unanimous consent is thus given the same shall operate as the order of the Senate, but any unanimous consent may be revoked by another" granted in the manner prescribed above upon one day's notice. Where a request is made for unanimous consent to vote on the passage of a Senate resolution, a quorum is not required under the rule, since it applies only to bills and joint resolutions.

The Presiding Officer can rule that the request for a quorum call is dilatory, but his decision is subject to appeal.

There is no limit to the number of requests that may be made during the course of a day; a request is generally held dilatory if no business has transpired since the last one, and it is not in order immediately after a roll call vote showing that a quorum is present. The reception of a message from the House has not been ruled as the transaction of business sufficient to justify a quorum call. The following have been ruled to be business: the ordering of engrossment and third reading of a joint resolution, presentation and reference of a communication, granting of permission to insert an article in the *Record,* objection to a bill under call of calendar under Rule VIII, the making of a motion or ordering of yeas and nays, voting on motions to recess, adjourn, lay on table, and on an appeal from the decision of the chair, the offering of an amendment, agreeing to a motion for an executive session, and submitting a report out of order.

If a quorum fails to develop on the first call of the roll, it is the custom for the Presiding Officer to direct the names of the absentees to be called again; on July 24, 1947, a recapitulation of a call was demanded and ordered. A motion may be made to request attendance of those absent, and instructions to compel their

[184] C.R., 77-1, pp. 2055-57 (daily edition).
[185] C.R., 78-1, p. 2103 (daily edition).

attendance may be added. Such a motion is not debatable. A quorum call on various occasions has been withdrawn by unanimous consent while the roll was being called; but when an announcement of no quorum has been made, it is not in order to vacate the call even by unanimous consent.

In the absence of a quorum, neither debate nor the transaction of business including motions (except the motion to adjourn) is in order;[186] it is not even in order to move to recess.

Voting: After all amendments to an original amendment to a bill have been disposed of the question recurs on the adoption of the amendment as amended, if any. After all amendments to a bill have been acted on the question recurs on the third reading and passage. Any one of the several methods of voting utilized by the Senate may be resorted to for final disposition of any amendment or bill, or question. The methods are: voice vote, division, and yea and nay. The Senate votes by roll call much more frequently than the House. It takes only about 6 to 10 minutes for a yea and nay vote in the Senate as contrasted to 25 to 45 minutes in the House. The yeas and nays may be ordered when the request is seconded, by 1/5 of a presumptive quorum, but frequently the Presiding Officer does not bother to count; he merely takes a glance at the "showing" of hands and orders the call; simultaneously the bells ring in both the Senate wing of the Capitol and the Senate Office Building. The names of the Senators are called in their alphabetical order. Voting and changes on each issue are in order until the decision has been announced by the chair.[187]

Unlike the House, the Senate may not go from one method to another, testing each, until the yea and nay method has been reached. In the case of a veto, a yea and nay vote is required as provided for in the Constitution. Otherwise, the Senators may utilize any one of the methods, but only one if the result is announced. After the result of a vote has been announced, a request for a division comes too late;[188] the same is true in the case of yeas and nays.[189] The announcement that the "ayes" (or nays) seem to have it is not a final vote. The yeas and nays may be demanded prior to announcement of the results of a division

---

[186] C.R., 80-2, p. 5232 (daily edition).
[187] Rule XII.
[188] C.R., 75-2, p. 2299 (daily edition).
[189] C.R., 75-1, p. 10266 (daily edition).

vote.[190] Likewise, the Senate has ordered the recapitulation of a close vote when its correctness was challenged.

Where less than a quorum votes and the number of pairs announced are not sufficient to make a quorum, it is the duty of the chair to order a quorum call; the vote is valid if a quorum was present, even if a quorum did not vote, provided a number of those not voting, sufficient to make a quorum, announced they were present but paired. "Pairing" is the common practice of both the House and Senate. This device has been developed in both houses to enable Representatives and Senators to register their opinion on any particular issue or issues when they are unavoidably absent from the chamber on public or private business. By the use of "pairs" a Representative or Senator favoring a particular issue and who is absent when a roll-call vote is taken on it, may make his opinion effective by contracting (pairing) with a colleague opposing the issue that neither of the parties will vote. "Pairs" are not counted as yeas or nays in the official tabulation on the roll call for the purpose of determining the adoption or rejection of the issues being voted on. For a further discussion of this practice, see pp. 299-300.

A Senator can change his vote at any time before the result is announced.[191] The roll call cannot be interrupted after a Senator's name has been called [192] and a response has been made. In the case of a tie the Vice President is permitted to vote.[193]

Rule XII, relating to voting, provides:

1. When the yeas and nays are ordered, the names of Senators shall be called alphabetically; and each Senator shall, without debate, declare his assent or dissent to the question, unless excused by the Senate; and no Senator shall be permitted to vote after the decision shall have been announced by the Presiding Officer, but may for sufficient reasons, with unanimous consent, change or withdraw his vote. No motion to suspend this rule shall be in order, nor shall the Presiding Officer entertain any request to suspend it by unanimous consent.

2. When a Senator declines to vote on call of his name, he shall be required to assign his reasons therefor, and having assigned them, the Presiding Officer shall submit the question to the Senate: "Shall the Senator, for the reasons assigned by him, be excused from voting?" which shall be decided without debate; and these proceedings shall be had after the roll call and before the result is announced; and any further proceedings in reference thereto shall be after such announcement.

[190] For precedent see C.R., 77-2, p. 8275 (daily edition).
[191] C.R., 77-1, p. 5186 (daily edition).
[192] Senate Journal, 74-1, p. 301; numerous other illustrations are available.
[193] Mr. Watkins, Senate Parliamentarian, has compiled in his volumes on precedents a list of all tie votes from March 4, 1921, to date.

3. No request by a Senator for unanimous consent for the taking of a final vote on a specified date upon the passage of a bill or joint resolution shall be submitted to the Senate for agreement thereto until, upon a roll call ordered for the purpose by the Presiding Officer, it shall be disclosed that a quorum of the Senate is present; and when a unanimous consent is thus given the same shall operate as the order of the Senate, but any unanimous consent may be revoked by another unanimous consent granted in the manner prescribed above upon one day's notice.[194]

Motion to Reconsider: After the Senate acts on an amendment or on a bill, or almost any question on which the Senate has voted, any Senator voting on the side that prevailed may offer a motion to reconsider the vote by which that action was taken. A Senator voting in the minority cannot move to reconsider a yea and nay vote;[195] if he did not vote he may.[196] If there were no yea and nay vote, any Senator may make the motion.[197]

The act of entering the motion is a privileged matter [198] but it must be made within "the next two days of actual session thereafter" to be in order.[199] Only one such motion is in order,[200] except by unanimous consent. When brought up for consideration, as contrasted to entering it, a majority vote is required for adoption; it is debatable, but not amendable.[201] Any negative action is final. To lay any motion to reconsider on the table, does not affect the status of the bill. Once entered, the consideration of a motion may be delayed indefinitely, but the Senate will hold up any matter still within its jurisdiction until the motion has been disposed of. The motion does not automatically come before the Senate.[202] It cannot be considered when an amendment is pending, but it may be entered and taken up immediately when no other business is pending. When the motion to reconsider which has been entered is taken up on motion it has the effect of displacing the unfinished business..[203]

A motion to reconsider a vote agreeing to an amendment to a bill which has been passed is not in order unless reconsideration of the vote on final passage is reconsidered.[204] It is in order to reconsider the passage of a House bill on which a conference has

---

[194] *Senate Manual*, p. 16.
[195] *Senate Journal*, 69-1, p. 544.
[196] *Senate Journal*, 71-2, p. 514.
[197] C.R., 76-3, p. 3812 (daily edition).
[198] C.R., 80-2, pp. 8497-8498 (daily edition).
[199] Rule XIII.
[200] C.R., 80-2, pp. 7449-7450 (daily edition).
[201] *Senate Journal*, 71-2, p. 250.
[202] C.R., 78-1, pp. 10182-10184 (daily edition).
[203] For decision of chair see Senate Proceedings for Mar. 4, 1938.
[204] *Senate Journal*, 69-1, pp. 342-345.

been requested if the Senate is in possession of the papers.[205] A motion to reconsider a bill transmitted to the House must be accompanied by a request for the return of papers, which is not debatable. In fact, consideration of the motion to reconsider is not in order where the Senate has lost jurisdiction of the matter. Bills, resolutions, reports, amendments, orders, or messages on which the Senate has acted and transmitted to the House of Representatives can be reconsidered only if they can be repossessed, by means of adopting a request for their return. Any attempt to reconsider a vote on a conference report that has been sent to the House must be accompanied by a motion requesting the House to return the same.[206]

Conference Reports and House Amendments: After a bill passes both houses of Congress it becomes a privileged matter. A Senate bill which passes the House with amendment, however, is not a complete product, ready for the President's signature. Before any bill is complete and ready for the White House, it must be approved by both houses in an identical form. A Senate bill which has passed the House with amendment or amendments, is messaged back to the Senate. Messages from the House of Representatives "may be received at any stage of proceedings, except while the Senate is dividing, or while the *Journal* is being read, or while a question of order or a motion to adjourn is pending."[207] When House amendments to a Senate bill are laid before the Senate, it is a privileged matter for immediate consideration [208] if no Senator has the floor, or if one has the floor and yields for that purpose; it takes precedence over the unfinished business but does not displace it—merely suspends;[209] such amendments are debatable and are considered separately, unless *en bloc* under unanimous consent procedure.

The order of precedence of motions on such pending business before the stage of disagreement has been reached, as listed by the Senate Parliamentarian, Charles Watkins, is:

1. To lay on table (which is not debatable).
2. Postpone indefinitely (which is debatable).
3. Postpone to a day certain (which is debatable).

[205] *Senate Journal*, 73-2, p. 34.
[206] *Senate Journal*, 71-2, p. 222.
[207] Rule XXVIII.
[208] See C.R., 75-1, p. 9116 (daily edition).
[209] See *Senate Journal*, GJ-B, p. 255.

4. To refer
   a. to a standing committee
   b. to a special committee
5. To amend.
6. To agree.
7. To disagree and ask for a conference.

In keeping with this list of motions, if no Senator makes any motion to the contrary, the question occurs on agreeing to the House amendment. If agreed to, this action clears the bill for the President. The Senate may amend the House amendment to the Senate bill, and send it back to the House for its concurrence.[210] But this type of procedure is seldom resorted to until after the bill has been sent to conference; it is not uncommon to resort to this cumbersome method for the disposition of any amendments reported in disagreement, which accompany the conference report on a bill. Generally speaking, when a Senate bill is messaged back to the Senate by the House with House amendments, if the House amendments are not controversial, the Senator in charge of the bill will request that the Senate agree to the House amendments, which action clears the bill for the President. If the amendments are controversial, a conference will be requested immediately, without attempting to send the bill from one House to the other until some kind of an accord can be reached. In the case of major or controversial bills, when one house adds various amendments to the version approved by the other house, the former requests a conference on the bill even before messaging it back for the latter's concurrence in the amendments. The Senate regularly at time of passage of a House appropriation bill with amendments insists on its amendments and asks for a conference with the House.[211] The question of sending a bill to conference and appointing conferees is debatable, and the motion may be displaced.

The Senate rules, like the rules of the House, have very little to say about conferences. Rule XXVII does stipulate that conference reports shall be in order "except when the *Journal* is being read or a question of order or a motion to adjourn is pending, or while the Senate is dividing; and when received the question of proceeding to the consideration of the report, if raised, shall be immediately put, and shall be determined without debate." [212] The

---

[210] A Senate amendment to a House amendment to a Senate bill may be amended in one further degree.
[211] C.R., 79-1, p. 3796, illustrates the case.
[212] Rule XXVII, paragraph 1.

Senate rule further deprives the conference committees of legislative power, but in practice this is frequently overlooked. It states that "Conferees shall not insert in their report matter not committed to them by either house, nor shall they strike from the bill matter agreed to by both houses." [213]   But many points of order against the insertion of new matter or the omission of matter in bills have been overruled.[214] Where both houses pass different bills by striking out the enacting clause and substituting a new bill, little limitation can be placed on their discretion, except as to germaneness or completely new subject matter. Rule XXVI paragraph (3a) provides that: "In any case in which a disagreement to an amendment in the nature of a substitute has been referred to conferees, it shall be in order for the conferees to report a substitute on the same subject matter; but they may not include in the report matter not committed to them by either house. They may, however, include in their report in any such case matter which is a germane modification of subjects in disagreement."

The chair has ruled that the conferees have very wide latitude and may make any germane amendment or modification. On April 2, 1948, a conference report on S. 1393, veterans' aid bill, was brought up and a point of order was sustained on the grounds that the conferees had exceeded their authority; an appeal from the decision of the chair was taken. A compromise was later reached and the appeal from the decision of the chair was vacated without ever being brought to a vote.[215]   In any case, "if new matter is inserted in the report, or if matter which was agreed to by both houses is stricken from the bill, a point of order may be made against the report, and if the point of order is sustained, the report shall be recommitted to the committee of conference." [216]

The presentation of a conference report to the Senate is privileged and may be made while another motion is pending; the motion to take up is not debatable. If a conference report is up for consideration under unanimous consent and the regular order is called for, it is in order to move to continue with the report, which suspends the consideration of the unfinished business; consideration of a conference report does not displace the unfinished business. The conference report itself is debatable. It may not

---

[213] Rule XXVII, paragraph 2.
[214] For illustration see proceedings for Feb. 3, 1927; Feb. 24, 1927; June 5, 1934, and Aug. 6, 1935.
[215] See Senate proceedings from April 2 to April 15, 1948.
[216] Rule XXVII.

be amended and cannot be recommittted if one house has already acted on it. If the report is rejected a further conference can be requested. If the motion to recommit is in order, it may embody instructions, but it is not in order to move to instruct conferees after the report is filed.[217] A motion to disagree to a report is not in order; it must be positive. The time to instruct conferees is between the time of agreeing or asking for conference and the time of appointing them.

After the conference report has been adopted (which is not amendable) the Senate will proceed to the consideration of amendments reported in disagreement, if any. They, too, must be approved by both houses in identical form before the bill is cleared for the President's signature. When bills in disagreement are reported for disposition in the Senate, the following motions are in order:

1. To recede (from its own amendment).
2. To adhere (to its own amendment, or to disagreement to House amendment).
3. To recede and concur.
4. To recede and concur with an amendment.
5. To insist and ask for further conference.

For further information on a general picture of the procedure for sending a bill to conference and the disposition of the same, see pp. 269-278.

Bills Read Three Times Before Passage: Hence, all bills introduced in the Senate or passed by the House and messaged to the Senate are faced with a heavily fortified parliamentary maze, which prescribe all the obstacles they must surmount before final approval by that body—just what can be done to push the bill along or what can be done to prohibit its enactment. Accordingly, every "bill and joint resolution shall receive three readings previous to its passage, which readings shall be on three different days, unless the Senate unanimously direct otherwise; and the Presiding Officer shall give notice at each reading whether it be the first, second, or third: *Provided,* That the first or second reading of each bill may be by title only, unless the Senate in any case shall otherwise order." No bill shall "be committed or amended until it shall have been twice read." "When a bill or resolution shall have been ordered to be read a third time, it shall not be in order

[217] C.R., 75-1, p. 12012 (daily edition).

to propose amendments, unless by unanimous consent," but it shall be in order to move its commitment at this stage.

"The Secretary of the Senate shall examine all bills, amendments, and joint resolutions before they go out of the possession of the Senate, and shall examine all bills and joint resolutions which shall have passed both houses, to see that the same are correctly enrolled, and, when signed by the Speaker of the House and the President of the Senate, shall forthwith present the same, when they shall have originated in the Senate, to the President of the United States and report the fact and date of such presentation to the Senate." [218]

Journal: All proceedings in the Senate Chamber are accounted for in the *Journal* and the *Congressional Record*. The *Journal* contains a briefly and accurately stated report of the Senate proceedings. "Messages of the President in full; titles of bills and joint resolutions, and such parts as shall be affected by proposed amendments; every vote, and a brief statement of the contents of each petition, memorial, or paper presented to the Senate, shall be entered." "The legislative, the executive, the confidential legislative proceedings, and the proceedings when sitting as a Court of Impeachment, shall each be recorded in a separate book."

Congressional Record: The *Congressional Record* contains a complete transcript of all proceedings in the Senate and House Chambers. The Appendix of the *Record* embodies speeches, reports, editorials, and papers, but not Senate or House proceedings, incorporated at the request of some Senator or Representative in pursuance of his request for "leave to print." The Daily Digest, the last section of the *Record*, gives a brief resumé of all legislative activity transpiring on Capitol Hill, including activity of the two chambers, committees of the two Houses, joint committee meetings, and the legislative program ahead.

[218] Rule XIV.

CHAPTER XI

Steps of Passage of a Bill Through the House and Senate

Introduction of a Bill: All bills and resolutions introduced in the House must be introduced by a Representative, Delegate, or Resident Commissioner even though the Administration, some private organization, pressure group, or individual is sponsoring the bill. Likewise, all bills and resolutions introduced in the Senate must be introduced by a Senator. A bill or resolution introduced in the House bears the name of the Representative introducing it, but only one name may be attached to a House measure. Bills and resolutions introduced in the Senate bear the name of the introducer or introducers; frequently, they bear the names of several Senators.

"All bills for raising revenue shall originate in the House of Representatives; but the Senate may propose or concur with amendments as on other bills," and this has been interpreted in practice to include appropriation bills. All other bills may originate in either chamber. All bills introduced in the House, including resolutions, carry a designation to show that they originated in the House as well as to distinguish their type, such as: "H.R."; "H.J.Res."; "H.Con.Res."; and "H.Res." Those introduced in the Senate bear the following designations: "S."; "S.J. Res."; "S.Con.Res."; and "S.Res." For further details on these see pp. 19-22.

Representatives and Senators may introduce as many bills and resolutions as they wish; precedents are against Senators introducing identical or duplicate bills.

The introduction of a bill or resolution in the House is very simple; the attention of the House is seldom called to it. The Member introducing a measure merely throws it in the "hopper" at the Speaker's desk. From the "hopper" the Parliamentarian of the House, under the supervision of the Speaker, receives and examines the measure and designates to which committee it shall

393

be referred; it is then recorded by different officials at the Speaker's desk and taken to the Bill Clerk's office, given a number, and sent to the Government Printing Office. After the bill is printed, copies are placed in the House and Senate Document Rooms for distribution and, at the same time, copies are sent to the committee to which it was referred.

In the Senate a little more attention is given to introduction than in the House. It is not uncommon during the morning hour for the Senator introducing a measure to make a brief speech on it. The Senator, however, may merely send the measure to the Clerk's desk without making any comment.

Legislation may be considered by the House or Senate committee having jurisdiction before a bill on the subject is introduced. For example, a message from the President referred to a committee may serve as a substitute for a bill on which that committee might hold hearings. A Congressman may merely introduce a petition, leaving it to a member of the committee concerned to introduce a bill after hearings on the subject have been held.

Reference of Bills and Resolutions to Committees: Public bills and resolutions introduced in the House and Senate or messaged from one body to the other are generally referred to the proper standing committees by the parliamentarians, under the supervision of their respective presiding officers, subject to the will of the membership. The references are made in pursuance of the applicable rules and precedents. A Senator may designate the committee to which he wishes a public bill referred, but his preference is without force unless approved by the Senate. Representatives and Senators introducing *private* bills and resolutions under the rules are authorized to designate the committee to which they wish the matter referred. If they fail so to designate, the Parliamentarian makes the reference. Under the Reorganization Act of 1946 in the House "the payment or adjudication of any private claim against the Government shall be referred, except by unanimous consent," to the Committee on Foreign Affairs or the Committee on the Judiciary. In the Senate all private claims, and private immigration bills are referred to the Judiciary Committee.

Either house may recall a bill or resolution from any one of its committees and re-refer it to another, or refer any bill or resolution in the first instance to any committee it sees fit, regardless of the rules and precedents.

In the House, according to the rule, bills and resolutions are read by title before they are referred to committees. In practice, nothing is said about any bill unless the Member making the introduction should call it to the attention of the House, provoking a discussion. In the Senate, bills and resolutions are read twice by title and referred to committees, usually by unanimous consent since the Senate generally recesses from day to day, avoiding the morning hour. In practice, bills have been introduced in the Senate and referred without being called to the attention of the Senators in session.

Committee Action on Bills: Bills or resolutions when referred become pending committee business and remain so for the duration of a Congress until the committee disposes of it, unless the House or Senate as the case may be should discharge the committee from further consideration. The committee is free either to refuse consideration of a bill, consider and vote it down, report it out just as introduced, amend and report it, or to report it after completely rewriting it.

Standing committees usually keep printed calendars of their pending business.

Committee Procedure: The following illustrates committee procedure: The bill is introduced and referred. The chairman of the committee to which the measure is referred, or in cooperation with other members of that group, decides when meeting shall be held to consider the pending business. (Rarely, the committee decides of its own accord, regardless of the will of the chairman, to hold meetings for the disposition of a particular bill.) At a called meeting, the chairman, or someone designated by him, presides and presents the pending business. The chairman generally designates the order of business. Members of the committee, having been recognized by the chairman, may present a motion that the committee immediately proceed with a particular bill.

Minor bills are usually disposed of quickly and without controversy. The clerk of the committee merely reads the bill and a vote is taken immediately on reporting the measure to the parent body. If the vote is in the affirmative, the chairman either accepts the responsibility of writing a report to accompany the bill or assigns some member of his committee to do so.

If the bill involves a "major" issue, it is generally decided beforehand when hearings will be started, and the date is announced. That day having arrived, the witnesses, called in by the committee or granted permission to appear upon request, testify pro and con on the enactment of the proposed legislation. Witnesses usually consist of representatives of the interested government departments and private citizens, either versed in that subject or interested, or both. The committee itself may take the initiative and invite or subpoena all witnesses.

Hearings having been concluded, the membership studies the bill in the light of the testimony. Committee meetings for such purpose are usually closed; they may consume several weeks, or, after a brief session under the directorship of the chairman, a vote on reporting it is taken. The chairman either writes the report to accompany the measure, or assigns some other member of the committee to do so, assuming the vote is in the affirmative.

A major bill having been approved, it is generally several days before the written report is available. Time is required for preparation. Each report bears a number (as House Report 10, to accompany H.R. 1050 or Senate Report 10, to accompany H.R. 1050), and is designed to give information on all actions taken by the committee on the measure; it explains the various sections of the proposal, as well as analyzes any amendments which the committee recommends, including an explanation of why certain portions of the original language were proposed to be stricken out, if any. The existing law to be affected by the bill if enacted is likewise cited, accompanied by an explanation of proposed changes in the law.

Generally, the House and Senate meet at 12 noon each day, when Congress is in session. The committees of the House and Senate [1] are not privileged to sit while their respective chambers are in session, except by special permission given by unanimous consent.

Bills Reported by Committee: Bills and resolutions receiving affirmative committee approval are reported. House committees report to the House and Senate committees report to the Senate.

---

[1] The House Rules Committee is authorized by the rules of the House to meet at any time, even though the House is in session.

When bills are reported they are either considered immediately or placed on a calendar of business. Each chamber has a distinct system. Measures reported and placed on a calendar remain the pending business until disposed of or until that Congress adjourns *sine die.*

Pending Business in House and Senate Printed on Calendars: The legislative calendars of the House and Senate are printed lists of bills, resolutions, messages, reports, and the like; they are primarily bills and resolutions. Each calendar gives the following information on each bill or resolution: a calendar number, derived according to the chronological order reported; the bill or resolution number; the name of the Representative or Senator and the committee reporting the measure; the date it was reported; and the report number. The name of the Representative introducing a House bill is carried on the bill until it passes the House; the same principle is applicable to bills introduced in the Senate. A bill having passed one body, the name of the introducer is stricken off.

While bills printed on all calendars are listed in the chronological order reported, they are not necessarily disposed of in that way. The order of disposition of House and Senate legislative business is dependent upon many factors, discussed in other chapters.

Calendars and House Procedure: *Calendars of Business:* This resumé will first trace the passage of a bill through the House, and then through the Senate. In the House there are five different legislative calendars; bills and resolutions are placed on each according to their nature. The calendars are: Union Calendar (Calendar on the Committee of the Whole House on the state of the Union) House Calendar, Unanimous Consent Calendar, Private Calendar (Calendar of the Committee of the Whole), and the Discharge Calendar.[2] In addition to the classification of legislative calendars, the House has established legislative days for consideration of business in particular categories such as, Calendar Wednesday, District of Columbia Day, Suspension of the Rules, Consent Calendar business, Private Calendar business, and Discharge Calendar business. As already stated the privileged status of business varies.

[2] Business on these last 3 calendars is considered on special legislative days.

All bills when reported to the House are printed on either the Union Calendar, House Calendar, or Private Calendar. Bills on Consent Calendar are at the same time on either the Union or House Calendars. Bills discharged from a standing committee in pursuance of the Discharge Rule procedure are printed on the "Discharge Calendar."

Business on the Union and House calendars is never considered according to the chronological order reported. Proposed legislation on these two calendars comes up either under unanimous consent procedure, in pursuance of a special rule reported by the Rules Committee or under the procedure of a special legislative day.[2a]

Proposed legislation on the Consent, Private, and Discharge calendars are usually considered in the order in which they appear on the calendars and on the first four Mondays of each month, depending on which is in order under the rules.

Some characteristics of each calendar are briefly as follows:

Union Calendar: The Union Calendar rule provides for "a Calendar of the Committee of the Whole House on the state of the Union, to which shall be referred bills raising revenue, general appropriation bills, and bills of a business character directly or indirectly appropriating money or property." The calendar takes this name because the bills listed on it are first considered in the Committee of the Whole House on the state of the Union and reported back to the House for its final approval. For discussion of Union Calendar, see pp. 202-205, 212-228.

House Calendar: The House Calendar rule provides for "a House Calendar, to which shall be referred all bills of a public character not raising revenue nor directly or indirectly appropriating money or property"; see pp. 205, 200-327.

Private Calendar: Private bills, proposed pieces of legislation involving individual claims against the government, or individual consideration under the immigration acts, and the like, are printed on the Private Calendar; see pp. 228-235.

Consent Calendar: Listed on this calendar are bills or resolutions which have already been reported and printed on the Union or House Calendars; they are actually put on this calendar at request of any Member, by filing a notice with the Clerk of the House to that effect. On the first and third Mondays of each

[2a] See p. 124.

month, the Speaker directs the clerk to call in numerical order the bills which have been on the Consent Calendar for three legislative days. When called, the measures are either passed over until the next time or quickly approved in the absence of objection. See pp. 228-231.

Discharge Calendar: The rule provides that any Member may file with the Clerk of the House a motion to discharge a committee from further consideration of a public bill or resolution which has been for thirty days in the committee or seven days before the Rules Committee. When 218 Members have signed the motion, it is entered in the *Journal,* printed with the signatures in the *Congressional Record,* and referred to the Calendar of Motions to Discharge Committees. Bills on the calendar are privileged business to be brought up for consideration on the second and fourth Mondays of each month. They are called in the order printed on the calendar, and when called up, they become the unfinished business of the House until final disposition. For details of this procedure see pp. 236-257.

Special Legislative Days and House Procedure: The House has established special legislative days in order to expedite certain types of unprivileged business. The special legislative days are Calendar Wednesday (every Wednesday), District of Columbia (second and fourth Mondays), and Suspension of Rules (first and third Mondays), Consent Calendar business (first and third Mondays), Private Calendar business (first and third Tuesdays), and Discharge Calendar business (second and fourth Mondays).

The business privileged for consideration in the House on the special legislative days is defined in each instance. For example, on Calendar Wednesday days "bills may be called up from either House or Union calendars excepting bills which are privileged under the rules, but bills called up from the Union Calendar shall be considered in Committee of the Whole House on the state of the Union."

Calendar Wednesday: The Calendar Wednesday rule was originally adopted to expedite the passage of non-privileged business. Under this procedure, emphasis is placed on the standing committees, giving each when called [3] a chance to bring up in the House any bills it desires over which it has jurisdiction, and which

---

[3] Under this procedure, committees are called according to their alphabetical listing under Rule X. See Rule XXIV, clause 7. For an alphabetical listing of all standing committees see p. 161.

are not privileged for consideration otherwise. Of course, the bills must have been reported and placed on either the House or Union calendars. For further details see pp. 257-262.

District of Columbia Day: The House has a standing committee (District of Columbia Committee) to handle all District of Columbia legislation. Likewise, two days each month are set aside for the disposition of this business. This rule provides that when the second and fourth Mondays shall be claimed by the Committee on the District of Columbia, after certain other business pending before the House has been transacted, the rest of that day shall "be set apart for the consideration of such business as may be presented by said Committee." See pp. 264-265.

Suspension of Rules: Suspension of Rules procedure gives the Speaker the power on two days every month to recognize any Representative to call up any bill pending before the House for consideration. The Speaker under this procedure, may recognize or refuse to recognize any Member or permit or refuse to permit the consideration of any particular piece of legislation. Bills thus called up may be debated for forty minutes, but amendments are not in order. To pass a bill under this procedure requires a two-thirds vote. See pp. 262-264.

Consent, Private, and Discharge Calendar Days: The disposition of business under any one of these three procedures has already been mentioned under discussion of the five calendars. Business on each of these calendars is privileged for consideration on two days of every month. See pp. 228-257.

Unanimous Consent and House Procedure: Most bills and resolutions presented to the House each year are disposed of under one of the above special procedures; that is, under the Private Calendar, Consent Calendar, Discharge Calendar, Calendar Wednesday, Suspension of Rules, or District of Columbia. Of course, to these should be added bills disposed of under unanimous consent as distinguished from the Consent Calendar business. Under this procedure some Member merely requests by unanimous consent that he be permitted to call up and consider out of the regular order of business, a certain bill or resolution. Measures called up under this procedure are passed "without objection."

Controversial Measures and House Procedure: For the disposition of legislation which requires some or much debate as distinguished from the special procedures mentioned above, the

House proceeds with general debate of the measure in the Committee of the Whole, followed by reading the bill or resolution in the Committee for amendments. The Committee then rises and reports its action, with recommendation back to the House. Immediately, if the Committee has concluded its consideration, the House votes first on the amendments reported and then to pass or to defeat the measure as the case may be.

Consideration under this procedure is possible because of the privileged status of the proposed legislation or in pursuance of a special rule reported by the Rules Committee and adopted by the House.[3a]

Procedure Generally: Rule XXIV proposes the daily order of business. This rule is practically ignored, however. Certain of its steps are adhered to every legislative day regardless of what business is in order; namely, prayer by the Chaplain and reading of the *Journal.*

After the regular routine business each morning, including the reading of the *Journal,* the House proceeds to the consideration of bills or resolutions if any are to be acted on that day. The order in which they are called varies as follows:

(1) on special calendar and special legislation days, bills and resolutions are called up in pursuance of the procedure defined by the rules in each instance, as pointed out above; (2) under unanimous consent bills are called up in pursuance of the requests made and granted by the House, regardless of the regular rules of procedure; (3) privileged bills, including general appropriation bills, general revenue bills, conference reports, special rules, and the like may be called up by the Members in charge of them at almost any time, interrupting other less privileged business, provided the Representative in charge is recognized by the Speaker; and (4) bills are regularly voted the next business in order, usually by adopting a special rule. (which is privileged business) to that effect, reported by the Rules Committee (any rule to call up a bill may be debated an hour before it is voted on).[3a]

Bills coming up under the fourth category are usually major or controversial pieces of legislation; they are generally not privileged for immediate consideration or provisions embodied therein are subject to points of order. Consequently, unless they can be brought up under the Suspension of the Rules (which requires a

3a See p. 124.

two-thirds vote for approval) or unless unanimous consent is granted in each instance to take them up out of the regular order of business, there is only one feasible way left for them to be brought up—that is by the adoption of a special rule reported by the House Rules Committee.

Appropriation measures, general revenue bills, and "controversial non-privileged proposals" comprise the important legislation enacted during each session. General appropriation and general revenue measures are privileged for consideration almost at any time. Special rules, therefore, are not needed in order to expedite their consideration. Special rules sometimes are essential to expedite their passage by waiving points of order against them or to define the conditions under which an amendment might be offered. The controversial non-privileged bills can usually get up only under a special rule. The fact that the Rules Committee can report a simple resolution to provide for the immediate consideration of such proposals or refuse to report one, making that proposed legislation dependent upon the will of that committee, makes the Rules Committee a very important organ in the House procedure. It is possible for that Committee to kill a bill by negative action.[3b] Of course, if it reports a resolution providing for the immediate consideration of a bill, that resolution (although it is privileged business and may be called up almost any time) must be approved by a majority vote of the House before the bill for which it provides consideration may be called up. The procedure for the consideration of each bill (the length of general debate, whether or not points of order shall be waived, or what amendments are in order) is defined in the resolution.

The Senate Committee on Rules is not so empowered. It does not report special rules for consideration of business; that committee concerns itself with the routine Senate and housekeeping matters, and reporting recommendations to amend the permanent rules of the Senate, as well as jurisdiction over some legislative subjects.

Consideration of Bill: House Procedure: The procedure for disposition of bills and resolutions (sometimes referred to as noncontroversial or unobjected to measures) called on Consent and Private Calendar days and bills called up under unanimous consent already mentioned, are passed by negative action; the Speaker merely announces that without objection the bill will be

3b See p. 124.

considered, and then "without objection the bill will be considered and passed." This action is taken in the absence of any general debate on the measures, and usually there is little or no discussion. The procedure for disposition of bills on the Discharge Calendar, under Suspension of the Rules, and Calendar Wednesday business is defined in each rule. Unanimous consent procedure is self-explanatory. Bills brought up in the House or in the House as in "the Committee of the Whole" are disposed of according to a defined procedure—under the one hour rule or under the five-minute rule, respectively. See Chapter IX for this procedure.

To get up for consideration appropriation, revenue, and "controversial non-privileged" measures is one thing; the disposition or actual consideration of them is another. Appropriation, revenue, and "major controversial non-privileged" measures are first debated under general debate and then read for amendments under the five-minute rule—all in the Committee of the Whole.

Public bills which raise revenue or make or authorize appropriations of money or property must be considered in the Committee of the Whole House on the state of the Union, under the rules of the House. In practice, nearly all bills of importance are thus considered.

The Committee of the Whole is in reality a form of procedure followed by the House when it is studying legislation, getting it into condition for a final verdict. The Committee of the Whole is merely the House membership resolved into a Committee. In the Committee of the Whole, the procedure is different from that in the House. A hundred Members instead of 218 compose a quorum; roll call votes may not be taken; bills may not be recommitted; they may not be passed; they may be studied and amended. All amendments added to a bill in the Committee of the Whole must be confirmed by the House before they become a part of that bill; and the bill must be passed by the House. The stages of consideration in the Committee of the Whole are: general debate, reading for amendment (under the five-minute rule), order to lay aside with a favorable recommendation, or to rise and report without resolution, and rise and report to the House with recommendation of passage.

The time for all general debate is at the disposition of the chairman and the ranking minority member of the committee handling the bill (or someone designated by them). The time is divided equally between the two. These two persons in charge are theoretically obligated to yield this time respectively to the members in favor of and in opposition to the measure, and to divide the time among the membership of the House so as to give the Representatives interested in the bill an opportunity to express their position on it. The seniority rule prevails in the House in yielding time for debate. The chairman generally opens the debate on a bill for the majority side and the ranking minority member opens the debate for the minority side. These two persons then yield the remainder of time for debate to the members of their committee first, after which any time left over is yielded generally to other Members of the House who have remarks to make.

At the conclusion of the general debate of a bill in the Committee of the Whole (during which time no amendments may be offered), the bill is read for amendments under the five-minute rule. That is, the Clerk reads the bill section by section (or paragraph by paragraph) and after each section is read, any Member who is recognized by the chair may offer an amendment to that portion of the bill, and he has five minutes to explain it; any Member opposed to the amendment may use five minutes to present his arguments against it. Again, the seniority rule prevails. The chairman is always given preferential recognition to offer an amendment or amendments (usually committee amendments), members of the committee next, and the general membership lastly. In reading the bill for amendments if no one has an amendment to offer or if no one seeks recognition, the Clerk proceeds to read uninterruptedly with consent of the House. Special arrangements for disposition of bills are frequently agreed upon by the House; for example: The bill may be considered as having been read, and amendments may then be offered to any part of the bill instead of by section. Sometimes a special rule excludes any amendments, in which case a vote on passage is taken immediately following the debate.

All amendments must not only be germane to the bill but to the section to which they are offered. (This procedure is different in the Senate. Amendments in the Senate are in order to any part of the bill as soon as it is called up for consideration, but committee amendments are disposed of first, and amendments do not have to be germane, except in the case of appropriation bills.) After disposing of all amendments, the question automatically recurs on third reading and passage of the bill. The Speaker puts the question.

Bills considered in the House as distinguished from the Committee of the Whole may not be read under the five-minute rule unless permission is granted under unanimous consent to consider them in the House "as in the Committee of the Whole." Bills considered in the House, as distinguished from the Committee of the Whole, are read under "the hour rule"; each member is entitled to an hour to debate each amendment offered by him. Bills are seldom considered under this procedure.

First Reading: According to the rules, bills and resolutions are read a first time when they are referred to committees; in practice, this step is omitted.

Second Reading: Bills not requiring consideration in the Committee of the Whole are read a second time in full in the House when called up for consideration after which they are open to debate and amendment, in general. Bills considered in the Committee of the Whole are read a second time in full in that Committee when they are read under the five-minute rule for amendments, and when reported out, with or without amendments, they are not read in full again (by title only), but are subject to further debate or amendment (under the hour rule) in the House unless the previous question is operating or is immediately ordered.

Engrossment and Third Reading: After the amending process has been concluded on House bills, the question is taken on ordering the engrossment and third reading at one vote. If decided in the affirmative, the reading a third time usually takes place at once by title; any Member may demand the reading in full of the engrossed copy, in which case the bill must be laid aside until engrossed.

Senate bills come to the House in an engrossed form and, therefore, in the case of their passage, the question is put on the third reading alone. When the question on engrossment and third reading of a House bill, or the third reading of a Senate bill, is decided in the negative the bill is lost just as if defeated on final passage. The question on engrossment and third reading is put by the Speaker as a matter of course without suggestion from the floor. After engrossment and third reading, the motion on passage of the bill is put.

Passage of Bill in House: If the question on the passage of a House bill is decided in the affirmative, the bill goes to the Senate for further action; if decided in the negative, the bill is dead unless that action is reconsidered. If the bill is a Senate bill and is passed without amendment, it is returned to Senate and made ready for the President's signature. The motion can be made to recommit it to committee for further study, just prior to moving the passage of bill.

Bills Passed by House are Messaged to Senate: House bills passed by the House are engrossed and messaged to the Senate. At this stage, the bill no longer bears the title "A Bill"; it is entitled "An Act."

Bills originating in the House and passed by it are messaged to the Senate and go through the same stages of procedure in the Senate as do bills which are introduced in the Senate.

Procedure for Passing House Bills in the Senate: *Bills referred to Committees:* In the Senate, House-passed bills, in accordance with the same rules that apply to bills introduced in the Senate, are referred by the Presiding Officer to a Senate standing committee. Senate committees are set up under a plan similar to that used by the House. The committees of the two chambers do not have identical jurisdiction in every instance. There are 19 House committees and only 15 Senate committees.

Bills Studied by Committees and Reported to Senate: A House-passed bill having been referred to a Senate standing committee becomes its pending business and is considered just as if it had been introduced in the Senate. (For review of committee procedure, see pp. 146-199.) If, however, a House committee holds exhaustive hearings on a bill, the Senate committee might or might not hold further hearings on it. Exhaustive public hearings are frequently held by both houses on a few bills during each session.

Senate committee consideration having been concluded on a bill (including amending, rewriting, substitution of a new bill, or reporting as referred to the committee) a vote is taken on reporting it. If the vote is in the affirmative, the measure is returned to the Senate with an accompanying report, and placed on the

Senate Calendar.   A vote in the negative kills the bill unless it is reconsidered.

Senate Calendar and Senate Procedure: Bills and resolutions reported to the Senate are listed on the Senate Calendar and remain the pending business until disposed of, either affirmatively or negatively, or until the end of that Congress.

The Senate procedure is by no means as complex as_ that of the House. The business of the Senate is not divided into classes and printed on a number of different calendars. The Senate Calendar, however, differentiates the pending business before the Senate in the following manner: "Unfinished Business," "Resolutions and Motions Over Under the Rule," "General Order," "Subjects on the Table," "Calendar of Special Orders," "Motions for Reconsideration," and "Executive Calendar" (consisting of Treaties and nominations).

"Unfinished Business" is a matter for continued consideration by the Senate, having been voted the order of business, and remains privileged each legislative day after the morning hour until its disposition, or until the Senate votes to displace it and take up something else.

"Resolutions and Motions Over Under the Rule" consist of resolutions or motions which were made during one legislative day but not laid on the table or referred; this business is in order for disposition during the morning hour at the beginning of the next legislative day.

Composing the "Calendar of General Orders" are all bills and resolutions reported by Senate committees or otherwise placed on the Senate Calendar but still awaiting Senate action.

Business listed under the subject, "On the Table" includes business placed there by request, and which at a later date may be called up for immediate consideration or for reference to a committee, according to the circumstances.

"Motions for Reconsideration" are not privileged; they must await determination by a majority of the Senators.

The "Calendar of Special Orders" is composed of what the title implies and these matters are decided without debate and take precedence *seriatim*.   They may be interrupted at any time after the morning hour by the unfinished business of the preceding day, since unfinished business is privileged after the morning hour. If no unfinished business is coming over from the preceding legislative day, the special order may be made the unfinished business.

The "Executive Calendar" consists of nominations and treaties which are usually disposed of in executive session.

Order of Business in the Senate: The procedure in the Senate is in accordance with its rules, customs, and practices. The daily order of business in the Senate follows: The Chaplain opens the session with a prayer, after which any of the other regular morning hour business is in order, but only at the beginning of each legislative day. When the Senate recesses from day to day, the first order of business is the unfinished business of the preceding calendar day unless by unanimous consent other business is entertained. The regular morning business consists of reading the *Journal* and disposing of reports, messages, and communications on the Presiding Officer's table, the presentation and introduction by Senators of petitions, memorials, bills, resolutions, and amendments. On each legislative day the unfinished business is privileged for immediate consideration at the conclusion of the morning hour. (See pp. 340-392.)

Bills are not always considered in the order in which they are reported and printed on the calendar but they may be. Some bills are called up for consideration from the floor when reported; some bills are called up from the calendar out of order when the Senate adopts a motion to that effect by a majority vote; other bills are called up in the order they are reported or listed on the calendar on days when the calendar is called for disposition of "unobjected-to bills." The latter method is used by the Senate for passing most of its bills.

When the calendar is called for disposition of "unobjected-to bills," the bills are disposed of with little or no debate; that is, they are passed over, defeated, or passed without objection and without discussion after any amendments to them have been adopted. Under the call of the calendar, the Senate proceeds under the five-minute rule and no Senator except by unanimous consent, may consume more than five minutes in discussion of the bill or amendment thereto.

Bills which the Senate moves to consider may or may not entail long debates, few or many amendments, and the taking of one or several roll calls. The Senate does not consider bills in the Committee of the Whole.

Consideration of Bills in the Senate: When bills or resolutions are presented to the Senate for consideration they are subject to debate and amendments, and are engrossed, read a third time, and passed. The debating and amending stages are not distinct and separate as generally is the case in the House. Amendments are in order immediately after the bill is called up, but committee amendments, if any, are first in order. Bills are not read for amendment under the five-minute rule as they are in the House. When the bill is presented to the Senate, it is immediately read in full or considered as having been so read; it is then ready to be debated and amended. Following the disposition of committee amendments it is in order for any Senator having received recognition, to offer an amendment. Also, any Senator may offer an amendment to any committee amendment when it is up for disposition. Amendments, however, may not be beyond the second degree, see 360-368.

House Bills Passed by the Senate Without Amendment: House bills and resolutions which are called up by the Senate and passed without amendment are returned to the House and enrolled on parchment paper for signature of the Speaker of the House, the President of the Senate, and the President of the United States. The signatures having been affixed the bill becomes law in the form it passed both houses.

House Bills Passed by the Senate With Amendment: House bills and resolutions having passed the Senate with amendments may be sent back to the House and placed on the Speaker's table; or the Senate may immediately request a conference and appoint conferees, and then send the message back to the House for its concurrence or action.

Back in the House, the message from the Senate is placed on the Speaker's table and remains there until further disposition. If the Senate amendments are controversial, the motion is usually made to take the bill from the Speaker's table with the Senate amendments thereto and send them to conference, by unanimous consent or by use of a special rule (see discussion of Conferences, pp. 269-278, 388-391). If the Senate amendments are minor or if the House has no opposition to them, they are agreed to and the bill is ready to be enrolled on parchment paper, signed by the Speaker, President of the Senate, and President of the United States.

According to the rules (which are usually ignored under unanimous consent procedure), House bills on the Speaker's table with Senate amendments which require consideration in the Committee of the Whole are referred by the Speaker informally to the standing committees, which first considered the bill, for further study. A point of order may be made against any procedure to the contrary. When reported back to the House by the committee, the amendments are first considered by the Committee of the Whole on the state of the Union, after which the House acts just as if it were a bill up for original consideration. This rule is usually by-passed under unanimous consent procedure or by use of special rule.

If the House bill, with the Senate amendments, does not require consideration in the Committee of the Whole the bill is called up directly from the Speaker's table and disposed of immediately by a majority vote.

Disposition of Senate Amendments by the House: Senate amendments to a House bill, when the bill is returned to the House and no conference has been requested by the Senate, are disposed of separately, unless *en bloc* by unanimous consent. The House may agree to each amendment, agree to each with amendments or disagree to each, and if the stage of disagreement is reached on any amendment, the House immediately asks for conference on the bill. If there is only one Senate amendment and the House agrees to it with an amendment, it goes back to the Senate for its concurrence in the Senate amendment as modified by the House amendment. Usually, however, as pointed out above, House bills passed by the Senate with controversial amendments are sent directly to conference without further consideration (for Conference Procedure see, pp. 269, 388). The chairman of the House committee handling the bill merely asks unanimous consent that the bill be taken from the Speaker's table, that the House disagree to the amendments of the Senate, and that the House ask for a conference on the bill.

Disposition of House Amendments by the Senate: The Senate disposes of House amendments to a Senate bill when the Member in charge of that bill gets recognition for that purpose.

All Senate bills with House amendments are given preferential consideration, and the Senate may agree to such House amendments separately or *en bloc*. If the Senate refuses to agree to such House amendments, a conference is requested on the bill to which the amendments have been added. If the Senate should agree to the House amendments with an amendment, the bill then goes back to the House for its concurrence in the amendment as modified by the Senate amendment. All amendments must be concurred in by both houses. A bill or resolution having thus been cleared is ready to be enrolled and signed by the Speaker, the President of the Senate, and the President of the United States. A Senate bill having cleared both houses, it is turned over to the Senate Enrolling Clerk to be placed on parchment paper.

Conference Committees: If the House and Senate decide to send a bill to conference, with or without instructions as to what they shall agree to or disagree to, the Speaker appoints the House conferees and the Presiding Officer of the Senate appoints the Senate conferees.

The House conferees appointed to handle a particular bill are usually the ranking majority and minority members of the standing committee which handled the bill in the House; likewise, the Senate conferees are the ranking Senators of the standing committee which handled the measure on the Senate side. For example: the House conferees on a revenue bill would be the top Democratic and Republican members of the Ways and Means Committee and the Senate conferees would be the top Democratic and Republican members of the Finance Committee. Sometimes exceptions are made, but conferees are usually selected according to their seniority rank on the particular standing committee or sub-committee.

The number of House and Senate conferees is not always the same, usually varying from three to nine each. There may be five Representatives and nine Senators, or vice versa. Each group votes separately as a unit with a majority ruling, in making determinations on conference reports.

The conferees are really "managers" for the House and Senate. Theoretically, they are selected to represent the will of the House and Senate and of the committees sponsoring the particular legislation.

The jurisdiction of any set of conferees extends to the differences in the forms in which the House and Senate passed the same bill. Conferees are not authorized to write new legislation. Theoretically, conferees must reach a compromise between the two extremes taken on a bill by the House and Senate. To illustrate: In an appropriation bill, if the House should provide $5,000 for a particular purpose and the Senate should provide $10,000 for the same purpose, it is assumed that the conferees will reach a compromise somewhere between the $5,000 figure and the $10,000 figure, or one of the two figures. If amendments are added to a bill by one chamber involving legislative or appropriation matters on which the other chamber took no position, the conferees of the latter mentioned body would theoretically have to accept the amendments or refuse to accept them. In practice, the conferees might even write a new bill.

When a Bill Goes to Conference: In pursuance of the rules of the two bodies, a bill is not sent to conference until the stage of "disagreement" has been reached. To illustrate: A bill originating in the House, having passed that body, goes to the Senate. The latter considers and passes it with an amendment or amendments. The bill is then sent back to the House and if that body refuses to accept the amendment or amendments added to the bill by the Senate, a conference will be asked. In practice, however, the Senate, upon adding a substantial amendment or amendments to a House-passed bill, does not necessarily wait to send the bill back to the House to see if that body will accept the Senate amendment or amendments; to the contrary, the Senate might immediately ask for a conference on the bill and appoints conferees. The bill is then messaged back to the House and the House agrees to a conference and appoints conferees. The stage of disagreement obtains on bills originating in the Senate under like conditions.

The time necessary to reach an agreement in conference varies from a few minutes to several weeks. When a complete conference has been held and an agreement reached, the conferees (managers for the House and Senate) embody their findings, compromises, or decisions in a report which is submitted to both the House and Senate, and which must be acted on affirmatively by each body. All amendments in disagreement must be disposed of (agreed to by each House in an identical form) if the bill is to be enacted. The report is known as a "Conference Report."

If all the amendments sent to conference are compromised, when that report has been agreed to by both chambers, the act as modified by the conferees is ready for the signatures of the Speaker of the House, the President of the Senate, and the President of the United States; the report may not be amended. If the conference report contains amendments reported in disagreement as well as the "agreements" (matters agreed upon) not only must that portion of the report which may not be amended (the agreements) be adopted by both Houses, but those amendments reported in disagreement by the conferees must also be disposed of before the bill is cleared to become law. The legislative chamber in which the bill originated could expedite the enactment of a bill at this stage by adopting the conference report and then receding and concurring in the amendments reported in disagreement, but if it adopts the conference report and refuses to recede and concur in the amendments reported in disagreement, then further disposition must be made on those amendments if the bill is to be enacted. If the legislative body in which the bill originated concurs with amendments in these amendments reported in disagreement, the bill then goes back to the other body. If the other chamber should accept such amendments to its amendments, the bill is then ready to become law as soon as the proper officials have signed it. In other words, all amendments added to a bill by one house which has already been passed by the other, must be put in a form acceptable to both bodies before the bill is cleared for enactment. If a deadlock is reached which cannot be broken, the bill will die at that stage.

The legislative chamber agreeing to a conference on a bill acts first on the Conference Report; the legislative chamber requesting the conference acts secondly.

Passage of a Senate Bill: The procedure in the enactment of a Senate bill is identical to that of the House bill, discussed above, except the bill originates in the Senate instead of in the House. Briefly, the bill is introduced in the Senate, referred to a Senate committee, studied by a Senate committee, reported back to the Senate, passed by the Senate, messaged to the House, referred by the House to a House committee, studied by the House committee, reported by the House committee to the House, considered by the House and passed with or without amendments. Any bill may be amended or defeated at any stage of this series. If the bill should be passed without amendment, it is then ready for enrollment on parchment paper and for the signatures of the Speaker of the House and the President of the Senate.

If a Senate bill passes the House with amendments the bill will be messaged back to the Senate and placed on the table of the President of the Senate. From there it will be called up and the Senate will either accept the House amendments, which makes the bill become law in the form in which it passed the House, or the bill will be sent to conference. In conference the conferees will iron out the differences between the House- and Senate-passed versions of the bill. House amendments to a Senate bill, if not sent to conference, are disposed of separately unless the request is made to dispose of them *en bloc,* at which time the Senate may agree to each, agree to each amended, or disagree to each. If the Senate agrees to House amendments with an amendment, it goes back to the House for its concurrence in the Senate amendment. If a state of disagreement is reached the bill will be sent to conference. (For details see discussion of "Conference Committees.")

Bills Passed by Both Houses Are Examined for Enrollment: The Committee on House Administration and the Senate Enrolling Clerk have the responsibility "of examining all bills and joint resolutions which shall have passed both houses to see that they are correctly enrolled" for signature by the Speaker and President of the Senate.

The Speaker and Vice President Sign the Bill: All bills (House or Senate) are first signed by the Speaker of the House of Representatives and then transmitted to the Senate where they are signed by the President of that body.

CHAPTER XII

Congress and The President

Introduction: The relationship between the President and Congress has been one of constant change. The Constitution establishes these two arms of the Government and defines their powers, but it does not provide for a mode of contact between them. In a sense they are independent of each other; yet, the pattern is a design of checks. The primary source of power the President has in dealing with Congress flows from: the charge to keep Congress posted from time to time on the state of the Union, and to make to it recommendations for the enactment of legislation including proposed expenditures; the veto he exercises over bills and resolutions approved by Congress; the prerogative of negotiating treaties which when ratified with the approval of the Senate become the law of the land, placing him in a position practically to control our foreign relations; the right to nominate persons to fill specified offices created by law; the position he occupies in case of emergencies and as Commander in Chief of the Army and Navy; the power he asserts as titular head of his party; and finally, the influence he commands because of his position in general.

The power of Congress in dealing with the President and the Administration is derived from its: authority to legislate—i.e., prerogative to determine policy, to set up offices of the Administration, and to decide on amounts to be spent for each purpose; the authorization to override the veto by a two-thirds vote; the right to reject recommendations of the President or to give him quite the opposite of what he requests; the right to pass on nominations and treaties; and the authority to impeach the President or any of his subordinates.

The position of the President as contrasted with that of Congress will not be discussed in accordance with the prerogatives mentioned above. These are more fully discussed in various volumes devoted to those subjects.

A brief description of the actual relations of these two arms of the Government are more immediate to the purpose of this volume. Thus, observations will be limited to some recent experiences between the President and Congress in pursuance of their respective Constitutional prerogatives.

The degree of accord with which the Congress and the Executive have been able to work has been dependent upon various factors. The attitude, personality, philosophy, and desires of the President himself are significant. Economic conditions, the political situation as to strength of the majority party, the international picture, the social attitude of the people—or at least what the people are led to believe these conditions are—have much to do with the determination of any harmony or any stresses and strains between the legislature and the Administration.

Legislative-administrative relations have not always been too good. One arm often tends to dominate the other to the extent that the latter is unable properly to perform its commonly accepted responsibilities and duties. A determined political personality in the White House tends to overshadow Congress in the performance of its duties prescribed in the Constitution; a determined political leadership in Congress might well restrain a free performance by the Executive and the Administration. History reveals each President and each Congress making their way to the extent of their own powers and prerogatives, fortified by the native ability of the President and of the leadership of Congress in each instance.

At times Congress has enjoyed the dominating role—at times, the Executive; the tendency of recent years has been toward a continuous expansion of the powers and prerogatives of the President and Administration at the expense of Congress.

With the expansion of government by legislation and the gargantuan growth of the Administration, the President and the Administration have assumed a major role in the determination of legislative policy. The problem nearly becomes one for the experts. It is much the case of the Administration concocting the policy and submitting it to the Congress for approval or rejection, with slight modifications. This situation has aggravated the relationships between the President and Congress.

Nevertheless, little or nothing has been done to establish a formal or legal machinery to stabilize these relationships. The offices involved have acted individually to set up certain procedures. The experience, however, has been one of "hit or miss," dependent upon the legislative and administrative leaders. All Presidents have used the methods of making official recommendations to Congress with varying success; all recent Presidents have exercised the veto in varying degrees; and the use of emergency powers have aided some Presidents in influencing the legislative program, particularly in recent years. Our involvements in international affairs in the last two or three decades have necessitated the President as director of our foreign policy to take a more dominant role in the determination of domestic affairs closely related thereto. As titular head of his political party he assumes the role of spokesman for the party, and hence his recommendations for legislative enactment carry much weight. The trend has been toward an executive determination of policy in all phases of our economic life. This condition has evolved even though Congress by constitutional mandate is charged with the power to make policy, or to legislate.

Within the last two decades a new relationship has grown up between the President and the leaders of Congress, even though it was slightly interrupted with the 80th Congress, the President being of one political faith and the party then in control in the House and Senate of another. This new association between the President and Congress grew out of the weekly conferences at the White House between the President and the Vice President, the Speaker, and the majority floor leaders of the House and Senate. These weekly conferences were started soon after Sam Rayburn became the majority floor leader of the House on January 3, 1937, to whom belongs much of the credit for this innovation. Little is known about the origin of these regular conferences, but reliable sources accredit Speaker Rayburn for the groundwork.

Actually the practice became necessary because of the strained relationships between President Franklin D. Roosevelt and his Congressional leaders. It was a common practice during the early part of the Speakership of William Bankhead for the Speaker to tell reporters at his "11 o'clock press conference" that there would be no message from the White House that day. When Congress would convene at noon, a message from the President would be on hand. This situation became embarrassing. Likewise, the President frequently submitted messages to Congress requesting far-reaching laws. This was even done without first consulting the leaders, and they often found themselves unable to sell such legislative proposals to their memberships; in fact, it became embarrassing at times to present them. The situation is illustrated by the recommendation to "pack the Supreme Court."

No official records have been kept of these weekly conferences. Apparently, however, they have been constructive as evidenced by subject matter considered and subsequent announcements made to the press.

The Congressional leaders at these meetings advise the President of the legislative schedule for the week ahead. The first topic of discussion, except in case of emergencies, is generally the pending program of the two houses. Other subjects for discussion include: future program, national and international problems, specific bills and proposed amendments thereto pending before Congress. The business transacted, of course, is always dependent upon the time and character of matters confronting the Government. Very controversial pieces of legislation are certain to provoke much conversation as to content and strategy for enactment. Such meetings have been used as a clearing house for legislative-administrative problems.

Naturally, the President as titular head of his party assumes a role of importance in making up the party's program. This extends to deciding on the kind of legislation the party will support as well as that which it will push above all others for enactment. To play this role, the President must keep in close contact with his party leaders, but not necessarily with the Congressional leadership. He might even ignore Congressional leaders and work closely with other party leaders, sufficient to hold the popular support of the voters electing his party to power. This, of course, inflicts "wounds on Capitol Hill" and finally will do hurt to his party's legislative program. Experience has taught this. Congressional leaders have been by-passed on different occasions. But at the cost of strained relations between the President and Congress.

The President as spokesman for the Administration has established endless procedures to bring its legislative recommendations to the attention of Congress. At times the Administration has not only made legislative recommendations but has tried to force the hands of Congress to bring about their enactment. In this capacity, the pressure by the Administration to influence the decisions of Congress are frequently articulated in the name of the people.

Professor E. P. Herring in discussing the influence wielded by the Administration wrote that:

The technique of the alert public relations expert is to forestall criticism and to present the best side of the case, to dramatize events, and to arrange situations that generate favorable news. This the Administration is doing. Those in opposition are outclassed, outguessed, and completely outstripped. They are left sputtering and protesting in the dust of the activities of the Administration.[1]

According to students of public opinion the Administration has been able to do this through its publicity programs. Professor James T. Young declared:

Few realize the immense volume of both information and propaganda regularly released from Federal offices. On March 2, 1938, a Member of the House of Representatives . . . stated that in 1936 over 669,000,000 pieces of mail, weighing over 91,000,000 pounds, were sent out by the executive departments of the Government at public expense. The paper and printing were estimated to have cost over $22,000,000.

Generally, little or no attention is given to the initiation of legislative or appropriation bills, a matter on which more emphasis could well be placed. It is an important stage of the legislative process. The President is charged by the Constitution to make recommendations. He is denied the power to initiate laws, a function given to Congress.

In colonial days, the governors of the colonies in their "heyday" exercised the power to originate laws, but later, because of dissatisfaction, this prerogative was reduced to the right to send messages only. The Founding Fathers, drawing heavily on the colonial experience, thus limited the President's power to the recommending of measures. This was obviously done to protect the independence of Congress, a principle more honored in the breach than the observance. In 1908 when a Cabinet officer essayed to send the draft of a proposed bill to the Senate that body arose in its dignity, ordered the bill sent back, and adopted a rule, now innocuous, ordering all gratuitous executive communications returned unless transmitted through the President.

Practice has reversed that action of the Senate, with the Administration extending its "arm" over the control of legislation. Today, administrative officials not only draft legislative proposals and submit them to Congress, but they use the prestige and facilities of the Administration to swing the public and Congressmen to their point of view. In the first session of the 75th Congress—

[1] *South Atlantic Quarterly* Vol. XLI, No. 2, p. 185.

a session selected at random—271 drafts of proposed bills were fed into the congressional hopper of the House after having been sent to that body by the heads of departments, bureaus, and commissions, attached to messages or communications by officials of the Administration. Nearly half of them became law during the same session, some of them having been slightly amended without losing their identity. Some of them were incorporated in bills in the form of amendments, which in turn became law. Others no doubt became law in subsequent sessions of Congress.

Under current practices very few bills are considered and enacted until they have been submitted to the division of the Administration concerned as well as the Bureau of the Budget for recommendations and approval; few are ever enacted with the opposition of the entire Administration. Sometimes divisions of the Administration are at variance over a single legislative proposal.

This development has been rapid and complete since the turn of the century. It is now an exception to the rule for Congress to enact bills before the standing committees concerned send the proposals to the appropriate division of the Administration for comment, which in turn clears with the Bureau of the Budget. This statement assumes that the bills were not sent up by some unit of the Administration in the first place, attached to a communication. One of the most dramatic utterances reflecting on this practice was made by Representative Monroney, during the debate on the Price Control Bill in 1941. He declared:

There is criticism attaching to the Gore Bill (a substitute for the committee bill), a blight that I am afraid may kill it, according to the popular conception on Capitol Hill, and that is that the Gore Bill originated in Congress. The Gore Bill was drafted by the gentleman from Tennessee (Mr. Gore) with the help of the Congressional legislative drafting service, and no person other than Members of Congress have had a hand in the direction and drafting of that bill.

More important than the part the Administration plays in initiating bills, is its part in influencing the enactment of such bills after they have been proposed to Congress Much if not most of the testimony before standing committees during each session on pending pieces of legislation is submitted by Government agencies and witnesses. In fact, nearly all of the testimony taken by the two appropriations committees, involving thousands of pages each session, is presented by various governmental officials. In the House that testimony is taken in closed session with only governmental officials and members of the committee present. The Senate in pursuance of the Reorganization Act holds most of its hearings on appropriation bills in open session.

Obviously all of the committees studying pending legislation must depend on governmental data and governmental statistics as a source of information on which to base legislation. Until recent years Congress has had very little staff of its own to study problems and prepare data. This statement excepts studies made by special investigating committees of Congress in connection with proposed legislation.

It should be emphasized that much of the work of the Administration is devoted to making studies and compiling data in connection with its legislative and appropriaton needs.

The Administration does not stop there. Their experts accompany many of the major bills at all stages through to enactment. Officials of the particular department concerned with a special piece of legislation attach themselves to Senators and Representatives primarily responsible for the proposed legislation more closely than "private lobbyists." Their influence no doubt is greater because they hold a sort of official position in the "governmental family." This has gone to the extent that the issue has been raised in debate on the floor of the two houses on various occasions. It has not been uncommon to find experts of the Administration instead of employees of the Congress sitting in the legislative chambers in advisory capacity to the Senators and Representatives when certain bills sponsored by the Administration were under consideration.

In addition to this role assumed by the Administration—drafting, recommending, and sponsoring legislation—it devotes much effort to creating a public climate that will be favorable to the proposed legislation, or working to cause public pressure to be brought on Congress.

Of the endless proposals recommended to Congress, the following observations will reveal some of the experiences of the Administration in recent years in getting its proposed legislative programs enacted. There will be no attempt to give an over-all review of all measures proposed; comments will be limited to the showing of a trend.

Vetoes Since 1900: Since 1900 the President and Congress have publicly disagreed often over the enactment of bills. The number of vetoes by the President each year during that time together with the number of vetoes overriden by Congress are as follows:

Congress	Session	Dates	Bills and Resolutions Enacted	Vetoes			
				Regular	Pocket	Total	Over-ridden
		(McKinley's Administration)					
56th......	1	(Dec. 4, 1899–June 7, 1900)..	968	2	2	4	....
	2	(Dec. 3, 1900–Mar. 3, 1901)..	972	2	29	31	....
		(T. Roosevelt's Administration)					
57th......	1	(Dec. 2, 1901–July 1, 1902)...	1,484	8	....	8	....
	2	(Dec. 1, 1902–Mar. 3, 1903)..	1,306	7	6	13	....
58th......	1	(Nov. 9, 1903–Dec. 7, 1903)..	1	....	....	....	....
	2	(Dec. 7, 1903–Apr. 28, 1904)..	2,198	....	....	....	....
	3	(Dec. 5, 1904–Mar. 3, 1905)..	1,842	....	2	2	....
59th......	1	(Dec. 4, 1905–June 30, 1906).	4,043	8	9	17	....
	2	(Dec. 3, 1906–Mar. 3, 1907)..	2,981	7	6	13	....
60th......	1	(Dec. 2, 1907–May 30, 1908).	270	3	....	3	1
	2	(Dec. 7, 1908–Mar. 3, 1909)..	376	9	17	26	....
		(Taft's Administration)					
61st......	1	(Mar. 15, 1909–Aug. 5, 1909).	19	....	....	....	....
	2	(Dec. 6, 1909–June 25, 1910).	528	3	3	6	....
	3	(Dec. 5, 1910–Mar. 3, 1911)..	336	5	2	7	....
62d.......	1	(Apr. 4, 1911–Aug. 22, 1911).	61	4	....	4	....
	2	(Dec. 4, 1911–Aug. 26, 1912).	461	13	2	15	....
	3	(Dec. 2, 1912–Mar. 3, 1913)..	194	5	2	7	1
		(Wilson's Administration)					
63d.......	1	(Apr. 7, 1913–Dec. 1, 1913)..	54	1	....	1	....
	2	(Dec. 1, 1913–Oct. 24, 1914)..	402	2	....	....	....
	3	(Dec. 7, 1914–Mar. 3, 1915)..	244	1	....	1	....
64th......	1	(Dec. 6, 1915–Sept. 8, 1916)..	485	2	1	3	....
	2	(Dec. 4, 1916–Mar. 3, 1917)..	199	2	1	3	1
65th......	1	(Apr. 2, 1917–Oct. 6, 1917)..	109	....	1	1	....
	2	(Dec. 3, 1917–Nov. 21, 1918).	212	5	....	5	....
	3	(Dec. 2, 1918–Mar. 3, 1919)..	131	....	....	....	....
66th......	1	(May 19, 1919–Nov. 19, 1919)	121	6	....	6	2
	2	(Dec. 1, 1919–June 5, 1920)..	292	5	3	8	....
	3	(Dec. 6, 1920–Mar. 3, 1921)..	181	9	5	14	3
		(Harding's Administration)					
67th......	1	(Apr. 11, 1921–Nov. 23, 1921)	152	....	....	....	....
	2	(Dec. 5, 1921–Sept. 22, 1922).	435	4	1	5	....
	3	(Nov. 20, 1922–Dec. 4, 1922).	4	....	....	....	....
	4	(Dec. 4, 1922–Mar. 3, 1923)..	340	1	....	1	....
		(Coolidge's Administration)					
68th......	1	(Dec. 3, 1923–June 7, 1924)..	393	3	....	3	1
	2	(Dec. 1, 1924–Mar. 3, 1925)..	603	....	4	4	....
69th......	1	(Dec. 7, 1925–July 3, 1926)...	896	2	5	7	....
	2	(Dec. 6, 1926–Mar. 3, 1927)..	527	2	2	4	....
70th......	1	(Dec. 5, 1927–May 29, 1928).	993	13	3	16	3
	2	(Dec. 3, 1928–Mar. 3, 1929)..	729	....	16	16	....
		(Hoover's Administration)					
71st......	1	(Apr. 15, 1929–Nov. 22, 1929)	44	....	....	....	....
	2	(Dec. 2, 1929–July 3, 1930)...	883	4	3	7	1
	3	(Dec. 1, 1930–Mar. 3, 1931)..	597	7	5	12	1
72d.......	1	(Dec. 7, 1931–July 16, 1932)..	525	7	1	8	....
	2	(Dec. 5, 1932–Mar. 3, 1933)..	318	3	7	10	1
		(F. Roosevelt's Administration)					
73d.......	1	(Mar. 9, 1933–June 15, 1933).	105	....	1	1	....
	2	(Jan. 3, 1934–June 18, 1934)..	871	19	53	72	1
74th......	1	(Jan. 3, 1935–Aug. 26, 1935)..	840	35	28	63	....
	2	(Jan. 3, 1936–June 20, 1936)..	882	49	36	85	1
75th......	1	(Jan. 5, 1937–Aug. 21, 1937)..	899	17	23	40	2
	2	(Nov. 15, 1937–Dec. 21, 1937)	5	....	....	....	....
	3	(Jan. 3, 1938–June 16, 1938)..	855	16	61	77	1
76th......	1	(Jan. 3, 1939–Aug. 5, 1939)...	719	18	40	58	....
	2	(Sept. 21, 1939–Nov. 3, 1939).	2	....	....	....	....
	3	(Jan. 3, 1940–Jan. 3, 1941)...	941	108	1	109	2

Congress	Session	Dates	Bills and Resolutions Enacted	Vetoes			
				Regular	Pocket	Total	Over-ridden
77th.......	1	(Jan. 3, 1941–Jan. 2, 1942)...	649	28	....	28	....
	2	(Jan. 5, 1942–Dec. 16, 1942)..	836	51	....	51	....
78th.......	1	(Jan. 6, 1943–Dec. 21, 1943)..	384	13	3	16	1
	2	(Jan. 10, 1944–Dec. 19, 1944).	773	15	14	29	1
		(F. ROOSEVELT'S-TRUMAN'S ADMINISTRATION)					
79th.......	1	(Jan. 3, 1945–Dec. 21, 1945)..	658	23	4	27	....
	2	(Jan. 14, 1946–Aug. 2, 1946)..	967	33	16	49	....
		(TRUMAN'S ADMINISTRATION)					
80th.......	1	(Jan. 3, 1947–Dec. 19, 1947)..	526	13	19	32	1
	2	(Jan. 6, 1948–Aug. 7, 1948)...	837	29	14	43	5

Veto messages, although submitted to Congress by the President, are usually prepared by the particular governmental agency concerned with the administration of the law. Of course, the President is not bound by any such procedure. Even after the agency concerned prepares a proposed veto message or report of approval, as the case may be, and submits it to the President, the whole matter is generally turned over to the Bureau of the Budget. There the proposed law is examined to see if it fits generally into the President's program. After clearing all of these hurdles, the bill comes back to the President for final action. Some bills do not involve all of this, and others are approved by Congress in the form recommended by the Administration in the first place.

The above table, however, does not show the complete picture. Some bills vetoed by the President have been enacted in modified forms and signed by the President, some of which were not totally to the liking of the President. Many of the veto messages were referred back to the standing committee of origin and permitted to die without further action. Portions of some bills which have been vetoed have been added as amendments to subsequent bills which became law. Thus it is not fair to say that since Congress failed to override the President's veto nothing further was ever done. In some instances that is true. Each time the President's veto was overridden, on the other hand, Congress repudiated the will of the Administration and wrote the proposed legislation into law, even though the Administration in return may have failed to give its complete support to the enforcement of that law.

Disposition of Nominations: In the case of nominations, the picture has been more clear-cut. Since 1930 the number of nominations submitted to the Senate, the number confirmed, the number withdrawn, and the number defeated are set out below in 5 categories:

NOMINATIONS SUBMITTED TO SENATE, 1929 TO DATE

Congress	Session	Dates	Number Sent to Senate	Number Confirmed	Number Withdrawn	Number Rejected	Number Unconfirmed
71st	1	(Apr. 15, 1929–Nov. 22, 1929)	3,728	3,551	5	2	170
	2	(Dec. 2, 1929–July 3, 1930)	8,459	8,354	61	2	42
	3	(Dec. 1, 1930–Mar. 3, 1931)	5,321	5,000	2	1	318
72d	1	(Dec. 7, 1931–July 16, 1932)	9,806	9,739	10	1	56
	2	(Dec. 5, 1932–Mar. 3, 1933)	2,903	1,167	9	....	1,727
Special Session of Senate alone.	....	(July 7–21, 1930)	7	3	....	....	4
73d	1	(Mar. 9, 1933–June 15, 1933)	1,256	1,253	2	....	1
	2	(Jan. 3, 1934–June 18, 1934)	7,822	7,758	15	3	46
Special Session of Senate alone.	....	(Mar. 4–6, 1933)	16	16	....	....	....
74th	1	(Jan. 3, 1935–Aug. 26, 1935)	14,998	14,925	25	13	35
	2	(Jan. 3, 1936–June 20, 1936)	7,489	7,361	26	2	100
75th	1	(Jan. 5, 1937–Aug. 21, 1937)	7,701	7,665	14	9	13
	2	(Nov. 15, 1937–Dec. 21, 1937)	1,386	1,344	....	....	42
	3	(Jan. 3, 1938–June 16, 1938)	6,243	6,184	6	18	35
76th	1	(Jan. 3, 1939–Aug. 5, 1939)	11,340	11,278	8	10	44
	2	(Sept. 21, 1939–Nov. 3, 1939)					
	3	(Jan. 3, 1940–Jan. 3, 1941)	17,732	17,661	8	11	52
77th	1	(Jan. 3, 1941–Jan. 2, 1942)	11,485	11,346	7	2	130
	2	(Jan. 5, 1942–Dec. 16, 1942)	12,859	12,791	26	3	39
78th	1	(Jan. 6, 1943–Dec. 21, 1943)	11,656	11,298	13	2	343
	2	(Jan. 10, 1944–Dec. 19, 1944)	10,119	10,073	18	4	24
79th	1	(Jan. 3, 1945–Dec. 21, 1945)	11,056	10,965	11	3	77
	2	(Jan. 14, 1946–Aug. 2, 1946)	25,966	25,585	6	....	375
80th	1	(Jan. 3, 1947–Dec. 19, 1947)	40,557	39,855	132	....	570
	2	(Jan. 6, 1948–Aug. 7, 1948)	26,084	14,941	21	....	11,122

Some of the nominations over which the most conflict occurred follow: in 1939 Harry Hopkins, as Secretary of Commerce, was confirmed by 58 yeas (53 Dem., 2 Rep., and 3 others) to 27 nays (21 Rep., 5 Dem., and 1 other). In the same year William S. Boyle, nominee for the District Attorney for the District of Nevada, was refused his appointment without a record vote, because it involved personal objections by Senator McCarran. The question of senatorial courtesy was raised in connection with the appointment of Floyd H. Roberts as judge of the western district of Virginia. Both Senator Glass and President Roosevelt wrote public letters to the press over the matter. The nomination was rejected by 9 yeas (8 Dem., 1 other) to 72 nays (50 Dem., 21 Rep., and 1 other). The action of the Senate on the appointment of Elmer D. Davies, as district judge, presented an unusual relationship. After the confirmation, in 1939, Senator Barbour of New Jersey, holding that the nomination had been disposed of unexpectedly, offered a motion to recall the nomination from the President, which was adopted. The following day the President replied that he was unable to accede to the request since the appointment had already been sent out.[2]

In 1940 the most discussed appointments were those of Secretary of War Stimson and Secretary of Navy Knox, both Republicans, to membership in President Roosevelt's cabinet. The nomination of Stimson was agreed to by 56 yeas (Dem. 45, Rep. 10, and others 1), to 28 nays (Dem. 14, Rep 12, and others 2). The nomination of Knox was confirmed by 56 yeas to 16 nays. The nomination of Thad Brown to the Federal Communications Commission was a subject for hearings before the Senate Committee on Interstate Commerce for 13 days and 686 pages of testimony were taken. Finally the nomination was withdrawn.

The procedure for disposition of nominations in 1941 was merely routine. A number of important nominations were confirmed, such as: Mr. Justice Stone to be Chief Justice, Robert Jackson and Senator Byrnes to be associate judges of the Supreme Court, Frank Walker to be Postmaster General, Dean G. Acheson to be Assistant Secretary of State, John G. Winant to be Ambassador to the Court of St. James, Rex Tugwell to be Governor of Puerto Rico, and Francis Biddle to be Attorney General.

The most contested nomination in 1942 was that of Judge

[2] See *American Political Science Review*, 76-1, Vol. XXXIII, Dec. 1939, p. 1043.

Meaney. It was opposed by many Senators on the ground that Meaney did not merit a federal judgeship. Senator Norris put up his most vigorous fight of the year opposing this nomination; but it was finally approved, after prolonged hearings, by a vote of 39 to 20.

One of the most debated nominations of 1943 was that of Admiral Land to the Maritime Commission, the proceedings of which took up some 48 pages of the *Congressional Record*. Generally, the disposition of nominations during that year was merely a routine matter—they were referred to the appropriate committees, studied briefly, reported to the Senate, and confirmed after little or no debate.

In 1944 nominations to top posts in the State Department created much conflict. Those of the Under Secretary of State and five Assistant Secretaries of State were contested. The Foreign Relations Committee having defeated a motion to ask President Roosevelt to withdraw them, ordered them reported; after two days of debate, the Senate confirmed the nominations of Joseph C. Grew to be Under Secretary of State (by a vote of 66 yeas to 7 nays) and of Nelson A. Rockefeller (by a vote of 62 yeas to 10 nays), William L. Clayton (by a vote of 52 to 19), James C. Dunn (by a vote of 62 to 10), Brig. Gen. Julius C. Holmes (by a vote of 61 yeas to 9 nays), and Archibald Mac-Liesh (by a vote of 43 yeas to 25 nays). The nomination of Leland Olds to be a member of the Federal Power Commission was fought, but confirmed.

In 1945 standing committees adversely reported 3 major nominations.[3] Only that of Aubrey W. Williams to be REA Administrator was rejected. The nomination of Raymond S. McKeough to be a member of the Maritime Commission was fought on the grounds that he was closely affiliated with the CIO-PAC. After heated debate the nomination was confirmed by a vote of 42 yeas to 34 nays. The nomination of Henry A. Wallace to be Secretary of Commerce was confirmed by 56 yeas to 32 nays, but only after Congress passed a bill to divorce certain lending agencies, including the RFC, from the Department of Commerce.

In 1946 the most warmly contested nomination of the session was that of Edwin W. Pauley to be Under Secretary of the Navy,

---

[3] Henry A. Wallace, to be Secretary of Commerce, was adversely reported by the Commerce Committee by a vote of 6 to 11; Aubrey W. Williams, to be REA administrator, was adversely reported by the Committee on Agriculture and Forestry by a vote of 8 to 12; and Raymond S. McKeough, to be a member of the Maritime Commission, was adversely reported by the Commerce Committee by a vote of 7 to 10.

submitted by President Truman. The nomination never came to a vote in the Senate; opposition grew so strong that the President finally withdrew it.

The most debated nomination of 1947 was that of David E. Lilienthal to be Chairman of the Atomic Energy Commission. The Senate debate alone involved 166 printed pages of the *Congressional Record;* the committee consideration was even more extensive. The nomination was confirmed on April 9, by a vote of 50 to 31, after a motion by Senator Bricker to recommit it for further investigation was rejected by a vote of 38 to 52.

"The nomination of Gordon R. Clapp to be a member of the Board of Directors of the TVA was confirmed on April 24 by a vote of 36 to 31. The Committee on Public Works had adversely reported the nomination on February 28 by a vote of 7 to 5.

"Senator O'Daniel contested the nomination of Joseph B. Dooley to be United States district judge on the ground that 'this man is personally obnoxious to me.' On July 1, 1947, however, the nomination was confirmed."

Action on all postmaster nominations was delayed until July of 1947. The Democrats insisted, meanwhile, that something should be done about reporting and confirming nominations of several hundred postmasters; the Republicans maintained that more study should be made before final action. Before the session was adjourned, however, most of the nominations were confirmed.[4]

Action of Treaties: A number of treaties have been submitted to the Senate and acted on during the last decade, some of which were of major importance but very few have produced much controversy. Some of them involved much debate. Note the following table:

TREATIES SUBMITTED TO THE SENATE *

Congress	Year	Number Submitted	Number Ratified	Number Withdrawn
71st	1929	41	37	1
72nd	1931	17	14	....
73rd	1933	21	18	....
74th	1935	28	27	1
75th	1937	39	35	1
76th	1939	31	27	3
77th	1941	13	12	....
78th	1943	11	7	....
79th	1945	19	17	1
80th	1947	46	23	15
Totals		266	217	22

[4] See *American Political Science Review*, Vol. XLII, p. 689.

In 1939 the Senate ratified a treaty between the United States and the Republic of Panama on which it placed much emphasis. In 1940, it ratified 13 treaties without amendment or reservation, returned two to the President, and left three pending on the Executive Calendar. Four noncontroversial treaties were ratified in 1942.

The time devoted by the Senate to treaties in 1942 and in 1943 was insignificant; but it did expend much energy on the question of treatymaking during 1943. In pursuance of a resolution introduced by Senator Vandenberg on July 6, (S.Res. 170), a special subcommittee composed of members of the Foreign Relations Committee was appointed to conduct an investigation of the United Nations Relief and Rehabilitation Draft Agreement which the Executive and the State Department had announced would "be executed by Executive agreement. It was to be done exclusively by the administrative arm of the Government, without reference to Congress." The committee found that the draft "did involve practically illimitable obligations on the United States almost in perpetuity, and that as drawn it was a treaty, or should have been. Certainly it was not an obligation such as could be concluded merely by Executive agreement." In pursuance of this investigation, the special subcommittee and certain officials of the State Department re-wrote the draft agreement, according to Senator Vandenberg "to eliminate from it those illimitable commitments which carried it into the realm of a treaty, and to bring it back into what we thought was the realm of an agreement. We succeeded in re-writing it to a point where it is now literally nothing more than the authorization of appropriation, and there is no commitment in the text to anything except the expenditure of such moneys as are specifically appropriated from time to time by Congress for this purpose." [5]

The longest debated issue of that session was the Connally peace machinery resolution (S. Res. 192), occupying ten days. Much emphasis in that prolonged debate was placed on "by and with the advice and consent of the Senate, to make treaties, provided two-thirds of the Senators present concur." It was con-

---

* The above table was prepared by the Executive Clerk of the Senate, Lewis W. Bailey.
    The number of treaties left pending on December 31, 1948, totaled 27 since 266 were submitted of which 217 were ratified and 22 withdrawn.
    Note no treaties received prior to the 71st Congress, nor action thereon, are given consideration in the above table. Two treaties in the above group failed of ratification but were retained in the Senate until withdrawn by the President during the 80th Congress.
[5] See C.R., 78-1, pp. 8903-8904 (daily edition).

tended that the treaty-making power is divisible; "that there are two functions which the Senate performs. One function is to advise, the other is to consent." This definition was emphasized by certain Senators to discredit the opinion advanced by the Solicitor of the State Department to the effect that a two-thirds vote on the resolution would not only be giving advice to the President as to a peace treaty following the war, but would be giving consent to any treaty made in pursuance of that resolution. The Senators handling the resolution insisted that regardless of the vote, Senators could not destroy the powers of the Senate to modify a treaty.

The Senate spent very little time in 1944 on the ratification of treaties; but there was some discussion of the treaty-making power in the disposition of the St. Lawrence Waterway proposal, as an amendment to the Rivers and Harbors Bill, which died in conference. The Foreign Relations Committee, on November 22, of that year, voted not to hold hearings on the Mexican-U. S. Water Treaty and the Anglo-American Oil Agreement, two controversial issues, until the beginning of the Seventy-ninth Congress (1945).

In 1945 the Senate spent much time on treaties. In the face of little or no opposition, it debated the UN charter for 220 pages of the *Congressional Record* and finally approved the treaty by a vote of 89 yeas to 2 nays. It debated the Mexican Water Treaty for 10 days, involving 187 pages of the *Record*, finally assenting to it by a vote of 76 yeas to 10 nays.

In 1946 the President transmitted nine treaties to the Senate, of which eight were agreed to. Four others which had been submitted the prior year, but left unfinished, were also approved. A few others received much attention by the Foreign Relations Committee, even though they were relatively noncontroversial. Most unusual during that session was the Senate's procedure in disposing of Senate Resolution 196 for participation in the World Court. The resolution was adopted in the absence of any treaty or communication from the Executive. Likewise, the Senate began consideration of the resolution in legislative session, and after debating it for some time, resolved into executive session so as to give the instrument more of a treaty sanction. In the end the resolution was adopted by a vote of 60 yeas to 2 nays, after approval of an amendment (by vote of 51 yeas to 12 nays) allowing the United States the right to refuse jurisdiction on questions deemed purely domestic.

Treaties consumed very little of the Senate's time during the session of 1947. The Inter-American Treaty of Reciprocal Assistance formulated at Rio de Janiero, Brazil on September 12, 1947, was ratified on December 8, by a vote of 72 to 1. Other treaties approved during that session included the one with China on Friendship, Commerce and Navigation; Italian, Roumanian, Bulgarian and Hungarian peace treaties; the protocol prolonging the international agreement regarding the regulation of production and marketing of sugar; and the Inter-American Coffee Agreement.

On April 17, Senator Vandenberg reported on behalf of the Committee on Foreign Relations, a resolution which was passed without objection, directing the Secretary of the Senate to return 19 obsolete treaties which in his message to the Senate of April 8, 1947,[6] the President had asked to have withdrawn.

Legislative Experiences: The legislative experiences of the President with Congress in recent years have not been uniform; at times Congress has given him everything he asked for; other times it has refused to do so. Some requests have been completely rejected; others have been granted in modified form. In the case of particular legislative proposals recommended by the President, some of the experiences, chronologically presented, have been as follows:

In 1939 the neutrality bill pushed by the Administration was finally enacted in a special session. In the regular first session of the 76th Congress, the House passed the bill after a genuine fight by 200 yeas (194 Dem., 4 Rep., 2 others) to 188 nays (153

[6] Mr. VANDENBERG. Mr. President, under the law and practice, whenever the President of the United States sends treaties to the Senate they remain on the calendar of the Senate Committee on Foreign Relations from one Congress to another. As a result, when the committee organized for the Eightieth Congress, I found innumerable old treaties carried currently on the calendar of the committee, some of them going back to as far as 1923. For instance, on the current calendar of the committee one treaty is still in the hands of a subcommittee consisting of the Senator from Idaho, Mr. Borah; the Senator from Wisconsin, Mr. La Follette; the Senator from Illinois, Mr. Glenn; the Senator from Arkansas, Mr. Robinson; and the Senator from Montana, Mr. Walsh.

"I find another treaty, Mr. President, which is still currently carried on the calendar and is in the hands of a subcommittee consisting of the Senator from Wisconsin, Mr. Duffy; the Senator from Indiana, Mr. Van Nuys; and the Senator from New Mexico, Mr. Cutting.

"It occurred to me that it would be a good idea to clean up the calendar, and, in accordance with instructions of the Committee on Foreign Relations, I addressed a communication to the Department of State, suggesting that it recommend some course of action to bring the calendar down to date. As a result, we received a Presidential message last week, recommending the return to the President of all treaties submitted prior to 1941." (C.R., 80-1, p. 3756—daily edition.)

Rep., 33 Dem., 2 others). In the Senate the Foreign Relations Committee refused to report it during that session. A special session (2nd session) was called in the latter part of the same year and the bill was passed and cleared through conference, but after much effort.[7]

In the third session of the 76th Congress (1940), the major legislative proposals were drafted in or recommended by the Administration. With occasional exceptions Congress played the primary role of looking into, slightly amending, or blocking the enactment of bills sent to it by the Administration. The two general tax bills of that year, legislation recommended by the Administration, were drafted under the supervision of the Ways and Means Committee and modified by the Senate. Treasury officials worked closely with the committees of both houses and followed the bills at all stages to enactment. Compromises were made but the shadows of the Administration were frequently visible in the determination of tax procedures and policies. Expressed sentiments on Capitol Hill to modify the trade agreements program were squelched when a resolution extending the program for 3 years was finally enacted without amendment. The House made 4 unsuccessful attempts to override the President's veto, but some were just barely short of the necessary 2/3 vote. The President's veto was overriden twice, once on a general bridge bill and again on a veterans' pension bill. The House rejected the President's Reorganization Plan IV, although it was not defeated since under the Reorganization Act of 1939 both houses were required to take affirmative action. A second river and harbors bill to replace one vetoed by the President was drafted and enacted.[8]

In 1941 (first session of the 77th Congress) the important measures of the session were recommended by the Administration. As stated in an article in the *American Political Science Review*, "The committees concerned held hearings on the measures, but most of the time in each instance was consumed by Administration officials testifying in support of the legislative or appropriation bills. Generally the testimony was presented convincingly, primarily because of the national emergency. The bills were then passed by each chamber nearly as reported. Should one chamber insist on writing in 'undesired' amendments, such provisions were

[7] See *American Political Science Review*, Vol. 33, pp. 1027-1043.
[8] See *American Political Science Review*, Vol. 35, No. 2, April 1941, pp. 302-303.

more than likely to be changed or wiped out by the other body, or at least modified in conference. Thus only a few paragraphs of legislation and hardly any entire public laws were finally enacted contrary to the will of the Administration. Of course, sometimes the various units of the Administration were in discord, at least not in accord, as to what a particular Administrative proposal should contain." [9]

In that year, Congress made significant changes in the Lease-Lend Act, the bill increasing the lending authority of the RFC by $1.5 billions, the first bill amending the Selective Service Act relative to age groups, and the bill requisitioning property for defense purposes. A bill to authorize wire-tapping was completely voted down in the House by 146 yeas (111 Dem., 35 Rep.), to 154 nays (56 Dem., 94 Rep., and 4 others). "Congressional initiative to amend the labor laws as applied to defense work, directly or indirectly, was killed on several occasions. Several times the House resorted to the use of riders on appropriation bills, and each attempt came to naught." The House did pass a much opposed labor bill, which died in the Senate.[10]

The President vetoed 28 bills. The Senate overrode his veto of the Strategic Defense Highway Bill by a vote of 57 yeas (41 Dem., 14 Rep., and 2 others), to 19 nays (13 Dem., 6 Rep.) but the House failed in its attempt by 251 yeas (137 Dem., 111 Rep., and 3 others), to 128 nays (88 Dem., 40 Rep.). All the other messages were referred to the appropriate committees without further action.[11]

In 1942 (77th Congress, 2nd Session) the President in the case of "strict war measures" continued to request what he wanted and got it. The same was true in noncontroversial measures. On other counts, there developed an estranged feeling between the two arms of government; Congress felt it had public support in this change of attitude. Certain proposals urged by the President were ignored. The President did enjoy the prestige of mapping out the general legislative program, and the Administration worked to get it enacted, but the President suffered some outstanding defeats.

On Sept. 25 of that year Senator Tobey in reflecting on the Administration pressure on Congress, stated:

[9] See *American Political Science Review*, Vol. 36, p. 300.
[10] See *American Political Science Review*, Vol. 36, pp. 301-302.
[11] See *American Political Science Review*, Vol. 36, p. 301.

Speaking of lobbyists, I should like to point out to the Senator that they come not only from farm organizations but from other sources as well. As a Member of the House for 6 years prior to coming to this body, I distinctly recall when a certain 'lame duck' Representative from Ohio was appointed by the Executive at $10,000 a year. His chief function was to cajole, importune, and threaten Members of the House to 'come across' and meet the demands of the Administration. As compared to the methods used then, the methods of farm leaders pale into insignificance.[12]

The most outstanding refusal by Congress during the session occurred over the $300,000,000 unemployment compensation benefits, requested by the President on January 19, 1942, with proposed legislation attached. The message was referred to the Ways and Means Committee. After public hearings, the committee ordered the bill tabled, in effect killed, on February 19. Members of the committee declared that it was not benefits the President wanted; he wanted control over the whole social security program. Again on March 4 of the same year, the President sent a supplemental estimate for $100,000,000 for the Federal Works Agency, to be used for war displacement insurance. This time the matter went to the House Appropriations Committee; hearings were held and the committee voted to table the estimate.

On February 19, the President's request on employment stabilization was voted down in the House by 104 to 252. Representative Beiter said: "This bill was introduced at the instance of the President of the United States, who made recommendations in two of his messages to the first session of this Congress." [13]

On November 2, he submitted a message requesting legislation to suspend for the duration of the emergency the operation of laws restricting free movement of persons, property, and information in and out of the United States. The President stated that, although many obstacles had been removed, restrictions still existed which impeded the war effort. The proposal was referred to the Ways and Means Committee, and hearings were held. The committee, however, could not agree with the President as to the need of such power. The proposal died in committee.

Again, the President sent a letter to the Vice President, as President of the Senate, opposing a piece of legislation. The Senate ignored the recommendation and passed the bill by a vote of 50 to 23. Senator Gillette stated:

[12] C.R., 77-2, p. 7721 (daily edition), Sept. 25, 1942.
[13] C.R., 77-2, p. 1483 (daily edition).

I was very much disturbed and somewhat agitated by the reading of the letter from the Chief Executive addressed to the Vice President, in opposition to the passage of this measure . . . I desire to say that this is a very unusual procedure in legislation, so far as my knowledge goes. The Chief Executive of the United States has a function with reference to legislation, and a duty which is laid upon him by the Constitution of the United States . . . I question that it is proper procedure for the President of the United States, when a measure is pending before the Senate of the United States, not to send a message to the Congress, but to send a letter to the presiding officer of the Senate, the Vice President of the United States, to be laid before the Senate, to influence our action in the matter which is before us.

The bill was never passed by the House.[14]

The message proposing legislation "placing a floor under prices of farm products," was most dramatic. It was submitted to Congress on September 7, as follows:

I ask the Congress to take this action by the first of October. Inaction on your part by that date will leave me with an inescapable responsibility to the people of this country to see to it that the war effort is no longer imperiled by a threat of economic chaos. In the event that the Congress should fail to act, and act adequately, I shall accept the responsibility, and I will act.[15]

This message was severely criticized in both houses by Democrats and Republicans; but the President got his legislation on October 2 of that year.

In 1943 (78th Congress, 1st Session) the relations continued much the same as in prior years, with Congress getting a bit more stern on particular issues. The President was not successful in his contest with Congress over several counts of importance to him. His veto was overridden and the Connally-Smith Anti-Strike Bill was enacted into law within less than 2 hours after the message reached the Capitol. The NYA was liquidated by a provision inserted in the Labor-Federal Security Appropriation Bill (H.R. 2935). The HOLC was liquidated by a provision of the Independent Offices Appropriation Bill. Against the will of the President, Congress appropriated $50,000 for the liquidation of the NRPB, to be abolished on August 31, 1943. The Bituminous Coal Act of 1937 was permitted to expire, after extension by two acts during that session for 30 and 90 days respectively. The Trade Agreements Act was extended but only after stirring some ill feeling. Senator Gillette warned against a message to

---

[14] C.R., 77-2, pp. 1647-1648 (daily edition).
[15] *House Doc.* 716 of 77th Congress; see also *American Political Science Review*, Vol. 37, pp. 302-305.

the Vice President urging a continuation of that act. He served notice that he would make a point of order if the practice were attempted again; he insisted that such communications should be made to Senators and presented by them to the Senate, not by the Vice President.

As reported in the *American Political Science Review,* during that year "there were conflicts within the Administration in which Congress participated. Representative Martin Dies took part in the removal of John Bovingdon from the OEW. Dies had accused Bovingdon of subversive activities, and had announced his intention to present an indictment against him. Before this was done, Leo Crowley removed him, and out of gratification over this action Dies stated: 'I have been certain for a number of years that there is a clique in Washington who are determined to change this country to some form of dictatorship. The clique, pursuant to their plans, has attempted to pack Government services with people like Bovingdon.' On July 29, Representative Taber asked that Milo Perkins be ousted from the BEW; and after the dispute between Vice President Wallace and Secretary of Commerce Jones, when the BEW was changed to OEW, Perkins disappeared from the scene.

"On the other hand, it is evident that the Administration had some effect on the removal of Representative Cox from the chairmanship of the special House committee investigating the Federal Communications Commission. The committee attempted to make some investigations and to get the records of some administrative agencies, which it was denied. In its attempt to investigate Harold E. Smith, Director of the Budget, over certain records, Mr. Smith announced that he had 'been directed by the President not to make the Bureau files available to the committee and not to testify if called as a witness.' Likewise, Chairman Fly of the FCC refused to testify. Finally, Representative Cox resigned." [16]

In 1944 (78th Congress, 2nd Session) the strained relations were definitely pronounced. The President mapped out the general legislative program in his annual Budget message and his message on the state of the Union. He did not get all that he requested. The tax bill of the year caused a break between Senator Barkley, majority floor leader of the Senate, and the President. The President vetoed the measure and Senator Barkley challenged his

[16] See *American Political Science Review,* Vol. 38, p. 316.

action, concluding ". . . If the Congress of the United States has any self-respect yet left, it will override the veto of the President . . ." He resigned his post as floor leader but was re-elected unanimously. The bill became law over the veto.

The soldier vote bill stirred up trouble. The Administration wanted a Federal-controlled ballot; Congress granted a State-controlled ballot; the President finally let the bill become law without his signature.

The Administration wanted the social security pay-roll tax increased. Congress passed a bill freezing the tax at 1% each on employers and employees during 1945. The President threatened to veto the measure but finally signed it.

The House Appropriations Committee in one of its reports, implying that Government agencies try to perpetuate themselves, wrote:

Members of the committee have been impressed with the considerable amount of correspondence received in connection with the appropriation for this Bureau [Children's Bureau] and the widespread interest in the demand that the appropriation be maintained at its present level, or increased. Such interest indicates that the public generally will give wholehearted support to every effort of the Bureau to carry on its duties within the amount appropriated; but government employees who are beneficiaries of the appropriation concerned should not be used in having the Congress or members of the Committee on Appropriations circulated on behalf of such appropriation.[17]

Various other reports accused the Administration of flouting the will of Congress in administering the laws.

In 1945 (79th Congress, 1st Session), Congress had the rare experience of dealing with two Presidents of the same political faith. The relations between President Roosevelt and Congress remained much the same as in the previous session; the case with Mr. Truman was different. The first months of the Truman Administration, after the death of Mr. Roosevelt, found Congress and the President in complete accord, Mr. Truman having been a Senator in the prior session. The latter part of the session found Congress in doubt as to continued good relationships between the two arms of the government. "The Administration's legislative program was submitted to Congress first by President Roosevelt in his state of the Union and Budget messages, and later by President Truman in his special message of September 6, 1945, together with a series of others."

[17] H.Rept. 1526, pp. 7-8; see also C.R., 78-2, pp. 5192-3 (daily edition), May 29, 1944.

The following picture is taken from the annual review article devoted to that session of Congress as carried in the *American Political Science Review*.

Perhaps the most pronounced conflict [during the year] between Congress and President Roosevelt came over the so-called Work or Fight bill (H.R. 1752), which passed both houses in different forms after much Administrative pressure in support thereof,[18] but which was finally killed after a conference report had been filed on the two passed versions.[19] In keeping with the same general program, President Roosevelt asked that Congress 'provide for the induction of nurses into the armed forces.' [20] A bill in pursuance of the request was passed by the House and reported to the Senate by the Committee on Military Affairs, but then it died on the Senate Calendar, without consideration. Mr. Roosevelt also urged Congress on two different occasions to enact peacetime universal military training.

In his message to Congress in the early part of the session, President Roosevelt outlined a far-reaching program, but at the time of his death Congress had not enacted the recommendations . . .

Before the close of the session, in spite of the rough sailing between Truman and Congress in the later months of the year, much of of the Administration's program was written into law, such as extension of the Trade Agreements Act (with an additional 50 per cent increase or decrease authorized), Bretton Woods Agreements, United Nations Charter, salary adjustment for federal employees, surplus property bill to set up a single administrator, reduction in taxes, reorganization of government agencies, financial control over government corporations, the extension of the Price Control Act, and more liberal credit and benefits to veterans. On the other hand, Congress either rejected or failed to approve several major proposals, in spite of persistent urging on the part of the President, who on one occasion made an appeal by radio directly to the people, over the heads of the Representatives and Senators. Still pending for further Congressional action were: unemployment compensation, full employment, FEPC, USES extension, fact-finding boards, health and medical care, minimum wage increase, housing, Presidential succession, liberalization of social security, St. Lawrence Waterway, Missouri Valley Authority, universal military training, and unification of armed forces.

The Administration was not unmindful of Congressional criticism when Senators and Representatives accused it of flouting the will of Congress in administering the laws. The OPA was influenced on various occasions no doubt, under the suspense of what Congress might do to it if it ignored the wishes publicly expressed in the halls of Congress; the same was true in connection with the transportation of servicemen, the demobilization program of the Army, and other activities.

"Lobbying" on the part of the Administration to get bills enacted, defeated, or modified was not uncommon, to say the least. The situation

[18] President Roosevelt recommended the legislation in his State of the Union message and various other subsequent communications, including personal letters to chairmen of the committees handling the bill.
[19] The House adopted the conference report by a vote of 167 to 160, but the Senate rejected it by a vote of 29 to 46, after several days of debate. The vote in the Senate showed 18 Democrats and 11 Republicans voting for the report and 21 Democrats, 24 Republicans, and 1 Progressive voting against it. Under unanimous consent, the House then returned the whole issue to the House Military Affairs Committee, and no further action was taken on it (see *Record* for Apr. 23, 1945).
[20] In his state of the Union message, he told Congress that "the need is too pressing to await the outcome of further efforts at recruiting."

became at one time so distasteful to the House leadership that Speaker Rayburn, in his press conference, when the bill to reorganize government agencies (H.R. 4129) was under consideration, warned administrative officials to stay away from Capitol Hill, and to stop lobbying to get their respective agencies exempted from the reorganization bill. He told the reporters he knew who the offenders were, and that if they did not desist he would call names.

The Administration's legislative program for the 79th Congress, Second Session, was submitted to Congress in his state of the Union and Budget message of January 21, 1946. Again, as reported in the *American Political Science Review:*

Mr. Truman, however, was not too successful in getting his recommendations enacted. Many bills introduced in pursuance of his recommendations were finally enacted, but most of them were modified, in varying degree, before becoming law. They include: control of atomic energy, the $3,750,-000,000 loan to Britain, return of employment services to States as of November 16, 1946; federal airport legislation, pay increase for government employees, full employment, veterans' emergency housing, extension of price control, ship sales bill, school lunch program, extension of the Second War Powers Act as modified, stock piling of strategic materials, Selective Service extension, veterans' benefits and federal aid for hospitals and public health centers. The Administrative Procedure Bill became law, and with the complete support of President Truman.

On the other hand, many important recommendations of the Administration were not enacted, including self government for the District of Columbia, educational aid, labor disputes fact-finding boards, fair employment practices, food nutrition relief, health and medical care, repeal of the Johnson Act, minimum wage increase, national housing program, Presidential succession, scientific research, extension of social security and health, small business, St. Lawrence Waterway, territories and insular possessions, unemployment compensation, unification of armed forces, expansion of crop insurance, Missouri Valley Authority, and universal military training.

The President on different occasions urged that Congress do something about increasing minimum wages, and the Senate passed such a bill (S. 1349), amended. The Senate-passed version, however, included the amendment affecting farm parity prices, which the President had designated as not acceptable to him . . . The House never gave the Senate-passed version any consideration, and a bill on the same subject reported to the House was never considered. Further, support for the parity amendment was just as strong in the House as it was in the Senate. Thus the bill was permitted to die without reaching the President.

Next to labor legislation, OPA extension was the most controversial and debated proposal of the session. The first bill (H.R. 6042), after prolonged consideration, was passed in a form unacceptable to the President. In vetoing it, Mr. Truman declared that it would destroy the price control and stabilization program. The House sustained the veto by 173-142. Of the 173 voting to override the veto, 68 were Democrats and 105 Republicans; of the 142 voting to sustain, 90 were Democrats, 50 were Republicans, with two other members voting in the affirmative. Congress subsequently

passed a second OPA extension, which the President also declared unacceptable, but which he signed since he felt it was that or nothing.
Various Representatives and Senators were rather critical of the President for not reducing the numbers of government personnel; and it was only after a definite plan for reduction had been reached that Congress cleared the bill providing for pay increases for government employees.

The annual review article in the *American Political Science Review* for the first session of the 80th Congress had the following to say of the relation between the President and Congress:

The relationship between the President and Congress took its tone from their differences in political faiths. As in all recent Congresses, nevertheless, the Administration formulated its program, sent it to the House and Senate, and urged its enactment. The program was submitted to the legislature primarily in three documents: the state of the Union message, the budget message for the fiscal year 1948, and the special message of November 17, 1947, on "interim aid for certain Western European countries and a program to curb inflation in the United States."
Some of the program was enacted substantially in the form recommended, some of it was ignored, while other parts of it were the subject of legislative enactment, but not necessarily to the taste of the Administration. A few major bills, having passed both houses, were vetoed, and the vetoes were sustained. By and large, the President was not too successful in getting what he asked for except in the case of his foreign policy.
The President's interim aid program "for certain Western European countries" became law on December 17 (P.L. 389) practically in the form requested. His recommendation for terminating certain emergency and war powers was approved on July 25. The presidential succession proposal, making the Speaker of the House the third in line, became law on July 18. The President was granted $400,000,000 for aid to Greece and Turkey. After many meetings and prolonged hearings, the bill to create a National Military Establishment by consolidating the various branches of the Armed Services became law. Other proposals of major importance written into law in close keeping with the Administration's recommendations included: re-incorporation of the Export Import Bank; extension of rent control; extension of the Commodity Credit Corporation to June 30, 1948; R.F.C. extension until June 30, 1948; extension of the Second War Powers and Export Control Acts; the Sugar Act of 1948; and the Armed Services Personnel Act.
A number of the President's recommendations were never enacted; some never passed the discussion stage. The "establishment of a well-integrated Department of Welfare" reached only the stage of introduction. Suggestions to "protect the civil rights of citizens" were barely mentioned. A bill to establish and carry out a national housing policy was reported in the Senate, but never passed that stage. Nothing was done to "set the stage for permanent farm welfare." Selective Service was permitted to expire as of March 31 without extension and before any action was taken on Universal Military Training. At the time of adjournment on December 19, Congress had acted on only one of the proposals of the President in his message of November 17. No bill was enacted by the end of the first session to carry out the ten recommendations in that message on his anti-inflation program. Congress did enact a bill (S.J.Res. 167) "to aid in the stabilization of commodity prices and to stabilize the United States economy" by voluntary

methods (P.L. 395). Finally, no legislation was forthcoming on educational aid (except for veterans), FEPC, extension of social security benefits, statehood for Hawaii, self government for the District of Columbia, the St. Lawrence waterway, and minimum wage increase.

Congress, in spite of the President, enacted bills on labor-management relations, freezing pay-roll taxes at one per cent until 1950, and portal-to-portal pay. Two of these issues provoked much controversy. The Taft-Hartley Labor Bill passed both houses after heated contests, and by large enough majorities to override a veto; the same was true in the case of the conference report, which was basically the Senate bill. The bill was duly vetoed, but there was little question that it would become law from the date the Senate first passed its version on May 13, 1947. There was question as to how it would be administered. The President had characterized the proposed law as "unworkable" and had added that it would "do serious harm to our country." This situation caused various members of Congress publicly to question the wisdom of the part the President had played before a final verdict by the House and Senate.

In the case of the Portal-to-Portal Pay Bill, the President finally signed the measure, but unwillingly; and he sent a message to Congress explaining his reasons for signing—an unusual procedure. In this message, he placed certain interpretations upon what the law meant. In reply, the Judiciary Committee issued a statement on the "full intent and purpose of the legislation." The Chief Executive's procedure was criticized. A Democratic Senator stated: "Mr. President, I want it understood that I do not believe that any statement by the President, when he either signs or vetoes an act of Congress, becomes any part of its legislative history."

The President vetoed several important bills which were not passed over his veto. Among them were the two bills "to reduce individual income tax payments." Congress was unable to override the veto in either instance; the House mustered a two-thirds vote in the second case, but the Senate failed by a vote of 57 yeas to 36 nays. Congress sustained the President's veto of S. 814, to provide price support for wool, but it took his reasons into consideration and then enacted another bill (S. 1498) which the President signed. The pocket veto of S. 526, Science Foundation Act, of August 6, 1947, was final; nothing further was done about it during the second portion of the session.

There was considerable comment in the two houses concerning pressure incited by the Administration and brought to bear on Congress to get certain funds or legislation. To illustrate: in the case of the "customs budget," the activity by the National Customs Service Association to get the full amount of the budget estimates appropriated was emphasized. This caused a considerable stir and incited much condemnation of administrative activity in the interest of self perpetuation. A comparative picture was exhibited in the case of funds for the soil conservation program carried in the Agriculture Appropriation Bill. As a result of an investigation by the House Committee on Expenditures in the Executive Departments into publicity and propaganda as relating to universal military training, a special report was made to the House which concluded: "On the basis of the evidence at hand, the War Department, its personnel, and civilian employees have gone beyond the limits of their proper duty of providing factual information to the people and the Congress and have engaged in propaganda supported by taxpayers' money to influence legislation now pending before the Congress."

REAPPORTIONMENTS OF REPRESENTATIVES SINCE 1787

States	1787	1790	1800	1810	1820	1830	1840	1850	1860	1870	1880	1890	1900	1910	1920*	1930	1940
Delaware	1	1	1	2	1	1	1	1	1	1	1	1	1	1	...	1	1
Pennsylvania	8	13	18	23	26	28	24	25	24	27	28	30	32	36	...	34	33
New Jersey	4	5	6	6	6	6	5	5	5	7	7	8	10	12	...	14	14
Georgia	3	2	4	6	7	9	8	8	7	9	10	11	11	12	...	10	10
Connecticut	5	7	7	7	6	6	4	4	4	4	4	5	5	5	...	6	6
Massachusetts	8	14	17	20	13	12	10	11	10	11	12	13	14	16	...	15	14
Maryland	6	8	9	9	9	8	6	6	5	6	6	6	6	6	...	6	6
South Carolina	5	6	8	9	9	9	7	6	4	5	7	7	7	7	...	6	6
New Hampshire	3	4	5	6	6	5	4	3	2	3	2	2	2	2	...	2	2
Virginia	10	19	22	23	22	21	15	13	11	9	10	10	10	10	...	9	9
New York	6	10	17	27	34	40	34	33	31	33	34	34	37	43	...	45	45
North Carolina	5	10	12	13	13	13	9	8	7	8	9	9	10	10	...	11	12
Rhode Island	1	2	2	2	2	2	2	2	2	2	2	2	2	3	...	2	2
Vermont		2	4	6	5	5	4	3	3	3	2	2	2	2	...	1	1
Kentucky		2	6	10	12	13	10	10	9	10	11	11	11	11	...	9	9
Tennessee			3	6	9	13	11	10	8	10	10	10	10	10	...	9	10
Ohio				6	14	19	21	21	19	20	21	21	21	22	...	24	23
Louisiana					3	3	4	4	5	6	6	6	7	8	...	8	8
Indiana					3	7	10	11	11	13	13	13	13	13	...	12	11
Mississippi					1	2	4	5	5	6	7	7	8	8	...	7	7
Illinois					1	3	7	9	14	19	20	22	25	27	...	27	26
Alabama					2	5	7	7	6	8	8	9	9	10	...	9	9
Maine					7	8	7	6	5	5	4	4	4	4	...	3	3
Missouri					1	2	5	7	9	13	14	15	16	16	...	13	13
Arkansas							1	2	3	4	5	6	7	7	...	7	7
Michigan							3	4	6	9	11	12	12	13	...	17	17
Florida								1	1	2	2	2	3	4	...	5	6
Iowa								2	6	9	11	11	11	11	...	9	8
Texas								2	4	6	11	13	16	18	...	21	21
Wisconsin								3	6	8	9	10	11	11	...	10	10
California								2	3	4	6	7	8	11	...	20	23
Minnesota									2	3	5	7	9	10	...	9	9
Oregon									1	1	1	2	2	3	...	3	4
Kansas									1	3	7	8	8	8	...	7	6
West Virginia									3	3	4	4	5	6	...	6	6
Nevada									1	1	1	1	1	1	...	1	1
Nebraska									1	1	3	6	6	6	...	5	4
Colorado										1	1	2	3	4	...	4	4
South Dakota												2	2	3	...	2	2
North Dakota												1	2	3	...	2	2
Montana												1	1	2	...	2	2
Washington												2	3	5	...	6	6
Idaho												1	1	2	...	2	2
Wyoming												1	1	1	...	1	1
Utah												1	1	2	...	2	2
Oklahoma													5	8	...	9	8
Arizona														1	...	1	2
New Mexico														1	...	1	2
Total	65	105	141	181	212	240	223	234	241	293	325	357	391	435	...	435	435

* No apportionment in 1920.

POLITICAL DIVISIONS OF THE U. S. SENATE AND HOUSE OF REPRESENTATIVES FROM 1855 (34th CONG.) TO 1949-51 (81st CONG.)

Congress	Senate					House of Representatives				
	Number of Senators	Democrats	Republicans	Other parties	Vacant	Number of Representatives	Democrats	Republicans	Other parties	Vacant
Thirty-fourth	62	42	15	5	......	234	83	108	43	......
Thirty-fifth	64	39	20	5	......	237	131	92	14	......
Thirty-sixth	66	38	26	2	......	237	101	113	23	......
Thirty-seventh	50	11	31	7	1	178	42	106	28	2
Thirty-eighth	51	12	39	......	......	183	80	103	......	......
Thirty-ninth	52	10	42	......	......	191	46	145	......	......
Fortieth	53	11	42	......	......	193	49	143	......	1
Forty-first	74	11	61	......	2	243	73	170	......	......
Forty-second	74	17	57	......	......	243	104	139	......	......
Forty-third	74	19	54	......	1	293	88	203	......	2
Forty-fourth	76	29	46	......	1	293	181	107	3	2
Forty-fifth	76	36	39	1	......	293	156	137	......	......
Forty-sixth	76	43	33	......	......	293	150	128	14	1
Forty-seventh	76	37	37	2	......	293	130	152	11	......
Forty-eighth	76	36	40	......	......	325	200	119	6	......
Forty-ninth	76	34	41	......	1	325	182	140	2	1
Fiftieth	76	37	39	......	......	325	170	151	4	......
Fifty-first	84	37	47	......	......	330	156	173	1	......
Fifty-second	88	39	47	2	......	333	231	88	14	......
Fifty-third	88	44	38	3	3	357	220	126	8	......
Fifty-fourth	88	39	44	5	......	357	104	246	7	......
Fifty-fifth	90	34	46	10	......	357	134	206	16	1
Fifty-sixth	90	26	53	11	......	357	163	185	9	......
Fifty-seventh	90	29	56	3	2	357	153	198	5	......
Fifty-eighth	90	32	58	......	......	386	178	207	......	1
Fifty-ninth	90	32	58	......	......	386	136	250	......	......
Sixtieth	92	29	61	......	2	386	164	222	......	......
Sixty-first	92	32	59	......	1	391	172	219	......	......
Sixty-second	92	42	49	......	1	391	228	162	1	......
Sixty-third	96	51	44	1	......	435	290	127	18	......
Sixty-fourth	96	56	39	1	......	435	231	193	8	3
Sixty-fifth	96	53	42	1	......	435	210	216	9	......
Sixty-sixth	96	47	48	1	......	435	191	237	7	......
Sixty-seventh	96	37	59	......	......	435	132	300	1	2
Sixty-eighth	96	43	51	2	......	435	207	225	3	......
Sixty-ninth	96	40	54	1	1	435	183	247	5	......
Seventieth	96	47	48	1	......	435	195	237	3	......
Seventy-first	96	39	56	1	......	435	163	267	1	4
Seventy-second	96	47	48	1	......	435	[1] 214	220	1	......
Seventy-third	96	59	36	1	......	435	313	117	5	......
Seventy-fourth	96	69	25	2	......	435	322	103	10	......
Seventy-fifth	96	75	17	4	......	435	333	89	13	......
Seventy-sixth	96	69	23	4	......	435	262	169	4	......
Seventy-seventh	96	66	28	2	......	435	267	162	6	......
Seventy-eighth	96	57	38	1	......	435	222	209	4	......
Seventy-ninth	96	57	38	1	......	435	243	190	2	......
Eightieth	96	45	51	......	......	435	188	246	1	......
Eighty-first	96	54	42	......	......	435	263	171	1	......

[1] Democrats organized House, due to Republican deaths.

BILLS DEBATED FOR THREE OR MORE PAGES OF CONGRESSIONAL RECORD *

(By Session from 1941 through 1947)

Pages Debated	77th Congress				78th Congress				79th Congress				80th Congress	
	First Session 1941		Second Session 1942		First Session 1943		Second Session 1944		First Session 1945		Second Session 1946		First Session 1947	
	House	Senate	House	Senate	House	Senate	House	Senate	House	Senate	House	Senate	House	Senate
3– 5	7	10	20	13	10	10	9	4	7	4	14	6	15	11
5– 10	20	14	26	16	16	13	12	15	30	15	25	11	26	14
10– 15	24	9	10	5	24	11	12	4	15	13	20	4	16	4
15– 20	9	7	13	2	7	5	10	3	7	2	16	7	13	8
20– 25	15	7	5	5	3	5	10	1	12	5	3	8	4	6
25– 30	9	5	6	5	8	3	2	2	8	3	7	3	5	4
30– 35	8	2	3	1	3	2	4	0	10	3	4	1	3	1
35– 40	3	2	4	0	5	0	1	2	1	1	3	0	4	5
40– 45	1	2	3	1	1	1	1	1	6	0	1	2	2	3
45– 50	3	1	1	0	1	1	1	1	3	2	2	1	3	1
50– 60	2	0	5	4	5	5	5	1	4	4	5	2	3	1
60– 70	1	2	1	2	4	1	3	2	5	3	3	2	3	3
70– 80	5	1	0	1	3	1	4	1	1	1	1	1	2	0
80– 90	0	0	1	0	1	0	1	0	0	2	2	1	1	0
90–100	1	0	1	1	2	1	0	2	2	2	1	0	0	0
100–125	3	1	0	3	4	6	3	2	6	2	0	2	3	1
125–150	1	1	2	1	2	0	0	1	1	2	1	0	1	5
150–175	2	0	0	3	1	1	1	1	0	1	2	0	2	2
175–200	1	1	1	0	0	0	1	1	1	0	2	1	1	0
200–300	1	0	0	0	1	2	2	3	1	1	1	2	1	1
300–400	0	0	0	0	0	0	0	0	0	0	0	3	0	0
400–500	0	0	0	0	0	0	0	0	0	0	0	1	0	0
500–600	0	1	0	0	0	0	0	0	0	0	0	0	0	1
Totals	116	67	102	63	101	68	86	47	120	66	113	58	108	71

* These data are subject to very slight error, but certainly not as much as 5 per cent. The difficulty of making such a tabulation invites the possibility of slight error.

SENATE OF THE UNITED STATES

EIGHTIETH CONGRESS
FIRST SESSION BEGAN JANUARY 3, 1947
SENATE IN ADJOURNMENT FROM JULY 27, TO NOVEMBER 17, 1947

No. 127

CALENDAR OF BUSINESS

Legislative Day, Monday, November 24, 1947
Calendar Day, Monday, December 1, 1947

GENERAL ORDERS
UNDER RULE VIII

ORDER No.	NUMBER AND AUTHOR OF BILL	TITLE	REPORTED BY
5	S. 27 Mr. McCarran	A bill to provide for suspending the enforcement of certain obligations against the operators of gold and silver mines who are forced to cease operations because of the war.	Jan. 15, 1947.—Mr. McCarran, Committee on the Judiciary, without amendment. (Report No. 4.)
45	S 865	A bill to provide for the striking of medals in lieu of coins for commemorative purposes.	Mar. 10, 1947.—Mr. Flanders, Committee on Banking and Currency, without amendment. (Report No. 49.)
55	S. 669 Mr. Capper (and others)	A bill to provide for the payment of a bonus of 30 cents per bushel on wheat and corn produced and sold between Jan. 1, 1945, and Apr. 18, 1946.	Mar. 19, 1947.—Mr. Capper, Committee on Agriculture and Forestry, without amendment. (Report No. 59.)

Sample Copy of the Heading of Title Page and a Part of Contents of Senate Calendar